AF674935

TĀRANĀTHA'S
HISTORY OF BUDDHISM IN INDIA

Tāranātha's
HISTORY OF BUDDHISM IN INDIA

Translated from Tibetan by

LAMA CHIMPA

ALAKA CHATTOPADHYAYA

Edited by

DEBIPRASAD CHATTOPADHYAYA

MOTILAL BANARSIDASS PUBLISHERS
PRIVATE LIMITED • DELHI

Reprint : Delhi, 1990, 1997, 2004, 2010
First Edition: Simla 1970

ISBN : 978-81-208-0696-2 (Cloth)
ISBN : 978-81-208-3470-5 (Paper)

MOTILAL BANARSIDASS
41 U.A. Bungalow Road, Jawahar Nagar, Delhi 110 007
8 Mahalaxmi Chamber, 22 Bhulabhai Desai Road, Mumbai 400 026
203 Royapettah High Road, Mylapore, Chennai 600 004
236, 9th Main III Block, Jayanagar, Bangalore 560 011
Sanas Plaza, 1302 Baji Rao Road, Pune 411 002
8 Camac Street, Kolkata 700 017
Ashok Rajpath, Patna 800 004
Chowk, Varanasi 221 001

Printed in India

By Jainendra Prakash Jain at Shri Jainendra Press,
A-45, Naraina, Phase-I, New Delhi 110 028
and Published by Narendra Prakash Jain for
Motilal Banarsidass Publishers Private Limited,
Bungalow Road, Delhi 110 007

In memory of the pioneers

V.P. VASIL'EV

and

A. SCHIEFNER

FRONTISPIECE

It was part of the original plan of this publication to add at the end of the book the entire xylograph of the Tibetan text (Potala 1946 edition, which is mainly followed in the present translation) in photo-offset reproduction. Unfortunately, the trial reproduction of the xylograph from the micro-film copy in possession of the editor proved a failure and the idea of reproducing the entire xylograph had to be abandoned. As the frontispiece of the book, however, are reproduced from half-tone blocks only the beginning and end of the xylograph. These include the title-page and Folios 1,139B and 140A—the last containing the colophon specially added to the Potala edition of the text.

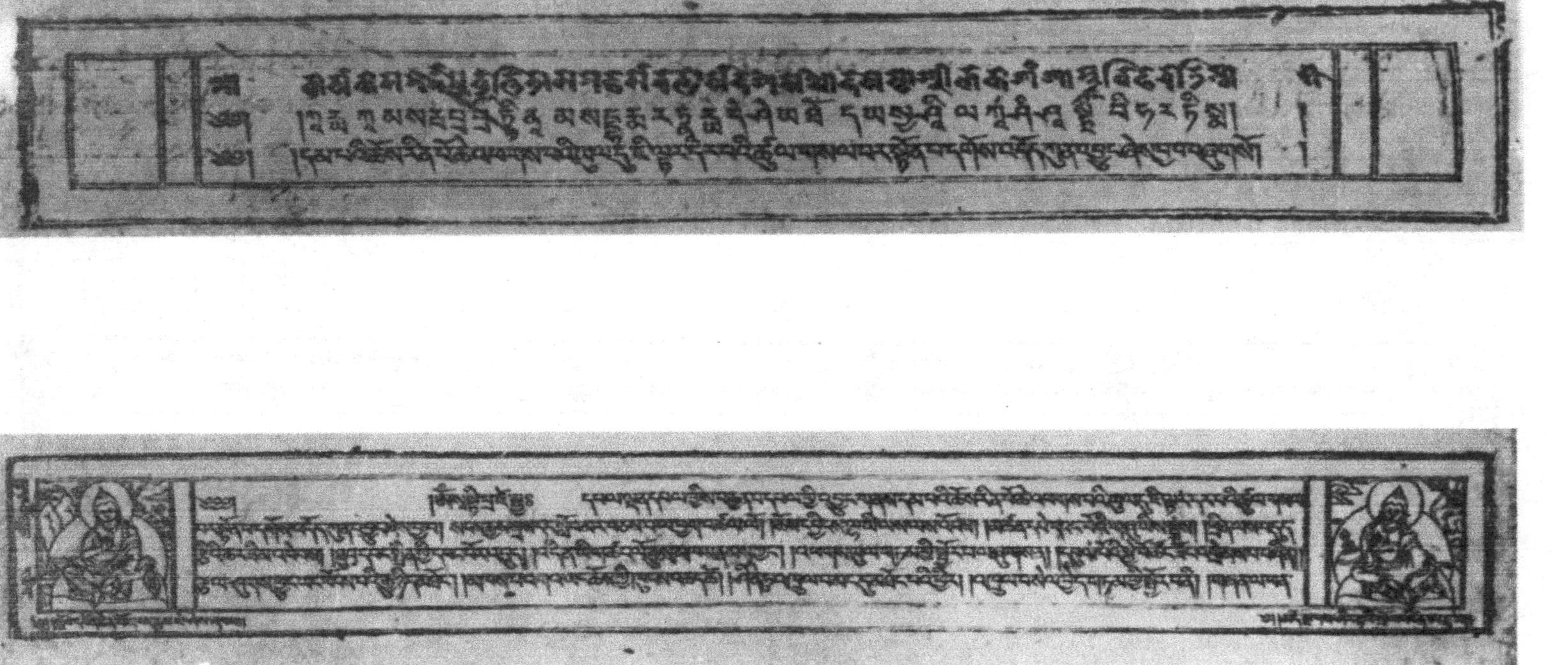

Top : Title page of the work (Potala edition). Bottom : Folio 1 of the same.
On the reverse side : Folios 139B & 140A, the latter containing the colophon of the Potala edition.

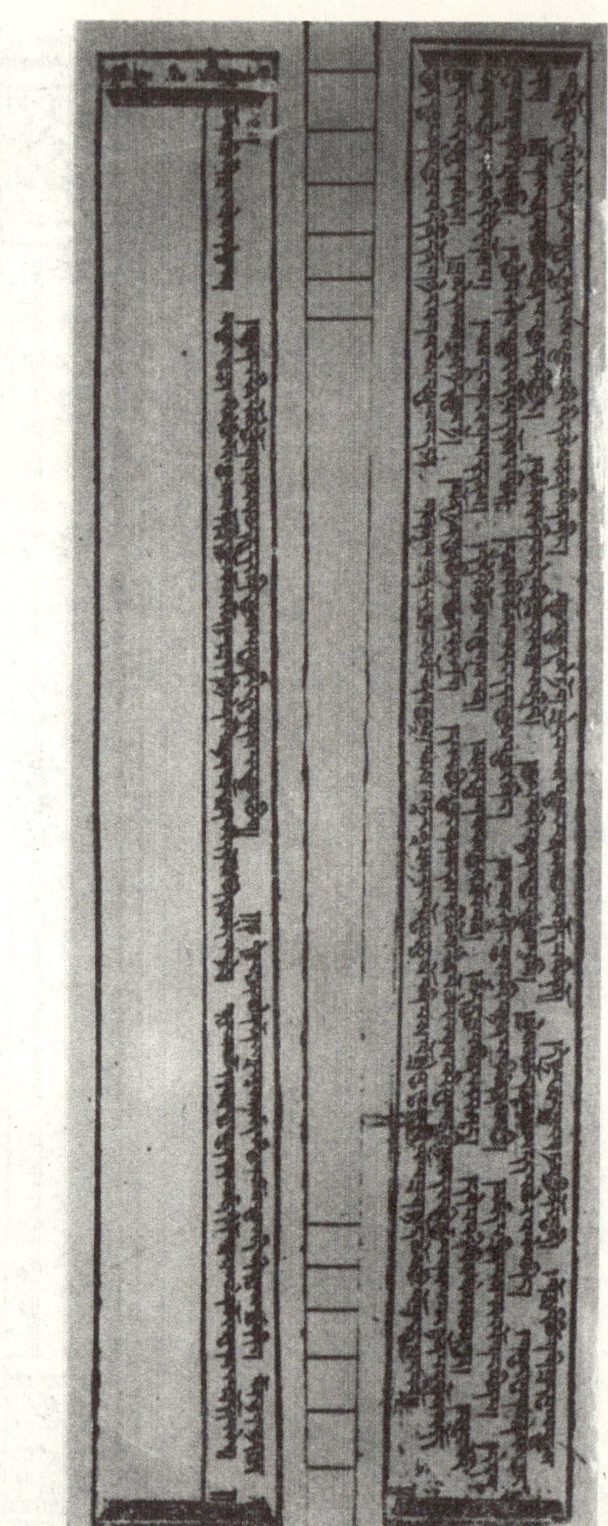

FOREWORD

When I walk on snow-laden paths of hills my each footprint appears clear, deep and distinct through which I can trace my path back without effort. But after a while due to wind and fresh snowfall all traces of my footsteps are wiped out in the snow. The residue is what sticks to my imagination. It is the same with the study of history. Every episode in it howsoever realistic, does fade with the sweep of time and occurrences of new events. Surviving evidences largely depend on interpretation of the historian whose reason emanates from intellect and as such has the glaring weakness of limitations of one's mind which are conditioned by the present environment.

The general attitudes and outward expressions of men of our time cannot be similar to those of the primitive society or even of the preceding generations. Thus, the logic of today recalling the events of the past times with indecisive evidences must surely be inaccurate in many ways.

The line of demarcation between history and legend is too thin to observe while writing; the two overlap each other unconsciously and unknowingly.

Faith and reason overpower each other throughout one's life, which results in contradiction, but the conflict never ceases in any sphere. As such, it is difficult to say if the author of a book of history is free from the influence of his faith in analysing the past.

I know many such persons who do not accept in their writings many episodes as historical in order to exhibit their rational mind and modern scholarship. But in the core of their hearts they believe the episodes *in toto* and do respect them. Such proclivities in authors are nothing short of dishonesty.

As we focus our vision on the historical perspective of our time interspersed with strong socio-economic bias of the historian for recording past events to suit their political ideologies, we can sense the real flaw in the cross currents of historical literature and that takes us into a land of phantasy.

In this situation I cannot claim Lama Târanâtha to be free from all those conditions which make me ponder, but I can unhesitatingly say that his rationality and honesty to his own findings are beyond cavil, a thing which held him high in the assessment of his contemporaries.

I entirely agree with V.P. Vasil'ev that the history of Tāranātha is not history as such but history in the sense of a document that calls for further research in history. Straightway, this notion of an acute historiographer claims for specialisation in the field of an independent discipline. We should not be oblivious of the fact that Tāranātha's work does not aim at revealing the past in the strict sense of a modern history, his work vouchsafes better and more clear understanding of the lineages and developments of the virtuous Buddhists with a view to strengthening the faith (*śraddhā*) in lineage of teachers as well as distinguishing the right lineages from the fake ones. We may thus assume the work to be a part or outcome of his own spiritual practices.

A reader of Tāranātha's work should bear in mind that he is reading a Buddhist treatise composed by a great devotee of Buddha who earnestly wishes to intensify faith in the lineage. But at the same time a reader may find in it useful material for historical purposes also. With this approach one may succeed in evaluating the work of Tāranātha in right perspective. It is also noteworthy that Tāranātha made an attempt to keep the episodes at conventional level. Tāranātha disavowed many well known legends specially with regard to the extraordinary length of the life-span of many personages and saw that the sequence of the lineages did not distort the chronology. But in one thing he remained an avowed Tibetan as he did not ignore or refute miracles (*ṛiddhi*). He admitted the power of *ṛiddhi* not as something supernatural but as perfectly natural. Such view is possible for a person who himself had possessed direct experience of it.

Lama Tāranātha was the most suitable person of his age to write an account of the development of Buddhist teachings in India due to following reasons:

1) He was vitally interested in writing accounts of the past and the lives of personages of lineages.

2) He had mastery over Sanskrit and also knew some of the Indian dialects prevalent at that time.

3) He had moreover access to the authentic works of Pandits, viz. Kṣemendrabhadra, Indradatta and Bhataghati.

For modern scholarship it would have been much better if

Târanâtha had translated all the source materials into Tibetan language instead of writing his account based on them. Besides, Târanâtha has also not thrown any light on the lives of the Pandits from whose works he has freely drawn. So, neither can we trace the lives and works of those Pandits who are mentioned by him nor have we any access to their works.

In his autobiography called *The Secret Biography* Lama Târanâtha records that without any formal instructions from any teacher he effortlessly acquired proficiency in various Indian languages. When he was just four years old, he overheard the conversation of Venerable Tenzin Ngawang with an Indian Zoki (Yogi) and he could understand the substance of it. He further says that because of his many previous births in India he had vivid recollection of geography and topography of the country and knowledge of various Indian languages since his childhood. At 16, he was prophesied by his personal deity (*iṣṭadeva*) that if he chose to go to Zanskar in Ladakh and Gar-Sha (presently in Himachal Pradesh) before he was twenty years old, he would accumulate merit to do immense service to the sentient beings. But since the prophecy remained unimplemented he thought his life work could not be so prolific. Further he tells that while in his twenties he once fell sick with constant bleeding through his nostrils for about three months. At that time in a dream he saw two Indian yogis. One of them named Jvâlânâtha gave him the name Târanâtha. "Târanâtha" is purely an Indian name. It does not correspond to his original Tibetan name.

It appears that in Târanâtha's time Indian pilgrims and other visitors used to trail the passes to reach the land of snow, although by that time very few Buddhist scholars were left in India. Most of the travellers who visited Tibet were not the followers of Buddhism. This is clear from Târanâtha's autobiography in which he refers to two Pandits, Purnananda and Paramananda who stayed with him for about ten days. He talks of their great erudition in various subjects. He learnt the episodes of the *Rāmāyaṇa* and *Mahābhārata* from them. Being persuaded by them to worship Hanumân, Târanâtha did not accede to their desire. The only likelihood of meeting with a Buddhist Yogi from Telangana (India) occurs in an allusion to such an ascetic Pandit Changaśrī who stayed for only two days with Târanâtha but who was in a hurry to go back to India. Changaśrī was considered as a Mahāyāna Buddhist scholar by Tāranātha. Although he did not visit India during his life time, yet it seems that he was known to many Indian scholars and rulers. Tāranātha tells in his *Autobiography* that he got a letter from Raja Balabhadra of Badua of the Vindhya Hills which was written in Sanskrit in the Gaudi script. The content of the letter is as follows:

"I hear that you are the only person in Himavat (snowland) who has preserved the tradition of Siddha Śāntigupta. I have also known from the Siddhas that you have had close relationship with me in other births. Therefore, I am sending you two "batol jarb" and two "Suryakanta".

A reply was sent by Tāranātha, the purport of which is as follows:

"When the Buddha's doctrine is languishing in India you are the only king who is reviving the *Saddharma* in the Vindhyas and the contiguous regions."

The name of the messenger who brought the letter and the gift from Raja Balabhadra is recorded as Illikhan.

The above episode is difficult to verify but it shows Tāranātha's contacts with Indian scholars and rulers. Among the works of Tāranātha we have no text translated by him, but he mentions in his Autobiography that he did translations of minor texts also. He relates to have studied several Sanskrit manuscripts belonging to Atisa which he found preserved in the Rading Monastery. His scholarship of Sanskrit is evidenced from many of his extensive works on the *Kālacakra Tantra* and other philosophical texts.

Till recent times Tibetan scholars did not take much notice of Tāranātha's *History of Buddhism in India*. Tāranātha is widely known in Tibet for his works on Tantra and Philosophy. It seems Tāranātha himself did not give importance to *History of Buddhism in India*, as he does not make any mention of it in his autobiography whereas he refers to most of his important works with details of time and circumstances which prompted him to write. But strangely modern scholars know Tāranātha by the present work alone, and despite the alleged limitation of Tāranātha as historian scholars invariably refer to Tāranātha's *History of Buddhism*.

I personally do not attach much importance to the fact whether Tāranātha's work is history or a religious document.

The importance of the work of Tāranātha which is modest in comparison to his other works lies in the fact that it has contributed extensively to the Indian Studies in general and the Buddhist Studies in particular in the recent time.

Tāranātha in his autobiography lays emphasis on his utter honesty, straightforwardness and impartiality in his writings for which he is proud. He also pays his deep respect to all the lineages of various Buddhist scholars. All these facts of Tāranātha are substantiated by his extensive works relating to a diversity of subjects ranging from his random Psalms and Verses (*dohās* and *gāthās*) to the most sophisticated philosophical and Tāntrika treatises, including commentaries of *sūtras* and *tantras* besides his original compositions.

Thus I can say with much confidence that *History of Buddhism in India* written by Tāranātha is a faithful recounting of Indian source materials to which Tāranātha had an access and there is no scope of distortion of facts in his narratives.

This English translation of Tāranātha's *History of Buddhism in India* belongs, indeed, to the class of finest translations of Tibetan works in English. The age-old tradition of Tibetan translation of treatises with one Pandit of the source language and one translator of the destination language and a third person for checking and editing has been faithfully preserved in the preparation of this work. Lama Chimpa, an erudite scholar of Tibetan studies who is also well-versed in English, has acted as the *Pandita*, Alaka Chattopadhyaya, an erudite scholar of English and History with copious grasp of the Tibetan language has worked as *lotsava* (translator). Further the work has been edited by a scholar of great eminence, Professor Debiprasad Chattopadhyaya, who worked as *Shuchain* (reviser). The supplementary notes and appendices have much enhanced the value of the present work. I am happy to know that the book which has been out of print for a long time is now being reprinted for the great benefit of scholars and students.

May all sentient beings be happy!

Sarnath
7th December, 89

S. Rinpoche

CONTENTS

Foreword xi

Preface xxiii

Acknowledegement xxxi

On Typography and abbreviations, etc 1

TĀRANĀTHA'S HISTORY OF BUDDHISM IN INDIA

Introductory 5

Benedictory Verse 5

Aim of the Work 5

Table of Contents 6

The Sources 19

Ch. 1.
Account of the Period of King Ajātaśatru 20

Ch. 2.
Account of the Period of King Subāhu 26

Ch. 3.
Account of the Period of King Sudhanu 29

Ch. 4.
Account of the Period of Ārya Upagupta 34

Ch. 5.
Account of the Period of Ārya Dhītika 45

Ch. 6.
Account of the Period of King Aśoka 50

Ch. 7.
Account of the Incidents During the Period of King Aśoka 68

Ch. 8.
Account of the Period of King Vigataśoka 76

Ch. 9.
Account of the Period of Kāśyapa, the Second 79

Ch. 10.
Account of the Period of Ārya Mahāloma and Others 82

Ch. 11.
Account of the Period of King Mahāpadma 85
Ch. 12.
Account of the Period of the Third Council 91
Ch. 13.
Account of the Period of the Beginning of the Extensive Propagation of the Mahāyāna 96
Ch. 14.
Account of the Period of Brāhmaṇa Rāhula 102
Ch. 15.
Account of the Period of the Doctrine Under the Leadership of Ārya Nāgārjuna 106
Ch. 16.
Account of the Period of the First Hostility to the Law and of its Restoration 120
Ch. 17.
Account of the Period of Ācārya Āryadeva and Others 123
Ch. 18.
Account of the Period of Ācārya Mātṛceṭa and Others 130
Ch. 19.
Account of the Period of the Renewed Hostility to the Doctrine and of its Restoration 137
Ch. 20.
Account of the Period of the Third Hostility to the Doctrine and of its Restoration 140
Ch. 21.
Account of the Period of the Final Activities of King Buddhapakṣa and of the period of King Karmacandra 144
Ch. 22.
Account of the Period of 'Brothers Ārya Asaṅga' [Asaṅga and Vasubandhu] 149
Ch. 23.
Account of the Period of Ācārya Dignāga and Others 176
Ch. 24.
Account of the Period of King Śila 196

Ch. 25.
Account of the Period of the Kings Cala, Pañcamasiṃha and Others 210
Ch. 26.
Account of the Period of Śrī Dharmakīrti 224
Ch. 27.
Account of the Period of King Govicandra and Others 249
Ch. 28.
Account of the Period of King Gopāla 257
Ch. 29.
Account of the Period of King Devapāla and His Son 265
Ch. 30.
Account of the Period of King Śrī Dharmapāla 274
Ch. 31.
Account of the Period of King Masurakṣita, King Vanapāla and the Great King Mahīpāla 284
Ch. 32.
Account of the Period of the Kings Mahāpāla and Śāmupāla 289
Ch. 33.
Account of the Period of King Canaka 294
Ch. 34.
Account of the Period of Kings Bheyapāla and Neyapāla 304
Ch. 35.
Account of the Period of Āmrapāla, Hastipāla and Kṣāntipāla 310
Ch. 36.
Account of the Period of King Rāmapāla 313
Ch. 37.
Account of the Period of the Four Sena Kings and Others 316

TĀRANĀTHA'S SUPPLEMENT TO THE HISTORY OF BUDDHISM IN INDIA

Ch. 38.
Account of the Succession of Teachers at Vikramaśila 325
Ch. 39.
Account of the Spread of the Doctrine in Ko-ki in the East 330

Ch. 40.
Account of the Introduction of the Law into the Smaller Islands and of its Revival in the South 332
Ch. 41.
Account of the Spread of the Doctrine in the South as Related in *The Garland of Flowers* 334
Ch. 42.
Some Discussion on the Four Sects 339
Ch. 43.
A Brief Discourse on the Origin of the Mantrayāna 343
Ch. 44.
The History of Image-makers 347

On the Sources etc 350
Epilogue 351
Colophon 352
Colophon of the Potala edition 352

SUPPLEMENTARY NOTES

1. The Patriarchs 355
2. The Aśoka Legends 361
3. Ten Prohibitions and the Second Council 367
4. Tiṣyarakṣitā & Kuṇāla Legend 373
5 Mahādeva and his Five Principles 375
6. Kaniṣka's Council : Yuan-Chuang & Bu-ston 377
7. Vararuci 381
8. Saraha 382
9. Nāgārjuna : Biographical 383
10. Nāgārjuna : Works 385
11. Āryadeva 387
12. Obermiller's Note on the Mādhyamika Ācārya-s and their different points of view 388
13. Nāgabodhi 389
14. Śākyamitra 389
15. Śabarapāda 390
16. Mātṛceta 390
17. Aśvaghoṣa & Mātṛceṭa 391
18. Śūra 392
19. Aśvaghoṣa 392
20. Lūi-pā 393
21. Asaṅga 393
22. Maitreya 394
23. Vasubandhu 395
24. Vasil'ev on the Two Vibhaṅgas 398
25. Dārika-pā 398
26. Sthiramati 399
27. Dignāga 400
28. Bhavya or Bhāvaviveka 401
29. Candrakīrti 401
30. Candragomī 402

31. Dharmapāla 403
32. Virū-pā 404
33. Śāntideva 405
34. Dombī Heruka 405
35. Vajraghaṇṭa 406
36. Ratnakīrti 406
37. Dharmakīrti 407
38. Kambala 408
39. Indrabhūti 409
40. Kukuri-pā 410
41. Saroruhavajra 410
42. Lalitavajra 411
43. Jālandhari-pā 412
44. Kṛṣṇācārī 412
45. Sahajalalita 413
46. Vinītadeva 414
47. Jñānagarbha 414
48. Buddhajñāna 415
49. Śāntarakṣita 415
50. Haribhadra 416
51. Yaśomitra 416
52. Śākyamitra 417
53. Kalyāṇamitra 417
54. Daṃṣṭrāsena 417
55. Mañjuśrīkīrti 418
56. Līlāvajra 418
57. Paṇḍita Rāhula 418
58. Kalyāṇagupta 419
59. Prabhākara 419
60. Buddhaguhya 419
61. Vairocanabhadra 421
62. Kamalaśīla 421
63. Dharmottara 422
64. Vimalamitra 422
65. Dharmākara 423
66. Ānandagarbha 423
67. Parahita 424
68. Jinamitra 425
69. Sarvajñadeva 425
70. Tilli-pā 426
71. Prajñāpālita ·426
72. Jetāri 426
73. Kālacakrapāda 427
74. Śānti-pā 428
75. Vāgīśvarakīrti 428
76. Nāro-pā 429
77. Bodhibhadra 429
78. Ratnavajra 430
79. Mahājana 430
80. Jñānaśrī 430
81. Amoghavajra 431
82. Vīryabhadra 431
83. Maṇikaśrī 432
84. Jñānavajra 432
85. Bhārata Paṇi 433
86. Abhayākaragupta 433
87. Śākyaśrī 434
88. Ratnarakṣita 435
89. Dīpaṃkarabhadra 436
90. Śrīdhara 436
91. Bhavabhadra 436
92. Durjayacandra 437
93. Tathāgatarakṣita 437
94. Kamalarakṣita 438
95. Khyuṅ-po-rnal-'byor 438
96. Vanaratna 440
97. Sahajasiddhi 441
98. The Turuṣka king 'Moon' (Fol 125B) 442
99. History of Image-makers 445

APPENDIX

A. Schiefner, *Foreword to the Introduction of the Russian Translation of Tāranātha's History of Buddhism in India by Professor Wassiljew (Vasil'ev)* 449

V. P. Vasil'ev, *Introduction to the Russian translation of Tāranātha's History of Buddhism in India* 453

Bibliography 471

Index

Errata

PREFACE

Born in A.D. 1575, Kun-dga'-sñiṅ-po (= Ānandagarbha), better known as Lama Tāranātha, wrote this work in 1608, i.e. at the age of 34, according to the Tibetan mode of calculating the age. This work is usually referred to as *rGya-gar-chos-'byuṅ*, which means "the history of Buddhism in India". But the brief title Tāranātha himself chose for it was *dGos-'dod-kun-'byuṅ*, literally "that which fulfils all desires". The corrupt Indian form in which the name occurs in the title-page of its Potalá edition (1946), namely *Kārya-kāma-sarva-pravṛtti-nāma*, is evidently intended to convey the same idea. Thus the history of Buddhism in India was for Tāranātha something more than mere history. It was also the *māhātmya* of Buddhism : the account was intrinsically auspicious, so much so that it led to the fulfilment of all desires. But there is nothing extraordinary about this. As Vasil'ev (spelt Wassiljew in German) rightly remarks, historiography for the Buddhists had always been an important mode of propagating their creed.

In Tibetan writings Tāranātha is usually mentioned as "Jo-naṅ Tāranātha" or "rje-btsun (= bhaṭṭāraka) Tāranātha of the Jo-naṅ sect". Jo-naṅ is the name of a place with a lofty *caitya* and a convent about a hundred miles to the north-west of the Tashi-lhun-po. The sect of Tibetan Buddhism which had Jo-naṅ as its stronghold came to be known as the Jo-naṅ-pa sect. The founder of this sect was Phyogs-las-rnam-rgyal (= Digvijayī), born in A.D. 1306. It appears that a pronounced enthusiasm for the Kālacakra Tantra constituted an important feature of its creed. Tāranātha himself, a later leader of the sect, was famous as an author of several works and "guide-books" (*khrid-yid*) on the Kālacakra doctrine, which Roerich wanted to analyse—a project unfortunately left unfinished by him.

The chief monastery of the Jo-naṅ-pa sect—rTag-brtan-phun-tshogs-gliṅ (= the perfect and eternally firm island)—had a printing establishment well-known in Tibet. The complete works of Tāranātha were published by it. A copy of this is preserved in the Tsybikov Collection, Institute of the Peoples of Asia (now renamed as the Institute of Oriental Studies), USSR. A. I. Vostrikov gives us the following information about Tāranātha's works from this collection.

The present history of Buddhism consisting of 143 folios is contained in the sixteenth volume of Tāranātha's collected works, the same volume also containing in 70 folios the work (written in A.D. 1600) with the brief title *bKa'-babs-bdun-ldan*, translated into German by A. Grünwedel. The first volume of the collected works contains a detailed autobiography of Tāranātha in 331 folios, the second volume contains a history of the Kālacakra system in 22 folios, the tenth volume contains a history of the Yamāntaka Tantra in 74 folios (its colophon giving the date of the composition as A.D. 1631) and the twelfth volume contains a history of the cult of Tārā in 20 folios. From these one can easily judge how voluminous a writer Tāranātha was and in what constituted his main interest.

By courtesy of the Institute of the Peoples of Asia, Leningrad, I obtained a microfilm copy of the so-called "secret" biography (*gsaṅ-ba'i-rnam-thar*) of Tāranātha written by himself: though brief, it is so full of the so-called mystic or occult experience and a quaint vision, that we had to give up our original idea of appending its translation to the present edition. Such mystic stuff is not easy to translate and, if translated at all, would not make much sense for the modern reader. Incidentally, in Northern Mongolia (Urga) the incarnations of Lama Tāranātha are supposed to have resided even in recent times!

The original printing blocks of Tāranātha's works were largely destroyed "during the persecution of the Jo-naṅ-pa sect in the time of the Fifth Dalai Lama (Ňag-bdaṅ-blo-bzaṅ-rgya-mtsho: A.D. 1617-1682) in the first half of the 17th century A.D. The Karma-pa and the Jo-naṅ-pa sects supported the ruler of Tsaṅ [i.e. a central province of Tibet of which the chief city is Shiga-tse, adjoining which stands the grand monastery of Tashi-lhun-po, the seat of the Tashi Lama] and thus incurred the enmity of Lhasa and of the dGe-lugs-pa sect [i e. the most dominant sect of Tibetan Buddhism usually referred to by the European authors as the Yellow Cap sect]. In the chief monastery of the (Jo-naṅ-pa) sect, rTag-brtan-phun-tshogs-gliṅ, were preserved the printing blocks of the works of Tāranātha. Many of the printing blocks were destroyed and the monastery itself was renamed [as dGa'-ldan-phun-tshogs-gliṅ]."

Apparently, over two centuries later the Lhasa rulers realised that at least Tāranātha's history of Buddhism in India was too precious to be allowed to remain out of circulation. Hence in 1946 a fresh edition of the work was prepared in Potala in 141 folios. The present translation follows mainly this edition, though it also takes note of the first letter-press edition of the Tibetan text published from St. Petersburg in 1868 as edited by A. Schiefner. There exists another letter-press edition of the work published from Varanasi in 1963 as edited by Chos-rje-bla-ma. This edition, however, appears to have been intended as a literal reproduction of the Potala edition of 1946.

Tāranātha's *History* is surely one of the most widely discussed works in contemporary Indology. The modern scholars owe their information of it mainly to A. Schiefner and V. P. Vasil'ev. Their German and Russian translations of the work appeared from St. Petersburg in 1869. As to their mutual relation and the circumstances that led them to take up these translations, it is best to follow their own statements. These are to be found appended to the present work. Readers are moreover likely to find the introduction of Vasil'ev to Tāranātha's *History* illuminating in many respects.

Schiefner's German and Vasil'ev's Russian apart, the only complete translation of Tāranātha's *History* exists in the Japanese language : the translation was done by Enga Teramoto, it contains 404 pages and was published from Tokyo in 1928 by Heigo Shuppan-sha. From a stray reference it appears that the great Indian linguist Harinath De started translating

Tāranātha's *History* directly from Tibetan into English and that at least some pages of this translation appeared in a journal called *The Herald*, January 1911. Any copy of this journal is hard to trace and it appears that this was one of the innumerable projects left unfinished by the great linguist. Only the other day, we received the heartening news that a few pages of this translation (? all that the great linguist translated) have been recovered and that these are going to be reprinted in the forthcoming issue of the *Journal of Ancient Indian History*, Calcutta University.

While preparing the present translation, our main purpose has been to make the work as intelligible as we could for the modern reader. This means much more than the task of transferring a text from one language into another. Tāranātha's statements could be made more intelligible only by annotating these extensively, and this mainly by way of collecting other materials that have some light to throw on his statements. The limitation of the annotations given by us is obvious and none can perhaps be more keenly aware of it than we are. We have dared to present this translation in spite of the obvious inadequacy of the annotations mainly with the hope of attracting the attention of the really great scholars from whom are expected profound comments. These alone would make the text more intelligible. As for our own annotations, we are anxious to be clear about a few points.

First, we have attempted to incorporate into our annotations practically all the important annotations of Vasil'ev and Schiefner. Though a hundred years old, these annotations contain much more than mere historic interest. These have often vital relevance for understanding Tāranātha properly. Secondly, we have, in our annotations, mentioned practically all the major points on which the present translation differs from those of Vasil'ev and Schiefner. Though fully aware of the rather severe comments of eminent Tibetologists like A.I. Vostrikov and E.E. Obermiller on the accuracy of the translations of both Vasil'ev and Schiefner, we are also aware that these translations substantially helped the later compilers of the standard Tibetan dictionaries like Jaschke and Das. Therefore, the purpose of pointing out where the present translation differs from that of Vasil'ev or Schiefner is not necessarily to claim greater accuracy in favour of the present translation. On the contrary, our own experience is that Tāranātha's Tibetan is often hard to understand and it is sometimes difficult to be sure of the exact sense he wants to convey, particularly because of some peculiar ambiguities of the classical Tibetan language. While presenting the present translation, the possibility of an alternative understanding of some of the passages is taken into consideration and it has been but our simple duty to mention such alternatives as actually suggested by the great pioneers. Thirdly, our annotations have sometimes assumed the form of long quotations from the writings of eminent modern scholars. The reason for quoting them at such length has simply been the anxiety to allow them to speak in their own language, so that the risk of misrepresenting their point could be eliminated.

It is not for us to answer the question how Tāranātha's account of Buddhism, in spite of being so overwhelmingly legendary, could also become one of the most widely discussed texts for the modern scholars working on diverse aspects of ancient and medieval Indian history and culture. Writers on the political history of India find themselves obliged to take note of Tāranātha's *History*, no less than those writing the history of Indian literature and Indian logic, not to speak of the investigators of the history of Buddhism itself. Apparently, along with all sorts of quaint stories, Tāranātha somehow or other managed to squeeze into this brief work a tremendous amount of solid historical data (and interesting Indian folklore) which are not easy to trace in other available sources. The very attempt to reconstruct a connected account from the time of Ajātaśatru to that of the Turuṣka invasion—in the background of which Tāranātha wants us to understand the history of Buddhism in India—appears to us to be an amazing intellectual performance, particularly when we remember that it was done in A.D. 1608 by a Tibetan scholar in his early thirties. Of course, as Vasil'ev rightly remarks, it is not to be taken as a finished history, but rather as a draft demanding a great deal of further investigation and that the importance of the work lies more particularly in its chapters covering the period intervening between the visit of Yuan-chuang and the virtual extinction of Buddhism in India.

Of the varied suggestions given by Tāranātha regarding this period, we may mention here only one. He left for us, though in his own way, clear indications of the factors that contributed to the decline and fall of Buddhism in India. Buddhism in its latest phase, as Tāranātha so vividly described it, almost completely surrendered precisely to those beliefs and practices, as a direct rejection of which the Buddha himself had preached his original creed. For all we know, it was a creed concerned above all with the fact of suffering and with the way out of suffering. As Stcherbatsky puts it, "It can hardly be said to represent a religion. Its more religious side, the teaching of a path, is utterly human. Man reaches salvation by his own efforts, through moral and intellectual perfection. Nor was there, for aught we know, very much of a worship in the Buddhism of that time. The community consisted of recluses possessing neither family nor property, assembling twice a month for open confession of their sins and engaged in the practice of austerity, meditation and philosophic discussions." The Buddha preached all these precisely because he had realised the futility of worshipping God or a host of demi-gods, offering sacrifices to them or trying to coerce them with magical rituals. For the Buddha himself, these beliefs and practices were characteristics of the *tīrthika*-s or outsiders. By contrast, Buddhism in its latest phase—if we are to trust Tāranātha—bowed down to all these beliefs and practices and thus became practically indistinguishable from popular Hinduism so-called. It assumed the form of being an elaborate worship of all sorts of gods and goddesses of the popular pantheon—often under new names, but sometimes caring not even to invent any new name for them—and of indulging in all sorts of ritual practices for which the

Buddha himself had expressed his unambiguous repulsion. Thus, e.g., the Vikramaśila-vihāra, the last grand centre of Buddhism established in India, had even the provision for a Bali-ācārya and a Homa-ācārya! Buddhajñānapāda, Tāranātha further tells us, persuaded king Dharmapāla to perform a *homa* for many years, during which period the king spent over nine lakh and two thousand *tolā*-s of silver—and all these were designed to make his dynasty last longer! And so on. Evidently, the memory of the human founder of the creed and even the vestige of his essentially human teachings were fully lost to the Buddhists and their patrons when Buddhism assumed such a queer form. The ideology, in short, passed into its opposite, and being left with no internal justification to survive as a distinct creed, the only thing on which it could then thrive was the fad of some big patron, the Pālas being about the last of them. With the withdrawal or collapse of this patronage, Buddhism as a religion had to go into pieces.

Sharing fully the creed in its latest phase, Tāranātha is of course not expected to have realised all these. As far as he understood, therefore, the end of the Vikramaśila and the Odantapurī meant the end of Buddhism in India: with the fall of these two monasteries the Buddhist ācārya-s ran hither and thither, seeking shelter in Kashmir, Nepal and the Ko-ki countries. He does not ask himself how can a creed, so long as it possesses any inner vitality, become virtually extinct from such a vast country only with the fall of two centres situated somewhere in Bihar.

The causes that contributed to the internal decay of Buddhism in India constitute indeed an extremely important subject for investigation. Our historians are yet to work these out fully. Could it, however, be that at least one of the important causes of this was the continued patronage of merchants, feudal chiefs and monarchs, primarily on which Buddhism thrived for centuries? Being himself a devout Buddhist, Tāranātha dilated much on the account of such patronage. His enthusiasm for the financiers of Buddhism was hardly less than that for its actual exponents. What he did not note—and what we do not surely expect him to note—is that nothing could be more ruinous for an ideology than to have drawn its sanction only from such patronage. That is the surest way of getting alienated from the heart of the people, of becoming completely parasitical and of being left with no vitality of its own.

The account of any genuine popular enthusiasm for Buddhism—particularly in its later phase—is conspicuous by its absence from Tāranātha's *History*. What could be the real implication of this ? Did the later leaders of Indian Buddhism—dreaming in their all-found monasteries mainly of the easy ways of attaining miraculous powers—really ceased to think of the relevance of any genuine popular support for their creed ? Or was it only the historian's blindness to notice their care for such popular support ? The chances in favour of the latter alternative are somewhat remote, for Tāranātha was much too saturated with the tradition of the later Indian Buddhists to overlook anything considered important by them.

It is obviously not the place for us to try to go into this question in greater detail. What is relevant instead is simply to note that the decline of Buddhism in India is too important a subject to remain unsettled, and in order to settle it we cannot afford to ignore Tāranātha : he was about the only historian to have compiled for us—in his own way though—a vast amount of relevant data concerning Indian Buddhism in its latest phase, which are not easy to trace elsewhere.

May 26, 1970. *Debiprasad Chattopadhyaya*

ACKNOWLEDGEMENT

Without the encouragement and active help in various forms of Professor Niharranjan Ray, Director, Indian Institute of Advanced Study, Simla, it would have been most difficult for me to complete this work. I cannot be explicit enough about my indebtedness to him.

It is because of the kindness of Professor V. V. Balabushevich, Head of the Indian Department, Institute of the Peoples of Asia (now renamed Institute of Oriental Studies), Academy of Sciences, USSR, that I received a complete microfilm copy of the Potala (1946) edition of Tāranātha's xylograph preserved in the Roerich Collection of the Institute. I also received a complete microfilm copy of Vasil'ev's Russian translation of Tāranātha's *History* from Dr. I. D. Serebryakov of the same Institute. I take this opportunity of expressing my sincere gratitude to Professor Balabushevich and Dr. Serebryakov for these precious gifts.

The present work embodies the labour of over five years of Professor Lama Chimpa of the Visvabharati University and Dr. Alaka Chattopadhyaya of the Vidyasagar College for Women, Calcutta. They had to revise the translation several times Entrusted with the work of editing it, I had to be most exacting. If they have not felt exasperated it is primarily because of their devotion to the work itself, though partly also because of their personal relation to me. Professor Lama Chimpa happens to be one of my dearest friends and Alaka is my wife.

This work also embodies a great deal of labour of two other friends of mine, without whose help the editing itself would have been impossible. They are Haridas Sinharay, Department of Sanskrit, Central Calcutta College, and Harish Chandra Gupta of the National Library, Calcutta. Haridas Sinharay helped me to compare the present translation with Schiefner's German and every scrap of Schiefner's German incorporated into the present work is translated by him. Exactly in the same way, Harish Chandra Gupta helped me to compare the present translation with the Russian translation of Vasil'ev and every scrap of Vasil'ev's Russian incorporated into the present work is translated by him. But even that was not enough. Haridas Sinharay spared himself of no drudgery in seeing the book through the press and Harish Chandra Gupta prepared the Index, along with Dr. N. N. Bhattacharyya, Department of Ancient Indian History, Calcutta University.

In the matter of preparing the list of works of the Buddhist *ācārya*-s given in the Supplementary Notes, I received substantial help from Mrinalkanti Gangopadhyaya, Department of Sanskrit, Vidyasagar College, Calcutta, who also helped me in preparing the press copy of the text.

To Harbans Mukhia and Pranabranjan Ray I am indebted for two Supplementary Notes, printed with acknowledgement to them.

I take this opportunity of expressing my grateful thanks also to my friend Dr Mahadevprasad Saha, who has shown keen interest in the work throughout its progress and has extended his kind cooperation all through. I had also to depend substantially on the help of my friend Rama Krishna Maitra particularly in seeing the book through the press.

It makes me hesitate much to mention another name here, not because the help I received from him is not substantial but because his stature as a scholar is indeed too great to be freely associated with those of humble workers like us. Nevertheless, objectivity demands that I mention his name. He is Dr Suniti Kumar Chatterji, our National Professor in Humanities. Taking advantage of his paternal affection for us, myself and Alaka intruded upon his valuable time whenever we felt that something about the work was beyond our own depth. If we have pestered him too much, it is because of the indulgence he is in the habit of allowing to all students of Indian studies.

In a somewhat similar way, we did exploit the paternal affection also of Dr. A. P. Banerjee-Sastri, without whose academic help the present work would have remained more incomplete and unsatisfactory than it is.

Debiprasad Chattopadhyaya

TYPOGRAPHY, ABBREVIATIONS, ETC

1. Tāranātha gives the Indian names in three forms, namely—
   i) both as transliterated in Tibetan script and as translated into Tibetan language,
   ii) only as transliterated in Tibetan script, and
   iii) only as translated into Tibetan language.

In the present translation, the first form is indicated by double asterisks at the beginning of the name, the second by a single asterisk and the third by none. Thus—

   i) ★★Muditābhabhadra. In the text *muditābabhadra ste kun-tu-dga'-ba-bzaṅ-po*—Fol 49A.
   ii) ★Kṛṣṇarāja. In the text *krisṇarāja*—Fol 49A.
   iii) Aśoka. In the text *mya-ṅan-med*—Fol 2A.

2. Where Tāranātha mentions the names only in Tibetan translations, their possible Indian equivalents are given in the text of the present translation, indicating at the same time in the notes the Tibetan forms in which these are actually given by Tāranātha. Only when such Indian equivalents differ from those suggested by Vasil'ev and/or Schiefner, the equivalents they suggest are mentioned in the notes. In other cases, the equivalents given in the present translation may be taken as being the same.

3. Indian words other than proper names also occur in the text as transliterated in Tibetan characters. To indicate these, a single asterisk is put at their beginning. Thus—

★ *paṇḍita*—Fol 23A
★ *śloka*—Fol 32A
★ *ṭaṅkā*—Fol 72B.

4. In the Tibetan text, the number and title of each chapter occur at its end in the form of a brief colophon. Vasil'ev follows only the modern European principle of putting the chapter heading at the beginning of each chapter. Roerich, however, in his translation of the *Biography of Dharmasvāmin* (Patna 1959) follows a principle which appears to be more satisfactory and hence is adopted here. Over and above giving the chapter heading in the European form, he adds at the end of each chapter the translation of the colophon as actually occurring in the text.

5. Folio-beginnings of the Potala edition of the xylograph—on which the present translation is based—are indicated by bold letters within square brackets.

6. References to the works in ***bsTan-'gyur*** (Tanjur) are according to Cordier's *Catalogue*.

7. Transliteration of Tibetan words is (broadly) based on the principles followed in *A Tibetan-English Dictionary* by S. C. Das.

8. Following are the main abbreviations used in the notes

BA—*The Blue Annals.*
Bu-ston—Bu-ston's *History of Buddhism* (tr Obermiller).
D—Das, S. C., *A Tibetan-English Dictionary.*
J—Jaschke, H. A., *A Tibetan-English Dictionary.*
Kg—*bKa'-'gyur* (Kanjur).
P-ed—Potala edition of Tāranātha's xylograph.
rG—rGyud-'grel.
S—Schiefner

Hence,

S-ed—Schiefner's edition of Tāranātha's text (1868)
S n— Schiefner's Note
S tr— Schiefner's translation.

Tār—Tāranātha
Tg—*bsTan-'gyur* (Tanjur)
V—Vasil'ev (in German, Wassiljew)

Hence,

V n—Vasil'ev's Note
V tr—Vasil'ev's translation.

For other authors and their works referred to in the notes, see *Bibliography*.

9. Comparatively longer annotations are given at the end of the book in the form of Supplementary Notes.

TĀRANĀTHA'S

History of Buddhism in India

(*tā-ra-nā-tha'i-rgya-gar-chos-'byuṅ-bshugs*)

INTRODUCTORY

[Fol 1]

oṃ svasti prajābhyaḥ

The clear exposition of how the precious gem of the True Doctrine—the glorious, the magnificent and the source of all glories—was spread in India (*ārya-deśa*), [is briefly] called the *dgos-'dod-kun-'byuṅ*.[1]

[BENEDICTORY VERSE]

Salutation to the Buddha and the Bodhisattvas along with their disciples. Salutation to the Greatest Sage (*munīndra*), who descends from the *dharmadhātu*[2] by the heavenly path and who—like the Lord of Clouds (*meghendra*)—decorated with the multi-coloured rainbow of *lakṣaṇa*-s[3] and *vyañjana*-s[4], showers the rain of nectar in the form of holy deeds.

[AIM OF THE WORK]

Even the learned (Tibetan) chroniclers and historians, when they come to discuss India, exhibit with their best efforts merely their poverty, like petty traders exhibiting their meagre stock. Some of the scholars, while trying to describe the origin of the Doctrine[5], are found to commit **[Fol 2A]** many a mistake. For the benefit of others, therefore, I am preparing this brief work with the mistakes eliminated.

1. Literally, 'that which fulfils all desires', hence translated by V as The Treasure of Wish-fulfilments. The title-page of the P-ed gives the (corrupt) Indian form of the short title as *Kārya-kāma-sarva-pravṛtti-nāma*, which suggests the same idea.
2. *chos-dbyiṅs*. The sphere or purview of religion—D 430.
3. The 32 holy marks of the Buddha—J 454.
4. The 80 physical perfections of the Buddha, described in the *Lalitavistara* as marks of secondary perfection—D 792.
5. The word *chos* is uniformly rendered as 'the Doctrine' (*dharma*), while *bstan-pa* as 'the Law' (*śāsana*).

[TABLE OF CONTENTS]

Here in brief is the necessary table of contents.

The descendants of the king Kṣemadarśin[6] (Ajātaśatru) were four—

Subāhu,[7]
Sudhanu,[8]
Mahendra[9] and
*Camaśa

And four of the successors[10] of Aśoka—

Vigataśoka,[11]
Vīrasena,[12]
Nanda[13] and
Mahāpadma.[14]

6. *mthoṅ-ldan-dge-ba.*
7. *lag-bzaṅ.* The reconstruction is after V & S It is difficult to guess the exact Indian names of the successors of Ajātaśatru that Tāranātha has in mind, particularly because the lists we come across in the *Mahāvaṃsa* and the *Purāṇa*-s do not concur.
8. *gshu-bzaṅ.*
9. *dbaṅ-chen.*
10. Aśoka's name is given in Tibetan as *mya-ṅan-med.* Tār is perhaps following here the prophecy of the *Mañjuśrī-mūla-tantra,* which is also followed by Bu-ston ii.118-9 and given in prose as follows : 'One hundred years after the Teacher will have passed away, in the city of Kusumapura there will appear the king Aśoka who will live 150 years and worship the monuments of the Buddha during 87 years. After him, the king named Vigataśoka will worship these monuments for 76 years. Thereafter, the king Vīrasena will rule for 70 years and will be succeeded by the king Nanda. The latter's reign will dure fiftysix years and his friend will be the *brāhmaṇa* Pāṇini. Then there will appear the king Candragupta, and after him his son called Bindusāra, who will rule for 70 years. The minister of these kings Cāṇakya, (owing to his deeds) will depart to hell.'
11. *mya-ṅan-bral.*
12. *dpa'-bo'i-sde.*
13. *dga'-bo.*
14. *padma-che-sde.*

Those who came in the *Candra dynasty were—

*Hari-,
*Akṣa-,
*Jaya-,
*Nema-,
*Phaṇī-,
*Bhaṃśa-(? Vaṃśa-),
*Sāla-, etc.

—to each of these is to be added *candra.

Then *Candragupta and Bindusāra[15] and his nephew[16] *Śrīcandra.

Then,

*Dharma-,
*Karma-,
*Vṛkṣa-,
*Vigama-,
*Kāma-,
*Siṃha-,[17]
*Bāla-,
*Vimala-,
*Govi-,
*Lalita-, etc.

—to each of these also is to be added *candra.

Without counting Bindusāra, there were nineteen bearing the name *candra. Among them,[18]

**Akṣacandra,
**Jayacandra,

15. *sñiṅ-po-thig-le.*

16. *tsha-bo* means both 'grandson' and 'nephew'. V & S take it here as nephew.

17. S-ed Siṃha, P-ed Piṅga. The former reading is followed, because in Fol 73B of P-ed also is mentioned Siṃha-candra (in transliteration) of the Candra Dynasty. V & S Siṃha.

18. P-ed : the names in the following list up to the Ten Candra-s occur both in translation and transliteration. S-ed : the names occur only in translation. But V says in his note that the text has these names in both forms.

**Dharmacandra,
**Karmacandra
**Vigama (-candra),
**Kāmacandra and
**Vimalacandra [Fol 2B]

—these were famed as the Seven *Candra-s.

**Candragupta, **Gobi (-candra) and **Lalitacandra, added to this list, make the famous Ten *Candra-s.

Those who came in the line of the *Pāla-s were fourteen—

*Gopāla-,
*Deva-,
*Rāsa-,
*Dharma-,
*Vana-,
*Mahī,
*Mahā,
*Śreṣṭha,
*Bheya
*Neya,
*Āmra,
*Hasti
*Rāma,
*Yakṣa,

—to all these is to be added *pāla.

The kings that came seperately[19] were—

Agnidatta,[20]
*Kaniṣka,
*Lakṣāśva
*Candanapāla,
*Śrīharṣa,
Śīla,[21]

19. *thor-bur-byuṅ-ba*. V translates 'temporarily' and explains 'not belonging to any dynasty or not having formed any and appearing in separate places'.

20. *mes-byin*.

21. *ṅaṅ-tshul*. V & S Śīla. See Bu-ston ii. 119.

Udayī, (Uttrāyana, Udayana),[22]
*Gauḍavardhana,
*Kanika,[23]
*Turuṣka,[24]
Turuṣka Mahāsammata,[25]
Buddhapakṣa,[26]
Gambhīrapakṣa,[27]
Cala,[28]
Caladhruva,[29]
*Viṣṇu,
Siṃha,[30]

22. S-ed *bde-spyod*, P-ed *bde-byed*. The former reading followed. In Fol 37A Tār gives the name as Uttrāyana, which, S says, is the usual form in which the name occurs in Tibetan works. In Tg *bde-spyod* is an equivalent of Udayī : mDo xciv. 27 *Suhṛllekha, ācārya-nāgārju-nena mitrāya udayirājñe prerita...lekha*; lit. reproduction mDo xxxiii. 32—*mahācārya-nāgārjunena mitrāya udayibhadrāya prerita lekha*. In both versions, the Tibetan equivalent of Udayī is *bde-spyod*. Obermiller (Bu-ston ii. 167) reconstructs *bde-spyod* as Udayana, which agrees with V & S. However, for the problem of identifying the Indian name of the addressee of Nāgārjuna's famous letter, see I-Tsing (Takakusu) 158f and 159n : Takakusu is inclined to identify the name as Sātavāhana, a corrupt form of which is Āntivāhana. cf also note 43 *infra*.
23. cf Fol 46A, where Tār says that this Kanika is not the same as king Kaniṣka, though this seems to go against the colophon of Mātṛceṭa's letter to Kaniṣka (Tg mDo xxxiii. 34 & xciv. 29), where the names Kanika and Kaniṣka occur interchangeably. For further discussion, see note 10 of chapter 18.
24. cf *Mañjuśrī-mūla-tantra* quoted by Bu-ston ii. 119, 'In the north, a king called Turuṣka is to live 300 years and after him he who is called Turuṣka Mahāsammata.'
25. *sog-po*, lit. the Mongol, Turuṣka, etc. V & S Śākya Mahāsammata. In Fol 53A, the name occurs as Turuṣka Mahāsammata.
26. *sans-rgyas-phyogs*.
27. *zab-mo'i-phyogs*. cf Bu-ston ii. 119.
28. *gyo-ba*. cf Bu-ston ii. 119.
29. *gyo-brtan* : *gyo* (to move), *brtan* (firm, the Pole Star, etc).
30. *sen-ge*. lit. 'the lion'.

*Bharśi (? Varṣa),[31]
Pañcamasiṃha,[32]
Prasanna,[33]
Pradyota,[34]
Mahāsena,[35]
Śākya Mahābala.[36]

In between the *Pala-s also came separately—

*Vasurakṣī (? Masurakiṣta)[37]
*Canaka,[38]
Śāmupāla,[39]
Kṣāntipāla,[40] etc.

There were four *Sena-s—

*Laba-,
*Kāsa- (? Kasa),
*Maṇita- and
*Rāthīka-.

31. The text has Bharśi. Can it be a corruption of Varṣa ? See J 386—the letter *bha* is sometimes written for *ba* (*va*) either from ignorance or in order to appear learned. Thus, Bhaṅgala for Baṅgala. However, both V & S Bharśa.
32. *seṅ-ge-lṅa*, lit. 'the five lions'. cf Bu-ston ii.118.
33. *gsal-ba*, lit. 'clear, bright' etc.
34. *rab-gsal*, lit. 'very clear'. Both V & S Prāditya. Roerich (BA ii.753) translates *rab-gsal* as Pradyota.
35. *sde-chen*, lit. 'the great group'.
36. *śakya-stobs-chen*. Both V & S Mahā Śākyabala.
37. P-ed Vasurakṣī. S-ed Masurakṣī. In Fol 111A the name is given as Masurakṣita in transliteration. V Masurakṣa. Tg (mDo cxxiii.33) contains a work called *Nīti-śāstra* attributed to Masurakṣa, *alias* Masurakṣī or Maṣa having the colophon : Masurakṣa-nīti (*masurakṣa'i lugs-kyi*).
38. *tsa-na-ka*. V & S Canaka, whose account is given in Fol 115A ff. This *tsa-na-ka* is not to be confused with *tsa-na-ka* (or Cāṇakya, see Bu-ston ii.119) mentioned in Fol 45B.
39. S-ed *gshoṅ-skyoṅ*, lit. Pātra-pāla. P-ed *shiṅ-skyoṅ*, lit. Kṣetrapāla. In Fol 113B the name occurs as Śāmupāla in transliteration, which agrees with V & S.
40. *bzod-pa-skyoṅ-ba*.

Those who ruled *Kāñcī etc in the south—

Śukla,[41]
Candraśobha,[42]
Sālavāhana (? Sātavāhana, Sālivāhana),[43]
Mahendra (? Maheśa),[44]
Śaṃkara (? Kṣemaṅkara, Udayana),[45]
Manoratha (? Manohara, Manojña),[46]
Bhoga-subāla,[47]
Candrasena,[48]
Kṣemaṅkarasiṃha (? Śaṃkarasiṃha),[49]
Vyāghra,[50]
*Budha,[51]
*Buddhaśuca,
Ṣaṇmukha,[52]
Sāgara,[53]

41. *dkar-po.*
42. *zla-mdses,* lit. 'the beautiful moon'.
43. P-ed *sā-la'i-bshon.* S-ed *sā-la'i-gshon.* The former means Sāla-vāhana, the latter Sāla-kumāra. V & S Salivāhana. In Fol 132A the name occurs as Sāla-vāhana both in translation and transliteration, perhaps as a corruption of Sātavāhana. Alberuni (Sachau i. 136) mentions Sātavāhana as Samalavāhana.
44. *dbaṅ-chen.* D 907 Mahendra. V & S Maheśa. In Fol 131A the name occurs as *dbaṅ-byed* (lit. 'one who subdues', 'one who accumulates power'.)
45. P-ed *sde-byed.* S-ed *bde-byed.* The former is an equivalent of Senakara, the latter of Śaṃkara or Kṣemaṅkara. In Fol 131A of P-ed also the name occurs as *bde-byed.* Hence this reading is followed. V & S Kṣemaṅkara.
46. *yid-'oṅ,* lit. 'handsome, delightful' etc. V & S Manoratha. Obermiller (Bu-ston ii. 96) reconstructs as Manojña. cf I-Tsing (Takakusu) xiii.
47. *loṅs-spyod-skra-bzaṅ,* lit. 'one who enjoys beautiful hair'. In Fol 131A the name occurs as Bhoga-subāla in transliteration.
48. *zla-ba'i-sde.*
49. *bde-byed-seṅ-ge.* V & S Kṣemaṅkarasiṃha.
50. *stag.* In Fol 131B the name occurs as Vyāghra-rāja in transliteration.
51. P-ed Buda, obviously a corruption of Budha, which occurs in Fol 131B.
52. *gdoṅ-drug,* lit. 'the six-faced one'. cf Fol 131B
53. *rgya-mtsho.*

Vikrama,[54]
Ujjayana,[55]
Śreṣṭha,[56]
Mahendra,[57]
Devarāja,[58]
Viśva,[59]
Śiśu,[60]
Pratāpa.[61]

The southern *brāhmaṇa*-s were—

Balamitra,[62]
Nāgaketu,[63]
Vardhamāla.[64]

The early great *ācārya*-s were—

*Gaggari,
Kumārānanda,[65]
Matikumāra,[66]
Bhadrānanda,[67] [Fol 3A]
Dānabhadra,[68]
*Laṅkādeva,

54. *rab-gnon*. But in Fol 131B, the name occurs as *rnam-gnon*, an equivalent of Vikrama.
55. *rgyal-mchog*. Both V & S Ujjayana, though S suggests Jinavara as an alternative.
56. *gtso-bo*.
57. *dbaṅ-chen*.
58. *lha-rgyal-po*.
59. *sna-tshogs*.
60. *byis-pa*.
61. *rab-gduṅ*.
62. *stobs-kyi-bśes-gñen*. In Fol 132A the name occurs as Balamitra in transliteration.
63. *klu'i-tog*. In Fol 132B the name occurs as Nāgaketu in transliteration.
64. *'phel-ba'i-phreṅ-ba*. In Fol 132B the name occurs as Vardhamāla in both transliteration and translation.
65. *gshon-nu-dga'*. In Fol 132B, Kumārānanda.
66. *blo-gshon*. In Fol 132B, Matikumāra.
67. *bzaṅ-po'i-kun-dga'*. In Fol 133A, Bhadrānanda.
68. *sbyin-bzaṅ*. In Fol 133A, Dānabhadra.

*Bahubhuja and
Madhyamati.[69]

If Madhyântika[70] is added to the very famous seven successors of the Teacher Jina, their number becomes eight.

The *arhat*-s who nourished the Law were—

Uttara,[71]
Yaśaḥ,[72]
Poṣada,[73]
Kâśyapa,[74]
Ślaṇavâsa,[75]
Mahâloma,[76]
Mahātyāga,[77]
Nandin,[78]
Dharmaśreṣṭhī,[79]
Pârśva,[80]
Aśvagupta[81] and
*Nanda.

69. *dbu-ma'i-blo.*
70. *ñi-ma-guṅ-ba.*
71. *bla-ma.*
72. *grags-pa.*
73. *bsos-byin.*
74. *'od-sruṅs.*
75. P-ed *yul-brlan.* In Fol 27A the name occurs as *yul-bslan-pa,* lit. 'one who unified the country'. In both places, S translates the name as Ślaṇavāsa, taking the word as a corruption of *sa-na-pa.* cf Bu-ston ii. 109, where Obermiller, on the evidence of Kg, reconstructs *yul-slan-pa* as Ślaṇavāsa. In Fol 5A, however, the Tibetan form of Śāṇavāsika occurs as *śa-na'i-gos-can.* V translates Ślaṇavāsa and says that it is nothing but an equivalent of Śaṇakavāsa.
76. *spu-chen-po.*
77. *gtoṅ-ba-chen-po.*
78. *dga'-ba-can.* Obermiller (Bu-ston ii. 109) reconstructs the name as Nandin.
79. *chos-kyi-tshoṅ-dpon,* lit. 'the pious merchant'. Both V & S Dharmaśreṣṭha. In Tg. (mDo lxxviii. 5 and xc. 9) Dharmaśreṣṭhin and Dharmaśreṣṭha are interchangeably mentioned.
80. *rtsibs-can.* Obermiller (Bu-ston ii. 108) takes *rtsibs* as Pārśva. V & S Pārśvika.
81. *rta-sbas.*

The great *bhaṭṭāraka*-s[82] were—

Uttara,[83]
Kāśyapa,[84]
Mahīśāsaka (? Bahuśāsaka),[85]
Dharmagupta,[86]
Suvarṣaka,[87]
Vatsīputra,[88]
Tâmraśāṭa,[89]
Vahuśruta,[90]
Dharmottara,[91]
Avantaka,[92]
Sañjaya,[93]

82. *btsun-pa-chen-po'i-sde-rnams*. S takes these as names of the 'schools' founded by the great *bhadanta*-s, ediventIy because of the use of the words *sde-rnams* in the text. But the same words occur in the list of the *brāhmaṇa*-s given immediately afterwards, where the sense of the 'school' is ruled out. It is, therefore, safer to take the words *sde-rnams* here as simply conveying the sense of the plural, though some of the names in the present list are those of the founders of the well-known eighteen sects (see Tāranātha Ch 42) while some other names here are not so. V translates *btsun-pa* as 'the elders' and adds in the note, 'By this term is meant the well-known persons of the Hīnayāna Buddhist hierarchy. They are below *arhat*-s, but they must be either from amongst the heads, founders of schools, propagators of the Doctrine or the authors.'
83.. *bla-ma*. cf Bu-ston ii. 96.
84. *'od-sruṅs*.
85. The text has *maṅ-ston* and *sa-ston*. Roerich (BA i. 28) takes both to mean Mahīśāsaka, though the literal meaning of the former seems to be Vahuśāsaka. S takes *maṅ-ston* as Sammitīyas and *sa-ston* as Mahīśāsakas. V Mahīśāsaka.
86. *chos-bsruṅs*.
87. *char-bzaṅ-'bebs*, lit. 'good shower'. V & S Suvarṣa.
88. *gnas-ma-bu*, lit. 'son of Vatsa'. S Vātsiputrīyas.
89. *gos-dmar-ba*, lit. 'one with red robe'. S Tāmraśāṭīyas.
90. *maṅ-thos*, lit. 'one with many listenings'. S Vahuśrutīyas.
91. *chos-mchog*.
92. *sruṅ-ba-pa*. D 717 Āvantaka. cf Bu-ston ii. 99.
93. *yaṅ-dag-rgyal-ba*, taken in Bu-ston ii. 109 as Sañjaya. S Jetavanīya, the usual Tibetan for which is *rgyal-byed-tshal-gnas-pa*—D 718 and Bu-ston ii. 99.

Sthavira,[94]
Dharmatrāta,[95]
Vasumitra,[96]
Ghoṣaka,[97]
Śrīlābha,[98]
Buddhadeva,[99]
Kumāralāta,[100]
Vāmana,[101]
*Kuṇāla,
Śubhaṅkara (? Kṣemaṅkara),[102]
Saṅghavardhana[103] and
Sambhūti (?).[104]

94. *gnas-brtan.*
95. *chos-skyob.*
96. *dbyig-bśes.* V Vasumitra. S Vasubandhu. But this name is not to be confused with that of the famous brother of Asaṅga, the usual Tibetan form of which is *dbyig-gñen.* Besides, in the *Table of Contents* Tār evidently includes Vasubandhu among the Six Jewels of Jambudvīpa. cf Fol 31B.
97. *dbyaṅs-sgrogs.*
98. *dpal-len.*
99. *saṅs-rgyas-lha.*
100. *gshon-nu-len,* lit. Kumāralābha. See Winternitz HIL ii. 268: 'Kumāralābha is only a wrong translation of the Chinese name given for Kumāralāta.—See Luders, *Bruchstucke der Kalpanāmaṇḍiṭikā des Kumāralāta,* Leipzig 1926, p. 20'. [cf Watters 1.244 : Kumāralabdha or Kou-mo-lo-lo-to.] S. C. Vidyabhusana HIL 248 overlooks this and accepts the form Kumāra-lābha or Kumāra-labdha. V & S Kumāra-lābha.
101. *mi'u-thuṅ.*
102. *dge-byed,* taken by both V & S as Śaṃkara, the usual Tibetan for which is *bde-byed.* The Tg contains a work by one *dge-byed* (rG lxxi. 106), the Sanskrit equivalent of which is given as Śubhaṅkara. But *dge-byed* may also be the Tibetan form of Kṣemaṅkara.
103. *dge-'dun-'phel.*
104. *bsam-rdsogs,* 'one with perfect thinking'. S Sambhūti and adds in the note : 'The Tibetan compound of *bsam-rdsogs* allows of such a translation. But I do not wish to commit to it as the safe one. A later Tibetan author has sought to translate it as Dhyāna-saṃskṛta —cf Thob-yig in the Asiatique Museum, No. 287, Fol 257a, line 3.'

The great *brāhmaṇa*-s who also worked for the Law were—

Jaya,[105]
Sujaya,[106]
Kalyāṇa,[107]
Siddha,[108]
Adarpa,[109]
*Rāghava,
Yaśasvin,[110]
*Paṇi (Pāṇini),
Vijña,[111]
Bhadra,[112]
Vararuci,[113]
*Śūdra,[114]
Kulika,[115]
Udbhaṭa [-siddhi-svāmin] (Mudgaragomin),[116]
Śaṃkara [-pati],[117]
Dhârmika (? Dharmika),[118]

105. *rgyal-ba*. cf Bu-ston ii. 116.
106. *legs-rgyal*. cf Bu-ston ii. 116.
107. *dge-ba*. cf Bu-ston ii. 116.
108. *grub-pa*. cf Bu-ston ii. 116.
109. *dregs-med*. cf Bu-ston ii. 116.
110. *grags-ldan*. V & S Yaśika. Obermiller (Bu-ston ii. 116) Yaśasvin.
111. *mkhas-pa*, lit. 'the learned'. V & S Kuśala. Obermiller (Bu-ston ii. 109) Vijña.
112. *bzaṅ-po*.
113. *mchog-sred*.
114. S Sūdra and adds in note that in Bu-ston [Fol 87] the name occurs as *dmaṅs-rigs* (lit. śūdra). P-ed Sūtra in transliteration. See Bu-ston ii. 116.
115. *rigs-ldan*. cf Bu-ston ii. 116.
116. *mtho-brtsun*, V & S Mudgaragomin. But it is an abbreviation of *mtho-brtsun-grub-rje* or Udbhaṭa-siddhisvāmin *alias* Mudgaragomin, the author of the *Viśeṣa-stava* (bsTod 1) and *Sarvajña-maheśvara-stotra-nāma* (bsTod 3). See Fol 34A.
117. *bde-byed*, an abbreviation of *bde-byed-bdag-po* or Śaṃkara-pati, the author of the *Devātiśaya-stotra* (bsTod 4). See Fol 34A. V & S Śaṃkara.
118. *chos-ldan*. cf Bu-ston ii. 116—Dharmika.

Vīrya (? Mahāvīrya),[119]
Su-viṣṇu,[120]
Madhu,[121]
*Supramadhu,
Vararuci, the second,[122]
Kāśijāta,[123]
*Canaka,
Vasunetra,[124]
*Śaṅku,
Bṛhaspati,[125]
*Makṣika,
*Vasunāga,
Bhadrapālita,[126]
Pūrṇa[127] and
Pūrṇabhadra.[128]

Most of the teachers of the Mahāyāna [**Fol 3B**] were so highly renowned that, even though not mentioned in this brief *Table of Contents*, they would be known from the subsequent account.

The Six Jewels of the Jambudvīpa[129] were extremely famous. Known as the Great Four were—

Śūra,[130]
Rāhula,[131]

119. *brtson-ldan*. cf Bu-ston ii. 116—Mahāvīrya. V Uddyogin.
120. *khyab-'jug-bzaṅ*, lit. Viṣṇu-bhadra. cf Bu-ston ii. 116. V Su-viṣṇu.
121. *sbraṅ-rtsi*.
122. *mchog-sred-gñis-pa*.
123. *gsal-ldan-skye*. cf Bu-ston ii. 116.
124. *nor-gyi-mig*. cf Bu-ston ii. 117.
125. *phur-bu*.
126. *bzaṅ-po-bskyaṅs*.
127. *gaṅ-ba*. cf Bu-ston ii. 117.
128. *gaṅ-ba-bzaṅ-po*. cf Bu-ston ii. 117.
129. Typically Tibetan form of referring to 'Nāgārjuna, Āryadeva, Asaṅga, Vasubandhu, Dignāga and Dharmakīrti'—See Fol 94A.
130. *dpa'-bo*.
131. *sgra-gcan-'dsin*.

Guṇaprabha[132] and
Dharmapāla[133]

Śāntideva[134] and *Candragomī were famed among the learned as 'the two wonderful teachers'.

In India, the two Uttama-s[135] were not famous. Only the Tibetans join their names to the list of the Six Jewels.

The twelve Tāntrika teachers of Vikramaśīla[136] were—

Jñānapāda,[137]
Dīpaṃkara-bhadra,[138]
*Laṅkā-jayabhadra,[139]
Śrīdhara,[140]
*Bha-va-bha (Bhavabhadra),[141]
Bhavyakīrti,[142]
*Līlāvajra,
Durjaya-candra,[143]
Samaya-vajra,[144]
Tathāgata-rakṣita[145]
Bodhibhadra[146] and

132. *yon-tan-'od.*
133. *chos-skyoṅ.*
134. *shi-ba-lha.*
135. *mchog-gñis.* V 'the two Supremes'.
136. *rnam-gnon-tshul.* The usual form for Vikramaśīla, however, is *rnam-gnon-ṅaṅ-tshul.*
137. *ye-śes-shabs.*
138. *mar-me-mdsad-bzaṅ-po.*
139. *laṅkā-rgyal-bzaṅ.* Jayabhadra of Laṅkā or Ceylon. Tg contains a number of works by him on Cakrasamvara: rG vii. 12; xiii. 22-3; 33; lxxvi. 16 & 20. Of these, the last was composed by him in Magadha.
140. *dpal-'dsin.*
141. In Fol 127A the name occurs as Bhavabhadra in transliteration.
142. *skal-ldan-grags-pa.*
143. *mi-thub-zla-ba.*
144. *dam-tshig-rdo-rje.* In Fol 127B the name is given as Kṛṣṇasamaya-vajra.
145. *de-bshin-gśegs-bsruṅs.*
146. *byaṅ-chub-bzaṅ-po.*

Kamalarakṣita.[147]

Next came various Tāntrika teachers like the Six Door-keeper Scholars.

The following account will be clearly understood and followed if all these are remembered.

[THE SOURCES]

The dependable sources of our knowledge of the royal chronology prior to the appearance of our Teacher Samyaksambuddha in this world are the *Vinayaśāstra*,[148] *Abhiniṣkramaṇa-sūtra*[149] and partly also the *Lalitavistara*, etc. In the *śāstra*-s of the *tīrthika*-s occur the genealogies of innumerable kings, sages and other persons belonging to the *satya*, *tretā*, *dvāpara* and *kali* aeons. However, these are not fully reliable, because these are mixed up with errors. Further, since these are not related to the history of the True Doctrine—and therefore are of no value to the seekers of truth in its purity—**[Fol 4A]** I am not mentioning all these here. Nevertheless, to name their authoritative sources : the **Bhārata* consisting of over a hundred thousand **śloka*-s, the **Rāmāyaṇa* containing a hundred thousand **śloka*-s, the ***Aṣṭādaśa-purāṇa* containing over a lakh of **śloka*-s, a poetical work consisting of 80,000[150] **śloka*-s called the **Raghuvaṃśam*, etc.

I am going to narrate here the account of only those who worked for the spread of the Law of the Teacher.

147. *padma-spuṅ-ba*. In Fol 128A the name occurs as Kamalarakṣita in transliteration.
148. *'dul-ba-luṅ*. V Vinayavastu.
149. *mṅon-par-'byuṅ-ba'i-mdo*. Kg—Sendai Cat. No. 301.
150. *stoṅ-phrag-brgyad-bcu*.

CHAPTER 1

ACCOUNT OF THE PERIOD OF KING AJĀTAŚATRU

At the time when the sayings of the Teacher Samyaksambuddha were collected,[1] the gods offered their praises, happiness and prosperity prevailed all over the human world,[2] both gods and men lived in bliss and the piety of king Kṣemadarśin[3]—also renowned as Ajātaśatru[4]—increased spontaneously. He brought under control without warfare all the five cities excepting only Vaiśālī.[5]

When the Tathāgata and his two disciples[6], along with

1. Does this refer to the First Council said to have taken place at Rājagṛha under the patronage of king Ajātaśatru ? The Pāli *Cullavagga* does not mention Ajātaśatru in its account of the First Council ; but the *Mahāvaṃsa*, the *Samanta-pāsādikā* etc do (See *2500 Years* 37). Bu-ston ii. 73ff gives an account of the First Council based on the *Vinaya-kṣudraka-vastu* (Kg 'Dul-ba xi—Sendai Cat. No 6), in which also Ajātaśatru figureş. As to the conditions that necessitated the First Council or 'the first collection of the sayings' of the Buddha, Yuan-chuang (See Watters ii. 37) refers to the general feeling of doubt and consternation and also of the deep sense of sorrow with which the people were overpowered during the Buddha's *nirvāṇa* ; the Pāli sources like the *Cullavagga* mention the general tendency to laxity expressed for example by Subhadda ; the *Vinaya-kṣudraka* (quoted by Bu-ston ii. 73) refers to the general contempt expressed by the gods who said, 'The Word of the Teacher is dispersing like smoke. The monks who possessed authority and power have likewise passed away. Therefore the three codes of scripture will never come to be expounded.'
2. *mi'i-'jig-rten*, i.e. as contrasted with *nāga-loka* etc.
3. *mthoṅ-ldan-dge-ba*. V tr 'the so-called Kṣemadarśin' and adds in the note, 'The Tibetan word should roughly mean gifted with auspicious vision'. The idea conveyed is, therefore, very near to *priyadarśin*.
4. *ma-skyes-dgra*.
5. *spoṅ-byed*. V & S Vṛji. But see D 802 and J 332. For other sources on Ajātaśatru's campaign against the Vṛjis, see Basham HDA 71ff.
6. Śāriputra and Maudgalyāyana, both of whom—as V adds in note—died before the Buddha.

1,68,000 *arhat*-s[7] went to eternal sleep and Mahâkāśyapa[8] also attained the *nirvāṇa*,[9]—everybody was plunged into great grief. All the *bhikṣu*-s, who saw the great Teacher in person, thought : 'Because of our own carelessness, we failed to attain distinction during the life-time of the Buddha.' And they resolved to devote themselves exclusively to the Doctrine. The venerable preceptors also did the same. The younger *bhikṣu*-s, who did not see the Teacher in person, thought : 'We are incapable of practising the Doctrine **[Fol 4B]** properly, because we could never see the Teacher himself. We are likely to be misguided if we do not exert ourselves for the Law.' Thus thinking they strove after virtue.

As a result, there greatly swelled the number of those who attained the 'four stages of perfection'.[10]

Ārya Ānanda[11] frequently preached to the 'four classes of followers'.[12] Also those who were proficient in the *piṭaka*-s

7. According to *Vinaya-kṣudraka* quoted by Bu-ston ii. 73, Śāriputra had 80,000 followers, Maudgalyāyana 70,000, while the Teacher himself 18,000 followers.
8. *'od-sruṅs-chen-po.*
9. V n 'Mahākāśyapa looked after the Law for about ten years.'
10. *'bras-bu-bshi-thob-pa.* See J 400—*'bras-bu*, reward of ascetic exercises, the various grades of perfection of which four are distinguished, viz. 1) *srotāpatti*—or as practised *srotāpanna*—, i.e. he who enters the stream (that takes from the external world to *nirvāṇa*), 2) *sakṛdāgāmin*, i.e. he who returns once more (for the period of a human birth), 3) *anāgāmin*, i.e. he who returns no more, being a candidate of *nirvāṇa*, 4) *arhanta*, the *arhat*, the finished saint.
    V tr 'the four fruits' and adds in the note, 'i.e. the stages of *srotāpannaka*, *sakṛdāgāmin*, *anāgāmin* and *arhat*.'
11. *kun-dga'-bo.* V n 'The title *ārya* (*'phags-pa*) is added to the early patriarchs counted in the succession of the seven.'
12. *'khor-rnam-pa-bshi.* See J 57—The attendants of Buddha's hearers divided into four classes (namely, in the earliest times)—1) *dge-sloṅ* (*bhikṣu*), 2) *dge-sloṅ-ma* (*bhikṣuṇī*), 3) *dge-bsñen* (*upāsaka*) and 4) *dge-bsñen-ma* (*upāsikā*). At a later period : 1) *maṅ-thos* (*śrāvaka*), 2) *raṅ-saṅs-rgyas* (*pratyeka-buddha*), 3) *byaṅ-chub-sems-dpa'* (*bodhisattva*), 4) *so-so'i-skye-bo-rnams* (*pṛthak-jana*), V n '*bhikṣu*, *bhikṣuṇī*, *sramaṇera* and *śramaṇerikā*.'

(*piṭaka-dhara*-s) expounded the Doctrine. Consequently, the ordained monks (*pravrajyita*-s) lived the life of strict moral care.

The Teacher entrusted Mahākāśyapa with the Law.[13] He entrusted *ārya* Ānanda with the Law. This was of special significance.[14]

The king and all the householders—and also the (other) kings, the merit of whose virtue was dffiicult to measure,—became disturbed with the multitude of worldly affairs (and) felt that previously they saw the foremost Teacher of the world while they now could see only his disciples. (Thus) they came to realise the preciousness of the *buddha*, *dharma* and *saṃgha* and went on worshipping these with great reverence. They storve after virtue and thus disappeared quarrels and conflicts.

It is said that in this way the world remained virtuous for about forty years.

On about the fifteenth year of *ārya* Ānanda's leadership of the Doctrine, the young Suvarṇavarṇa[15] attained *arhat*-hood. His account is already given in the *Suvarṇavarṇa-avadāna*.[16]

At that time king Ajātaśatru thought : 'If even a person like Suvarṇavarṇa could smoothly and without difficulty be led to *arhat*-hood by Ānanda, he must be a *śrāvaka*[17] like the Buddha himself.'—Thus thinking, he worshipped for five years with all sorts of gifts five thousand *arhat*-s[18], inclusive of *ārya* Ānanda.

Then came to *Magadha from the [Fol 5A] city of *Kimmilimālā[19] of the south a *brāhmaṇa* belonging to the

13. See Supplementary Note No 1 for Tār's account of Ānanda and of the succession of the patriarchs as throwing light on his sources.
14. V omits this sentence in his translation.
15. *gser-mdog-gi-rtogs-brjod.* V & S Kanakavarṇa.
16. Tg mDo xc 17 *Suvarṇavarṇa-avadāna*.
17. *ñan-thos.*
18. *dgra-bcom-pa.*
19. S Kimmilimālā and adds in note, which is also quoted by V 'Whether here the northern city of Kimpila (which is decidedly a corruption of Kāmpilla)—also mentioned by Vasil'ev in *Vinaya* vol iii—is to be understood or whether it is Krimilā, cannot be decided.'

vicious *Bharadvāja family.[20] He was a great expert in magic and entered into a competition of magic power with the monks.

In the presence of the king and other people, he conjured up four hills made of gold, silver, crystal and **vaidūrya*. Each of these had four pleasure-gardens full of jewels. Each of the gardens had four lotus ponds full of all sorts of birds.

Ārya Ānanda conjured up hordes of wild elephants that could not be destroyed. They devoured the lotuses and devastated the ponds. The trees fell down by a strong blast of wind. Nothing remained of the hills or of their boundaries because of terrible thunder shower.

Ārya Ānanda transformed his own body into five hundred bodies. From some of them emitted lustre, some others started showering rain and some others showed the four-fold performances[21] in the sky. From the upper parts of certain other bodies came out fire and from their lower parts came out streams of water.

Thus he showed many assorted[22] magical feats like these.

[The *brāhmaṇa* of the] vicious *Bharadvāja family and the assembled people were full of reverence. As a result of the elaborate exposition of the Doctrine [by *ārya* Ānanda], eighty thousand people, including five hundred *brāhmaṇa*-s like *Bharadvāja and others, were led to truth within seven days.

On another occasion, when *ārya* Ānanda was residing at

20. V & S '*brāhmaṇa* Bharadvāja belonging to the line of Jambhala.' But this seems to be far-fetched. The text has *gnod-pa-can*, meaning 'the vicious', which also fits the context. Besides, Bharadvāja being a well-known *brāhmaṇa gotra* is itself suggestive of a line of descent. S & V mention Jambhala perhaps because of reading the word as *dsam-bha-la*, meaning Jambhala, the god of riches or Pluto—see D 1048.
21. *spyod-lam-bshi*, the four postures of sitting, lying, standing and walking—J 335.
22. *ya-ma-zuṅ*.

Jetavana,[23] the householder called Śaṇavāsika[24] lavishly entertained the *saṃgha*-s for five years. After this, he was ordained (*pravrajyita*), being instructed by the *ārya* [Ānanda]. In course of time, he became proficient in the three *piṭaka*-s and eventually attained *arhat*-hood, free from the two-fold obscurations.[25]

[Fol 5B] In this way on various occasions [*ārya* Ānanda] led to *arhat*-hood about ten thousand monks. He resided in the middle of the *Gaṅgā river, where it flowed between the two lands, [viz. Vaiśālī and Magadha], so that the *Licchavis of Vaiśālī and king Ajātaśatru of *Magadha could be equally favoured with his relics. Being prayed for ordination (*upasampadā*)[26] by five hundred sages, he miraculously created an island in the middle of the river. With his supernatural power he got the *bhikṣu*-s to congregate there and within an hour led the five hundred sages from the stage of *upasampadā* to

23. *rgyal-byed-kyi-tshal*. V n "Bu-ston fol 95 *'od-ma'i-tshal* or Venuvana."

24. *śa-na'i-gos-can*. V Śaṇavāsa. Variously mentioned as Śaṇika, Śaṇavāsa, Śoṇavāsī, Śānavāsika and Śāṇavāsika. Yuan-chuang (See Watters i. 120) explains the significance of the name with special reference to his robes. Yuan-chuang was shown the robe which by that time 'suffered some diminution and this was proof to disbelievers.'

25. *gñis-ka'i-cha-las-rnam-par-grol-ba*, i.e. *ubhayato-bhāga-vimukti* or deliverance from both *kleśa-āvaraṇa* and *jñeya-āvaraṇa* by the force of *samādhi*. See N. S. Sastri, *Vāhyārtha-siddhi* (Namgyal Institute of Tibetology, July 1967) pp 12 & 34. cf also D 333. Dutt EMB 267—the *arhat*-s are distinguished into two categories, of which the higher one comprises of those who have attained emancipation by two means, viz. by perfecting himself in the Eight Releases from thought-construction and by acquisition of the highest knowledge. They are called *ubhato-bhāga-vimukta-arhat*-s. The lower category comprises of *arhat*-s who practise 'only the first four meditations and not the higher ones nor the releases.'
V tr 'He became proficient first in the three *piṭaka*-s and then in the two forms of *arhat*-hood and attained absolute salvation.' In the note he explains the two forms of *arhat*-hood as with and without abode. S follows this interpretation.

26. *bsñen-par-rdsogs-pa*. See D 511.

arhat-hood. That is why, these five hundred were famed as the five hundred *madhyāhnika*-s, [i.e. the five hundred that reached *arhat*-hood during mid-day] or the five hundred *madhyāntika*-s [i.e. the five hundred that reached *arhat*-hood in mid-stream].[27] The foremost of them was known as Mahā-madhyāntika or Mahā-madhyāhnika.[28]

After this, he [Ānanda] attained *nirvāṇa* and the relics of his mortal body were burnt by self-kindled fire. The ashes of his bones assumed the form of two balls of gems and were carried by the waves to the two shores of the river. The northern one was taken by the Vṛjis[29] and the southern one by Ajātaśatru. They built *caitya*-s[30] [containing these relics] in their respective countries.

Ānanda served the Law for forty years. The next year Ajātaśatru also died. After being born for a while in the hell,[31] he died again there and was reborn in heaven. He listened to the doctrine from *ārya* Śāṇavāsika and entered the stream [i.e. attained the first stage of perfection, viz. that of *srotāpatti*]. Thus it is said.[32]

The first chapter containing the account of the period of king Ajātaśatru.

27. cf Bu-ston ii. 89ff
28. V & S n : Both the Tibetan words *ñi-ma-guṅ-pa* and *chu-dbus-pa* appear to be based on Pali *majjhantiko*.
29. *spoṅ-byed-pa*. V 'the inhabitants of Vaiśālī'.
30. Yuan-chwang was shown these *caitya*-s. See Watters ii. 80 : 'Here (i.e. the Śvetapura monastery near Vaiśālī) were two topes, one on the north and one on the south side of the river, to mark the spots at which Ānanda on going into extinction, gave one half of his bodily relics to Magadha and the other half to Veśāli.' Fa-hien gives practically the same legend of Ānanda's *nirvāṇa*—See Legge 75f.
31. Here at last Tāranātha shows that he is not totally unaware of the dark deeds of the king. Interestingly, Kg contains a work called *Ajātaśatru-Kaukṛtya-Vinodana*—see Bu-ston i. 41.
32. The typical Tibetan way of referring to something as a hearsay, about the authenticity of which the author himself takes no responsibility. The expression corresponds to the Chinese *huo-yue*—See Watters ii. 97.

CHAPTER 2

ACCOUNT OF THE PERIOD OF KING SUBĀHU

After that, Subâhu, son of king Ajātaśatru, ascended the throne and worshipped the Law of the Buddha for about seventeen[1] years.

At that time, *ārya* Śāṇavāsika looked after the Law for a brief period. However, during this period mainly *ārya* Madhyāntika,[2] residing in *Vārāṇasi, expounded the *āgama*-s to the 'four classes of followers' and preached the doctrine to the householders and *brāhmaṇa*-s.

Once upon a time, many *brāhmaṇa*-s and householders of *Vārāṇasi **[Fol 6A]** became annoyed with the *bhikṣu*-s, who were begging for alms. They said to them, 'Is there no other place to get the alms from ? Has *Vārāṇasi alone any surplus to offer ? And if we feed you, are you not obliged to give us something in return ?'

On hearing all these, *ārya* Madhyāntika, along with his ten thousand *arhat* followers, flew through the sky and reached *Uśira[3] hill on the north. There a householder, called *Aja, arranged for the congregation of the *saṃgha*-s all around[4]

1. V & S 'ten years', because S-ed has *lo-bcu* (ten years) ; but the P-ed has *lo-bcu-bdun* (seventeen years).
2. V & S Madhyāntika (passim), though in the text occurs *ñi-ma-guṅ-pa*, literally 'the person of the mid-day' or madhyāhnika.
3. V n (quoted by S) : 'It is said in the *Vinaya* that the Buddha, before his *nirvāṇa*, had left Ānanda in Rohitaka and himself went towards the north along with Vajrapāṇi. The first object which appeared to him from afar was the Uśira mountain. The Buddha predicted that hundred years after him there would be an arena for the religious people there in the Tāmasa forest on this mountain. Yuan-chuang also speaks of the cloister Tāmasavana in the kingdom of Tehi-ma-po-ti.' Cf Watters ii. 308 ; BA i. 23 ; Bu-ston ii. 109.
4. *phyogs-bshi'i*, lit. 'of the four directions', an equivalent of Sanskrit *cāturdiśika*.

and entertained them for one year. Forty-four thousand *arhat*-s assembled there. For this reason, the Law was spread more extensively in the north.

In this way, Madhyāntika preached the Doctrine for three years in *Uśira.

At that time, *ārya* Śāṇavāsika resided at Śrāvastī.[5] As the result of his preaching the Doctrine to the 'four classes of followers', the number of the *arhat*-s there reached nearly a thousand.

Earlier, during the time of king Ajātaśatru, there lived two persons who, though *brāhmaṇa* by birth, were extremely tough, wicked, sinful and were indifferent to the purity and impurity of food. They used to kill all sorts of animals. They were called *Paṇa and *Nava.[6]

They committed theft in some houses and were therefore punished by the king.[7] This made them extremely angry. So they offered midday meals to many *arhat*-s and prayed, 'By virtue of this act, may we be reborn as *yakṣa*-s and plunder[8] the king and people of *Magadha'.

After some time, these two persons died in an epidemic **[Fol 6B]** and were reborn as *yakṣa*-s. On the seventh or eighth year of the reign of king Subāhu, they became very powerful *yakṣa*-s of *Magadha and caused a terrible epidemic to spread in the country. A large number of persons and cattle perished. But the epidemic did not subside.

When the astronomers came to know the cause of this [epidemic], the citizens of *Magadha succeeded in inviting Śāṇavāsika from Śrāvastī and entreated him to overpower the two *yakṣa*-s.

He [Śāṇavāsika] came to the *Gurva hill[9] and took shelter in the cave in which these two *yakṣa*-s were residing. At

5. *mñan-yod*.
6. V & S Napa. S-ed Napa. P-ed Nava.
7. V & S 'their hands were chopped off'. This translation is because S-ed has *lag-pa-bcad-pa*, instead of which P-ed has *chad-pas-bcad-pa* (punishment).
8. V tr 'take revenge on'.
9. A corruption of Gurupāda, which was the other name of Kukkuṭapāda—see Watters ii. 143.

that time, these *yakṣa*-s had gone to other *yakṣa*-s and were called back by a friend of theirs, who was also a *yakṣa*.

On returning, they smashed in a terrible fury the stones that formed the cave. But there emerged another cave and *ārya* Śāṇavāsika was seen sitting within it. This happened thrice. Then these two [*yakṣa*-s] set fire [to the cave]. But the *arhat* covered all the ten directions with greater flames. The two *yakṣa*-s got scared and tried to escape. But they could find no way out because of the flames all around. When they surrendered to Śāṇavāsika, the flames got extinguished. After this, he [Śāṇavāsika] preached the Doctrine to them. They became full of great devotion and were led to *śaraṇa-gamana* and *śikṣā*.[10]

Immediately after this, the epidemic came to an end. Thousands of *brāhmaṇa*-s and householders thus witnessed the miraculous power [of Śāṇavāsika].

The second chapter containing the account of the period of king Subāhu.

10. *bslab-pa'i-gnas*—see D 1324, V n 'i.e. the promise to respect the Doctrine and to learn its dogmas. Even today, this is the attitude that the lay devotees adopt to Buddhism.'

CHAPTER 3

ACCOUNT OF THE PERIOD OF KING SUDHANU

After the death of this king [Subāhu], his son Sudhanu succeeded him. At that time there took place the conversion of Kashmir by Madhyāntika.[1]

By his miraculous power, Madhyāntika went to Kashmir and settled on the shore of a lake where lived the Nāgas.[2] The furious Nāga king *Auduṣṭa[3] and his attendants, **[Fol 7A]** caused a terrible storm[4] and rain, but could not shake even a

1. For legends of the conversion of Kashmir by Madhyāntika given by Yuan-chuang and others, see Watters i. 230,239,260ff. cf also Bu-ston ii. 89 ; BA i. 23. V n 'For the spread of Buddhism in Kashmir, see L. Feer in *Journal Asiatique*, December 1865. We do not think that it is necessary to regard the arrival of Madhyāntika here as a pure historical fact. The beginning of the introduction of the religion in all the countries has always been considered earlier than the facts actually taking place. For example, in this history itself, we find a reference to the prevalence of mysticism at a time when it was still not there in India. In China, in Tibet and in Ceylon—everywhere the appearance of Buddhism is attributed to an earlier date in various histories.' S quotes this note.
2. cf Watters i. 264-5.
3. S n 'In other sources, the name of the *nāga-rāja* is stated otherwise—cf. L. Feer in *Journal Asiatique* 1865, p. 498ff.' Przyluski 5 : the name given as Hu-lu-t'u in the Vinaya of the Mūla-sarvāstivādīs. BA i. 23 Auduṣṭa. cf Watters i. 229-30, 'We read in the *Sarvata Vinaya* that the Buddha on a certain occasion near the end of his career, took with him his attendant *yakṣa* named Vajrapāṇi and went through the air to the country beyond the Indus to subdue and convert this dragon (Apalāla)...In a Vinaya treatise apparently from Pāli sources, we read of a dragon called Alāpalu in Kapin (Kashmir), who is overcome and converted by the great *arhat* Madhyāntika (Majjhantika) who had come as an apostle to introduce Buddhism. This legend seems to be a version of the story here narrated (by Yuan-chuang : Watters i. 229), Majjhantika taking the place of the Buddha.'
4. S omits 'storm', though both S-ed and P-ed have *rdsi-char-drag-po* (rain and storm).

corner of his [Madhyântika's] robe. The rain of weapons let loose by them changed into a shower of flowers. So the Nāga king appeared in person and asked, 'Oh *ārya*, what exactly do you want ?'

He replied, 'Give me a plot of land.'

'How much of land ?'

'Just enough for a seat with legs crossed.'[5]

'So let it be yours.'

With his miraculous power, he covered nine valleys of Kashmir by his single sitting posture.

The Nâga asked, 'How many attendants are there with the *ārya* ?'

'Five hundred.'

'If it is less even by one, I shall take back the land.'

The Teacher [Buddha] had predicted[6] that this place was going to be fit for *vipaśyanā*.[7] [Madhyāntika] thought : '*Brāhmaṇa*-s and householders should also be made to settle here, because the donors and donees should exist together.' Thus thinking, he brought to Kashmir five hundred Madhyântika

5. *skyil-kruṅ*, the posture of sitting cross-legged—J 27.
6. On this prophecy, see Watters i, 264. Przyluski 5 notes a contradiction on this point in the Vinaya of the Mūla-sarvāstivadī-s : 'Speaking to Vajrapāṇi at the spot where the monastery of the Dark Forest was to be set up, the Buddha says, "For the study of *śamatha* this will be the best place." And when he travels through Kashmir, the Buddha says with reference to the place where Madhyāntika was later to subdue the *nāga* Hu-lu-t'u, "The most important of the monasteries for the cultivation of *vipaśyanā* shall be established there." Later, showing to Ānanda the future site of the Naṭa-Bhaṭa monastery in the country of Mathurā, he makes the following prediction : "Among the habitations of those who practise the methods of *śamatha* and *vipaśyanā*, this will be the premier one," It will be seen to what extent these compilers were negligent and without scruple. After having attributed to the Buddha two prophecies destined to exalt the monasteries of the northern region, they have carelessly reproduced an ancient text that contradicts the previous assertion !'
7. *lhag-mthoṅ*. V n 'Contemplation in which the mind is engrossed in metaphysical thought.' cf J 474—implies an absolute inexcitability of mind and a deadening of it against any impression from without,

followers[8] from *Uśira and also many a hundred-thousand *brāhmaṇa*-s and householders highly devoted to the Doctrine from *Vārāṇasī. After this, there gradually assembled a large number of persons from various directions.

Even during the lifetime of Madhyāntika himself, the country [Kashmir] became ornamented with a large number of *saṃgha*-s living in nine big towns, many hilly villages, one palace and twelve monasteries. From there he went to the Gandhamādana[9] mountain with his miraculous power and, accompanied by the people of Kashmir, subdued the Nāgas there with charmed fire.

[The Nāgas] promised to give him that quantity of saffron[10] [field] which could be covered by the shadow of his [stretched out] robe. Then the *arhat* enlarged his robe with miraculous power and all the people [i.e. his followers] collected the saffron [? saplings[11]]. In a moment [they] returned to Kashmir.

By converting Kashmir **[Fol 7B]** into a saffron-producing land, he told them, 'This is going to be the main source for increasing your wealth.'

Thus saying, he converted all the inhabitants of Kashmir into the followers of the Law and attained *nirvāṇa*.

It is said that he preached the Doctrine in Kashmir for about twenty years.

At the time of Madhyāntika's departure for Kashmir, *ārya* Śāṇavāsika preached the Doctrine to the 'four classes of followers' in the six cities.

After reigning for twentythree years, king Sudhanu passed

combined with an absorption in the idea of Buddha or which in the end amounts to the same thing, in the idea of emptiness and nothingness. This is the aim to which the contemplating Buddhist aspires, when placing an image of Buddha as *rten* (*caitya*) before him, he looks at it immovably, until every other thought is lost and no sensual impressions from the outer world any longer reach or affect his mind.

8. cf Watters i. 267
9. *ri-spos-ṅad-ldan*. cf Watters i. 262, for the legend of Madhyāntika bringing saffron from Gandhamādana to Kashmir.
10. *gur-gum*.
11. V adds 'on which the shadow fell.'

away. Then his officers and attendants, numbering two thousand[12] in all, received ordination (*pravrajyā*) under Śāṇavāsika. Along with numerous people including them, he spent the rainy season[13] (*varṣā-vāsa*) in the crematorium of Śītavana.[14] During the *pravāraṇa*,[15] he took them to show the crematorium itself. This led them to attain the *aśuci-samādhi*.[16] Purifying their mind of all desires, it instantly led them to *arhat*-hood.

After this, Upagupta,[17] son of Gupta[18] the incense-seller, had the realisation of the Truth immediately after being ordained (*upasampadā*). Within seven days, he attained the *ubhayato-bhāga-vimukta arhat*-hood.[19]

12. S 'one thousand', though both S-ed and P-ed have *gñis-stoṅ* (two thousand). V 'about two thousand.'
13. *dbyar-gnas*, literally 'summer residence'. S also takes it in this sense. V tr '*varṣaka* time'. For such rendering of the *varṣā-vāsa*, however, see Watters i. 144-5. cf also Legge 10 n ; I-Tsing (Takakusu) 85f.
14. *bsil-ba'i-tshal.*
15. *dgag-dbye*. V 'period of permission'. V n 'a kind of festival at the end of the rainy season when the monks were allowed to come out. In Vinaya also, there is a separate section on it.' cf J 94 ; I-Tsing (Takakusu) 86f.
16. *mi-sdug-pa'i-tiṅ-ṅe-'dsin*. J 293 'contemplating one's self and the world as a foul putrid carcass. V n 'Here it means artificial representation to oneself of every surrounding thing and finally of the whole world in the form of a deadbody, which blackens, decays—in 9 forms in all. These representations are sometimes three-fold : initial, purifying and the final. That is why there is a reference to the corresponding representations here.'
17. *ñe-sbas*. In the account of Tār, Upagupta, the apostle of Mathurā, is converted by Śāṇavāsika, who is also an apostle of Mathurā. Thus, he follows here what Przyluski calls the tradition recorded in the *Aśokāvadāna*, described by him as 'Eulogy and Illustriousness of the Church of Mathurā' (Przyluski 3, 7). By contrast, according to the tradition of Kashmir, as recorded in the Vinaya of the Mūla-sarvāsti-vādī-s, Upagupta is converted by Madhyāntika, the apostle of Kashmir (*ib* 3). This, as Przyluski argues, is the result of the later tendency of the monks of Kashmir to glorify their own centre. cf the prophecy of Ānanda in *Vinaya-kṣudraka* quoted by Bu-ston ii. 88-9.
18. S omits Gupta. But both S-ed and P-ed have *sbas-pa* (gupta). cf Przyluski 4 ; Bu-ston ii. 88-9.
19. V 'salvation in both forms of *arhat*-hood.'

Entrusting Upagupta with the Law, he [Śāṇavāsika] himself attained *nirvāṇa* in *Campā.

The number of those who realised the Truth as a result of Śāṇavāsika's preaching amounted to about a lakh and the number of the *arhat*-s also reached about ten thousand.

According to the tradition of Kashmir, Madhyāntika also must be counted as one in the succession of teachers who were entrusted with the Law, because while living in the *madhyadeśa* he looked after the Law for fifteen years. At that time, the disciples of *ārya* Śāṇavāsika were few in number. Only after Madhyāntika's departure for Kashmir, Śāṇavāsika looked after the Law. **[Fol 8A]** Therefore, it is said that the successors of (those entrusted with) the Law should be counted as eight.

According to others, the Teacher had himself predicted that Madhyāntika was to convert Kashmir. So Ānanda directly instructed him to do so. However, Ānanda entrusted only Śāṇavāsika with the Law. Therefore, only seven are to be counted in this line of succession. The Tibetans follow this view.[20]

The third chapter containing the account of the period of king Sudhanu.

20. See Supplementary Note 1 (on the patriarchs).

CHAPTER 4

ACCOUNT OF THE PERIOD OF ĀRYA UPAGUPTA

Then Upagupta crossed the *Gaṅgā and proceeded to the north. He reached Videha,[1] a country on the western side of *Tirahuti.[2] There he resided in a monastery built by a householder called *Vasusāra, who was entertaining the *saṃgha*-s all around. He (Upagupta) spent the rainy season there, and, because of his preachings during these three months [of *varṣā-vāsa*], the number of those who attained *arhat*-hood became one thousand. After this, he went to the great mountain *Gandhāra[3] and led many people to [the realisation of] truth by preaching the Doctrine.

From there he went next to the city of Mathurā on the north-western border of the *madhya-deśa*. During that time, at the portal of Mathurā[4] where people used to assemble, the Malla chiefs[5]—the merchants *Naṭa and *Bhaṇṭa[6]—were talking to each other. They praised *ārya* Upagupta and thought how much desirable it would have been if *ārya* Upagupta took his residence at the monastery built by them on the *Śira[7] hill during the time of *ārya* Śāṇavāsika.

1. *lus-'phags.*
2. i.e. Tīrabhukti. Tār throughout refers to it as Tirahuti.
3. S-ed Gandha, P-ed Gandhāra. S n 'it is definitely Gandhamādana.'
4. *bcom-brlag.*
5. *gyad-kyi-gtso-bo.* J 74 *gyad*, an equivalent of Sanskrit Malla, the name of a people. V tr *gtso-bo* as 'chief' and *gyad* as 'Malla'. Hence the expression is rendered by him as 'the Malla chiefs—the merchants Naṭa and Bhaṭa'. cf Bu-ston ii. 88, 'Naṭa and Paṭa, sons of a merchant'; Watters ii. 44.
6. P-ed Bhaṇṭa.
7. cf Watters i. 308 : 'In some books the hill on which was the Naṭabaṭa *vihāra* occupied by Upagupta is called Śira or Uśira, although we also have mention of the Uśira hill without any reference to a cave or monastery. This Uśira hill was at the side of the Urumuṇḍa

They saw then *ārya* Upagupta coming from a distance and they said, 'Ah, this one coming here from afar and looking self-controlled and brilliant must be *ārya* Upagupta.'

[Fol 8B] Saying this to each other, they moved forward to welcome him, bowed down before him and addressed him thus, 'Art thou *ārya* Upagupta ?'

'So am I known in this world', said he.

They offered him the Naṭa-bhaṭika *vihāra*[8] on the mount *Śira fully furnished with all requirements. When he preached the Doctrine there, many ordained monks and householders were led to the realisation of the Truth.

On another occasion, as he was preaching the Doctrine to several lakhs of people, the evil Māra[9] showered rice[10] on the city.

This drew many people away from the congregation [to the city]. Others went on listening to the sermons. On the second

hill and the latter name may have included the two hills and the wood or forest adjoining.' Bu-ston ii. 88 mentions the hill as Muruṇḍa ; in BA i. 23 it is called Śīrṣa-parvata.

8. *gar-mkhan-dpa'-bo'i-gtsug-lag-khaṅ.* V & S Naṭa-bhaṭika *vihāra.* V n 'In the Tibetan-Sanskrit Dictionary, we find the word Naṭa corresponding to the Tibetan word *gar-mkhan.* But the Tibetan word *dpa'-bo,* "knight", does not have any suitable equivalent, which should mean *bhaṭa.*' For other names in which this monastery was mentioned, see Watters i. 309 : 'This Upagupta monastery is apparently the Cream Village *vihāra* of a Vinaya treatise, one of the many Buddhist establishments mentioned as being in the Mathurā district. It may also perhaps be the Guhā-vihāra of the Lion Pillar Inscriptions. We find it called the Naṭika-saṃghārāma, and the Naṭa-baṭa (or Naṭi-baṭi) vihāra, as already stated, and the Naṭa-bhaṭikāraṇyāyatana of the *Divyāvadāna.*'

9. *bdud-sdig-can.* S Māra-Pāpīya. cf BA i. 23 : Upagupta subduing Māra, the sinner. The account of the conversion of Māra by Upagupta, argues Przyluski 7, was evidently designed in the *Aśokāvadāna* to glorify Upagupta : 'The Buddha had not certainly converted Māra, the personification of evil. He had done this in order to leave to Upagupta the glory of carrying this difficult enterprise to a successful conclusion.'

10. S fruit, but both S-ed and P-ed have *'bras* (rice) and not *'bras-bu* (fruit). V bread.

day, when [Māra] showered clothes, many more people went away to the city. In the same way, there was a shower of silver on the third, of gold on the fourth and of *sapta-ratna*[11] on the fifth day. The number of listeners was reduced to insignificance.

On the sixth[12] day, Māra himself assumed the form of a celestial dancer[13]. His wife,[14] sons and daughters appeared as celestial singers and dancers and thus there entered the city thirtysix males and females in the guise of celestial actors. Distracted by the magic of the dance and sweet tunes of vocal and instrumental music [everybody left the congregation] and there was none left to listen to the Doctrine[15].

Then *ārya* Upagupta himself went to the city. 'Ah, the foremost ones, how wonderful is your performance ! I have garlands to offer you.' Thus saying he put garlands on the heads and necks of all of them.

By the miraculous power of the *ārya*, the bodies of the evil one and of his associates immediately turned into aged, decayed and ugly ones, wearing tattered rags **[Fol 9A]** with decomposed corpses on their heads and rotten dead dogs hanging from their necks. There was stink all around. He turned the whole scene into a nauseating one. The people, who were yet to be free from passion, covered their noses and turned back in anger, fear and disgust.

Then Upagupta asked, 'Oh evil one, why did you harm my followers ?'

11. *rin-po-che-sna-bdun.*
12. S 'seventh day', but both S-ed and P-ed have *ñi-ma-drug-pa* (sixth day).
13. V 'celestial actor' and adds in the note, 'i.e. not a simple actor. It appears that this word should mean something more than a good actor. We will find later a reference to celestial architects and painters.'
14. V & S omit 'wife', because S-ed does not contain *chuṅ-ma*, which occurs in P-ed.
15. V tr 'And with their performances, magical arts, melodious songs and music so captivated (lit. transformed) the hearts of all, that not a single (person) was left to listen to the Doctrine.'

'Forgive us, please, oh *ārya*, and free us from our fetters.'

Upagupta said, 'I shall do this if you do not try to harm my followers [any more].'

'I shall do no harm even though I perish.'

Immediately, Māra's body resumed its usual form. He said, 'I caused injuries with all my power to *Gautama while he was in Bodhimaṇḍa[16] (Vajrāsana). Yet he remained undisturbed in his meditation on compassion. But in spite of being the followers of *Gautama, you are violent and aggressive. You, *ārya*, have put us under fetters as soon as we tried the slightest joke.'

Then Upagupta, preaching the Doctrine even to the evil Māra, said, 'I had vision only of the *dharma-kāya*[17] of the Teacher, but I never saw him in his *rūpa-kāya*.[18] You, however, have seen him, oh evil one. Therefore, show me his physical form.'

When he (Māra) assumed the physical form of the Teacher, *ārya* Upagupta became full of profound reverence. His hairs stood on end in ecstasy, his eyes were full of tears. He placed his folded hands on his head and said, 'I bow down to the Buddha.'

Unable to bear this, the evil Māra fell down unconscious and then vanished.

Thus was born a great reverence in all the people, who, as a result of the merit of their past virtue, **[Fol 9B]** assembled there from all directions. As a consequence of his preaching the Doctrine throughout the sixth night [beginning] from that of the showering of rice, eighteen lakhs of people were led to the realisation of the Truth on the seventh day.

He (Upagupta) spent the rest of his life in the Naṭa-bhaṭika

16. *byaṅ-chub-sñiṅ-po*. See J 374 & D 884. Yuan-chuang (Watters ii. 114-5) 'The name is derived from the fact that here the 1000 Buddhas of this *kalpa* go into the *vajra-samādhi* ; as they attain *bodhi* at this spot, it is also called the Bodhi Arena (*tao-ch'ang*, i.e. Bodhimaṇḍala or Bodhimaṇḍa.)'

17. *chos-kyi-sku*.

18. *gzugs-kyi-sku*.

vihāra. There was a cave there, eighteen cubits[19] in length, twelve in breadth and six in height. Each of the ordained monks who attained *arhat*-hood by virtue of his preaching, used to throw one wooden chip four inches long into the cave. In this way, the cave was so filled up with such wooden chips that no passage remained and, after some time, when *ārya* Upagupta attained the *pari-nirvāṇa*, his body was cremated with these.[20] His relics were collected together and, it is said, it was taken away by the gods.

The Teacher himself had predicted that he (Upagupta) was to be a Buddha without the *lakṣaṇa*-s.[21] This meant that though without the *lakṣaṇa*-s and *vyañjana*-s of the Buddha, he was similar to the Buddha in his compassion for the living beings. After the *nirvāṇa* of the Tathāgata, nobody surpassed him in compassion for the living beings.

The period during which Upagupta served the Law was mainly the period of nine years' rule over most of the regions of Aparântaka[22] by king Mahendra, son of king Sudhanu, and the

19. *khru,* literally the measure from the elbow to the extremity of the middle finger. But D 172 takes it roughly as a cubit. Similarly, *sor* literally means the finger, but D 1286 takes *sor-bshi-pa* as roughly equivalent to 4 inches in measure. BA i. 23 gives the measurement of the cave as 18 cubics in length and 12 cubics in width. For other measurements of the cave, see Watters i. 307 : 'Connected with the monastery was the cave in which the disciples converted by Upagupta's teaching, on their attainment of *arhat*-ship, deposited each a slip of wood or bamboo...Its dimensions vary in different books, one authority making it 18 *chou* (*chou* : 1·5 ft.) by 12 *chou* wide and 7 *chou* high. In our pilgrim's (Yuan-chuang's) description, we should probably regard "above 20 feet high" as a mistake for "above 20 feet long", other writers giving the length as 24 or 27 feet, the height being about 9 or 10 feet.'

20. cf Watters i. 307, 'When he (Upagupta) died, all the tallies deposited by these *arhat*-s were taken away and used at his cremation. Yet Yuan-chuang would have us believe that he saw them still filling up the cave !'

21. *a-lakṣaṇa-buddha.* cf Watters i. 311 ; Bu-ston ii. 89. Przyluski 7 quotes the prediction as occurring in the *Aśokāvadāna.*

22. *ñi-'og-gi-rgyal-khams.* See D 481 & J 187.

period of twentytwo years' rule by his (Mahendra's) son *Camaśa.

Now, there lived in eastern India an *arhat* named Uttara.[23] King Mahendra had great reverence for him. The people of *Bagala[24] built for him a monastery in the region of Kukkuṭapāla[25] and offered it to him. It became famous as Kukkuṭa-ārāma.[26] As a result of his many sermons to numerous people belonging to the 'four classes of followers' of Aparântaka, **[Fol 10A]** a large number of them were led to the attainment of the 'four stages of perfection'.

His foremost disciple was *arhat* Yaśaḥ[27].

Shortly after king *Camaśa had ascended the throne after the death of king Mahendra, there lived in *Magadha a *brāhmaṇa*-woman called *Jaḥsā, who was then about one hundred and twenty years old. She had three sons, called Jaya, Sujaya and Kalyāṇa.

The first of them was a worshipper of the god Mahādeva,[28]

23. *bla-ma*. cf Watters ii. 224-5.
24. P-ed Bagala, S-ed Baṃgala. S 'people of Bagala', V 'people of the whole country.'
25. *bya-gag-skyoṅ-ba'i-ljoṅs*. S n 'The word-for-word translation of the Tibetan text should be Kukkuṭa-pāda. Other sources ascribe the building of the *vihāra* to king Aśoka.' But S-ed also has *skyoṅ-ba*, lit. 'pāla'. Przyluski 173f Kukkuṭa-pāda. V 'a monastery equipped with birds'. cf Watters ii. 143ff, where Yuan-chuang refers to it as the Kukkuṭa-pāda or Guru-pāda Hill : 'The mountain here called by our pilgrim as Cock's Foot and Sage's Foot is also called Wolf's Traces, i.e. perhaps Koka-pāda.' Watters' note 'The Wolf's Traces Mountain was apparently part of Gṛdhrakūṭa.'
26. *bya-gag-gi-kun-dga'-ra-ba*, literally 'the bird grove'. cf Watters ii. 98f : both Yuan-chuang and Fa-hien place the monastery to the south-east of Pāṭaliputra. According to Yuan-chuang it was built by Aśoka. Watters adds, 'There was an earlier Kukkuṭārāma near Pāṭaliputra, probably only huts in the park. Aśoka may have built a monastery on this ancient site. There was also another Kukkuṭārāma near Kauśāmbī in the Buddha's time.'
27. *grags-pa*.
28. *lha-chen-po-dbaṅ-phyug*. V & S Maheśvara.

the second of the sage Kapila[29] and the third of Samyak-sambuddha. They studied their respective doctrines thoroughly and used to argue among themselves every day in the same house.

Their mother once said, 'I provide you with food and clothing, leaving you nothing more to want. Why, then, do you always argue ?' They replied, 'We do not argue for the sake of food etc. What we argue about are the right teacher and the right doctrine.'

Their mother said, 'If you fail to discriminate with your own intellect between the right and wrong teacher or doctrine better ask other scholars about these.'

Obeying the mother, they went about many places and made enquiries. They failed to find anybody who could convince them. At last they came to *arhat* Uttara and each of them placed his view elaborately before him.

Jaya and Sujaya first narrated how Mahādeva was praised for destroying Tripura and how Kapila had the terrible power of cursing. But the *śramaṇa* *Gautama could not curse and therefore it was obvious that his penance was fruitless. He could not overpower the *asura*[30] and hence his might was limited.

To this, the *arhat* [**Fol 10B**] replied,

> 'What does penance mean to one that allows the mind to be agitated with anger and leads it to curse others ? Even the evil, immoral and violent *ḍākinī*-s and *rākṣasa*-s can curse. It is extremely foolish to try to kill those who, even without being killed, chained or beaten, are inevitably going to die. That is like a stupid person who threatens the setting sun with his stick and boasts that he has driven it away. Listen further, Oh *brāhmaṇa*-s : The Buddha strives for the welfare of the world. Non-violence is his Doctrine. He who has faith in him

29. *ser-skya.*
30. V tr 'the masses', because, as he says in the note, he reads the word as *lta-min* (instead of *lha-min*, which occurs in the text).

and follows him, always speaks of non-violence. Working ever for others' welfare, he attains enlightenment. Being non-violent, he always acts in the virtuous way. He teaches also his followers to act for the welfare [of others]. One listening to his words—be one a *brāhmaṇa* or *śramaṇa*—can never find any harm in these. Such are the maxims of universal virtue. [By contrast], the religion of Mahādeva is of one who is cruel and loves to live in the crematorium, eats the flesh, fat and marrow of the human body and by nature is violent and revels in killing. His doctrine, being the doctrine of violence, is defiled. Even to have faith in it amounts to the practice of violence. How can any sensible person have reverence for it? If mere courage is virtue, why are not the lions and tigers worshipped? Tranquillity of mind alone is real virtue.'

(This passage occurs in the text in the form of a verse)

Such was the first sermon [of the *arhat*]. Thereafter he delivered other **[Fol 11A]** sermons illustrating the difference between virtue and vice in five hundred ways. These two *brāhmaṇa*-s also realised the truth of all these and were filled with great reverence for the *tri-ratna*. The young *brāhmaṇa* Kalyāṇa, who was already devout, became all the more devoted.

Thus, agreeing among themselves, the three went back to their home and addressed their mother, 'All of us have realised the virtue of the Buddha. So each of us want to build a temple for placing the image of the Teacher. Show us, mother, the land for these.'

When the mother showed them the places, the *brāhmaṇa* Jaya built a temple for the image [of the Buddha] at *Vārāṇasī, the place of the Turning of the Wheel (*dharma-cakra-pravartana*).

The *vihāra*-s in which the Teacher had himself lived, being essentially supernatural phenomena, had to disappear with the withdrawal of the miracle [i.e. the Buddha's *nirvāṇa*]. In the eyes of mortals, however, there was then no trace of these because of destruction, devastation and other causes [lit. evils].

The *brāhmaṇa* Sujaya built a temple with the image [of the Buddha] in Veṇuvana[31] in Rājagṛha.[32] Kalyāṇa, the youngest *brāhmaṇa*, built the *Gandhola of Vajrāsana[33] with the Mahābodhi[34] in it. Those who built this were celestial architects appearing in human form. [At the time of making the image] the *brāhmaṇa* Kalyāṇa and the celestial architects shut themselves within the temple with the materials for making the Mahābodhi. Nobody was permitted to enter it for seven days. On the sixth day, the mother of the three *brāhmaṇa* brothers came and knocked at the door. 'It is now not more than six days and the door can be opened only tomorrow morning', [they said from inside the temple]. The mother said, 'I am going to die tonight. In the world today, I alone survive who personally have seen **[Fol 11B]** the Buddha. Therefore, others in the future will not be able to determine whether the image is in the likeness of the Tathāgata or not. So you must open the door.'[35]

When she had said thus and the door was opened, the architects vanished. A close examination of the image showed overall likeness with the Teacher. However, there were discrepancies

31. *'od-ma'i-tshal.*
32. *rgyal-po'i-khab.*
33. *rdo-rje-gdan.*
34. *byaṅ-chub-chen-po.*
35. cf Watters ii. 116 for other legends about the making of the image : 'The pilgrim (Yuan-chuang) goes on to tell the wonderful story of the image of Buddha made by Maitreya in the disguise of a Brahmin. This artist asked only for scented clay, and a lamp and to be left alone in the Temple for six months. When this time was up, except four days (not four months as in some texts), the people became curious, and opened the door to see. They found the beautiful likeness complete, except for one little piece about the right breast, but the artist had disappeared.' For Chag lo-tsa-ba's account of the legend, see Roerich SW 525ff.

in three aspects. These were : no halo radiated from it, it was not preaching the Doctrine and, except for sitting, it did not show the three other attitudes. That is why it is [generally] said that this image resembled the real Buddha. Since full seven days could not be devoted to the construction of the image, its iconographical lacuna consisted, according to some, in the toe of the right foot ; according to others, it was in the curl of the hair turning towards the right. So it appears that these two were later added to the image. But it is known that the **paṇḍita*-s say that [the iconographical] lacunae consisted in the lack of hair on the body and the failure to make the robe remain without touching the body. **Paṇḍita* Kṣemendra-bhadra[36] is of the same opinion.

36. *sa-dbaṅ-bzaṅ-po*. An authority frequently referred to by Tār, whose historical work forms one of the most important sources of his own history. Unfortunately, Tār nowhere gives the Indian form of his name nor mentions the title of his historical work. V & S reconstruct the original Indian name as Kṣemendra and add in the note that he was the same Kṣemendra as mentioned by Burnouf 555. In Fol 22A, Tār mentions another of his own sources as *Kalpalatā*. Przyluski thinks that it must be another work by the same author and this *Kalpalatā* is nothing but an abbreviated form of the well-known *Avadāna-kalpalatā* by Kṣemendra (*Bibliotheca Indica*, Calcutta 1940). Therefore, referring to the other lost historical work by *sa-dbaṅ-bzaṅ-po*, Przyluski 108 argues, 'The historical work of Kṣemendra mentioned by Tāranātha has not come down to us for all we know. But there cannot have been any doubt regarding the identity of its author. He is the celebrated Kashmirian writer who lived in the eleventh century.' Assuming this, it is relevant to ask : could this lost work of Kṣemendra be the same as the *Nṛpāvalī*, mentioned by Kalhaṇa as one of his own sources ? cf Keith 161, 'The polymath Kṣemendra had written a *Nṛpāvalī* which Kalhaṇa censures for want of care, but which probably was a careful summary of his sources, and, therefore, is a real loss.' Peculiarly, however, in Fol 139A, Tār speaks of the same writer as a scholar of Magadha (*magadha'i paṇḍita*). Besides, it needs to be noted that the name *sa-dbaṅ-bzaṅ-po* also occurs in the Tg,—though evidently as that of some other author—where the Sanskrit equivalent of the name is given as Mahīndrabhadra or Bhūmīndrabhadra (mDo xciv. 1) and as (*paṇḍita śrī*) Mahīndrabhadra (of Nepal) (mDo cxvi. 6).

On the same night, the *brāhmaṇī* *Jahsā died without falling ill.

Soon afterwards, *brāhmaṇa* Kalyāṇa, while travelling, found a self-radiating gem called *Aśmagarbha. He thought, 'Had I found this before making the Mahābodhi, it could have been used for the eye-balls of the image. But, alas, I could not find it then.' Immediately, there spontaneously appeared holes in the places of the eye-balls of the image. When he was about to break it [i.e. the gem] into two, there spontaneously appeared another similar one. These two were grafted in the places of the eye-balls. Similarly was found another self-radiating gem called *Indranīla. This was placed in-between the brows[37] of the image.

Till the time of king *Rāthika, the interior of the temple of the Mahābodhi remained illuminated with the rays of the gems during the night.

[Fol 12A] Then the three *brāhmaṇa* brothers arranged for the maintenance of five hundred *bhikṣu*-s in each of these three temples. They worshipped the *saṃgha*-s all around with the necessary provisions.

The fourth chapter containing the account of the period of ārya Upagupta.

37. *mdsod-spu.* D 1051—a circle of hair between the eyebrows in the middle of the forehead, one of the particular marks of a Buddha from which he sends forth divine rays of light.

CHAPTER 5

ACCOUNT OF THE PERIOD OF ĀRYA DHĪTIKA

Ārya Upagupta entrusted *ārya* *Dhitika with the Law. His account is as follows.

In Ujjayinī[1] there lived a fabulously rich *brāhmaṇa*. He had a son called *Dhītika who was very intelligent and straightforward. After he completed the study of the four Vedas and the eighteen branches of learning, his father, feeling happy, wanted to see him settled and get married. But he said, 'I have no desire for a home. Permit me, please, to get ordained.'

His father said, 'If you are determined to get ordained, do not do it before I die. And look after these five hundred *brāhmaṇa* attendants.'

Obeying his father, he lived in the house a chaste life,[2] teaching the five hundred *brāhmaṇa*-s the practice of non-violence.[3]

After sometime, when his father died, he gave away all the properties to the *śramaṇa*-s and *brāhmaṇa*-s. Along with his five hundred *brāhmaṇa* followers, he assumed the robe of the travelling mendicant and went through sixteen big cities.[4] There he asked the most famous *tīrthika*-s and *brāhmaṇa*-s about the path of pure moral conduct, but received no satisfactory answer. At last he went to Mathurā, approached *ārya* Upagupta and asked him the same questions. [From him he learnt the right answers]. He received with great reverence the ordination of *pravrajyā* **[Fol 12B]** and *upasampadā* [under Upagupta].

1. *'phags-rgyal.*
2. *tshaṅs-spyod.* See D 1021. V n 'This for the first time indicates the attempt of Buddhism to unite with those leading a mundane life from which subsequently arose the Bodhisattvas.'
3. V tr 'instructed these five hundred *brāhmaṇa*-s without any cruelty (or pressure on them)'.
4. *groṅ-khyer-chen-po-bcu-drug*, i.e. the *ṣoḍaśa-janapada*-s.

By virtue of Upagupta's seven-fold sermons, the five hundred *brāhmaṇa*-s attained *arhat*-hood only within seven days. Ārya *Dhītika established himself in the *aṣṭa-vimokṣa-samādhi.*[5] He roused great reverence for the Buddha's Law among the leading *brāhmaṇa*-s of different places. He delivered the sermons to the 'four classes of followers' in six cities, after *ārya* Upagupta entrusted him with the Law. Thus spreading extensively the Law of the Buddha, he led the living beings to bliss.

Once upon a time, there lived in the country called *Thogar[6] a king named *Mi-nar.[7] In this country, everybody worshipped the sky-god. Besides this, they knew no distinction between virtue and vice. During their festivals, they worshipped the sky-god with great smoke by burning grains, clothes, jewels and fragrant woods. Along with his five hundred *arhat* followers, *ārya* *Dhītika once flew through the sky, appeared at the place of their worship and took his seat at the altar there. They took him as the sky-god, bowed down at his feet and worshipped him elaborately. When, however, he preached the Doctrine, about a thousand people—including their king—were led to the realisation of the Truth. Innumerable people were brought to the path of *śaraṇa-gamana* and *śikṣā.*

He spent the three months of the rainy season there. As a result, the number of *bhikṣu*-s greatly increased. Even the number of those who attained *arhat*-hood reached about a thousand. Thereafter, the route between this country and Kashmir cleared up and thus many *sthavira*-s of Kashmir came to this place and the Law was widely spread.

During the time of this king **[Fol 13A]** and his son called *I-ma-sya,[8] about fifty big monasteries were filled with a large number of *saṃgha*-s.

5. *rnam-par-thar-pa-brgyad-la-bsam-gtan-pa.* See *Mahāvyutpatti* (Calcutta 1944) Pt. iii. p. 288.
6. Tukhāristān. V & S Tukhāra. For the spread of Buddhism in Tukhāristan, see Litvinsky in *Kushan Studies in USSR* 57ff.
7. S n 'the name is very close to that of Menandros—see Lassen ii. 323ff'.
8. S n 'Is it reminiscent of Hermaios ?' V n 'see Lassen ii. 337'

Also in *Kāmarūpa in the east, there lived a *brāhmaṇa* called *Siddha, who was as wealthy as a great king and had thousands of attendants. He used to worship the sun. Once, while he was worshipping the sun, *ārya* *Dhītika, by his miraculous power, made himself emerge as it were from the solar region and sat in front of him, radiating lustre. Taking him to be the sun-god, he [Siddha] bowed down to him and worshipped him. He [Dhītika] delivered sermons to him. When the *brāhmaṇa* was full of reverence, the *ārya* revealed his real self and preached the Doctrine over again. The *brāhmaṇa* realised the Truth and with great reverence built a *vihāra* called Mahācaitya.[9] He also lavishly entertained the *saṃgha*-s all around. Thus the Law of the Buddha was widely spread in *Kāmarūpa.[10]

At that time, in *Mālava on the west, there was a *brāhmaṇa* called Adarpa,[11] who ruled as an uncrowned king. Every day he performed a sacrifice with the flesh and blood of a thousand slaughtered goats. He had also a thousand altars for sacrifice. All his *brāhmaṇa* attendants had to perform the *Aja-medha sacrifice according to their own capacities and all those who were not *brāhmaṇa*-s were employed to collect the materials for the sacrifice. He once wanted to perform the *Go-medha sacrifice and invited *Bhṛku-rākṣasa [Bhṛgu], **[Fol 13B]** belonging to the Bhṛgu family[12] for performing the sacrifice. He collected ten thousand white cows, invited many *brāhmaṇa*-s and arranged everything for the sacrifice.

When he started performing the sacrifice, *ārya* *Dhītika appeared at the altar. In spite of their best efforts, the sacrificial fire could not be kindled nor could the cows be slaughtered in

9. *mchod-rten-chen-po.* V Mahāstūpa.

10. According to Yuan-chuang, however, Kāmarūpa was almost unaware of Buddhism. See Watters ii. 186 : 'they worshipped the *deva*-s and did not believe in Buddhism. So there had never been a Buddhist monastery in the land and whatever Buddhists there were in it performed their acts of devotion secretly.'

11. *dregs-med.*

12. *ṅan-spoṅ-gi-rigs.*

any way. It was even impossible to hurt these. Though the *brāhmaṇa*-s tried to recite the Vedas[13] and *mantra*-s, they could utter no sound.

*Bhṛku-rākṣasa said, 'The real obstacle to the performance of the sacrifice is being caused by the influence of this *śramaṇa*.' Though everybody threw stones, sticks and dust at him, they saw these being turned into flowers and sandal-powder. This made them full of reverence for him. They bowed down at his feet and prayed for forgiveness.

'Oh *ārya*, what dost thou command ?'

The *ārya* said, 'Listen, oh *brāhmaṇa*-s, what are you going to attain by this sinful and evil sacrifice ? [Instead of this] offer gifts and strive after virtue. Cows[14] are deities of the *brāhmaṇa* families. How can it be proper for one who behaves like a human being[15] to kill the gods and the parents ?[16] The cow's flesh is always impure and the *brāhmaṇa*-s do not even touch it. Is it not an insult to the gods [to offer it] ? Oh sages, renounce this sinful religion. What are you going to achieve by this sacrifice designed for the purpose of eating meat ?[17] It is debasing the *mantra*-s to feed oneself with the help of the Black Art.'[18]

In these ways, when he preached the Doctrine elaborately, they were full of remorse because of their sin.

13. *rig-byed.*
14. The text has *bdag* (self), perhaps a corruption of *ba-dag* (cow).
15. The text has *me* (fire), perhaps a corruption of *mi* (man). S takes the word as *ma* (implying the sense of the negative), which hardly gives a clear meaning in this context.
16. S tr 'As you yourselves are gods of the *brāhmaṇa* families and should fulfil the filial duties, why should you, as gods, have to do with the murder of your parents ?' V tr 'If I (i.e. we), being a god of the *brāhmaṇa*-s, am obliged to perform (some) filial duties, what is the use of killing gods and parents ?' Such translations hardly give a coherent meaning, though, accepting the textual readings proposed in notes 14 & 15 above, the passage becomes quite intelligible.
17. V tr 'If you are prejudiced against using meat as a food, what will you achieve (what is the justification) by this sacrificial oblation ?'
18. V tr 'The *mantra*-s to which miraculous power is attributed are illusions of the world.'

Ashamed of their own conduct, they hung their heads low and humbly asked how to atone for the sin. As taught by the *ārya*, all the *brāhmaṇa*-s were brought to the path of *śaraṇa-gamana* and *pañca-śikṣā*.[19] **[Fol 14A]** They built a big temple on the ruins of the *ārāma* of the house-holder Ghoṣila[20] and strove after the wonderful seven-fold merit.[21]

In this way, the Law was widely spread in that country. This happened shortly after the birth of king Aśoka. After this, he [Dhītika] gradually converted about five hundred *brāhmaṇa*-s into the devotees of the *ratna*-s. He looked after the Law of the Buddha for a long time and thus caused welfare to the living beings.

After entrusting *ārya* Kṛṣṇa[22] with the Law, he attained *nirvāṇa* in Ujjayinī in the *Mālava country.

The fifth chapter containing the account of the period of ārya Dhītika.

19. N. Dutt EMB 151 : of the ten *śila*-s or *śikṣā-pada*-s, only the first five were specially intended for the lay devotees.
20. *gdaṅs-can*. V & S Ghoṣavat. V n 'The sweet-voiced.' However, for the Ghoṣilārāma or Ghoṣitārāma, see Watters i. 369-370.
21. *bsod-nams-bdun*.
22. *'phags-pa-nag-po*. V & S *ārya* Kāla. V n 'It can be Kṛṣṇa, the Chinese form of which is Mi-tsche-kia.'

CHAPTER 6

ACCOUNT OF THE PERIOD OF KING AŚOKA

At that time, king Aśoka[1] attained his youth. His account is as follows.

In *Campāraṇa[2] of the border-land[3], there was a king called *Nemita[4] of the solar dynasty, who, with five hundred ministers and great wealth, ruled the northern lands. He had from the first [wife] six sons, called Kalyāṇa,[5] Rathika,[6] Śaṅkhika[7] Dhanika[8], Padmaka[9] and the sixth called Kanaka.[10]

1. *mya-ṅan-med* For Przyluski's view concerning the possible sources from which Tār compiles the legends of Aśoka, see Supplementary Note 2. V n 'In the Buddhist works, there is a prediction by the Buddha that 100 years after his death there will be a *cakravartin* named Aśoka—having the surname Peacock (*maurya*)—who, by building 84,000 monuments, will spread the power of Buddha. This prediction, therefore, refers to the *dharma-rāja* Aśoka, whom the European scholars regard as Aśoka the second. He could have lived not later than 100 (or 110 or 116) years after Buddha.'
2. Campā, the capital of Aṅga, was also called Campāraṇya—D. C. Sircar CGEIL 109. S sees in this the contraction of two names, Campā and Karṇa. V quotes S. cf Watters ii. 181f.
3. V tr 'belonging to the Tha-ru tribe' and adds in note that S translates *tha-ru* as border-land.
4. In the standard account, Aśoka is considered a son of Bindusāra, whom, along with Candragupta, Tār seems to relegate to another line—Fol 2A.
5. *dge-ba-can*. V Lakṣmaṇa. It is tempting to conjecture if Tār has in mind the name of Susīma or Sumana. From Tār's list of Aśoka's brothers, the absence of the names of Tissa Ekavihārika and Vītaśoka appears to be particularly conspicuous—see C. D. Chatterjee in JAIH i. 117ff; Przyluski 121 and Watters ii. 94f. Vītaśoka appears in Tār as the grandson and successor of Aśoka—Fol 26A.
6. *śiṅ-rta-can*.
7. *duṅ-can*.
8. *nor-can*.
9. *padma-can*.
10. P-ed *gser-can*, 'one possessing gold'. S-ed *ser-can* (D 1279—brass), reconstructed by V & S as Anūpa.

Later on, the king united with the wife of a merchant[11] and she conceived. The king's mother died and on the day the mourning was over this merchant's wife gave birth to a son. [The king said] 'Let he be called Aśoka, because he is born on the day when the period of mourning came to an end.' So he was thus named.

On growing up, he became an adept in the sixty arts, eight-fold divination and the arts of writing and reading palms. At that time, **[Fol 14B]** in the presence of many people, the ministers enquired of the *brāhmaṇa* astrologers : 'Which one of the king's sons is going to be the king ?'

[The astrologers answered] 'He who eats the best food, wears the best clothes and sits on the best seat.'

On being confidentially enquired by two of the foremost ministers, it was told that by best food was meant cooked rice, by best clothes were meant the coarse ones and by the best seat the ground. Since the other sons of the king lived the life of luxury while Aśoka had ordinary food and clothes, it was known that Aśoka was going to be the king.

Meanwhile, peoples of the hilly countries like Nepal and *Khasya[12] revolted. Aśoka was sent with the army to subdue them. Without difficulty Aśoka subdued the hilly races, imposed levy and annual tax on them, realised ransom from them and offered these to the king.

11. V tr 'the wife (i.e. the daughter of some) merchant'. However, see C. D. Chatterjee in JAIH i.119—according to the commentary on the *Mahāvaṃsa*, Aśoka and his co-uterine brothers Tissa and Vītaśoka were born of queen Dharmā, a princess of a Moriyan royal family, while, in the *Avadāna* texts, of Subhadrāṅgī, a certain *brāhmaṇa* lady of Campā. 'Aśoka', adds C. D. Chatterjee, 'was the heir apparent and not Susīma or Sumana, whichever might have been his real name. But in the *Avadāna* texts, Aśoka has been represented as the usurper ! Susīma might have been the eldest son of Bindusāra ; but that did not justify his claim to the throne, judging by the law of succession followed in the Moriyan royal family.'
12. 'Khasa, a Himalayan people, including the ancestors of the modern Khakkas of Kashmir'—Sircar CGEIL 83. According to the *Aśokāvadāna*, however, Aśoka, during his youth, subdued the country of the Khasas and Takṣaśilā (instead of Nepal)—Przyluski 111.

The king said, 'I am highly pleased with your intelligence, might and bravery. I shall give you whatever you want.'

[Aśoka said] 'My brothers here are going to harm me. Therefore, please give me the city of *Pāṭaliputra[13] as my own place along with the other things that I need.'

He (Nemita) granted him all these. In this city were built five hundred gardens and a thousand girls with musical instruments surrounded him the whole day and night and satisfied his lust.

*Camaśa, king of *Magadha, died at that time. Though he had twelve sons, none of them could retain the kingdom when placed on the throne. His *brāhmaṇa* minister called Gambhīra-Śīla[14] ruled for a few years. During that time there developed enmity between him and king *Nemita. In the long-drawn battle fought on the bank of the *Gaṅgā, the six elder sons [Fol 15A] of the king took part. King *Nemita died at that time. Considering that the news of the king's death might boost up the morale of the *Magadhans, this was kept suppressed and the administration of the kingdom was carried on by two ministers. However, since on the seventh day the people of the city came to know all about this, they started disobeying the two ministers.

[The ministers thought] 'So now is the time of the prediction of the *brāhmaṇa*-s coming true.' Thus thinking, they invited Aśoka and installed him on the throne.[15]

After conquering *Magadha, on the day when each of the six elder sons of the king took possession of a city, they heard that Aśoka had been installed on the throne. On receiving this news, instead of returning towards the north of the *Gaṅgā,

13. Yuan-chuang (Watters ii. 88) : 'In the 100th year after the Buddha's *nirvāṇa*, king Aśoka, the great-grandson of king Bimbisāra, transferred his capital from Rājagṛha to Pāṭaliputra.'

14. *ṅaṅ-tshul-zab-pa.*

15. According to the *Dīpavaṃsa* and *Mahāvaṃsa*, Aśoka, when acting as the vice-regent at Ujjayinī, came to know of Bindusāra's death and hence proceeded to Pāṭaliputra to seize the throne—Bongard-Levin & Volkova 6.

the sons of the king, along with five hundred ministers, established their own rule in the five cities like Rājagṛha etc, while the sixth of them established his rule in *Aṅga.

The king's first son followed the 'secret doctrine of the Lokāyata,'[16] the second worshipped Mahādeva, the third Viṣṇu,[17] the fourth the secret [doctrine of the] Vedānta,[18] the fifth the Digambara Kaṇaka[19] and the sixth the *brahmacārī brāhmaṇa* *Kuśa-putra[20] [? Kauśika]. Each of them established his own centre.

Following the advice of the anchorite of the *Bhṛku [Bhṛgu] family, the worshipper of *ḍākinī*-s and *rākṣasa*-s, Aśoka accepted for his deity the mother goddesses of the crematorium including *Umā-devī. Indulging as he did in lust for several years, he came to be known as *Kāmāśoka.

Having once a clash of opinions with the elder brothers, he (Aśoka) went on fighting them for several years. **[Fol 15B]** At last, he killed his six brothers[21] along with the five hundred ministers. He attacked many other cities and brought under his rule the whole territory from the Himālaya to the Vindhya.

As he grew extremely haughty and cruel, he felt no peace of mind or even an appetite without performing a violent

16. *'jig-rten-rgyaṅ-phan-gyi-gsaṅ-tshig.*
17. *khyab-'jug.*
18. *rig-byed-mtha'.*
19. *gcer-bu-pa-gser-can.* V & S Nirgrantha Piṅgala. V n 'cf Burnouf 360. In the text *gser-can,* which, according to S, is a corruption of *gser-skya.*'
20. *kuśa'i-bu,* lit. 'son of Kuśa'. V tr 'the Brahmanical teaching of the *brāhmaṇa* Kauśika.'
21. C. D. Chatterjee in JAIH i. 118f observes that though Aśoka's claim to the throne was quite legitimate, in the Pāli chronicles, he 'was dubbed Caṇḍāśoka...for conducting a fratricidal war, in the course of which all his step-brothers were killed.' The *Avadāna* texts go further and claim that the name Caṇḍāśoka 'had its origin ... in the slaughter, after torturing mercilessly, all those who, by mistake, entered the Hell of which he was the creator. Indeed...the flight of *kalpanā* (imagination) cannot be higher than this !' Evidently, the motive behind all these fabrications was to add a dramatic background to the later pious career of the king.

action. On each morning, he ordered for punishments like killing, beating and chaining. Soothed only by these, he could sit peacefully for his meal. Kṣemendrabhadra says, 'There are many such accounts of the aggressiveness of the king. But I am not relating all these here, because that is unnecessary.' I have myself heard many Indian legends. These also I am not recording here.

Led by the false knowledge of the *brāhmaṇa*-s, he decided to perform animal sacrifice. The anchorite of the *Bhṛku [Bhṛgu] family Gokarṇa[22] in particular said, 'If you perform a sacrifice of ten thousand human beings, your empire will expand and you will also attain liberation.'

Thus advised, he got the sacrificial house built.[23] He searched everywhere for a person that could slaughter ten thousand men. For sometime, however, none could be found like this. At last he found a Caṇḍāla[24] of *Tirahuti and ordered him, 'I am going to send to this house all those that are to be slaughtered. Go on slaughtering anybody that enters this house till the number reaches ten thousand.' The king himself took the oath of worshipping Umā[25] in this form.

22. *ba-lan-rna-ba*. cf Watters ii.89—According to other legends 'king Aśoka had burnt to death 500 ladies of his harem, and his chief minister Rādhagupta (called also Anuruddha) reminding him that such proceedings were unseemly of a king, recommended His Majesty to institute a place of punishment under a proper official. The king took the advice and caused a jail or place of punishment to be constructed, with a handsome attractive building with trees and tanks like a city.'

23. Usually referred to as Aśoka's Hell. Both Fa-hien and Yuan-chuang were shown its relics. cf Watters ii. 90 : 'Fa-hien's account is not taken from the *Divyāvadāna*, but it agrees with that work in placing the site of the Hell near the tope erected by Aśoka over Ajātaśatru's share of Buddha's relics. Yuan-chuang also seems to have found the site near and to the north of the Relic Tope as Fa-hien describes.' cf Przyluski 127ff.

24. In the *Divyāvadāna*, he is called Caṇḍa-giri (in Chinese O-shan or Wicked Hill)—Watters ii. 90. *Aśokāvadāna* mentions him as Caṇḍa Girika, but considers him to have been a merchant—Przyluski 118 & 127.

25. *bka'-thub-zlog-ma*.

After slaughtering one or two thousand men, when this killer was going somewhere outside the city, a *bhikṣu*,[26] with the hope of changing his conduct, told him about the sin of killing animals and of many details of the [punishments given in the] hell. However, the killer totally misunderstood all these virtuous **[Fol 16A]** words and thought[27] : 'I have so long been killing by chopping off the heads of men. From what the *bhikṣu* says, it now appears that I can as well kill them in various other ways like burning, cutting to pieces and taking off the skin [as the *bhikṣu* describes the scenes of the hell].'

So he continued to kill in these ways many other men and about five thousand persons were slaughtered in that sacrificial house. At that time, the king's former name was changed into *Caṇḍāla *Aśoka.

Now at that time, a disciple of *arhat* Yaśaḥ entered the house by mistake. He was well-versed in the scriptures, was placed in the *yoga-mārga* and was a novice[28] (*śramaṇera*). When the killer was about to strike him with the sword, he enquired the cause thereof. He [the killer] told him about what had happened before.

26. Watters ii. 90—the *bhikṣu* belonged to Ke-tu-ma monastery. According to other sources, he was from Kukkuṭārāma *vihāra* ; Bālapaṇḍita was either his name or the text he recited—Przyluski 127ff.
27. V tr 'However (these virtuous words) could not arouse even a grain of virtue in him, and he, on the contrary, thought...'
28. In the *Aśokāvadāna* his name is given as Samudra—Przyluski 120. cf Watters ii. 90—his name in Chinese form : Hai, meaning 'the sea'. Interestingly, Tār does not mention his name and refers to him simply as a *śramaṇera*, though he is supposed to have been responsible for the epoch-making event of converting Aśoka. Comments Przyluski 120-1 : 'Having been in use for a long time, the figure of Samudra afterwards lost its prominence and his name fell into oblivion. Ere long it was found that this anonymity was not without its advantage. It was an edifying spectacle to see the most powerful of monarchs to have been converted by an ordinary monk. The moment the value of this contrast was realised, it was sought to be accentuated. In the account of Tāranātha as in the Ceylonese chronicles, it is no longer an ordinary *bhikṣu* that converts the great king ; it is a novice, a little *śramaṇera*.'

'So, kill me after seven days. I shall not move out till then and shall stay in this sacrificial house.' When he said this, the killer agreed.

Witnessing the sacrificial place full of blood, flesh, bones, intestines, etc, he directly realised the sixteen truths[29] like impermanence and, before the expiry of seven days, attained *arhat*-hood. He also acquired the miraculous power (*ṛddhi*).

On the day of the expiry of these seven days, the killer thought : 'None like him had entered this house before. Therefore, I am going to kill him in a new way.' Thus thinking, he filled an enormous cauldron with *til oil, put the novice[30] in it and placed it on fire. In spite of the fire burning for the whole day and night, not even the slightest damage was done to his body.[31]

On receiving this news, the king was surprised **[Fol 16B]** and he came to the sacrificial house to see this. The killer ran towards him with the sword. The king asked him the reason for this. [The killer said] 'Oh king, it is your own vow that anybody entering this house must be killed till the number reaches ten thousand.'

The king said, 'But, then, you have yourself entered the house before me. So I must kill you first.'

While the two were thus arguing among themselves, the novice showed the miraculous feats like showering rain, causing lightning, moving in the sky, etc. Both the king and the killer were full of great reverence and bowed down at his feet and the seed of enlightenment germinated within them.

29. *bden-pa'i-rnam-pa-bcu-drug*. See *Mahāvyutpatti* (Calcutta 1944) Pt. iii. p. 275-6. cf Yuan-chuang (Watters ii. 90), 'At that time, one of the king's concubines arrived to undergo punishment for misconduct. She was at once pounded to atoms in the presence of the *bhikṣu*. The latter now made the most of his respite, and by zealous application became an *arhat*.'

30. *dge-tshul*, lit, *śramaṇera*. It is apparently strange to refer to him thus even after his attainment of *arhat*-hood. In the next chapter also, Sudarśana prays for ordination after attaining *arhat*-hood.

31. Yuan-chuang describes the scene differently—see Watters ii. 89.

He (the novice) delivered the sermon and the king became extremely repentant for his sins and at once demolished the sacrificial house. He asked the novice how to atone for the sin.

'Oh king, I am incapable of telling you the means of atoning for your sins. In the Kukkuṭārāma in the east, there lives an *upādhyāya arhat* called Yaśaḥ-dhvaja[32], who will be able to tell you about the ways of atoning for your sins.'

Accordingly, the king sent the message to the *arhat* : 'Oh *ārya*, please come to *Pāṭaliputra and relieve me of my sins. If, oh *ārya*, you cannot come here, I shall go to you.'

Realising that the arrival there of the king himself would have meant harm to many people, the *arhat* Yaśaḥ himself came to *Pāṭaliputra. There, he delivered the sermons to the king during every day, and, during every night, he delivered the sermons to the 'four classes of followers' at the monastery.

From the time of meeting **[Fol 17A]** *arhat* Yaśaḥ, the king was full of great reverence and started spending the day and night in pious acts. He worshipped thirty thousand *bhikṣu*-s every day.

When *arhat* Yaśaḥ was living in other places like *Magadha etc, the king once sent five hundred merchants to collect gems from the treasure island[33]. Their voyage was successful and they were returning with the cargo of various gems. When they halted for rest on this side of the sea [? Indian coast], the Nāgas sent waves to carry away their merchandise. They had to return depending on other sources of livelihood. It was rumoured in *Pāṭaliputra that the merchants were going to be back within seven days. Since nobody heard about what actually had happened to them, all sorts of people including the *brāhmaṇa*-s and *parivrājaka*-s collected to see the colour and

32. In Tār's account, from now on Yaśaḥ becomes the adviser of Aśoka. For other legends connecting Aśoka with Upagupta, see Watters ii. 91 and Przyluski 69ff.

33. *nor-bu'i-gliṅ.* cf Przyluski 111-2.

other wonderful qualities of the gems. On the seventh day, when the king along with the people came to the garden, they saw the merchants returning only with their upper garments on and looking exhausted. Everybody was amazed by this unexpected sight and burst into laughter.

The king asked the cause of this. The merchants told their story and said, 'Oh lord, if you do not take some measure to subdue the Nāgas, nobody from now on will be willing to go to collect the gems. Oh king, please take some measure.'

The king felt highly disturbed and consulted the wise men about the possible measures. The *brāhmaṇa*-s and *parivrājaka*-s **[Fol 17B]** knew of none. But an *arhat*[34] with six *abhijñāna*-s thought, 'The possible measure should be suggested [in the form of the prediction] by a deity. If the *arhat* himself does it, the people may take him as being partial to the *bhikṣu*-s. Even the king will feel sceptical and the *tīrthika*-s would slander.' With this consideration, he said, 'Oh great king, there certainly is a measure. But this will be predicted tonight by your tutelary deity.'

Early in the morning, the king heard the tutelary deity residing above[35] saying, 'Oh king, worship the Buddha elaborately. The Nāgas will be subdued.' And the tutelary deity residing below[36] said, 'Oh king, worship the *saṃgha*-s of the *arhat*-s. [The Nāgas] will be subdued.'

In the morning, the king got the people assembled together, told them about the predictions and asked, 'What should be done now ?'. The ministers said, 'Please ask the *arhat* himself who foretold this yesterday.' He was summoned and questioned. [The *arhat* thought] 'Let me adopt some means of convincing them.'

He wrote on a small piece of copper-plate, 'Oh Nāgas,

34. Though in Tār, the usual adviser of Aśoka is Yaśaḥ, in his account of subduing the *nāga*-s another *arhat*—mentioned as Indra in the *Avadānakalpalatā*—acts as his counsellor : see Przyluski 111.

35. *khyim-gyi-nam-mkha'-la-gnas-pa'i-lha*, lit. 'tutelary deity in the upper sphere of the house'.

36. *sa-la-gnas-pa'i-lha*, lit. 'tutelary deity on the ground'.

listen to the command of king Aśoka. Return to the merchants the gems that you have taken away', etc. And he threw the copper-plate into the *Gaṅgā. On the top of a lofty pillar of stone at the broad cross-road of the city, he also placed a pot made of **aṣṭa-dhātu* containing golden images of both the king and the Nāga.

On the next morning, it was found that the copper-plate was thrown back at the gate of the king's palace by the storm and rain caused by the furious Nāgas and that the king's image was bowing down before that of the Nāga.

[Fol 18A] On being questioned by the king, the *arhat* said, 'The accumulated merit of the Nāga is at present greater than that of the king. For increasing your own merit, please worship the Buddha and the *saṃgha*.'

The king, feeling inspired, started worshipping the images[37] and *caitya*-s seven times more than before. In a moment, the *arhat* went to the realm of the Nāgas and of the gods and invited all the *arhat*-s. The king also built a very big house for the festival. When the *arhat* rang the **gandi*,[38] the *arhat*-s assembled even from Sumeru[39] and its surroundings. (The king) worshipped with all the requisites the *saṃgha* of sixty thousand *arhat*-s for three months. During this period, the king's image raised itself gradually day by day and in fortyfive days became as high as that of the Nāga. After this, the image of the Nāga went on stooping down every day. And on the next fortyfifth day, it was found that the image of the Nāga was bowing down at the feet of the king's image.

The people were full of great wonder : 'Ah, such then is the result of worshipping the Jewels (*tri-ratna*).'

37. *sku-gzugs*, lit. 'image'. Przyluski 109 takes this as a reference to the worship of the image of the Buddha and argues that Tār's source here 'points to the Kashmirian period at the earliest, for before the rise of the Graeco-Bactrian School of Art (of Gandhāra) artists avoided building images of the Buddha.' However, Yuan-chuang saw images of the Buddha which he believed were made during the time of Prasenajit and Udayana—Watters i. 384. cf also I-Tsing 190.

38. D 214—the gong or bell to call monks to monastic services.

39. *ri-rab*.

When the same copper-plate was again thrown into the *Gaṅgā, the messenger of the Nāga appeared in human guise on the next day and said, 'The gems are deposited back on the seashore. Please send the merchants to bring these.'

As the king was about to do so, the same *arhat* said, 'That will not be a great wonder. **[Fol 18B]** Better send them the message that within seven days they are to bring the gems here on their own shoulders. That will be a great wonder.'

This being done, on the seventh day when the king was surrounded by a large number of people, the Nāgas, in the guise of merchants, brought the gems and touched the king's feet. It was a grand spectacle for the people and a great festival was organised to celebrate it.

The king became an adept in the magic spell of *yakṣa-ratha*[40] and with this raised a four-divison army of the *yakṣa*-s—with horses as big as elephants and men as tall as the **tāla* trees, etc. He brought under his rule without bloodshed all the countries including those to the south of the Vindhya. And he conquered the northern Himālayas, the snowy ranges beyond Li-yul,[41] the entire land of *Jambudvīpa bounded by seas on east, south and west, and also fifty small islands.

Arhat Yaśaḥ then explained to him the prediction of the Teacher Samyak-sambuddha thus : '[You are to] decorate the surface of the earth with *caitya*-s containing the relics of the Tathāgata.'

So he felt the need of finding the relics[42] of the Teacher.

40. *gnod-sbyin-śiṅ-rta'i-rigs-sṅags.* S n 'The *Mañjuśrī-mūla-tantra* refers to the *yakṣa-ratha-siddhi.*' cf Chag lo-tsā-ba (Roerich SW 537) : 'He propitiated the great *yakṣa* called Ratha.'

41. D 1213 Kaṃsadeśa or Khoten. In Tg *Arhat-saṃghavardhana-vyākaraṇa* (mDo xciv. 44) and *Kaṃsa-deśa-vyākaraṇa* (mDo xciv. 45) contain a history of Li-yul, with a descriptive enumeration of the *vihāra*-s and religious sects there and also an account of Kustana, the first king of Li-yul, from whose name was derived the name Khoten. For Kustana and Khoten, see Watters ii. 295ff ; I-Tsing (Takakusu) liii & 20 and Legge 16ff & 109.

42. For legends of finding the relics, see Przyluski 109ff ; Watters ii. 20f and C. D. Chatterjee in JAIH i. 124.

The relic which was received by king Ajātaśatru as his share was securely preserved, buried under the great *caitya* of Rājagṛha. The king and *arhat* Yaśaḥ, along with the people, went there to recover it. Reaching the place, they dug the ground three men deep and saw a burning iron-wheel so swiftly turning round that it was not possible to go near it.

On the advice of a local old woman **[Fol 19A]**, they went to a hilly stream about three *yojana*-s to the west. When the course of its flow was diverted, the wheel stopped turning and the fire on it got extinguished. After the ground was dug further, a copper-plate was found containing the inscription: 'Here lies the relic of the Tathāgata, one big *Magadhan *droṇa* in measure. In the future, a certain poor king would dig it out.'

Seeing this, Aśoka arrogantly thought, 'So the person to discover it cannot be myself, because he is supposed to be a poor one. Therefore, he must be somebody else.' Thus he was about to return.

However, being requested by the *arhat*, he dug the ground again seven men deep and at last found the relic, which was originally only one big *Magadhan *droṇa* in measure but had now increased to measure six *khala*-s. It was preserved in the innermost of seven chests, placed one within the other, of which the outermost one was made of iron. The chests were studded with self-radiating gems placed at their four corners. Each of these gems could illumine as far as a *yojana*. All these were arranged in the form of offerings [of lighted lamps]. The value of each gem was so much that the entire property throughout the whole empire of Aśoka could not equal it. Knowing this, his arrogance was removed.

He took only one big *droṇa* of the relic and kept the rest hidden as before, rediverted the hidden stream so that the iron-wheel started revolving and the fire burning as before. This was again covered up [with earth].

Employing the powerful *yakṣa*-s as messengers and assistants, he sent out command to the people of the different places, and, only in the course of a day and night, built the *caitya*-s of the eight holy places,[43] [Fol 19B] and the *caitya*-s surrounding Vajrāsana and those that were spread all over *Jambudvipa as far as Li-yul in the north,—a total of eighty-four thousand *caitya*-s[44] containing the relics of the Muni. Then he sent out his command everywhere that daily worship was to be conducted in each of these *caitya*-s with thousands of lamps, incense and garlands. The Bodhi Tree was worshipped with scented water and *pañca-amṛta*[45] filled in ten thousand pitchers made of gold, silver and **vaidurya*, and from some distance it was worshipped with ten thousand incense burners and lamps. For three months, he worshipped with all offerings at *Pāṭaliputra sixty thousand *arhat*-s, who had been invited and offered high seats of honour (lit. 'placed in the sky'). He worshipped the *saṃgha*-s, the *ārya-śaikṣa*-[46] and the *pṛthak-jana*-s[47], who were offered seats on the ground. At the end, he offered to each monk robes worth a lakh. On the same night, the king, along with his attendants, started on the shoulders of the most powerful *yakṣa*-s for visiting the *caitya*-s and, in seven days, completed his pilgrimage of the *caitya*-s raised all over *Jambudvipa in

43. i.e. 1) Lumbinī Garden, Kapilāvastu ; 2) Bodhi Tree near the Nairañjanā river, Magadha ; 3) Vārāṇasī ; 4) Jetavana, Śrāvastī ; 5) Kānyakubja ; 6) Rājagṛha ; 7) Vaiśālī and 8) Kuśīnagara. See Takakusu *I-Tsing* 108n. There exists a work by Śrī-Harṣadeva, king of Kashmir, called *Aṣṭa-mahā-sthāna-caitya-vandanā-stava*—Tg, bsTod 57. Another work in Tg is attributed to Nāgārjuna called *Aṣṭa-mahā-sthāna-caitya-stotra*, bsTod 24-5.

44. cf Watters ii. 92 'The 84,000 topes set up by Aśoka are generally said to have been for the distribution of the Buddha's relics taken for the purpose by the king from seven of the eight topes erected by the original recipients. But they are also said to have been made for the worship of the 84,000 aphorisms of Buddhism or sections of the Law'. cf Legge 69n : 'the bones of the human body are supposed to consist of 84,000 atoms, and hence the legend of Aśoka's wish to build 84,000 topes, one over each atom of Śākyamuni's skeleton '

45. *bdud-rtsi-lna*. See Roerich SW 512-13.

46. *'phags-pa-slob-pa*. J 587—the venerable preceptors, more than *bhikṣu*-s but less than *arhat*-s.

47. *so-so'i-skye-bo*. D 1283—a layman, a man in his natural state, i.e. one not yet enlightened.

honour of the Jewels. Everywhere he increased the offerings ten-fold and offered golden ornaments to each of the *caitya*-s (containing the relics) of the Buddha and of the *śrāvaka*-s. He lavishly decorated the Bodhi Tree with all kinds of gems.

On the eighth day, the king repeatedly prayed, 'Let me, by virtue of these pious acts, attain enlightenment and become the supreme among men.' **[Fol 20A]** And he asked the people to join him earnestly in this prayer.

But most of the people started saying that though the king was making a great deal of labour, it was going to bear little fruit. Some others said that as there was nothing called the *anuttara-bodhi* (highest enlightenment), how the prayer of the king could be fulfilled ?

On hearing all these the king said, 'If this prayer of mine is going to be fulfilled, let the great earth shake and flowers shower from the sky.' Immediately after he said this, the earth shook and the sky showered flowers. As a result, faith grew in these people and they also joined the prayer.

He worshipped the *bhikṣu*-s for three months during the consecration of the *caitya*-s. When this was over, there accidentally remained behind[48] many ordinary *bhikṣu*-s. The king made a big offering to them in the garden and showed particular respect to an aged monk, who sat at the head of the row.[49] This aged monk was extremely foolish and was of little learning.

He could not recite even a single **śloka*, while among the younger *bhikṣu*-s there were many *piṭaka-dhara*-s.

After the feast, the monks occupying lower seats asked the aged monk, 'Do you know why the king is making special offering to you ?'

The aged one said, 'I do not know it'.

They said, 'But we know this. The king will presently come to you for listening to your sermons. You will have to deliver a sermon.'

48. *glo-bur-du-lhags-pa*. S 'who suddenly appeared'.
49. *vṛddhāsana*. cf I-Tsing (Takakusu) 35ff.

This greatly hurt the feelings of the aged monk and he said, 'I received ordination sixty years back. Yet I do not know even a single *śloka. [Fol 20B] Only if I could guess this before, I would have found another monk capable of delivering the sermon and would have offered all the good food to him. However, I have already eaten all these. Now, what is to be done ?'

Thus he felt sad. The deity of the garden thought, 'It would be highly improper if the king fails to show respect to this monk.' So he came to this monk in human guise and said, 'If the king approaches you for sermons, you should say : "Oh great king, since even this earth with its mountains is afterall momentary, what is there to think about the kingdom ? Oh great king, you should meditate on this." '

Then came the king and, presenting him with a set of robes of golden colour, sat down to listen to the sermon. As the king was already full of reverence, when the aged monk repeated all these, he thought that this was the fundamental truth and felt ecstasy to think over its significance.

The deity of the garden again told the aged monk, 'Do not allow the offerings of the devotee to go waste.'[50] So he [the aged monk] took instructions from an *ācārya* and, concentrating intensely on it, attained *arhat*-hood in three months. He spent the rainy season in the Pārijāṭa-vana of the Tuṣita [lit. the region of the 33 gods] and returned again to the *saṃgha*-s and to the people of *Pāṭaliputra. The robes which he received from the king were fragrant with the scent of Pārijāta and it spread all around. On being asked by the other monks, he said all that had happened and this astonished all.

The king also eventually heard all these. [He thought] 'The attainment of *arhat*-hood even by an utterly foolish monk is due to the merit of the Doctrine [Fol 21A] and to my gift of the robes.' Impressed by the blessings derived by others from his gifts, he lavishly entertained again three lakhs

50. P-ed *chud-zod* (waste), S-ed *chuṅ* (little). V & S 'Do not accept even a grain of food offered by the devotee.'

of monks for five years[51] : he offered excellent food and robes to the *saṃgha*-s of the *arhat*-s during the first part of the day, to the *saṃgha*-s of the venerable preceptors (*ārya-śaikṣa*-s) during the second part of the day and to the *saṃgha*-s of the *pṛthak-jana*-s during the third part of the day.

Towards the end of his life the king took the vow to donate one hundred crores of gold to the *saṃgha*-s of each of [the following countries, viz.] Aparāntaka, Kashmir and *Thogar.[52] He donated in full to the *saṃgha*-s of Kashmir and *Thogar and also made offerings of other things equal in amount. When, however, four crores of gold and other materials remained to be donated to the *saṃgha*-s of Aparāntaka [to complete the promised sum of one hundred crores], the king fell seriously ill. His nephew[53] Vāsavadatta,[54] the treasurer of the royal gold, disobeyed the king and refused to pay the remaining gold to the *saṃgha*-s [of Aparāntaka].

At that time, the king had half a handful[55] of *āmalaka*-s before him for quenching his thirst. He offered these with great reverence to the *arhat*-s who at that time had come to him. All the *arhat*-s unanimously exclaimed, 'Oh king, the virtue of this gift is much greater than that of the donation of ninetysix crores of gold which you had made while you were ruling.'

51. *pañcavārṣika*. cf Przyluski 109 & 122. For Fa-hien's detailed description, see Legge 22f.
52. Przyluski 109 argues that this reference to Tukhāristān indicates that Tār is drawing here on much later legends, because Tukhāristān 'opened itself to Buddhism only after the Kuṣānas'. But Tār apparently believes that Buddhism was introduced into Tukhāristān much earlier—see Fol 12B, the account of Dhītika. For archaeological evidences of Buddhism in Tukhāristān, see Litvinsky in *Kushan Studies in USSR* 57ff.
53. *tsha-bo*. V & S grandson.
54. *nor-lhas-byin*.
55. *skyu-ru-ra-sñim-pa-phyed*, lit. 'half an *añjali* of *āmalaka*-s'. But the usual legend is about half an *āmalaka*. cf Przyluski 65 ; Watters ii. 100.

An attendant maid was once fanning him with a *cāmara*,[56] the handle of which was studded with jewels. She felt sleepy by the midday heat and the *cāmara* fell down from her hand on the body of the king. The king thought, 'Previously even the great kings **[Fol 21B]** used to wash my feet. Even the lowest of the servants is insulting me now in this way.' Thus he died with anger in mind.

Because of this anger, he had to be reborn as a Nāga in a big lake of *Pāṭaliputra.

It is said that *arhat* Yaśaḥ thought : 'Where is the pious great king reborn ?' And he came to know that he was reborn in the lake as a Nāga. The *arhat* went to the shore of this lake. He (the Nāga) came upon the surface of the lake and sat in front of the *arhat* in a very pleasant manner, as had been his old habit. When he was about to eat the birds and other animals, the *arhat* preached the Doctrine and said, 'Oh great king, beware !' Immediately he stopped eating and died. He was reborn among the gods in the Tuṣita.

From the time the king acquired reverence for the Law of the Buddha, started building numerous temples and monasteries all over his kingdom and spread the Law of the Buddha in all directions—from then on his former name was changed and he became famous as **Dharma-Aśoka.

When he failed to donate to the *bhikṣu*-s of Aparāntaka more than ninety-six crores of gold, one of his wise ministers told him, 'Oh king, there is a way out. Make a gift of this entire kingdom worth a hundred crores of gold to the *saṃgha*.' Accordingly, the king donated the kingdom to the *saṃgha*. For the sake of enhancing the king's virtue, the *saṃgha* ruled the kingdom for only two days, after which they (the ministers) took back the kingdom in exchange of immeasurable gold and wealth offered to the *saṃgha*. And then **[Fol 22A]** Aśoka's grandson[57] Vigataśoka[58] was placed on the throne.

56. *rṅa-yal*.
57. *tsha-bo*.
58. *mya-ṅan-bral*.

In the history compiled by Kṣemendrabhadra, is given this biography in an orderly form. (The account is also found) in the *Śrāvaka Piṭaka*-s[59] and along with the *Aśoka-avadāna*, *Aśoka-vinīta-avadāna*, *Aśokena-nāga-vinīta-avadāna*, *Caitya-avadāna*, *Utsava-avadāna*, *Svarṇa-dāna-avadāna*. These six, along with the *Kuṇāla-avadāna*, make the total of seven. Of these, the second and the seventh are translated in Tibet. I have seen the others in their Indian originals. Certain incidents like that of the 'gift of gold' are to be found also in the *Kalpa-latā*.[60]

The sixth chapter containing the account of the period of king Aśoka.

59. See Supplementary Note 2.
60. *dpag-bsam-'khri-śiṅ*, evidently the *Avadāna-kalpalatā* (Bib. Ind., Calcutta 1940). Incidentally, in Tg (mDo xciii), the Tibetan form of the name of the author Kṣemendra is given as *dge-ba'i-dbaṅ-po* and not as *sa-dbaṅ-bzaṅ-po*—see note 36 of ch. 4.

CHAPTER 7

ACCOUNT OF THE INCIDENTS DURING THE PERIOD OF KING AŚOKA

Before entrusting *ārya* Kṛṣṇa[1] with the Law, *ārya* *Dhītika was ill for a long time. He resided then in *Kauśāmbī in the *Mālava country. He was to deliver sermons to the 'four classes of followers.' However, the monks of Vaiśālī (said), 'How can we expect sermons on the True Law from a *sthavira* who is himself sick ?' And they refused to go to him. While violating the Ten Prohibitions[2], they claimed : 'Such is the Doctrine, such is the Vinaya and such is the Law of the Teacher.'

Seven hundred *arhat*-s[3]—including *arhat* Yaśaḥ[4]—felt annoyed and organised the Second Council for the collection of the sayings (of the Buddha) at the *Kusumpurī *vihāra* under the patronage of king Nandin,[5] a *Licchavi by birth.

1. V & S Kāla. V n 'According to the Chinese histories, Dhītika was born in Mathurā and preached in Central India, while Kāla (Chinese Mi-tsche-kia) was born in Central India and was the head of 8,000 ascetics.'
2. For the Ten Prohibitions and the Second Council, see Supplementary Note 3.
3. On the Second Council being a council of 700 *arhat*-s, see Bu-ston ii. 94 ; Watters ii. 73ff ; BA i. 24. According to the *Cullavagga* xii. 2.9 and *Vinaya-Kṣudraka* (quoted by Bu-ston ii. 94), all of them were the disciples of Ānanda.
4. On the part played by Yaśaḥ (variously mentioned as Yaśa, Yaśoda, Yaśano, Yaśaḥ—Watters ii. 74) in summoning the Second Council, see Bu-ston ii. 91ff ; Watters ii. 73ff ; *Cullavagga* xii. 1.1 (where he is mentioned as the son of Kākaṇḍaka) ; etc. Tār glosses over the account of the organised hostility of the Vaiśālī monks against Yaśaḥ : *Cullavagga* xii. 1.7—they expelled Yaśaḥ ; *Vinaya-Kṣudraka* (see Bu-ston ii. 94)—they tried to bribe his followers ; etc. Hence, Yaśaḥ had to go round various places for mobilising support in favour of himself.
5. *dga'-byed.* See Supplementary Note 3.

[Fol 22B] Now, about those seven hundred *arhat*-s. At the time of the demarcation[6] of the six cities, (even) among those who belonged only to the region of Vaiśālī there were *ubhayato-bhāga-vimukta* and *vahuśruta arhat*-s. Hence this Second Council was a representative[7] (lit. 'collection of parts' or 'composite') one. Since a full description of it is given in the *Kṣudra-āgama*[8] and is accordingly well-known, I am not describing it here.

That this Second Council took place at this time is stated by *Bhāḍaghāṭi[9] and Kṣemendrabhadra and we take it to be in accordance with our view, because the *Vinaya* current in Tibet states that the Second Council took place one hundred and ten years after the Teacher's *nirvāṇa*.

According to the *Vinaya* of the other sects, the Second Council took place two hundred and ten or two hundred and twenty years after the Teacher's *nirvāṇa*. Many historical works were produced in India for bringing the two versions into agreement. Though these make *ārya* *Dhītika and others the contemporaries of Aśoka, (at the same time) according to these the Second Council took place after the *nirvāṇa* of Mahāsudarśana[10] and the death of king Aśoka.

In the *Kṣudra-āgama* is said, 'When he [Kṛṣṇa] entrusted Mahāsudarśana with the Law, even the great elephants[11] [the

6. *mtshams-bcad-pa*. V n—it should be understood here in the sense of 'demarcation'.
7. *cha-śas-kyi-bsdu-ba*, lit. 'collection of parts'. According to the *Cullavagga*, this Council referred the matter to a committee consisting of four monks from the east and four from the west; *bhikṣu* Ajita was appointed the seat-regulator and Sabbakāmī (Sarvakāmin) was elected to preside over the Council. The *Vinaya-kṣudraka* (quoted by Bu-ston ii. 91ff) asserts that Yaśaḥ first mobilised for himself the support of *arhat* Sarvakāmin of Śāḍha from the city of Śoṇaka, of Dhanika from Saṃkāśya, of Kubjita from Pāṭaliputra, of Ajita from Śrughna, of Sambhūtà from Mahiṣmatī and of Revata from Sahaja. cf also Watters ii. 76 on the Council being representative.
8. *luṅ-phran-tshegs*, the *Vinaya-kṣudraka-vastu* (Kg Dul-va xi 2, xii, xiii) Sendai No. 6.
9. S-ed Bhaṭaghaṭi. P-ed Bhāḍaghāṭi.
10. *legs-mthoṅ-chen-po*.
11. *glaṅ-po-chen-po*. Rockhill LB 170n—the seven early patriarchs are

patriarchs] had attained *parinirvāṇa* and at that time (*de'i-tshe*) one hundred and ten years had passed after the *nirvāṇa* of the Teacher.' There is some confusion about the meaning of these words.

The Indian particle **yadācit*, according to the ways of analysing the compound, is used in both the senses of 'at which time' (*gaṅ-gi-tshe*) and 'at that time' (*de'i-tshe*).[12] **[Fol 23A]** In the present context, it should be translated as 'at which time' [i.e roughly this period].[13]

The *guru* **paṇḍita* said, 'To speak of two hundred and twenty years is the same as to speak of one hundred and ten years, because the former counts a half year as one year.' In the metrical composition of **paṇḍita* Indradatta[14] [is said] : 'After the *nirvāṇa* of the Jina, on the fiftieth year came Upagupta and the succession of the Leadership of the Order came to its end on the hundred and tenth year. After that was born Aśoka.' We also come across the comment on this : 'This does not agree with the prediction. Further, it contradicts the main Indian sources. Therefore, though it appears quite all right and justified, it is in fact baseless.'

In *Aṅga in the east, there lived a very rich householder. In his house there was a tree that grew as the result of his virtue. It gave fruits in the form of gems. He had no son. So he worshipped the images of Mahādeva, Viṣṇu and Kṛṣṇa.[15] As a result, a son was born to him, who was given the name Kṛṣṇa.

On growing up, he had the desire for a sea-voyage and reached the treasure island with five hundred merchants in a ship. His voyage was successful. Thus he made six smooth and

designated in the Tibetan Vinaya as elephants, i.e. mighty ones. V tr 'the great teachers (lit. elephants)'.

12. i.e. the former roughly refers to a period whereas the latter specifies it.
13. S n 'So imagines Tāranātha. One can easily see how far he was versed in Sanskrit. The word *yadācit* is, indeed, a Tibetan fabrication.' But the comment is hardly justified, for the meaning of the word suggested by Tār can as well be justified by the rules of Sanskrit grammar.
14. *dbaṅ-po*ₛ*-byin*. See Fol 139A, where the title of his work is mentioned as the *Buddha-purāṇa*.
15. V Kāla.

successful voyages within a short time and became known everywhere as a virtuous merchant. In the meanwhile his parents died and he became a devotee of *ārya* *Dhītika. A number of merchants came to him from the far north and requested him to make another voyage with them. **[Fol 23B]** He said, 'I have never heard of one making seven successful voyages. So I cannot go.' But on the strong insistence of others, he had to make the voyage at last.

They reached the treasure island and were returning with the ships loaded with gems. They saw an island covered with green forest raised above the sea and thought of having some rest there. As they reached the place, the *rākṣasī* called Krauñcikumārī[16]—a kind of sea-demon—captured the merchants. The leader of the merchants (Kṛṣṇa) prayed to *ārya* *Dhītika. The deities favouring him reached this message to *ārya* *Dhītika. By his miraculous power, *ārya* *Dhītika appeared in the island. The *rākṣasī*-s were scared by his halo and ran away. Thus the merchants safely returned to *Jambudvīpa.

After this the merchants entertained the neighbouring *saṃgha*-s for three years with all their wealth. They got themselves ordained, received *upasampadā* under *ārya* *Dhītika and eventually attained *arhat*-hood.

Later on, at the time of *ārya* *Dhītika's *nirvāṇa*, *ārya* Kṛṣṇa was entrusted with the Law. Though coming from a leading merchant family, he became an ordained monk. His sermons to the 'four classes of followers' maintained the tradition of leading them to 'the four stages of perfection.'

There was then in Kashmir a monk called Vatsa[17] born in a

16. *khruṅ-khruṅ-gshon-nu-ma.*
17. *gnas-pa*, lit. *sthira*. S reconstructs the name as Vatsa, which is adopted here, because the view under discussion appears to be that of the Vātsīputrīyas. See Stcherbatsky BL i. 32 ; N. Dutt AMB 17n ; Vallee-Poussin in ERE iv. 184 & n. V n 'We do not know if this Vatsa should be considered as the same person as Vatsīputra, from whom originated the well-known school of the Vātsīputrīyas, one of the earliest to be separated from the Sthaviras.' Incidentally, the Tibetan form of Vatsa as forming part of the Vātsīputrīyas is *gnas-ma*.

brāhmaṇa family. He was cruel, wicked and, though vastly learned, was in favour of the doctrine of the (permanent) soul (*ātmaka-vāda*). He went around corrupting the common monks with the wrong view. This resulted in minor controversies within the *saṃgha*. So in the *Puṣkariṇī-vihāra in *Maru, the *saṃgha*-s congregated from all around, *yakṣa* Kapila providing them for their maintenance. **[Fol 24A]** The expiatory rite was performed there. He (Kṛṣṇa) repeatedly preached the doctrine of impermanence (lit. denial of soul, *anātma-vāda*) to all the *saṃgha*-s. When three months were almost over, he purified the minds of those monks who were previously influenced by the doctrine of the soul as preached by *sthavira* Vatsa and led everybody to the realisation of truth. At last even *sthavira* Vatsa himself was brought to the right view.

At that time, in the island of *Siṅgala [Siṃhala] there lived the king Āsana-Siṃha-Koṣa.[18] As he was holding his court, a merchant from *Jambudvīpa presented him a wooden image of the Teacher. He asked, 'What is this ?' [The merchant] described to him the greatness [of the leaders] from the Teacher to *ārya* Kṛṣṇa. The king felt eager to see *ārya* Kṛṣṇa and to listen to the true Doctrine. He sent a messenger. The messenger reached the *ārya* and the *ārya*, along with his five hundred followers, flew through the sky by his miraculous power. Clinging to his robe, the messenger also reached the border of *Siṃhala. The messenger was sent (to the king) and the king, along with others, came to welcome them. They proceeded towards the capital, showing on their way various miracles like radiating multi-coloured rays. He (Kṛṣṇa) preached the Doctrine for three months in that island, filled it with monasteries and *saṃgha*-s and led many people to the 'four stages of perfection.'

Though the island had been blessed before by the Teacher's feet, after the Teacher's *nirvāṇa* the Law there gradually faded away. **[Fol 24B]** But *ārya* Kṛṣṇa spread it extensively again.

18. This reconstruction is after V & S. The text has *khri-ldan-seṅ-ge-mdsod-pa* However, assuming *khri-ldan* not forming part of the name itself, the passage may be translated as, 'The throne of the Siṃhala island was at that time occupied by Siṃha-koṣa.'

At last, he (Kṛṣṇa) entrusted *ārya* Sudarśana with the Law, who was a *kṣatriya* by birth and who attained *nirvāṇa* in *Kuśavana in the north.

Now about *ārya* Sudarśana.

There lived a very prosperous person called Darśana,[19] born in the Pāṇḍu[20] family of the *kṣatriya*-s in *Bharukaccha in the west. His son was named Sudarśana. When he grew up, he had in fifty gardens fifty charming damsels, each of them with five female attendants and five female musicians. Everyday, he used to have flowers worth five thousand golden **paṇa*-s, not to speak of his other riches. In fact, he was as wealthy as the gods.

While proceeding to the garden accompanied by his attendants, he once saw an *arhat* called *Śukāyana, who was going towards the city along with his large body of followers. Filled with great reverence, he (Sudarśana) bowed down at his feet and sat nearby. When the *arhat* (Śukāyana) preached the Doctrine, he attained *arhat*-hood while sitting on the same place.

He prayed for ordination. The *arhat* said that one living in the house was unfit for ordination. Hence, there was no scope for it. (And the *arhat* Śukāyana added), 'However, you may ask your father.'

So he prayed to his father (for the permission of) getting ordained. This made the father furious, who was about to bind him with iron chains. At that moment, he raised himself up in the sky and showed miracles like radiating lustre, etc. His father was full of reverence and said, 'Oh son, since you are possessed of such excellences, please get yourself ordained and have mercy for me also.' **[Fol 25A]** Then he received the ordination and, as the result of his preaching the Doctrine to the father, the father also realised the Truth.

After this, he accepted *ārya* Kṛṣṇa as the *ācārya* and stayed with him for a long time. After the *nirvāṇa* of *ārya* Kṛṣṇa, the

19. *mthoṅ-ba.*
20. *skya-seṅ.*

great Sudarśana maintained discipline among the 'four classes of followers.'[21]

There lived then in the region of *Sindhu in the west a powerful *yakṣiṇī* called *Hiṅgalācī, who wielded great magical power. She caused terrible epidemics in different countries. When the people tried to escape, she assumed a dreadful form and blocked their roads. The people offered her everyday a sacrifice consisting of food drawn by a cart of six oxen, and also a man and a woman and a good horse.

Then *ārya* Sudarśana realised that it was time to subdue her. So he received his alms of cooked food (*piṇḍa*) from a village of *Sindhu and started eating it at her place. The *yakṣiṇī* took him as a monk who had lost his way. When the slop-water fell on the ground, she became furious and showered stones and weapons at him. But as the *arhat* remained absorbed in meditation on compassion, these turned into a shower of flowers. By the will-power of the *ārya*, there broke out fire all around. As the *yakṣiṇī* herself began to be burnt by it, she got scared and took refuge to the *ārya*. He preached the Doctrine to her and led her to *śikṣā*. [Since then] no sacrifice of flesh and blood is offered to her till now

[**Fol 25B**] Realising that after him there would be none to do it, he subdued about five hundred Nāgas and Yakṣas, who had no respect for the Law. The *ārya* next toured the southern countries extensively, filled these with monasteries and *saṃgha*-s and established the Law of the Buddha in many small islands. He spread the Doctrine also in Mahā-cīna[22] and other places, though in a limited form.

Thus causing bliss to innumerable people, he attained *nirvāṇa* 'without any corporeal residue'.[23]

21. V n 'According to the Chinese historians, the seventh patriarch is called Buddhanandī and he was a native of northern India. Kṛṣṇa (or Kāla) met him in a market and reminded him of the Buddha's prophecy to Ānanda that 300 years after his *nirvāṇa*, Buddhanandī will spread the Doctrine in the north.'

22. *rgya-yu'-chen-po*. See J 106.

23. *phuṅ-po-lhag-ma-med-pa'i-dbyiṅs*, N. Dutt AMB 79 *nirupādhi-śeṣa—nirvāṇa-dhātu*.

The childhood of king Aśoka synchronised with the latter part of the life of *ārya* *Dhītika. The Law was looked after by *ārya* Kṛṣṇa when Aśoka was following his career of sin and by *ārya* Sudarśana when he (Aśoka) became *dharma-rāja*.[24]

After the *nirvāṇa* of the great Sudarśana, the king (Aśoka) also passed away.

From *ārya* Ānanda to Sudarśana, there exist *avadāna*-s about each (of the patriarchs). I have given here their gist based on the selections from these by Kṣemendrabhadra.

These successors maintained the Law fully and their contributions are in a manner comparable to those of the Buddha himself. Many *arhat*-s appeared after them, yet the contribution of none of them could match that of the Teacher himself and that of these patriarchs.

The seventh chapter containing the account of the incidents of the period of king Aśoka.

24. *chos-kyi-rgyal-po.*

CHAPTER 8

ACCOUNT OF THE PERIOD OF KING VIGATAŚOKA

King Aśoka had eleven sons, among whom the best was *Kuṇāla. He was given the name *Kuṇāla by a sage, because he had eyes like those of the *Kuṇāla birds of the Himālaya. When he became well-versed in all arts, **[Fol 26A]** a queen of Aśoka called Tiṣyarakṣitā[1] became erotically attached to him and tried to seduce him.[2] Being very chaste, he did not respond. Tiṣyarakṣitā was extremely angry.

Aśoka was once sick with violent vomitting and purgations. Tiṣyarakṣitā came to know that a common man of the hilly region was similarly sick. She got him killed and his abdomen opened. It was found that within his stomach there was a hideous looking insect with many limbs. She understood that its movement up and down was causing the vomitting and purgation. It could not be killed by any medicine other than white garlic. So Tiṣyarakṣitā gave the king the medicine of white garlic. The *kṣatriya*-s did not take garlic. But the king took it on medical consideration and was cured.

When the king wanted to grant her whatever she desired, she said, 'Not now ; I shall ask for it some other time.'

Prince *Kuṇāla was once sent with the army to suppress the revolt of king Kuñjarakarṇa[3] in the far north-western country called *Aśmaparānta.[4] When he subdued the king,

1. *skar-rgyal-bsruṅs-ma.*
2. For legends of Tiṣyarakṣitā, see Supplementary Note 4.
3. *glaṅ-po'i-rna-ba,* lit. the ear of an elephant or of a cow. V & S Gokarṇa. In the *Kuṇāla-avadāna* (Bongard-Levin & Volkova verse 85 f) and *Avadāna-kalpalatā,* the name occurs as Kuñjarakarṇa.
4. By Aśmaparānta, Tār refers to Takṣaśilā—see, e.g. Fol 32A, though the usual Tibetan form of Takṣaśilā is *rdo-'jog.* In Chinese sources, it is variously mentioned as 'cut off head' (*śilā* understood as *śiras*), 'severed rock', 'chiselled rock', 'the rock of the Takkas' etc—Watters i. 241 ; Legge 32.

Tiṣyarakṣitā said to Aśoka, 'Lord, it is now the time to fulfil your promise. Give me the power to rule for seven days.'

This was granted. She wrote a letter ordering to pluck off the eyes of *Kuṇāla, stole the king's seal, put it on the letter and sent it with a messenger to *Aśmaparānta. In spite of reading the letter, the king of that country hesitated to pluck off *Kuṇāla's eyes. *Kuṇāla himself read the letter and taking it as the king's order was about to offer his own eyes, when (the king of Aśmaparānta) said, 'Pluck off only one of your eyes, and hand it over to me.' **[Fol 26B]** He did so.[5]

An *arhat* had already foretold all these to him and preached to him many aspects of the Doctrine, like that of impermanence, etc. As he remembered the significance of all these while handing over one of his eyes, he attained the *srotāpatti* stage. He then left all his attendants and wandered about in different places with a *vīṇā* in his hands.

At last he reached the elephant-stable of (the king of) *Pāṭaliputra. A wise elephant recognised and saluted him.[6] But the men there could not recognise him. In the early morning, the elephant-keepers told him, 'Play the *vīṇā*.' When he played the *vīṇā* and gave out the **gamaka*, the king listened to it from his gorgeous palace and the sound reminded him of his son. In the morning, he made enquiries and found his son.

After he came to know the reason for all these, he became furious and ordered : 'Put Tiṣyarakṣitā in a house made of lacquer and set fire to it.' But *Kuṇāla dissuaded him from doing this.[7]

5. Yuan-chuang reports (Watters i. 245-6) : 'On the north side of the south hill to the south-east of the capital (Takṣaśilā) was a tope about 100 feet high erected by king Aśoka on the spot where his son prince Kuṇāla had his eyes torn out by the guile of his step-mother ; the blind came here to pray, and many had their prayers answered by restoration of sight.'
6. Kṣemendra narrates this legend of the elephant recognising Kuṇāla, though it does not occur in the *Divyāvadāna*—Bongard-Levin & Volkova 4.
7. 'According to the *Divyāvadāna*, Aśoka severely punished queen Tiṣyarakṣitā and the people of Takṣaśilā ... In Kṣemendra's poem,

'If I have the same compassion for Tiṣyarakṣitā that I have for my own son and if I am free from all anger, let me get back my eye as before.' —The moment he prayed like this he received back the eye[8] more beautiful than the older one.

He next took up ordination and attained *arhat*-hood. That is why, though it was his turn to be the king, his son Vigataśoka[9] was placed on the throne.

Now, there lived a *brāhmaṇa* called *Rāghava[10] in *Oḍiviśa. He was wealthy and became a follower of the Three Jewels. In his dream, he received the following inspiration from the deity: 'In the next morning, a monk will come to beg at your house. He is powerful and is possessed of miraculous power. So he will be able to make the neighbouring *ārya*-s assemble. Pray to him.'

[Fol 27A] In the morning, *arhat* Poṣada[11] came to his house. When he (Rāghava) prayed to him, he got about eighty thousand *arhat*-s assemble there and they were entertained for three years. The deities favouring the Law showered gems[12] on his house. During the rest of his life he used to satisfy one lakh of beggars[13] every day.

The eighth chapter containing the account of the period of king Vigataśoka.

the king, full of kindness, forgives the guilty ... According to one of the versions, Aśoka executed Tiṣyarakṣitā' (*ib.*). cf also Watters ii. 295.

8. Though, according to the *Divyāvadāna* and Kṣemendra's poem, Kuṇāla received back his eye-sight by virtue of his truthfulness (*satyādhiṣṭhāna*), according to other sources (see Beal BRWW 139-41), he was actually cured by *arhat* Ghoṣa. Watters i.246 : 'Ghoṣa, the name of the *arhat* who restored eye-sight to Kuṇāla, was also the name of a physician of this district (Takṣaśilā), who was celebrated as an occulist.'
9. V n 'According to Lassen ii.271, the son of Kuṇāla is named Saṃpati. The account given in the Chinese history of Aśoka agrees with this.' cf Bongard-Levin & Volkova 6.
10. cf Bu-ston ii.116.
11. *bsos-byin.*
12. S 'flowers.' But the text has *rin-po-ce* (*ratna*).
13. V & S *bhikṣu*. But the text has *sloṅ-ba-po*, i.e. beggars (D 1301) not in the sense of the monks, for which the usual Tibetan is *dge-sloṅ*.

CHAPTER 9

ACCOUNT OF THE PERIOD OF KĀŚYAPA, THE SECOND

Now,[1] *arhat* Kāśyapa,[2] born in *Gandhāra in the north, was working for the welfare of the living beings with 'the threefold deeds of the Law.'[3] At that time king Vīrasena,[4] son of king Vigataśoka, obtained inexhaustible treasure without causing the least harm to the living beings by propitiating the goddess Śrī,[5] the consort of Kuvera.[6] He entertained for three years the monks all around and worshipped all the *caitya*-s in the world with a hundred items of offerings for each.

In Mathurā a *brāhmaṇa* called Yaśasvī,[7] who was highly devoted to the Law, built a monastery called Śarāvatī[8] and an *arhat* named Ślaṇavāsa[9] preached the Doctrine there to a large number of monks assembled from the four directions. He entertained about a hundred thousand monks.

In *Maruda[10] there lived the son of a merchant called Mahādeva.[11] He committed the three deadly sins[12] namely

1. *de'i-rjes-su*, lit. 'after that'.
2. *'od-sruṅs*.
3. *bstan-pa'i-bya-ba-rnam-pa-gsum*. V n 'teaching, debating and composing.'
4. *dpa'-bo'i-sde*. S-ed *dbaṅ-po'i-sde*, hence S translates the name in the note as Indrasena, though retaining the form Vīrasena in the text. In the *Table of Contents*, S-ed also gives the form *dpa'-bo'i-sde*, lit. *vīra-sena*, which occurs in both the places in P-ed. cf Bu-ston ii. 118.
5. *lha-mo-dpal*. S Lakṣmī.
6. *rnam-thos-sras*. S Vaiśravaṇa,
7. *grags-ldan*. V & S Yaśika. Obermiller (Bu-ston ii. 116) Yaśasvin.
8. *'dam-bu-can*.
9. *yul-bslan-pa*. S. Ślaṇavāsa.
10. V n 'According to Palladius, Maruda. S thinks that the name of this kingdom might have originated from the name of Maruṇḍa king.'
11. On Mahādeva, his alleged sins and the five principles preached by him as related in the Abhidharma treatises, see Supplementary Note 5.
12. *mtshams-med-gsum*, See J 455; D 1039; *Mahāvyutpatti* Part iii, p. 312.

killing his father, killing his mother and killing an *arhat*. Depressed in mind, he left for Kashmir where, carefully concealing his misdeeds, he became a monk. As he had a keen intellect, [Fol 27B] he acquired mastery of the three Piṭaka-s, felt remorse for his sins and strove by himself after meditation in a monastery. Being blessed by the power of Māra, he was taken by all for an *arhat* and thus his prestige grew more and more. He went to the Śarāvatī monastery[13] with a large number of his monk-followers. The monks there used to recite by turn the *Prātimokṣa-sūtra*.[14] When it was Mahādeva's turn to recite, at the end of the recital he added :

> 'All the gods are deceived by ignorance. The path is made of mere verbal tradition. Those with doubt are being converted [into the Law] by others. Such is the Law of the Buddha.'

As he recited thus, the *ārya*-s and older *bhikṣu*-s said, 'This does not form part of the *sūtra*.' Most of the younger *bhikṣu*-s sided with Mahādeva. Thus there arose a quarrel.

On many other occasions also, he similarly distorted the meaning of the *sūtra*-s. After his death, another monk called Bhadra,[15] who is considered to have been a veritable incarnation of the evil Māra, raised many doubts by way of challenging the sayings [of the Buddha]. He preached the five principles,[16] namely of 1) rejoinder,[17] 2) ignorance,[18] 3) doubt,[19] 4) critical

13. V n 'Palladius mentions Pāṭaliputra instead of Śarāvatī as the place of this incident.' cf Watters i. 269ff ; Bu-ston ii.109.
14. *so-sor-thar-pa'i-mdo* (Sendai No. 2)
15. *bzaṅ-po*. cf Bu-ston ii.96, where Mahādeva is not mentioned in connection with the controversies leading to the Third Council (under Kaniṣka). Instead of that, Bu-ston quotes the *Tarkajvālā* of Bhāvaviveka : 'Māra, the Evil One, having assumed the form of a monk named Bhadra, showed many miraculous apparitions, sowed disunion amongst the clergy and brought confusion into the Teaching.'
16. See Supplementary Note 5.
17. *gshan-la-lan-gdab-pa*. Roerich (BA i. 28) translates 'advice to others.'
18. *ma-śes-pa*.
19. *yid-gñis*. V double-mindedness. Roerich (BA i. 29) doubt (*vimati*).

examination[20] and 5) fortifying one's own thesis.[21] [He said] that these formed the Law of the Teacher.

Thus there arose many differences of opinion concerning the understanding of the sayings of the Teacher. Irregularities and conflicts resulted from the various doubts and uncertainties.[22] As the preachers of the various *sūtra*-s preached these in different languages of the different regions, the sayings were gradually corrupted, the letters becoming shorter or longer due to the influence of the different dialects and modes of writing.[23]

The *arhat*-s and other scholars [**Fol 28A**] tried to resolve these conflicts. However, because of the influence of Māra on the common monks, the controversies could not be resolved.

Only after the death of Mahādeva and Bhadra, the monks realised their real character.

After the *nirvāṇa* of *arhat* Kāśyapa, the second, *ārya* Mahāloma[24] and *ārya* Nandin[25] worked for the Law in **Mathurā.

The ninth chapter containing the account of the period of Kāśyapa, the second.

20. *yoṅs-su-brtag-pa.* V full conviction. Roerich (BA i. 29) careful investigation (*parikalpa*).
21. *bdag-ñid-gso-bar-byed-pa.* Roerich (BA i. 29) self-maintenance.
22. S tr 'Conflict became manifold from the doubts and misunderstandings.'
23. cf Bu-ston ii. 96-7. See Supplementary Note 6.
24. *spu-chen-po.*
25. *dga'-ba-can.*

CHAPTER 10

ACCOUNT OF THE PERIOD OF ĀRYA MAHĀLOMA AND OTHERS

King Vīrasena died shortly after *ārya* Mahāloma and *ārya* Nandin started to look after the Law. His son Nanda[1] ascended the throne and ruled the kingdom for twentynine years. He brought the *piśāca* *Pi-lu-pa[2] under control and, as a result, whenever he stretched his palms to the sky, these were filled with gems.

There lived then a *brāhmaṇa* called Vijña[3] in Suvarṇa-droṇa.[4] He got the monks of the four directions to assemble and entertained them for seven years. After that, the king of *Kāśī-vārāṇasī worshipped the monks and maintained them for many years.

Now, a vastly learned monk called Nāga repeatedly praised the five principles [of Bhadra] and intensified the disputes among the *saṃgha*-s. This led to the split of the *saṃgha*-s into four sects. So *ārya* Dharmaśreṣṭhī,[5] after attaining *arhat*-hood,

1. *dga'-bo.*
2. V Pilu. Tg (rG xliii.152) contains a work called *Piśāca-pilupāla-sādhana* attributed to Prajñāpāla or Prajñāpālita.
3. *mkhas-pa.* V Kuśala. But see Obermiller—Bu-ston ii. 109.
4. *gser-bre.* cf Bu-ston ii. 109. V n 'This kingdom is mentioned in the Vinaya Vol *ge* 144. It lies on the path traversed by the Buddha from Sa-la'i-sto-bas to Sāketana (*gnas-bcas*). This kingdom was thus called, because the Brahmins measured gold which Śākyamuni, in his previous birth—when he was still a Bodhisattva—distributed in weight of units of *droṇa* (*bre*).'
5. *chos-kyi-tshoṅ-dpon.* V & S Dharmaśreṣṭha. But *tshoṅ-dpon* means 'the leading merchant.' The *Vinaya-stotra* (mDo xc.9, commented upon by Vinītadeva—mDo lxxviii.5 lit. repro. xc.10) attributed to him in Tg mentions his name as *ācārya bhadanta* Dharmaśreṣṭhin, (Index Mongolian giving the equivalent of the name as Dharma Sārthavāha).

left the disputing groups of *saṃgha*-s and went towards the north accompanied by the peace-loving monks.

The *brāhmaṇa* *Pāṇini[6] was a friend of king Nanda. He was born in the *Bhiruka-vana in the west. He asked the palmist whether he was going to be an expert in grammar. The prediction was in the negative. **[Fol 28B]** With a sharp knife, he changed the lines of his own palm, studied grammar under all the grammarians of the world, worked hard and acquired great proficiency. Yet he remained dissatisfied.

By intense propitiation, he received the vision of the tutelary deity. The deity appeared before him and uttered **a*, **i*, **u*, and he acquired knowledge of all words in the three worlds.

The 'outsiders'[7] (*vāhya*-s or *tīrthika*-s) consider him as the *īśvara*. But the 'outsiders' have no basis for this. The 'insiders'[8] consider him as Avalokiteśvara. This is based on the prophecy of the *Mañjuśrī-mūla-tantra*[9]: "*Pāṇini, the son of a *brāhmaṇa*, will certainly attain the *śrāvaka-bodhi*. I have predicted that he would be the great *lokeśvara* (Avalokiteśvara) by his own words (lit. charms)'.

He composed a grammatical work called **Paṇi-vyākaraṇa*, containing a thousand **śloka*-s and a commentary on it containing another thousand **śloka*-s. Thus, he composed two thousand **śloka*-s [10] in all. These are supposed to be the basis of all grammatical works.

6. The usual form in which Tār mentions the name is Paṇi.
7. *phyi pa*, i.e. the non-Buddhist.
8. *naṅ-pa*, i.e. the Buddhist.
9. Obermiller (Bu-ston ii. 167) translates the passage—

    Pāṇini, the *brāhmaṇa*'s son,
    Has been prophesised by me
    To attain the enlightenment of the *śrāvaka*-s
    And he shall likewise secure the charm
    For propitiating the High Lord of the Universe.

    Interestingly, Pāṇini's grammar, as preserved in Tg (mDo cxxxv.1) is mentioned as being revealed by *ārya* Avalokiteśvara to Pāṇini.
10. The colophon of the *Pāṇini-vyākaraṇa-sūtra*, as preserved in Tg (mDo cxxxv.1) says that it contains 2000 *śloka*-s.

There existed no written treatise on grammar before him, nor was there any system (of grammar). It is said that older grammarians used to learn a lot of grammar only by way of collecting stray rules from different fragmentary works.[11] But in Tibet, the **Indra-vyākaraṇa* is believed to be older[12] than this. If it is really older, it must have been a celestial composition. However, it is certain that in India (*ārya-deśa*) it could not have been an earlier work. This will be explained later.

The *Candra-vyākaraṇa*[13] translated in Tibet is in agreement with that of *Paṇi. The *Kalāpa-vyākaraṇa*[14] agrees with the [grammatical] system of *Indra. So say the **paṇḍita*-s.[15] That is why, it is said that persons with a thorough mastery of all the implications of the **Paṇi-vyākaraṇa* are very rare, these implications being extremely extensive.[16] **[Fol 29A]**

The tenth chapter containing the account of the period of ārya Mahāloma and others.

11. V & S add : 'and they were regarded as highly learned.' This is perhaps because of the word *grags-so* in the text, taken in the present translation as : 'It is said.'
12. cf Bu-ston ii. 166f on the *Indra-vyākaraṇa* being earlier than that of Pāṇini.
13. Tg (mDo cxvi. 1) *Candra-vyākaraṇa-sūtra-nāma* by *mahācārya* Candragomipāda.
14. see Fol 39B
15. V tr 'our *paṇḍita*.'
16. For Bu-ston's view of the history of the grammatical literature, see Bu-ston ii. 166f. V quotes this in his note.

CHAPTER 11

ACCOUNT OF THE PERIOD OF KING MAHĀPADMA.

There was a king named Agnidatta[1] in Vanāyu[2] on the northern frontier. He entertained for over thirty years about three thousand *ārya*-s, inclusive of *arhat* Dharmaśreṣṭhī.

When *ārya* Mahātyāga[3] was looking after the Law in the *madhya-deśa*, Mahāpadma,[4] son of king Nanda, entertained all the *saṃgha-s* in Kusumapura.[5] A *bhikṣu* called Sthiramati,[6] who was a follower of *sthavira* Nāga,[7] provoked at that time wider controversies by propagating the five principles (of Bhadra) over again. Thus the four sects began gradually to divide into eighteen.

King Mahāpadma had two friends, the *brāhmaṇa* Bhadra and the *brāhmaṇa* Vararuci[8]. Both of them entertained the *saṃgha*-s extensively.

The *brāhmaṇa* Bhadra could visit any kingdom by his magic power and acquire all the wealth of the non-human beings

1. *me-byin.* V n quoted by S 'In the *Vinaya-kṣudraka* there is a legend about a king called Agnidatta, who was born out of fire after the death of his mother. According to the Tibetan Vinaya, he was a contemporary of the Buddha. He reigned in Parāntaka and he was afraid that his possible disrespect for Gautama was to cause discontent among the people and officers. Buddha passes through his place from Mathurā *via* Otala for going to Pañcāla.' cf the prophecy quoted by Bu-ston ii. 110 : 'In the border woodland, in the royal palace called The Peaceful, the king named Agnidatta is to worship the relics and the disciples of the Buddha. In that country, more than 3,000 *arhat*-s are to arise,'
2. *nags-kyi-sa*, lit. *vana-bhūmi.*
3. *gtoṅ-ba-chen-po.*
4. *padma-chen-po.*
5. *groṅ-khyer-me-tog.*
6. *yid-brtan-pa*—not the famous author and disciple of Vasubandhu, whom Tār discusses in Fol 65A-B.
7. *gnas-brtan-klu.*
8. *mchog-sred.* See Supplementary Note 7.

(? *yakṣa*-s, *nāga*-s etc). With this he daily entertained with all requisites about eighteen hundred *brāhmaṇa*-s, two thousand monks and other wandering mendicants and beggars—ten thousand in all.

Vararuci had a pair of charmed sandals made of leaves. Wearing these, he used to acquire precious things from the realm of the gods and the Nāgas and with these he satisfied the needy persons.

But there once developed hostility between him and the king. The king was apprehensive of being harmed by his black magic. So he sent an agent to kill him. **[Fol 29B]** Wearing his pair of sandals, he escaped to Ujjayinī.[9] At last a woman employed by the king seduced him and robbed him of his pair of sandals. He thus became unable to escape and was murdered by the killer. The king then built twentyfour monasteries to atone for the sin of killing a *brāhmaṇa*. By providing these with all the necessaries, he made these the prosperous centres of the Doctrine.

According to some, the Third Council[10] took place during this time. Obviously, however, this cannot be fully true.

It is said that this Vararuci prepared[11] a number of copies of the *Vibhāṣā*[12] and distributed these among the preachers of

9. *'phags-rgyal.*
10. Tār gives his account of the Third Council in Fol 31Af
11. *bris*, lit. 'wrote'. V 'wrote (i.e. did not compose but copied or ordered to be copied).'
12. *bye-brag-tu-bśad-pa.* V n 'Under the title *Vibhāṣā*, there are two works in Chinese translation, the first comprising 14 and the second 200 chapters. Both of these are ascribed to Kātyāyana, who is said to have lived during the time of the Buddha and to have collected together or explained the words of the Buddha in answer to the questions of Śāriputra, the 500 *arhat*-s and others. The first of these works is very unusual, but the second is nothing more than a detailed commentary on the *Jñānaprasthāna*—the first of the seven Abhidharma-s of which the *Vibhāṣā* is in a certain sense a summary. With reference to these works we find mention in these as well as in other sources that Kātyāyana lived 300 years after the *parinirvāṇa* of the Buddha and that the first *Vibhāṣā* was composed by *arhat*

the Doctrine and that, though certain written works containing the sayings (of the Teacher) existed even during the lifetime of the Teacher himself, only henceforth began the practice of writing of the commentaries in the form of the *śāstra*-s.

But the word *vibhāṣā* is to be taken here in the sense of detailed exposition.[13] Thus also were explained the precepts of the Teacher on the basis of the exact words uttered by him before. In this way was spread the significance of the sayings. Hence, from the point of view of the *śāstra*-s, nothing was composed as being more easily understandable than the *sūtra*-s.

This *Vibhāṣā* was composed for the welfare of the living beings of the later period. According to some, this was composed collectively by the *arhat*-s during the time of Upagupta. According to others, this was composed by Yaśaḥ, Sarvakāma[14] and others. The Tibetans think that it was composed by five hundred *arhat*-s like Sarvakāma, Kubjita[15] and others in the north of the Vindhyas in the Naṭa-bhaṭika *vihāra*. Such a view is clearly the result of mixing up the two views just mentioned. In any case, it is a collection of the sayings (of the Teacher) by the *arhat*-s[16] **[Fol 30A]**, which, after being orally transmitted through the succession of the *sthavira*-s, was later committed to writing.

According to the Vaibhāṣikas, the Seven *Abhi*-s[17] (i.e. the

Shi-to-pan-ni and the second by 500 *arhat*-s called to Kashmir by the Gandhāra king Kaniṣka 400 years (according to another tradition of this *Vibhāṣā*, 600 years) after the Buddha. Among the compilers were Pārśva and Vasumitra. It is clear that the Vaibhāṣikas, the followers of this work, wanted this work to be associated with the name of the Buddha. The Sautrāntikas, however, being opposed to the Vaibhāṣikas, had no ground to conceal the truth (i.e. these works were much posterior to the Buddha). One must have this fact before one's eyes as one follows the text of Tāranātha further.'

13. *don-ni-shib-mor-bśad-pa.*
14. *thams-cad-'dod.*
15. *skur-po.*
16. P-ed *de-dag-gi*, lit. 'of the *arhat*-s'. S-ed *de-dag-gis*, 'by the *arhat*-s'. The latter reading followed.
17. These are 1) *Dharma-skandha* of Śāriputra, 2) *Prajñapti-śāstra* of

seven *Abhidharma* treatises) are but the sayings (of the Teacher). Therefore, the *Vibhāṣā* was the first of the commentaries on the significance (of the sayings). According to the Sautrāntikas, even the Seven *Abhi*-s were really composed by the *śrāvaka-pṛthagjana*-s,[18] though falsely propagated as the sayings of the Teacher compiled by Śāriputra[19] and others. Thus the Seven marked the beginning of the commentaries on *śāstra*-s.[20]

Some of the *ācārya*-s say that the Seven were originally the sayings of the Teacher, though it may be that into these

Maudgalyāyana, 3) *Dhātu-kāya* by Pūrṇa, 4) *Vijñāna-kāya* by Devaśarman, 5) *Jñāna-prasthāna* of Kātyāyana, 6) *Prakaraṇa-pāda* of Vasumitra and 7) *Saṃgīti-paryāya* by Mahākauṣṭhila.—see Bu-ston i. 49.

18. *ñan-thos-so-so-skye-bo.*

19. *śā-ri-bu.*

20. V n 'Here is what is stated in the first Chinese *Vibhāṣā*. Who composed this *sūtra* ?—Buddha. Why ?—Because it contains the most profound wisdom, the most treasured essence of the teaching ; it explains all boundaries of omniscience. And, who, except Buddha, can possess such boundaries ! Why has it been said that it is composed ?—This *sūtra* was pronounced in reply to the questions of Śāriputra, 500 *bhikṣu*-s and magic enquirers. Why is it said that Kātyāyana composed this *sūtra* ?—Because this *ārya* committed it to memory, mastered it and considerably propagated it by preaching. He took a vow for 500 Buddhas to compile the Abhidharma. What is meant by the Abhidharma of Buddha ?—Buddha preached various fragmentary teachings at various places and Kātyāyana, as a result of his previous desire, arranged these in sections and articles'.
cf Bu-ston i. 49f 'The Kashmirian Vaibhāṣikas regard these seven works as belonging to the Word of the Buddha. They say that they contain sermons delivered by the teacher at various time, at different places and to diverse persons separately, the *arhat*-s and *śrāvaka*-s having subsequently collected them ... The Sautrāntikas and the other (schools) say, that the Abhidharma is included in both the Sūtras and the Vinaya, or otherwise, has been expounded at intervals, and that no mistake is made (by admitting such an order). As to the seven works, (the schools just mentioned) regard them as exegetical treatises. The contents of these works are rendered, in abridged form, by the *Mahāvibhāṣā*, which in its turn is condensed in the *Abhidharma-koṣa* and other treatises.'

were later interpolated the words of the *śrāvaka-pṛthagjana*-s, i.e. somewhat like the collection of the *sūtra*-s of the different sects. The portions of these (*Abhidharma*-s) that contradict the three *pramāṇa*-s[21] are to be considered as interpolations. Just as there is an *Abhidharma-piṭaka* of Mahāyāna, so also there could have been one of the *śrāvaka*-s. It should be admitted that there is coherence in the significance of the three *piṭaka*-s. Since there exist as separate works two other *piṭaka*-s of the *śrāvaka*-s, there is no reason to think that they had no *Abhidharma*.

The last view appears to be correct. So we may accept it here. The statement (to the contrary) made by the great *ācārya* Vasubandhu[22] seems to have been influenced by his tendency to follow the Sautrāntika view.

Again, there are some who think that these (seven *Abhidharma*-s of the *śrāvaka*-s)[23] are not at all the words of the Teacher and these contain many errors. So these could have been actually composed by Śāriputra and others. Such a view is extremely foolish, because the Venerable Two (Śāriputra and Maudgalyāyana) attained *nirvāṇa* before the Teacher. **[Fol 30B]**

During the lifetime of the Teacher, commentaries on the significance of the sayings were not prepared at all. It is, therefore, too much to imagine that commentaries distorting the significance of his sayings were already written while the Teacher himself was alive.

To keep ourselves confined to the Law of our Buddha : the difference between the sayings and the commentaries on the significance of these is as follows. The former were compiled

21. i.e. a) consistency with the teaching of the Buddha (*raṅ-tshig-sṅa-phyi-mi-'gal-ba*), b) freedom from internal contradiction (*luṅ-daṅ-sṅa-phyi-mi-'gal-ba*) and c) not refuted by independent argument, i.e. logically sound (*rigs-pa-daṅ-sṅa-phyi-mi-'gal-ba*).
22. *dbyig-gñen*.
23. V 'it (i.e. the *Vibhāṣā*)'. The literal translation of the cryptic sentence is : "there are some who think (?) not the sayings".

during his lifetime while the latter were composed after his *nirvāṇa*.

If even the Venerable Two and others are viewed as having distorted the significance of the sayings, it will be impossible to trace anybody as being 'duly authorised'[24] mentioned (in the following prediction): 'It is almost the period of the termination of the duly authorised ones.' If even the *arhat*-s are considered to have been without the realisation of the Truth, it will have to be admitted that none realised the Truth following the path of the *śrāvaka*-s. This will amount to deliberate insults to the great *arhat*-s produced by the spiritual power of the Buddha. Therefore, such a view could only be the result of the influence of Māra.

Shortly after the period of king Mahāpadma, Candrarakṣita[25] became the king of *Oḍiviśa. It is said that *ārya* Mañjuśrī came to his house in the guise of a monk, preached some Mahāyāna doctrines and left a book there. According to the followers of the *sūtra*,[26] it was the *Prajñā-pāramitā-aṣṭa-sāhasrikā*.[27] According to the followers of *tantra*, it was the ***Tattva-saṃgraha*.[28] However, the point is not of major significance, though in my opinion the former view is right. This was the first appearance of the Mahāyāna in the human world after the Teacher's *nirvāṇa*. **[Fol 31A]**.

The eleventh chapter containing the account of the period of king Mahāpadma.

24. *dbaṅ-gyur-skye-bo.*
25. *zla-ba-sruṅ-ba.* V & S Candragupta. But V adds in note 'literally, the protector of the moon, can also be Candrarakṣita (?), because the name of Candragupta in the Candra-vaṃśa is written as *zla-ba-sbas-pa*.'
26. *mdo-lugs-pa.* V & S Sautrāntika. The usual Tibetan form of Sautrāntika is *mdo-sde-ba.*
27. *śes-rab-kyi-pha-rol-tu-phyin-pa-brgyad-stoṅ-pa.* Kg Sendai No 12.
28. Kg—Sendai No 479 *Sarva-tathāgata-tattvasaṃgraha-nāma-mahāyāna sūtra.*

CHAPTER 12

ACCOUNT OF THE PERIOD OF THE THIRD COUNCIL

Now, there was a king called Siṃha[1] in Kashmir. He received ordination and was called Sudarśana.[2] He then attained *arhat*-hood and preached the Doctrine in Kashmir.

King *Kaniṣka of *Jalandhara[3] heard about him, became full of respect and came towards Kashmir in the north. He listened to the Doctrine from *ārya* Siṃha Sudarśana, worshipped extensively all the *caitya*-s in the north and also lavishly entertained the *saṃgha*-s of the four directions.

At that time, there was a monk called Sañjaya.[4] He was taken as an *arhat*. He preached the Doctrine extensively, became very influential and received enormous wealth from the *brāhmaṇa*-s and householders. As a result the Doctrine was discussed by the *saṃgha* of two lakhs of monks.[5]

The monks were then already divided into eighteen sects, but lived without much controversies.

In Kashmir there was a *brāhmaṇa* called *Śūdra[6] who possessed inconceivable wealth. *Bhaṭṭāraka* Dharmatrāta,[7] the

1. *seṅ-ge.*
2. *legs-mthoṅ.* cf BA i. 24-5 'Ārya Kṛṣṇa ... entrusted the Doctrine to *ārya* Sudarśana ... At that time three hundred years had elapsed since the *parinirvāṇa* of the Blessed One. King Aśoka having died, Sudarśana was reborn in Kāshmīra. His parents gave him the name of Siṃha. Having taken up ordination in the religious order of the Blessed One, he attained the stage of *arhat*-ship. About that time, a king from the country of Uttarāpatha, named Kaniṣka, visited Kāshmīra in order to meet Siṃha.'
3. cf Bu-ston ii. 97—Kaniṣka, king of Jalandhara.
4. *yaṅ-dag-rgyal-ba-can.* V Saṃjayin. cf Bu-ston ii. 109, where Saṃjaya (along with Vijña) mentioned as belonging to Sāketana.
5. lit. two lakhs of *saṃgha*-s. V accepts this meaning.
6. V & S Śūdra. cf Bu-ston ii. 116 *dmaṅs-rigs*, lit. *śūdra*. However, both in S-ed and P-ed, the name occurs as Sūtra in transliteration.
7. *chos-skyob,* whose *Udānavarga* (Tg mDo lxxi. 1, lit. repro. of Kg—Sendai No 326) is considered as an *āgama* (bka') by the Vaibhāṣikas.

Vaibhāṣika, along with his attendants, and the first Sautrāntika *mahā-bhaṭṭāraka* Sthavira[8] of Kashmir, along with his five thousand attendant-monks, continued to receive his patronage and thus the *Tri-piṭaka* was extensively propagated.

The scriptures of the Sautrāntikas, at this period, were the series of *āgama* works[9] (*āgama-grantha-mālā*), the *Piṭakadhara-muṣṭi*,[10] etc.

From the east there came then an *arhat* called *ārya* Pārśva,[11] who had reached the limit of scriptural knowledge. **[Fol 31B]**. He recited some extremely rare *sūtra*-s like the *Suvarṇamālā-avadāna*,[12] and the one containing the prediction received in dream by king *Kri-Kri,[13]—works that he received from some profoundly learned *sthavira*-s.

Hearing (these), king *Kaniṣka got a large number of monks assembled in the Karṇikavana monastery[14] of Kashmir and, according to the Kashmiris, the Third Council then took place.

8. *gnas-brtan.*
9. *luṅ-dpe'l-phreṅ-ba.* V & S *Dṛṣṭānta-mūlāgama.* Tg (mDo xciv. 41) contains a work called *Dṛṣṭānta-mālya.*
10. *sde-snod-'dsin-pa'l-dpe-mkhyud.* V n 'We will in vain search in Chinese language—in which alone the *āgama*-s are preserved in their complete form—some works corresponding to these titles. But if we think that Tāranātha uses here not the exact titles of books but has in view their content, these works could be *Madhyama-āgama*, which always makes use of comparison, and *Saṃyukta-āgama*, which expounds the view of the creation of the universe. Otherwise, these works are already lost and the *āgama*-s available are much later additions.
11. *rtsibs-logs.* cf Bu-ston ii. 108 and BA i. 25.
12. *gser-phreṅ-can-gyl-rtogs-brjod.* Tg mDo xc. 17.
13. This dream-prediction is found in *Ārya-svapna-nirdeśa-nāma-mahā-yāna-sūtra*—Kg Sendai No. 48. Bu-ston ii. 98 quotes the dream and its significance : 'Oh great monarch, in thy dream thou hast seen how 18 men were pulling at a piece of cloth. This means that the teaching of the Buddha Śākyamuni will be split into 18 sects. But the cloth—that is (the Doctrine of) Salvation—will not be torn asunder. This passage likewise proves that (the canonical texts acknowledged by the 18 sects, represent all of them the Words of the Buddha.'
14. *rna-rgyan-nags or rna-rgyan-gyi-nags.* BA i. 25 Karṇikavana. Bu-ston ii. 97—Kuvana monastery. V Kuṇḍalavana-vihāra.

According to others, this council took place in the *Kuvana *vihāra*,—a monastery of *Jalandhara. Most of the scholars accept the latter view.

According to the Tibetans, this council took place in an assembly of five hundred *arhat*-s, five hundred *bodhisattava*-s[15] and five hundred common (*pṛthagjana*) **paṇḍita*-s.[16] Although this does not go against the Mahāyāna tradition (it needs to be noted that) at that time the great Buddhist scholars were called *mahā-bhaṭṭāraka*-s rather than **paṇḍita*-s.[17] So the use of the word **paṇḍita* with five hundred is not exactly correct.

A stray page containing the later portion of an Indian work on the succession of the hierarchs is translated by Kumāraśrī of 'Gos.[18] In this also are mentioned four hundred *bhaṭṭāraka*-s like *Vasumitra and others.[19] So this is proper. However, it will be wrong to identify this *Vasumitra with the

15. N. Dutt AMB 40 'The reference to the existence of a class of monks called *bodhisattva*-s at the time of Kaniṣka's council is also significant. For we read in the *Divyāvadāna* p. 261 of the existence of a class of monks called *bodhisattva-jātika*, along with a hint that they were not looked upon with favour by the Hīnayānists.' *Ib.* 40n 'Two or three days after the first ordination according to the *prātimokṣa* rules, the monks pass through a special ordination according to the *Brahmajāla-sūtra* and become *bodhisattva*.'
16. Bu-ston ii. 97 'The members of the Council were 500 *arhat*-s with Pūrṇika at their head, 500 *bodhisattva*-s, Vasumitra and others, and 250 or 10,000 ordinary *paṇḍita*-s.'
17. Vidyabhusana HIL 271f '*Paṇḍita* was a degree which was conferred by the Vikramaśīla university on its successful candidates. It is not known what the title the university of Nālandā conferred on its distinguished students. Perhaps, in that university,' too, the title *paṇḍita* was recognised.'
18. i.e. the author of *The Blue Annals*, briefly referred to as 'Gos lo-tsā-ba. The passage is quoted in BA i.24-5 and it is added : 'The above passage was discovered by me in a single leaf of an Indian manuscript which contained an account of the hierarchy of the Doctrine.'
19. The passage, as quoted in BA i.25, is : 'At the *vihāra* of Karṇikavana in Kāshmīra, 500 *arhat*-s headed by *ārya* Pārśva, 400 venerables headed by Vasumitra and 500 *bodhisattva*-s recited the Abhidharma.'

great Vaibhāṣika *ācārya* Vasumitra.[20] Further, since these relate to the Law of the *śrāvaka*-s, it is desirable to follow the *śrāvaka* tradition here. It is said (in the *śrāvaka* tradition) that five hundred *arhat*-s and five thousand *mahā-bhaṭṭāraka*-s, well-versed in the *Tri-piṭaka*, took part in this council. Five hundred *arhat*-s are mentioned here in order to glorify the Law. As a matter of fact **[Fol 32A]** the number of *arhat*-s was smaller. The number could have been five hundred including those who attained the *srotāpatti* and other stages.

Before Mahādeva and Bhadra, the number of those that attained the stages (of spiritual perfection) everyday was quite considerable. Because of the damage done to the Law by these two, controversies started among the monks and they became more keen on debate than on meditation. As a result, the number of those that attained spiritual perfection sharply dropped. That is why, at the time of the Third Council there were only a few *arhat*-s.

During the latter part of king Vīrasena's life, throughout the lives of kings Nanda and Mahāpadma and the first part of the life of king *Kaniṣka, the controversies among the monks continued. The controversies were most acute for sixtythree years.

20. Yuan-chuang also says that Vasumitra figured prominently in Kaniṣka's Council. Referring to this name, Watters i.273f comments : 'Vasumitra, here as in other places, is a name common to several illustrious Buddhists in the early periods of the Church.' Thus : 1) a personal disciple of the Buddha, 2) author of the *Abhidharma-prakaraṇapāda-śāstra* and *Abhidharma-dhātukāyapāda-śāstra* and probably also of a brief work commented upon by Dharmatrāta, 3) author of *Ārya-vasumitra-bodhisattva-saṅgīti-śāstra*, 4) the author of the treatises translated in Chinese as *Chih-pu-yi-lun* and *Yi-pu-tsung-lun*, 5) commentator on Vasubandhu's *Abhidharmakoṣa-śāstra*. Vasumitra mentioned in connection with Kaniṣka's Council is supposed to have headed the 500 *arhat*-s who, in this Council, composed the *Abhidharma-mahā-vibhāṣā-śāstra*. 'But', comments Watters, 'there is nothing either in this treatise or the *Saṅgīti-śāstra* to show that these works were written at the time of Kaniṣka, nor is there anything in either to show that it was wholly or in part the work of Vasumitra.'

If to these are added the minor controversies of the earlier and later periods, these went on for about a hundred years.

The controversies subsided at the Third Council, when all those belonging to the eighteen sects jointly purified the Law and codified the *Vinaya.* Also those portions of the *Sūtra-piṭaka* and the *Abhidharma* which were not codified before received codification and those portions which were already codified were revised.[21]

During the time of all these, some of the Mahāyāna scriptures reached the human world. A few monks who attained the *anutpattikadharma-kṣānti*[22] stage preached these a little. However, since this did not become very extensive, the *śrāvaka*-s did not contest it.

The twelfth chapter containing the account of the Third Council.

21. cf Bu-ston ii.101 on the time of the codification of the *piṭaka*-s.
22. N. Dutt AMB 40 'It may be a development of the Hīnayānic *anutpādajñāna* (further non-origin of *āśrava*-s and hence rebirth) and *kṣaya-jñāna,* but it bore a completely different sense in the Mahāyāna scriptures.' V & S tr 'those who had attained the practice in the teaching of "not to be born again." '

CHAPTER 13

ACCOUNT OF THE PERIOD OF THE BEGINNING OF THE EXTENSIVE PROPAGATION OF THE MAHĀYĀNA

After the Third Council, king *Kaniṣka passed away.

There lived a very wealthy householder called *Jaṭi[1] in *Aśmaparānta in the north, near the Thogar country **[Fol 32B]** to the west of Kashmir. He used to worship all the *caitya*-s in the north. He invited Vasumitra, the Vaibhāṣika[2] *bhaṭṭāraka*, from the region of *Maru in the west and *bhaṭṭāraka* Ghoṣaka[3] from the Thogar country. He entertained three lakhs of monks for twelve years. At the end of this, he prayed for *anuttara-bodhi* and as, the sign of the prayer being fulfilled, the offerings of flowers and lamps remained fresh and burning throughout the year and, moreover, the sandal-powder and the flowers offered (in the course of the prayer) remained suspended in the air. The earth shook and there came the sound of music, and so on.

In the Puṣkalāvatī[4] Palace, king *Kaniṣka's son entertained

1. cf the prophecy quoted by Bu-ston ii. 109-10: 'On the northern borderland, in the city of Takṣaśilā, a householder named Jaṭānika will appear. He will pay homage to my body and my disciples and, after one thousand aeons, in the age of Good Luck, in the world called Mahāvyūha-svalaṃkṛta, he is to become the Buddha Samantaprabha.'
2. V Sarvāstivādin. But the text has *bye-brag-tu-smra-ba*, the usual Tibetan for Vaibhāṣika, that of Sarvāstivādī being *thams-cad-yod-pa.*
3. Litvinsky in *Kushan Studies in USSR* p. 64 'The famous Buddhist theologian Ghoṣaka was born in Tukhāristān. He was one of the leading figures at the Buddhist Council in Puruṣapura and author of the commentary composed there on the *Abhidharma-vibhāṣā*. Ghoṣaka returned to Tukhāristān after the Council. This theologian was accordingly a follower of the Vaibhāṣika school, later divided into branch schools, one of which, called the Western Vaibhāṣika school, was connected with "the country of Balhika" or Balkh. The traditions of this school may even be traceable to Ghoṣaka.'
4. *rgyas-ldan*. Obermiller in Bu-ston ii. 110 translates as Vistaravatī, cf

for five years one hundred *ārya*-s and *arhat*-s and ten thousand other monks.

There lived a *brāhmaṇa* called *Viduḥ in Kusumapura in the east. He prepared many copies of the *Tri-piṭaka* and donated these to the monks. Each of the three *piṭaka*-s contains a hundred thousand **śloka*-s. He prepared a thousand copies of each of these. He also provided lavishly each monk with materials for worship.

In the city of *Pāṭaliputra there lived an *arhat* called *ārya* *Aśvagupta,[5] who was an *a-samaya-vimukta*[6] *arhat* and who devoted himself to the *aṣṭa-vimokṣa-samādhi*.[7] As a result of his preaching the Doctrine, *ārya* Nandamitra[8] and some others attained *arhat*-hood and many were led to realise the Truth.

There was a king called *Lakṣāśva in the west. He also extensively worked for the Law of the Buddha.

In *Saurāṣṭra in the south-west, there lived a *brāhmaṇa* called Kulika.[9] **[Fol 33A]** There lived then a *mahā-sthavira* *arhat* called *Nanda, who was born in *Aṅga and was well-versed in Mahāyāna. On hearing about him, he (Kulika) invited him to learn from him the Mahāyāna.

Watters i. 214 Puṣkaravatī, the ancient capital of Gandhāra. According to Yuan-chuang, it was here that Vasumitra and Dharmatrāta composed the treatises on Abhidharma.

5. cf prophecy quoted by Bu-ston ii. 109 'In the city of Pāṭaliputra, in the Mārgārāma, there will be a monk called Aśvagupta.'
6. *dus-mi-sbyor*. D 634—one of the twenty stages a monk of the Śrāvaka school reaches, (delivered at a wrong time). V 'whose salvation does not depend upon time' and adds in note 'the highest stage of *arhat*-hood.'
7. *rnam-par-thar-pa-brgyad*. Bu-ston ii. 91—eight degrees of liberation (from materiality). But see note 5 of Ch. 5
8. *dga'-ba'i-bśes-gñen*. Tg (mDo xc. 19) contains a work called *Ārya-nandamitra-avadāna*, author not known. cf Bu-ston ii. 105, where this work is quoted.
9. *rigs-ldan*. Mentioned in the *Mañjuśrī-mūla-tantra*—see Bu-ston ii. 116.

At that time there appeared all at once innumerable *kalyāṇa-mitra*-s in different places capable of preaching the Mahāyāna. All of them attained the *dharma-srota-anugata-nāma-samādhi*[10] as a result of listening to the Doctrine separately from *ārya* Avalokiteśvara, Guhyapati[11], Mañjuśrī[12], Maitreya[13] and others.[14]

There were about five hundred preachers of the Doctrine like *mahābhaṭṭāraka* *Avitarka, *Vigatarāgadvaja, *Divyākara-gupta, *Rāhulamitra, *Jñānatala, *mahā-upāsaka* *Saṅgatala and others. From the lands of the gods, Nāgas, Gandharvas, Rākṣasas etc—but particularly from the land of the Nāgas[15]—, were obtained most of the *sūtra*-s like *Ārya-ratnakūṭa-dharma-paryāya-śata-sāhasrikā*[16], *Sannipāta-sāhasrikā*[17], *Ārya-avataṃ-saka-dharmaparyāya-śata-sāhasrikā*[18] containing one thousand chapters, *Ārya-laṅkāvatāra-pañcaviṃśati-sāhasrikā*,[19] *Ghana-vyūha-dvādaśa-sāhasrikā*[20], *Dharma-sañcaya-(gāthā)-dvādaśa-sāhasrikā*,[21] etc.

Most of these *ācārya*-s were invited by the *brāhmaṇa* (Kulika). When king *Lakṣāśva heard about this, he was full of great reverence. Desirous of inviting these five hundred preachers of the Doctrine, he asked his ministers, 'What is the number of the preachers of the Doctrine ?'

10. *chos-kyi-rgyun-gyi-tiṅ-ne-'dsin.* cf D 431 & Bu-ston ii. 141. V *'samādhi* of continuation of teaching.' V n 'The *Mahāvyutpatti* does not give the name of this *samādhi.* But from the meaning it can be concluded that by being immersed in this *samādhi,* one can listen to the teaching of those whom the Buddha himself taught.'
11. *gsaṅ-ba'i-bdag-po.*
12. *'jam-dpal.*
13. *byams-pa.*
14. cf Bu-ston ii. 101f on the rehearsal of the Mahāyāna scriptures.
15. Bu-ston ii. 124—Śrīmān obtains Mahāyāna texts from the land of the *nāga*-s and is henceforth called Nāgārjuna.
16. *'phags-pa-dkon-mchog-brtsegs-pa-chos-kyi-rnam-grans-'bum.*
17. *'dus-pa-stoṅ-yod-pa.*
18. *'phags-pa-phal-bo-che-chos-kyi-rnam-grans-'bum.*
19. *'phags-pa-laṅkāra-gśegs-pa-ñi-khri-lṅa-stoṅ-pa.*
20. *rgyan-stug-po-stoṅ-phrag-bcu-gñis-pa.*
21. *chos-yaṅ-dag-par-sdud-pa-stoṅ-phrag-bcu-gñis.*

'Five hundred'.

[Fol 33B] 'What is the number of the listeners to the Doctrine ?'

'Five hundred'.

So the king thought, though there were many preachers of the Doctrine, the listeners to it were few. Thinking thus, he built five hundred temples on the top of the mount *Abhu (Ābu). To each of these he invited one teacher and provided (each) with all the necessaries. From among his own attendants he selected five hundred intelligent and highly devout persons, got them ordained and engaged them to listen to the Mahāyāna.

After this, the king felt desirous of having copies of the scriptures.

The king asked, 'How voluminous are the Mahāyāna *piṭaka*-s ?'

'Normally these cannot be measured. However, what we now possess run to one hundred lakhs (of *śloka*-s).'

The king said, 'So this is enormous. Still, let us have more copies.' Saying this, he got all these copied and donated the copies to the monks. These works were later brought to Śrī *Nalendra.

These three groups of the followers of the Mahāyāna, consisting of five hundred each, were profoundly versed in a large number of *sūtra*-s, were sharply intelligent and attained the stage of forgiveness (*kṣānti-prāpta*).[22] They possessed fore-knowledge (*abhijñāna*)[23] and had the capacity of showing some miraculous feats[24] to the people. Thus was spread the fame of Mahāyāna in all directions.

Failing to understand its significance, the *śrāvaka-s* slandered the Mahāyāna as something different from the sayings of the Buddha.

All the Mahāyānī-s were followers of the path of

22. *bzod-pa-thob-pa.*

23. *mṅon-par-śes-pa.* D 365—certain gifts of supernatural perception, of which six kinds are enumerated.

24. *rdsu-'phrul.* D 1058—*ṛddhi.*

yogacaryā.[25] Because they were all originally ordained in the eighteen sects, they lived among the followers thereof. There lived (thus) only a few Mahāyānī-s among thousands of *śrāvaka*-s. Still the *śrāvaka*-s could not dominate them.

There lived at that time in *Magadha, two *brāhmaṇa* brothers called Udbhṭa-siddhi-svāmin[26] and Śaṃkara-pati[27]. **[Fol 34A]** They used to worship Mahādeva as their tutelary deity. Both of them were proficient in the philosophy of the *tīrthika*-s as well as of the Buddhists. But Udbhaṭa remained doubtful [of Buddhism] and even considered Mahādeva as superior, while Śaṃkarapati had reverence only for the Buddha. Inspired by the words of their mother and having acquired the miraculous power of moving swiftly,[28] they went to *Kailāsa, the king among the mountains. In this mountain resided Mahādeva. They saw his white riding bull and also *Umā-devī plucking the flowers. At last they saw Mahādeva himself, sitting on his throne and preaching religion. Gaṇeśa[29] led the two [brothers] by both hands to Mahādeva.

When five hundred *arhat*-s came flying from the Mānasa-sarovara,[30] Mahādeva bowed down to them, washed their feet, offered them food and listened to the Doctrine from them. So he [Udbhaṭa] realised that the Buddha was superior. Still he made enquiries and was told by Mahādeva, 'Only the path of the Buddha leads to salvation, which is not to be found anywhere else.'

The two felt fully satisfied and returned to their own place. They renounced the dress of the *brāhmaṇa* and took the vow of

25. *rnal-'byor-spyod-pa-sems-tsam-pa. sems-tsam-pa* usually means the Yogācāra doctrine, which cannot be referred to in the present context.
26. *mtho-btsun-grub-rje*. Tg contains the *Viśeṣa-stava* (bsTod 1) and the *Sarvajña-maheśvara-stotra* (bsTod 3) by *ācārya* Udbhaṭa-siddhi-svāmin, *alias* Mudgaragomin.
27. *bde-byed-bdag-po*. Tg contains the *Devātiśaya-stotra* (bsTod 4—lit. repro. mDo xxxiii. 100) by *ācārya* Śaṃkarapati.
28. *rkaṅ-mgyogs-bsgrubs. dūratvagāmī-siddhi*—D 359-60.
29. *tshogs-kyi-bdag-po*.
30. *yid-kyi-mtsho*.

the *upāsaka bhaṭṭāraka*. They studied the scriptures of all the vehicles (*yāna*-s) and became great scholars. Udbhaṭa composed the *Viśeṣa-stava* and Śaṃkara the *Devātiśaya-stotra* with a view to show the excellence of the Buddhists and the inferiority of the *tīrthika*-s. Beginning from the market-place up to the king's palace, these were extensively propagated. Most of the people of the country recited these as songs.

[Fol 34B] Udbhaṭa and his brother provided five hundred *śrāvaka* monks with livelihood in Vajrāsana and entertained five hundred followers of the Mahāyāna at *Nalendra.

*Nalendra, the birth-place of Śāriputra, was also the place where Śāriputra, along with eighty thousand *arhat*-s, later attained *nirvāṇa*.

In the meanwhile, the *brāhmaṇa* settlement there fell into ruins. Only the *caitya* of Śāriputra remained. King Aśoka elaborately worshipped it and built a large temple of the Buddha there. The first five hundred *ācārya*-s of the Mahāyāna discussed among themselves and came to know that if the Mahāyāna was preached at the place of Śāriputra, it was going to be extensively spread. However, if it was preached at the place of Maudgalyāyana, [the Buddhists] were going to be very powerful without greatly spreading the Doctrine.

So the two *ācārya*-s—the *brāhmaṇa* brothers—built[31] eight temples [at Nālandā] and placed there all the scriptures of the Mahāyāna. Thus Aśoka was the founder of the first *vihāra* at *Nalendra. The five hundred *ācārya*-s along with Udbhaṭa and his brother enlarged the centre. Rāhulabhadra spread the Doctrine [of Mahāyāna] still further and Nāgārjuna made it most extensive.

The thirteenth chapter containing the account of the period of the beginning of the extensive spread of the Mahāyāna.

31. Bu-ston ii. 107 'the teachers Udbhaṭasiddhisvāmin and Śaṃkarasvāmin became possessed of the intention of making an image of the Mahābodhi at Magadha, when the latter arose from a pile of sandalwood instead.'

CHAPTER 14

ACCOUNT OF THE PERIOD OF BRĀHMANA RĀHULA

Now, *Candana-pāla was ruling the kingdom of Aparāntaka. This king lived up to the age of one hundred and fifty and it is said that he ruled the kingdom for one hundred and twenty years. Except for the account of his grand worship of the temples and the *saṃgha*-s, [Fol 35A] nothing much is known about his activities for the Law of the Buddha.

At that time, the *brāhmaṇa* *Indra-dhruva, a friend of the king, propitiated Indra and succeeded in attaining his desired object. He thus received the knowledge of the 'science of words' (grammar). When he took down in writing all that he (Indra) had said, the work became known as the **Indra-vyākaraṇa*.[1] This contains twentyfive thousand **śloka*-s. It is also called 'The Grammar Revealed by the Deity.'[2]

About the time the king ascended the throne, the great *ācārya brāhmaṇa* Rāhulabhadra[3] came to *Nalendra. He was ordained by *bhaṭṭāraka* Kṛṣṇa and listened to the *piṭaka*-s of the *śrāvaka*-s. In some of the sources it is said that he received ordination under *bhaṭṭāraka* Rāhulaprabha with Kṛṣṇa acting as the *upādhyāya*. But this Kṛṣṇa is not the same as (Kṛṣṇa) belonging to the line of the hierarchs.

He (Rāhulabhadra) listened to the Doctrine from *ācārya* *Avitarka and other *ācārya*-s of Mahāyāna. However, he learned the *sūtra*-s and *tantra*-s mainly from the tutelary deities like Guhyapati and others and he spread the system of the Mādhyamikas. Contemporary of this *ācārya* were the eight *mahā-bhaṭṭā-*

1. cf Bu-ston ii. 166ff.
2. *lhas-bstan-pa'i-brda-sprod-pa.*
3. *alias* Rāhula or Saraha, usually considered as the preceptor under whom Nāgārjuna received ordination. See S. Pathak in IHQ xxx. 93. S. K. De in HB i. 348 argues that by Rāhula or Saraha a number of different persons are referred to.

raka-s of the Mādhyamika system like *bhaṭṭāraka* *Kamalagarbha, *Ghanasa[4] and others.

Bhaṭṭāraka *Prakāśadharmamaṇi received the vision of *ārya* Sarvanivāraṇa-viṣkambhī[5] and thus attained the stage of *anutpattikadharma-kṣānti*. He brought from the nether world (the Mahāyāna work) *Ārya-mahāsannipāta-dharmaparyāya-śata-sāhasrikā*,[6] containing one thousand chapters.

Moreover, the first five hundred *ācārya*-s (of Mahāyāna), along with their numerous disciples, brought many *sūtra*-s **[Fol 35B]** and *tantra*-s that were not known before. Since then there appeared three forms of the *tantra*-s, namely *kriyā*, *caryā* and *yoga*, and also a few works on the *anuttara-tantra* like the *Guhyasamāja*,[7] *Buddhasamayoga*[8] and *Māyājāla*[9] etc.

About this time, there lived in the city of Sāketa[10] a monk called Mahāvīrya,[11] in the city of *Vārāṇasī the Vaibhāṣika *mahā-bhaṭṭāraka* Buddhadeva[12] and in Kashmir the Sautrāntika *mahā-ācārya bhaṭṭāraka* Śrīlābha[13]. *Bhaṭṭāraka* Dharmatrāta,[14] Ghoṣaka,[15] Vasumitra and Buddhadeva,—these four were famed as the four great Vaibhāṣika *ācārya*-s and, it is said, each of them had about a lakh of disciples. These great *ācārya*-s propagated the principal works of the Vaibhāṣikas as the *Trayamiśraṇa-mālā*[16] and *Śata-upadeśa*.[17]

4. S-ed Ghanasa, P-ed Ghanasāla. The former reading followed.
5. *'phags-pa-sgrib-pa-rnam-sel.*
6. *'phags-pa-'dus-pa-chen-po-chos-kyi-rnam-grańs-'bum.* V 'the book on Mahāsamāja containing a hundred thousand sections and 1000 chapters'.
7. *gsań-ba-'dus-pa.*
8. *sańs-rgyas-mñam-sbyor.*
9. *sgyu-'phrul-dvra-ba.*
10. *gnas-bcas.* V Sāketana.
11. *brtson-'grus-chen-po.*
12. *sańs-rgyas-lha.*
13. *dpal-len.*
14. *chos-skyob.*
15. *dbyańs-sgrog.*
16. *luń-ni-spel-ma-gsum-gyi-phreń-ba.* V 'the garland of three mixtures'.
17. *gdams-ńag-brgya-pa.* V 'hundred *upadeśa*-s'.

This Dharmatrāta is not to be taken as the other Dharmatrāta who compiled the *Udānavarga*.[18] This Vasumitra should not be confused with two others of the same name viz. one Vasumitra who composed the *prakaraṇa-śāstra*[19] and the other Vasumitra who was the author of the *Samaya-bheda-paracana-cakra*.[20]

In the account of the *ārya*-s of the Guhyasamāja, *Visukalpa, the king of *Oḍiviśa, is to be taken as a contemporary of king *Candana-pāla. There lived then a *brāhmaṇa* called Dharmika[21] in *Kuru. He built one hundred and eight temples of the Buddha around this region and made these the centres for all the Mahāyāna teachers of the time.

[Fol 36A] There lived a very prosperous *brāhmaṇa* called Vīrya[22] in the city of *Hastināpurī. He also built one hundred and eight temples and made these the centres for one hundred and eight teachers of the *Vinaya*.

At that time, king *Haricandra, the first king of the *Candra dynasty, was ruling *Bhaṅgala (Bengal) in the east. He attained *siddhi* by following the Mantrayāna. His entire palace was built of five kinds of gems. On the outer walls of the palace were reflected the three worlds. In prosperity he was comparable to the gods. Along with a thousand attendants, he attained the *vidyādhara-sthāna*.[23] Śrī *Saraha,[24] *alias* the great *brāhmaṇa*

18. Tg mDo lxxi. 1.
19. See Note 20, Chapter 12.
20. *gshuṅ-lugs-kyl-bye-brag-bkod-pa'i-'khor-lo.* Tg (mDo xc. 11).
21. *chos-ldan.* cf Bu-ston ii. 116.
22. *brtson-ldan.* V Yogins. Obermiller (in Bu-ston ii. 116) Mahāvīrya. V n 'S remarks that both the names Dhārmika and Yogin are found in the *Mañjuśrī-mūla-tantra* Fol 343 and that they can be taken as simple epithets.'
23. *rig-pa-'dsin-'pa'i-gnas.* D 1179 *rig-'dsin* or *vidyādhara*, a kind of spirit to whom a high degree of wisdom is attributed by the Tantras ; all these spirits are alleged to reside in the magical forest and to spend their time in perfect enjoyment with women who are equally accomplished.
24. For works in Tg attributed to Saraha *alias* Rāhula, see Supplementary Note 8.

Rāhula, was at that time still following the practices of the *brāhmaṇa*-s[25]. The five hundred *ācārya*-s of *yoga-caryā* (previously mentioned) also lived at this time. Excepting the *Prajñā-pāramtiā-śata-sāhasrikā*, almost all the Mahāyāna *sūtra*-s were obtained during his lifetime.

The fourteenth chapter containing the account of the period of brāhmaṇa Rāhula.

25. *bram-ze'i-spyod-pa.*

CHAPTER 15

ACCOUNT OF THE PERIOD OF THE DOCTRINE UNDER THE LEADERSHIP OF ĀRYA NĀGĀRJUNA

After that, *ācārya* Nāgārjuna[1] nourished the Law and spread extensively the Mādhyamika system.[2] He greatly helped also the *śrāvaka*-s, particularly by expelling from the monastery those *bhikṣu*-s and *śramaṇera*-s who had violated their discipline and yet became much influential within the *saṃgha*-s. It is said that they numbered about eight[3] thousand.

He was accepted as the leader of all the sects.

About this time, the three Yogācāris[4]—namely *bhaṭṭāraka* Nanda, *bhaṭṭāraka* Paramasena[5] and *bhaṭṭāraka* Samyaksatya,[6] —adhering to the standpoint of Yogācāra, wrote some treatises. In the "exposition of the *ālaya-vijñāna*"[7] **[Fol 36B]** these three *bhaṭṭāraka*-s are mentioned as the early Yogācāris. Therefore, the 'Asaṅga brothers' are to be considered as the later Yogācāris. Thus it is clearly said that they [Asaṅga and his brother] were not their followers.

With the help of the art of alchemy, he [Nāgārjuna] maintained for many years five hundred teachers of the Mahāyāna doctrine at Śrī *Nalendra. Then he brought under control *devī* *Caṇḍikā.

The goddess once proposed to take him to heaven through the sky. He said, 'I have no intention to go to the heavenly

1. *klu-sgrub.* See Supplementary Note 9.
2. *dbu-ma'i-tshul-lugs.*
3. S 'five thousand'. But the text has *stoṅ-phrag-brgyad,* i.e. 'eight thousand'.
4. *rnal-'byor-spyod-pa-ba.*
5. *dam-pa'i-sde.*
6. *yaṅ-dag-bden-pa.*
7. *mṅon-par-kun-gshi'i-bśad-pa.*

sphere. I have invoked you for maintaining the *saṃgha*-s of the Mahāyāna as long as the Law exists.'

Thus told, she settled in the western vicinity of *Nalendra in the guise of a noble *vaiśya* lady. On the high stone wall of the temple of Mañjuśrī, the *ācārya* nailed a peg of *khadira* wood as big as could be carried by one man. He gave her the order, 'You must provide the *saṃgha*-s with livelihood as long as this peg is not reduced to dust.'

She maintained the *saṃgha*-s for twelve years with all the needful. At last a wicked *śramaṇera*, then acting as a steward,[8] made passes at her and proposed to her repeatedly. She made no response. However, she once said, 'We shall be united when the *khadira* peg is reduced to dust.' The wicked *śramaṇera* set fire to the *khadira* peg and, when it was reduced to ashes, the goddess also vanished.

The *ācārya* established one hundred and eight centres of Mahāyāna in the hundred and eight temples. In each of these, he placed the image of Mahākāla[9] **[Fol 37A]** and instead of her (i.e. Caṇḍikā) asked Mahākāla to maintain (the followers of) the Law. Moreover, when the Bodhi Tree of Vajrāsana was being damaged by elephants, he built two lofty stone-pillars behind it and for many years there was no more damage. As, however, there was damage again, he established on the top of each pillar the image of Mahākāla riding a lion and holding a club in his hand. This proved effective for many years; but the damage started again. So he built a stone wall surrounding it and also one hundred and eight *caitya*-s with images outside [the wall].

He also built the boundary wall of the Śrī Dhānyakaṭaka[10] *caitya* and, within this boundary wall, built one hundred and eight temples.

When the eastern side of Vajrāsana was severely damaged by the river, he placed seven huge blocks of stone in the form of a dam on which were sculptured the images of the Buddha

8. *shal-ta-ba*. see D 1089.
9. *nag-po-chen-po*.
10. *dpal-ldan-'bras-spuṅs*. See N. Dutt AMB 22f & 42 ; Watters ii. 216ff.

with their faces turned back. This stopped the damage caused by water. (The images) were called the Seven Sages of the Dam. The word *chu-lon* simply means a dam (*chu-rags*). It is, therefore, extremely foolish to say that these constituted the 'reflection' (*'dra-len*), because the images were reflected on the water. It also goes flatly against the *Vinaya-āgama* to say that this took place at the time of the conversion of king *Uttrāyaṇa. On these two points one [presumably some historian referred to] shows one's own nature [i.e. ignorance].[11]

During this time, king *Muñja[12] of *Oḍiviśa, along with his thousand attendants, attained the Vidyādhara-kāya. In the west, king *Bhojadeva,[13] along with his thousand attendants, vanished in *Dodhahari[14] in a region of *Mālava. And so on. Thus, there was none who did not attain *siddhi* after entering the Mantrayāna.

Now, when the *Prajñā-pāramitā-śata-sāhasrikā* and many *dhāraṇī*-s were brought by the *ācārya* (Nāgārjuna), **[Fol 37B]** the *śrāvaka*-s said that these were composed by Nāgārjuna himself. After this no more *sūtra* work on the Mahāyāna appeared.

He composed five fundamental treatises[15] to silence the contesting *śrāvaka*-s who believed in the external reality. According to the Tibetan account, the *Nyāyālaṃkāra-nāma-śāstra*[16] written by *bhikṣu* Śaṃkara in refutation of the Mahāyāna contains twelve lakhs of **śloka*-s. But this is a verbal error. Three Indian historical works agree in asserting that it contains twelve thousand **śloka*-s.

11. V tr 'These two presumptions clearly show the foolishness of the compilers.'
12. Evidently not the famous royal author Muñja of the 10th century—Keith 53n.
13. Evidently not the royal author Bhojadeva (of Mālava), the nephew of Muñja and belonging to the 11th century.
14. S-ed Toḍahari.
15. For the large number of works in Tg attributed to Nāgārjuna, see Supplementary Note 10. Bu-ston i. 50-1, however, speaks of six fundamental works of Nāgārjuna : *Śūnyatā-saptati*, *Prajñā-mūla*, *Yukti-ṣaṣṭikā*, *Vigraha-vyāvartanī*, *Vaidalya-sūtra* and *Vyavahāra-siddhi*.
16. *rig-pa'i-rgyan-shes-bya-ba'i-bstan-bcos*. cf Bu-ston ii. 124 'At that

He built many temples in the eastern countries like *Paṭavesa or *Pukhaṅ, *Oḍiviśa, *Bhaṅgala, *Rāḍha, etc. At that time, *Suviṣṇu,[17] a *brāhmaṇa* of *Magadha, built one hundred and eight temples at Śrī *Nalendra. He made these the centres for the *mātṛkā-dhara*-s[18] so that the *Abhidharma* of both Mahāyāna and Hīnayāna were not lost.

In the latter part of his life, *ārya* Nāgārjuna went to the south. After converting king Udayana,[19] he nourished the Law for many years. In *Drāvalī of the south, there lived two *brāhmaṇa*-s possessing enormous wealth. They were called *Madhu and *Supramadhu.[20] A debate took place between the *ācārya* and these two *brāhmaṇa*-s. Their knowledge even of the Brahmanical scriptures—such as the four Vedas and 'the eighteen branches of knowledge—could not be equal to a hundredth part of that of the *ācārya*.

Then the two *brāhmaṇa*-s asked, 'Why should you, the son of a *brāhmaṇa* and versed in the three Vedas and a great scholar of all *sāstra*-s, be still a *śramaṇera* of *Śākya ?'[21] Thus asked, he praised the Doctrine and not the Vedas. So the *brāhmaṇa*-s became full of great reverence and worshipped the Mahāyāna. **[Fol 38A]** The *ācārya* gave them the magic spell. The one attained *siddhi* of goddess Sarasvatī[22] and the other of goddess Vasudhārā.[23] Each of them maintained two hundred and fifty preachers of the Mahāyāna. The first of them could copy

time, a monk named Śaṃkara, having composed a treatise called *Nyāyālaṃkāra*, consisting of 1,200,000 *śloka*-s, refuted everyone. In order to subdue (this monk, Nāgārjuna) expounded the Doctrine at Nālandā.'

17. cf Bu-ston ii. 116.
18. *ma-mo-'dsin-pa*. D 949 *mātṛkādhara*, holder of the *mātṛkā* or the mystic diagram.
19. V n 'In the text *bde-byed*, Śaṃkara. But S reads it as *bde-spyod*.' See note 22 of Introduction.
20. Bu-ston ii. 116 Madhu and Madhubhadra.
21. V tr 'Why have you become a Buddhist ?'
22. *dbyaṅs-can-ma*.
23. *nor-rgyun-ma*.

the *Prajñā-pāramitā-śata-sāhasrikā* in one, two, three or a few days. In this way he donated many copies of the scriptures to the monks. The second of them worshipped the monks with all the necessaries.

Thus, this *ācarya* nourished the True Doctrine in every way, i.e. by listening, expounding, meditating, building temples, providing the *saṃgha*-s with livelihood, causing welfare even to the living beings other than men, silencing the challenge of the *tīrthika*-s etc. His contribution to the Mahāyāna is, therefore, incomparable.

In the 'History of Seven Versions of the Words of the Buddha which is Comparable to the Mine of Jewels',[24] I have already given the full biography of *ārya* Nāgārjuna and of the great *brāhmaṇa*[25]. These can be known from there.

King Udayana lived for one hundred and fifty years.

According to one calculation, this *ācarya* lived for seventy one years less than six hundred years ; according to another, twentynine years less than that [i.e. less than six hundred years].

On the basis of the first calculation, he should have lived for two hundred years in the *madhya-deśa*,[26], two hundred years in the south and one hundred and twenty-nine years in Śrī Parvata.[27] This appears to be a rough account. But my **paṇḍita* teachers say that in this a half year was counted as a full year. On the basis of the second [calculation], he lived in Śrī Parvata for one hundred and seventy one years, the other periods being the same [as in the first calculation].

From the time he became a *rasāyana-siddha*,[28] **[Fol 38B]** his complexion looked like that of a gem. As the result of his meditation in the Śrī Parvata, he attained the first *bhūmi*[29]

24. Briefly referred to as the *bKa'-babs-bdun-ldan*.
25. i.e. Rāhulabhadra or Saraha—see Fol 36A.
26. V Magadha. The text has *yul-dbus*.
27. *dpal-gyi-ri*. See Watters ii. 208.
28. *bcud-len-grub-pa*. See D 359 on *dṅos-grub* ; *rasāyana-siddhi* is the fifth form of *siddhi*.
29. i.e. the first of the ten *bhūmi*-s called the *pramuditā* or beatitude—D 1257. cf Watters ii. 206. V n 'According to others, the eighth *bhūmi*'.

and his body was ornamented with thirtytwo auspicious signs.[30]

Ācārya brāhmaṇa Vararuci, a friend of this *ācārya*, was once acting as the royal priest of king Udayana.[31]. The youngest queen of this king had some knowledge of grammar.[32] But the king had no knowledge [of it]. While having a water sport in the garden, the king splashed water at her.[33] She said : **mā-mo-da-ka-siñca*,[34] (*māmodakaṃ siñca*), which, rendered into Tibetan, means : 'Do not throw water at me.' However, influenced by the southern dialect, the king understood this to mean : 'Give me a cake of peas fried in **til* oil.' When he offered this, the queen thought that it was better to die than to live with a king as stupid as an ox. And she was about to seek death by drowning herself. The king stopped her and then started learning grammar. Though he learned a great deal from *brāhmaṇa* Vararuci, for what was left for him to learn he studied under *ācārya* *Saptavarman.[35]

Now, the account of *ācārya* Vararuci.

When *ārya* Nāgārjuna was the *upādhyāya* of *Nalendra, he had a friend in *Rā-ra[36] [? Rāḍa] in the east of *Magadha, who was a *brāhmaṇa*, was extremely devoted to the Law of the Buddha and was very diligent in the six-fold duties.[37] He spent

30. V n 'which are the characteristic marks of the Buddha alone. According to one legend, Nāgārjuna placed himself on the same level as the Buddha and probably the reference to the Buddha alone possessing the 32 marks dates from this period.'
31. Though both S-ed and P-ed give the name as *bde-byed*, the correct form appears to be *bde-spyod*, which is found in Bu-ston ii. 167. Hence the Indian original could be Udayī or Udayana.
32. V 'Sanskrit grammar.' But the word for Sanskrit does not occur in the text.
33. See Sachau i. 136 for Al-beruni's version of the story, where the name of the king occurs as Samalvāhana, 'i.e. in the classical language Sātavāhana.'
34. The story occurs in the *Kathā-sarit-sāgara* vi.114.
35. In Tg, the *Kalāpa-sūtra* (mDo cxvi.9) is attributed to Śarvavarman, Sarvavarman, Saptavarman, Īśvaravarman or *dbaṅ-phyug ço-cha*.
36. V & S Chagala, perhaps because *ra* in Tibetan means the goat.
37. S-ed *drug-la* (six), P-ed *drug-pa* (sixth). The former reading followed.

twelve years chanting the *mantra* of *ārya* Avalokiteśvara. After this, he performed a rite with a fire offering (*homa*) costing four lakhs of gold. This made *ārya* Avalokiteśvara appear before him in person and ask, 'What do you desire ?'

'I desire to work for the welfare of every living being with the eightfold great supernatural powers (*aṣṭa-mahā-siddhi*[38]). Please employ Mahākāla to my service.' Being thus prayed, he [Avalokiteśvara] granted [this].

[Fol 39A] After this, Vararuci acquired the *siddhi*-s. For the purpose of working for the welfare of the living beings, with each of the eight *siddhi*-s like the *guṭikā* etc, he got initiated a thousand *siddha*-s. All these eight thousand *siddha*-s accepted him as their *guru* and acquired proficiency in all the branches of knowledge without any study.

He then went to the west and lived in the country of the very prosperous king *Śāntivāhana.[39] There also he worked for the welfare of every living being with *mantra* and *tantra*. When he went to *Vārāṇasī, the king then ruling there was *Bhīmaśukla. Also in his kingdom he worked extensively for the welfare of the living beings. To this period belongs the account of *Kālidāsa.

After this, he proceeded to the south, where king Udayana[40] wanted to learn grammar. But no *ācārya* could be found who had a complete mastery of the grammar of *Paṇi (Pāṇini). He came to know that the Nāga king[41] *Śeṣa was thoroughly proficient in *Paṇi. *Brāhmaṇa* Vararuci, with his magic power, coerced him (Śeṣa) to come and engaged him to compose a work of one lakh **śloka*-s as an extensive commentary on the

38. *grub-pa-chen-po-brgyad*. See D 359.
39. S suggests the possibility of this being the same as Sātavāhana. V n 'Lassen thinks that Vararuci was a contemporary of Vikramāditya.' See Watters ii. 207.
40. *bde-byed*.
41. In Tibetan writings, Pāṇini's commentator Patañjali is referred to as the Nāga king called Śeṣa. In Tg (mDo cxxxv. 2 & cxxxvi.1—the translation of Patañjali's *Mahābhāṣya*), Patañjali is called *nāga-rāja* Vāsuki-putra Śeṣa. cf also Bu-ston ii. 167.

whole of *Paṇi. The *ācārya* used to take these [whatever Śeṣa said] down in writing, and in-between the two of them there was a partitioning screen. When twentyfive thousand **śloka*-s were completed, the *ācārya* felt curious to see how the other looked. So he raised the screen and saw there a large snake yawning.[42] The Nāga went away out of shame. After this, the *ācārya* himself started to compose the commentary further, but he could not write more than twelve thousand verses. These two taken together are called the 'Grammar Taught by the Nāga.'[43]

He next taught many branches of learning like grammar [**Fol 39B**] and it is said that after this Mahākāla took him on his shoulders to the Pārijāta grove on top of mount Sumeru.[44]

But king Udayana, dissatisfied with *ācārya* Vararuci's commentary, employed *brāhmaṇa* *Saptavarman to invoke 'the six-faced youth' [Ṣaṇmukha-kumāra, i. e. the deity Kārtika]. When he (Saptavarman) attained *siddhi*, [Kārtika] asked, 'What do you desire ?' 'I desire to learn the *Indra-vyākaraṇa.' Being thus prayed, he [Kārtika] said, **si-ddho-va-rṇa-sa-ma-mnā-ya* (*siddho varṇa-samāmnāyaḥ*).[45] And the moment this was uttered, he [Saptavarman] acquired the full knowledge of the entire science of words.

According to the older Tibetan tradition, the portion preceding the fourth chapter of **Kalāpa* [-*vyākaraṇa*] was revealed by the Six-faced Youth. The word **kalāpa*[46] is used in the sense of a collection. Hence, it refers to the collection of many

42. S-ed *bsgyiṅs-pa* (yawning). P-ed *bskyiṅs-pa*, which appears to be a corruption. V tr 'coiled'.

43. According to this legend, therefore, Patañjali's *Mahābhāṣya* was composed partially by Vararuci. According to Bu-ston ii.168, however, Vararuci contributed to the completion of the *Kalāpa-vyākaraṇa.*

44. *ri-rab*.

45. In fact, this is the opening *sūtra* of the *Kalāpa-vyākaraṇa*. cf Bu-ston ii.168.

46. cf Bu-ston ii.168.

colours in the peacock's tail. In the present context, however, it is not used in this sense, because the **Kalāpa* was composed by *Saptavarman himself. Collection here only means the compilation of all useful parts in one place. Similarly, it is an error to say that the real name of the *ācārya* was Īśvara-varman.[47] The error results from the verbal corruption **sarva-varman*. *Saptavarman means *dbun-pa'i-go-cha* [i.e. (One with) Seven Armour].

Next is the account of *Kālidāsa.

When *brāhmaṇa* Vararuci was living in the royal temple of king *Bhīmaśukla of *Vārāṇasī, the king wanted to offer [in marriage] princess Vāsantī[48] to the *brāhmaṇa* Vararuci. Vāsantī arrogantly said, 'I am a greater scholar than Vararuci and therefore cannot serve him.' So Vararuci thought, 'I must befool her.' He said, 'Let me then ask my learned teacher who is a hundred times more intelligent than me. The king would better offer Vāsantī to him.'

[Fol 40A] Now, there lived a handsome shepherd in *Magadha. He [Vararuci] saw him cutting with an axe the branch of a tree while sitting on it and so knew him to be a big fool. He [Vararuci] took him along and for a few days arranged for his bathing, anointing, etc. He was made to wear the dress of a *brāhmaṇa* **paṇḍita* and the only words he was made to memorise were: **oṃ svasti*.

'When you find the king holding his court, offer flowers to him and just say: **oṃ svasti*. If anybody else asks any question, do not try to answer.'

While trying to carry out these instructions, after offering flowers to the king he said : **u-śa-ṭa-ra*. The *ācārya* [Vararuci] explained the significance of these four letters as follows :

**umayā sahito rudraḥ*
śaṃkara-sahito viṣṇuḥ
ṭaṅkāraḥ śūlapāṇiśca
rakṣantu śiva sarvadā

47. *dbaṅ-phyug-go-cha.*
48. *dpyid-ldan-ma.*

Thus he construed a benedictory verse [out of the letters]. Translated into Tibetan it means : Umā along with Rudra, Śaṃkara along with Viṣṇu and Śūlapāṇi with his sound of the bow—let Śiva protect thee for ever.'

Then Vāsanti asked him many questions concerning the import of words etc, but he did not reply. Vararuci said, 'Why should a profound scholar like my teacher at all answer the questions of a woman ?' Befooling her in this way, *brāhmaṇa* Vararuci fled to the south.

When he [Kālidāsa] was taken to the temple, he said nothing. At last he was highly delighted to see the picture of a cow among those of various animals painted on the outer wall of the temple. Thus he revealed his real self as a shepherd.

'Alas ! this is just a cowherd !' **[Fol 40B]** She cried and realised that she had been cheated. [And she thought] 'However, if he has intelligence, I am going to teach him grammar.'

By examining him, however, she found him to be an utter fool. Vāsanti became angry and sent him to collect flowers everyday.

There was in *Magadha an image of goddess Kāli[49] made by a celestial sculptor. He used to worship her every day with profuse flowers and great reverence. Once in the early morning he went to collect flowers for the worship to be performed by Vāsanti. One of her maids wanted to have some fun. She concealed herself behind the image, chewing a ball of areca nut. When the cowherd finished his usual prayers, the maid put into his hand the remnants of her chewing. He thought that the goddess herself had presented this to him. So he swallowed it. Immediately dawned in him unlimited knowledge of logic and grammar and he became a great poet.

He took a **padma* flower in his right hand, an **utpala* in his left and [thought] : 'Though the **padma* is beautiful, its stem is rough. Though the **utpala* is small, its stem is soft. Which of the two does she prefer ?' Thinking thus, [he addressed Vāsanti]

49. *lha-mo-nag-mo.*

I have in my right hand a *padma and in the left an *utpala.
The stem of one is rough, of the other soft.
Tell me, oh lotus-eyed one, which one do you want?'

When this was said, she realised that he had become learned and showed him high respect. From his great reverence for the goddess Klāī he came to be known as *Kālidāsa or the servant of Kālī. From then on he became the crowning jewel of all the poets.

He composed "the eight *dūta*-s",[50] like the *Meghadūta*[51] etc and also voluminous poetical works like the *Kumārasambhava*.[52] [Fol 41A] Both he and *Saptavarman were *tīrthika*-s by conviction. During their time, *arhat* Saṃghavardhana[53] lived in Li-yul. Among the Vaibhāṣika *ācārya*-s of the time were *ācārya* Vāmana[54] of Thogar, *Kuṇāla of Kashmir, Śubhaṅkara[55] [? Kṣemaṅkara] of central Aparāntaka, *ācārya* Saṃghavardhana of the east etc. Among the Sautrāntika *ācārya*-s was *bhaṭṭāraka*. Kumāralāta[56] in the west. All of them had innumerable followers.

50. For the imitations of the *Meghadūta*, see IHQ iii.273ff.

51. Apart from the Tibetan translation of the *Meghadūta* (mDo cxvii.8), the Tg contains a work called *Maṅgalāṣṭaka* (rG lxxxvi.93) attributed to *kavi-mahā Kālidāsa* of India and two *stuti*-s to Sarasvatī (rG lxxi.399 & lxxxii.57) attributed to *Kālidāsa* or *mahā-paṇḍita Kālidāsa* born in south India.

52. *gshon-nu-'byuṅ-ba.*

53. *dge-'dun-'phel.* According to ancient belief, two works in the Tg are by the oriental Turk Saṃghavardhana and written in Li-yul. These are the *Arhat-saṃghavardhana-vyākaraṇa* (mDo xciv.44) and *Kaṃsa-deśa-vyākaraṇa* (mDo xciv.45). See note 41 ch 6.

54. *mi'u-thuṅ.* Author of the *Kāśikā* commentary on Pāṇini's grammar. cf I-Tsing (Takakusu) ii, xiii, lvii, 176n.

55. *dge-byed.* Śubhaṅkara ? V & S Kṣemaṅkara. Tg contains two works attributed to Śubhaṅkara (rG lxxi.106 & 163).

56. *gshon-nu-len*, lit. Kumāralābha, a corruption of Kumāralāta—see note 10^ of Introduction. Yuan-chuang (Watters ii.286) refers to him as a native of Takṣaśilā. He composed some tens of treatises which were widely known and read and he was the founder of the

King *Haricandra,[57] along with his attendants, attained the rainbow-body.[58] He had no son. His nephew[59] was *Akṣa-candra, whose son was *Jaya-candra. They used to rule during this period. Though these two had reverence for the True Doctrine, I have come across no particular account of their contribution to the Law.

King *Haribhadra of the south attained *guṭikā-siddhi* with his thousand attendants.

From the early spread of Mahāyāna up to this period, every hundred in a thousand [Mahāyānists] became *vidyādhara-siddha*-s.[60]

About this time, first appeared the religion of the *mleccha*-s. According to some, this appeared when *bhaṭṭāraka* Śrīlābha of Kashmir passed away. According to some others, he [? the founder of the *mleccha* religion] was a disciple of *bhaṭṭāraka* *Kuṇāla and was called Kumārasena[61]. In spite of listening to many *sūtra*-s[62] and being well-versed in the scriptures, he had no faith [in the Doctrine]. He was expelled from the *saṃgha*, because of his violation of the vow. This agitated him highly. He resolved to found a religion as a rival of the law of the Buddha.[63] So he went to the country called *Śulika beyond Thogar, **[Fol 41B]** concealed himself under the name

Sautrāntika school : 'In his time, Aśvaghoṣa in the east, Deva in the south, Nāgārjuna in the west and Kumāralābha in the north were called the Four Shinning Suns.'

57. V Haribhadra.
58. *ja'-lus*. D 454—the body of a saint vanishing in the rainbow or in the manner of the colours of the rainbow.
59. *tsha-bo*, nephew or grandson. V takes it here in the sense of nephew.
60. *rig-pa-'dsin-pa-grub-po*—perhaps refers to the attainment of a high degree of wisdom, like that of the *ḍākinī*-s.
61. *gshon-nu'i-sde*.
62. V tr 'a Sautrāntika.' The text has *mdo-sde-'dsin-pa*, which is more likely to mean a *sūtradhara*.
63. S tr 'There was a very learned but unbeliever Sautrāntika, Kumārasena by name. He had been driven out of the *saṃgha*, as he transgressed the Law. It agitated him highly and he decided to found a school in order to refute the Law of the Buddha.'

*Mā-ma-thar, changed his robes, composed the *mleccha* scripture preaching violence and kept it concealed in the place of *Bi-śli-mi-lil,[64] the great demon among the *asura*-s. By the grace of Māra, he attained many magical powers like that of winning wars, etc.

At that time, a girl born in the *brāhmaṇa* family[65] in *Khorāsāna used to collect flowers everyday. A part of these she used to offer to the gods and another part she used to sell to others. A cat once came out of the heap of flowers and merged into her body. As a consequence, she conceived. At the time (of delivery) she gave birth to a healthy son. On growing up, he used to beat all children of his own age and kill all sorts of animals. So the ruler of the country banished him to the forest. Even there he enslaved anybody that he came across, killed the wild animals and offered their flesh, bones and skin to the people. On knowing this, the king made enquiries. He replied, 'I am not a *brāhmaṇa*, nor am I a *kṣatriya*, *vaiśya* or *śūdra*. There is none to teach me the conduct appropriate for my birth. That is why, I am angry and violent. If anybody teaches me the conduct appropriate for my birth, I shall act accordingly.'

He was asked, 'Who is going to teach you the conduct appropriate for your birth ?' He answered, 'I shall search for him myself'. Guided by Māra in his dream, he found the work that was previously concealed. He read it, became full of reverence for it and thought : 'But who can teach me according to it ?' Directed by Māra, he met *Mā-ma-thar and received instructions from him. Immediately he acquired magic powers.

[Fol 42A] Along with a thousand attendants, he became the sage of the *mleccha*-s under the name *Bai-kham-pa. He went to the region in the vicinity of *Makha city. As a consequence of his preaching there the false religion to the *brāhmaṇa*-s and *kṣatriya*-s, there came into being the royal dynasties of *Sai-da and *Tu-ru-ṣka.

64. S-ed B: sli-mli.
65. V omits 'born in the *brāhmaṇa* family,' though the text has *bram-ze'i-rigs-kyi*.

This teacher came to be known as *Ardho. Thus originated the religion of the *mleccha*-s.

The fifteenth chapter containing the account of the period of the Law under the leadership of ārya Nāgārjuna.

CHAPTER 16

ACCOUNT OF THE PERIOD OF THE FIRST HOSTILITY TO THE LAW AND OF ITS RESTORATION

The two kings *Akṣa-candra and *Jaya-candra ruled the kingdom of Aparāntaka. They were very powerful and had reverence for the Three Jewels. That is why, they are counted among the seven *Candra kings.

*Jayacandra's son was *Nema-candra. His son was *Phaṇi-candra. His son was *Bhaṃśa-candra [? Vaṃśa-candra]. His son was *Sāla-candra. None of them was very powerful. Therefore, they are counted neither among the seven nor among the ten *Candras.

Soon after *Nema-candra ruled the kingdom, *brāhmaṇa* *Puṣyamitra, the royal priest, revolted against the king and assumed power.

At that time, an old woman related to this *brāhmaṇa* went to *Nalendra on some errand. As the **gaṅdi* was rung, she heard [the sound] **phaṭ-ṭā-ya.*[1] coming out of it. [She enquired about its significance.] The *brāhmaṇa* experts on sound said that it meant : 'Smash the skull of the wicked *tīrthika*-s into pieces.

The earlier Tibetan account of this is said to have been as follows. This [*gaṅdi*] is the crown of the Three Jewels worshipped by the *deva*-s, Nāgas and the sages. When it is struck, the brains of the wicked *tīrthika*-s get dried up.

The [Tibetan] word *'gems*, describing the significance of the sound of the **gaṅdi*, should properly be *'gems-pa*, i.e. 'to smash into many pieces.' **[Fol 42B]** It must be the equivalent of an Indian word. It is ridiculous to suggest that it is originally the Tibetan word *'gems*[2] and further that it is to be taken in the sense of drying up.

1. It seems that Tār has in mind the Bengali word *pnāṭāo.*
2. Is Tār referring here to the view of Bu-ston, who in ii.136 describes

Then the *brāhmaṇa* king *Puṣyamitra, along with other *tīrthika*-s, started war and thus burnt down numerous monasteries from the *madhya-deśa* to *Jalandhara. They also killed a number of vastly learned monks. But most of them fled to other countries. As a result, within five years the Doctrine was extinct in the north.[3]

As it was predicted, the first five hundred years constituted the period of the flourish of the Law of the Teacher and the next five hundred years the period of its decay.

Accordingly, the period preceding Nāgārjuna's leadership of the Law in the *madhya-deśa* was the period of flourish according to the prophecy,[4] because it was the period of the increasing activity like building temples, etc.

The period of Nāgārjuna's work for the welfare of the living beings in the south was the period of the beginning of the *mleccha* religion. It is clear that when he was residing at *Śrī Parvata these damages were done by the *brāhmaṇa* king *Puṣyamitra. So this appears to be the beginning of the decline [of the Doctrine].

After that, king *Phaṇicandra was ruling in *Magadha. During this time, in *Gauḍa of *Bhaṅgala in the east, there was the king *Gauḍa-vardhana with great power and wealth. He rebuilt the monasteries previously damaged and thus helped the centres to increase.

Sthavira Sambhūti[5] extensively propagated the *Śrāvaka-piṭaka*-s, established sixty centres in *Magadha and thus contributed greatly to the Law. At that time, there lived in *Mol-ta-na[6]

the sound by the Tibetan word *'gems* ? D 44 *'gems* : 'lit. whose brains have been confounded ; to stun, to surprise, to confound, to overthrow in argument.'

3. V & S tr 'He (Puṣyamitra) himself died in the north after five years.' The text has the word *de-ñid*, meaning both 'himself' and 'the *tattva*'.
4. *luṅ-gi-bstan-pa*. D 1215.
5. *bsam-rdsogs*.
6. S Multan. cf Watters ii.254-5—Maula-sthāna, the older name of modern Multan.

in the west in the city of *Ba-ga-da a follower of the *mleccha* teacher, [Fol 43A] the Persian-Tartar king *Ha-la-lu.[7] He had the great might of about a hundred thousand strong cavalry. It is said that this was the first arrival of the *mleccha*-s in India.

Towards the end of the life of king *Bhaṃśa-candra [? Vaṃśa-candra] and during the period of *Sāla-candra, there lived a *brāhmaṇa* called *Kāśi-jāta[8] in the east. He used to worship with reverence all the surviving earlier centres and, in particular, he provided sixty-four teachers with livelihood, each with ten listeners to the Doctrine in the city of *Sva-na-ra-gha-bo[9] of *Bhaṅgala. Thus he worked for the restoration of the Law which was damaged.

All these happened during *ācārya* Nāgārjuna's stay at Śrī Parvata or shortly after that.

The sixteenth chapter containing the account of the period of the first hostility to the Law and of its restoration.

7. V & S Hallu.
8. cf Bu-ston ii.116.
9. Could it be Sonārgāon, the old capital of the Dacca district ? cf Watters ii.188.

CHAPTER 17

ACCOUNT OF THE PERIOD OF ĀCĀRYA ĀRYADEVA

Then there lived king *Candragupta, son of king *Sāla-candra.[1] Being very powerful, he is counted among the ten *Candra-s. He used to follow virtue and vice indiscriminately. But he is not counted among the seven *Candra-s,[2] because he did not take refuge to the Buddha.

During the reign of this king, *ācārya* *Āryadeva[3] and *ācārya* **Nā-gā-ha-va[4] (Nāgāhvāya) elaborately served the Law at Śrī *Nalendra.

According to the Tibetan tradition, *ācārya* *Āryadeva was miraculously born of a lotus in the pleasure garden of the king of the *Siṃhala island.[5] The king reared him up as a son. He eventually became a disciple of *ācārya* Nāgārjuna and, it is said, that during the lifetime of *ācārya* Nāgārjuna, he subdued Durdharṣakāla[6], the *tīrthika*. It is added by some that he was the same as *siddha* *Karṇa-ri-pā[7] and he attained the rain-bow body during Nāgārjuna's lifetime.

1. S-ed *de-nas-rgyal-po-sā-la-candra'i-bu-candra-gupta-ste* . . . P-ed *de-nas-rgyal-po-sā-la-candra-gupta-ste-zla-ba-sbas-pa*. The former reading followed. The latter means: 'Then king Sāla-Candra-gupta, i.e. Candragupta.'
2. V n 'Lassen mentions two Candragupta-s from the Gupta (and not Candra) dynasty. One of these reigned after A.D. 171 and the other after A.D. 230, and was also called Vikramāditya.'
3. For works attributed to Āryadeva (*'phags-pa-lha*) see Supplementary Note 11.
4. see Fol 45B, where he is also called Tathāgatabhadra. cf Bu-ston ii.113.
5. For the same account, see Bu-ston ii.130.
6. *thub-dka'-nag-po*, lit. 'Black, the Unconquerable.' The reconstruction is after V & S. Other possible Indian forms—Ajita-kṛṣṇa, Durdharṣa-kṛṣṇa. The Indian form of Mātṛceṭa's name before his conversion is not easily traced.
7. Perhaps Kāṇeripāda (*alias* Āryadeva).

[Fol 43B] In this land of Tibet, a story irrespective of being true or untrue, if once circulated among the people, nobody will listen to anything else, even though that be a firm truth. However, the truth should be stated here, even at the risk of incurring displeasure.

In the commentary called the *Catuḥśataka-vṛtti*[8], *ācārya* Candrakīrti also holds that he [Āryadeva] was the son of the king of the *Siṃhala island. The original sources of the history of *ārya-deśa* concur.[9] To follow these sources : A son with auspicious marks was born of *Pañcaśṛṅga, the king of *Śiṃhala. Though placed on the throne when grown up, he felt strongly inclined to accept ordination. From *upādhyāya* *Hemadeva he received *pravrajyā* and *upasampadā*.

After completing the study of the entire *Tri-piṭaka*, he came to *Jambudvīpa on pilgrimage to the temples and *caitya*-s of the different regions. He met Nāgārjuna shortly before he [Nāgārjuna] left for Śrī Parvata from the country of king Udayana. At Śrī Parvata, he sat at the feet of the *ācārya* and received various magical powers, like *rasāyana*, etc. He was entrusted with substantial responsibility of the Law.

After *ācārya* Nāgārjuna passed away, he [Āryadeva] worked for the welfare of the living beings by way of studying and meditating[10] in the adjacent lands [of Śrī Parvata] in the south. He built twenty-four monasteries with wealth obtained from the deities of mountains and trees, etc. He made each of these the centres of Mahāyāna and employed *yakṣiṇī* Subhagā[11] to maintain these.

There lived at that time a *brāhmaṇa* called Durdharṣa-kāla[12]

8. Tg (mDo xxiv.2) *Bodhisattva-yogacaryā-catuḥśataka-ṭīkā* by *mahā-ācārya* Candrakīrti, a commentary on Āryadeva's *Catuḥśataka-śāstra-kārikā-nāma* (mDo xviii.1, where Āryadeva is mentioned as born in the Siṃhala island and as the spiritual son of *ārya* Nāgapāda, i.e. Nāgārjuna).
9. Watters i.320, ii.100ff & ii.200ff for Yuan-chuang's account of Āryadeva, referred to as Deva Bodhisattva.
10. S-ed *sgom-pa*, which is followed here. P-ed *slob-ma* (disciple).
11. *skal-ba-bzaṅ-mo*.
12. *thub-dka'-nag-po*.

in the city of *Khorta in *Nalinī[13] in the east. **[Fol 44A]** He went around different places and defeated in debate the Law of the Buddha. When he arrived at Śrī *Nalendra, the Buddhists there, unable to face him in debate, wrote a letter of invitation to *ācārya* *Āryadeva and made offerings to Mahākāla. From the heart of the miraculously created [lit. self-created] stone-image of Mahākāla, there came out a crow. The letter was tied to its neck, it flew to the south and delivered the letter to the *ācārya*. The *ācārya* knew that it was time to defeat him [Durdharṣakāla] and arrived there with the enchanted object for swift transport.[14]

On the way, he met a *tīrthika* woman who needed an eye of a learned *bhikṣu* to complete the materials required for her *siddhi*. On being asked for it, he gave her one of his eyes.[15] He reached *Nalendra within a *prahara* and there—with the help of a shameless (*kākola*) *upāsaka*, a cat (*viḍāla*) and a jar full of black oil (*taila-ghaṭa*)—he subdued the sister **paṇḍita* (*bhaginī-paṇḍita*), the parrot (*śuka*) and the chalk (*khaḍika*) of the *tīrthika*-s.[16] He encircled the place with magic charm and covered it with tattered rags, etc. Hence Maheśvara could not enter his [Durdharṣakāla's] heart.[17] Though he went on arguing for a long time, the *ācārya* defeated him thrice. Then

13. S-ed Nalina. P-ed Nalinī.
14. Reference to the *dūratva-gāmi-siddhi*—see D 359.
15. cf Bu-ston ii.130 : 'On the way there the goddess of a tree begged him to grant her an eye, and he accordingly presented her with one of his eyes. Thereafter, as he had vanquished the heretic, (the monks said) : Who is this one-eyed ? Āryadeva replied—

    The Terrific One (Maheśvara), though he has three eyes,
    Cannot perceive the Absolute Truth ;
    Indra, though endowed with 1000 eyes,
    Is likewise unable to see it.
    But Āryadeva, who has only one eye,
    Has the intuition of the True Essence
    Of all the three Spheres of Existence.'

16. V tr 'He reached Nalendra within a *prahara* and found that the *bhaginī-paṇḍita*, *śuka* and *khaḍika* of the *tīrthika*-s had been subdued by *upāsaka kākola*, *viḍāla* and *taila-ghaṭa*.'
17. V tr 'So that Maheśvara could not enter the place of the contest.'

he tried to escape through the sky with the help of his magic spell. The *ācārya* arrested him and bound him with magic spell. When he was kept imprisoned within a temple, he started reading the scriptural works there and came across a prediction[18] about himself contained in the *sūtra*-s. He then became repentant for his past activities against the Law and was full of reverence for the Buddha. He accepted ordination **[Fol 44B]** and soon became a master of the *Tri-piṭaka*.

After this, *ācārya* *Āryadeva stayed at *Nalendra for a long time. At last he went again to the south and worked extensively for the welfare of all living beings. In *Raṅganātha near *Kāñci, he substantially entrusted Rāhulabhadra[19] with the responsibility of the Law and passed away.

During the time of *ācārya* *Āryadeva, the southern *ācārya* Nāgāhvāya,[20] whose real name was *Tathāgatabhadra, was invited by the Nāgas. Seven times he visited the realm of the Nāgas. A considerable number of the Mahāyāna *sūtra*-s was expounded by him and he clarified some aspects of the Vijñāna-madhya.[21]

The *Trikāya-stotra*,[22] now existing in Tibetan translation, was also composed by this very *ācārya*. Specially [important]

But the text has *rgyud*, which, it is difficult to take in the sense of 'the place of contest'.

18. For a prophecy quoted from the *Mañjuśrī-mūla-tantra*, see Bu-ston ii.112-3. See Note 22 of Ch. 18 for another prophecy quoted by I-Tsing. But F. W. Thomas in ERE viii.496 argues that the account of Āryadeva converting Mātṛceṭa involves an anachronism and is therefore to be rejected. Bu-ston ii.136 considers Mātṛceṭa to have been a pupil of Āryadeva.
19. *sgra-gcan-'dsin-bzaṅ-po*.
20. *klu-bos*.
21. *rnam-rig-gi-dbu-ma*. V tr *'madhyama* of Yogācāra'. But see Obermiller's note on the different standpoints of the Mādhyamika-ācārya-s, Bu-ston ii.135 n, quoted in our Supplementary Note 12.
22. *sku-gsum-la-bstod-pa*. In Tg, however, the *Kāyatraya-stotra* (bsTod 15) is attributed to Nāgārjuna and the author of the *Kāyatraya-stotra-nāma-vivaraṇa* (bsTod 16) is not mentioned. See also BA i.1 & note.

is the *śāstra* called *Hṛdaya-stotra*[23] composed by this *ācārya*. At that time in most of the southern cities like *Vidyānagara, even the children sang the verses of the *Tathāgata-hṛdaya-sūtra*.[24]

Thus spreading the Law extensively, he spent a long time at *Nalendra as the *upādhyāya*. This *ācārya* was also a disciple of Nāgārjuna.

In *Bhaṅgala in the east, an old *brāhmaṇa* couple had a son. As they were poor, *ācārya* Nāgārjuna gave them a lot of gold. So they became full of reverence and all the three of them became his disciples. The son became an attendant of the *ācārya* and a *rasāyana-siddha*. He received ordination and became a master of the three *piṭaka*-s. He was none else than *ācārya* Nāgabodhi.

He served *ācārya* Nāgārjuna as long as he lived. **[Fol 45A]** After he [Nāgārjuna] passed away, *ācārya* Nāgabodhi sat in a deep cave on one side of Śrī Parvata and, as a result of concentrated meditation for twelve years, attained the *mahāmudrā-siddhi*.[25] He stayed there and had the life as long as that of the sun and moon. He had two different names, **Nāgabodhi[26] and **Nāgabuddhi.[27]

Now, there lived a *siddha* called *Siṅ-khi-pā.[28] [His account is as follows].

When *ācārya* Nāgārjuna was staying on the mountain *Uśira in the north with a thousand disciples, he had an extremely dull-witted disciple, who could not memorise even a single verse in the course of many days. (Nāgārjuna) jokingly told

23. *sñiṅ-po'i-bstod-pa.*
24. *de-bshin-gśegs-pa'i-sñiṅ-po'i-mdo.*
25. *phyag-rgya-chen-po-mchog-gi-dṅos-grub.*
26. The colophon of Tg rG xlv.34 mentions Nāgārjuna as a synonym of Nāgārjunagarbha and also of Nāgabodhi (*klu'i-byaṅ-chub*) !
27. For works attributed to Nāgabuddhi (*alias* Nāgamati and Nāgabodhi), see Supplementary Note 13.
28. S n also quoted by V 'The name is certainly derived from Śṛṅgin, as it is testified by the Tibetan translation of it as *rwa-can*, i.e. the horned one.'

him, 'Meditate on having horn on your own head'. He meditated accordingly. Because of his intense concentration, there soon appeared visible horns on his head, which in no time reached the roof of the cave of his dwelling. The *ācārya* came to know of his power of concentration and made him sit on the meditation of being without horn on his head. And his horns disappeared. Giving him some instructions on *niṣpanna-krama*,[29] he [Nāgārjuna] asked him to meditate. So in a short time, he attained the *mahāmudrā-siddhi*.

Then the *ācārya*, along with his followers, practised the *pārada-rasāyana* for six months. After attaining success in this, when he distributed the alchemical pills to the disciples, he [One With Horns] touched the pill to his head and turned away without accepting it. The *ācārya* wanted to know the reason for this. [He said] 'Oh *ācārya*, I am not in need of it. If you need it yourself, please get some jars filled with water.'

Accordingly, a thousand big wine jars were filled with water and the whole forest looked as if full of jars. He [One With Horns] put a drop of urine **[Fol 45B]** into each of the jars and all these became full of alchemical gold. *Ācārya* Nāgārjuna kept all these concealed into a solitary cave of an inaccessible hill with the prayer that these should be of benefit for the living beings of the future.

This dull-witted one, who attained *siddhi*, came to be called *Siṅ-khi-pā, that is One With Horns.

Now about *ācārya* *Śākya-mitra,[30] the great. He was also surely a disciple of *ācārya* Nāgārjuna. However, his account is not read or heard of.

The account of the *mahā-siddha* Śabari-pa[31] is already given by me in my 'Account of the Jewels.'[32]

29. V n 'the final stage of contemplation.'
30. *śākya-bśes-gñen*. For works of Śākyamitra, see Supplementary Note 14.
31. For works of Śabari-pa or *ri-khrod*, see Supplementary Note 15.
32. *rin-chen-'byuṅ-gnas-lta-bu'i-gtam*.

Though it is said that *siddha* *Mātaṅgī[33] was a disciple of *ācārya* Nāgārjuna and his disciple [Āryadeva], he could not have lived at that time [i.e. the time of Nāgārjuna and Āryadeva]. He could have had their vision later.[34]

The seventeenth chapter containing the account of the period of ārya Āryadeva and others.

33. In Tg the *Kurukullā-sādhana* (rG lxxiv.46) is attributed to Mātaṅgipāda *alias* Mātaṅga.
34. *phyis-shal-mthoṅ-ba'o.* V tr 'We shall discuss him later.'

CHAPTER 18

ACCOUNT OF THE PERIOD OF ĀCĀRYA MĀTṚCEṬA AND OTHERS

Then, Bindusāra, son of king *Candragupta, ruled *Gauḍa for thirtyfive years.

*Canaka,[1] a *brāhmaṇa* minister,[2] propitiated Mahākrodhabhairava[3] and had a direct vision [of the deity]. This greatly increased his magical power. When the king fought wars and conquered all the lands between the eastern and western oceans, he [Canaka] killed the kings and ministers of sixteen big *janapada*-s[4] with *abhicāra*.[5] He killed about three thousand persons and magically induced insanity in ten thousand persons.

He committed a grave sin by injuring a large number of persons by beating, torturing, stifling and making them dumb. As a result of this sin he had a disease which decomposed his body into pieces. Then he died and was reborn in hell.

[**Fol 46A**] During the reign of this king was built the monastery called Kusuma-alaṃkāra[6] in Kusumapura. The great *ācārya* Mātṛceṭa[7] resided there and extensively propagated both the Hīnayāna and Mahāyāna doctrines. During

1. Obermiller (Bu-ston ii.119) Cāṇakya. In the Tg *Cāṇakya-nīti-śāstra* (mDo cxxiii.32) is attributed to Caṇaka or Cāṇakya.
2. P-ed *slob-dpon*, lit. *ācārya*. S-ed *blon-po*, lit. minister. The latter reading followed.
3. V Yamāntaka.
4. *groṅ-khyer-chen-po-bcu-drug*.
5. *mṅon-spyod*.
6. *me-tog-gis-brgyan-pa*, lit. 'decorated with flowers'. Anesaki in ERE ii.159—this Kusumapura : modern Patna. cf Sircar CGAIL 152. But see Watters i.341f.
7. *ma-khol*. For works attributed to Mātṛceṭa and Pitṛceṭa (*pha-khol*), see Supplementary Note 16.

the latter half of *ācārya* Mātṛceṭa's life, *Śrīcandra, son of the younger brother of Bindusāra, ascended the throne. He built a temple of *ārya* Avalokiteśvara and maintained there two thousand Mahāyāna monks.

[During this time] Rāhulabhadra became the *upādhyāya* of Śrī *Nalendra and built there fourteen *gandhola*-s[8] and made these fourteen different centres for the Doctrine. Many years after the reign of king *Śrī-candra, in *Di-li[9] (Delhi) and *Mālava in the west, king *Kaṇika ascended the throne at a young age. He became extremely prosperous by discovering twentyeight mines of gems. In each of the four directions, he built a temple. In these he continuously entertained thirty thousand monks of both Hīnayāna and Mahāyāna. From this one should know that this *Kanika is not[10] the same person as king *Kaniṣka.

This *ācārya* Mātṛceṭa was the same as the *brāhmaṇa* Durdharṣakāla mentioned a little earlier. The same person was known under the following different names[11] :

8. *dri-gtsaṅ-khaṅ*. D 213 & 653 : the principal chapel in a monastery ; the great temple of Buddha at Gayā was called Mahā-gandhola-caitya.
9. V Ti-li. S-ed Ti-li : P-ed Di-li. The latter followed.
10. The text has *mi-gcig-pa*, which means 'not the same' as well as 'one man'. V & S accept the first meaning and translate the sentence as, 'This Kanika is not the same person as king Kaniṣka.' In his *Table of Contents*, Tār clearly mentions Kanika and Kaniṣka as separate kings. However, as evidenced by Mātṛceṭa's letter to Kaniṣka (see note 24 of this chapter), Kanika appears to be but another name of Kaniṣka. Vidyabhusana in JASB 1910. 477ff doubts that Kanika, to whom this letter was sent, was identical with the Kushana King Kaniṣka. F. W. Thomas in IA xxxii.345ff & ERE viii.495, Anesaki in ERE ii.159 and Winternitz HIL ii.270n argue against such an untenable view. cf Watters ii.104—Kaniṣka also referred to as Kanita.
11. Though the Tibetan colophon of Mātṛceṭa's *Stotra-śata-pañcāśatka* (Tg bsTod 38) attributes it to Aśvaghoṣa, the modern scholars are generally inclined to consider the identification of the two as due to some confusion : Anesaki in ERE ii.159-60 ; F. W. Thomas in ERE viii.495 ; Winternitz HIL ii.270. Their main points are : 1) I-Tsing

Śūra,[12] Aśvaghoṣa,[13] Mātṛceṭa, Pitṛceṭa,[14] Durdharṣa, Dhārmika Subhūti,[15] *Maticitra,[16] etc.

Now, in the city called *Khorta[17] there lived a merchant who had ten daughters. All of them established themselves in *śaraṇa-gamana* and *pañcaśikṣā* and used to worship the Jewels. All the daughters were married to nobles of the different parts of the country. The youngest of them was married to a very wealthy *brāhmaṇa* called *Saṃghaguhya.[18] A son was once born to her [Fol 46B] and was called Kāla. He thoroughly studied the Vedas along with all their branches. Because of his devotion to the parents he was known as Mātṛceṭa and Pitṛceṭa. He became thoroughly proficient in *mantra*,

clearly knew the two as separate poets, 2) Aśvaghoṣa figured in the court of Kaniṣka while Mātṛceṭa, on the ground of his old age, declined to go there. For further discussion of the question, see Supplementary Note 17.

12. *dpa'-bo*. For the works attributed to Ārya-śūra or Śūra, see Supplementary Note 18. Winternitz ii.276 argues : 'the poet probably belongs to the 4th century A.D.' on the ground.that the frescoes of Ajantā (6th cen. AD) quote verses of his *Jātakamālā* and that his work was translated into Chinese in A.D. 434.
13. *rta-dbyaṅs*. For the name Aśvaghoṣa, see Watters ii. 103f. For the works attributed to him, see Supplementary Note 19.
14. *pha-khol*. See Supplementary Note 16.
15. *chos-ldan-rab-'byor*. V Dhārmika Subhūti. cf Anesaki in ERE ii.159. 'The *Vajrasūci*, a refutation of the caste-system bears the name of Aśvaghoṣa as its author ; but the same text in the Chinese translation (Nanjio No. 1303) is ascribed to Fa-Hien, literally Law-famed. This name is usually rendered as Dharmayaśas, but may be Dhārmika Subhūti, literally Lawful Glory'. In Tg the following works are attributed to Dhārmika Subhūti : *Bodhisattva-caryā (-saṃgraha)-pradīpa-ratnamālā-nāma* (mDo xxx.31), *Saddharma-smṛti-upasthāna-kārikā* (mDo xxxiii.38 & xciv.24), *Daśakuśala-karma-patha-nirdeśa* (mDo xxxiii.40 & xciv.21).
16. See note 7 of this chapter. cf F. W. Thomas in ERE viii.495-6.
17. F. W. Thomas in ERE viii.495 : does this refer to Gauḍa ?
18. In Tg, the *Aṣṭāṅga-hṛdaya* (mDo cxviii.4) and its auto-commentary (mDo cxviii.5 and cxix) are attributed to *mahā-vaidya* Pitṛceṭa (*pha-khol*), *alias mahā-vaidya* Vāgbhaṭa, son of *vaidya-pati* Saṃghaguhya, *alias* Saṃghagupta or Siṃhagupta,

tantra and debate. He received direct precepts from god Mahādeva.[19]

Proud of being proficient in logic, he defeated in debate the Buddhists in *Oḍiviśa, *Gauḍa, *Tīrahuti, *Kāmarūpa and other places. He converted some into *tīrthika*-s, deprived others of their power and humiliated still others by compelling them to bow down before the *tīrthika*-s and in many other ways.

The mother thought, 'If he goes to *Nalendra, the masters of logic and *vidyā-mantra* would make him feel humble and convert him into a follower of the Doctrine.'

And she said, 'If the Buddhists of the other places are comparable to the hairs growing on the ear of a horse, the Buddhists of *Magadha are comparable to the body of the horse. Without defeating the Buddhists of *Magadha, none can earn fame in debate.'

How he went to *Magadha and received ordination is already narrated. When he became a *sthavira* proficient in the *piṭaka*-s, *āryā* [*Tārā-devī*] instructed him in a dream : 'Compose many *stotra*-s to the Buddha. That will remove the defilement caused by your past sins against the Doctrine.' Thus instructed, he composed the *stotra* called 'Praise for the Praiseworthy'[20] to atone for his sins. It is said that besides

19. I-Tsing (Takakusu) 157 : 'Previously as a follower of another religion, when born as man, Mātṛceṭa had been an ascetic, and had worshipped Maheśvara-deva. When a worshipper of this deity, he had composed hymns in his praise.'

20. Tg bsTod 29 : *Varṇanārhavarṇane-bhagavato-buddhasya-stotre'śakya-stava-nāma* by Mitracita (Maticitra orMātṛceṭa). cf I-Tsing (Takakusu) 157 : 'He composed first a hymn consisting of four hundred *śloka*-s (i.e. the *Varṇanārha-varṇana*) and afterwards another of one hundred and fifty (i.e. the *Śata-pañcāśatka*) ... These charming compositions are equal in beauty to the heavenly flowers, and high principles which they contain rival in dignity the lofty peaks of a mountain. Consequently in India, all who compose hymns imitate his style, considering him the father of literature. ... Throughout India, everyone who becomes a monk is taught Mātṛceṭa's two hymns as soon as he can recite the five and ten precepts (śīla). This course is adopted by both the Mahāyāna and Hīnayāna schools'.

this, he composed a hundred *stotra*-s to the Buddha. Best among these is the *Śata-pañcāśatka-stotra.*[21]

When Mātṛceṭa became a follower of the Law of the Buddha [**Fol 47A**], a large number of *tīrthika*-s and *brāhmaṇa*-s accepted ordination in the monasteries of four directions.

Among the *brāhmaṇa*-s, Durdharṣakāla was the foremost and most accomplished. When even he was seen to renounce his own views like brushing off the dust from the shoes and to accept the Law of the Buddha, [others thought] the Doctrine of the Buddha was surely most wonderful. As a result, in Śrī *Nalendra alone more than a thousand *brāhmaṇa*-s and an equal number of *tīrthika*-s took up ordination.

Being exceedingly virtuous, this *ācārya* used to receive everyday a lot of food while going round for alms in the city. Thus he relieved five hundred monks from the worry of livelihood. He led two hundred and fifty of them to devote themselves to meditation and the other two hundred and fifty to studies.

As the Jina himself predicted[22] the composition of these, the *stotra*-s of this *ācārya* bring the same blessings as the words of the Buddha. These *stotra*-s became very popular and were recited even by the singers, dancers and jesters. As a result, all the people of the country became naturally devoted to the Buddha. Thus through these *stotra*-s[23] he proved himself extremely helpful for the spread of the Law.

21. bsTod 38 in Tg, where it is attributed to Aśvaghoṣa. But see F. W. Thomas in ERE viii.497 : this hymn of Mātṛceṭa was translated by I-Tsing into Chinese. The originals of both *Varṇanārha-varṇana* and *Śata-pañcāśatka* are found in fragments among the "MS Trouvailles from Chinese Turkstan".

22. See I-Tsing (Takakusu) 156f : 'A nightingale in the wood, seeing the Buddha ... began to utter its melodious notes ... The Buddha, looking back to his disciples, said, "The bird, trasnported with joy at sight of me, unconsciously utters its melodious notes. On account of this good deed, after my *nirvāṇa* this bird shall be born in human form, and named Mātṛceṭa, and he shall praise my virtues with true appreciation." '

23. V 'he (Aśvaghoṣa).' V seems throughout to accept Tāranātha's identification of Mātṛceṭa with Aśvaghoṣa.

Towards the latter part of his life, king *Kanika sent a messenger to this *ācārya* and invited him. He was then too old to go to the king. Still he helped the king to remain firm in the Doctrine by writing a letter to him[24] and also by sending his own disciple Jñānapriya[25] for preaching the Doctrine to the king as his *ācārya*.

He resolved to compose a work in which, instead of depending merely on the written works like the *sūtra*-s etc, he intended to depend also on the oral tradition of the *upādhyāya*-s and *ācārya*-s **[Fol 47B]** and narrate each of the ten *Jātaka*-s ten times in accordance with the ten *pāramitā*-s.[26] After completing thirty four of these, he passed away.

According to another account, he thought : 'Just as the Bodhisattva offered his own body to a tigress, I can also do the same. It is not a difficult task.' Thus, on coming across in a similar way a famished tigress followed by her cubs, when he was about to offer his own body, he had a little hesitation. [Hence he realised the real greatness of the Bodhisattva and] he became more profoundly reverent for the Buddha. With

24. *Mahārāja-kaniṣka-lekha* (mDo xxxiii.34 & xciv.29) by Mātṛceṭa or Maticitra. The colophon : 'letter sent by *ācārya* Maticitra to *mahārāja* Kaniṣka,' though in the Tibetan form this name occurs as Kanika. The corrector of the translation Śrīkūṭa says that this probably refers to the Kuṣāna king Kaniṣka. It is translated by F. W. Thomas in IA xxxii.345f, who, in ERE xiii.496, comments, 'Undoubtedly, the most interesting of Mātṛceṭa's writings is the epistle to king Kaniṣka ... Beginning with excuses for not accepting the great king's invitation and for boldness in offering advice, he proceeds to counsel the young sovereign as to his moral policy, the concluding 20 out of 85 verses containing a pathetic appeal on behalf of the dumb animals and deprecating the chase. The latter topic was familiar on Buddhist lips, as we may see from the Edicts of Āśoka. The whole epistle is full of mildness, gracious courtesy and moral worth ; that it is an old man's writing appears on the surface.'
25. *ye-śes-sñan-pa*.
26. S-ed *bcu-phrag-bcu*, which is followed here. P-ed *phrag-bcu* (ten) is missing. Tār evidently refers here to the *Jātakamālā* of Āryaśūra—Śūra being for him only another name of Mātṛceṭa or Aśvaghoṣa.

his own blood, he wrote the Seventy *praṇidhāna*-s.[27] He offered a little blood to the tigress, which gave some strength to her weak body [and thus enabled her to be strong enough to devour him]. Then he offered his body to them.

According to others, he who did this was actually *ācārya* Parahitaghoṣa-āraṇyaka[28] and who was much later than *ācārya* Mātṛceṭa.

He[29] composed many other *śāstra*-s like the *Prajñā-pāramitā-saṃgraha.*[30] He showed equal compassion for the monks of both Mahāyāna and Hīnayāna and was not partial to the Mahāyānī-s. Hence the Śrāvakas also had great respect for him. He belonged to all the Buddhists and hence had a very high reputation.

Ācārya Rāhulabhadra,[31] though a *śūdra* by birth, was all-perfect in physical charm and wealth. He received ordination at *Nalendra and became a monk proficient in the three *piṭaka*-s. Sitting at the feet of *ācārya* *Āryadeva, he realised the truth. When he resided at *Nalendra, a huge pot raised by him to the sky used to be filled with delicious food. Thus he provided many *saṃgha*-s with livelihood. At last in *Dhiṅkoṭa he had the direct vision of Amitābha Buddha.

[Fol 48A] He passed away facing Sukhāvatī. I have already written about him in my 'Account of Tārādevī.'[32]

The eighteenth chapter containing the account of the period of ācārya Mātṛceṭa and others.

27. P-ed *bdun-cu-pa,* (lit. seventy) *smon-lam* (lit. *praṇidhāna*). S 'a prayer consisting of seventy *śloka*-s.' Tg contains *Praṇidhāna-saptati-nāma-gāthā* (mDo xxxiii.53 & cxxxvi.38) by *ācārya bhaṭṭāraka* Parahitaghoṣa Āraṇyaka.
28. *gshan-la-phan-pa'i-dbyaṅs-dgon-pa-ba.* V & S Parahita Svarakāntāra. But see note 27.
29. V 'he (Aśvaghoṣa) ...'
30. *śer-phyin-bsdus-pa.* Does Tār refer here to the *Ārya-prajñā-pāramitā-saṃgraha-kārikā-vivaraṇa* of Triratnadāsa (mDo xiv.3) ? See F. W. Thomas in ERE viii.496—the tradition identifying Triratnadāsa with Mātṛceṭa.
31. *sgra-gcan-'dsin-bzaṅ-po.*
32. *sgrol-ma'i-lo-rgyus.*

CHAPTER 19

ACCOUNT OF THE PERIOD OF THE RENEWED HOSTILITY TO THE DOCTRINE AND OF ITS RESTORATION

After that, in the east [ruled] *Dharma-candra, son of king *Śrī-candra.

He also extensively worshipped the Law of the Buddha. He had a *brāhmaṇa* minister called *Vasunetra,[1] who had a great reverence for the Law of the Buddha and who attained direct vision of *ārya* Avalokiteśvara.

He [Vasunetra] obtained from the Nāgas various medicines and cured all diseases all over the kingdom of Aparāntaka. Thrice did he establish equality by writing off everybody's debts.

At that time there lived in Kashmir a king called *Turuṣka.[2] He lived for a hundred years and was highly religious.

During the reign of *Dharmacandra, there ruled in *Moltan and *Lahore king *Ban-de-ro, *alias* *Khuni-ma-mpta, the Persian king. Between this king and king *Dharmacandra, there took place repeated wars and treaties of peace. Once, during a period of peace, some greedy monks were used as messengers to each other by both sides. The Persian king sent presents of horses and jewels to the king of *madhya-deśa*. In return, the latter sent presents of elephants and fine silk to the Persian king.

*Dharma-candra, king of Aparāntaka, once sent to the Persian king a present of highly precious and very fine silken robe made without any stitch.[3] Unfortunately, because of

1. cf the prophecy quoted from *Mañjuśrī-mūla-tantra* by Bu-ston ii.117f.
2. *Ibid* ii.119, according to which Turuṣka lives for 300 years.
3. *srubs-med-pa*.

faulty weaving there appeared something like a foot-print[4] on that part of the robe which covered the chest. [Fol 48B] This roused suspicion of black magic. On another occasion, he [Dharmacandra] wanted to send some fruits as a present. A *brāhmaṇa* wrote charmed circles on pieces of birch-bark and left these in the sun [to dry]. [One of these] was carried by the wind into the opening of the flower that turned into a banana bunch. He [Dharmacandra] sent to the Persian king the present of fruits including this [banana bunch] in a box containing melted butter [as the preserver]. When the charmed circle was found inside the fruit, [the Persian king] became convinced of the use of black magic.

So he [the Persian king] destroyed *Magadha by the *Turuṣka army, ruined many temples and heavily damaged Śrī *Nalendra. Even the ordained monks fled away.

After this, *Dharmacandra passed away. He was succeeded by one of his nephews, who, however, submitted to the *Turuṣkas and remained powerless.

Buddhapakṣa,[5] son of *Dharmacandra's maternal uncle, was the king of *Vārāṇasī. He sent a number of Sautrāntika *ācārya*-s to China.[6] In return for this kindness, the Chinese king sent to king Buddhapakṣa presents of precious articles. These were carried by ten thousand persons, of whom one hundred carried gold.

With this wealth, he [Buddhapakṣa] pleased the kings, big and small, as well as the feudatory lords and chiefs of the western and central regions, mobilised them in a war against the Persian king and killed many Persian heroes including king *Khuni-ma-mpta.

King Buddhapakṣa sent orders to most of the kingdoms of Aparāntaka and of the west to reconstruct all the damaged temples and to invite the monks back. In Śrī *Nalendra

4. V 'print of a horse-hoof'. cf Sachau ii.11 for Al-beruni's account of similar stories.

5. *sans-rgyas-phyogs*. cf Bu-ston ii.119.

6. *rgya-nag*.

[**Fol 49A**] eightyfour centres of the Doctrine were established. Of these, seventyone were established by the king himself and the remaining ones by the queen and the ministers.

There lived then the later *Maticitra,[7] who had direct vision of Mañjuśrī. He became the *guru* of the king. [The king] entertained the monks on top of the royal palace and fed the *tīrthika*-s outside the gate. Thus he restored the Law that had been damaged before.

The nineteenth chapter containing the account of renewed hostility to the Doctrine and of its restoration.

7. *maticitra phyi-ma-gcig*. V n 'Perhaps the author or even the historians before him finding various legends about Mātṛceṭa, assume several persons instead of one. Apparently, there should not be any doubt that this later Mātṛceṭa is the same Aśvaghoṣa, who is referred to in the ancient Chinese biography. And thus, was the king Buddhapakṣa same as Vikramāditya, the liberator of India from the Indo-Scythians ? But we do not find any reference in the Chinese histories that they rendered aid to the Indian kings, though it has been mentioned that during the first Han dynasty, the Chinese spent much on gifts. The reference to the first introduction of Buddhism into China after A.D. 64 is conjectural ; it began to spread there in the fourth century.' But Takakusu(I-Tsing) p. xvii : Buddhism first introduced into China in A.D. 67, the date of the arrival of the first Indian *śramaṇa*-s,—Kāśyapa, Mātaṅga, etc—who were invited by the Chinese Emperor Ming-ti (A.D. 58-75).

CHAPTER 20

ACCOUNT OF THE PERIOD OF THE THIRD HOSTILITY TO THE DOCTRINE AND OF ITS RESTORATION

Then, in the country of *Kṛṣṇarāja in the south, there lived an exponent of the Prajñā-pāramitā called *ācārya* *Mālikabuddhi. He established in the *madhya-deśa* twentyone big centres of the Doctrine, built one thousand *caitya*-s containing the images of deities, extensively propagated the Prajñā-pāramitā for twenty years and was at last murdered by the *Turuṣka robbers. His blood flowed in the form of milk, flowers came out from within his heart and filled the sky.

In the same country was born *ācārya* **Muditābhabhadra,[1] whose words [lit. throat] were ornamented with thousands of *sūtra*-s, who acquired the twelve *dhūta-guṇa*-s[2] and attained the stage of *anutpattikadharma-kṣānti*. He also rebuilt the *caitya*-s previously damaged, surrounded each with ten new *caitya*-s and led all the householders and *brāhmaṇa*-s to the reverence [for the Buddha].

At that time there were many ordained monks in the *madhya-deśa* who did not properly observe the vows. **[Fol 49B]** He helped those who agreed to atone for their violation of the vows, while those who refused to do so were expelled by him. So [the expelled ones] became hostile to this great monk and started slandering him. Thus he felt worried and prayed to *ārya* Samantabhadra[3] and received his direct vision. He prayed, 'Please take me to a place where I can work for the welfare of all living beings.'

1. V & S Muditābhabhadra, which occurs in S-ed. P-ed Muditābabhadra.
2. *sbyaṅs-ba'i-yon-tan-bcu-gñis.* D 939—talents or qualifications kept up, used or practised ; ascetic practices. cf. I-Tsing (Takakusu) 56-57, 57n.
3. *kun-tu-bzaṅ-po.*

[Samantabhadra] said, 'Hold the corner of my robes.' The moment he held it, he reached Li-yul. Working there for the welfare of the living beings for many years, he passed away.

In these ways, the Doctrine was extensively spread for forty years.

*Kakutsiddha,[4] a minister of the king,[5] built a temple at Śrī *Nalendra. During its consecration he arranged for a great ceremonial feast for the people. At that time, two beggars with *tīrthika* views came to beg. The young naughty *śramaṇera*-s threw slops at them, kept them pressed inside door panels and set ferocious dogs on them. These two became very angry. One of them went on arranging for their livelihood and the other engaged himself to the *sūrya-sādhanā*.[6]

For nine years, he sat in a deep pit dug into the earth and pursued the *sādhanā*. Yet he failed to attain *siddhi*. So he wanted to come out of the pit.

His companion asked, 'Have you attained *siddhi* in the spell ?' He said, 'Not yet.'

The other said, 'In spite of famine conditions all around, I have obtained livelihood for you with great difficulty. So, if you come out without acquiring *mantra-siddhi*, I shall immediately chop off your head.'

Saying this he brandished a sharp knife. This made him afraid and he continued in the *sādhanā* for three more years. Thus he attained *siddhi* through the endeavour of twelve years.

He performed a sacrifice (*yajña*)[7] and scattered the charmed ashes all around. **[Fol 50A]** This immediately resulted in a miraculously produced fire. It consumed all the eightyfour temples, the centres of the Buddha's Doctrine.

The fire started burning the scriptural works that were kept in the *Dharmagañja of *Śrī *Nalendra, particularly in the big temples called *Ratnasāgara, *Ratnodadhi and *Ratnaraṇ-

4. P-ed Kakudasiddha (?). V Kakudasiṃha. Vidyabhusana HIL 516 gives the name as Kakudasiddha from Sum-pa.
5. S 'a *kṣatriya* minister of the king.' But V does not mention *kṣatriya*.
6. *ñi-ma-sgrub-pa.*
7. *sbyin-sreg,*

ḍaka,[8] in which were preserved all the works of Mahāyāna *piṭaka*-s. At that time, from certain works kept in the upper floor of the nine-storeyed *Ratnodadhi temple, came out water to extinguish the fire. The works to which this water reached remained unburnt.

It is said that these [unburnt] works, on being examined later, were found to be works of the five esoteric *tantra*-s.[9] According to others, these were works only on the Guhyasamāja. In any case, these works belonged to the class of *anuttara-tantra*[10] and there is no difference of opinion on the Guhyasamāja being included in these.

Many temples in other places were also burnt and the two *tīrthika*-s, apprehending punishment from the king, escaped to *Ha-sa-ma [Assam] in the north. But they were themselves burnt by the self-kindled fire produced in their body by their sins.

The vastly learned monks living in all directions then assembled and wrote out the scriptural works from what remained of these in their memory as well as in the form of written works.

The temples damaged by the fire were reconstructed by king Buddhapakṣa, the *brāhmaṇa* *Śaṅku,[11] the *brāhmaṇa* Bṛhaspati[12] and many householders who were full of reverence.

Of the fifteen parts of the Mahāyāna *piṭaka*-s that came to the human world, **[Fol 50B]** two parts were destroyed during each of the two hostilities to the Doctrine that had taken place before this incident [i.e. four parts in all were previously destroyed], one part of these was lost without any act of hostility,

8. S-ed Ratnaraṇḍaka. S Ratnakaraṇḍaka. Vidyabhusana HIL 516, depending on Sum-pa, gives the name as Ratnarañjaka.
9. ? *tantra*-s of the insiders. The text has *naṅ-rgyud-sde-lṅa*. V tr 'five sections of the *tantra*-s of the "insiders" (? internal *tantra*-s).'
10. V *anuttara-yoga*.
11. Tg contains the *Siddha-garuḍa-śāstra* (rG lxxi.405) attributed to *brāhmaṇa* Śaṅku.
12. *phur-bu*. Tg contains four works attributed to *brāhmaṇa* Bṛhaspati—rG lxxi.396 ; 397 ; lxxvii-lxxx ; mDo cxxiii.25.

nine parts were destroyed by this hostile fire. Only one part of these now survives.

This [surviving part] includes the fortynine chapters of *Ārya-ratnakūṭa-samāja*,[13] which originally contained one thousand chapters. Similarly survived thirty eight of the one thousand chapters of the *Avataṃsaka*,[14] only nine of the thousand chapters of the *Mahā-samāja*[15] and only one small chapter viz. the *Tathāgata-hṛdaya*[16] of the *Laṅkāvatāra*.[17] These are only a few examples.

The twentieth chapter containing the account of the third hostility to the Doctrine and of its restoration.

13. *'phags-pa-dkon-mchog-brtsegs-pa-'dus-pa.*
14. *phal-bo-che.* V Buddha-avataṃsaka.
15. *'dus-pa-chen-po.*
16. *de-bshin-gśegs-pa'i-sñiṅ-po.* V 'heart of Tathāgata'.
17. *laṅkāra-gśegs-pa.*

CHAPTER 21

ACCOUNT OF THE PERIOD OF THE FINAL ACTIVITIES OF KING BUDDHAPAKṢA AND OF THE PERIOD OF KING KARMACANDRA

Now, near the coast of the ocean, on the top of a hill in the country of *Oḍiviśa in the east, king Buddhapakṣa, in the latter part of his life, built a temple called Ratnagiri.[1] He prepared three copies of each of the scriptural works of the Mahāyāna and Hīnayāna and kept these in this temple. He established there eight great centres for the Doctrine and maintained[2] five hundred monks.

A monastery called Devagiri[3] was built on the model of Ratnagiri on a hill on the sea coast near *Bhaṅgala.[4] His [Buddhapakṣa's] minister built the temple there and the *brāhmaṇa* *Śaṅku arranged for [the copies] of the scriptural works. The *brāhmaṇa* Bṛhaspati provided it with all the articles of worship and the queen maintained the monks and the centre of the Doctrine.

Now about the *brāhmaṇa* *Śaṅku.

In *Puṇḍravardhana, which was situated between *Magadha and *Bhaṅgala, there lived a wealthy *brāhmaṇa* called *Saro along with his seven brothers. **[Fol 51A]** He tried to subdue the Nāgas by acquiring the spells of Mahādeva. But they could not be subdued. The entire *brāhmaṇa* family, inclusive of the seven brothers, died of the bite of poisonous snake.

The *brāhmaṇa* had a son named *Śaṅku. Out of love for him, his relatives kept a large number of mongoose on the ground floor of the building. Outside the building, they kept

1. *rin-chen-ri-bo.*
2. P-ed *'tshogs-pa* (collected). S-ed *'tsho-ba* (maintained). The latter reading followed.
3. *lha'i-ri-bo.*
4. V Baṅgala.

the animals called *śela-s[5] that killed the snakes. On the top of the building, they kept a number of peacocks and thus ensured protection against the snakes. They tried also to master the spell as well as to obtain other articles to subdue the snakes.

After this, the Nāgas once appeared and made the loud sound : **phuṭ*.[6] This scared the peacocks which flew away. The **śela* animals were driven into their holes by a terrible storm. A very lean snake scaled up the building by one of its corners, entered the room and bit *Śaṅku to death.

His wife[7] took out the dead body, put it into a small raft and floated on the *Gaṅgā for three days, saying : 'Who can bring him back to life !'

During these three days, the shepherds [on the bank] jeered at her. Then appeared a woman, who uttered spell on some water, washed his body with it and brought him back to life.

Returning to his place, he enquired about what had been going on. He was told that the *brāhmaṇa* *Śaṅku had died seven days back and that all his household articles were being offered to the *brāhmaṇa*-s. He entered the house and, failing to believe what was happening, wondered if it was real or only a magic show. Thus he was afraid.

At last he realised what had happened and felt happy. Then **[Fol 51B]** he searched for spells to subdue the Nāgas. He once witnessed [the following] : A woman came to work in the field and uttered a spell. Suddenly there appeared a snake from where nobody knew and touched with its mouth the foot of her little son, who immediately died as it were. But when her

5. S *śaila*. S n : 'In the text, there is *sela*, which is evidently derived from the Sanskrit *śaila*. Yet I cannot ascertain which animal of the hill is here referred to.' But could it be a corrupt form of the Bengali word *śeyāla* (শেয়াল) or *śyāla* (শ্যাল) ?
6. *phutkāra* ? See Monier-Williams 718.
7. cf the folklore of Behulā (*Manasūmaṅgala*), where also the name Śaṅku or Śaṃkara-gāruḍi occurs as an expert in the spell against snake.

work in the field was over, a snake appeared and the moment it bit the foot of the child, the child came back to life.[8]

Realising that she was a *ḍākinī*, [Śaṅku] fell at her feet and said, 'Teach me, please, the spell.'

'You are not fit to receive the spell and it is difficult to obtain the articles for the rite.' Though she refused thus, as he remained clinging to the earth and went on urging her, she consented.

The article required for the rite was eight palmful of thickened milk (*kṣīra*) of perfectly black bitch. After obtaining this, he asked for the spell. She chanted the charm a number of times and asked *Śaṅku to drink it.

Six handfuls of this filled his stomach and he could not drink any more. Then she said, 'If you fail to take this [remaining milk], the snake will kill you first and after that will kill many others.'

With this threat, she forced him to drink more. He swallowed another handful, but, with his best efforts, could not swallow the remaining handful. So the *ḍākinī* said, 'Did I not tell you at the very beginning that you were unfit for it? You can now subdue and bring under your control the seven classes of Nāgas. But you will not be able to do this with the Vāsuki-s.[9] So you are going to die in the future of the bite of Vāsuki-nāga.'

Wielding great magic power, the *brāhmaṇa* then became very strong. He commanded the Nāgas to do whatever he liked, both good and evil. **[Fol 52A]** Everyday he arranged for the recital of the scriptures by the *brāhmaṇa*-s, offered them gifts and performed other pious acts. Every night, he used to go to the pleasure garden and satisfy the five-fold lust in the company of the female Nāgas. He built with **aṣṭa-dhātu* a temple near *Puṇḍravardhana of *bhaṭṭārikā āryā* Tārā-devi and elaborately worshipped there the Three Jewels.

There was among the female Nāgas an attendant of the

8. cf the washer-woman Netā in the folklore of Behulā (*Manasāmaṅgala*).
9. *nor-rgyas*.

Nāga king Vāsuki. The *brāhmaṇa* did not know of her identity and remained careless. She bit him on his forehead and escaped.

Then [the *brāhmaṇa*] told his servant, 'Go and fetch "white cuttle-fish bone."[10] While returning with it, you must not look back, must not listen to others and must not speak.' With these instructions, he sent the servant with the enchanted material for swift transport.

As he [the servant] was coming back, somebody called him from behind. He did not respond at first.

'I am a physician. I can cure the diseases and also cases of poisoning',—being thus told, he looked back and saw a *brāhmaṇa* carrying a medicine chest, who said, 'Show me the medicine you are carrying.'

He [the servant] showed him the white cuttle-fish bone. Immediately the *brāhmaṇa* threw it on the ground and vanished.

After meeting *Śaṅku, he [the servant] reported this. [Śaṅku] said, 'Bring it along with the earth on which it has fallen.'

But he failed to collect it, because when he reached the place it was already flooded by the sea caused by the magic power of the Nāgas. Thus died *Śaṅku.

Such a[11] *brāhmaṇa* *Śaṅku built a stone pillar called the Garuḍa-stambha[12] in Khagendra in the south. Cases of poisoning were cured immediately after offering worship to it. **[Fol 52B]** Drinking or bathing in the water with which this pillar was washed, effected cure of leprosy.[13]

Now about *brāhmaṇa* Bṛhaspati.

As he was an adept in the *Kurukullā[14] spell, the king asked him 'Show me *Takṣaka, the king of the Nāgas.' He threw a stone into the sea after chanting the *Kurukullā spell. Then the sea started boiling and at its centre emerged the dome

10. *rgya-mtsho'i-lbu-ba.* lit. sea-foam. See Monier-Williams 718 : 'supposed to be indurated foam of the sea.'
11. *de-lta-bu* (similar). V tr 'such a *brāhmaṇa* Śaṅku.'
12. *nam-mkha'-ldiṅ-gi-mchod-sdoṅ.*
13. *klu-nad,* lit. *nāga-roga.* D 45.
14. V Kurukulli.

of the palace of the Nāgas. The king along with his attendants saw this. But the Nāga could not be shown. [By the mere sight of the dome] many men and cattle died of the Nāga poisoning, and everything disappeared again into the sea.

This *brāhmaṇa* Bṛhaspati built many temples of the Buddha in the city of *Kaṭaka in *Oḍiviśa and he arranged for the entertainment of a large number of *saṃgha*-s.

King Buddhapakṣa. After him *Karmacandra, the nephew of *Dharmacandra. During their time came *ācārya* Rāmapriya,[15] *ācārya* Aśvaghoṣa the junior,[16] Rāhulamitra[17] the disciple of Rāhulabhadra and his [Rāhulamitra's] disciple Nāgamitra.[18] They spread the Mahāyāna. However, from the commentary on *Stotra-śata-pañcāśatka*[19] now current in Tibet, it is clear that the commentator *ācārya* Rāmapriya[20] came after Dignāga and others. Therefore, [the *ācārya*] of this period had similarity only in name with [the *ācārya*] of that period.

The twentyfirst chapter containing the account of the period of the final activities of king Buddhapakṣa and of the period of king Karmacandra.

15. *dga'-byed-sñan-pa.* V Nandapriya.
16. *rta-dbyaṅs-chuṅ-ba.*
17. *sgra-gcan-'dsin-bśes-gñen.* Tg contains a work attributed to *siddha mahācārya* Rāhulaśrīmitra—rG xxxiii.22.
18. *klu'i-bśes-gñen.* Tg contains *Kāyatrayāvatāramukha-nāma* (mDo xxix 1) attributed to Nāgamitra. Another work (mDo xxxiii.83 & lxi.8) is a commentary by *ācārya* Jñānacandra on a work by Nāgamitra, which, however, is not traced in Tg.
19. *Śatapañcāśatka-nāma-stotra-ṭikā* (bsTod 39) by *bhikṣu* Rāmapriya.
20. V Nandapriya.

CHAPTER 22

ACCOUNT OF THE PERIOD OF 'BROTHERS ĀRYA ASAṄGA'

[ASANGA & VASUBANDHU]

After this, about the time of king *Karmacandra.

Gambhīrapakṣa,[1] son of king Buddhapakṣa, established his capital in Pañcāla.[2] He ruled for a period of about forty years. **[Fol 53A]** In Kashmir, *Turuṣka Mahāsammata, son of king *Turuṣka,[3] lived for one hundred and fifty years. He had a vision of Krodha-amṛta-kuṇḍalī.[4] He also ruled for about one hundred years. He brought under his rule Kashmir, Thogar, *Gajni, etc. He used to worship the Jewels. Specially in *Gajni, he built a great *caitya* containing the tooth [relic] of the Buddha.[5] He employed *bhikṣu*-s and *bhikṣuṇī*-s, *upāsaka*-s and *upāsikā*-s—a thousand each—for maintaining the religious services of the *caitya*. He built an immensely large number of various types of images.

Bhikṣu *Jīvākara and *upāsaka* Dharmavardhana,[6] along with

1. *zab-mo'i-phyogs*. cf Bu-ston ii.119.
2. *lṅa-len*.
3. cf Bu-ston ii.119. V & S 'Mahāsammata, son of king Turuṣka.'
4. *khro-bo-bdud-rtsi-'khyil-ba*. S Krodhāmṛtāvarta. V n 'Kg vol. *sha* fol 220 has *Amṛta-kuṇḍali-āgama*.'
5. *saṅs-rgyas-kyi-tshems*. cf prophecy quoted by Bu-ston ii.110 : 'In the northern border-land, in the village Hiṅgala, the teeth of the Buddha will be greatly worshipped and many monks endowed with the highest morality will appear.'
6. *chos-'phel*. cf prophecy quoted by Bu-ston ii.110 : 'In the north, in the place called Vistaravatī many *brāhmaṇa*-s and householders devoted to the Doctrine are to appear ... And in that place, a devotee of the laity called Dharmavardhana (*chos-'phel*) possessed of miraculous powers will likewise appear. In the north, moreover, a Mahāyānist monk called Jīvaka (*'tsho-byed*) will arise. He will restore the monuments of the Buddha, that will have undergone destruction and richly decorate them with gold and the like.'

five thousand *bhikṣu*-s and five thousand *upāsaka*-s meditated on the significance of the Prajñā-pāramitā and enjoyed the bliss of Tathāgata-sādhana. [Among them] hundreds of *bhikṣu*-s and *upāsaka*-s attained *ṛddhi*. The practice of the ten virtues also became extensive.

After twelve years of king Gambhīrapakṣa's reign, king *Karmacandra passed away. His son *Vṛkṣacandra ascended the throne. Since he was not very powerful, *Jaleruha, king of *Oḍiśa [Oḍiviśa] conquered most of the eastern region.

The period of the rule of these kings synchronised with the period of the second half of the life of *mahā-bhikṣu* *Arhat,[7] with the period of *ārya* Asaṅga's[8] activities for the welfare of the living beings and with the period of the earlier career of *ācārya* Vasubandhu,[9] Buddhadāsa[10] and Saṃghadāsa.[11]

7. cf prophecy quoted by Bu-ston ii.112—

'At the time which is to come
A monk called Arhat is to appear.
He is to know the meaning of the secret charms,
Become versed in the *tantra*-s and greatly learned.
By uttering the charm of the Yakṣa-s
He will secure a precious vessel.'

8. *thogs-med.*
9. *dbyig-gñen.* Bu-ston ii.145 gives the following meaning of the name: he 'was possessed of the wealth (*vasu*) of the Highest Wisdom and, having propagated the Doctrine out of mercy, had become the friend (*bandhu*) of the living beings.'
10. *saṅs-rgyas-'baṅs.* Watters i.353f: Yuan-chuang mentions one Buddhadāsa as the author of the *Mahāvibhāṣā*; but Watters comments—'as this work was a book of the Sarvāstivādin school of the Hīnayāna, its author cannot have been the Buddhadāsa, who was a contemporary of Vasubandhu and a disciple of his brother Asaṅga. Very little seems to be known about any *śāstra* writer with the name Buddhadāsa and there is no author with this name in the catalogues of Buddhist books known in China and Japan.' Neither any work is attributed to him in Tg.
11. *dge-'dun-'baṅs.* Tg does not contain any work by Saṃghadāsa, but contains two works by his disciples *vajrayānācārya* Guhyadatta (rG lxxxi.27) and *śrī ārya* Viśākhadeva or Sagadeva (mDo lxxxix.1: *Vinaya-kārikā* or *Puṣpamālā*).

[Fol 53B] *Ācārya* Nāgamitra lived for a long time. His disciple was Saṃgharakṣita.[12]

Not that the esoteric Yoga and Anuttara Tantras were not prevalent among the fortunate people before their time. Shortly after the spread of the Mahāyāna doctrine, there were a hundred thousand *vidyādhara*-s. Most of them, like those of *Urgyana who attained the stage of the *vidyādhara*, attained it by the help of the *anuttara-mārga*. However [during this earlier period] *mantra-yāna* was preached to groups of hundred or thousand fortunate people by Guhyapati[13] and others who suddenly appeared before them. They attained the rainbow-bodies and left nothing in the form of preaching.

People of the earlier generations had the capacity of tenaciously keeping the secret. Therefore, nobody could know them as practising the Guhya-mantra so long as they did not attain the *vidyādhara-siddhi*. All those who attained *mahā-ṛddhi*[14] used to vanish into the sky. Only after this, others wondered : 'Ah, so they were practising the *mantra*-s !' That is why, there was nothing in the form of teachings imparted in the preceptor-disciple tradition.

Beginning with the period of the spread of Mahāyāna, the study of the rituals and spells of the *kriyā* and *caryā* Tantra was quite considerable. However, because these were being studied under extreme secrecy, outside the *guhya-mantracārī*-s themselves, nobody knew who was practising what. Therefore, they could perform the rites and attain *siddhi* without any difficulty.

[Fol 54A] Therefore, it is clearly well-known that the tradition of teachings coming down in preceptor-disciple succession began from the time of *Saraha and Nāgārjuna 'the father and son'[15] [i.e. Nāgārjuna and Āryadeva] up to *siddha* *Śabari-pā.[16] Before this, no *ācārya* is known to have entered

12. *dge-'dun-sruṅ-ba.*
13. *gsaṅ-ba'i-bdag-po.*
14. V *mahā-māyā.*
15. V tr 'Saraha, the teacher of Nāgārjuna with his pupils.'
16. See Supplementary Note 15.

the tradition of transmitting *anuttara guhya-mantra*.[17] Though in the *Caryā-saṃgraha-pradīpa*[18] are mentioned *Padmavajra[19] and *Kambala-pā[20] as the original authorities [of the *mantra-yāna*], the former did not obviously work for the welfare of the living beings in *ārya-deśa* and I have not come across any account of the latter.[21] Hence it is said that there exists practically nothing in the form of the commentary on the *anuttara-tantra*[22] before what was written on the *anuttara-śāstra*-s by the Great Brāhmaṇa,[23] Nāgārjuna 'the father and son' and others. Besides, even these treatises are not as well-known as the collection of the Mādhyamika *śāstra*-s.[24] These were entrusted only to Nāgabodhi, who attained the *vidyādhara-sthāna* and these were made extensively available later on during the period of

17. V *anuttara-yoga.*
18. *spyod-bsdus-sgron-me*—Tg mDo xxxi.23 & mDo xxxiii.2 by Dīpaṃkara-śrī-jñāna.
19. On the view of Padmavajra being one of the earliest teachers of *tantra*, see BA i.356ff—a view sought to be vigorously refuted by Tār in Fol 136Af. Tg contains a number of Tāntrika works attributed to *ācārya mahāpaṇḍita śrī* Padmavajra (rG xxiv.5), *siddhācārya* Padmavajra (rG xi), *mahācārya* Padmavajra (rG xlviii.115) ; in certain other works in Tg, the author Padmavajra is only a synonym of Saroruhavajra (rG xxi.1 ; xxi.2 ; etc). In the list of the 84 *siddhācārya*-s, we come across one Paṅkaja-pā—a disciple of Nāgārjuna ; another *siddhācārya* called Saraha-pā belonged to the period of king Dharmapāla—see R. Sankrityayana *Purātattva-nivandhāvali* 147ff.
20. The usual Tibetan form of the name is Lva-va-pā (see BA i.362). Lva-va means blanket, *kambala*. He was thus called because he 'used to wear only one piece of blanket as his raiment'—D 1203. In Fol 96B, Tār relates how Lva-va-pā and Saroruhavajra brought the Hevajra Tantra. In the account of the 84 *siddhācārya*-s, Kambala-pā is mentioned as belonging to Oḍiviśa, as being a disciple of Vajraghaṇṭa and as being preceptor of the *siddha* king Indrabhūti—see R. Sankrityayana *op. cit.* 162.
21. Assuming the identity of Lva-va-pā and Kambala-pā, this statement of Tār is strange, because in Fol 96Bf he gives an account of Lva-va-pā. Does Tār think the two to have been different ?
22. V *anuttara yoga.*
23. i.e. Saraha or Rāhula.
24. V *madhyama-vidyāgaṇa.*

king *Deva-pāla and his son. Hence the absence of any remote succession accounts for the purity of the *Ārya* and *Buddhakapāla*[25] [*Tantras*], as in Tibet there is no corruption of the works in circulation [bccause these are copies from] the sealed texts.[26]

From then on, for two hundred years the Tantras of *kriyā* and *caryā* were extensively propagated and openly practised. However, before the attainment of *siddhi*, nobody openly practised the *yoga* and *anuttara-yoga* Tantras. Still, these were more extensively spread and various commentaries **[Fol 54B]** were composed on these, compared to the earlier period. Some great and famous *siddha*-s appeared at this time. At this time also lived *ācārya* Paramāśva,[27] *mahā-ācārya* *Lui-pā,[28] *siddha* *Ca-rba-bi-pā[29] and others. Their account is clearly given in other works.

25. In Tg several works on the Buddhakapāla-tantra are attributed to Saraha *alias* Rāhulabhadra : rG xxiv.4 ; 7 ; 9.
26. V tr 'Here is the reason why the (account of) succession of Anuttara-yoga known under the name of Sacred Sections—of Buddhakapāla and others—appeared separately and not at a very early period. It does not matter, for example, as to what (happened) in Tibet, to the pure (*yaṅ-dag-snaṅ-gi-chos*) teaching and the uncorrupted books found out in treasures.'
27. In Tg *Śrī-paramasvarūpa-mahāsukhapada-vajra-nāma-samādhi* (rG lxxiv.27) is attributed to *ācārya* Paramāśva.
28. S n 'His name is written as Lu-yi-pā, but more often as Lūi-pā and he has the surname *ña-lto-ba*, fish-belly, perhaps equal to *matsyodara*. This may recall to one the names Matsyendra, Matsyanātha, Mīnanātha—on which names I refer to the St. Petersburg Dictionary. The last name is mentioned there besides Carpaṭi, many works by whom are preserved in Tg.' V quotes this note and adds : 'In the account of the 84 *siddha*-s included in *Thob-yig*, Lūi-pā is the first. He attained the *mahā-mudrā siddhi* by studying the Cakrasaṃvara system. On the bank of the Gaṅgā in Baṅgala, he lived by eating the intestine of fishes left by the fishermen. This is how the name Lūi-pā has been derived.' For works attributed to Lui-pā, see Supplementary Note 21.
29. V & S Carpaṭipāda, In Tg the *Lokeśvara-stotra* (rG lxviii.29),

Now, about *ācārya* *Arhat. During the period of king *Karmacandra he practised asceticism and became a master of the three *piṭaka*-s. Engaging himself in the *mahā-koṣa-kalaśa-sādhana*,[30] he gradually attained success. In *Vārāṇasī, he discovered from under the earth a jar one *yojana* deep and full of gems. With this he used to provide tens of thousands of monks.

He once forgot to keep the jar protected and, during the night, the *yakṣa*-s stole [the gems] away. In the morning, opening it for the provision of the monks, he found it empty. This monk, with his spells and great miraculous power, summoned the great gods like Brahmā and others and started coercing them to force the *yakṣa*-s to appear and thus got the treasure jar refilled. People knew of the coming of the gods from signs like the shaking of the earth, shower of flowers and the fragrance continuing for seven days.

He entertained the monks for about forty years. He alone could see the treasure jar, while others saw him only digging the ground.[31]

Now, the account of 'Brothers *ārya* Asaṅga.'

In the past, during the time of king *Gauḍavardhana, there lived a monk with a mastery of the three *piṭaka*-s. He followed *ārya* Avalokiteśvara as his tutelary deity. He once had a difference with another monk, deeply wounded his sentiments and started arguing with him. **[Fol 55A]** He arrogantly abused the other and said, 'You are a person with a female

Ārya-avalokiteśvarasya-carpaṭi-racita-stotra (rG lxviii.31) and *Sarva-siddhikara-nāma* (rG lxxxvi.8) are atributed to him, where his name occurs as Ca-ra-pa-tri, Car-pa-ti'i-pāda and Carya-ḍi-pā. V n 'he is not mentioned among the 84 *siddha*-s'. But this is not correct. In the list of the 84 *siddha*-s, Carpaṭi occurs as the 59th one : he is also called Pacari and is described as the resident of Campā, a Kāhār by caste and the preceptor of Mīna-pā—see R. Sankrityayana *op. cit.* 152 & 200.

30. *gter-gyi-bum-pa-chen-po*. D 525 *gter*, the wishing pot, which yields whatever precious object is sought. cf the prophecy quoted in Note 7 of this chapter.

31. V n 'S remarks that this legend has been taken from the *Mūla-tantra*.'

brain.' *Ārya* Avalokiteśvara then told him, 'As the result of this act of yours, you are going to have repeated births as a woman. However, I shall continue to be your *kalyāṇa-mitra*, so long as you do not attain enlightenment.'

When reborn as a woman during the time of king Buddhapakṣa, she was *brāhmaṇī* **Prakāśaśīlā.[32] Possessing as she did the memory of the past life, she used to understand from her very early age the collection of the *sūtra*-s and the *abhidharma*-s by mere reading or listening. She always worshipped *ārya* Avalokiteśvara, was instinctively placed in the path of the ten-fold virtue and had the inner capacity of a *bodhisattva*.

However, it will be a mistake to believe that she was a nun.[33] On growing up she united with a *kṣatriya* and gave birth to a son with auspicious marks. She performed the rites for making the son keenly intelligent.[34]

As the son grew up, he received from his mother sound instructions in eighteen branches of learning like writing, arithmetic, the eight-fold examination,[35] grammar, debate, medicine, fine arts, etc, and he became highly proficient in all these.

When he enquired about the profession appropriate for his birth, [his mother told him], 'You are not born, my son, to follow the profession of your birth. You are born for spreading the Doctrine. Therefore, take up ordination and devote yourself to learning and meditation.'

32. Bu-ston ii.137 gives the name as *gsal-ba'i-tshul-khrims*, reconstructed by Obermiller as Prasannaśīlā. Tār does not mention Asaṅga's place of birth. According to Yuan-chuang, the two brothers were natives of Gandhāra—Watters i.357.

33. V & S tr 'However, her wish to become a nun was not fulfilled.' This is perhaps because of taking the word *'dod* in the sense of wish, though the word also means 'to believe'. Besides, *'khrul-pa* in the text clearly means mistake.

34. *blo-rno-ba'i-cho-ga*. cf Bu-ston ii.137 'The mother drew on their tongues the letter *ā* and performed all the other rites in order to secure for them an acute intellectual faculty.'

35. *brtag-pa-brgyad*. J 225.

Accordingly, he went in for ordination and spent a year serving the *upādhyāya*, *ācārya* and the *saṃgha*.

[Fol 55B] He spent five years in studying [the scriptures] after receiving the *upasampadā*. Every year, he memorised a hundred thousand **śloka*-s and grasped their significance. Thus, it was not difficult for him to have a general understanding of the three *piṭaka*-s and most of the *Mahāyāna sūtra*-s. However, finding it difficult to understand the *Prajñāpāramitā-sūtra* without being confused by its verbal repetitions,[36] he concentrated on having a vision of the tutelary deity. For this purpose, he received *abhiṣeka* from *ācārya* *Arhat,[37] about whom we have discussed before. The flower offered at this time reached *jina* Ajita [Maitreyanātha]. However, the nature of the Tantra and the *maṇḍala* of the *abhiṣeka* are not clear, though the latter appears to have been the *māyājāla-maṇḍala*, because this *ācārya* practised the *maitreya-sādhana*[38] with the *māyājāla-tantra*.[39]. This is said by [my] *paṇḍita* teacher.[40]

Then in a cave of the *Gur-pa-parvata,[41] which is mentioned in the scriptures as the *Kukkuṭapāda-parvata,[42] he spent three years propitiating *ārya* Maitreya. But he felt disheartened by the absence of any sign [of success] and came out [of the cave].[43] He noticed that in the course of a long time the stones were worn out by birds' wings, though these wings touched the stones only when in the morning the birds, which had their nests on the rocks, went out in search of food

36. *brjod-bya-ma-zlos.*
37. According to Yuan-chuang, Asaṅga began as a Mahīśāsaka and afterwards became a Mahāyānī—Watters i.357.
38. see Tg *Ārya-maitreya-sādhana* (rG lxxi.345) by *ārya* Asaṅga.
39. Tg contains a considerable number of works on Māyājāla-tantra—see Lalou 39.
40. *bla-ma paṇḍita.* Tār apparently refers to some of his Indian teacher, without mentioning his name.
41. S n 'According to Yuan-chuang, the mountain was called Gurupāda, becaus^ Kāśyapa lived there.' See note 9, ch. 2.
42. cf Bu-ston ii.137.
43. *Ib.* ii.137f.

and once when in the evening they returned to their nests. 'So, I have lost assiduity'—thinking thus, he continued the propitiation for three more years.

Similarly, he came out again. Noticing the stones eroded by drops of water, he propitiated for another three years and again came out. This time, he saw an old man rubbing a piece of iron with soft cotton and saying, 'I am going to prepare fine needles out of this. I have already prepared so many needles by rubbing iron with cotton.' And he showed a box full of needles.

[**Fol 56A**] So he propitiated for three more years. In this way, twelve years passed by ; but he saw no sign of success. Disappointed, he came out and went away.

In a city he came across a bitch, infested with worms on the lower half of her body, furiously scratching her wound.[44] The sight made him full of compassion. He thought : 'If these worms are not removed, the bitch is going to die. But if removed, the worms are going to die. So I am going to place the worms on a piece of flesh cut off from my own body.'

He brought a shaving razor from the city called *Acintya,[45] placed his begging bowl and staff on a sitting mat, slashed the thigh of his own body and, with his eyes shut, stretched his hands to catch the worms. Failing to reach the worms, he opened his eyes and saw there neither the worms nor the bitch. He saw instead *bhaṭṭāraka* Maitreya with the halo of *lakṣaṇa*-s and *vyañjana*-s. To him he said with tears flowing from his eyes :

> 'Oh my father, my unique refuge,
> I have exerted myself in a hundred different ways,
> But nevertheless no result was to be seen.
> Wherefore have the rain-clouds and the might of
> the ocean,

44. The text has *mi* (man). S tr 'biting men' and V tr 'licking the people'. But this word may be a corruption of *rma* (wound), which seems to give a better sense. cf Bu-ston ii.138 'As he was about to go away, he saw a dog ; the lower part of its body was eaten by worms, but the upper part (was still free) and it was barking and biting.'

45. Bu-ston ii.138 also mentions the city as Acintya.

Come only now, when, tormented by violent pain
I am no longer thirsting ?'[46]

[Maitreya] answered,

'Though the king of the gods sends down rain,
A bad seed is unable to grow
Though the Buddhas may appear [in this world]
He who is unworthy cannot partake of the bliss.'[47]

'I have been throughout present near you',[continued Maitreya] 'but remaining under obscurations as you did by your own *karma*, you have failed to see me. The obscuration of your sin is now removed by the accumulated power of your previous repetition of the charm along with your present great compassion as expressed in the rigorous form of cutting off the flesh of your own body. That is why, you can now see me. Now, take me up on your shoulder and carry me to the city to show me to the people there.'

When he was being thus shown, others saw nothing. **[Fol 56B]** Only a woman wine-seller saw him carry a pup. As a result, she later became enormously rich. A poor porter saw only the toes. As a result, he reached the stage of *samādhi* and attained *sādhāraṇa-siddhi*. The *ācārya* immediately attained the *srotaḥ-anugata-nāma-samādhi*.[48]

[Maitreya asked,] 'What do you desire ?'

'I have the desire to spread the Mahāyāna.'

'Then catch hold of the corner of my robe'.

The moment he [the *ācārya*] caught it, he reached the Tuṣita. In the older marginal note on the *Bhūmi*-s[49] it is said

46. This translation of the passage is taken from Obermiller, Bu-ston ii.138.

47. *Abhisamaya-alaṃkāra* viii.10. Tr Obermiller—Bu-ston ii.138.

48. *chos-rgyun-gyi-tiṅ-ṅe-'dsin*. See D 431. V *'samādhi* of stream of faith.'

49. *sa-sde*, an abbreviated form of referring to Asaṅga's work on the Yogacaryā-bhūmi in five divisions, viz. *Bahubhūmika-vastu*, *Nirṇaya-saṃgraha*, *Vastu-saṃgraha*, *Paryāya-saṃgraha* and *Vivaraṇa-saṃgraha*—see Bu-ston i.54ff. For works of Asaṅga, see Supplementary Note 21.

that he spent six months in Tuṣita. According to some others, he spent fifteen human years in Tuṣita. Different views like these are current. However, according to the popular belief prevalent in India and Tibet, he spent fifty human years [in Tuṣita]. This calculation of fifty years appears to be based on counting every half year as one year, for the Indians say that he actually spent twentyfive years there.[50]

In Tuṣita, he listened to the Mahāyāna doctrine in its entirety from Ajitanātha [Maitreyanātha] and learnt the real significance of the whole collection of *sūtra*-s. Then he listened to the 'Five Works of Maitreya'.[51] While doing this he attained *samādhi* on each aspect of these Five-fold Teachings separately at the very moment he listened to it.

After this, when he returned to the earth[52] and worked for the welfare of all living beings, he was already in possession of *paracitta-abhijñāna*[53] and he could, along with his attendants, cover in a day—or even in one *prahara*—the distance which ordinarily took one month or half a month to cover.[54]

Though over ninety years old,[55] he remained at the same youthful stage when he first received the vision of Maitreya. He had thirty-two auspicious marks on his body **[Fol 57A]** and he clearly acquired the quality of reaching the stage of 'the *ārya* who attained the *bhūmi*.'[56] 'He had no selfish idea even in dreams and he practised meditation in all forms. He

50. V tr 'The Indians affirm that considering a year as half year, he spent 25 years'.
51. *byams-pa'i-chos-lṅa*. Bu-ston i.53f : these five works are the *Sūtrālaṃkāra*, *Madhyānta-vibhaṅga*, *Dharma-dharmatā-vibhaṅga*, *Uttaratantra* and *Abhisamaya-alaṃkāra*. See also Supplementary Note 22.
52. For Yuan-chuang's account, see Watters i.355ff.
53. *mṅon-śes* D 365.
54. ref. to *dūratva-gāmi-siddhi*.
55. V n 'According to the *Mūla-tantra*, he was born 900 years after the death of Buddha and lived for 150 years. But if a year is taken to be a half, it will come to be less.'
56. *sa-thob-pa'i-'phags-pa*. Though the text has *yon-tan-mṅon-gyur* (lit. the sixth *bhūmi* called *abhimukti*—D 1257), the passage is translated differently, because Tār shortly says that Asaṅga reached the third *bhūmi*.

was very tender, humble and, at the same time, extremely firm. He had a sharp intellect for defeating those who followed the wrong doctrines or the wrong practices. He is to be considered as one who reached the third *bhūmi*,[57] because he followed the principles in their purity like 'Having no satiation in listening [to the Doctrine] and preaching the Doctrine without consideration of material benefit'.[58]

This *ācārya* built a *vihāra* in the forest called *Veluvana[59] in *Magadha. Residing in it, he used to preach the profound significance of the Mahāyāna doctrine to eight disciples who observed the moral vows and were vastly learned. All of them attained *kṣānti*,[60] acquired the miraculous power of attracting the public veneration and were vastly learned in the *sūtra*-s. Hence, the place became famous as the Dharmāṅkura-vihāra.[61]

In this place, he put in written form the Five Works of Maitreya. Here he also wrote most of his treatises[62] like the *Abhidharma-samuccaya*,[63] the *Mahāyāna-saṃgraha*,[64] the *Five*

57. *sa-gsum-pa*, i.e. the third *bhūmi* called *'od-byed-pa* or *prabhākarī*—D 1257. cf Bu-ston ii.140f. V n 'Buddhism divides Bodhisattvas (just like *arhat*-s) into learners and non-learners, the former pass through ten stages called *bhūmi*-s. The third stage referred to is *prabhākarī*.'
58. *thos-pas-mi-ṅoms-ñid-daṅ-ni* / *zaṅ-ziṅ-med-par-chos-sbyin-daṅ* //
59. V & S Piluvana, which occurs in S-ed. P-ed Veluvana. cf Watters i.354.
60. *bzod-pa*—D 1112.
61. *chos-kyi-myu-gu'i-dgon-pa*. S n Dharmāṅkura-araṇya. But *dgon-pa* means both monastery and wilderness—D 275. V n 'Dharmāṅkura-araṇya. According to Yuan-chuang, it was located in the east of Ayodhyā, in Prayāga, in an *āmra*-forest.'
62. See Supplementary Note 21.
63. V n *'chos-mṅon-pa-kun-las-btus-pa* (Tg mDo lvi.2). It is also called higher one, as distinguished from the Abhidharma of Vasubandhu or the lower one (*mṅon-pa-goṅ-'og*). Here *ārya* Asaṅga wanted to employ the Hīnayāna teaching for the Mahāyāna. That is why the eight treatises are presented with their titles changed. The contents constitute an abridgement of the first two sections of the Yogacaryābhūmi.'
64. *theg-pa-chen-po-bsdus-pa*. Tg mDo lvi.1. V n 'Abridgement of Mahāyāna based on the Sandhinirmocana. It explains the ten qualities of the words of Buddha.' cf Bu-ston i.56.

Bhūmi-s,[65] the exposition of the *Abhisamaya-alaṃkāra*.[66]

After this, under the patronage of king Gambhīrapakṣa[67] the monks of the four directions assembled in the monastery of *U-sma-pu-ri[68] [Uṣmapurī] in the city of *Sa-ga-ri[69] in the near-west.[70] In this assembly, *ārya* Aṣaṅga delivered many sermons according to the understanding of each. He expounded the three *piṭaka*-s of the *śrāvaka*-s and the collection of about five hundred *Mahāyāna-sūtra*-s. **[Fol 57B]** For leading everybody to the ultimate truth, he introduced to them the Mahāyāna views. The number of those whose knowledge was enriched by the understanding of the *sūtra*-s reached beyond a thousand.

Though the Mahāyāna had extensively spread in the early period, with the passage of time the capacity to understand it became feeble. It [also] suffered by the three hostilities[71] to it. At the time of the appearance of this *ācārya*, though there were many monks following the Mahāyāna, there was none to understand the Mahāyāna fully. Many of them could recite a few *sūtra*-s, though without understanding their real significance. As the result of the preaching of the Doctrine there by the *ācārya* himself and his eight foremost disciples,[72] the

65. V 'Yogacaryā-bhūmi in five sections.' V n 'In all 45,000 *śloka*-s in 150 chapters. The five sections are : 1) *Yogacaryā-bhūmi* itself, 2) Systematic exposition explaining the essence of existence, 3) a survey of the fundamentals of the Sūtra-s and Vinaya, 4) Terminologies and 5) Explanations.'
66. No commentary on *Abhisamaya-alaṃkāra* by Asaṅga is traced in Tg. Haribhadra, in his introductory verse of the *Abhisamayālaṃkārāloka* (mDo vi.1) refers to Asaṅga's commentary on *Abhisamayālaṃkāra* called the *Tattvaviniścaya*, but Tsoṅ-kha-pa does not accept this as Asaṅga's work—see Obermiller Bu-ston ii.140 n.
67. *zab-mo-phyogs.*
68. V Uṣmapura.
69. V '? Sāgar, Saugar ?'
70. V 'not far from the west (of India).'
71. V 'three-fold enmities (to the Doctrine).' cf Bu-ston ii.136-7.
72. Yuan-chuang mentions Buddhasiṃha as 'a great scholar, who was a friend and disciple of Asaṅga'—Watters i.358.

Mahāyāna, which once declined, was again spread in all directions and acquired fame.[73]

King Gambhīrapakṣa used then to recite the *Prajñā-pāramitā-sūtra* everyday.[74] He thought : This *ācārya* is famed as an *ārya* and as capable of reading others' thoughts. If this is true, I shall also praise his qualities. If, however, this is false, people are being deceived and hence I should make him humble by challenging him publicly.—Thinking thus, he consulted about five hundred of his trusted men, inclusive of his ministers and the *brāhmaṇa*-s.[75]

In the courtyard of his palace, he invited this *ācārya* and his disciples to a public gathering and offered them food and robes lavishly. He kept concealed within a room a black buffalo with a whitewash on it. He filled with filth a golden jar, put honey on its top, covered it up with a piece of cloth and took it up on his hands.

He asked, 'What is there in that room ? What am I holding in my hands ?'

[Fol 58A] [The *ācārya*] said what these actually were.

'Even persons of petty wisdom are found to have the little power of knowing what is kept concealed. But can he read the thoughts of others ?'—Thinking thus, the king [mentally] devised six questions in all. Three of these were related to the words and three to the significance of the *Prajñā-pāramitā-sūtra*. He mentally questioned the *ācārya* about these. The *ācārya* offered correct replies and in accordance with these composed small works like the *Tri-svabhāva-nirdeśa*.[76]

The three questions related to the words were :

1. 'Since, to the question, "What is referred to by the word *bodhisattva* ?" it is replied, "The *bodhisattva* is not something

73. V tr 'The news spread everywhere that the Mahāyāna, which once declined, was again spread in all directions.'

74. S tr 'used to listen to the recital of (*Prajñā-pāramitā-sūtra*).' The text has *kha-ton-du-byed-do*, 'to read with devotion'—D 694.

75. V tr 'He consulted (his) ministers, *brāhmaṇa*-s and five hundred trusted men.'

76. In Tg, *Tri-svabhāva-nirdeśa* (mDo lviii.4) is attributed to Vasubandhu.

visible"—is this not useless as a definition ?'[77]

2. 'To what is applied the analogy of a huge bird—as huge as covering five hundred *yojana*-s ?'

3. 'What is meant by "the boundary with an unseen destination"—when, without seeing the sign of the hill or the forest, it is said that the sea is very near ?'

To these three [the answers were] :

The first is indicative of the *adhyātma-śūnyatā* [which, being internal, is invisible like the *bodhisattva*].

The second is indicative of the great power of pious acts.

The third is indicative of the *mahā-dharma-uttama* [i.e. the unseen limit which, when crossed, the *pṛthak-jana* becomes an *ārya*].

The three questions related to significance were :

1. Does the *ālaya-vijñāna*[78] objectively exist ?[79]
2. When it is said that everything is nature-less (*a-svabhāva*), does it not imply that even nature-lessness is without its own nature (*svabhāva*) ?
3. When it is said that emptiness (*śūnyatā*) itself does not make everything empty, what is meant by the emptiness which does not make everything empty and by the cause of not making empty ?

[His answers were]:

First, it [i.e. the *ālaya-vijñāna*] has relative [pragmatic] reality (*saṃvṛti satya*) but no absolute reality (*pāramārthika satya*).[80]

Secondly, the nature-less is conceived in three ways. Therefore, what is nature-less is again divided into two, namely as having its own nature and as having no such nature.

Thirdly, [Fol 58B] by the emptiness of that which cannot make everything empty is simply meant the concept of emptiness itself. By the cause of [making everything empty] is meant the negation of any rule according to which that which was

77. V tr 'is it not one of the undefined theories ?'
78. S-ed *kun-śes-rnam-par-śes-pa*. S suggests that it should have been *kun-gshi-rnam-par-śes-pa*, which actually occurs in P-ed.
79. V tr 'Does the universal cause (*ālaya*) exist as an object or not ?'
80. V tr 'Relatively, this is the thing ; but absolutely this does not constitute the concept (idea) in the cognitions of the mind.'

previously existing ceases later to have its existence. Thus is refuted the view that something previously existing ceases later to have existence.[81]

In these ways, he answered [the three] questions relating to significance.

This amazed the king and the assembled people. Thus making the king feel humble, the *ācārya* led him to establish twentyfive centres of the Mahāyāna doctrine. One hundred *bhikṣu*-s and a large number of *upāsaka*-s were accommodated in each of these. During his stay in this place, he also converted his younger brother Vasubandhu. But the account of this will be given later.

There lived then a *brāhmaṇa* called *Basunāga in *Kṛṣṇarāja in the south. He heard that an *ārya* called Asaṅga, having received instructions from Jina Ajita, was spreading the Mahāyāna over again. Along with his five hundred attendants, the *brāhmaṇa* himself came to *madhya-deśa*. He worshipped the *caitya*-s of the eight holy places[82] and requested the *ācārya* to come to the south and lead the *brāhmaṇa*-s and householders to the virtuous path.

Along with the *brāhmaṇa* and his attendants, the *ācārya* was about to proceed [to the south] accompanied by twentyfive of his own followers, when a messenger came with the news that the *brāhmaṇa*'s mother was ill. The *brāhmaṇa* became anxious to proceed quickly and the *ācārya* said, 'If the *brāhmaṇa* wants it, we can reach very quickly.' [The *brāhmaṇa*] said, 'Please do it.' Then they entered the path and the *ācārya*, along with the *brāhmaṇa* and the attendants, [miraculously] reached *Kṛṣṇarāja by the same afternoon. *Kṛṣṇarāja was situated in *Triliṅga and was at a distance of three months. It was reached only in two *prahara*-s.

[**Fol 59A**] Also, when invited by the merchant *Dhanarakṣita of *Urgyana in the west, the *ācārya*, accompanied by the

81. V tr 'The emptiness, which makes emptiness, has the sense of taking the form of emptiness—and in reducing it (to causes) are refuted (the concepts) that (there is something which) previously existed.'

82. V 'eight great places'.

merchant and the attendants, covered the entire distance between *Magadha and *Urgyana in the course of a single day. He stayed and preached the Doctrine for a long time in both *Kṛṣṇarāja and *Urgyana and propagated the Mahāyāna among a large number of persons. In both these places, he built a hundred *caitya*-s and twentyfive temples and established in each of these a centre of the Mahāyāna doctrine. Similarly, were built [by him] a hundred *caitya*-s and twentyfive centres of the Doctrine also in *Magadha.

He was once preaching the Doctrine to a feudatory prince in a non-Buddhist[83] city of India near *Ayodhyā. There was then a settlement of the Garlogs[84] nearby. At the time the *ācārya* was preaching, the Garlog army attacked them. He advised those who were listening to the Doctrine to remain patient. So they sat in meditation. All the arrows thrown by them [i.e. the Garlogs] turned into dust. Even when the chief of the Garlogs hit the *ācārya* with a sword, no harm was done to him and the sword broke into a hundred pieces. In spite of all the insults, they remained unmoved. So they [the Garlogs] bowed down in great reverence and went away.

Because this *ācārya* could know the minds of others, he explained while preaching all the points about which the pupils were ignorant or doubtful. Therefore, there was none who listened to the Doctrine from the *ācārya* and yet did not become learned.

[Fol 59B] There was practically no Mahāyānī of that time who did not listen to at least one *sūtra* from him.

This *ācārya* established one hundred centres of the Doctrine from his personal resources and maintained at least two hundred students in each of these. Speaking in general, the number of

83. *mtha'-'khob*, meaning either 'border country' or 'barbarous (i.e. non-Buddhist) country'. S & V accept the former sense.

84. D 217 & J 68. Roerich SW 516n 'Gar-log or Qarluq, name of a Central Asian Turkish tribe. This is the usual Tibetan translation of the Sanskrit Turuṣka. About the Gar-log in Tibetan literature, see H. Hoffmann, *Die-Qarluq in cer. Tibetaischen-Literatur*, ORIENS iii,2,1950, pp 190-208.'

disciples who listened to the Doctrine from him could not be counted. All of them followed his views with great reverence. Thousands of them attained the *bhūmi* and the *yoga-mārga*. He taught in every way without showing any bias for any *sūtra* or *siddhānta*. That is why, even the *śrāvaka*-s of the time respected him highly. Many *śrāvaka*-s learnt their own *sūtra*-s and *abhidharma* [from him.][85]

Having acquired proficiency in the *Gandhāri *mantra*,[86] he used to visit the Tuṣita and, in a moment's time, could reach distant places. Because of his proficiency in the Kalpa-vidyā-mantra,[87] he could read others' thoughts.

'He was of strong moral conduct and vastly learned. It is a great wonder that he was still an adept in the Vidyā-mantra !' —the others [Hīnayānis] used to say—'His only fault was that of entering the Mahāyāna.'

Before him, even during the time of the most extensive spread of the Mahāyāna, the number of the Mahāyāna monks did not reach ten thousand. Even in the days of Nāgārjuna, most of the monks were *śrāvaka*-s. During the time of this *ācārya*, the number of Mahāyāna monks reached tens of thousands. Because of these reasons, it is said that he became the foremost [preacher] of the Mahāyāna Law. Still, the number of the disciples who were constantly attached to this *ācārya* did not exceed twentyfive.[88] All of them were of strong moral conduct [Fol 60A], vastly learned in the Piṭaka-s and their tutelary deities removed all their doubts. All of them attained *kṣānti*.[89]

85. V n 'From this it can be inferred that even *ārya* Asaṅga did not separate out Mahāyāna from the general teaching of Buddhism. Even Vasubandhu was more a Śrāvaka than a Mahāyānist.'
86. D 213—a Buddhist *mantra* or charm, which has the power of enabling one to move in space. V n 'S has traced in Tg (Vol *du* of Tantras) two works bearing the title *Vajra-gandhāri-sādhana*.'
87. *rtog-byed-kyi-rig-sṅags*.
88. V n 'probably this was then the real circle of Mahāyānists.'
89. V 'freedom from rebirth.'

He spent twelve years in Śrī *Nalendra[90] during the latter part of his life, when, in the winter,[91] the *tīrthika*-s came everyday to challenge him in debate. He refuted their views and thus humbled them. Then he preached the Doctrine to them. He conferred ordination on about a thousand [converted] *tīrthika*-s. He reformed according to the Doctrine all the monks of all the monasteries who had fallen from the right view, right conduct (*śīla*), right practices (*caryā*) and right observances (*vidhi*) and made them extremely pure.

At last he passed away in the city of Rājagṛha,[92] where his disciples built a *caitya* with his relics.

Now, about the younger brother Vasubandhu.

According to some in Tibet, he was a twin brother of *ārya* Asaṅga. I find others calling him 'a brother by faith'. But the Indian scholars do not say so.

His father was a *brāhmaṇa* versed in the three Vedas. He was born the year after *ācārya ārya* Asaṅga's ordination. The two *ācārya*-s were real brothers, because they were born of the same mother.[93] From the performance of the rite for making him keenly intelligent to the stage of being vastly learned and of being established in meditation, his account is the same as that of his elder brother Asaṅga.

He was ordained in Śrī *Nalendra and thoroughly studied the three *Śrāvaka-piṭaka*-s. Moreover, he went to Kashmir and studied mainly under *ācārya* *Saṃghabhadra[94] for a deep

90. V n 'According to Yuan-chuang, *ārya* Asaṅga appears only in Gandhāra and Ayodhyā. But later on, the legends about Nālandā connected all the Buddhist celebrities, including *ārya* Asaṅga, to this centre.'
91. *dgun-gyi-dus.*
92. *rgyal-po'i-khab.* Bu-ston does not mention the place where Asaṅga died. From other sources it appears to have been Puruṣapura—Watters i.358.
93. cf Bu-ston ii.137 : 'From her union with a *kṣatriya,* (a son named) Asaṅga, and (later on) from another union with a *brāhmaṇa* (a second son named) Vasubandhu were born.'
94. Bu-ston ii.142-3 : 'Vasubandhu received his education in the school of Saṃghabhadra in Kashmir ... After that he resolved to go back to India ... and came to Nālandā'. In Tg the *Abhidharmakoṣa-śāstra-*

understanding of the Abhidharma and for learning the views of the eighteen schools and all the branches of knowledge. After learning the *Vibhāṣā*, the scriptural works of the eighteen schools—particularly where the *Vinaya*-s and *Sūtra*-s of the different schools differed—[**Fol 60B**] and all the works of the six systems of *tīrthika* philosophy and the technique of debate in its entirety, he became a great scholar.

He explained there [in Kashmir] for a number of years the *Śrāvaka-piṭaka*-s and distinguished between what was right and wrong in these.

When he was returning to the *madhya-deśa*, the robbers and *yakṣa*-s on the way could not stop him.[95] Thus he reached *Magadha. Here also he lived for a number of years preaching in a highly learned manner the scriptural works to many *śrāvaka* monks.

At that time he read the *Five Bhūmi*-s, [the *Yogacaryābhūmi* in five sections], the work of *ārya* Asaṅga, but failed to understand the Mahāyāna. He did not believe that [*ārya* Asaṅga] received these from his tutelary deity. And it is said that he remarked :

> 'Alas ! Though Asaṅga meditated for twelve years in the forest, instead of attaining success in his meditation he has composed a work [useless in sense but heavy enough] to be an elephant's load.'[96]

In any case, Vasubandhu said something sarcastic about Asaṅga. Hearing this, his elder brother *ārya* [Asaṅga] thought : 'It is time to convert[97] him.' He made a monk to

kārikā-bhāṣya (mDo lxiv.2) is attributed to *ācārya* Saṃghabhadra *alias* Saṃgamaśrībhadra of Kashmir, a student of *ācārya* Vinītabhadra. Another work, the *Ārya-mūla-sarvāstivādi-śramaṇera-kārikā* (mDo xc.1) is attributed to *ācārya* Nāgārjuna and equally to Saṃghabhadra of Kashmir ! In Fol 63B, the name is given as *'dus-bzaṅ*.

95. cf Bu-stom ii. 143 for the story in more details.

96. Bu-ston ii. 143—Obermiller translates the verse more freely.

97. This story of Vasubandhu's conversion is practically the same as given by Bu-ston ii. 143. But see Watters i, 358 : 'In other works, Asaṅga uses the pretext of fatal sickness to bring his brother from Ayodhyā

memorise the *Akṣayamati-nirdeśa-sūtra*[98] and another the *Daśa-bhūmi-sūtra.*[99] He sent them to the younger brother with the instruction : 'While reciting, recite first the *Akṣayamati* and then the *Daśabhūmi-sūtra*'.

The two [went to Vasubandhu] and in the evening [one of them] recited the *Akṣayamati*. [Vasubandhu] thought : 'The Mahāyāna appears to be logically well-founded. However, will it not lead to indolence ?'[100] When, in the morning, [the other monk] recited the *Daśabhūmi-sūtra*, [Vasubandhu] realised that [the Mahāyāna] was sound both in theory and practice. [He thought] 'So I have committed a great sin by showing disrespect to the Mahāyāna', and he wanted to get a razor to cut off the tongue[101] that had uttered these disparaging remarks.

[Fol 61A] The two monks said, 'Why should you cut off the tongue for this ? Your brother knows how to absolve you of the sin. You better go to the *ārya* and pray to him.'

So he went to *ārya* Asaṅga.

The account of his conversion as current in Tibet[102] today is as follows :

After [Vasubandhu] studied all the Mahāyāna scriptures, when the two brothers discussed the Doctrine, the younger one showed signs of keener intelligence. The elder one, though without such a quick grasp, could evolve better answers. On being asked about it, [he said] 'I am answering after learning these from my tutelary deity.' The younger brother also prayed to have a vision of him. [Asaṅga said] 'You are not

to visit him at Puruṣapura and there reasons with him and converts him to Mahāyāna.'

98. *blo-gros-mi-zad-pas-bstan-pa'i-mdo.* Kg mDo Vol *ma* xvi. 4.

99. *sa-bcu-pa'i-mdo.* Kg Vol *ji* xxxvii.l. Commentary on it by Vasu-bandhu—Tg mDo xxxiv.14, *Ārya-daśabhūmi-vyākhyāna.*

100. V 'confusion'. But the text has *gyel-lam,* 'slumbering, indolence'– D 1155.

101. cf Watters i.358.

102. cf Bu-ston ii.143-4.

yet fortunate enough for it.' After this, he preached to him the way of atoning for the sin. Thus it is said.

In the Indian account, however, I have not come across all these. Nor do these appear to be coherent. [Vasubandhu] listened to the *Mahāyāna-sūtra*-s from *ārya* Asaṅga. It was not proper for decent people in the good old days to argue with one's own preceptor, nor to show one's greater skill after learning a treatise by oneself, i.e. without any systematic instruction from the preceptor. Therefore, assuming that in decent society one could not argue with one's own preceptor, how can it be said that he [Vasubandhu] had argued with *ārya* Asaṅga? [Further] it was known to all that Asaṅga received the scriptures from Maitreya. Therefore, it does not appear to be coherent to say that Vasubandhu was ignorant of it, asked about it and that *ārya* Asaṅga concealed it from his younger brother with the remark, 'I am answering after consulting a tutelary deity.'

Accordingly, the Indian version is as follows:

To continue the previous account—When [Vasubandhu] asked about the means of atoning for the sin, the *ārya* consulted Jina Ajita **[Fol 61B]** and said [to Vasubandhu], 'Preach the Mahāyāna doctrine extensively. Prepare commentaries on many *sūtra*-s. Recite for a hundred thousand times the *Uṣṇīṣa-vijayā-dhāraṇī*.'[103]

Thus instructed, he learnt all the *Mahāyāna-sūtra*-s after listening to these only once from his elder brother. He received instructions on *mantra* from a *mantra-ācārya* and chanted five hundred *dhāraṇī-sūtra*-s.[104] He attained *siddhi* by chanting the *Guhyapati-dhāraṇī*[105] and realised the ultimate truth. He excelled in meditation and memorised all the teachings of the Buddha that survived then in the human realm.

It is said that after the *nirvāṇa* of the Teacher, there was

103. *gtsug-tor-rnam-par-rgyal-ma'i-rig-sṅags.* V n 'In Kg Vol *pha* there are ten works relating to this *dhāraṇī*'. Tg also contains two works related to *Uṣṇīṣa-vijayā*—rG lxxxvi 51 & 52.

104. *gzuṅs-mdo.*

105. *gsaṅ-ba'i-bdag-po'i-rig-sṅags.*

none as profoundly learned in the scriptures as *ācārya* Vasubandhu. To mention these separately: [he learned] each of the five hundred *sūtra*-s of the Śrāvaka Tripiṭaka containing three lakhs of *śloka*-s, the collection of fortynine *Ārya-ratnakūṭa-samāja*, the *Avataṃsaka* and the *Samāja-ratna*.[106] Besides these he learned the five hundred big or small *Mahāyāna-sūtra*-s like the *Prajñā-pāramitā-śata-sāhasrikā* and also five hundred *dhāraṇī*-s. He learned all these word for word and also their significance. Normally it took a whole year to read all these.[107] However, placing himself in a tub of **til*-oil, he could read all these uninterruptedly in fifteen days and nights. He used to read everyday in an hour[108] or two the whole of the *Prajñā-pāramitā-aṣṭa-sāhasrikā*.[109]

When this *ācārya* entered the Mahāyāna, about five hundred scholars of the Śrāvaka Piṭakas also entered the Mahāyāna.

[Fol 62A] After the passing away of *ārya* Asaṅga, he became the *upādhyāya* of Śrī *Nalendra. Everyday, he used to recite various religious works, confer the *pravrajyā* and *upasampadā* on others according to their different requirements, himself acted as the *upādhyāya* and the *ācārya* in the *pravrajyā* and *bhikṣu-dīkṣā* [of others], [helped others to] rectify their faults by voluntary confession, himself continuously observed the ten-fold duties of the monk and helped thousands of others to observe their ten-fold duties fully. On special occasions he explained for twenty continuous *prahara*-s[110] the incomparable religious significance of the *Mahāyāna-sūtra*-s. In the evening he dispelled differences of opinion by discussing the scriptures and by summing up the essence of the Doctrine. He listened

106. *'dus-pa-rin-po-che*—D 687. S n 'It is certainly the *Mahā-samaya-sūtra*'.
107. V tr 'He read these once every year'.
108. chu-tshod—D 419 *daṇḍa*, lit. the measure of time by a water-clock, the Indian hour.
109. V tr 'The 8,000-*prajñā-pāramitā* repeated by him every month could ordinarily be read (by him) in one or two quarters of an hour'.
110. *thun*—D 580 *yāma*, *prahara*, period of three hours, etc.

to the Doctrine from the tutelary deity even in the short sleep[111] of one *prahara* at midnight and sat in deep meditation at dawn. In the intervals of all these activities, he composed treatises and defeated the *tīrthika*-s in debate. He wrote[112] fifty commentaries expounding the short and long Mahāyāna and Hīnayāna *sūtra*-s, like the *Prajñā-pāramitā-pañcaviṃśati-sāhasrikā*, the *Akṣayamati-nirdeśa*, *Daśabhūmaka*, *Buddha-anusmṛti*,[113] *Pañcamudrā-sūtra*,[114] *Pratītya-samutpāda-sūtra*, *Sūtrālaṃkāra*, *Vibhaṅgadvaya*[115] etc. He also wrote eight original **prakaraṇa*-s.[116]

He recited the *Uṣṇīṣa-vijayā-[-dhāraṇī]* for a hundred thousand times and acquired mastery of this charm. After that he had a direct vision of Guhyapati and attained the stage of perfect meditation.

Three commentaries composed by this *ācarya* like the *Pratītya-samutpāda-sūtra-ṭīkā* [Fol 62B] are counted in this country [Tibet] as included in the eight **prakaraṇa*-s.[117] However, a commentary is not a *prakaraṇa* and it is difficult to characterise the *Vyākhyā-yukti* as a *prakaraṇa*. By *prakaraṇa* is meant a short treatise discussing a specific and important topic. When a large work like the *Sūtrālaṃkāra* cannot be called [a *prakaraṇa*], how can its commentary [which is bigger in volume] be called one ? Nor can it be said that, among the

111. P-ed *mnal-ba'i-ṅaṅ-la*, 'while asleep'. S-ed *mnal-ba'i-dad-las*, which, as S says in note, appears to him as inexplicable.

112 *dbyig-gñen*. For works attributed to Vasubandhu, see Supplementary Note 23.

113. *dkon-mchog-rjes-dran*, lit *Ratna-anusmṛti*. Does Tār refer to Vasubandhu's *Buddha-anusmṛti-ṭīkā* (mDo xxxiv. 7 of Tg) ?

114. *phyag-rgya-lṅa'i-mdo*.

115. V 'the two Vibhaṅga-s'. V n—see Supplementary Note 24.

116. *raṅ-rkaṅ*, lit. 'on his own feet', hence translated as 'original'. Bu-ston i. 56f mentions the eight treatises of Vasubandhu, of which the last three are commentaries. These eight are : *Triṃśaka-kārikā-prakaraṇa*, *Viṃśaka-kārikā-prakaraṇa*, *Pañcaskandha-prakaraṇa*, *Vyākhyā-yukti*, *Karma-siddhi-prakaraṇa*, and the commentaries on *Sūtrālaṃkāra*, *Pratītyasamutpāda-sūtra* and *Madhyānta-vibhaṅga*.

117. Does this refer to the view of Bu-ston ? see note 116.

eight *prakaraṇa*-s, some contain the word *prakaraṇa* in the title while others do not.

This *ācārya* did not visit any non-Buddhist[118] part of the country nor any distant land. He stayed mostly in *Magadha. He filled the whole of *Magadha with centres of the Doctrine by way of reconstructing those that were previously damaged and building one hundred and eight new centres of the Mahāyāna doctrine.

He once visited *Gauḍa in the east. When he preached many *sūtra*-s to a congregation of numerous citizens there, the gods showered golden flowers. Even the beggars collected golden flowers one *mahā-droṇa* in quantity. Here also he established one hundred and eight centres of the Doctrine.

A *brāhmaṇa* called *Makṣika of *Oḍiviśa invited him. He entertained there twelve thousand Mahāyāna monks for three months. In the house of this *brāhmaṇa* were revealed five mines of gems. He [Vasubandhu] made the *brāhmaṇa*-s, householders and kings of the place full of reverence and established one hundred and eight centres of the Doctrine. Moreover, the number of the centres of the Doctrine built under the instruction of this *ācārya* in the south and other places **[Fol 63A]** equals[119] to those already mentioned. It is said that altogether these made a total of six hundred and fifty four.

The number of monks during this time was greater than that of *ācārya ārya* Asaṅga. It is said that the total number of monks all over the country came to about sixty thousand. The number of monks who stayed with this *ācārya* and accompanied him in his travels was about a thousand. All of them observed the moral discipline and were vastly learned.

Wherever the *ācārya* stayed, he used to receive articles of worship [even] from non-human beings [i.e. Nāgas, Yakṣas, etc] and the miraculous phenomena like the finding of mines of gems used to take place. By virtue of his supernatural

118. *mtha'-'khob.* V borderland.

119. V n 'i.e. 324 centres established in Magadha, Gauḍa and Oḍiviśa.'

fore-knowledge, he rightly answered all questions [concerning] both good and evil.

When the fire broke out in the city of Rājagṛha, he extinguished it by his solemn prayer. With his solemn prayer, again, he brought under control the epidemic that broke out in the city of Jananta.[120] By virtue of his *vidyā-mantra*, he controlled his own longevity. There is no end to the miraculous anecdotes like these.

He defeated about five hundred *tīrthika* rivals in all [i.e. before and after entering the Mahāyāna]. In all he brought five thousand *brāhmaṇa*-s and *tīrthika*-s to the Law of the Buddha.

At last, he went to Nepal[121] accompanied by a thousand *ācārya*-s. There also he established the centres of the Doctrine and vastly increased the number of the monks.

Finding a *bhaṭṭāraka* with religious robes living in his house and ploughing his field, he felt shocked and said, 'The Law of the Teacher is degenerated.' So he preached the Doctrine among the monks, [**Fol 63B**] thrice chanted the *Uṣṇīṣa-vijayā-dhāraṇī* in the reverse order[122] and died there.[123] This was described as the setting of the sun of the Doctrine for the time being. His disciples built a *caitya* there.

According to the account current in Tibet, when he composed the *Abhidharmakoṣa* and sent it to Saṃghabhadra[124] in Kashmir, he [Saṃghabhadra] was pleased. But when the commentary was shown to him, he felt displeased and came to *Magadha to argue with him [Vasubandhu]. By that time, *ācārya* Vasubandhu had left for Nepal.

Such an account of pleasing and displeasing Saṃghabhadra with the *Abhidharmakoṣa* and its commentary may be correct. But in India it is not clearly said that Saṃghabhadra actually

120. *mthar-skyes*. V Janantapura. V n 'S assumes that the name Yanantapura is derived from Jayantapura'.
121. *bal-yul*.
122. cf Bu-ston ii. 145.
123. But see Watters i. 359—according to the Chinese biography of Vasubandhu, he died at Ayodhyā at the age of 80.
124. *'dus-bzaṅ*.

came to *Magadha. Even assuming that he came there, it is clear that this must have taken place earlier. It is also clear that by the time of Vasubandhu's departure for Nepal, many years had elapsed after the passing away of Saṃghabhadra.[125]

After receiving the ordination, *ācārya* Asaṅga worked for the Doctrine for seventyfive years. In the prediction, 'He will live for one hundred and fifty years'—each year is to be counted as a half-year. This agrees with his religious career.

It is certain that he [? Vasubandhu] worked for the welfare of the living beings for over thirty years. In the opinion of some of the Indians this was over forty years. *Ācārya* Vasubandhu lived up to the age of nearly one hundred years. He worked for the welfare of the living beings for many years during the life-time of *ārya* Asaṅga and for about twentyfive years after the *ārya.*

It is said that this great *ācārya* [Vasubandhu] was a contemporary of the Tibetan king Lha-tho-tho-ri-gñan-btsan.[126] This seems to be correct. **[Fol 64A]**

The twentysecond chapter containing the account of the period of Brothers ārya Asaṅga.

125. But see Watters i. 324f for a totally different account of Saṃghabhadra and his relation with Vasubandhu.

126. On Lha-tho-tho-ri, see A. Chattopadhyaya AT 179. V n 'Lha-tho-tho--ri was the fifth of the earlier successive kings before Sroṅ-btsan-sgam-po. Therefore, he would have lived not earlier than A.D. 450. For understanding how the later Buddhists exaggerate the stories about their celebrities and distort their biographies, it will be worthwhile to compare the biography of Vasubandhu given by me in the first part of my work on Buddhism with the account of Yuan-chuang. According to my own account, he lived during the reign of Vikramāditya and his successor Prāditya and established three centres in all. He died at the age of 80. According to his (Yuan-chuang's) account of the biography, not Siṃhabhadra (probably Saṃghabhadra) but Vasubandhu was older. But the two accounts agree in this that he (Vasubandhu) died in Ayodhyā, and hence Nālandā—and even Nepal, Gauḍa. Oḍiviśa—linked themselves to him later on,'

CHAPTER 23

ACCOUNT OF THE PERIOD OF ĀCĀRYA DIGNĀGA AND OTHERS

During the latter half of the life of the great *ācārya* Vasubandhu and after the death of king Gambhīrapakṣa, there lived an extremely powerful king called *Śrīharṣa. He was born in *Maru in the west. He conquered all the kingdoms of the western region. Later, he became respectful to the Law of the Buddha and accepted *ācārya* Guṇaprabha[1] as his preceptor.

Roughly in the same period, there ruled in the east king *Vigamacandra, a descendant of king *Vṛkṣacandra, and his [i.e. Vigamacandra's] son *Kāmacandra. Both these kings had great power and wealth. They delighted in making gifts and ruled the kingdom righteously. But they did not take refuge to the Three Jewels. They showed respect to both the

1. *yon-tan-'od.* The commentary on the *Bodhisattva-bhūmi* attributed to Guṇaprabha in Tg (mDo liv.5 &6) mentions him as the preceptor of king Harṣavardhana Śīlāditya of Thāneśvara. The *Vinaya-sūtra-vṛtti-abhidhānasya-vyākhyā* (Tg mDo lxxxiii-lxxxiv) mentions the author as Guṇaprabha of Mathurā, who belonged to the Mūla-sarvāstivāda sect and who composed this commentary in the *mahā-vihāra* Śrī-Siñā (Śrī Siñjā ?) during the earlier period of the reign of Harṣavardhana Śīlāditya of Thāneśvara. The Tg also contains the *Vinaya-sūtra* (mDo lxxxii.1) and its auto-commentary (mDo lxxxviii) by Guṇaprabha. Bu-ston ii.160 refers to him as a *brāhmaṇa* and as a great authority in the Vinaya of the Mūla-sarvāstivādī-s, but rejects as an anachronism the view that he was a disciple of Upagupta or Sudarśana. The *Ekottara-karmaśataka* attributed to him in Tg (mDo lxxxii.2) is, according to some, the work of Vinītadeva (Bu-ston ii.160). Tg (mDo lxxxv-lxxxvi) contains a commentary on his *Vinaya-sūtra* by his disciple Dharmamitra of Tukhāristān, the great expert in Vinaya and belonging to the Mūla-sarvāstivāda sect. For Guṇaprabha, see also I-Tsing (Takakusu) lviii-lix & 181 ; Watters i. 323f.

insiders and outsiders and had special reverence for the Nirgranthas.

It is said that at this time, Kashmir was ruled by Mahāsammata.[2]

This was the period when, in the east, *ācārya* Sthiramati[3] and Dignāga[4] worked for the welfare of the living beings and, in the west, Buddhadāsa,[5] the disciple of *ārya* Asaṅga, worked for the welfare of the living beings in the latter part of his life. This was also the zenith of Guṇaprabha's career, and the time when in Kashmir *bhaṭṭāraka* Saṃghadāsa[6] also extensively worked for the welfare of the living beings, when *ācārya* Dharmadāsa[7] used to visit the different countries to preach the Doctrine and *ācārya* Buddhapālita[8] went to the south. This was the period of the earlier career of Bhavya[9] and Vimuktasena.[10]

[Fol 64B] In *Oḍiviśa, during this period also lived *Nāgeśa, son of king *Jaleruha and his *brāhmaṇa* minister *Nāgakeśa. While ruling for seven years, he became extremely powerful. As a result, even *Vigamacandra submitted to him.

2. *maṅ-pos-bkur-ba.*
3. *blo-gros-brtan-pa,* cf Bu-ston ii.147ff, one of the four outstanding disciples of Vasubandhu who surpassed even Vasubandhu. Yuan-chuang mentions him as one of his own contemporaries—see Watters ii.109,168f ; cf I-Tsing (Takakusu) lviii, 181 & 225.
4. *phyogs-kyi-glaṅ-po.* lit *dik-hastin.* see Watters ii.211f on the name.
5. *saṅs-rgyas-'baṅs,* said to have been an uncle of Vimuktasena (Tg mDo i.2). cf Watters i.353 & 359.
6. *dge-'dun-'baṅs.* Tg mentions *vajrayānācārya* Guhyadatta (rG lxxxi.27) and Viśākhadeva (mDo lxxxix.1) as his disciples, but contains no work by him.
7. *chos-'baṅs.*
8. *saṅs-rgyas-bskyaṅs.*
9. *legs-ldan.* Bhavya or Bhāvaviveka, *alias* Nirāloka (*snaṅ-bral*)—colophon of mDo xviii.9 of Tg.
10. *rnam-grol-sde.*

Ācārya *Lo-yi-pā[11] converted[12] them and led them to renounce the kingdom. After they attained *siddhi*, the king was called *Dārika-pā[13] and his minister *Diṅgi-pā.[14]

Ācārya Triratnadāsa[15] was a contemporary of *ācārya* Bhavya. Also in *Oḍiviśa a *brāhmaṇa* called *Bhadrapālita worked extensively for the Law.

Among them, king *Śriharṣa was incomparable as a king. He wanted to wreck the religion of the *mleccha*-s. In a small place near *Maul-tan,[16] he built a **masita*, that is a big monastery of the *mleccha*-s. The whole of it was made only of wood. He invited all the *mleccha* teachers there, lavishly offered gifts to them for several months and made them collect all their scriptural works there. Then he set fire to it, and, as a result, twelve thousand experts of the doctrine of the *mleccha*-s perished.

At that time, there lived in *Khorosan only a weaver well-versed in the *mleccha* religion. From him the *mleccha*-s of the later period gradually grew in number. As a result of this wreck [of the *mleccha* religion] by this king, there remained for about one hundred years only a few to follow the religion of the Persians and Turuṣkas.[17]

11. In Tg the name occurs variously as Lo-yi-pā, Lū-yi-pā, Lū-hi-pāda, Lū-i-pā, Lū-yi-shabs ; also as *ña'i-rgyu-ma-za-ba* (lit. 'one who eats the intestines of fishes' ; hence Matsyāntrāda ; *ña-lto-pa* or Matsyodara ; Mīna. See Supplementary Note 20.
12. P-ed *btul* (to subdue or convert), S-ed *bskul* (to inspire).
13. Mentioned also as Dāri-pāda and Dārika-pāda. See Supplementary Note 25.
14. As reviser of Lūi-pā's *Buddhodaya-nāma* (Tg rG lxxiii.62) is mentioned Deki-pā, Dheṅkī, Dhanakuṭṭi, Dhaki, Diṅka-pā, Deṅgi-pā, Diṅga-pā, Idiṅgi-pā, Tenki-pā, Teṅgi-pā, Śrī Taṅki-pāda.
15. *dkon-mchog-gsum-gyi-'baṅs*. The following are attributed in Tg to Triratnadāsa or Ratnadāsa : *Bhagavat-śākyamuni-stotra* (bsTod 43), *Guṇāparyanta-stotra* (bsTod 44 & mDo xxxiii.96) and *Ārya-prajñā-pāramitā-saṃgraha-kārikā-vivarana* (mDo xiv.3). cf Watters ii.213.
16. S Maulasthāna. Watters ii.254 modern Multan. It is of interest to note that Tg contains a work called *Nāgānanda-nāma-nāṭaka* (mDo xcii.3) the author of which is probably Harṣadeva of Kanauj.
17. S Śākeras, V Sakas. V n '*sog-po*, this is how the Mongolians are now called by the Tibetans'.

After this, to atone for his sin he built a big monastery at each of the places, like *Maru, *Mālava, *Mewār, *Pituva and *Citavara. In each of these, he maintained a thousand monks. As a result, the Doctrine was widely spread.

[Fol 65A] Now, about *mahā-ācārya* Guṇaprabha.

He was born in a *brāhmaṇa* family of Mathurā. After thoroughly studying the Vedas and all the *śāstra*-s, he received in a monastery there the *pravrajyā* and *upasampadā* ordination. Under *mahā-ācārya* Vasubandhu, he studied the Śrāvaka Tripiṭaka and many *Mahāyāna-sūtra*-s and became a scholar in the Vinayas and all the scriptures of the different sects. He used continuously to recite from his memory the 'collection of a hundred thousand Vinayas'.[18]

He resided in a monastery called *Agrapurī in Mathurā. Along with him there lived five thousand monks. They immediately rectified even the slightest transgressions of the vow, and thus purified their conduct, as it was done in the good old days when the *arhat*-s were looking after the Law. Among them many were vastly learned in the *sūtra*-s and Abhidharmas and about five hundred of them regularly recited [lit knew by heart] the 'collection of a hundred thousand Vinayas.'[19]

As a royal punishment, the eyes of a minister of king *Śrī-harṣa, called *Mātaṅgarāja, were once plucked off. By the power of the resolute prayer of the *ācārya*, resulting from his pure moral conduct, he got back the eyes. Being the preceptor of the king, he used to receive everyday immeasurable wealth and he immediately converted these into virtue [i.e. spent on virtuous purposes]. He never allowed himself to fall from the ascetic practices (*dhūta-guṇa*-s).

Now about *ācārya* Sthiramati.[20]

When *ācārya* Vasubandhu recited the *śāstra* viz. 'The Collection of a Hundred Thousand Śloka-s in Ninetynine Sections', **[Fol 65B]** an intelligent dove that lived in the edge of

18. *'dul-ba-'bum-sde.*
19. S 'hundred thousand Hīnayāna sections'. But the text has *'dul-ba-'bum-sde.*
20. For works of Sthiramati, see Supplementary Note 26.

the beams listened to it with great reverence. After its death, it was reborn as the son of a merchant in *Daṇḍakāraṇya in the south.[21]

Immediately after birth, he asked 'Where is the *ācarya* ?'

When asked, 'Which *ācarya* ?' he replied, 'Vasubandhu of *Magadha.' On enquiries being made to the merchants of that place, they said 'Yes [that an *ācarya* like that was there]'.[22]

So, at the age of seven he was sent to *ācarya* Vasubandhu. He studied the branches of learning and, without difficulty, became wise.

He had a handful of beans, wanted to eat these in the temple of Tārā and thought that it was not proper to eat without offering to the *āryā*. He offered a few beans, which rolled back. He thought : 'It will not be proper for me to eat so long as the *āryā* does not accept it'. He went on offering till the beans were exhausted. Being a child afterall, he broke into tears. The *āryā* directly appeared before him and said, 'Do not weep. You have my blessings.' Immediately, his intelligence became limitless. The image also came to be known as *Māṣa-Tārā (i.e. Tārā with Beans).[23]

He eventually became a *sthavira* with a mastery of the three *piṭaka*-s. He became a scholar specially of the *abhidharma* of both Mahāyāna and Hīnayāna. He used regularly to recite the *Ārya Ratnakūṭa*. In all his actions, he used to be led by the predictions of *āryā* Tārā. He wrote commentaries on the *Ratnakūṭa-samāja-ūnapañcāśaka* and the *Mūla-madhyamaka*.

Shortly after the passing away of *ācarya* Vasubandhu, he defeated many *tīrthika* challengers like *Viṣṭa-pāla[24] and others

21. Bu-ston ii.147 gives practically the same account, though adding that at that time Vasubandhu resided at the Bhaga-vihāra and differing from Tār in maintaining that Sthiramati was born the son of a Śūdra.

22. V tr : When asked, 'Which *ācarya* ?', he replied, 'Vasubandhu' and was told that he (Vasubandhu) resided in Magadha. cf Bu-ston ii.147.

23. cf Bu-ston ii.147-8.

24. S Veṣṭa-pāla.

and became famous as the master of debate. He wrote glosses on most of the commentaries composed by *ācārya* Vasubandhu [**Fol 66A**] and composed many commentaries on his original works. It is said that he also wrote a commentary on the *Abhidharmakoṣa*. But I am not sure whether it was done by this *ācārya*.[25]

It is said that during his time as most of the centres of the Doctrine established by the previous *ācārya*-s had become defunct, this *ācārya* established a hundred centres of the Doctrine.

Now about *ācārya* Dignāga.

He was born in a *brāhmaṇa* family in the city of *Siṅga-vakta[26] near *Kāñci in the south. There lived at that time an *upādhyāya* belonging to the Vātsīputrīya[27] sect called **Nāga-datta, who was profoundly learned in all the doctrines of the *tīrthika*-s. [Dignāga] received *pravrajyā* under him and became a scholar of the Śrāvaka Tripiṭakas. He prayed to this *upādhyāya* for *upadeśa*. He [the *upādhyāya*] instructed him to seek the 'indescribable self'.[28] In spite of searching for it with an intense critical effort, he could not find anything like that. So he used to throw open all the windows during the day and used to light lamps all around during the night and, denuding himself, he repeatedly examined himself from all sides, both in and out.[29]

One of his friends found him doing so and reported it to the *upādhyāya*. Questioned by the *upādhyāya*, he said, 'Oh *upādhyāya*, because of my weak intellect and little insight, I fail to see what

25. However, Tg contains *Abhidharmakoṣa-bhāṣya-ṭikā Tattvārtha-nāma* (mDo cxxix-cxxx) by Sthiramati, a commentary on Vasubandhu's commentary on the *Abhidharmakoṣa*.
26. S Siṃha-vaktra and adds in note that the text has Siṃha-vakta.
27. *gnas-ma-bu*. cf Stcherbatsky BL i.32 'This sect admitted the existence of a real personality as something different from the elements of which it is composed.' cf also Stcherbatsky *Central Conception* ... 31.
28. *brjod-du-med-pa'i-bdag*. cf Bu-ston ii.149 'the principle of the Ego, which was said to be inexpressible as being neither identical with the groups of elements nor differing from them.'
29. cf Bu-ston ii.149f.

you instruct me to seek. Therefore, suspecting that it is covered by some obscuration, I am searching for it in this way.'

It was an indirect refutation of him [the *upādhyāya*]. So the *upādhyāya* became angry and said, 'You are trying to find fault with my doctrine. Therefore, you leave this place.'

[Fol 66B] Thus he [*upādhyāya*] drove away somebody whom it was not right to drive away. He [Dignāga] could defeat him with arguments ; but since this was not proper, he bowed down before him and went away.

Eventually, he went to *ācārya* Vasubandhu and listened to all the Piṭakas of the Mahāyāna and Hinayāna and thus became proficient in five hundred *sūtra*-s,—those of the Mahāyāna, Hinayāna—and even the *dhāraṇī*-s. It is said that he specially received *vidyā-mantra* from a *mantra-ācārya*, attained *siddhi* and had the direct vision of *ārya* Mañjuśrī. He listened to the Doctrine [from Mañjuśrī] to his heart's content.

In a very solitary place of a forest in *Oḍiviśa, he sat in the cave of a hill called *Bhoṭa-śela[30] and attained *samādhi* with intense concentration.

After some years there took place at Śrī *Nalendra a big debate with the *tīrthika*-s. Among them there was a *brāhmaṇa* called *Sudurjaya, who had the vision of the deity he propitiated. He learnt the technique of debate extremely well and it was most difficult to defeat him. Failing to compete in debate, the Buddhists invited *ācārya* Dignāga from the east. He thrice defeated that *tīrthika* and converted all the assembled *tīrthika*-s to the Law of the Buddha after defeating them individually. He explained many *sūtra*-s to the monks there, propagated the *Abhidharma* more extensively, wrote many works on Vijñāna-vāda and on logic.[31] It is said that he wrote one hundred works in all.

After this, he returned again to *Oḍiviśa **[Fol 67A]** and devoted himself to meditation.

There he resolved to compose the logical treatise called

30. S-ed. Bhora-śaila.

31. For works of Dignāga, see Supplementary Note 27.

Pramāṇa-samuccaya, in which he wanted to unite his previous scattered products of extraordinary keen intellect and he wrote the opening verse embodying his resolution :

'I salute him who is the personified Logic,
Who pursues the weal of the living beings,
The Teacher, the Blessed One, the Protector,
And, in order to demonstrate the means of Logical Proof,
I shall unite here under one head
The different fragments from all my other treatises.'[32]

When he had written this with a piece of chalk[33] [on the rock], the earth shook, a light blazed forth and a thunderous sound was heard.

A *brāhmaṇa* called Kṛṣṇa[34] realised the significance of these signs. When the *ācārya* had gone out for alms, he [Kṛṣṇa] came and wiped the words off.

Similarly, he wiped off for the second time.

He [Dignāga] wrote it for the third time, and added : 'Know this to be extremely important. Therefore, you must not wipe it, if you are wiping just for the fun of it. If, however, you think it to be wrong and want to have a debate, appear in person.'

After this, when he went out for alms, [the *brāhmaṇa*] came to wipe it. But noticing the note, he kept on waiting. The *ācārya* returned and, staking their respective creeds, entered into a debate. The *tīrthika* was repeatelly defeated. He [Dignāga] said, 'You have now to accept the Law of the Buddha.' At this, he [Kṛṣṇa] threw enchanted dust, which burnt the belongings of the *ācārya* and even the *ācārya* himself narrowly escaped the fire.

The *tīrthika* fled.

The *ācārya* thought : 'How can I be fit to work for the

32. Tr Obermiller Bu-ston ii.150.
33. Bu-ston ii.150 'Accordingly in the cavern known by his name, he wrote on the side of a rock'...
34. *nag-po*. cf Bu-ston ii.150 'a heretical teacher called Kṛṣṇa-muni-rāja.'

welfare of others when I fail to bring welfare even to a single person like this!' Thinking thus, when he was about to renounce his *citta-utpādana*, **[Fol 67B]** *ārya* Mañjuśrī appeared before him and said, 'Oh son, do not do it. Do not do it. Wrong ideas result from evil company. Know it for certain that the *tīrthika*-s can do no harm to your treatise. I shall remain your *kalyāṇa-mitra*, as long as you do not attain Buddhahood. In the future [your treatise] will be the only eye of all the *śāstra*-s.'

Then the *ācārya* said, 'I cannot bear this unbearable distress. My mind is revelling in wrong conduct. It is so difficult to encounter a venerable soul, —but how does it help me if you are not giving me your blessings in spite of already appearing before me?'

When he said this, [Mañjuśrī answered] 'Oh son, do not be depressed. I shall protect you from all dangers.' Saying this, he disappeared.

Then he [Dignāga] composed the *śāstra* excellently.

He was once slightly indisposed. After his [daily round of] alms in the city he entered a forest which he saw, felt sleepy and fell asleep. In his dreams, he had visions of many Buddhas and he attained many *samādhi*-s. The gods showered flowers around him, all the flowers of the forest bowed at his feet and the elephants provided him with cool shadow.

The king of the country, along with his attendants, while roaming there for pleasure, witnessed this scene. He felt amazed, woke him up with the sound of musical instruments and asked, 'Are you Dignāga?'

'So am I called.'

Then the king fell at his feet.

After this, he [Dignāga] went to the south. **[Fol 68A]** He defeated the *tīrthika* rivals of different places and reconstructed most of the damaged centres of the Doctrine established by the earlier *ācārya*-s.

Now, the king of *Oḍiviśa had a minister called *Bhadrapālita, who acted as the royal treasurer. [Dignāga] made him a follower of the Law of the Buddha. That *brāhmaṇa*

[Bhadrapālita] built sixteen big monasteries, each accommodating a large number of monks. In each of these monasteries were established various centres for the Doctrine.

As a mark of his pure moral conduct, this *brāhmaṇa* had a *haritaka*[35] tree in his garden. It was called the *Muṣṭi-haritaka and it cured all diseases and thus benefitted a large number of people. The tree was once drying up. So the *ācārya* offered prayers for saving it and it was revived in seven days.

By defeating most of the *tīrthika* rivals in debate, he acquired the fame of being the leading logician.[36] The devout followers of his creed filled the four directions. But he had not even a novice as his attendant. He had little desire of his own, was always self-content and, after devoting his whole life to twelve ascetic practices,[37] he passed away in a solitary forest of *Oḍiviśa.

Now about *bhaṭṭāraka* Saṃghadāsa.

He was a disciple of *ācārya* Vasubandhu. By caste a *brāhmaṇa*, he was born in the south and belonged [originally] to the Sarvāstivādī sect. He spent a long time in Vajrāsana and established there twentyfour centres of Vinaya and Abhidharma. **[Fol 68B]** He went to Kashmir in response to the invitation from king *Turuṣka *Mahāsammata. He built the *vihāra* called Ratnagupta[38] and *Kumbhakuṇḍalī.[39] After extensively propagating the Mahāyāna doctrine, he passed away in that country. Formerly, the Law of the Mahāyāna was not much in vogue in Kashmir. During the time of the brothers Asaṅga [i.e. Asaṅga and his brother] it was spread there, though in a limited form. From the time of this *ācārya*, it began gradually to spread more and more.

35. *a-ru-ra.*
36. *rtsod-pa'i-khyu-mchog.* V n 'lit. the bull of debate'.
37. *sbyaṅs-pa'i-yon-tan-bcu-gñis*, lit. *dvādaśa-dhūtaguṇa*—D 939. But V tr 'twelve subjects of learning.'
38. *rin-chen-sbas-pa.*
39. V & S Kumbhakuṇḍala.

Now about *ācārya* Dharmadāsa.

Born in *Bhaṅgala in the east, he was a disciple of Asaṅga and his brother. He went round the countries all around and built in each direction a temple of *ārya* Mañjuśrī. He is said to have prepared a commentary on the entire *Yogacaryā-bhūmi*.

Now about *ācārya* Buddhapālita.

Born in a place called Haṃsakrīḍa[40] in *Tambala in the south, he received there the *pravrajyā* and became vastly learned in the scriptures. Under *ācārya* Saṃgharakṣita,[41] a disciple of *ārya* Nāgamitra,[42], he learnt the original works of *ācārya* Nāgārjuna. He attained the highest knowledge through intense meditation. He had a direct vision of *ārya* Mañjuśrī and he delivered many sermons on the Doctrine while residing in the *Dantapurī[43] monastery in the south. He expounded[44] many scriptural works composed by the '*ārya*-s father and son' [i.e. Nāgārjuna and Āryadeva], *ācārya* Śūra etc.

At last he practised Guṭikā-siddhi and attained success.

Now about *ācārya* Bhavya.[45]

Born in a noble Kṣatriya family in *Malya-ra of the south **[Fol 69A]** he received *pravrajyā* there and became a scholar of the Tripiṭakas. He came to the *madhya-deśa* and learnt under *ācārya* Saṃgharakṣita many *sūtra*-s of the Mahāyāna and the teachings of Nāgārjuna. He went back to the south and received the vision of Vajrapāṇi. He attained *viśiṣṭa-samādhi*,[46] became the head of about fifty monasteries in the south and delivered many lessons on the Doctrine. He studied the works of *ācārya* Buddhapālita after the latter had passed away. Taking his stand on the views of Nāgārjuna, he resolved to compose a commentary refuting the views of the earlier

40. *naṅ-pas-rtse-ba.*
41. *dge-'dun-sruṅ-ba.*
42. *klu'i-bśes-gñen.*
43. S-ed Dantapurī. P-ed Daṇṭapurī.
44. Tg contains only *Buddhapālitā-mūlamadhyamaka-vṛtti* (mDo xvii.20) by Buddhapālita.
45. See Supplementary Note 28 for the works of Bhavya or Bhāvaviveka.
46. *tiṅ-ṅe-'dsin-khyab-par-can.*

ācārya-s as expressed in their expositions of the *Madhyamaka-mūla*. Thus he wrote commentaries on some *sūtra*-s. At last he also practised Guṭikā-siddhi and attained success.

Both these *ācārya*-s [Bhavya and Buddhapālita], after leaving their mortal bodies, went to the Vidyādhara-sthāna.[47]

Now, these two *ācārya*-s composed the basic texts on the Mādhyamika doctrine of nature-lessness (*svabhāva-hīna-vāda*). The number of disciples of Buddhapālita was not very large, while *ācārya* Bhavya had a large number of disciples and, because he had thousands of monks as his followers, his views were more extensively spread.

Before the appearance of these two *ācārya*-s, all the Mahāyānī-s were under the same Law. But these two *ācārya*-s [thought], 'The doctrines of *ārya* Nāgārjuna and of *ārya* Asaṅga are fundamentally different. The doctrine of Asaṅga is not indicative of the path of the Mādhyamika. It is merely the doctrine of *vijñāna*. **[Fol 69B]** What we uphold is the real view of *ārya* Nāgārjuna.'

Saying this, they refuted the position of the others. As a result after the passing away of Bhavya, the Mahāyānī-s were split into two groups and started having controversies among themselves.

In this [controversy], *ācārya* Sthiramati wrote the work explaining the *Madhyamaka-mūla* from the standpoint of *vijñāna*.[48] When copies of this work reached the south, the disciples of Bhavya objected to it. So they came to *Nalendra and had a debate with the disciples of Sthiramati. The followers of the doctrine of nature-lessness claim that in this debate the disciples of Bhavya were victorious. But this debate should be viewed as similar to that between *Candragomī and Candrakīrti.

Many Tibetans say that Buddhapālita was a disciple of *ārya* Nāgārjuna during the first half of his [Nāgārjuna's] life, while

47. V n 'i.e. changed their usual human bodies into celestial bodies'. cf Watters ii.223f.

48. *dbu-ma-rtsa-ba'i-dgoṅs-pa-rnam-rig-tu-'grel-'pa'i-rnam-bśad.* See Supplementary Note 12.

Bhavya was his disciple during the second half of his life, that they entered into a controversy and that Buddhapālita was reborn as Candrakīrti. All these are, however, irrational and groundless. Others reject all these and try to resolve the difficulty with the claim : 'These [*ācārya*-s] were direct disciples of *ācārya* Nāgārjuna. Nāgārjuna acted as the *upādhyāya* at the *upasampadā* of Bhavya. Candrakīrti was the direct disciple of Āryadeva.' But how could the doctrines of these two differ even during the lifetime of Āryadeva, on whom both equally depended ? How can a person with a critical faculty believe all these ?

Now about *ārya* Vimuktasena.[49]

Born near Jvālā-guhā[50] situated between the *madhya-deśa* and the south, he was the nephew of *ācārya* Buddhadāsa.[51] **[Fol 70A]** The *ārya* received ordination of the *Kaurukullaka sect.[52] Being a scholar of the doctrine of this sect, he had reverence for the Mahāyāna and so he went to *ācārya* Vasubandhu. After listening to the Prajñā-pāramitā, he fully memorised the entire *Prajñā-pāramitā-sūtra*. However, failing to listen to his instructions, he became the last disciple of *ācārya* Saṃgharakṣita and received from him the instructions on the Prajñā-pāramitā.

According to the account current in Tibet, this *ācārya* was a disciple of *ācārya* Vasubandhu[53] and surpassed him as a scholar in Prajñā-pāramitā. According to some Indians, he was a

49. cf Bu-ston ii.155f : 'He was the principal of many great monasteries, belonged (at first) to the sect of the Kaurukullakas and was the nephew of the teacher Buddhadāsa. He attained the stage of joy (*rab-tu-dga'-ba=pramuditā*).' Practically the same is said in the colophons of his *Ārya-pañcaviṃśati-sāhasrikā-prajñāpāramitopadeśa-śāstra-abhisamaya-alaṃkāra-kārikā-vārtika* (mDo ii.1) and *vṛtti* (mDo i.2). Obermiller Bu-ston ii.156n—Tsoṅ-kha-pa in his *gSer-phreṅ* expresses doubt as regards the authorship of *Abhisamaya-alaṃkāra-vārtika*.

50. *'bar-ba'i-phug*.

51. V wrongly translates the name here as Buddhapālita.

52. see note 49 above.

53. V n 'i.e. he was not his contemporary, which is probable.'

disciple of Dignāga and could not have touched the feet of Vasubandhu ; he listened to the *Prajñā-pāramitā-abhisamaya* from *ācārya* Dharmadāsa, though he received instructions on it from Bhavya. However, from the account most widely spread in the *ārya-deśa*, it appears that he was the last disciple of Vasubandhu. Among the followers of this *ācārya* the following account is current.

Feeling tired of too many scriptural works, he wanted to remove his weariness in the meditation on the Prajñā-pāramitā. As a result of this meditation, he had a special form of bliss. He had no doubt about the significance [of the Prajñā-pāramitā]. Still he felt disturbed by certain discrepancies between the wordings of a *sūtra* and those of certain parts of the *Abhisamaya-alaṃkāra*. At that time, *ārya* Maitreya instructed him in dream : 'Go to the monastery of Vārāṇasī, where you will attain great success.' **[Fol 70B]** As he went there in the morning, he met *upāsaka* Śāntivarman,[54] who was renowned for his gift of the gab[55] and who brought the text of the [*Pañca-*]*viṃśati-sāhasrikā-aṣṭa-adhyāya*[56] from *Potala in the south. He found [on the basis of this] the wordings of the *sūtra* to agree with those of [*Abhisamaya-*]*alaṃkāra* and felt relieved. He composed a work explaining the *Sūtra-aṣṭa-adhyāya* and *Abhisamaya-alaṃkāra* from the Mādhyamika standpoint of nature-lessness. In this he synthesised all the *sūtra*-s and *alaṃkāra*-s. Such [a work] did not exist before this *ācārya*, because the [*Pañca-*]*viṃśati-sāhasrikā-āloka*[57] says, 'This was not realised before by others.'

Later on, he became the preceptor of a feudatory ruler in the east and, as the head of twentyfour monasteries, he assiduously read and taught the Prajñā-pāramitā. Among the listeners to the *Prajñā-pāramitā-sūtra*, the number of only the *bhikṣu*-s exceeded thousands within a short period. About

54. *shi-ba'i-go-cha.*
55. P-ed *lcags-kyi-byin-pa-can.* S-ed *ljags-kyi-byin-pa.* (*lcags*=armour, *ljags*=gab). The latter reading followed.
56. V 'Twenty thousand *pāramitā*-s in eight sections.' But in the note, he says *Pañca-viṃśati-sāhaśrikā.*
57. *ñi-khri-snaṅ-ba-*

thirty years passed like this. Both in India and Tibet, this *ācārya* is famed as one who reached the first stage of saintly perfection [*prathama-bhūmi*).[58]

According to some, he was not really an *ārya*, for he was still in the *yoga-mārga*. Still he was called an *ārya* because he reached a stage very near it. According to some others, he was really a *pṛthak-jana* and the word *ārya* is only a part of his name Ārya-vimuktasena : just as the word Buddha in the name of king Buddha-pakṣa is not taken by any for the Buddha himself. According to still others, he was a *bodhisattva*, who had previously traversed the path of the Hina[-yāna].

There are many anecdotes like these. But I have come across no difference of opinion in the matter of viewing him as a great and wonderful person. How could one know whether internally he was a *pṛthak-jana* or an *ārya* in spiritual perfection ? His conduct and teachings were obviously those of a pious *pṛthak-jana*.

Now about *ācārya* Triratnadāsa.

[Fol 71A] He listened to the *Abhidharma-piṭaka* from *ācārya* Vasubandhu, studied under many *piṭaka-dhara* scholars of different places and was a close friend of Dignāga. He also became a disciple of Dignāga, because he studied the Prajñā-pāramitā under him. It is said that in wisdom he was equalto Dignāga. He composed[59] the commentary on the *Aṣṭa-sāhasrikā* [*-prajñā-pāramitā-*] *saṃgraha*. Dignāga also prepared a work[60] on the precise meaning of the *Guṇāparyanta-stotra* written by him.

According to some historians of the Doctrine, *ācārya* Triratnadāsa was but another name of *ācārya* Śūra,[61] and further Śūra and Dignāga were mutual preceptors and disciples, inasmuch as he [Dignāga] appended the *Miśraka-stotra* to

58. Bu-ston ii.155 also refers to the stage of *pramuditā* (the first stage), though the colophon of mDo ii.1 refers to his attainment of the sixth *bhūmi*, called *adhimukti*.
59. See note 15 of this chapter.
60. Tg bsTod 46=mDo xxxiii.97 *Guṇāparyanta-stotra-ṭikā* by Dignāga.
61. V Śūra (Aśvaghoṣa).

[Śūra's] *Stotra-śata-pañcāśatka*.[62] Such a statement must be due either to listening to a wrong history or to the wrong recording of what was rightly told. In any case, the statement is fanciful. Besides, in the *Miśraka-stotra* of Dignāga are either analysed the compounds of the *Stotra-śata-pañcāśatka* or are merely clarified its significance.[63] Therefore, it simply formed a commentary. The works of these two *ācārya*-s are to be understood as different.

Later on, this *ācārya* [Triratnadāsa] went to the south and, as the head of several monasteries, preached the Doctrine to many people. He went to *Drabala,[64] established fifty new and large centres for the Doctrine and for a long time added lustre to the Law. He eventually brought a *yakṣiṇī* under control and went to the great mountain called The Hundred Flowers.[65] **[Fol 71B]** During the same period, *upāsaka* Śāntivarman also went to *Potala.[66]

62. V n 'Mātṛceṭa (i.e. Aśvaghoṣa himself).' Evidently, Tār also has here in mind the same idea of identification of Mātṛceṭa, Aśvaghoṣa and Śūra. In Tg, *Miśraka-stotra* (bsTod 41) is attributed to Dignāga and Mātṛceṭa, while *Śatapañcāśatka-stotra* (bsTod 38) to Aśvaghoṣa. cf F. W. Thomas in ERE viii.496, who quotes I-Tsing in this connection.
63. In Tg, the commentary (bsTod 39) on *Satapañcāśatka-stotra* is attributed to Rāmapriya. cf I-Tsing (Takakusu) 151, who attributes the *stotra* to Mātṛceṭa, and comments, 'There are many who have written commentaries on them, nor are the imitations of them few. Bodhisattva Jina (Dignāga) himself composed such an imitation. He added one verse before each of the one hundred and fifty verses, so that they became altogether three hundred verses, called the Mixed Hymns. A celebrated priest of the Deer Park, Śākyadeva by name, again added one verse to each of Jina's, and consequently they amounted to four hundred and fifty verses, called the Doubly Mixed Hymns.'
64. S-ed Dvravali.
65. *me-tog-brgya-pa*. V Śatapuṣpa. V n 'which, S remarks, can be the same as Śatruñjaya.' see Sircar CGEIL 104
66. D 785—Potala or Potalaka, the residence of Avalokiteśvara and *āryā* Tārā on a hill situated in a harbour somewhere in the Indian Ocean. cf Watters ii.229ff.

This *upāsaka* attained most of the marks of *siddhi* by propitiating *ārya* Avalokiteśvara in a forest of *Puṇḍravardhana. A king called *Śubhasāra saw in his dream as if *ārya* Avalokiteśvara was invited and brought to his country and immediately Jambudvīpa was rid of famine and epidemic and prosperity was restored there. [And it was predicted that] for this purpose, the same *upāsaka* dwelling in the forest had to be sent to the *Potala mountain.

The king summoned the *upāsaka* and gave him a pearl necklace, the letter of invitation and *paṇa*-s (money) for travelling expenses. The *upāsaka* thought : 'The journey being long and full of hazards is likely to involve the risk of life. Since, however, he is requesting me to go to the abode of the tutelary deity, it will not be proper to disobey him.' Thinking thus, he started with the road-guide[67] on his way to *Potala. He reached the Śrī Dhānyakaṭaka[68] *caitya* in the island of *Dhanaśrī. While moving from there to *Potala, he had to go through a subterranean way a little and then by a route over the earth, which, though existing at that time, is now under the sea. That is why people these days cannot use this route.

Then he failed to cross a great river on the way. Following the road-guide, he prayed to Tārā and an old woman appeared with a boat and took him across. Further on, failing to cross another sea, when he prayed to Bhṛkuṭi, a girl with a raft appeared and took him across. Then he reached the fringe of a forest and could not pass through it because of a forest fire. When he prayed to Hayagrīva **[Fol 72A]** it rained and the fire was extinguished. Lightning showed him the way. Again, he could not proceed because the path was cut off by a ravine many *yojana*-s deep. When he prayed to Eka-jaṭī, a huge serpent appeared and served as a bridge, enabling him to

67. *lam-yig*—D 1210. Interestingly, Tg contains a work, attributed to Śrīmat Potalaka Bhaṭṭāraka (Avalokiteśvara), with the title *Potalaka-gamana-mārga-patrikā* (rG lxxii.51).

68. *'bras-spuṅs.* Roerich in BA ii.754—Amarāvatī in the Sattenapalle Talluka of Guntur District, Madras. cf Watters ii.214ff.

cross it. Then his path was obstructed by many apes, as big as elephants. When he prayed to Amoghapāśa, these huge apes gave him the way and brought delicious food for him.

From there he reached the foot of *Potala but could not climb up the rocky hill. When he prayed to *ārya* Avalokiteśvara, there came down a ladder made of canes. With this he climbed up. Because of dense fog he failed to see the way. When he prayed for a long time, the fog cleared up. He saw the image of Tārā at the third stage of the hill and on its middle the image of Bhṛkuṭī. Reaching the top of the hill [he saw] nothing but some flowers remaining scattered in an empty place. He sat in a corner there and prayed for a month. Then appeared a woman who said, 'Ārya has arrived. Come along.' Saying this, she took him along and opened one thousand doors of the palace one after the other. With the opening of each door, he attained a stage of *samādhi*. Then he saw *ārya* Pañcadeva.[69] He offered flowers to him and placed before him the king's letter and offerings. When he prayed to him to visit the Jambudvīpa, he [*ārya*] accepted it, gave the *upāsaka* a large sum of **paṇa*-s as his travelling expenses and said, 'On your way back, spend these for your maintenance. I shall come when these **paṇa*-s [**Fol 72B**] are exhausted.' Thus saying he directed him the route back. He had direct vision of the goddesses whose images were there in the middle and on the third stages of the hill. Of the fifteen days of his journey back, when the fourteenth day arrived, he felt delighted to see the hills of *Puṇḍravardhana and spent the remaining **paṇa*-s in purchasing food and drink in excess, which he consumed.

Before reaching the city of the king, when he reached the place of his own meditation [i.e. the forest], all his **paṇa*-s were spent out. He sat there and expected the *ārya* at day-break. But he [Avalokiteśvara] did not appear. As he fell asleep at midnight, he woke up by the sound of musical instruments.

69. *lha-lṅa.* V & S 'five deities'. V n 'probably the deities meant here are those of body, word, heart, merit and fate.'

Noticing the gods worshipping in the sky, he asked 'Whom are you worshipping ?' [The gods said] 'Oh thou foolish son of Jambudvīpa, the *ārya* has arrived along with his attendants on the tree on which you are leaning back.' Then he saw the Pañcadeva himself[70] sitting on the tree. He bowed down to him and prayed, 'Please come to the country of the king.'

'That would have happened, had all your **paṇa*-s been not exhausted. I shall now remain here in this way.'

As this message was sent to the king, the king felt displeased and it is said that he did not offer any reward to the *upāsaka.* A temple was built in that forest and it came to be known as that of *Khasarpaṇa.

It is said that [the name] *Khasarpaṇa was derived from the fact that he 'came through the sky' or because he 'came when the **paṇa*-s were exhausted.'[71] But it is better to use it in the sense of coming through the sky. In the alternative interpretation, *Kharsa is an equivalent for 'the price of food' and **paṇa* means gold and silver coins,[72] which is now called **taṅkā.* Thus the name means, 'Coin as the price for food.'

[Fol 73A] Thus it is commonly known in India.

According to the account of the *[Pañca]-viṃśati-sāhasrikā-aṣṭa-adhyāya*, there is no mention of [the *upāsaka*] being sent by the king. Thrice he went to *Potala by himself. His first visit was in the form of a personal pilgrimage. On the second occasion, he was sent by the monks of *Vārāṇasī for solving the problem of the discrepancy [in wordings] between *Abhisamaya-alaṃkāra* and the *sūtra.* However, instead of raising this topic, he invited *ārya* *Khasarpaṇa himself. [After he came to Vārāṇasī] *Khasarpaṇa, on being prayed [to solve

70. V & S 'five deities themselves'.

71. S tr 'It is said that the name is Khasarpaṇa, or "moving through the sky", because Avalokiteśvara came through the sky. Others maintain that it means "the exhausting of the *paṇa*-s", as he (Avalokiteśvara) arrived after the *paṇa-s* were exhausted.'

72. The derivation suggested : *khasarpaṇa=karṣas* & *paṇa=karṣāpaṇa* or *kārṣāpaṇa. karṣa*, a weight of gold and silver, about 280 gr.

the problem] said, 'I am only an incarnation [of Avalokiteśvara and not Avalokiteśvara himself]. So I do not know it.' When he [the *upāsaka*] went to *Potala for the third time with the purpose of solving the problem, he brought back with him the *Aṣṭa-adhyāya*.

It is said that *ārya* *Khasarpaṇa Pañcadeva[73] personally appeared before him and directly received the offerings made by him. When the robbers, greedy for the wealth of this *upāsaka*, were about to kill him, he thought that this was but the inevitable result of his past actions and said, 'Place my head on the hand of [the image of the] *ārya*.' The robbers did accordingly. Tears came out of the eyes [of the image] of the *ārya* and entered into the hole of his [*upāsaka's*] skull[74] and it turned into a relic. From then on, he [*ārya*] does not accept any direct offering. Thus it is said.

The twentythird chapter containing the account of the period of ācārya Dignāga and others.

73. S 'the five *ārya* Khasarpaṇa gods'. V 'the five deities Khasarpaṇa.'
74. S-ed *klad-khu-sa-ru*. V & S tr 'and as the forehead fell on the earth, it became a relic'. P-ed *klad-khuṅ-du* : 'entered into the hole of his skull.'

CHAPTER 24

ACCOUNT OF THE PERIOD OF KING ŚĪLA

After king *Śrīharṣa, his son Śīla[1] became the king.

He was previously (i.e. in his previous birth) a monk well-versed in the three *piṭaka*-s. He went to beg at the palace of a certain king where a grand festival was going on. But he received no alms and was turned out by the gate-keepers. He fasted and, while dying of hunger, prayed, 'May I become a king, worship the Three Jewels and [**Fol 73B**] satisfy the ordained monks with food.'

As a result, he became a very prosperous king and offered good food to the monks of the four directions.

He built a palace in the city called *La-tā and lived for one hundred and forty years. He ruled for about a hundred years. He ascended the throne towards the end of Guṇaprabha's life.

In the east there was a very powerful king called Siṃha,[2] belonging to the *Licchavi line. During his time was born *ācārya* *Candragomī.

King *Bharṣa [? Varṣa], son of king Siṃha, also ruled for a long time.

In the *Candra dynasty, king *Siddhacandra ascended the throne. Because of his limited power, he had to obey the orders of kings Siṃha and *Bharṣa.

This was the period of the second half of the lives of Bhavya and *ārya* Vimuktasena and the period of the latter half of *ācārya* Sūryagupta,[3] of Paramasena,[4] a disciple of Vimuktasena,

1. *nan-tshul.*
2. *sen-ge.*
3. *ñi-ma-sbas.* Evidently not the logician Ravigupta who belonged to a much later period (Stcherbatsky BL i.43f) and who is mentioned in Tibetan as *ñi-ma-bsruṅ-ba* (author mDo civ.1 & cviii.3). We have in Tg a number of works on Tārāsādhana (rG xxvi.3 ; 4 ; 5 : 6 ; 7 ; 8 ; lxxii.47 ; lxxxii.51) by one Sūryagupta of Kashmir, whose name in Tibetan is given as *ñi-ma-sbas.* Tār in Fol 74A mentions him as Tārā-siddha. Hence, the reconstruction of the name here as Ravigupta by V appears to be unacceptable.
4. *mchog-sde.* V & S Varasena.

and of *Kamalabuddhi, a disciple of Buddhapālita.

Ārya Candramaṇi,[5] a disciple of Guṇaprabha, and Jayadeva,[6] the *upādhyāya* of *Nalendra, were contemporaries. In the south also lived *ācārya* Candrakīrti.[7] This was about the period of the first part of the lives of *ācārya* Dharmapāla,[8] *ācārya* Śāntideva[9] and of *siddha* *Viru-pā. Evidently, *ārya* *Saga-deva[10] also lived during this period, because in the *Puṣpa-mālā-tantra*,[11] translated by lo-tsā-ba Prajñākīrti[12] of sñel-tsor, is said : 'It [*Puṣpa mālā*] was composed by *ārya* *Saga-deva, a disciple of *ārya* Saṅghadāsa.' Hence it is necessary to determine whether he was a Śrāvaka *arhat* or not.

[**Fol 74A**] Of these [*ācārya*-s] belonging to this period, I have not heard the account of Paramasena and *Kamala-buddhi. I have not come across any detailed account of Candramaṇi beyond that he was the preceptor of king Śīla.

Now about Sūryagupta.

He held that the views of *ācārya* Nāgārjuna were the same as those of Asaṅga. In both Kashmir and *Magadha he built twelve big centres for the Doctrine. He employed the *yakṣa*-s to collect the materials required for these. He protected all the 'insiders' from the eightfold dangers.[13] He was also a

5. *zla-ba'i-nor-bu.*
6. *rgyal-ba'i-lha.* Tg contains a commentary by Dīpaṃkara-śrī-jñāna (rG xlviii. 145) on Jayadeva's *Mūlāpatti*, which however is not traced in Tg.
7. *zla-ba-grags-pa.*
8. *chos-skyoṅ.* see Fol 80B.
9. *shi-ba-lha.*
10. *sa-ga-lha.* V & S Viśākhadeva, which is another name by which he was known. See next note.
11. Tg mDo lxxxix.1 *Ārya-mūla-sarvāstivāda-vinaya-kārikā Puṣpa-mālā-nāma* by *saga-lha* (Sagadeva or Viśākhadeva), a disciple of *mahā-vinayadhara ārya* Saṃghadāsa. cf BA i.82.
12. *śes-rab-grags.*
13. viz. dangers from lion, elephant, fire, snake, robber, chains (prison), water and flesh-eater (*śa-za*). Tg contains several works on *Aṣṭa-bhaya-trāṇa* (rG lxviii.46 by Lakṣmīṅkarā ; rG lxxi.38 by Atīśa ; etc).

bhikṣu proficient in magic spells and was Tārā-siddha. His account is to be known from other sources.

Also Jayadeva, a scholar of many *śāstra*-s, lived for a long time in *Nalendra as a *mahā-ācārya*. I have not come across any detailed account of him.

At that time the tooth[14] relic of the Buddha reached *Ha-sa-ma [Assam] in the north. The poet Guhyadatta,[15] a disciple of *ācārya* Saṅghadāsa, and *Ratnamati,[16] a disciple of Dharmadāsa,[17] along with hundreds of thousands of others belonging to 'the four classes of followers' who acted according to the Doctrine, began to worship the tooth-relic. The tradition of this (worship) still continues in *Pu-khaṅ.[18]

Now about Śrī Candrakīrti.

He was born in *Samanta[19] in the south. He mastered all the branches of knowledge at an early age, was ordained in the same place in the south and became a scholar of all the *piṭaka*-s. He learnt all the *śāstra*-s and *upadeśa*-s of Nāgārjuna **[Fol 74B]** from many disciples[20] of Bhavya and from *Kamalabuddhi, a disciple of Buddhapālita.[21] He became the master-scholar among scholars and the *upādhyāya* of Śrī *Nalendra.

He extensively propagated the doctrine of Buddhapālita by composing[22] the *Mūla* [i.e. the *Mūla-madhyamaka-vṛtti-*

14. *mche-ba*. D 435, tooth—though generally the canine tooth.
15. *gsaṅ-ba-byin*. Tg contains *Rakta-yamāntaka-pañcadevābhisamaya-siddhi Mañjarī-nāma* (rG lxxxi.27) and *Sapta-kumārikā-avadāna* (mDo xxxiii.42=mDo xc.20) by Guhyadatta, a disciple of Saṅghadāsa.
16. The name is mentioned in the colophon of Tg mDo cxvi.16.
17. *chos-'baṅs*.
18. See Fol 129A.
19. The colophon of Tg mDo xxiv.1 mentions the birth-place of Candrakīrti as Samata (Samanta). cf Bu-ston ii.134—Samana.
20. S 'a disciple', but the text has *maṅ-po* (many).
21. S tr 'from Kamalabuddhi, a disciple of Bhavya as well as of Buddhapālita.'
22. For works of Candrakīrti, see Supplementary Note 29. Bu-ston ii.134f—'the most celebrated of his works, those which resemble the sun and the moon', are the *Prasannapadā* (commentary on the *Mūla-madhyamaka*) and *Pradīpa-uddyotana* (commentary on *Guhya-samāja-tantra*).

Prasannapadā-nāma], the *Avatāra* [i.e. the *Madhyamaka-avatāra-kārikā-nāma*], the *Catah* [i.e. the *Bodhisattva-yoga-caryā-catuḥ-śataka-ṭīkā*],—these three and the *Yukti-ṣaṣṭikā-vṛtti*.

By milking the milch cow drawn on a picture, he used to satisfy the entire *saṃgha* with thickened milk (*kṣīra*). Even the stone-pillar could not obstruct the movement of his hand. He could freely move through the wall.[23] He showed many wonderful feats like these and defeated many *tīrthika* opponents.

At last he went to the south (again) and in the country called *Koṅ-ku-na[24] defeated many *tīrthika* rivals, converted most of the *brāhmaṇa*-s and householders into the followers of the Law and established many big centres for the Doctrine.

According to the *mantra-ācārya*-s, he again spent a long time in the *Manu-bhaṅga hill, strove after the highest *siddhi* following the *mantra-yāna* and attained the rainbow-body.

According to the Tibetan account, he lived for three hundred years and showed marvellous feats like driving away the *Turuṣka army while riding a stone-lion.

The latter (account) could have been true. As for the former, however, if he did attain the rainbow-body, he must have had become immortal. As such, the question of [living for] three hundred years does not arise. Obviously, it can neither be claimed that he lived [for three hundred years] in this world with his mortal body.

Now about *ācārya* *Candragomī.

In the east, [Fol 75A] in *Varendra, there lived a **paṇḍita* who attained the vision of *ārya* Avalokiteśvara. He entered into a debate with a *tīrthika* Lokāyata[25] teacher. He defeated his [*tīrthika's*] views no doubt; yet [the *tīrthika* claimed] that arguments depended on intellect and hence one with keener intellect gained victory. [So he said]

'There is no direct evidence for anterior and posterior existence. So I do not admit this.'

23. cf Bu-ston ii.134.
24. P-ed Goṅ-ku-na. S-ed Koṅ-ku-na. The latter reading followed.
25. *rgyaṅ-'phen-pa*.

Being thus told, he kept the king and others as witnesses and said, 'I am going to be reborn. Put a mark on my forehead.'

He placed on his forehead a mark of vermilion cut deep into the flesh. Putting a pearl into his mouth, he (the *paṇḍita*) died on the spot.

His corpse was kept in a covered copper-vessel and it was sealed by the king.

According to his promise to be reborn as the son of a *kṣatriya* **paṇḍita* called *Viśeṣaka, a son with auspicious marks was born to the latter. His forehead was found to have the mark of vermilion and within his mouth was found the pearl. On being examined by the king and others, the deadbody was found to have no mark of vermilion on the forehead and the place where the pearl was kept was found empty. It is said that the same *tīrthika* then believed in the past and future existence.

Immediately after being born, the child bowed down before the mother and said, 'I hope you did not suffer much[26] during these ten months.' The mother thought it was ominous for a new-born baby to speak and so she said, 'Stop talking.'

He did not speak for seven years and passed for one dumb.

At that time a *tīrthika* rival composed an extremely difficult [**Fol 75B**] treatise in verse. The purport of this poetry was the refutation of the views of the Buddhists. [Copies of it] were offered to the king and scholars.

A copy reached the house of *Viśeṣaka. In spite of examining it for a long time, he could not understand even its literal meaning, not to speak of refuting it. Pondering on it, he went out of the house for some work. The seven years old *Candragomī examined the poem, understood its purport and found no difficulty in refuting it. He explained its purport in the form of a short gloss and also wrote verses in refutation of it.

As the father returned home and found this piece of writing, he asked *Candragomī's mother whether any one had come to the house.

26. V & S tr 'I hope you did not faint during these ten months.' This is perhaps because of misreading *'o-brgyal-ba* (suffer) as *brgyal-ba* (faint).

'Nobody came. This dumb boy was reading and writing.'

On being questioned by the father, the son kept dumb, looking at the mother's face.

The mother said, 'Speak out.'

Then he said, 'I wrote this' and added, 'It is not at all difficult to defeat this rival.'

The next morning, a debate was organised between *Candragomī and the *tīrthika* teacher. *Candragomī was declared victorious and he received a grand reward.

Thus by himself he acquired proficiency in grammar, logic and all other general branches of knowledge without studying these [under anybody]. His fame was spread in all directions.

He then received the *śaraṇa-gamana* and the five *śikṣā*-s from a Mahāyāna teacher and learnt by heart most of the *Sūtra*-s and the *Abhidharma-piṭaka* [**Fol 76A**] after listening to these only once from *mahā-ācārya* Sthiramati. He received instructions from a *vidyādhara ācārya* called Aśoka,[27] attained *siddhi* in magic spells and had direct vision of *ārya* Avalokiteśvara and Tārā. Thus he became a profound scholar.

He next composed[28] many treatises on medicine, prosody, fine arts[29] etc, in the land of king *Bharṣa [? Varṣa] in the east. He excelled particularly in treatises on grammar.

He next married princess *Tārā and received a province from the king.[30]

He once heard a female attendant addressing her as *Tārā and he thought that it was not proper to live [the conjugal life] with anybody bearing the same name as that of the tutelary deity. So the *ācārya* was about to leave for some other place.

The king came to know of this and said, 'If he does not live with my daughter, put him into a box and throw it into

27. *mya-ṅan-med-pa*. Tg contains a number of Tāntrika treatises attributed to Aśoka or Aśokaśrī—rG lxi.13 ; 16-22 ; lxxi.359 ; lxxxi.18.

28. For works of Candragomī, see Supplementary Note 30.

29. V architecture. The Indian equivalent seems to be *śilpa-sthāna-vidyā* —Roerich SW 506n.

30. cf Bu-ston ii.132.

the *Gaṅgā.[31] This was done as ordered by the king. The *ācārya* prayed to *bhaṭṭārikā āryā* Tārā[32] and was drifted to an island at the confluence of the *Gaṅgā on the sea.

According to some, this island was miraculously created by the *āryā* and it was called the *Candradvīpa, because *Candragomī lived there. It is said that the island still exists and is large enough to have seven thousand villages.

While residing on the island, he set up the stone images of *ārya* Avalokiteśvara and [*āryā*] Tārā. The fishermen first heard about these and gradually other people also collected there and it grew into a city.

[Fol 76B] Instructed by *ārya* Avalokiteśvara, he became a **gomī*[33] *upāsaka*. His own name was *Candra. Thus he came to be known as *Candragomī.

The merchants took him to the *Siṅ-ga-la (Siṃhala) island which was infested with *nāga-roga*[34] (leprosy). As he built the temple of *ārya* Siṃhanāda,[35] the disease was miraculously stamped out. Here also he widely spread the knowledge of the fine arts, medicine and other branches of learning. Thus he caused welfare in various forms to the simple folk of this small island. He also preached there—though partly—the Mahāyāna doctrine. With the wealth obtained from the Yakṣa ruler of the place, he built there many centres for the Doctrine.

He then returned to the south of *Jambudvīpa. In the temple of *brāhmaṇa* Vararuci, he came across the image[36] of

31. *Ib.*
32. *sgrol-ma.*
33. V & S '*gomī* or *upāsaka*'. S n 'unless *gomī* was not a special form of *upāsaka*'. But Roerich BA i.297—vows of *gomī*, 'abstaining from sexual life'.
34. *klu-nad.* In Tg a work called *Kuṣṭha-cikitsopāya* (rG lix.151) is ascribed to Candragomī.
35. Tg contains *Siṃhanāda-sādhana* (rG lxxi.24=lxviii.165) ascribed to Candragomī.
36. The text is obscure. It has the word *bkod-pa*, lit. 'form'. Hence S translates 'image' (Aufban). But V tr 'In the temple of (founded by) Vararuci, he came across the tenets of grammar heard from the Nāga and a commentary on Pāṇini composed by Śeṣa Nāga.'

[Vararuci] listening to grammar from the Nāga and the commentary on *Paṇi grammar as expounded by *Śeṣa-nāga.

[He thought] A commentary should be brief in words, profound in significance, without repetition and complete. But the naive Nāga [prepared a commentary which is] verbose, poor in purport, full of repetitions and is incomplete.

Thus criticising [the Nāga], he composed a commentary on *Paṇi.[37] It is called the *Candra-vyākaraṇa and is complete in all the sections. 'This work, though brief, is clear and complete,' —even this comment was a harsh criticism of the Nāga.

Then he went to Śrī *Nalendra, the mine of learning.

At that time, those among the *paṇḍita-s of *Nalendra who were capable of arguing with the *tīrthika*-s preached the Doctrine outside the boundary walls while those who were incapable of this preached within. Candrakīrti, who was then the *upādhyāya*, was once preaching outside [the boundary wall]. *Candragomī reached there and stood listening.

[Fol 77A] Usually those who wanted to challenge did like this [i.e. remained standing]. Others either did not listen at all or listened with reverence. So Candrakīrti thought, 'Is he an opponent calling for a debate ?' And he asked 'Where do you come from ?'

'I am coming from the south' [Candragomī] said.

On being asked, 'What subjects do you know ?' he said, 'I know the three, viz. *Paṇi grammar, the *Stuti-śata-pañcāśikā*[38] and the *Nāma-saṃgīti*.'[39]

Thus, though in words he did not express pride in so far as he said that he knew nothing beyond these three treatises, by implication he claimed that he knew all about grammar, *sūtra* and *tantra*.[40]

[Candrakīrti] thought, 'So, is this *Candragomī ?' and asked him accordingly.

37. cf Bu-ston ii.133. For grammatical works attributed to Candragomī, see Supplementary Note 30.
38. bsTod 38.
39. Tg rG lix=lx.
40. cf Bu-ston ii.132.

'Thus I am known in this world'.

'Then it is not appropriate for a great scholar to appear like a flash of lightning. He should be properly welcomed by the *saṃgha*. So, please return to the city for the time being.'

*Candragomī said, 'I am only an *upāsaka*. How can I be welcomed by the *saṃgha* ?'

Candrakīrti said, 'There is a way out. An image of *ārya* Mañjuśrī will be invited. Please come fanning the image with a *cāmara*.[41] The *saṃgha* will welcome the image of Mañjuśrī.'

When this was arranged, there came three chariots in the middle one of which was placed [the image of] *ārya* Mañjuśrī, Candrakīrti waving the *cāmara* from the right and *Candragomī from the left. The *saṃgha* welcomed from the front. Numerous people gathered to see this. The image appeared as real Mañjughoṣa to *Candragomī who offered the *stuti* : 'Oh Mañjughoṣa, though thou art eulogised by tens of millions [Fol 77B] of *tathāgata*-s of the ten directions…'

The image of Mañjuśrī turned its face sideways, as if listening to him. The people said, 'Look ! look ! what the image is doing !' So it (the image) remained fixed. Hence it was called the Ārya with the Neck Turned Left.[42] *Candragomī's reverence became most profound.

As the charioteer failed to pull back, his chariot moved before that of Candrakīrti.[43] Candrakīrti thought, 'He is highly insolent and hence I must have a debate with him.'[44]

In this [debate], following the views of Asaṅga, *Candragomī defended the doctrine of *vijñāna*. Following the *śāstra*-s of Nāgārjuna as interpreted by Buddhapālita and others, Candrakīrti defended the doctrine of nature-lessness (*svabhāva-hīnatā*). For seven years they went on arguing with each other. A large number of people was always present to listen to this

41. *rṅa-yab.*
42. cf Bu-ston ii.133.
43. V tr 'Candragomī, swept by the power of reverence, did not control the wheel and went ahead of Candrakīrti, who thought...'
44. S tr 'and he wishes to have a debate with me'. But the text has *bdag-gis-rtsod-par-bya'o*, 'I must have a debate with him'.

debate. Even the local boys and girls understood it partially and they sang :[45]

> 'Ah, the *śāstra* of *ārya* Nāgārjuna is medicine
> for some, but poison for others. The *śāstra*
> of Ajita and *ārya* Asaṅga is nectar for all.'[46]

Once, towards the end of the debate[47] [the following happened].

*Candragomī used to sit in the temple of Avalokiteśvara and to receive from him during the night answers to the arguments put forth by Candrakīrti during the day. In the (next) morning he used to offer these answers, which Candrakīrti could not refute. This went on for many months. So Candrakīrti thought : 'Somebody must be teaching him these arguments.' Thinking thus, he followed *Candragomī **[Fol 78A]** to the temple. From outside the door, he overheard the stone-image of *ārya* Avalokiteśvara teaching the Doctrine to *Candragomī, much in the manner in which an *ācārya* teaches his disciple.

'So is not the *ārya* showing partiality ?'[48]—Saying this Candrakīrti opened the door and he [Avalokiteśvara] immediately turned himself into a stone-image [again]. Its finger remained raised in the posture of teaching the Doctrine. From then on, it came to be known as 'the *ārya* with the fore-finger raised.'

And thus the debate came to its end.[49]

Being earnestly prayed to by Candrakīrti, Avalokiteśvara told him in a dream, 'You are already blessed by Mañjughoṣa

45. S tr 'started taking sides'. V tr 'partially'.
46. V tr 'Ah ! Of the works of *ārya* Nāgārjuna,
    Some are a medicine and the others poison.
    But the works of Ajita (Maitreya) and *ārya* Asaṅga
    Are only a nectar for all people.'
47. cf Bu-ston ii.134. See Roerich SW 549 for Chag lo-tsā-ba's account of the same.
48. V & S tr 'Candrakīrti opened the door to see whether the *ārya* was nearby.' But the text has *ñe-riṅ,* which should better be taken here as 'partial'—D487.
49. V n 'Because Candrakīrti considered it impossible to argue with divinity.'

and as such you are not in need of my blessings. So I have bestowed some blessings on *Candragomī.'

Such is the generally prevalent account. But the followers of the Guhyasamāja claim that on being prayed for another vision [by Candrakīrti, Avalokiteśvara] said, 'Meditate on the Guhya-samāja.' After seven days of meditation, he had the vision of the coral-red body of Avalokiteśvara at the western gate of the *maṇḍala.*

After this he [Candragomī] stayed at *Nalendra and preached[50] the Doctrine to many. He came across there an excellent verse treatise on grammar called the *Samantabhadra*[51] by Candrakīrti. He realised that his own work on grammar was not of much poetical worth. He thought that it was not going to cause welfare to the living beings and threw the work into a well. But *bhaṭṭārikā āryā* Tārā told him, 'You worked on this with the noble intention of causing welfare to the living beings. In the future it will be immensely useful for the intelligent living beings. Since Candrakīrti is proud of his scholarship, **[Fol 78B]** it [his work] will be of limited use for others. So you take out your book from the well.'

As a result of this prediction,[52] he took it out of the well. Those who drank water from this well were immediately filled with great wisdom. From then on, that [work] of *Candra remains widely prevalent until now. All the 'insiders' and 'outsiders' study it. But the *Samantabhadra* was soon lost, the existence of the book is hardly known today.

After this, he (Candragomī) composed treatises on hundred subjects like fine arts, grammar, logic, medicine, prosody, dramaturgy, dictionary, poetics, astronomy, etc.

When he was teaching all these to the pupils, *āryā* Tārā told him :

50. P-ed *bskul.* S-ed *bstan.* The latter followed.

51. In Tg *Vyākaraṇa-liṅgāvatāra* (mDo cxxiv.4) of Thon-mi-sambhoṭa, section 6 of which is the *Samantabhadra-vyākaraṇa* attributed to Candrakīrti. cf Bu-ston ii.133.

52. *luṅ-bstan.* V instruction.

> 'Better read the works like the *Daśabhūmaka*, *Candrapradīpa*, *Gaṇḍālaṃkāra*, *Laṅkāvatāra* and the *Prajñā-[pāramitā-sūtra]* of the Jinas. What is the use of your construing verses on trivial subjects.?'[53]

Thus instructed, he curtailed the teaching of secular knowledge[54] and continuously studied and preached these five wonderful *sūtra*-s. He also prepared the gists of these *sūtra*-s

It is said that in all he composed four hundred and thirty-two separate works, of which one hundred and eight were *stotra*-s, one hundred and eight treatises on esoteric knowledge, one hundred and eight treatises on secular knowledge and one hundred and eight on the fine arts. In the work called the **Pradīpa-mālā* [*Pradīpa-mālā-śāstra*] were shown all the stages of the path (*mārgakrama*) of the Bodhisattva. But this is not now much in circulation.[55]

[Fol 79A] It is said that in the Drāviḍa[56] country and in the *Siṅ-ga-la island, its teachings are still existing. All the Mahāyāna *paṇḍita*-s that came after him studied his *Saṃvara-viṃśaka* [*Bodhisattva-saṃvara-viṃśaka*[57]] and the *Kāya-traya-avatāra*.[58] The *Tārā-sādhana-śataka* and the *Avalokiteśvara-sādhana-śataka* of this *ācārya* are extant in Tibetan translations. Thus it is clear that, generally speaking, he composed a large number of treatises.

53. Given in verse. V tr 'Read (teach) Prajñāpāramitā-(sūtra-s), on ten *bhūmi*-s
And Candrapradīpa, the mother of victors,
Gaṇḍālaṃkāra and Laṅkāvatāra !
Why should you engage yourself to prosody
And useless and false composition ?'
54. V 'external sciences'.
55. *cher-ma-dar*. S tr 'But the text is no longer extant'.
56. *'gro-ldiṅ*. V & S Dramila.
57. mDo lxi.12.
58. cf Bu-ston ii.133. Tg has a number of works on Kāyatraya (by Nāgārjuna—bsTod 15 ; by Nāgamitra—mDo xxxix.1 ; by Jñānacandra—mDo xxix.2 ; an anonymous one—bsTod 16); but no such work is attributed to Candragomī.

Now, an old and poor woman had a beautiful daughter. Having no means to arrange for her marriage, she went round begging in various places. On reaching *Nalendra, she heard about the enormous wealth of Candrakīrti and went to beg of him.

[Candrakīrti said] 'Being only a *bhikṣu*, I do not possess much wealth. The little that I have is necessary for the temples and the *saṃgha*. *Candragomī lives in that house. Go there and beg.'

Thus instructed, when the old woman went to *Candragomī and begged, he had nothing but a set of robes on him and a copy of the *Ārya-aṣṭa-sāhasrikā-*[*-prajñā-pāramitā*]. There was a picture of Tārā drawn on the wall. Moved by the compassion for the pauper, he earnestly prayed to her [Tārā] with eyes full of tears. It [the picture] became real Tārā, took off all her ornaments made of various jewels—inclusive of an invaluable gem—and gave all these to the *ācārya*. He also gave all these to her.

[The old woman] was full of joy. Bereft of all the ornaments the image came to be known as Tārā without ornaments.'[59] **[Fol 79B]** The empty places caused by the removal of the ornaments were aflame.

Working thus for the welfare of the living beings, he at last resolved to go to *Potala and sailed to the island of *Dhanaśrī from *Jambudvīpa.

*Śeṣa-nāga, to avenge the harsh criticisms of the past, sent huge tidal waves in the sea and his ship was about to be wrecked. From inside the sea, came the voice : Throw out *Candragomī.[60]

When he prayed to Tārā, the company of the five—the *āryā* herself and her attendants—came flying there on the back of Garuḍa.[61] The Nāgas fled in terror. The ship safely reached *Dhanaśrī.

59. Chag lo-tsā-ba was shown the image—Roerich SW 558.

60. *phyuṅ-shig* (to expel, to throw out). V tr 'Candragomī come out.' S tr 'Candragomī will be saved.'

61. *mkha'-ldiṅ*.

In the Dhānyakaṭaka *caitya* there, he worshipped Tārā and *ārya* Avalokiteśvara and built a hundred temples for each of them. He went to the *Potala hill and is still living there without renouncing his mortal body. To his disciple, he sent a letter,—the *Śiṣya-lekha*.[62] This was sent through the merchants of *Potala to prince Ratnakīrti,[63] who was previously ordained but who eventually renounced it.[64] It is said that after receiving the *Śiṣya-lekha* he went on acting according to the Doctrine.

The period of the first half of the lives of Śrī Candrakīrti and *Candragomī is to be understood as the period of the reign of kings Siṃha and *Bharṣa [? Varṣa] and also the first half of the life of Dharmapāla. The period of the meeting of Candrakīrti and *Candragomī at *Nalendra was the period of the second half of their lives. It was also the period of *ācārya* Dharmapāla's activities for the welfare of the living beings and the period of king Pañcamasiṃha.

The twentyfourth chapter containing the account of the period of king Śīla.

62. Tg mDo xxxiii.33 *Śiṣya-lekha* addressed to Vīra Ratnakīrti, *alias* the royal prince Ratnakīrti, a disciple of Candragomī,

63. *rin-chen-grags-pa*. But Bu-ston ii.133 : 'At that time, there was (in Nālandā) a pupil, a monk of the *kṣatriya* race, who had trespassed, and had committed many sinful deeds. In order to subdue (this monk, Candragomī) wrote the *Śiṣya-lekha*.'

64. The text has *rab-tu-byuṅ-ba-babs-pa-shig*, lit. 'one who had fallen from the stage of ordination.' In the two commentaries on the *Śiṣya-lekha*, two different reasons are given for Ratnakīrti's renunciation of ordination. Vairocanamitra in the *Śiṣya-lekha-ṭippaṇa* (Tibetan Tripiṭaka, Vol 129, p. 227, last folio, line 4) says that when Ratnakīrti was being led by the minister to ascend the throne, Candragomī sent this letter to him. But Prajñākaramati in the *Śiṣya-lekha-vṛtti* (*Ib.*, Vol. 129, p. 278, first folio, line 4) gives a more romantic reason for this. According to him, Ratnakīrti renounced the vow of ordination and made love to a princess ; for the purpose of bringing him back to the vow of the ordained, Candragomī wrote this letter to him. V & S misunderstand Tār and translate—'Ratnakīrti, the time of whose ordination was near ...'

CHAPTER 25

ACCOUNT OF THE PERIOD OF THE KINGS CALA, PANCAMASIMHA AND OTHERS

After the passing away of kings *Bharṣa [? Varṣa] **[Fol 80A]** and *Siddhacandra,[1] the king called Cala[2] of *Mālava[3] in the west became very powerful. He could vie with king Śīla.[4] He reigned for about thirty years and died at the same time as king Śīla.

In the east, king Pañcamasiṃha, son of *Bharṣa [?], was extremely powerful. King *Bālacandra, son of king *Siddhacandra[5] was driven out of *Bhaṅgala and he reigned in *Tīrahuti.

King Pañcamasiṃha brought under his rule the territory upto Tibet in the north, *Triliṅga in the south, *Vārāṇasī in the west and the sea in the east.

This was the period of Paramasena's[6] disciple Vinītasena[7] [? Vinayasena], of *bhaṭṭāraka* Vimuktasena[8] of *Magadha, of Guṇaprabha's disciple Guṇamati,[9] an expert in the Abhidharma,

1. V Siṃhacandra.
2. *gyo-ba.*
3. S-ed *ma-mkhar*, P-ed Mālava. S Mātṛkoṭa. V n 'probably Mecca'.
4. S tr 'He ruled in union with Śīla'. Could this be because of reading *bdo-ba* as *bde-ba* ?
5. V Siṃhacandra.
6. *mchog-sde.* V & S Prasena, though V suggests as alternative Vīrasena. In Fol 73B, S reconstructs the same name as Varasena.
7. *dul-ba'i-sde.*
8. *grol-sde.* V Muktasena. V n 'This Muktasena (*btsun-pa-grol-sde*) or may be Mokṣasena, is clearly distinguished by the author from Vimuktasena (*rnam-grol-sde*), mentioned in the previous chapter. Besides, in Tg there is a commentary on the Abhisamaya attributed to '*phags-pa-grol-ba'i-sde* and another commentary attributed to *btsun-pa-rnam-grol-sde*.' However, in Fol 80B Tār says that he has not found any detailed account of this *bhadanta* Vimuktasena.
9. *yon-tan-blo-gros.* cf Watters ii.165 & 246—mentioned by Yuan-chuang as a contemporary of Sthiramati, cf I-Tsing (Takakusu) lviii, lix, 181.

of *ācārya* Dharmapāla, of Īśvarasena,[10] of Sarvajñamitra[11] of Kashmir and of king Praṣanna,[12] the younger son of king *Bharṣa of *Magadha. His (Prasanna's) kingdom, though small in area, was highly prosperous.

There was a king called Puṣpa[13] who conquered all the territories bordering the Vindhya mountain [14] in the south.

King Cala built temples in each of the four sides of his palace. For twelve years he used to offer to anybody that approached him from the 'four classes of followers' the excellent gift of the three, i.e. food, clothes and money. Their number reached about two lakhs[15] in all.

King Pañcamasiṃha had reverence for both 'insiders' and 'outsiders'. For the insiders, he established about twenty[16] centres for the Doctrine and built many *caitya*-s.

Now about king Prasanna.

[Fol 80B] He had reverence for all the scholars of Śrī *Nalendra like Candrakīrti[17] and *Candragomī. He donated one hundred and eight[18] golden[19] jars filled with pearls to the funds[20] of this centre for the Doctrine. He made special offerings to all the temples and *caitya*-s of *Magadha.

I have not come across any detailed account of Vinītasena and *bhaṭṭāraka*[21] Vimuktasena.[22]

It is said that in a certain temple Vinītasena built an image of Ajitanātha who told him, 'To facilitate your work

10. *dbaṅ-phyug-sde.*
11. *thams-cad-mkhyen-pa'i-bśes-gñen.* In Tg are attributed to him rG xxvi. 10-13 ; 40 ; lxxi.379.
12. *gsal-ba.*
13. *me-tog.* V & S Puṣpa, though V suggests the alternative Kusuma.
14. *ri-bo-'bigs-byed.*
15. *'bum-phrag-gñis* (two lakhs). V 'about twenty thousand'.
16. *ñi-śu* (twenty). V twentyfive.
17. V Dharmakīrti. Is it a misprint ?
18. *brgya-rtsa-brgyad.* V 'one hundred'.
19. *gser-gyi-bum-pa* (golden jar). V omits golden.
20. S-ed *thes* (benefit), P-ed *thebs* (fund).
21. *btsun-pa* (*bhaṭṭāraka*). S *ārya.*
22. V Muktasena.

for the welfare of the living beings, build also [an image] of *āryā* Tārā.'[23] Thus instructed, he invited *Candragomī and built it. Apprehensive of the *Turuṣkas, these two images were later brought to Devagiri,[24] which remained[25] there since then.[26]

Similarly it is said of *bhaṭṭāraka* Vimuktasena[27] that he propitiated Ajitanātha for ten years. Yet he had no sign of success. So he asked *ācārya* Candrakīrti what was to be done. He (Candrakīrti) advised him to perform a *homa*[28] for removing the obscurations caused by sin. After offering twelve lakhs of *homa*-s, he received the vision [of Ajitanātha] in the *kuṇḍa*.[29]

Now about *ācārya* Guṇamati.

After acquiring proficiency in all the branches of learning, he composed[30] a gloss[31] on the commentary of the *Abhidharmakoṣa* and [a commentary] on the *Madhyamaka-mūla*, in which, following Sthiramati, he refuted the views of Bhavya.

*Sampradūtaḥ, a disciple of Bhavya, was his contemporary. A debate (between the two) lasted for a long time in *Balapurī in the east and, it is said, that in this Guṇamati was victorious.

Now about *ācārya* Dharmapāla.[32]

23. S adds 'who is my companion'.
24. *lha'i-ri-bo.*
25. V 'remained (? remains)'.
26. *phyis-'byuṅ* (afterwards). V 'until recent (? present) time'. S 'till recent times'.
27. V Muktasena.
28. *sbyin-sreg.*
29. *thab.*
30. In Tg *Pratītya-samutpādādi-vibhaṅga-nirdeśa-ṭīkā* (mDo xxxvi.2) and *Vyākhyā-yukti-ṭīkā* (mDo lx) are attributed to Guṇamati. cf Watters i.324.
31. V & S 'he composed a commentary on the *Abhidharmakoṣa*'. This is perhaps because they overlook *'grel-bśad* (*ṭippaṇī*, secondary commentary) of the text.
32. *chos-skyoṅ.* cf Watters ii,109—Yuan-chuang's preceptor Śīlabhadra received ordination under Dharmapāla. Surely not the *guru* of Suvarṇadvīpa who was much later—cf A. Chattopadhyaya AT 84ff. See Supplementary Note 31.

He was born in the south in a family of bards. Already in the period when still an *upāsaka* [**Fol 81A**] he became highly renowned as a bard and acquired proficieney in most of the *śāstra*-s of the 'insiders' and 'outsiders'. He received ordination under *ācārya* Dharmadāsa and listened to the Vinaya from him. Thus he became a great scholar and came to the *madhya-deśa*.

From *ācārya* Dignāga, he listened over again to the Piṭakas along with all the auxiliary branches of study and became supreme among the scholars. He used to recite a hundred major *sūtra*-s. He went to Vajrāsana and offered many eulogies to the tutelary deities. He propitiated *bodhisattva* Ākāśagarbha[33] and received his vision as appearing on top of the *bodhi* tree. From then on, he constantly listened to the Doctrine from *ārya* Ākāśagarbha.

He preached the Doctrine at Vajrāsana for over thirty years and succeeded Śrī Candrakīrti as the *upādhyāya* of Śrī *Nalendra. In these places he could make those pupils that fell from the main path of the Bodhisattva atone for their transgressions in the presence of *ārya* Ākāśagarbha either directly or in dream. It is said that receiving wealth from the treasury of *ārya* Ākāśa, he met all the needs. Thus, for his own maintenance and the maintenance of the *saṃgha*, he used to beg from Ākāśa instead of begging from the donors. He used to silence the *tīrthika* opponents by the power of Krodhanīla-daṇḍa.[34]

He composed a commentary on the *Madhyamaka-catuḥ-śatikā*[35] from the Vijñāna-vāda standpoint. This commentary [**Fol 81B**] was composed at Vajrāsana and was clearly enough earlier than Candrakīrti's *Catuḥ-śataka-ṭīkā*.[36]

33. *nam-mkha'i-sñiṅ-po.*

34. *khro-bo-dbyug-pa-sṅon-po.*

35. Such a commentary by the earlier Dharmapāla is not traced in Tg, though in Tg *madhyamaka* commentaries are attributed to the later Dharmapāla of Suvarṇadvīpa, the *guru* of Atīśa.

36. *Bodhisattva-yoga caryā-catuḥ-śataka-ṭīkā* mDo xxiv.2.

It is said that he (Dharmapāla) went to the Suvarṇadvīpa in the east towards the end of his life.[37] He attained proficiency in alchemy and at last departed for the abode of the gods. He was the *upādhyāya* of *Nalendra for only a brief period. After him Jayadeva[38] became the *upādhyāya*. His [Jayadeva's] disciples were Śāntideva[39] and *Virū-pā.

Now, about the account of the latter (Virū-pā).[40]

While studying in the monastery of *Nalendra, he once went to *Devīkoṭa.[41] A woman gave him an **utpala* flower and a cowrie.[42] As he accepted these, people took pity on him and said, 'Ah ! Poor fellow ! He is marked by the *ḍākinī*-s.'[43] When he asked them the cause for this, they said, 'Throw these away.' He tried to throw these off, but these remained stuck to his hands and he could not get rid of these.

Then he met an 'insider' *ḍākinī* and said, 'Please save me.' She said, 'Whoever among us—be she an insider or an outsider—first offers the flower, acquires the right.'

'Is there then no way out ?'

'You will be saved if you can move beyond five *yojana*-s (today)'.

Thus told, he moved on till the evening but could not reach it. He went to an inn, crept under an upturned earthen cauldron and meditated on the void. During the night the *ḍākinī*-s called everybody there. Failing to find the person marked, they searched for him again and again. They could

37. See Supplementary Note 32.
38. *rgyal-ba'i-lha* See note 6 of ch 24.
39. *shi-ba-lha.*
40. BA refers to him as the preceptor of Dombi Heruka (i.206) and as receiving initiation from Lakṣmīṅkarā, sister of Indrabhūti (i.390). The great Avadhūti-pā or Paiṇḍapātika received initiation from Virū-pā (i.390) and another disciple of Virū-pā was *ḍākinī* Sukha-siddhā (ii.731). In Tg Virū-pā is also mentioned as Bi-ru-byed-pa or Birba-pā. For his works, see Supplementary Note 32.
41. *lha-mo-mkhar* in Tibetan. Tg (rG vi.3) refers to the place as situated in eastern India. cf D. C. Sircar CGEIL 104.
42. *'gron-bu.*
43. *mkha'-'gro-ma.*

not find out Virū-pā and so they dispersed at the break of day.

Escaping from that place, he went back to *Nalendra and became a **paṇḍita*. [**Fol 82A**] He then thought, 'Now is the time to subdue the witches.'

So he went to the Śrī Parvata[44] in the south. He received (the spell of) Yamāri from *ācārya* Nāgabodhi[45] and meditated on it. Thus he received the vision [of the deity]. It is said that after further prolonged meditation, he became as (powerful) as Śrī Mahākrodha.[46]

From there he went to *Devīkoṭa again. The same 'outsider' *ḍākinī*-s said, 'The person marked by us long ago has come.' They came in the night in fearful forms and wanted to gobble him up. He then drew up the Yamāri-maṇḍala and the *ḍākinī*-s fell unconscious and were about to die. Keeping them bound under the oath (? of doing no more harm), he returned again to *Nalendra. From then on, he took up *caryā*. His remaining account is to be found elsewhere.

Now about Śāntideva.

He was born as a son of a king in *Saurāṣṭra.[47] Because of his past merit he had in his dream the vision of Mañjuśrī from his early age. On growing up, when he was about to ascend the throne, he saw in a dream the throne already occupied by Mañjuśrī, who said, 'Oh son ! This seat is mine, I am your *kalyāṇamitra*. It will be highly improper for you to sit on the same throne with me.'[48]

In the dream he (also) saw *ārya* Tārā, in the guise of his own mother, pouring hot water on his head. When he asked the cause of this, she said, 'Kingdom is nothing but the unbearable boiling water of hell. I am consecrating you with this.'

So he realised that it was not proper for him to accept the

44. *dpal-gyi-ri.*
45. *klu'i-byaṅ-chub.*
46. *dpal-khro-bo-chen-po.*
47. cf Bu-ston ii.161f,
48. *Ib.*

kingdom. In the night just before the day of his coronation [**Fol 82B**] he ran away.

After walking for twentyone days, he reached a spring on the fringe of a forest. As he was about to drink the water, a woman appeared and asked him not to drink that water, and offered sweeter water instead. She led him to a Yogī living in the cave of a forest. He received *samyak-upadeśa* from him, attained *samādhi* and incomparable knowledge through meditation.

The Yogī was none but Mañjuśrī and this woman none but Tārā. Since then he had always the vision of Mañjuśrī.

From there he went towards the east[49] and lived among the attendants of king Pañcamasiṃha. As he was skilled in all arts and was extremely intelligent, he was requested to become a minister. He accepted the post for the time being.

As a mark of the *āyudha*[50] of his tutelary deity, he used to keep a wooden sword constantly hanging by his side. He spread there the fine arts[51] that were not known before. He also helped (the king) to rule the kingdom according to the Doctrine.

This made the other ministers jealous, who reported to the king that this man was a cheat. Even his sword was made of nothing but wood.[52]

So all the ministers had to show their swords to the king. The *ācārya* told the king, 'Oh Lord ! If I draw it out, it will do you harm.' Thus told, the king became all the more suspicious and said, 'Let it harm. Nevertheless, show it to me.'

'In that case, please shut up your right eye and have a look at it with the left.'

Thus shown, the left eye of the king was destroyed by the lustre of the sword. From then on he was known as a *siddha*.

49. *śar-phyogs* (east). V south. Is it a misprint ?
50. *phyag-mtshan*. S symbol.
51. *bzo'i-gnas*.
52. S-ed *ral-gri-yaṅ-śiṅ-las-med-do*. P-ed *ral...las-mad-do*. (*med*=not ; *mad*=truly). The latter reading followed. V & S 'and his sword was not made of wood'. cf Bu-ston ii.164.

With great wealth and honour he (the king) tried to persuade him to stay on. He told the king, 'Look after the kingdom according to the Doctrine and establish twenty centres for the insiders.'

[Fol 83A] Instructing him thus, he went to the *madhya-deśa*, received ordination under *upādhyāya* Jayadeva and had the name Śāntideva. He lived there in the company of the **paṇḍita*-s and used to eat five *mahā-droṇa*-s[53] of rice at each meal, though inwardly he was always meditating and listening to the Doctrine from *ārya* Mañjuśrī.

He composed[54] the magnificent works called the *Śikṣā-samuccaya* and *Sūtra-samuccaya*, studying the Doctrine in its entirety. Outwardly he appeared to sleep day and night[55] and to do nothing of the three—i.e. listening (*śravaṇa*), cogitating (*manana*) and meditating (*dhyāna*).

[The other *paṇḍita*-s] discussed among themselves and decided to drive him away, as he was causing drainage to the materials reverentially donated to the *saṃgha* : 'If we recite the *sūtra*-s by turn, he will have to go away of himself.'

When this was arranged and it was Śāntideva's turn to recite the *sūtra*, he at first did not agree to do so. On being repeatedly pressed, he said, 'So you prepare a seat for me and I shall recite.'

This made some of them doubtful, but most of them assembled with the idea of humiliating him. The *ācārya* sat on the *siṃhāsana*[56] and asked, 'Should I recite the existing ones or something new ?'

53. *bre-bo-che.*
54. For works attributed to Śāntideva, see Supplementary Note 33.
55. cf Bu-ston ii.162. Obermiller's note : '*bhusuku*=*bhuj* (eat), *sup* (sleep) and ?' But H. P. Sastri (*Prācīn Bāṅglār Gaurava* 30) suggests the following etymology of *bhu-su-ku* :

*bhu*ñjāno'pi prabhāsvaraḥ
*su*pto'pi prabhāsvaraḥ
*ku*ṭīṃ gato'pi prabhāsvaraḥ.

56. cf Watters i.347 'The Lion's Throne of the Buddhists was originally

For sizing him up, everybody said, 'Recite something new.' Then he started reciting the *Bodhisattva-caryā-avatāra.* During the recital, he came to the verse : 'When existence and non-existence cease to be present before the intellect..'[57] While uttering these he rose up in the sky. His body was no longer visible, but his voice continued [to be heard uninterruptedly]. Thus he completed the recitation of the *Caryāvatāra.*

The *śrutidhara* **paṇḍita*-s **[Fol 83B]** retained this in their memory.[58]

According to the Kashmirians, this work contained more than a thousand **śloka*-s and the benedictory verse was added by them [i.e. the *śrutidhara paṇḍita*-s]. According to the Easterners, the work did not contain more than seven hundred **śloka*-s and the benedictory verse was taken from the *Mūla-madhyamaka.* Further, it did not originally contain the chapters on Pratividhāna and Prajñā. According to the [scholars of the] *madhya-deśa*, it did not contain the benedictory verse and the verse stating the resolution ; and the **śloka*-s of the Sanskrit original, when actually counted, give the total of one thousand.

All these create confusion.

According to the ancient Tibetan account [after disappearing into the air, Śāntideva] lived in Śrī Dakṣiṇa.[59] However, on hearing that he was living in the city of *Kaliṅga in *Triliṅga, three **paṇḍita*-s went there and requested him to return to *Nalendra. But he did not agree.

'But then, how are we to learn the *Śikṣā-samuccaya* and

the seat reserved for the Buddha, as leader of the congregation, in the chapels and halls of the monasteries ; and afterwards, it became the throne or seat of the chief *bhikṣu* of a place'.

57 *yadā na bhāvo nābhāvo mateḥ saṃtiṣṭhate puraḥ |*
tadānyagatyabhāvena nirālamvā praśāmyati ||
—verse 35 of ch ix. (Bib. Ind. Series, p. 194).

58. cf Bu-ston ii.162ff.

59. *dpal-yon-can.* cf Bu-ston ii,163 'near the sanctuary of Śrī Dakṣiṇa'. S Dakṣi-nagara.

the *Sūtra-samuccaya* ? Again, where are the three works ?'[60]

On being thus prayed he said, 'The *Śikṣā* and *Sūtra* written in fine **paṇḍita* script on birch bark are to be found in the window-sill of my cell. The *Caryāvatāra* is to be accepted as retained in the memory of the scholars of the *madhya*[*-deśa*].'

There was a monastery in the forest and he lived there with five hundred monks. This forest was full of deer, etc. With his magic power, he used to devour the flesh of the animals that entered his cell. Other monks noticed the animals entering the cell of the *ācārya* but did not see these coming out of it. It was also noticed that the animals were getting reduced in number. Through the window some of them saw him **[Fol 84A]** eating the flesh of these. When the members of the *saṃgha* started accusing him, the animals came back to life; these emerged from the cell stronger than before and went away. Then he left the place in spite of being entreated by them to stay on.

He renounced the marks of *pravrajyā* and followed the *Ucchuṣma *caryā*.[61]

Now, somewhere in the south there was a conflict between the 'insiders' and 'outsiders'. When the insiders failed in the contest of [miraculous] power, the *ācārya* reached the place. It was found that the slop thrown at him started boiling as soon as it touched his body.[62] So they knew that he possessed miraculous power. On being requested to enter the contest of [miraculous] power with the *tīrthika*-s, he agreed to this.

The *tīrthika*-s [63] drew an enormous *maṇḍala* in the sky with coloured stone dust. He immediately caused a strong blast of wind which threw the *tīrthika*-s along with their *maṇḍala*

60. V tr 'But, then, what sort of works are the *Śikṣā-samuccaya* and *Sūtra-samuccaya*, which, it is said, have been seen ? Which of the three copies (of *Caryāvatāra*) is purer (i.e. more faithful) ?'
61. cf Bu-ston ii.165. Tg contains a number of works on Ucchuṣma-sādhana (rG xliii.161 ; lxx.129 ; 309 ; lxxii.38 ; 39 [41] ; 47 .
62. cf Bu-ston ii.165.
63. Bu-ston ii.165 mentions instead a heretical teacher called Śaṃkara-deva, who drew the magic circle of Maheśvara in the sky.

beyond a place where there was a river. The wind was about to blow off also those that favoured the *tīrthika*-s, but it did no harm at all to the king and others who were in favour of the 'insiders'.

This defeat of the *tīrthika*-s helped the Doctrine to spread and the place became famous as that of 'the victory over the *tīrthika*-s'[64]

This account is highly reliable, because it is mentioned in all the basic sources. By the influence of time, however, the name of the place is changed. So it cannot be identified now.

Further, according to the Tibetan account, when five hundred *pāṣaṇḍika*-s[65] were cut off from their livelihood, he gave them food and drink obtained by his miraculous power **[Fol 84B]** and thus led them to the Doctrine, He also did the same for a thousand beggars. It is said that he once went to a battle-field and stopped the war with his miraculous power.

Thus his seven wonderful acts were : having the vision of the tutelary deity, bringing prosperity to *Nalendra, silencing [others] in debate, converting the *pāṣaṇḍika*-s, the beggars, the king and the *tīrthika*-s.

Now about Sarvajñamitra.[66]

He was an extra[67] (? marital) son of a king of Kashmir. When he was a baby, his mother left him on the terrace and went to pluck flowers. The baby was picked up by a vulture and put on the roof of a **gaṇḍola* of Śrī *Nalendra in the *madhya-deśa*. He was reared up by the **paṇḍita*-s and, on growing up, became a sharply intelligent monk well-versed in the *piṭaka*-s. He propitiated *bhaṭṭārikā āryā* Tārā and received her vision along with enormous wealth. He distributed all these and was eventually left with nothing more to donate. He thought : 'If I stay here, many persons asking for alms will

64. S Jita-tīrtha. Obermiller Bu-ston ii.165 : 'the spot where the heretics were vanquished.'
65. cf Bu-ston ii.164.
66. See note 11 of this chapter.
67. *zur-bu*.

have to return with empty hands.'[68] So he went far into the south.

On the way he came across an old and blind *brāhmaṇa* being led by the son and he asked him, 'Where are you going ?'

The *brāhmaṇa* said, 'I have heard about one called Sarvajñamitra of *Nalendra who satisfies all the beggars. So I am going to him and beg.'

'That person is none but myself. But I have come here, because all my wealth is exhausted.'

Hearing this, he (the *brāhmaṇa*) was afflicted with great sorrow. (Sarvajñamitra) felt boundless compassion for him.

[Fol 85A] There was a king called *Saraṇa [?] passionately attached to the false views. Being a follower of the vicious *ācarya*-s he wanted to purchase one hundred and eight men for offering them to sacrificial fire so that he could thereby suck all their longevity and power and thus attain liberation. He procured one hundred and seven persons and was searching for the remaining one.

Hearing this the *ācarya* decided to sell himself in order to help the *brāhmaṇa* and told him, 'Do not feel sad. I shall bring wealth for you.'

He went to the city and asked, 'Anybody here to purchase a man ?' So the king purchased him and gave him gold equal in weight to that of the *ācarya's* own body. The *ācarya* gave the gold to the *brāhmaṇa*, who felt happy and went away.

When the *ācarya* entered the royal prison, the others there said, 'We could have perhaps been saved but for your coming. We are now going to be burned soon.' Thus they were afflicted with grief.

In the night a heap of wood—as huge as a hill—was piled up in a wide field and these hundred and eight persons were kept bound within it. The *ācarya*-s with false views performed the ritual. When fire was set to the pile of woods the hundred and seven persons started wailing. This filled the *ācarya* with boundless compassion and he earnestly prayed to *āryā* Tārā. The *bhaṭṭārikā* appeared before them and a stream of nectar

68. *rkaṅ-stoṅ*, lit. 'empty feet'.

flowed from her hand. People saw nothing elsewhere excepting rains coming down in the shape of a yoke only on the burning woods. The fire was extinguished and the place became a lake.

[Fol 85B] The king felt amazed and worshipped the *ācārya* with reverence. He released the persons with rewards. In spite of receiving great reverence from the king, he could not convert him (the king) to the right view and the true Doctrine was not spread.

Thus a long time was spent. The *ācārya* felt disheartened and prayed to *bhaṭṭārikā āryā* Tārā : 'Please send me back to my birth-place.'

She said, 'Catch hold of the corner of my clothes and shut your eyes.' Immediately after he closed his eyes, she said, 'Open your eyes.' On opening his eyes, he saw that he had reached a beautiful land decorated[69] with a magnificent palace, which he had never seen before.

He asked, 'Why did you bring me here instead of taking me to *Nalendra ?'

'This is your birth-place.'

He stayed there and built a big temple for Tārā. He preached the Doctrine extensively and led the people to bliss.

He was a disciple of Sūryagupta.[70] The *mahā-siddha* *Dombi-heruka[71] and *mahā-siddha* Vajraghaṇṭa[72] roughly belonged to his period. Though they were contemporaries, some of them were a little earlier, some a little later.

*Dombi-heruka attained *siddhi* about ten years after that of *Virū-pā. About ten years later Ghaṇṭa attained *siddhi.*

*Sukhadeva,[73] son of a leading merchant and a disciple of *ācārya* *Candragomī, belonged to this period. During his own

69. *brgyan-pa.* The word does not occur in S-ed and hence S tr does not contain 'decorated with'.

70. V Ravigupta.

71. For works of Dombi Heruka, see Supplementary Note 34.

72. *rdo-rje-dril-bu.* BA ii.754 mentions him as an early authority on Kālacakra. For works of Vajraghaṇṭa, see Supplementary Note 35.

73. Tg contains a work (author not mentioned) with the title *Śreṣṭhi-putra-sukhadeva-siddhi-lābha-ākhyāna* (mDo cxxiii.42).

business transaction, he purchased from a *tīrthika* a damaged image of the Buddha made of *gośīrṣa-candana*.[74] Princess *Saṅkajati[75] was once seriously ill and the physicians said that *gośīrṣa-candana* was the only remedy for it. Since, however, that was not available, they gave up [the hope of curing her].

The merchant asked the king, 'If I can cure her **[Fol 86A]** will you give her to me [in marriage] ?' The king promised to do so. He then prepared a paste of the *gośīrṣa-candana*, anointed her body with it and also made her swallow it. This cured her and she was given to *Sukhadeva.

He (Sukhadeva) thought, 'It is good that the disease is cured. But it is difficult to atone for the sin [of thus using the Buddha image].' So he asked *ācārya* *Candragomī about the way of atoning for the sin. He (Candragomī) gave him the *upadeśa* of Avalokiteśvara and led him to propitiate him. *Sukhadeva, son of the leading merchant, along with his wife attained *siddhi* after receiving the vision of the *ārya*.

The twentyfifth chapter containing the account of the period of kings Cala, Pañcamasiṃha and others.

74. *tsana-dana-sa-mchog*. D 1257 *hari-candana*. V & S *go-śīrṣa-candana*. cf Legge 38n 'Gośīrṣa Candana or sandal-wood from Cow's Head mountain, a species of copper-brown sandal-wood, said to be produced most abundantly on a mountain of (the fabulous continent) Ullarakuru, north of mount Meru, which resembles in shape the head of a cow'.

75. S Śaṅkhajāti.

CHAPTER 26

ACCOUNT OF THE PERIOD OF ŚRĪ DHARMAKĪRTI

After the death of king Cala, his younger brother Caladhruva[1] reigned for twenty years. He conquered most of the western regions. His son *Viṣṇurāja also reigned for many years.

When he (Viṣṇurāja) was residing in *Pālanagara[2] situated in *Hala in the west, five hundred ascetic *brāhmaṇa*-s like the great sages of the past lived in a hermitage. The king killed the birds and deer of the hermitage and diverting the course of the river destroyed the abodes of the *ṛṣi*-s. By their curse, water gushed out from beneath his palace which drowned (? the palace).

The king then ruling over the *madhya-deśa* and most of the eastern region was Pradyota,[3] son of king Prasanna. His son was *Mahāśyani (Mahāsena[4]). In the north ruled king Pradyota's brother *Śākya-mahābala[5], who lived in the city of *Haridvāra but whose command extended up to Kashmir.

*Vimalacandra, son of king *Bālacandra[6], ruled *Bhaṃgala, *Kāmarūpa [**Fol 86B**] and *Tirahuti—these three regions.

Among these kings, Caladhruva and *Viṣṇurāja looked after the kingdom peacefully and reigned in accordance with the Doctrine. Beyond this nothing more is known about their activities for the Law. The others extensively worshipped the Law.

Pradyota and *Mahāśyani (Mahāsena) had special reverence for Śrī Dharmakīrti.[7] King *Śākya-mahābala worshipped

1. *gyo-ba-brtan-pa.*
2. S-ed Bālanagara, P-ed Pālanagara. V & S Bālanagara.
3. *gsal-ba.* V & S Prāditya,
4. In the Table of Contents the Tibetan form of the name occurs as *sde-chen*, i.e. Mahāsena.
5. V & S Mahā-śākyabala.
6. S-ed B[illegible]lacandra, P-ed Śālaca Table of Contents—Bālacandra.
7. *chos-kyi-grags-pa.*

Vasumitra,[8] the great exponent of the Abhidharma. King *Vimalacandra worshipped *paṇḍita *Amarasiṃha[9] and Ratnakīrti[10] as well as the Mādhyamika Śrīgupta,[11] a disciple of *Sampradūta.

Generally speaking, though during this period the Law of the Buddha was widely spread, yet compared to the time of 'brothers Asaṅga' [i.e. Asaṅga and his brother] and of Dignāga, in all the eastern and southern regions the tīrthika-s prospered and the Buddhists were going down.

Now, during the time of king Pañcamasiṃha, there lived two brothers[12] who were the ācārya-s of the tīrthika-s. One of them was called *Datta-trai (Dattātreya). He was specially in favour of *samādhi*. The second was *Saṅgarācārya[13] (Śaṃkarācārya), who propitiated *Mahādeva. He chanted spells on a jar placed behind a curtain.[14] From within the jar emerged *Mahādeva up to his neck and taught him the art of debate.

In *Bhaṃgala he entered into debates. The elders among the *bhikṣu*-s said, 'It is difficult to defeat him. So *ācārya* Dharmapāla[15] or *Candragomī or Candrakīrti should be invited to contest in debate.' The younger *paṇḍita-s did not listen to this and said, 'The prestige of the local *paṇḍita-s will go down if a debater is brought from somewhere else. **[Fol 87A]** We are more skilled than they are.'

Inflated with vanity, they entered into debate with *Śaṃkarācārya. In this the Buddhists were defeated and, as

8. *dbyig-gi-bśes-gñen.*
9. Apart from the *Amarakoṣa* (mDo cxvii.1), Tg contains *Amarasiṃha-gītikā* (rG xlviii.12).
10. *rin-chen-grags.* For works of Ratnakīrti, see Supplementary Note 36.
11. *dpal-sbas.* Tg contains *Tattvāvatāra-vṛtti* (mDo xxix.3) and *Śrī-ratna-mañjarī-nāma-ṭīkā* (rG xx.17) attributed to Śrīgupta.
12. S-ed does not contain *spun* (brothers).
13. Tār throughout gives the corrupt form Saṅgarācārya.
14. V tr 'covered with a lid'.
15. V Dharmapālita.

a result, everything belonging to the twentyfive centres of the Doctrine was lost to the *tīrthika*-s and the centres were deserted. About five hundred *upāsaka*-s had to enter the path of the *tīrthika*-s.

Similarly, in *Oḍiviśa also *Śaṃkarācārya's *brāhmaṇa* disciple *Bhaṭṭa Ācārya did the same. The daughter of Brahmā (Sarasvatī) made him an expert in logic. Many debates between the insiders and outsiders took place there.

There lived then an insider **paṇḍita* called *Kuliśaśreṣṭha, highly skilled in grammar and logic. As before, he also arrogantly entered the debate by staking the [respective] creeds. The *tīrihika* became victorious and destroyed many temples of the insiders. They robbed in particular the centres for the Doctrine and took away the *deva-dāsa*-s (*vihāra*-slaves). During this latter incident, Dharmapāla and the Candra *bhaṭṭāraka*-s (Candrakīrti and Candragomī) were no longer alive.

In the south, there were then two leading *tīrthika* debaters, the famous *brāhmaṇa* **Kumāralīla[16] and **Kaṇadaroru.[17] The latter was a follower of Mahādeva and an observer of the *go-vrata*.[18] In many debates in the south they defeated the disciples of Buddhapālita, Bhavya, Dharmadāsa, Dignāga[19] and others. Also, none belonging to the Śrāvaka *saṃgha* could face them in debate. As a result, there were many incidents of the property and followers[20] of the insiders being robbed by the *tīrthika brāhmaṇa*-s.

[Fol 87B] These incidents belonged to a period little later than the one we have been discussing. During this period, *Devaśrama,[21] a disciple of *ācārya* Dharmapāla, composed

16. V Kumārila. Tār throughout gives the name as *gshon-nu-rol-pa*, lit. 'the sporting *kumāra*' and argues that the correct Indian form should be Kumāralīla and not Kumārila.
17. *gzegs-ma-sgra-sgrog*. Kaṇanāda ?
18. *ba-lan-gi-brtul*.
19. V omits Dignāga, but the text has *phyogs-kyi-glan-po*.
20. *mna'-'bans*. S slaves.
21. Could it be a corruption of Devaśarman or Devaśarmā, one of the eight famous Mādhyamika authors and commentators mentioned in the colophon of mDo xvii.6 ?

the Maohyamaka commentary called the Bright White[22] with the idea of refuting Candrakīrti. This *ācārya* was victorious in debate with some of the *tīrthika*-s in the south. He converted king *Sālavāhana into a follower of the Law of the Buddha. He also built many *caitya*-s and temples and established a centre for the Doctrine.

Siddha *Gorakṣa[23] belonged to the period of this king.

I have not come across any detailed account of *ācārya* *Amarasiṃha. Whatever little exists about it, is to be found elsewhere.

It is said that Ratnakīrti composed a commentary on the *Madhyamaka-avatāra*.[24] Vasumitra also composed a commentary on the *Abhidharmakoṣa*.[25] He was the author of the work called *Samaya-bheda-uparacana-cakra*,[26] the main treatise on the eighteen sects.

Before the time of *mahā-ācārya* Vasubandhu,[27] all the eighteen sects were in tact. At the time of the early hostility

22. *dkar-po-rnam-par-'char-ba.* V & S *Sitābhyudaya.* But no work with this title is traced in Tg.
23. In Tg *Vāyutattva-bhāvanopadeśa* (rG xlviii 51) is attributed to him. V n 'According to the account of the 84 *siddha*-s, Gorakṣa or Anaṅgavajra was the son of king *sa-skyoṅ* ('the protector of the land', Gopāla ?) in eastern India. As a punishment, his hands and feet were chopped off. But after attaining *siddhi*, he got these back. Even now, the sound of his *ḍamaru* is sometimes heard.'
24. No such work is traced in Tg.
25. V n 'This work, too, is not there in Tg. But whatever is preserved in Chinese translation cannot belong to the present Vasumitra, because it is regarded as one of the seven principal Abhidharmas.'
26. mDo xc.11. cf BA i.30. V n '*Samaya-bhedoparacana-cakra* is the same as translated by me in the first volume of my work on Buddhism. But if the period under discussion, as we assume, is close to that of Yuan-chuang, who translated this work into Chinese, how could it be possible that in the Chinese language there are two still earlier translations (of the same commentary on *Abhidharmakoṣa*) ? It can, therefore, be considered that the author is making a mistake in taking the composer of the commentary on the *Abhidharmakoṣa* for the same person as Vasumitra who wrote about the sects—more so because we find one Vasumitra belonging to a much earlier period.'
27. *dbyig-gñen.*

to the Law, some of the sects were weakened and impoverished. After that, because of controversies among them and because of misfortune and other reasons, the three sects of the Mahāsāṅghikas called the Pūrvaśaila, Aparaśaila and the Haimavat became extinct. The two sects of the Sarvāstivādins, namely the Kāśyapīyas and the Vibhajyavādins became extinct. The three sects of the Sthaviravādins, namely the Mahāvihāravāsins, Sammitīyas and the Āvantakas became extinct. Only the remaining sects thrived.

[Fol 88A] The practice of the Śrāvaka Law was indeed to degenerate (? according to prediction) after five hundred years. But there are still many who uphold the theoretical views of the Śrāvakas.

According to some of the historians of the Doctrine, the downfall of the Śrāvakas took place shortly after the propagation of the Mahāyāna. Though with the establishment of the Mahāyāna the influence of the Śrāvakas gradually decreased, it will be fanciful to think that during this period their number became insignificant. It is strange for one to write something for showing off knowledge to others without oneself possessing even little knowledge of the subject.

Now about Śrī Dharmakīrti.[28]

According to all the earlier scholars, he was born in the kingdom of Cūḍāmaṇi[29] in the south. But no place with such a name is to be found these days. All the insiders and outsiders know well that the birth-place of Śrī Dharmakīrti was *Trimalaya. Therefore, this place must have been known as the kingdom of Cūḍāmaṇi in the older days.

It is clear that he was born shortly after king Pañcamasiṃha and king Prasanna[30] and others ascended the throne. His father was a *brāhmaṇa tīrthika parivrājaka* called

28. For works of Dharmakīrti, see Supplementary Note 37.
29. *rgyal-dbaṅ-gtsug-gi-nor-bu*. Lit. Jinendra-cūḍāmaṇi. Bu-ston ii.152: "the southern kingdom of Cūḍāmaṇi."
30. *gsal-ba*. V & S Prāditya. But S takes *gsal-ba* in the Table of Contents as Prasanna.

*Ro-ru-nanda.[31] Thus was he born as his son.

Having a very sharp intellect, he thoroughly studied from his early childhood the fine arts, the Vedas with all their *aṅga*-s, medicine, grammar and all the *tīrthika* philosophies. Already at the age of sixteen or eighteen, he became a mature scholar of all the *tīrthika* philosophies. When he was being highly praised by the *brāhmaṇa*-s, **[Fol 88B]** he studied some Buddhist scriptures and realised that his own preceptor was full of faults and his own *śāstra*-s were repulsive. Finding the Buddha and the True Doctrine as opposed to these, he was full of reverence. He changed his dress into that of an *upāsaka* of the insiders.

On being asked by *brāhmaṇa*-s the reason for this, he praised the Buddha. So he was driven out of his place. From there he went to the *madhya-deśa*, received ordination under *ācārya* Dharmapāla[32] and became a scholar of all the three *piṭaka*-s. He learnt by heart the *sūtra*-s and *dhāraṇī*-s, five hundred in all.

He remained dissatisfied even after studying many works on logic. He listened to the *Pramāṇa-samuccaya* from Īśvara-sena,[33] a disciple of Dignāga, and after listening to it only once, became equal to Īśvarasena. On listening to it for the second time, he became equal to Dignāga. On listening to it for the third time, he realised that even Īśvarasena was wrong and could not fully understand the real implications of Dignāga. Realising this, he enumerated all these [i.e. the short-comings in Īśvarasena's understanding] to the *ācārya* himself (Īśvarasena). He (Īśvarasena) was delighted and said, 'You have become equal to Dignāga. Compose a commentary on the *Pramāṇa-samuccaya*, pointing out all the erroneous views.'

Thus he received the *ācārya*'s permission. After this, he received proper *abhiṣeka* also from the *mantra-vajrācārya*-s. Propitiating the tutelary deity, he had the vision of Heruka.

31. S-ed Ro-ru-nanda. P-ed Ro-ñan-ndra. The former followed.

32 *chos-skyoṅ*. Bu-ston ii.152 does not mention the name of the *ācārya* under whom he was ordained.

33. *dbaṅ-phyug-sde*. For a more elaborate account, see Bu-ston ii.152.

[Heruka] asked, 'What do you desire ?'

'I desire to have an all-round victory.'

[**Fol 89A**] Heruka said, '**Hā*, **hā*, **hum*' and vanished. He then composed the eulogy called the *Stava-daṇḍaka.*[34]

According to some, the *vajrācārya* of this *ācārya* was *Dārika. According to others, he was Vajraghaṇṭa. But the proper view seems to be of those who say that he was *Diṅgi,[35] that there exists a composition called the *Śrī-cakra-saṃvara-sādhana*[36] by this *ācārya* and that the *Vajrasattva-sādhana*, which is generally believed to have been composed by *Lū-yi-pā was also a composition of this *ācārya.*[37]

He then wanted to learn the secret teachings of the *tīrthika* systems. In the disguise of a servant, he went to the south, enquired about the scholar of the *tīrthika* systems. [He was told about] the *brāhmaṇa* Kumāralīla,[38] who, as a scholar of all the systems, was without any rival.

gShon-nu-ma-len (i.e Kumārila) is either a wrong rendering into Tibetan of the name *Kumāralīla or the translation of a wrong spelling of his name.

He is also said[39] to have been a maternal uncle of Dharma-kīrti. But nothing like this is known in India. Further, the story of tying a chord on the second toe of the wife of the *brāhmaṇa* while stealing the secret teachings of the systems is not known in India. Though it may appear as true, it is actually far from it.

Kumāralīla received from the king great power and he possessed excellent fields of **śālu* (*śāli*) rice, a large number of

34. Tg contains *Śrī-vajraḍākasya-stava-daṇḍaka-nāma* (rG xii.23) attributed to Dharmakīrti.
35. V & S Tiṅgi.
36. See note 14 of ch. 23.
37. Tg contains a number of works on Vajrasattva-sādhana by Lūi-pā (rG xiii.1), Kukkurī-pā (rG xxiii.22), *ācārya* Candrakīrti (rG xxxiii 18), *guru* Abhijña Vajrāsana (rG xlviii.147), *ācārya* Padma (rG lxxi.342) and *ācārya* Harisiṃha (rG lxxxvi.29).
38. *gshon-nu-rol-pa.*
39. Tār seems to reject here the account given by Bu-ston ii.153.

cows and buffaloes, five hundred each of male and female servants and a large number of hired persons. This *ācārya* (Dharmakīrti) did everything there, both indoor and outdoor, and by himself performed the work of fifty male and fifty female servants.

[Fol 89B] Kumāralīla, along with his wife, was highly pleased with him.

'What do you desire ?'

'I desire to listen to philosophy.'

Thus he began to listen to everything that Kumāralīla preached to his disciples. But some of the secret teachings were not taught to anybody other than the son and the wife. He learnt these by pleasing the son and the wife with his efficient services to them. Thus he learnt all the secrets of philosophy. When there was nothing more for him to learn about the technique of refuting others, he even found out from the other disciples the appropriate fees for the lessons. He also calculated the amount needed as the fee for learning a new argument.

He thought that since the *brāhmaṇa*-s were greedy, it was improper for him not to offer any fee. He had with him five hundred silver **paṇa*-s, which he had received as the salary for his services. He took seven thousand golden coins from a local *yakṣa*. He offered the gold to Kumāralīla and with the silver gave a grand feast to the *brāhmaṇa*-s. The same night he ran away.

There was a palace in a big commercial centre called *Kākaguhā. A king called *Drumaripu lived there. He (Dharmakīrti) put up a notice on its gate : 'Does anybody want a debate ?'

The *brāhmaṇa* *Kaṇagupta,[40] a follower of Kaṇāda's view, and five hundred experts in the six systems of philosophy assembled there and argued with him for three months. He defeated all the five hundred of them one by one and converted them into the followers of the Buddha's Law. He led the king to

40. Both S-ed & P-ed Kaṇagupta. V & S Kaṇādagupta.

order fifty wealthy *brāhmaṇa*-s among them to establish each a centre for the Doctrine of the insiders.

[Fol 90A] As he came to know this, Kumāralīla felt furious and himself came to argue accompanied by five hundred *brāhmaṇa*-s. He demanded of the king, 'Should I be victorious, Dharmakīrti is to be killed. If Dharmakīrti be victorious, I should be killed.'

But the *ācārya* said, 'In case of Kumāralīla's victory, the king should himself decide whether to convert me into a *tīrthika* or to kill me or to beat me or to bind me. But in case I win, he should not kill Kumāralīla. Instead of that he [i.e. Kumārila] should be converted into a follower of the Law of the Buddha.'

Thus he staked the Law and the debate started.

Kumāralīla had five hundred theses [lit. vows] of his own. He refuted each of these with a hundred arguments. Then even Kumāralīla started worshipping the insiders. The five hundred *brāhmaṇa*-s also realised that only the Law of the Buddha was correct. Thus they received ordination in the Law of the Buddha.

He also defeated the *nirgrantha* *Rāhuvratī, the *mīmāṃsaka* *Bhṛṅgāraguhya, the *brāhmaṇa* *Kumārānanda, the *tīrthika* leader of debate *Kaṇādaroru and all other rivals who lived in the Vindhyācala.

He next went to *Dravalī and, by ringing a bell, proclaimed : 'Is there anybody in this place capable of entering into a debate ?' Most of the *tīrthika*-s ran away while some admitted that they were not capable of it. He rebuilt there all the older centres of the Doctrine which had been damaged. He sat on meditation in a solitary forest.

[Fol 90B] At that time, *Śaṃkarācārya sent a message to Śrī *Nalendra announcing that he wanted to have a debate. They [the monks of Nālandā] postponed the debate to the next year and thus took time to invite Dharmakīrti from the south.

When it was time for the debate, king Pradyota[41] got

41. *rab-gsal*. S Prasanna. V Prāditya.

the Buddhists, the *brāhmaṇa*-s and other *tīrthika*-s to assemble in *Vārāṇasī. On the eve of the debate between *Śaṃkarācārya and Śrī Dharmakīrti, *Śaṃkara declared to the people in the presence of the king : 'In case of our victory, we shall decide whether to drown him into the *Gaṅgā or to convert him into a *tīrthika*. In case of his victory, I shall kill myself by jumping into the *Gaṅgā.'

Saying this, he started the debate. Dharmakīrti defeated *Śaṃkarācārya repeatedly. At last he was reduced to a position from where there was nothing more to say. When *Śaṃkarācārya was about to jump into the *Gaṅgā, the *ācārya* tried to stop him. But he did not listen to this. He told his own disciple *Bhaṭṭa *Ācārya, 'Go on arguing and defeat this man with shaven head. Even if you do not win, I shall be reborn as your son and shall go on fighting him.'

Saying this he jumped into the *Gaṅgā and died.

He (Dharmakīrti) converted many of his (Śaṃkara's) disciples into the followers of the Law of the Buddha, who by vow were *parivrājaka brahmacārī*-s. Others ran away.

The next year he was born as a son of *Bhaṭṭa *Ācārya. For three years *Bhaṭṭa *Ācārya propitiated the god and for three more years pondered on the views of the insiders and on the arguments with which to refute these. On the seventh year, he entered into debate by staking his own creed as before. And *Bhaṭṭa *Ācārya was completely defeated.

[Fol 91A] In spite of the *ācārya* (Dharmakīrti) trying to stop it, he paid no heed to it, jumped into the *Gaṅgā and killed himself. Along with the other *brāhmaṇa*-s who were devoted to their own philosophies, his elder son[42] *Bhaṭṭa *Ācārya the second, and [the son in the form of] *Śaṃkarācārya reborn, fled far to the east. Five hundred honest *brāhmaṇa*-s were ordained into the Law and another five hundred took refuge to the Three Jewels.

42, *thu-bo* (elder). V & S younger.

Now, there lived then a *brāhmaṇa* called Pūrṇa[43] in *Magadha and another *brāhmaṇa* called Pūrṇabhadra[44] in Mathurā. They were extremely powerful, enormously rich and highly proficient in logic. They received the blessings of their own deities like Sarasvatī and Viṣṇu. These persons also entered into debate sooner or later, were defeated by the arguments of the *ācārya* and were converted into Buddhists. Each of these two *brāhmaṇa*-s established fifty centres for the Doctrine of the insiders in *Magadha and Mathurā. In this way, this (the *ācārya*'s) fame was spread all over the earth.

Then he spent a long time in the forest called Ṛṣi *Mātaṅga near *Magadha and attained *siddhi* in many magic spells.

There lived in the Vindhyācala the son of king Puṣpa[45] called Utphullapuṣpa.[46] He ruled over thirty lakhs of villages and his wealth was comparable to that of the gods. While wandering about, the *ācārya* at last reached the king's palace. The king asked, 'Who are you ?'

He replied,

> 'Who else can I be, who am victorious in all countries,—like Dignāga in wisdom, like Candragomī in the purity of speech **[Fol 91B]** and skilled in prosody coming down from the poet Śūra ?'[47]

'So, are you Dharmakīrti ?'

'Thus I am known in this world.'

This king also built many monasteries and Dharmakīrti lived there. He composed his Seven Treatises on *pramāṇa*. On the gate of the palace of the king he wrote :

> 'If Dharmakīrti's words ever set like the sun,
> The Doctrine will either fall asleep or die
> And the false doctrine will replace it.'

After he propagated the Law of the Buddha for a long time, there was a congregation in that region of about ten thousand

43. *gaṅ-ba*. cf Bu-ston ii.117.
44. *gaṅ-ba-bzaṅ-po*. cf Bu-ston ii.117.
45. *n.e-tog*.
46. *me-tog-kun-tu-rgyas-pa*. cf Bu-ston ii.153f.
47. cf Bu-ston ii.154. Obermiller translates the passage rather freely.

monks. He established about fifty[48] centres for the Doctrine. From there he went to the border-land[49] *Gujiratha. He converted many *brāhmaṇa*-s and *tīrthika*-s into the Law of the Buddha. He built a temple called *Gotapurī.[50]

There were many *tīrthika*-s in that country. They set fire to the cloister of the *ācārya* and he was surrounded by flames. He then took resort to the tutelary deity, chanted the secret spell and flew through the sky to the royal palace of that country at a distance of about a *yojana*. Everybody felt amazed.

What is now current as the *stotra* of the eighty *siddha*-s[51] cannot be considered reliable. Still it is clear that the account of his flying through the sky after defeating his opponents etc is based on this.

At that time *Śaṃkarācārya reborn acquired a sharper intellect and a greater skill in debate than before. **[Fol 92A]** He had now the full vision of the god (Mahādeva) on the jar. At the age of fifteen or sixteen he came to *Vārāṇasī with the desire of entering into a debate with Śrī Dharmakīrti. He made king *Mahāśyani (? Mahāsena) to proclaim this in all directions by ringing the bell. So the *ācārya* was invited from the south. Five thousand *brāhmaṇa*-s, along with the king, gathered there in a big assembly. As before, staking their respective creeds, they entered into the debate and, being miserably defeated, he (Śaṃkara) killed himself as before by jumping into the *Gaṅgā in spite of attempts being made to prevent this.

Their own doctrine being thus properly refuted, many *brāhmaṇa*-s took up ordination and many others became *upāsaka*-s.

From Kashmir came three great *brāhmaṇa ācārya*-s called *Vidyāsiṃha,[52] *Devavidyākara and *Devasiṃha. They approa-

48. *lṅa-bcu* (fifty). V 'five hundred'. S fifty.
49. *mtha'-'khob*. V & S border-land.
50. S n 'Can it be Gauḍapurī or Gauḍapura ?'
51. *grub-thob-brgyad-bcu'i-bstod-pa*. But Tg contains *Caturaśīti-siddha-pravṛtti* (rG lxxxvi.l) by Abhayaśrī of Campāran.
52. Is the name reminiscent of Deva-vidyā-siṃha, the teacher of Thon-mi-saṃbhoṭa ?—see A. Chattopadhyaya AT 202ff.

ched Śrī Dharmakīrti and raised many honest doubts about the philosophy[53] (of the Buddhists). Dharmakīrti also pointed to them the correct solutions. They were full of reverence for the insiders and took resort to *śaraṇa-gamana* and *pañca-śikṣā*. They listened to the philosophy and specially studied the Seven Treatises on *pramāṇa* until they became great scholars.

They went back to Kashmir in the north and extensively propagated Dharmakīrti's system of logic. It is said that the second one of them lived for a long time in *Vārāṇasī.

He (Dharmakīrti) went again to the south and removed by his arguments the obstacles because of which in certain areas the Law of the Buddha could not be spread or had become degenerated. **[Fol 92B]** He converted the kings, ministers and others into the followers of the Doctrine and led them to establish innumerable *saṃgha*-s and centres for the Doctrine.

The number of temples built by the *ācārya* himself was about a hundred, while the number of those built by others under his inspiration could not be counted. It is said that the total number of the *bhikṣu*-s and *upāsaka*-s who, inspired by this *ācārya*, became the followers of the Law of the Buddha reached one lakh. But this number is mostly of those for whom he directly acted as the *upādhyāya* or *ācārya*. As a matter of fact, the whole world was full of his disciples related to him through his teachings. Yet it is said that the number of his personal attendants never exceeded five.

Towards the end of his life the same *Śaṃkarācārya was born again as the son of *Bhaṭṭa *Ācārya the second[54] and in intelligence became stronger than before. His god (Mahādeva) appeared before him in person and gave him lessons. Sometimes he (Mahādeva) even merged into his body and taught him some hitherto unknown arguments. At the age of twelve,

53. V tr 'frankly raised many objections to Dharmakīrti'. S tr 'laid before him with sharp intellect many controversial points of their systems'.

54. S tr 'as the younger son of the same Bhaṭṭa Ācārya'. V tr 'as the son of the last (junior ?) Bhadra Ācārya'. V n 'Here he is called Bhadra and not Bhaṭṭa'.

he wanted to enter into a debate with Śrī Dharmakīrti. The *brāhmaṇa*-s told him, 'It is better for the time being to debate with others, whom you are sure to defeat. But it is hard to defeat Dharmakīrti.'

He said, 'Without defeating him there can be no real fame in debate.'

Saying this, he went to the south and started debate with this agreement that the defeated one had to accept the other's creed. Śrī Dharmakīrti became victorious and converted him into a follower of the Law of the Buddha.

It is said that in the south, he (Śaṃkara) used to worship the Law of the Buddha as a *brāhmaṇa* **[Fol 93A]** following the practices of an *upāsaka*. The temple built[55] by him still exists.

At last he (Dharmakīrti) built a temple in *Kaliṅga, converted many persons to the Doctrine and passed away. His body was carried to the crematorium by holy persons [56] and, when it was burnt, there came a profuse shower of flowers. Fragrance and sweet sound of music persisted all around for seven days. His relics assumed the form of a crystal ball and there was no sign of any bone left. Even now, periodic festivals are observed in honour of it.

It is said that this *ācārya* was a contemporary of the Tibetan king Sroṅ-btsan-sgam-po.[57] This is clearly true.

According to the Tibetan account, at the time of his composition of the Seven Treatises, he was so deeply engrossed in the subject-matter of these that even when **tikta* (bitter) was put into the curry, he could not detect it. After he finished composing the treatises, on being enquired about it by the king, he said, 'Oh king, if there is anybody condemned to death by you, get him dressed up in white clothes and give him a pot full

55. S n quoted by V 'cf Lassen iv. 618ff and Breal in *Journal Asiatique* 1862, pp 497ff'.

56. *tshaṅs-pa-mtshuṅs-par-spyod-pa*. V & S 'who in their conduct were comparable to Brahmā himself'. But see D 1021 & J 545.

57. cf A. Chattopadhyaya AT 180ff: born in A.D. 569 (according to another tradition in A.D. 629).

of oil and a half-burnt stick. Tell him that even if a drop of oil is spilled from it or if (the stick) touches (his cloth and thus it gets smeared by the charcoal), he would be immediately killed. Keep somebody with a brandished sword just behind him. Now, if you ask him to go round the palace once and in various places of the palace you arrange for musical and other performances, and (after he completes his round) if you question him, he will not be able to tell you that there was any song, dance, musical instrument, etc. The reason for this is that he was fully engrossed in one thought (i.e. about his own life).'

This (Tibetan account) has the appearance of being convincing from the point of view of the following verse of the [*Bodhi-*] *caryāvatāra*[58] : 'If a pot full of mustard oil be given...' **[Fol 93B]** Still this account cannot be really true. The composition of the Seven Treatises was the result of his free choice, and, in the prsence of his disciples, these were composed in the monastery. Why should he write these in one corner of the palace, like the clerk writing the royal decree ? It is well-known that his intellect was so clear that he could answer ten opponents at a time. How could he be differentiated from the fools if, while concentrating on the subject-matter of his works, he failed to observe anything else ?

Further, the following story[59] also is palpably wrong. After composing the Seven Treatises (according to the story) he distributed these to the **paṇḍita*-s. Most of them failed to understand these. Only a few who understood felt jealous, said that these were not good enough and tied these to the tail of a dog. (Dharmakīrti) said, 'As the dogs move about in all sorts of roads, so will my work spread everywhere.' And he added one *śloka* at the beginning of the work : 'Most of the people are fond of the banal...'

After this, he carefully explained the Seven Treatises to

58. *Bodhicaryāvatāra* vii.70 (Bib. Ind. ed. p. 133)
tailapātradharo yadvadasihastairadhiṣṭhitaḥ /
skhalite maraṇatrāsāttatparaḥ syāttathā vratī //
59. This story strongly doubted by Tār is found in Bu-ston ii.154.

ācārya Devendrabuddhi[60] and *Śākyabuddhi[61] and asked Devendrabuddhi to complete the remaining portion of his auto-commentary. He (Devendrabuddhi) composed it for the first time and showed it to him. He (Dharmakīrti) washed it with water. When he composed it over again, he burnt it in fire. Again, he composed it and added, 'It is mainly my misfortune. Time is running out. I have briefly composed this *pañjikā* for the sake of (my) practice.' When he offered it (to Dharmakīrti, the latter said), 'From the point of view of the style, the use of words and of the deeper significance, it is still incomplete. But, as explaining the literal meaning, it is on the whole satisfactory,'—and allowed it to remain.

[Fol 94A] (Dharmakīrti) thought : 'Nobody in the future will understand my logic.' So at the end of the commentary he added the verse : 'Like the rivers merging into the ocean, it will disappear in my own self.'[62]

According to some others, Devendrabuddhi's disciple was *Śākyabuddhi and that the latter composed a gloss on it. And this is correct. It is said that his (Śākyabuddhi's) disciple was Prabhābuddhi.[63] According to others, *Yamāri[64]

60. *lha-dbaṅ-blo*. In Tg 2-4 *parivarta* of *Pramāṇavārtika-vṛtti* (mDo xcv.18) is attributed to Devendrabuddhi ; this portion also occurs as a separate work as mDo xcvi.

61. Apart from this work on the *Pramaṇavārtika* (mDo xcvii & xcviii), in Tg are attributed to Śākyabuddhi *Ārya-gayāśirṣasūtra-miśraka-vyākhyā* (mDo xxxiv.13) and *Ārya-daśabhūmi-sūtra-nidāna-bhāṣya* (mDo xxxvii.2).

62. cf Bu-ston ii.155 ; Stcherbatsky BL i.36.

63. *'od-kyi-blo* cf Bu-ston ii.155 : 'The pupil of Devendrabuddhi was Śākyabuddhi, who composed a sub-commentary. It is said that the pupil of this latter teacher was Prabhābuddhi. Some say that Yamāri was a pupil of Dharmakīrti himself, that (the author of) the *Pramāṇavārtika-alaṃkāra* obtained instructions from the dead-body (of Dharmakīrti), that the pupil (of this author) was Vinītadeva and the pupil of the latter Dharmottara. But in the commentary it is said that Dharmottara was the pupil of Dharmākaradatta and Kalyāṇarakṣita. Yamāri has composed a sub-commentary on the *Pramāṇavārtika-alaṃkāra*. Vinītadeva and Śaṃkarānanda have written commentaries on the Seven Treatises. So runs the tradition'.

64. Tg contains *Pramāṇavārtika-alaṃkāra-ṭikā-supariśuddha-nāma* (mDo

was the direct disciple of Dharmakīrti. Alaṃkāra-upādhyāya[65] is also mentioned as his direct disciple. To agree to this, one has to admit that he received the precepts from the dead-body (of the *ācārya*), and so on. All these are chronologically baseless.

Further, (it is improper) to say that Dharmakīrti beat the victory-drum seventeen times, because it was not the custom of the vow-holding insiders to beat the victory-drum. It is said that a *nirgrantha* with a spear in his hand came for a debate and declared : 'He who will be defeated in the debate will be killed with this spear.' Dharmakīrti did not himself argue with him and he was defeated by Devendrabuddhi. However, it is improper for a *nirgrantha* to have the desire of subduing the opponent in a way which goes against his principles. Such an incident is absolutely unknown to the scholars and it shows only poverty of the knowledge of history. Therefore, it is fictitious.

Similarly, it is said that, among the Six Jewels the three—namely Nāgārjuna, Asaṅga and Dignāga—were the composers of original treatises, while the other three—namely Āryadeva, Vasubandhu and Dharmakīrti—were the composers of commentaries. They are called the Six Jewels, because all of them added equal glory to the Law in ways appropriate for their own times.

The *brāhmaṇa* Śaṃkarānanda[66] belonged to a much later period **[Fol 94B]** and as such it is a gross error to write that he was a direct disciple of Dharmakīrti. The *siddha yogī*-s of the

civ.2-cvii) attributed to *śrī paṇḍtia* Yamāri. Apart from this enormous treatise on logic, Tg also contains his *Devī-vasudhārā-stotra* (rG lxxii.48).

65. i.e. Prajñākaragupta—see Fol 113B. Tg contains *Pramāṇavārtika-alaṃkāra* (mDo xcix-c) by *mahācārya* Prajñākaragupta, *alias* Alaṃkāra-upādhyāya, a disciple of both *brāhmaṇa* Śaṃkarānanda and Yamāri.

66. *bde-byed-dga'-ba*, *alias* Śaṃkaramudita. Tg contains his *Pramāṇa-vārtika-ṭīkā* (mDo ciii), *Samvandha-parīkṣānusāra* (mDo cxii.2), *Apohasiddhi* (mDo cxii.22) and *Pratibandha-siddhi* (mDo cxii.21).

period were *mahā-ācārya* *Lva-va-pā,[67] the middle *Indra-bhūti,[68] *Kuku-rāja,[69] *ācārya* Saroruha-vajra,[70] *Lalita-vajra[71]

67. S-ed Va-va-pā. Vn : 'Va-va-pā is also called Kambala, Kambhalī and Śrī-prabhada. S thinks that the word *va-va-pā* has been wrongly formed from Lva-va-pā or La-va-pa. According to the account of the 84 *siddha*-s, he first reigned in Kaṅ-karova, then after leaving the throne and propitiating Mahā-mudrā, he set off for Urgyana in the kingdom of Malapurī. There in the province of Karavīra, he settled himself in Sanava desert in Tala (Puk-tse ?) cave, carrying with him black *va-va*, which was gobbled up by some witches. He captured all the witches and shaved their heads. When the spirits wanted to throw a rock at him, he raised his finger and the rock remained suspended in the air.' For works of Kambala-pā or Lva-va-pā, see Supplementary Note 38.

68. *alias* Indranāla or *brgya-byin-sdoṅ-po*. The adjective 'middle' (*bar-ba*) is apparently peculiar. Indrabhūti, the famous king of Oḍḍīyāna, is usually mentioned as a contemporary of Lva-va-pā– see BA i.362 & Tār Fol 95Bf. However, BA i.359: 'The adepts of the (Guhya-) samāja--tantra agree that the *Guhya-samāja-tantra* had been preached by the Munīndra himself, following a request of Indrabhūti, the great king of Oḍḍīyāna, at the time when the Buddha had manifested himself in Oḍḍīyāna and initiated (the king).' The lineage mentioned is : Indra-bhūti—Nāga-yoginī—Viśukalpa—*mahā-brāhmaṇa* Saraha—*ācārya* Nāgārjuna—Śākyamitra—Āryadeva, Nāgabodhi, Candrakīrti, etc. Do we have a reference here to some tradition according to which there was an early Indrabhūti, a contemporary of the Buddha ? Assuming this, Indrabhūti, the contemporary of Lva-va-pā was a later one. For works attributed to Indrabhūti, see Supplementary Note 39.

69. P-ed Ku-ku-rāja. S-ed Kukura-rāja. V n : 'In the account of the 84 *siddha*-s there is one Kukuri-pā, who was a *brāhmaṇa* in Kapila-bhargu (?). [R. Sankrityayana reads Kapila(-vastu) : *Purātattva-nivandhāvali* p. 150] kingdom.' For works attributed to Kukuri-pā, see Supplementary Note 40.

70. *mtsho-skyes-rdo-rje*. S 'Louts-vajra'. V n : 'According to the account of the 84 *siddha-s*, *mtsho-skyes-rdo-rje* is called Sagha and was the elder son of king Indrabhūti in Gañja kingdom. Renouncing the throne, he left for Śrī-dhana, where he was attended by Yogi (?) Rāma, who later settled in Devagiri.' For works attributed to Saroruha-vajra or Padma-vajra, see Supplementary Note 41.

71. For works attributed to Lalitavajra, see Supplementary Note 42.

and others. Roughly speaking, they were contemporaries. There were many bearing the name *Padma-vajra. Padma[72] of this period was the middle one. The word *mtsho-skyes* (literally, the lake-born) has many (Indian) equivalents. Here this should be taken as *Saroruha.[73]

Among them, *ācārya* *Kuku-rāja,[74] 'the king of dogs', was very famous. In some histories, his name occurs as *Kutā-rāja.[75] He was most famous among the older *yogī*-s. During the day he used to preach the Doctrine in the guise of a dog to a thousand *vīra*-s and *yoginī*-s. In the night, he used to go to the crematorium and with them observe the esoteric rites like *gaṇa-cakra*. After practising this for twelve years, he ultimately attained the *mahā-mudrā-siddhi*. He expounded five esoteric Tantras[76] and many *yoga* Tantras. It is said that he attained *siddhi* by the *Guhya-candra-tilaka-tantra*.[77]

Now about *ācārya* *Lalita-vajra. He was a **paṇḍita* of *Nalendra. He followed the *Vairocana-māyñjāla-tantra*[78] and took resort to *ārya* Mañjuśrī as his tutelary deity. He asked his own preceptor, 'What is *bhairava-sādhana* etc as belonging to the Vajra-bhairava?'[79] Thus asked, he (the preceptor) said, 'All these do not exist in the human realm. So I do not know these. You should propitiate your tutelary deity for knowing these.'

[Fol 95A] He earnestly propitiated *ārya* Mañjuśrī and, after about twenty years, received the vision and the blessings of

72. *mtsho-skyes.*
73. V tr 'Though there were many *mtsho-skyes-rdo-rje*, the one referred to here is the middle one and of the many words corresponding to (the Tibetan word) *mtsho-skyes* (born of the lake i.e. lotus), here this should be taken as Saroruha.'
74. V & S Kukura-rāja, which occurs in S-ed.
75. i.e. *kuttā-rāja.*
76. *nañ-rgyud-sde*, which may be translated as '*tantra*-s of the insiders'. S tr 'five chapters of the Buddhist Tantras'. V tr 'he extensively preached Buddhist Tantras and Yoga Tantras.'
77. *Śrī-candra-guhya-tilaka-nāma-mahā-tantra-rāja*—Kg Sendai 477
78. *rnam-par-snañ-mdsad-sgyu-'phrul-dra-ba'i-rgyud,*
79. V tr 'What are the *tantra*-s of Vajrabhairava, Bhairava and others ?'

the Tantra. He also attained a number of *sādhāraṇa-siddhi*-s. (Mañjuśrī) instructed him: 'Bring the Yamāri Tantra from the Dharma-gañja[80] of *Urgyana.'[81] So he went to *Urgyana and had a contest of (magic) power with a number of *tīrthika yoginī*-s[82] there. He fell unconscious by their magic stare. Receiving back his consciousness, he prayed to the Vajra-yoginī-s. He received the vision of Vajra-vetālā, who conferred on him the *abhiṣeka* of the Yamāri-maṇḍala. He then meditated on the *sampanna-krama* of four *yoga*-s for two and a half months[83] and attained the *mahā-siddhi*. As a mark of this, he subdued a wild and violent buffalo, attracted it towards himself and rode on it. He also practised the Vidyā-vrata. He then wanted to take from the *Dharma-gañja of *Urgyana the Yamāri and other Tantras for the welfare of all future living beings. The *ḍākinī*-s said, 'You can take as much as you can commit to memory in seven days.' He prayed to his tutelary deity and committed to memory the *Kṛṣṇa-yamāri-tantra*, which was the body-speech-mind of all the Tathāgatas,[84] the Tri-kalpa,[85] the Sapta-kalpa[86] and many other fragmentary *dhāraṇī*-s and longer Kalpa-kramas. And he extensively propagated these in the Jambudvīpa.

[Fol 95B] In the land of the petty *tīrthika* feudatory chief *Naravarmā in the west, he had a contest of magic-power with the *tīrthika*-s. Some of the leading *tīrthika*-s swallowed a *droṇa* (measure) of poison each. The *ācārya* swallowed a quantity of poison which could be carried by ten men. He next swallowed two wine-jars of quicksilver. Still he remained unaffected. This king was full of reverence. He entered the path of the insiders and built a temple for Mañjughoṣa.

In the city of *Hastināpura he destroyed one day a group

80. *chos-kyi-mdsod*. V '(from the library of) Dharmagañja'.
81. S Udyāna.
82. P-ed *rnal-'byor-pa*. S-ed *rnal-'byor-ma*. Hence S tr '*yoginī-s*'.
83. *phyed-daṅ-gsum*. S tr 'after the third half month'.
84. *Sarva-tathāgata-kāya-vāk-citta-kṛṣṇa-yamāri-nāma-tantra*.
85. rG lxxxi.11-13—collectively called *Kalpatraya*.
86. Tg *Sapta-kalpa-vṛtti* (rG lxxxi.14) attributed to Lalitavajra.

of *tīrthika tāntrika*-s by turning the Yamāri-cakra. In *Bagala[87] —in a part of *Varendra in the east—a *nāga* called *Vikrīḍa was causing much damage to the insiders. He subdued him too with a *homa*. Immediately, the lake in which the *nāga* dwelled dried up. Thus he subdued thousands of *tīrthika*-s and Pārasikas[88] etc who were hostile to the Law. He also subdued about five hundred wicked sub-human beings with *abhicāra* and thus caused welfare to the living beings. At last he attained the rainbow-body.

His disciple *Līlāvajra committed to writing the works of the *ācārya*. But the *Yamāntakodaya* and the *Śānti-krodha vikrīḍita* etc were composed by Līlāvajra the great.

There are many anecdotes about contests in magic of *Lva-va-pā, *Lalitavajra, *Indrabhūti and others. After attaining *siddhi* both *Lva-va-pā and *Lalitavajra went towards *Urgyana in the west. There was an impassable hill called *Muruṇḍaka. These two *ācārya*-s discussed among themselves : 'With whose *ṛddhi* can we cross over it ?'

[Fol 96A] *Lalitavajra said, 'This time let us cross it with my *ṛddhi*. On our way back, it will be done with your *ṛddhi*.'

Then *Lalitavajra himself assumed the form of Yamāri and, with the sword—the *āyudha* of Yamāri—pierced the hill from the peak to the foot. Thus was opened a very narrow path. After they moved through it, the hill became as it was before.

*Indrabhūti was then attaining the *sādhāraṇa-siddhi* in *Urgyana. As he came to know that a *siddhācārya* called *Lalitavajra had just arrived, the king moved forward with the people to welcome him. Since it was necessary to massage each foot of the *ācārya* with two hands, he (Indrabhūti) started massaging with four hands. Then the *ācārya* created four legs of his own. The king had eight hands. The *ācārya* produced eight (legs). The king (produced) sixteen (hands), the *ācārya* (produced) sixteen (legs). The king had no power

87. V & S Bagla, which occurs in S-ed. P-ed Bagala.
88. *stag-gzig*. D 548 a corruption of the name Tajik, by which Persia and Persians are known to Tibetans.

beyond creating sixteen hands like the gods.[89] So he started massaging (one leg) with one hand each. The *ācārya* eventually created one hundred legs. Thus was smashed the pride of the king.[90]

On their way back towards the east, the two *ācārya*-s *Lva-va-pā and *Lalita stopped for one night again in front of the *Muruṇḍaka hill. *La-va-pā said, 'The hill is very high. We shall have to cross it tomorrow early morning.' A little after midnight, *Lva-va-pā made the hill vanish with his power of *samādhi* and the two moved easily as over a flat ground. In the early morning, *Lalitavajra looked back and found that they had already crossed the hill. It is said that this astonished him much **[Fol 96B]** and he bowed down to the feet of *Lva-va-pā.

According to the account widely current in the *ārya-deśa*, the foremost *yogī* *Virū-pā meditated on the path of Yamāri and attained *siddhi* under the blessings of Vajra-vārāhī. He became as great a *yogī* as Yamāri himself. And hence he could indeed preach all the Tantras. But it was the practice of the *siddha*-s to preach according to the capacity of the disciples. So he brought the *Rakta-yamāri-tantra*[91] according to the prediction of *bhagavan* himself. He wrote down the *sādhana* and the *upadeśa*[92] (on it). His disciple *Dombi *Heruka brought the *Kurukullā-kalpa and the *Aralli-tantra.[93] By

89. V & S tr 'As he had a vision of a sixteen-handed god only, the king could not bring forth any more'.

90. V n : 'According to the account of the 84 *siddha*-s, Urgyana had about 500,000 towns and was divided into two portions : in one, called Sambhala, reigned Indrabhūti, and in the other called Laṅkāpurī, reigned Jalendra, whose son was married to Indrabhūti's sister Lakṣmīṅkarā, who had become a sorceress. After this, Indrabhūti himself passed on the throne to his son and in 12 years attained *mahā-siddhi*. After having preached the Doctrine, he went to heaven.'

91. *bcom-ldan-'das*. J 147 & D 329 an usual epithet of the Buddha.

92. Tg contains *Rakta-yamāri-sādhana* (rG xlii.96) and *Rakta-yamāntaka-sādhana* (rG xliii.97) attributed to Virū-pā.

93. V n : 'In Kg vol *ṅa* there are two Arali Tantras (Vajra-arali and Rigi-arali Tantras).'

his *abhijñāna*, he learnt the real significance of the Tantras, discussed with the *jñāna-ḍākinī*-s, understood the essence of the *Hevajra-tantra*[94] and composed many *śāstra*-s like the *Nairātmā-devī-sādhana*[95] and the *Sahaja-siddhi.*[96] He also conferred *abhiṣeka* on his own disciples.

After this, the two *ācārya*-s *Lva-va-pā and Saroruha brought the *Hevajra-tantra.* *Lva-va-pā composed a *śāstra* called the **Svasaṃveda-prakṛta*, having *sampanna-krama* as its main subject-matter. Saroruha composed among others the *śāstra* on the *utpanna-krama-sādhana.* Siddha Saroruha was the first to bring the *Hevajra-pitṛ-sādhana.*

I have not read or heard any clear account of Śrī-gupta, the Mādhyamika *mahācārya* of the east.

At the time there lived in the south *Kamalagomī, a *siddha* of Avalokiteśvara. In a monastery in the south, there was then a monk, who was an expert in the three *piṭaka*-s [**Fol 97A**] and who meditated on the Mahāyāna. *Upāsaka* *Kamalagomī was his attendant. This *Kamalagomī was previously not a follower of the Law and he was not even aware of *karma.* In front of the gate of a monastery he found a silver-plate with something written on it. He gladly picked it up and misused it by way of offering it to some local harlots.

Now, the *ācārya bhikṣu* whom he served used to have his meal early and to keep himself shut within the cell till the evening. Once this *upāsaka* asked him, 'Why do you keep yourself thus shut from the morning to the evening ?'

'Oh son, what is the use of your asking this ?'

'I want to follow the *ācārya*'s practice and meditate on the same.'

'Oh son, I practise nothing special. I simply go to the

94. *Hevajra-tantra-rāja-nāma.*

95. In Tg *Nairātmā-yoginī-sādhana* (rG xxii.17) is attributed to Dombi Heruka. There are four more works on Nairātmā-sādhana (lxx.156 ; 157 ; lxxi.88 ; 336) whose author is not mentioned. rG xxii.23 is attributed to Kṛṣṇa-paṇḍita.

96. Tg contains *Śrī-sahaja-siddhi-nāma* (rG xlvi.8) attributed to Dombi Heruka, See also Supplementary Note 34.

*Potala hill to listen to the Doctrine from *ārya* Avalokiteśvara and I open the door after coming back.'

'Please take me along with you.'

Being thus prayed, (the *ācārya*) said, 'I should better ask the *ārya* about this.'

The next day, the *ācārya* came back and was asked (by the attendant about what had happened). The *ācārya* was mildly annoyed and said, 'Oh son, you have made me a messenger for a sinner !' The attendant asked, 'Why ?' The *ācārya* said, 'When I spoke to the *ārya* about you, the *ārya* asked me not to carry any message from a sinner. You have ruined the copy of the *Ārya-prajñā-pāramitā* inscribed on a silver-plate. So you will not have the good fortune to go to *Potala.'

Thus told, he realised that this was the silver-plate he had found earlier. Afraid of his own sin, **[Fol 97B]** he said, 'Oh *ācārya*, please find out from the *ārya* how to atone for this sin.'

The next day, he (*ācārya*) asked the *ārya* about it. Avalokiteśvara gave him a *sādhana* of very deep significance. The *ācārya* gave it to the *upāsaka*, who sat in a solitary forest and entered the *sādhana* with intense concentration. About twelve years passed by. Then a crow brought a lump of rice for eating it on the branch of a tree. It fell in front of *Kamalagomī. During the last twelve years, he had no cooked food to eat. So he felt like eating it and hence had a strong desire of eating rice.[97] Accordingly he went out for begging in the city. Unfortunately, however, he received nothing for a few days. At last he received a little quantity (of rice) and proceeded to the forest, carrying it in an earthen pot. On examination, he realised that the mind of one desirous of eating rice was actually nature-less (*svabhāva-hīna*). Then he clearly understood *śūnyatā* and saw before him *ārya* Avalokiteśvara along with his retinue sitting with a halo round him. He immediately threw the pot of rice on the ground and this made

97. S-ed *zos-pa* (ate). P-ed *mos-pa* (desired to eat). S tr 'So he had a strong desire to eat and he ate it up. Upon this a strong desire for rice grew in him.'

the earth shake. A piece of this broken pot fell on the head of the *nāga* king Vāsuki[98], who examined it and found out how this happened. The daughter of the *nāga* king Vāsuki, along with her five hundred attendants, came there to worship with nine items of delicious food. But as he had given up the desire of eating rice, he turned his back at these.

To convert the *nāga*-s, he went later to the realm of the *nāga*-s. He also worked extensively in the human realm for causing welfare to all the living beings. At last, he went to *Potala.

The twentysixth chapter containing the account of the period of Śrī Dharmakīrti.

98. *klu'i-rgyal-po-nor-rgyas.*

CHAPTER 27

ACCOUNT OF THE PERIOD OF KING GOBICANDRA AND OTHERS

[Fol 98A] Now, even after the death of *Viṣṇurāja, the old dynastic line of the *Mālavas continued without interruption.

*Bharthari[1] was then the king. A sister of this king was married to *Vimalacandra and king *Govicandra[2] was born of the union. He (Gobicandra) either ascended the throne or was about to ascend it at about the time of Dharmakīrti's passing away. These two kings were converted by *siddha* *Jalandhari-pā[3] and *ācārya* Kṛṣṇācārya.[4] But the account of this is to be found elsewhere.

There lived also at that time *siddha* *Tanti-pā[5]. In the city of *Arvanti[6] [? Avantī] in *Mālava, there was a weaver family which for a long time maintained itself by this profession. He (Tanti-pā of this family) had many sons and grandsons so that the weaver family became a large one. As he grew old and became incapable of working, he was maintained by turn in the houses of his sons. He ultimately became an object of ridicule for all. The sons told him, 'Do not worry for your livelihood and stay in a solitary place.' A hut was built for him in a corner of the garden of his eldest son and he lived there.

1. S n quoted by V : 'Is it not a corruption of Bhartṛhari ?'
2. S n quoted by V : 'cf Lassen iii.860, Gobicandra'.
3. For works attributed to Jalandhari-pā, see Supplementary Note 43.
4. *nag-po-spyod-pa-pa.* V & S Kṛṣṇācārin. cf Bu-ston ii.120 ; BA ii.754. For works attributed to *nag-po-spyod-pa-pa*, Kāhnapāda, Kṛṣṇapāda, Kṛṣṇācārya, Kṛṣṇapaṇḍita, Kānha-pā, nag-po('i)-shabs, etc, see Supplementary Note 44.
5. Tg contains *Caturyoga-bhāvana-nāma* (rG xlviii.54) attributed to *ācārya* Tantipāda.
6. S n 'surely Avantī'. V quotes this note.

His sons used to send him the daily food by turn from their own houses.

Siddha *Jalandhari-pā once arrived there in the guise of a simple *yogī* and asked for the night's shelter from the eldest son of the weaver, who honoured him with a little gift and sent him to the garden. After the lamp was lighted in the evening, the old man noticed a guest there. In the early morning, he asked, 'Who is there ?'

'I am a travelling *yogī*. **[Fol 98B]** But who are you ?'

'I am the father of these weavers. I am kept concealed here, for I have grown too old to be presented before others. You *yogī*-s are distinguished for mental purity. Kindly bless me.'

The *ācārya* found him worthy of blessings and immediately he drew the miraculous *maṇḍala*, conferred on him the *abhiṣeka*, gave him some instruction of profound significance and went away. The old man meditated intensely following the preceptor's instruction and, after a few years, *bhaṭṭārikā* Vajrayoginī appeared before him in person. When she put her hand on his head, he immediately attained the Mahāmudrā-siddhi.

For sometime, however, he kept this as a secret.

His eldest son had once a number of guests, who kept him so busy that he forgot to send food to the father. Late in the evening, he remembered this and sent a maid with the food. She heard the sound of songs and music and she came to know that it was coming from the hut. She peeped through the door, saw the body of the old man radiating lustre and twelve gods and goddesses worshipping him with offerings. It is said that they vanished immediately after the door was opened.

Thus it was known that he had attained *siddhi*. But on being questioned about it, he did not admit of anything and only said that by the blessings of a *yogī* he had regained some strength of the body.

So he started again the work of the weaver, singing all the time. He met Kṛṣṇācārya during this time. But the account of this is to be found elsewhere.

Once upon a time, the people of that country were about

to slaughter thousands of goats for worshipping Durgā[7] and other mother-goddesses. **[Fol 99A]** By the magic spell of the *ācārya*, these goats were turned into jackals. The people felt doubt and went away. He then feigned to have tumbled on the altar of Durgā, who appeared before him and asked, 'Oh *siddha*, what do you desire ?' He ordered her not to accept worship in the form of slaughtered animals. So till now, she is being worshipped there only with 'the three white things' (i.e. curd, milk and butter).

After this, he sang many *vajra* songs and went away, nobody knew where.

After *Gobicandra, his paternal cousin[8] *Lalitacandra[9] became the ruler. He ruled peacefully for many years. Kṛṣṇācārya, during the latter half of his life, converted the king and his minister and led them to attain *siddhi*. *Lalitacandra was thus the last king of the *Candra dynasty. After him, though many *kṣatriya*-s were born in the *Candra line, none of them actually ruled the country.

In *Bhaṃgala, *Oḍiviśa, etc—the five regions in the east—those who were born in the royal family lived as ministers, *brāhmaṇa*-s, rich merchants, etc and were lords in their respective spheres. But there was no king as such ruling the state.

During this preiod lived *siddha-rāja* Sahajalalita[10] and Vinītadeva[11], the *ācārya* of Śrī *Nalendra.

He (Vinītadeva) composed commentaries on the Seven Treatises on *pramāṇa*.

Also lived during this period *Śubhamitra, the expert in the *sūtra*-s.[12]

7. *dka'-zlog-ma.* V & S Umā.
8. *pha-tshan-gyi-spun-zla.* S cousin. V uncle.
9. *rol-pa'i-zla-ba.*
10. *lhan-skyes-rol-pa.* V & S Sahajavilāsa. For works attributed to Sahajalalita, see Supplementary Note 45.
11. *dul-ba-lha.* Vidyabhusana HIL 320 places him in c A.D. 700. For works attributed to him, see Supplementary Note 46.
12. *mdo-sde-'dsin-pa*, which means both 'expert in the *sūtra*-s' and Sautrāntika—D 676. It may be tempting to conjecture that Tār refers

[Moreover] *ācārya* Śīlapālita,[13] Śāntisoma and others, who propagated the *sūtra*-s and the *vinaya* from the Vijñāna[-vāda] standpoint[14] lived then. Ācārya Kambala-pā, the author of the *Prajñāpāramitā-nava*[15] and *mahācārya* [Fol 99B] Jñānagarbha,[16] a disciple of Śrīgupta, and others accepted the Mādhyamika doctrine of nature-lessness (*svabhāva-hīna*).

In *Hacipura[17] in *Bhaṃgala in the east, there lived *upāsaka bhaṭṭāraka* A-svabhāva.[18] He elaborately expounded the Vijñāna-mādhyamika[19] view.

here to the Sautrāntika author Kalyāṇamitra, from the Tibetan equivalent of whose name (*dge-legs-bśes-gñen*) Tār can as well reconstruct Śubhamitra. But such a conjecture would not be justified primarily because of two reasons. First, Tār seems to give here a list of *ācārya*-s who adhered to the stand-point of *vijñāna* (Vijñānavādī-s). Secondly, the Sautrāntika author on the Vinaya is mentioned by him later in Fol 105A by the Tibetan equivalent of the name. Therefore, it is better not to identify the present Śubhamitra (mentioned in transliteration) with the Sautrāntika Kalyāṇamitra, though no work of this Śubhamitra is traced in Tg.

13. *tshul-khrims-bskyaṅs*. In Tg *Āgama-kṣudraka-vyākhyāna* (mDo lxxxi.1 : commentary on Kg 'Dul-ba, vol *tha* & *da*) is attributed to *ācārya* Śīlapālita, a disciple of *paṇḍita guru* Dharmottara.
14. *rnam-rig*, which means both '*nyāya*' and '*vijñāna*'—J 314, D 761. In the present context, the latter meaning seems to make better sense. S tr "...the Sautrāntika Śubhamitra and the *ācārya* Śīlapālita, Śāntisoma and others, who composed the *nyāya-siddhānta* from its very basis and propagated the *sūtra*-s and *vinaya*." V tr "The Sautrāntika Śubhamitra, *ācārya* Śīlapālita, Śāntisoma and other followers of the system (of Yogācāra) of the idealists (nyāya-siddhānta) ; they propagated the *sūtra*-s and *vinaya*".
15. In Tg *Bhagavatī-prajñāpāramitā-nava-śloka-piṇḍārtha* (mDo xvi.3) along with a commentary on it (mDo xvi.4) are attributed to *mahācārya* Kambala.
16. *ye-śes-sñiṅ-po* cf BA i.34, where he is mentioned as a disciple of Śrīgupta. For works attributed to him, see Supplementary Note 47.
17. S n also quoted by V : 'Is it Hājipura, which appears in Tibetan Geography also as being on the bank of the river Gaṇḍakī ?'
18. *ṅo-bo-ñid-med-pa*. In Tg are attributed to him *Mahāyāna-sūtrālaṃkāra-ṭīkā* (mDo xlv.3), *Mahāyāna-saṃgraha-upanibandhana* (mDo lvi.4) and a commentary (mDo cxxviii.3) on Kambala-pā's *Āloka-mālā-prakaraṇa* (mDo cxxviii.3).
19. *rnam-riṅ-gi-dbu-ma*. S *nyāya-madhyamaka*. V 'the idealist Madhyamaka (*nyāya-madhyamaka*) !' But see Supplementary Note 12.

In Thogar lived the *mahā-vinayadhara* Vaibhāṣika[20] *ācārya* **Dharmamitra.[21] In *Maru in the west, lived the *mahā-vinayadhara* Puṇyakīrti.[22] In *Citavara lived Śāntiprabha,[23] an expert in the Vinaya and in Kashmir lived Mātṛceṭa,[24] also an expert in the Vinaya.

Apart from them, I have not come across any detailed account of others.

Now about *ācārya* Jñānagarbha. He was born in *Oḍiviśa and became a great **paṇḍita*. He listened to the Doctrine from *ācārya* Śrīgupta in *Bhaṃgala. He became famous as a great Mādhyamika follower of the views of Bhavya. He propitiated for a long time *ārya* Avalokiteśvara, at last had the vision of him as moving the Cintāmaṇi-cakra[25] and attained *abhijñāna*. He recited many *sūtra*-s from his memory and defeated the *tīrthika*-s.

Now about *upāsaka bhaṭṭāraka* A-svabhāva.

Born in a family of merchants, he became a follower of the Mahāyāna quite early in life. He received the vision of *ārya* Mañjuśrī and could recite from his memory about fifty *sūtra*-s. He never deviated from the ten-fold virtue. He preached the Doctrine to a thousand *upāsaka*-s and a thousand *upāsikā*-s. He once went towards *Kāmarūpa. His disciples reached a place on the den of a poisonous Ajagara snake. It was then asleep. They set up their camp by the road, which woke up the poisonous snake. **[Fol 100A]** It sniffed the human smell, swallowed some of the *upāsaka*-s and bit many others. Those

20. *bye-brag-tu-smra-ba*, the usual Tibetan for Vaibhāṣika. V 'of Vibhajyavāda school.' But Tg clearly mentions Dharmamitra as a Vaibhāṣika from Tukhāristān—see next note.
21. In Tg the colophon of the *Vinaya-sūtra-ṭīkā* (mDo lxxxv-lxxxvi) attributed to him mentions him as *ārya-mūla-sarvāstivādi-mahā-vinayadhara-tukhāra-vaibhāṣika-ācārya* Dharmamitra, the student of Guṇaprabha. cf Bu-ston ii.161 : 'he is considered by some to have been the pupil of Guṇaprabha.'
22. *bsod-nams-grags.*
23. *shi-ba-'od.*
24. *ma-khol.*
25. *yid-bshin-nor-bu'i-'khor-los-bsgyur-ba.*

who tried to escape fell down reeling by its poisonous breath.

He (A-svabhāva) earnestly prayed to *bhaṭṭārikā āryā* Tārā and composed a long eulogy to her. This caused intense pain to the poisonous snake. It vomitted out two *upāsaka*-s and fled off. When he sprinkled water charmed with Tārā-mantra on those who were swallowed or bitten or turned unconscious by the poisonous snake, the poison came out from the wound of their bodies. And thus they recovered.

On another occasion, the *ācārya* himself was attacked by a poisonous snake. As he threw a flower charmed with the Tārā-mantra, it vomitted out before the *ācārya* many pearls called **sarva-mukti* and went away. He had also the miraculous power to extinguish the forest fire with Tārā-mantra, etc.

A brief account of Dharmamitra is to be found elsewhere. It is worse than a grave mistake to say that this Dharmamitra, the direct disciple of Guṇaprabha, was the same as the Dharmamitra who composed the commentary called the *Prasphuṭa-padā*.[26] Such a view, if assumed to be true, will lead us to consider *ārya* Vimuktasena and Haribhadra[27] as contemporaries.

During this time, there arose various important disputes in the east. Though unlike the previous period there was no debate in big scale inspired by the spirit of contest leading to big victories and defeats, many minor controversies took place during this period. For the insiders it should have been easier to debate, because by this time they could depend on Dharmakīrti's *śāstra*. Due to the influence of time, however, the number of scholars diminished **[Fol 100B]** and, because of the increase of the number of the *tīrthika* rivals, the insider debators in the smaller monasteries were passing through anxious time.

There was a monastery called the *Piṇḍa-vihāra[28] in the

26. *Abhisamayālaṃkāra-kārikā-prajñāpāramitopadeśa-śāstra-ṭīkā Prasphuṭa-padā-nāma* (mDo viii 1).
27. *seṅ-ge-bzaṅ-po.*
28. The Piṇḍaka-vihāra mentioned by Yuan-chuang is, however, in the north—Watters i.130.

city of *Caṭighābo[29] in *Bhaṃgala. A number of *tīrthika* debators announced that they were going to have a debate there on the following morning. (The monks) felt uncertain about their own capacity. An old woman turned up at that time and said, 'While having the debate, put on caps with pointed tops like thorns. And that will bring you victory.' They acted accordingly and won victory. In other places also, they became victorious in a similar way. From then on, the **paṇḍita*-s adopted the practice of wearing pointed caps. During the period of the seven *Pāla-s and of the four *Sena-s, all the Mahāyāna **paṇḍita*-s used to wear pointed caps. Before this time, however, there was no such practice[30].

Before the great *ācārya* Dharmakīrti, the Law of the Buddha was as bright as the sun. After him, generally speaking, there were many great *upādhyāya*-s who worked excellently for the Law. But there was practically none equal to the older *ācārya*-s. By the influence of time, the Law also was not as bright as before.

The greatest Tāntrika *ācārya*-s belonged to the period between that of *ārya* Asaṅga and this one. But since the *anuttara-dharma* was spread only among the fortunate, the ordinary people were unaware of it. From this period on, the spread of the *yoga* and *anuttara tantra* gradually increased. During an intermediate period, the *yoga tantra* remained widely prevalent, but the exposition of and meditation on the *caryā* and *kriyā tantra*-s gradually went down. As a result, during the time of the seven **[Fol 101A]** *Pāla kings, among the Tāntrika Vajrācārya-s the number of those who attained some *siddhi* gradually increased.

About this period, there was a feudatory chief called **Prakāśacandra, who was born in the line of the *Candras and who attained *siddhi*. He propagated the *yoga tantra* extensively.

29. Is it modern Chittagong ? S n also quoted by V : 'In the Tibetan Geography p. 81 it is called Catigom.'

30. V n 'These are the caps which are now called the *paṇḍita* caps.' cf Vidyabhusana HIL 271.

Further, more than half of those who were famous among the insiders as the eighty-four *siddhācārya*-s came after the period of Dharmakīrti and before king *Canaka. Their account will be presently given.

During the period of the Six Jewels, the Mahāyāna *ācārya*-s were great scholars of the Doctrine and the *saṃgha*-s remained disciplined. In spite of this, however, the Śrāvaka *saṃgha*-s were larger in number.

From this period on, the Law became gradually weaker in the south and there eventually became extinct. In other areas also it went on decaying. However, during the period of the seven *Pālas, in the Aparāntaka countries like *Magadha, *Bhaṃgala and *Oḍiviśa and in the country of Kashmir (the Law) was extensively spread. In other places, it survived in a scattered and feeble form.[31] In the small country of Nepal, it became very widespread. In these lands where the Law was spread, it was spread mainly in the form of Mantra and Mahāyāna.

The Śrāvakas also maintained their popularity. But the nobler sections of the people consisting of the kings and others were above all devoted to the Mahāyāna. In the older times, the Mahāyānīs studied mainly the *sūtra*-s and the commentaries only secondarily. Later on, this mode was reversed and, excepting the *Prajñā-pāramitā*, they mainly studied the *śāstra*-s composed by the *ācārya*-s.

The twentyseventh chapter containing the account of the period of king Gobicandra and others.

31, V & S tr 'excepting in a few pockets, it did not survive.'

CHAPTER 28

ACCOUNT OF THE PERIOD OF KING GOPĀLA

Near a forest of Puṇḍravardhana on the border of the *madhya-deśa* and the east, **[Fol 101B]** there lived a very beautiful girl born in a Kṣatriya family. As a result of her union with a deity of the tree, a son with auspicious marks was born of her.[1] When he grew up into a boy, he found a large self-radiating gem by digging the ground at the foot of the tree which was the abode of the deity. With it [? as the *ācārya*'s fee] he received *abhiṣeka* from an *ācārya* with instructions to propitiate the goddess *Cundā.[2] He propitiated her. He always kept concealed with himself a small wooden club, the *āyudha* of his tutelary deity. The goddess once appeared in dream and blessed him.

From there he went to the temple of *ārya* *Khasarpaṇa and prayed, 'May I obtain a kingdom.' He (Khasarpaṇa) predicted, 'Move towards the east and you will obtain a kingdom.'

So he moved towards the east.

At that time there was no king in *Bhaṃgala for many years. As a result, the people there were passing through a disturbed and unhappy period. The chiefs of the country met in an assembly, discussed among themselves and elected a king to rule the country properly.

1. cf Bu-ston ii.156.
2. S n 'In vol *ru* of the Tantras, Tg contains *Cundā-sādhana*, which also appears in the manuscript in Paris under the title *Sādhana-mālā-tantra* Fol 81'. V quotes this note and adds, 'It also exists in China and portions of it will be translated by us, when we analyse the Tantras.' In Tg *Cundā-sādhana* occurs four times without mentioning the author : rG lxx.109 ; lxxi.41 ; 215 ; 217. There is also a work with the title *Ārya-cundā-sādhana* (rG lxxxvi.36) attributed to Buddhakīrti. The reference to Vol *ru* by S & V seems to be a misprint ; it should be read as *lu*.

There was an evil and powerful *nāginī*. A king with magic power made her the queen. According to some, she was the queen of *Gobicandra, according to others of *Lalitacandra. In any case she used to kill every night anybody who was appointed the king during the day. Thus she killed all those that were appointed as kings.[3] However, since there could be no welfare to the kingdom without a king, every morning somebody was appointed king, who was killed during the night. His dead body was taken out early in the morning. This was going on for several years and everybody in the country had to wait for his turn. Thus passed some years.

Then the person who had attained *siddhi* of goddess *Cundā entered a house and found everybody there plunged in grief. On enquiring the reason for this, he came to know that it was the turn for their son to be the king on the next day. He said, 'I shall go as his substitute, if I am paid for it.' This made them very happy and, receiving the payment from them, he became the king on the next day.

At midnight, the *nāginī* in the form of a *rākṣasī* **[Fol 102A]** came as usual to kill [lit. devour] him. He struck her with the *āyudha* of the tutelary deity and she died immediately.

On the next morning, the corpse-bearers came and, finding that he was not dead, were highly astonished. As the substitute for others, he was elected king everyday for seven successive days. Then everybody realised that he was highly pious and appointed him as the permanent king and gave him the name *Gopāla.

During the first part of his life, he ruled *Bhaṃgala. In the latter part, he also conquered *Magadha.[4] He built the *Nalendra *vihāra* near *Odantapurī.[5] In these two big provinces, he established many monasteries and thus extensively served the Law.

3. S n 'One may compare here Lassen ii.809 note, where a *vetāla* kills the kings.'

4. V n 'Lassen iii.721 places the beginning of the reign at about A.D.810'.

5. V tr 'He built a temple named Nalendra in the vicinity of Odantapurī'. cf Bu-ston ii.156.

According to Indradatta,[6] this king was appointed to his kingdom on the year following the death of *ācārya* Cārin[7] [? Kṛṣṇācārī]. According to Kṣemendrabhadra, this took place seven years after that.

He ruled for fortyfive years. During the time of this king, *ācārya* Śākyaprabha,[8] a disciple of Śāntiprabha and Puṇyakīrti,[9] was born in the west and worked for the welfare of the living beings in Kashmir. Specially prominent in Kashmir were also the great *Dānaśīla,[10] Viśeṣamitra,[11] Prajñāvarman[12] and *ācārya* Śūra,[13] an expert in Vinaya. In the east lived *ācārya* Jñānagarbha.

6. *dbaṅ-po-byin*. See Fol 139A, where his work is mentioned as *Buddha-purāṇa*.
7. *spyod-pa-pa*, lit. 'one who practises mysticism' D 809. V & S '*ācārya* Mīmāṃsaka.' But could it be nag-po-spyod-pa-pa, i.e. Kṛṣṇācārya or Kṛṣṇācārin ? See Fol 105A.
8. *śākya-'od*. Tg contains *Ārya-mūla-sarvāstivāda-śramaṇera-kārikā* (mDo lxxxix.2) along with its auto-commentary called *Prabhāvatī* (mDo lxxxix.3) by Śākyaprabha. Bu-ston ii.161 quotes from *Prabhāvatī* in which the author 'himself says that he is the pupil of Puṇyakīrti and Śāntiprabha'.
9. *bsod-nams-grags*. cf Bu-ston ii.161, where *Prabhāvatī* is quoted as mentioning Puṇyakīrti as one 'who resided in Magadha, was the ornament of that country and greatly famed'.
10. One of the early Indian *ācārya*-s to have visited Tibet and to have taken part in the first large-scale Tibetan translation of Indian texts under the patronage of king Khri-lde-sroṅ-btsan—see A. Chattopadhyaya AT 262f. Dānaśīla is mentioned as one of the compilers of the *Mahāvyutpatti* (mDo cxxiii.44) and in Tg about a hundred works are preserved as translated by him.
11. *khyad-par-bśes-gñen*. Tg contains *Vinaya-saṃgraha* (mDo lxxiv.2) attributed to him.
12. *śes-rab-go-cha*. Tg contains *Viśeṣastava-ṭīkā* (bsTod 2) and *Devātiśaya-stotra-ṭīkā* (bsTod 5) attributed to *ācārya* Prajñāvarman of Bengal. Besides, it contains a commentary (mDo lxxi.2-lxxii.1) on the Udānavarga (Kg Sendai 326) of *arhat* Dharmatrāta, where the commentator is mentioned as *sarvāstivādī ācārya* Prajñāvarman, born in Kabargya (Kāpaṭya ?) of Bhaṃgala and a disciple of *ācārya* Bodhivarman of Kapadhya (Kāpaṭya ?).
13. *dpa'-bo*. Tg contains *Pratimokṣa-sūtra-paddhati* (mDo lxxiii-lxxiv.1), commentary on Kg *Pratimokṣa-sūtra* (Sendai No 2) attributed to *ācārya* Śūra.

It is nothing but showing ignorance to say that Buddhajñāna's[14] disciple was Jñānagarbha, and this in spite of admitting that Bhavya, Avalokitavrata[15] (? Avalokiteśvaravrata), Buddhajñānapāda, Jñānagarbha, Śāntijīva (Śāntarakṣita)[16] and others belonged to the tradition of the Svātantrika-Mādhyamikas,[17] but without knowing of Haribhadra's[18] commentary, the *Aṣṭa-sāhasrikā-vṛhat-ṭīkā*,[19] and of Śāntarakṣita's [commentary on] *Madhyamaka-alaṃkāra*[20] and without knowing moreover that Buddhajñāna was a disciple of Haribhadra.[21] **[Fol 102B]**

To this period belonged Śākyamati,[22], Śīlabhadra,[23] prince

14. *sańs-rgyas-ye-śes.* cf Bu-ston ii.159f : a disciple of Haribhadra and a preceptor of Guṇamitra. cf also BA i.367ff for the Tāntrika career of Buddhajñāna. See Supplementary Note 48.
15. *spyan-ras-gzigs-brtul-shugs.* Tg contains *Prajñā-pradīpa-ṭīkā* (mDo xx-xxii), commentary on Bhāvaviveka's *Prajñā-pradīpa-mūla-madhyamaka-vṛtti* (mDo xviii.8), attributed to Avalokitavrata, born in Sāketa in a *brāhmaṇa* family.
16. *shi-ba-'tsho.* cf A. Chattopadhyaya AT 228ff. For works of Śāntarakṣita, see Supplementary Note 49.
17. *dbu-ma-rań-rgyud-pa'i-brgyud-pa.*
18. *seń-bzań (seń-ge-bzań-po).* V & S Siṃhabhadra. For his works, see Supplementary Note 50.
19. Tg mDo vi.
20. Tg mDo xxviii.5. See Supplementary Note 50.
21. See colophon of Tg mDo viii.3, where Buddha-śrī-jñāna is mentioned as the principal disciple of Haribhadra.
    V tr the passage : 'Those who assume that Bhavya, Avalokitavrata, Buddhajñānapāda, Jñānagarbha and Śāntarakṣita were *mādhyamika-svātantrikas* and who—without seeing any commentary on 8000 Pāramitās by Haribhadra or any commentary on *Madhyamaka-alaṃkāra* by Śāntarakṣita and forgetting that Buddhajñāna was the pupil of Haribhadra—consider Prajñāgarbha (? Jñānagarbha) as the pupil of Buddhajñāna, only give a proof of their greatest folly.'
22. *śākya-blo-gros.* Tg contains *Ārya-gayāśīrṣa-sūtra-miśraka-vyākhyā* (mDo xxxiv.13), *Ārya-daśabhūmi-sūtra-nidāna-bhāṣya* (mDo xxxvii.2) and *Pramāṇa-vārtika-ṭīkā* (mDo xcvii-xcviii) attributed to Śākyamati.
23. *ńań-tshul-bzań-po*, the preceptor of Yuan-chuang and a disciple of Dharmapāla. See Watters ii.109 ; I-Tsing (Takakusu) xiv, lviii, 181. Tg contains *Ārya-buddha-bhūmi-vyākhyāna* (mDo xxxvi.3) attributed to Śīlabhadra. It is a commentary on Kg Sendai 275.

Yaśomitra,[24] *paṇḍita Pṛthivībandhu[25] and others.

Kashmir was then ruled by *Hri *Harṣadeva[26] (Śrī Harṣadeva). The *siddhācārya*-s belonging to this period are to be known from the previous account.

It is particularly clear that *Virū-pā the junior, lived between this king (Gopāla)[27] and *Devapāla. In the *Kaccha country in the west, there ruled the king called *Vibharaṭṭa. His daughter became the queen of *Devapāla. And so was born their son *Rāsapāla.[28] During the period of this *Vibharaṭṭa, lived *Virū-pā the junior. The king had a shrine for both the insiders and outsiders. The king himself was devoted to the insiders, but his ministers were devoted to the outsiders. While building the temple, he placed in it the statues of standard human size of the gods of both the insiders and outsiders. The Buddhists asked him to build separate temples, but the *tīrthika*-s wanted him to build a united one and the ministers endorsed this.

*Virū-pā the junior was invited to consecrate this temple. He performed no special rite, but simply said, '**Āisa*, **āisa*.'[29] In Tibetan, this means *sog-sog*, (i.e 'come, come'). As he said this, all the images of the temple assembled in the corridor. He next said, 'Sit down'. And all the gods sat down on the floor. He then took a jar full of water and sprinkled the water on the head of the gods. As a result of this, the gods of the insiders suddenly stood up and entered the temple, laughing

24. *rgyal-sras-grags-pa'i-bśes-gñen*. For works of Yaśomitra, see Supplementary Note 51.
25. *sa'i-rtsa-lags*. Tg contains *Saddharma-puṇḍarika-vṛtti* (mDo xli.2), a commentary on Kg Sendai 113, attributed to him.
26. Tg contains *Suprabhāta-stotra* (bsTod 56) and *Aṣṭa-mahāsthāna-caitya-vandanā-stava* (bsTod 57) attributed to Śrī Harṣadeva, king of Kashmir, the corrupt form of whose name also occurs as Śrī Hirisadeva.
27. V tr 'the king (Gopāla or Śrī Harṣadeva ?)'
28. S n also quoted by V : 'Is it not a corruption of Rājyapāla ? See Lassen iii.730ff.'
29. Distinctly the words in Bengali dialect *āisa, āisa* (আইস, আইস).

loudly. The gods of the outsiders remained in the corridor, with their heads hung low. This temple called *Amṛta-kumbha still exists.

During this period also lived the great *ācarya* Kaudālika,[30] the author of the wonderful treatises.

During the period of this *Gopāla or *Devapāla, **[Fol 103A]** was also built the Śrī *Odantapurī *vihāra*. There was somewhere in *Magadha a *tīrthika yogī* of a very simple nature called Narada (? Nārada)[31], an adept in magic spells. For attaining the *vetāla-siddhi*, he needed an assistant who had to be truthful, physically strong, free from all diseases, having the nine marks of the *vīra*, highly intelligent, courageous, free from deceptions and an expert in all the fine arts. He found none with these qualities excepting an insider *upāsaka* whom he met. He requested the *upāsaka*, 'Assist me in my *sādhana*.' (The *upāsaka*) replied, 'I am not going to assist a *tīrthika* in his *sādhana*.'

'You need not be a follower of the *tīrthika*. Inexhaustible wealth will be obtained (from this *sādhana*), with which you can spread the Doctrine.'

'So, I shall go and ask of my *ācarya*.'

Receiving the permission from the *ācarya*, he became the assistant for the *sādhana*. When the time of the *siddhi* was

30. *tog-rtse-ba-che-ba*. V & S Mahā-koṭali. Tg contains *Acintya-kramopadeśa-nāma* (rG xlvi.13), *Ātma-yoga-nāma* (rG lxxxvi.7), *Sarva-devatā-niṣpannakrama-mārga-nāma* (rG xlviii.70) and *Citta-tattvopadeśa-nāma* (rG xlviii.82) attributed to Kaudālika (Kuddālipāda, Koṭali, Kotali, Kuddali, *alias* Gudhari, Guḍarī or Ghadhari). V n 'The Indian name Koṭali has been derived by S on the basis of the account of the 84 *siddha*-s in which he, in addition to his Tibetan name is also called Kotali. According to this account, when Kotali was digging on a hill, he met Śānti, who instructed him to meditate on the six *pāramitā*-s. In the terminology of his occupation, soul is the hill, concentration the hands, the shovel which destroys the barrier is negation, etc.'

31. P-ed Narada ? V & S Narada. Tg (mDo cxxiii.34) contains a work called *Sāmudrika-nāma-tanu-lakṣaṇa-parīkṣā*—said to be the original work on *tanu-vicāraṇa-śāstra*—attributed to Narada.

near, he (Narada) said, 'When the *vetāla* sticks out its tongue, you must immediately catch it. If you are able to catch it on the first chance, the *mahā-siddhi* will be attained. (If you are able to catch it) on the second chance, there will be the middle *siddhi* and on the third chance the lowest *siddhi*. If you fail to catch it even on the third chance, it (the *vetāla*) will first devour the two of us and will then make the whole country almost empty.'

The *upāsaka* could catch it neither on the first nor on the second chance. Then he waited with his own mouth placed on that of the *vetāla*. On the third chance, he caught it with his teeth. The tongue turned into a sword and the corpse itself into gold.

When the *upāsaka* took the sword and waved it, he began to fly in the sky. The *tīrthika* said, 'I have performed the ritual for the sake of the sword. So give this to me.'

'I shall be back after having some entertaining sights.' Saying this, he went above the top of the Sumeru, circled it and its four *dvīpa*-s as well as the *upa-dvīpa*-s and within a moment came back and gave the sword to him.

[Fol 103B] He (Narada) said, 'Take this corpse turned into gold. Take off those portions (of the corpse) that were its flesh, without touching those that were its bones. If you do not spend it for evil purposes like wine and women and if you go on spending it for your own maintenance and for virtuous acts, the part of the body that you slice off during the day will be replaced during the night. It will thus be inexhaustible.'

Saying this, with the sword in his hand he flew to the realm of the gods.

The *upāsaka* built the great *Odantapurī monastery with the gold from the corpse. *Otaṇḍa (Oḍanta)[32] means 'flying'

32. Tār has possibly the Indian word *uḍanta*, or *uḍḍīna* or *uḍḍayana* in mind. But the actual name of the monastery could have been Udaṇḍapurī (see Lalou 221, Kern *Geschichte* ii.545). In colophon of Tg mDo cxxiii.35, the name occurs as Otantras-purī (*alias* Otanta-purī) or Odantapurī, Udaṇḍapurī.

(*'phur-byed*), for the *upāsaka* flew in the sky over the Sumeru[33] along with its four *dvīpa*-s, saw these with his own eyes and built the monastery on that model. This *upāsaka* is famous as *Uḍya-upāsaka.[34]

This monastery does not owe itself to the grace of any king or minister. The architects, sculptors and artists that worked for the construction of the temple and its images were paid and maintained from the money obtained in exchange of the gold received from the *vetāla*. Maintaining five hundred *bhikṣu*-s and five hundred *upāsaka*-s from this gold alone, the *upāsaka* himself looked after this centre for the Doctrine as long as he lived. At the time of his death, he buried this gold under the earth with the prayer : 'Though this gold will not be useful for anybody right now, let this be of use for the benefit of the living beings of the future.' Saying this, he entrusted *Devapāla with this centre for the Doctrine.

The twentyeighth chapter containing the account of the period of king Gopāla.

33. *ri-rab.*
34. S n also quoted by V 'See Wilson, *Works*, ii.18'.

CHAPTER 29

ACCOUNT OF THE PERIOD OF KING DEVAPĀLA AND HIS SON

Now about king *Devapāla.

According to some, he was the son of a Nāga. But as he was blessed by the *kula-mantra* of *Gopāla's line of descent, he is considered to have been his (Gopāla's) son. However, the current account is as follows :

The youngest queen of king *Gopāla asked from a *brāhmaṇa* adept in magic charms the means of bringing the king under her power (*vaśikaraṇa*). (The *brāhmaṇa*) secured a medical herb from the Himālaya,[1] charmed it with magic spell, mixed it with food, sealed it and said, 'Serve it to the king.' She sent it through her maid.

[Fol 104A] (The maid) slipped on the bank of a river and it (herb) fell into the water. Carried by the water, it reached the *nāga-loka*. The Nāga king Samudrapāla[2] swallowed it and, under its influence, came in the guise of the king, united with the queen and she conceived. As the king was then about to punish her, she said, 'On such and such occasion, the king himself came.'

(The king said,) 'So let this be examined.'[3]

A son was born and at the time of offering worship on that occasion there emerged the hood of a Nāga. Also a ring was seen on the finger of the son which was found to have the Nāga

1. *ri-bo-gaṅs-can.*
2. *rgya-mtsho-skyoṅ.* V & S Sāgarapāla.
3. S tr : 'As she was about to be punished on the orders of the king, he (*nāga*) said, let the king himself come and probe into the matter once again.'
   V tr : 'As she was about to be punished by the king, he said that he would himself come at the time of delivery and investigate.'

script on it. So it was realised that he was the son of a Nāga king and he was reared up.[4]

After Gopāla's death, he ascended the throne and became more powerful than the previous king. He brought *Varendra in the east under his rule. He wanted to build a wonderful monastery and he built the *Somapurī[5].

According to most of the histories current in Tibet, the astrologers told the king, 'Prepare a wick with the clothes of *śramaṇa*-s and *brāhmaṇa*-s, obtain oil from the houses of kings and merchants, get a lamp from the hermitage, light it, put it before the tutelary deity and pray. After this, you should build the monastery where the incarnation of the Protector of the Doctrine (*dharma-pāla*) will drop the lamp. That will gradually bring prosperity to the king and blessedness all around.'

These being done, there appeared a crow which picked up the lamp and dropped it into a lake. This made him depressed. In the night, however, the five-headed Nāga king appeared before him and said, 'I am your father. I shall drain the lake dry so that you can build there. Arrange for grand weekly[6] offerings there.'

This was done and in twentyone days the lake got dried up and the monastery was built. Thus it was built (according to the current account).

4. Bu-ston ii.156 gives practically the same account, though, according to him, the king thus born of the union of Gopāla's wife and the Nāga king was Śrīmat Dharmapāla and not Devapāla. In Bu-ston's account, Devapāla was the grandson of Dharmapāla and the father of Mahīpāla and Haribhadra a contemporary of the latter. At the same time, Bu-ston ii.158 knows, 'In the Great Commentary on the Aṣṭasāhasrikā (by Haribhadra), it is said that this work was composed at the monastery of Trikaṭuka, under the patronship of Śrīmad Dharmapāla.' According to the account of Tār, Devapāla's son was Rāsapāla, whose son was Dharmapāla, the patron of Haribhadra and Jñānapāda.

5. Bu-ston ii.156f gives practically the same legend, though the monastery thus built was Odantapurī, not Somapurī.

6. *shag-bdun-bdun-na.* S 'for seven days', V 'seven weeks'.

[Fol 104B] In the account of the building of the Samudragupta[7] temple in Kashmir, a black man said in a dream, 'Worship Mahākāla[8] and the Yakṣa-s will dry up the lake.' Except this, the other details (of the above legend) are same. So it is better not to connect this legend with *Somapurī.

Similarly, the (above) account of the birth of *Devapāla is largely the same as that of Sahajalalita.[9] So it needs to be examined whether one is modelled on the other.

This famous *Somapurī is also said to be the new *Somapurī.

Inspired by a *yogī* called *Śiromaṇi, the king raised a big army to wage war on *Oḍiviśa and other places, which were previously the centres of the insiders, but by this period which came under the influence of the *tīrthika*-s only. When he crossed the country *Rā-rā,[10] he saw a black man coming slowly from a distance. On being questioned who he was, he said, 'I am Mahākāla. Remove the sand dune from this place and you will find a temple. To destroy the temples of the *tīrthika*-s you will have to do nothing else than surround this temple with the army and play the musical instruments very loudly.'

Then he (Devapāla) removed the sand dune and found a wonderful temple made of stone. The name of this was Śrī Trikaṭuka[11] *vihāra*. According to some account, from this monastery came out a *bhikṣu* who was absorbed in deep meditation and who enquired about Buddha Kāśyapa and king *Kṛkin.

'It is now the period of the Law of Śākyamuni.' Being told this, he showed many miracles and attained *nirvāṇa*.[12] Thus it is said.

Everything being done according to the prediction (of Mahākāla), all the temples of the *tīrthika-s* automatically fell

7. *rgya-mtsho-sbas-pa.* V & S 'a temple concealed inside a lake'.
8. *nag-po-chen-po.*
9. *lhan-skyes-rol-pa.*
10. S Chagala. V 'Rā-ra (Chagala)'. Does Tār refer here to Rāḍha ?
11. *dpal-tsha-ba-gsum.*
12. V n 'Detailed account of such *bhikṣu*-s who had given themselves to meditation even in the period of the previous creations of the universe is not rare in Buddhist works.'

into ruins. Thus in all about forty great centres of the *tīrthika-s* were ruined. Some of these were in *Bhaṃgala and *Varendra.

[Fol 105A] He then conquered the whole of *Oḍiviśa.

To the period of this king belonged Kṛṣṇācārya the junior,[13] who was a follower of *ācārya* Kṛṣṇācārya and a great **paṇḍita* of the three, namely the [Cakra-]sambara, Hevajra and Yamāri. He meditated on the Cakra-sambara in a place near *Nalendra and received the instruction from a *ḍakinī* to attain *vasu-siddhi* at the place of a goddess of *Kāmaru. He went there, found a chest, opened it and saw an ornamented **ḍamaru*. The moment he took it up, his feet were no longer touching the earth. Whenever he played it loudly, five hundred *siddhayogī*-s and *yoginī*-s appeared from nobody knew where and became his attendants.

He worked for the welfare of the living beings for a long time. At last he went to *Gaṅgāsāgara and passed away, though nobody knew when and how.

He composed many treatises like the exposition of the Sambara. As he had a very long life, he lived for some time even after king *Dharmapāla.

To this period also belonged Śākyamitra,[14] a disciple of *ācārya* Śākyaprabha.[15] And moreover lived during this period Kalyāṇamitra,[16] the expert in Vinaya, Sumatiśīla[17], **Daṃstrāsena,[18] Jñānacandra,[19] Vajrāyudha,[20] Mañjuśrīkīrti,[21]

13. *nag-po-spyod-pa-chuṅ-ba*, A Tāntrika work (rG xvii.3) is attributed to him in Tg.
14. *śākya-bśes-gñen*. For works attributed to him, see Supplementary Note 52.
15. cf Bu-ston ii.161.
16. *dge-legs-bśes-gñen*. For works attributed to him, see Supplementary Note 53.
17. *blo-bzaṅ-ṅaṅ-tshul*. In Tg *Karma-siddha-ṭīkā* (mDo lxi.2—a commentary on Vasubandhu's *Karma-siddha-prakaraṇa*) is attributed to him.
18. *mche-ba'i-sde*. For his works, see Supplementary Note 54.
19. *ye-śes-zla-ba*. In Tg two commentaries on Nāgamitra's works are attributed to him. These are *Kāya-traya-vṛtti* (mDo xxix.2) and *Yoga-caryā-bhāvanā-tātparyārtha-nirdeśa* (mDo xxxiii.83—lxi.8).
20. *rdo-rje-mtshon-cha*. In Tg *Śrī-jñāna-guṇa-phala-nāma-stuti* (rG lxviii. 19) is attributed to him.
21. *'jam-dpal-grags-pa*. For his works, see Supplementary Note 55.

Jñānadatta,[22] *Vajradeva,[23] *bhaṭṭāraka* Avalokitavrata[24] of the south and *ācārya* *Dhanamitra and others of Kashmir.

Ācārya Haribhadra[25] became a **paṇḍita* during the period of this king and he worked for the welfare of the living beings appropriately. But since during the period of King *Dharmapāla his activities greatly increased, these will be discussed later.

It is clear that *ācārya* Bodhisattva[26] who went to Tibet must have lived sometime between king *Gopāla and king *Dharmapāla. **[Fol 105B]** Relying on most of the Tibetan accounts some claim that during his life the nine successive Tibetan kings[27] had passed away. Assuming this, one has to claim that he even touched the feet of Asaṅga and his brother. That is quite incredible. It is a well-known fact that he was identical with *mahā-upādhyāya* Śāntarakṣita, the author of the *Madhyamaka-alaṃkāra*. Let us accept this for the time being, because all the great Tibetan scholars are agreed on this point.

According to their version, he became a great **paṇḍita* already during the period of *Gopāla and worked for the welfare of the living beings specially during the period of this king [i.e. Devapāla]. In the work called *bka'-yan-dag-pa'i-tshad-ma*[28] by Lha-btsan-po Khri-sroṅ-lde-btsan,[29] it is said, 'The name of *upādhyāya* Bodhisattva is mentioned as Dharma-śānti-ghoṣa.'

There is no contradiction in the same person being referred

22. *ye-śes-byin*. In Tg *Ārya-caturdharmaka-vyākhyāna-ṭīkā* (mDo xxxiv. 11) is attributed to him.
23. In Tg *Lokeśvara-śataka-stotra* (rG lxviii.32) is attributed to *kavi śrī* Vajradeva.
24. See note 15 of Ch. 28.
25. S Siṃhabhadra. V Haribhadra.
26. e.i Śāntarakṣita. cf A. Chattopadhyaya AT 228ff.
27. *bod-kyi-rgyal-rabs-dgu*. V & S 'the ninth Tibetan king'.
28. i.e. *Samyak-vāk-pramāṇodhṛta-sūtra* (mDo cxxiv.8) attributed to Khri-sroṅ-lde-btsan.
29. cf A. Chattopadhyaya AT 212ff.

to by several names. One of his names must have been Śāntirakṣita, because the word *rakṣita*, forming part of the name Śāntirakṣita, was added to the names of his disciples, called 'The Seven Selected Ones.'[30] But there is also the view that Śāntirakṣita, the commentator of Jñānagarbha's *Mādhyamika-satya-dvaya*,[31] was identical[32] with Śāntirakṣita, the author of the *Madhyamaka-alaṃkāra*. Therefore, it is necessary to examine which of the two views is correct.

Since the commentary on the *Yoga-tantra-tattva-saṃgraha*[33] was prepared by Śākyamitra in Kośala, it was called *Kośala-alaṃkāra*.[34] In this commentary is said that he was instructed by eleven *guru*-s. In the latter part of his life, he went to Kashmir and extensively worked for the welfare of the living beings.

Now about Vajrāyudha.

He composed the *stotra* for Mañjuśrī called the *gaṅ-blo-mar-grags-pa*.[35] Five hundred different *paṇḍita-s composed this *stotra* separately and the circumstance of the words and meaning of all these being identical is to be viewed as due to the miracle of the deity (Mañjuśrī).

Now about Mañjuśrīkīrti.

He composed the great commentary on the *Nāma-saṃgīti*.[36] He directly perceived the *maṇḍala* of Dharma-dhātu and

30. *sad-mi-mi-bdun*. The first group of Tibetan monk-scholars trained by Sāntarakṣita—see A. Chattopadhyaya AT 244f.

31. Tg contains his *Satya-dvaya-vibhaṅga* (mDo xxviii.1) along with its auto-commentary (mDo xxviii.2).

32. *mi-gcig-pa*, meaning both 'the same man' and 'not one'. V & S 'was not identical.' See mDo xxviii.3 Śāntarakṣita's commentary on mDo xxviii.2.

33. V n 'Kg Vol *ña* Tantras 1-109 : *Sarva-tathāgata-tattva-saṃgraha-nāma-mahāyāna-sūtra*, a Mahāyāna-sūtra which contains the essence of all *tathāgata*-s.'

34. Tg contains *Kosalālaṃkāra-tattva-saṃgraha-ṭīkā* (rG l-li.1) by Śākyamitra.

35. rG lxviii.19 (see note 20 of this chapter). S n 'The book opens with the words *gaṅ-blo-mar-grags-pa* (lit. 'one who is without intellect') and hence referred to by this name'.

36. See Supplementary Note 56.

Vāgīśvara[37] [Fol 106A] and became a great Vajrācārya. A careful study of this commentary shows that he was one of those who crossed the Ocean of the Knowledge of the *śāstra*-s. I find that a fairly extensive account of him was previously current in Tibet, though I have not liked it much. But those who are interested in it may look up the Ship of Yoga (*Yoga-gru-gziṅs* : *Yoga-pota*) by the great scholar Bu-ston.

Now about *Vajradeva.

He was a householder and by profession a highly successful bard. He went to Nepal and came across a degraded *tīrthika yoginī* with many perverse practices. He wrote a poem deriding her. By her curse, he was afflicted with leprosy. He prayed to *ārya* Avalokiteśvara and composed each day a verse of praise in *sragdharā* metre. Thus in about three months he received the vision of *ārya* Avalokiteśvara, got cured of the disease and his poem[38] which consisted of about a hundred verses remained everywhere in *ārya-deśa* as a model of excellent poetry.

King *Devapāla ruled for fortyeight years.

After him, his son *Rāsapāla ruled for twelve years. Since he did practically nothing new for the Law, he is not counted among the Seven *Pālas.

During this period Līlāvajra,[39] the *ācārya* of *Urgyana, spent ten years in Śrī *Nalendra, delivered many sermons on the Tantra-yāna and composed the commentary on the *Nāma-saṃgīti*.[40]

There lived then one bearing the same name as that of *ācārya* Vasubandhu. He delivered many sermons on the Abhidharma-piṭaka.

Among them, now about *ācārya* Līlāvajra.

37. V tr 'He was a great *vajra-ācārya*, who perceived *dharma-dhātu* in Vāgīśvara-maṇḍala (one having the power on the words, i.e. Mañjuśrī).' S tr 'He was a *vajrācārya* who had personally perceived the Dharma-dhātu-vāgīśvara-maṇḍala.'

38. i.e. *Lokeśvaraśataka*—see note 23 of this chapter. cf Winternitz ii.377.

39. *sgeg-pa'i-rdo-rje*. For his works, see Supplementary Note 36.

40. Tg rG lviii.2.

He was born in a place called *Ṣiṣa[41]. [**Fol 106B**] was ordained in *Urgyana and was a follower of the Vijñāna-mādhyamika[42] philosophy. After becoming a scholar in all the branches of knowledge, he meditated on Ārya-mañjuśrī-nāma-saṃgīti in a small island called *Madhima in *Urgyana. When he was about to attain the *siddhi* of *ārya* Mañjuśrī, the face of the picture of Mañjuśrī radiated bright lustre and kept the island illuminated for many days. Hence he was called Sūrya-vat[43] (the sun-like). A certain heretic felt the need for the five sense-organs of an insider **paṇḍita* as materials for his rituals. He came to kill this *ācārya*. He [Līlāvajra] went on changing his own form into that of an elephant,[44] horse, girl and boy. So he could not spot him and went away. Hence he was called Viśva-rūpa[45] (one with all sorts of forms).

During the latter part of his life, he extensively worked for the welfare of the living beings in *Urgyana. After this, he attained the rainbow-body or *vajra-kāya.*

His ordained name was Śrī-varabodhi-bhāgyavān.[46] His esoteric (Tāntrika) name was Līlāvajra. Thus the name of the author of the works composed by him is differently mentioned as Līlāvajra, Sūryavat, Viśvarūpa, Śrī-varabodhi-bhāgyavān, etc.[47]

During this time, a son of a Caṇḍāla had the vision of (lit, met) Āryadeva[48] and under his blessings received the knowledge of the Doctrine without much effort. He meditated and attained *siddhi.* He received all the Tantra-śāstras of Nāgārjuna

41. S-ed Si-ṣa. P-ed Siṣa. V & S Śaṃśa. cf BA i.367—he was born in *nor-bu-gliṅ*, Maṇidvīpa.
42. *rnam-rig-dbu-ma-pa.* S *'nyāya-madhyamaka'.*
43. *ñi-ma-daṅ-'dra-ba.* V 'Sūrya-sadṛśa ?'
44. *glaṅ-po,* meaning both elephant and ox. S ox. V cow.
45. *sna-tshogs-kyi-gzugs.*
46. *dpal-ldan-byaṅ-chub-mchog-gi-skal-ba-daṅ-ldan-pa.*
47. See Supplementary Note 57.
48. V n 'According to Tāntrika teaching, it is possible to call a certain person from among the dead and receive from him a lost Tantra or initiation up to any extent. This is how the Tāntrikas explain the later appearance of their books, which nevertheless, according to

'the father and son.'[49] He also expounded some of these. This one was *Mātaṅgī-pā.[50]

Ācārya Rakṣita-pāda[51] of *Koṅkana[52] composed the *Pradīpodyotana*[53] under the direct instruction of Candrakīrti.[54]

Similarly, **paṇḍita* Rāhula[55] also met Nāgabodhi. This was only the beginning of the Dharma-viśiṣṭa-maṇḍala.[56]

[Fol 107A] Afterwards during the four later *Pālas, this was widely spread. Hence it is said, 'The two—namely the sun and the moon in the sky—while on the earth shone the two[57] [? the two works entitled the *Pradīpodyotana*].'

The twentyninth chapter containing the account of the period of Devapāla and his son.

their belief, were preached during (the lifetime of) Buddha. By the way, it is highly probable that there was some real person bearing the name Āryadeva and that later on—for giving him importance—he was described as identical with the famous pupil of Nāgārjuna'.

49. V n 'This explains why there occur in Tibetan translation such works of Nāgārjuna and Āryadeva, which are not at all mentioned by the Chinese.'

50. Tg rG lxxiv.46 *Kurukullā-sādhana* by Mātaṅgī-pāda.

51. *sruṅ-ba'i-shabs.* In Tg *Caturmukha-samaya-siddhi-sādhana* (rG lxxxii. 73) and *Karma-vidhi* (rG lxxiv. 10) are attributed to *mahācārya* Rakṣita.

52. cf BA i.368, 'at a distance of about 300 *yojana-s* south of Magadha, there was a thick forest in the region known as Kaṃ-ko-na. In a part of this forest resided the *ācārya* Rakṣita-pāda, a disciple of the *ācārya* Nāgārjuna.'

53. In Tg *Pradīpodyotana-nāma-ṭīkā* (rG xxviii. 1) is attributed to Candrakīrti. This apart, Tg contains *Pradīpodyotana* by Āryadeva (rG xxx & xxxi—the latter an abridged version), Lakṣmīṃkarā (rG xxix. 5) and Karuṇaśrī-pāda (rG xxix. 3).

54. V adds '(called from the other world)'.

55. *sgra-gcan-'dsin.* For his works, see Supplementary Note 57.

56. *chos-'phags-skor-mgo.* S 'the circle of the elites of the Doctrine'.

57. V adds '(i.e. the two works entitled the *Pradīpodyotana*)'. S n 'It appears that this was written on the title of both the works referred to as the *Pradīpodyotana*, one of which was by Candrakīrti and the other by Āryadeva'.

CHAPTER 30

ACCOUNT OF THE PERIOD OF KING ŚRĪ DHARMAPĀLA

After this, *Dharmapāla, the son of that king (Rāsapāla), ascended the throne. He ruled for sixtyfour years. He conquered also *Kīmarūpa, *Tīrahuti, *Gauḍa and other places. Thus his empire was very large and his command was extended in the east up to the sea, in the west up to *Di-li[1] (Delhi), in the north up to *Jalandhara and in the south up to the heart of the Vindhyācala.

He accepted as his preceptors Haribhadra and Jñānapāda and filled all directions with the Prajñā-pāramitā and the Śrī Guhya-samāja. The **pan̩ḍita*-s versed in the Guhya-samāja and the Prajñā-pāramitā were offered the highest seats of honour etc.

Round about the period when this king ascended the throne, *siddhācārya* *Kukuri-pā[2] appeared in *Bhaṃgala and worked for the welfare of the living beings. His account is given elsewhere.

Immediately after ascending the throne, the king invited the teachers of the Prajñā-pāramitā. He had great reverence for Haribhadra[3] in particular. This king built in all about fifty centres for the Doctrine, of which thirtyfive were centres for the study of the Prajñā-pāramitā. He also built the Śrī *Vikramaśīla[4] *vihāra*.

1. V Tili, as occuring in S-ed. P-ed Dili.
2. V & S Kukura. V n 'Kukura or Kukkura (Ku-khu-ri-pā) was a Brahmin in the kingdom of Kapila-bhargu. He attained *sādhāraṇa-siddhi* and was among the 33 gods. The bitch reared up by him, after becoming a *ḍākinī*, advised him to attain *paramā-siddhi* and he combined art with spiritual power.'
3. S Siṃhabhadra.
4. S n 'With noteworthy tenacity, the Tibetans retain the form Vikramalaśīla and I have allowed this form to remain in my text.'

It was built in the north of *Magadha on the bank of the *Gaṅgā on the top of a hillock.[5] The central temple in it had a human-size statue of the Mahābodhi. Around it, there were fiftythree smaller temples of Guhya Tantra and fiftyfour common temples. **[Fol 107B]** Thus he built [the monastery with a] total of one hundred and eight temples and the boundary walls. He lavishly provided with food and clothes one hundred and fourteen persons, namely one hundred and eight **paṇḍita*-s and the Bali-ācārya, Pratiṣṭhāna-ācārya, Homa-ācārya, Mūṣika-pāla,[6] Kapota-pāla and the supervisor of the *deva-dāsa*-s. For each of them he made provisions that was sufficient for four. Every month he organised a festival for those that listened to the Doctrine and also made excellent gifts to them.

The chief of this centre was also to look after *Nalendra. Each **paṇḍita* regularly explained there a special aspect of the Doctrine. Though there was no separate material provision for the different centres, these in fact amounted to one hundred and eight centres.

According to some, this king was an incarnation of *ācārya* *Kambala-pā. But it is difficult to accept this. It is said that a certain master of the Piṭaka, after attaining power through prayer, was reborn as the king for the purpose of propagating the Prajñā-pāramitā. Since the time of this king, the Prajñā-pāramitā was extensively propagated. Regarding the propagation of the *Prajñā-pāramitā-sūtra* in the different regions, it was predicted[7] in it that this was to be propagated first in the *madhya-deśa*, then in the south, then again in the *madhya-deśa*,

5. *magadha'i-byaṅ-ṅos* ('north of Magadha'). V tr 'on the top of a hill on the northern bank of the river Gaṅgā'.

6. P-ed *byi-ba-sruṅ-ba*, (*byi-ba*=mouse). S-ed *bya-ba-bsruṅ-ba* (*bya-ba*= instructions). S tr 'the protector of duties (or instructions)'. V tr 'Protector (? from) (of) mice'. V n 'I have read *byi-ba-sruṅ-ba*. S reads *bya-ba-bsruṅ-ba*'.

7. S tr 'In the chapter on the *bhūmi-parīkṣaṇa* of *the Prajñā-pāramitā-sūtra* it was predicted—' V tr 'In the *Prajñā-pāramitā-sūtra* it was predicted—'

then in the north and from the north to the distant north. Of this prediction, the period of the spread from the south to the *madhya-deśa* again is to be identified as the period of this king. According to some, in the *sūtra* itself it was said that (the Prajñā-pāramitā) was to be spread again in the *madhya-deśa* after its spread in the north. Such a view is the result of not studying the *sūtra*-s properly.

During the period of this king, western India was ruled by king *Cakrāyudha, which can be clearly seen in the brief inscription on the stone-pillar of Jayasena.

[Fol 108A] On a rough calculation, he (Dharmapāla) was a contemporary of the Tibetan king Khri-sroṅ-lde-btsan.[8]

During the period of this king (Dharmapāla) lived the great logician Kalyāṇagupta,[9] Haribhadra, Sundaravyūha[10] Sāgaramegha,[11] Prabhākara,[12] Pūrṇavardhana,[13] the great *vajrācārya* Buddhajñānapāda and his famous disciples, namely Buddhaguhya[14] and Buddhaśānti,[15] and, in Kashmir, *ācārya* Padmākaraghoṣa,[16] the logician Dharmākaradatta[17] and

8. Petech in IHQ supplement xiii, xv, 77-82 gives the date of this Tibetan king as A.D. 755-797. cf A Chattopadhyaya AT 212ff & 250ff.
9. *dge-sruṅ*. See Supplementary Note 58.
10. *mdses-bkod*. Tg contains *Gāthādvaya-vyākhyāna* (mDo xxxvii.5) by him, a commentary on Kg mDo Vol. *pa* xiii.2.
11. *rgya-mtsho-sprin*. Tg contains *Yogacaryā-bhūmi-bodhisattva-bhūmi-vyākhyā* (mDo lv) attributed to Sāgaramegha (Samudramegha).
12. *'od-zer*. See Supplementary Note 59.
13. *gaṅ-ba-spel-(ba)*. Tg contains a commentary on *Abhidharmakoṣa* (mDo lxvii-lxviii) and an abridged version of the same (mDo lxx.3) attributed to him.
14. *saṅs-rgyas-gsaṅ-ba*. See Supplementary Note 60.
15. *saṅs-rgyas-shi-ba*. Tg contains *Deśanāstava-vṛtti* (bsTod 49) attributed to him.
16. *padma-'byuṅ-gnas-dbyaṅs*. In Tg *Bhikṣu-varṣāgrapṛcchā* (mDo xc.21) is attributed to Padmākaraghoṣa, though it is usually considered to be a work of Padmasambhava—see Roerich BA i.30n & Obermiller Bu-ston ii.*intro*.4.
17. *chos-'byuṅ-byin*. Vidyabhusana HIL 329—he was a disciple of Dharmākaradatta of Kashmir and of Kalyāṇarakṣita.

Siṃhamukha[18], the expert in Vinaya.

Among them now about *ācārya* Haribhadra.

He took up ordination though coming from a royal family and was a profound scholar in many *śāstra*-s. He listened to the exposition of the Madhyamaka works from *ācārya* Śānti-rakṣita. From *upādhyāya* Vairocanabhadra[19] he listened to the Prajñā-pāramitā along with the *Abhisamaya-alaṃkāra-śāstra-upadeśa*. After this, he propitiated Jina Ajita in the *Khasar-paṇi forest in the east. He received his vision in dream and asked, 'There exist now many commentaries on the Prajñā-pāramitā composed from different philosophical view-points. Which of these should be followed ?' He then received the permission : 'Compile those parts of these that are acceptable.'

Shortly after this, king *Dharmapāla invited him. He lived in the **Trikaṭuka monastery and preached the Prajñā-pāramitā to thousands of listeners. He composed many *śāstra*-s like the *Aṣṭa-sāhasrikā-mahā-ṭīkā*.

[Fol 108B] He passed away more than twenty years after king *Dharmapāla ascended the throne.

Now about *ācārya* Sāgaramegha.

He had a vision of Jina Ajita. It is said that being instructed by him to compose the commentary on the *Yogacaryā-bhūmi* in five sections, he composed a commentary on the whole of it. However, his commentary on the Bodhisattva-bhūmi[20] is most famous.

18. *seṅ-ge gdoṅ-can*. Bu-ston ii.161 doubts the tradition according to which he was a disciple of Śākyaprabha.

19. *rnam-snaṅ-mdsad-bzaṅ-po*. See Supplementary Note 61.

20. V n : 'This work of Sāgaramegha is available in Tg. *Bodhisattva-bhūmi* is the second part (the first part being Śrāvaka-bhūmi) of the first of the five divisions of the Yogacaryā-bhūmi and contains 6,750 *śloka*-s. It is partly identical with Sūtrālaṃkāra. It expounds : 1) about the traditions of peoples, 2) about the origin of thought, 3) causing welfare to self and others, 4) about the value of the absolute, 5) about Buddha and his Doctrine, 6) about perfection, 7) about *bodhi*, 8) about powers, 9)—14) about the six *pāramitā*-s, each examined in nine ways.'

Regarding Padmākaraghoṣa, I think that he was the same as *upādhyāya* Lo-dri.[21]

Now about *mahācārya* Buddhajñānapāda.

He may be considered as the foremost disciple of Haribhadra. He attained *siddhi* and started preaching the Doctrine round about the period when Haribhadra passed away. After some years, he became the king's preceptor. Shortly after this, he consecrated the *Vikramaśila (monastery) and was appointed the Vajrācārya there. Beginning with the time when this *ācārya* started working for the welfare of the living beings and up to the time of his passing away, he used to receive every night seven hundred golden **paṇa*-s from *ārya* *Jambhala and three hundred pearl necklaces from the goddess Vasudhārā. By the grace of these deities, every morning the buyer for these turned up. He used to spend before each evening all the money obtained therefrom in pious acts. He spent the time thus. He used to offer lamps as big as the chariot-wheel —seven each for the nineteen deities of the Guhya-samāja and three each for the eight Bodhisattvas and the six Krodhas. He used to offer fifteen *naivedya*-s to the fifteen guardians of the horizons, each *naivedya* being raised by two men. He used similarly to offer many other articles of worship and to satisfy the disciples who listened to the Doctrine **[Fol 109A]** and the ordained monks and all sorts of supplicants. Thus he worked for the perpetual spread of the Law.

He told king *Dharmapāla, 'There are indications of the ruin of the dynasty during the rule of your grandson (*tsha-bo*). Perform the great *homa* so that the dynasty may last long and the Doctrine also may be extensively spread.'

Accordingly, he (Dharmapāla) got the *homa* performed for many years by the *vajradhara*-s with this *ācārya* as their chief and offered during this articles worth nine lakh and two thousand **tolā*-s of silver.

He (the *ācārya*) predicted [to the king] : 'Twelve of your

21. *lo-dri=varṣa-pṛcchā*. As author of *Bhikṣu-varṣāgrapṛcchā* (see note 16 above), Padmākaraghoṣa is also referred to as *upādhyāya* Lo-dri.

successors will be kings, and up to your fifth descendant in particular, many countries will be under their rule and the Law also will be extensively spread.' This prediction came true. The details of his life are to be found elsewhere.

In a temple of Vajrāsana there was then a large silver-image of *Heruka[22] and many treatises on Tantra.[23] Some of the Śrāvaka *Sendhava-s[24] of *Siṅga island (Ceylon) and other places said that these were composed by Māra.[25] So they burnt these and smashed the image into pieces and used the pieces as ordinary money.

From *Bhaṃgala people used to come to *Vikramaśila for offering worship. (The Śrāvaka Sendhavas told them), 'That which is called Mahāyāna is only a source of livelihood for those who follow the wrong view. Therefore, keep clear of these so-called preachers of the True Doctrine.' In this way, they used to draw people towards themselves. Later on, the king came to know all these and was about to punish the *Siṅgala islanders. But the *ācārya* saved them at last.

This *ācārya* also explained in a limited form the three *Kri-yogas (*kriyā-yoga*-s). **[Fol 109B]** But he preached most extensively the five Tantras of the insiders, namely the Samāja, Māyājāla, Buddha-samayoga, Candra-guhya-tilaka-and Mañjuśrī-krodha. Special emphasis was put on the teachings of the Guhya-samāja and so it was very widely spread.

The *ācārya* had a disciple called Praśāntamitra.[26] He was an excellent **paṇḍita* of the Abhidharma, Prajñā-pāramitā and the three *Kri-yogas. He lived *ad libitum*[27]. But recognising him as fortunate, *ācārya* Jñānapāda conferred *abhiṣeka* on him,

22. *shig* (one). V tr 'large silver images of Heruka.'
23. *sṅags* (mantra or tantra). V tr 'many secret treatises.'
24. D 1276—*sendhava*, probably Tibetanised form of the word *siddha*.
25. Chag lo-tsā-ba (Roerich SW 531f) also found the predominance of the Śrāvakas in Vajrāsana.
26. *rab-shi-bśes-gñen*. Tg contains three Tāntrika works by him—rG xxv. 3 ; lvi.3 ; lvi.4.
27. *ci-bder-gnas-pa*. D 381—placed as they liked ; name of a section of Tāntrika Buddhists in the monastery of Vikramaśīla during Atīśa's time. V 'he lived calmly.'

who, by meditating, received the vision of Yamāri and brought the powerful and malignant[28] *yakṣa* under control, obtained from him whatever wealth he wanted and distributed it to the needy. Employing the *yakṣa* to work for him, he built to the south of *Nalendra a monastery called the Amṛtākara[29]. At last he attained the *vidyādhara* state in mortal body.

Now about Kṣatriya Rāhulabhadra.

He studied in a centre of learning and received the degree of **paṇḍita*. But he was not very sharp in intellect. The *ācārya* [Buddhajñānapāda] conferred *abhiṣeka* on him and blessed him. For a long time he practised the Guhya-samāja on the bank of a river near the *Sindhu in the west, attained the vision of Pañcagotra Tathāgata[30] and became a direct *siddha* of Guhyapati. He went to the Draviḍa country, instead of[31] working for the welfare of the living beings only in Jambudvīpa. There he delivered many sermons on the Guhyatantra. He obtained wealth from the Nāgas and from this he used to pay everyday a golden **dināra* as the daily wage to each of the five hundred workers employed in the construction of a temple.

[Fol 110A] [Thus] he built a big temple of Guhya-samāja. He attained the *vidyādhara* state in the mortal body and entered the sea to subdue the Nāgas. He still lives there.

Ācārya Buddhaguhya and Buddhaśānti were disciples of *ācārya* Buddhajñānapāda during the first part of his life. They listened to many *guhya-mantra*-s in general from the *ācārya* himself and from many other Vajradharas. They became special adepts in the three Tantra-s of *kriyā*, *caryā* and *yoga* and attained *siddhi* in the *yoga-tantra*.

Now about Buddhaguhya.

He propitiated *ārya* Mañjuśrī somewhere in Vārāṇasī. As

28. S-ed *snod-nas* (pitcher). P-ed *gnod-gnas* (malignant). S tr 'attained control over all the treasures of the *yakṣa*-s with excellent wealth'.
29. *bdud-rtsi'i-'byuṅ-gnas*, lit. 'the source of nectar'.
30. *de-bshin-gśegs-pa-rigs-lṅa*. V n : 'Vairocana, Akṣobhya, Amitābha, Ratnākara, Amoghasiddhi'.
31. *cher-ma-mdsad*, lit. 'not working extensively'. S tr 'He extensively worked for the welfare of the living beings in Jambudvīpa...'

a result, the picture of the deity smiled. The article for the *siddhi*—namely ghee from red and yellow cows—started boiling. The withered flowers blossomed again. So he knew these as marks of approaching *siddhi*. But he remained hesitant for a while, thinking whether first to swallow the ghee or offer the flowers. At that moment, a *yakṣinī* causing obstruction slapped on the face of the *ācārya*, which made him unconscious for a little while. On regaining consciousness, (he saw) the picture of the deity covered with dust, the flowers withered and the ghee spilt on the ground. He wiped off the dust, put the flowers on the head [of the image] and swallowed the ghee that remained. This made his body free from all diseases, light and strong. Also his intellect became sharp and he was endowed with *abhijñāna*.

Without the aid of these articles and the picture of the deity, by meditation alone Buddhaśānti **[Fol 110B]** attained the same qualities as Buddhaguhya.

Then the two together went to the *Potala hill. At the foot of the hill, *āryā* Tārā sat preaching the Doctrine to the Nāgas. But they saw only an old woman tending a big herd of cows. When they reached the middle of the hill, the goddess Bhṛkuṭi was preaching the Doctrine to the group of Asuras and Yakṣas. But they saw a girl tending a big herd of goats and sheep. When they reached the top of the hill, there was nothing but a stone image of *ārya* Avalokiteśvara. Thus it is said.

But Buddhaśānti thought, 'Why should this place be full of such trivial objects ? So all these are due to the defects of my vision. They must be Tārā and others.' With this deep conviction, he earnestly prayed to them. Thus he acquired as the general quality the miraculous power of transforming anything at will and also the extraordinary quality of boundless *abhijñāna* and with this he learnt all the *śāstra*-s that he never studied before. He realised the nature of everything as but void (literally, like the *ākāśa*).

But Buddhaguhya prayed with no such conviction and he attained only the miraculous power of moving without his feet touching the earth. Then the old woman instructed him, 'Go to the Ti-se [Kailāsa] of the Himālayas and meditate there.'

On their way back[32] (from Potala), he asked Buddhaśānti, 'What sort of *siddhi* did you attain ?' He (Buddhaśānti) told him all that had happened. He felt somewhat jealous to know that his companion had attained greater *siddhi*. Immediately he lost even the *siddhi* of moving without touching the earth. It is said that after expiating for it for a long time, he regained the *siddhi*. Then he preached the Doctrine for a few years at *Vārāṇasi **[Fol 111A]** and, being instructed by *ārya* Mañjuśrī as before, he went to the mount Ti-se,[33] meditated there and had the repeated vision of Vajradhātu-mahā-maṇḍala.[34] He could even speak with *ārya* Mañjuśrī personally as it were.

He employed all the sub-human beings to his service and acquired the power of *karma-sambhāra*[35] and the *sādhāraṇa-siddhi*-s.

At that time, the Tibetan king Khri-sroṅ-lde-btsan sent *Mañjuśrī of dBus[36] and others to invite him (Buddhaguhya). But he did not go there, because the permission for this was refused by (the god) Mañjuśrī.[37] So he preached to them (i.e. Tibetans) the three *Kri-yoga-s (*kriyā-yoga*-s).

He composed the *Vajra-dhātu-yogāvatāra*,[38] *Vairocanā-bhisambodhi-tantra-ṭīkā*[39] and the *Dhyānottara-paṭala-ṭīkā*[40].

32. *tshur-'oṅs-pa-na*, lit. 'on the way back'. S tr 'reaching there'.
33. one of Buddhaguhya's work (rG lxviii.238) is said to have been composed in the Himālaya.
34. *rdo-rje-dbyiṅs* (*vajradhātu*—see Tg rG lvii.1 & li.2). S Dharmadhātu.
35. *las-tshogs*. V & S *kriyā-gaṇa*.
36. *dBus*, i.e. central Tibet.
37. Tg contains *Bhoṭa-svāmi-dāsa-lekha* (mDo xciv.39), a letter sent by Buddhaguhya to Khri-sroṅ-lde-btsan, the king of Tibet and his subjects, the Tibetan devotees.
38. No work exactly with this title is traced in Tg—see Supplementary Note 60.
39. Tg rC lxiv.1 and its auto-commentary rG lxiv.2.
40. rG lxvi.1.

There are many brief commentaries on his writings. Though he did not attain the *parama-siddhi*, his body became invisible.

Though it is said that Buddhaśānti also lived in Ti-se, it is clear that he went to *Urgyana.

Evidently, *ācārya* *Kamalaśila[41] also lived during the period of this king. Therefore, I do not consider him as prior or posterior to this king.

The thirtieth chapter containing the account of the period of king Śrī Dharmapāla.

41. See Supplementary Note 62.

CHAPTER 31

ACCOUNT OF THE PERIOD OF KING MASURAKṢITA, KING VANAPĀLA AND THE GREAT KING MAHĪPĀLA

*Masurakṣita [? Vasurakṣī],[1] a son-in-law of king *Dharmapāla, then ruled for about eight years. After him *Vanapāla, a son of king *Dharmapāla, ruled for about ten years. To their period belonged *ācārya* Dharmottara[2] the logician, *Dharmamitra, *Vimalamitra,[3] *Dharmākara[4] and others.

These two kings extensively worshipped the Doctrine. **[Fol 111B]** But since they 'left no mark of their hands' (i.e. did not construct any new monastery etc), they are not counted among the Seven *Pālas.

After them, *Mahīpāla, the son of king *Vanapāla, ruled the kingdom for fiftytwo years. Roughly speaking, the time of the death of this king was the same as that of the Tibetan king Khri-ral (Ral-pa-can).[5]

During the reign of this king lived *ācārya* Ānandagarbha,[6] the Mādhyamika-prāsaṅgika[7] Aśvaghoṣa,[8] who wrote Saṃvṛti and Paramārtha *Bodhicittabhāvanā-krama*,[9] *ācārya* Parahita,[10]

1. Here the text has Masurakṣita, though in the *Table of Contents* the name occurs as Vasurakṣī. V Masurakṣita.
2. *chos-mchog*. See Supplementary Note 63.
3. See Supplementary Note 64.
4. See Supplementary Note 65.
5. A.D. 806-841. See A. Chattopadhyaya AT 250ff.
6. *kun-dga'-sñiṅ-po*. See Supplementary Note 66.
7. *dbu-ma-thal-'gyur-ba*. S 'follower of the Mādhyamika'.
8. *rta-dbyaṅs*.
9. In Tg are attributed to Aśvaghoṣa (who belonged to the period of king Mahāpāla of Bengal: Lalou 187) *Paramārtha-bodhicitta-bhāvanākrama-varṇa-saṃgraha* (mDo xxx.5 & xxxiii.54) and *Saṃvṛti-bodhicittabhāvanopadeśa-varṇa-saṃgraha* (mDo xxx.4 & xxxiii.55).
10. *gshan-la-phan-pa*. See supplementary Note 67.

ācārya Candrapadma[11] and others. It is further clear that *ācārya* Jñānadatta[12] and Jñānakīrti[13] and others also belonged to this period. Also lived in Kashmir during this period *Jinamitra,[14] the expert in the Vinaya, *Sarvajñadeva,[15] *Dānaśīla[16] and others. It is clear that these three went also to Tibet.[17] Siddha *Tillipa[18] also belonged to this period. His account is to be found elsewhere.

Now about *ācārya* Ānandagarbha.

Born in a Vaiśya family in *Magadha, he belonged to the Mahāsāṃghika sect. In philosophy, he was a Vijñāna-madhyamaka.[19] He studied the five branches of knowledge[20] in *Vikramaśīla.

He came to know that in *Bhaṃgala the disciples of *siddharāja* **Prakāśacandra were preaching all the Yoga-tantras and so he went there. He met many *ācārya*-s like Subhūtipālita[21] and others and became a scholar in all the Yoga-tantras. Then he remained firm in the *dvādaśa-dhūta-guṇa*,[22] meditated in a forest and had the vision of Vajradhātu-mahā-maṇḍala.[23] He also received instructions to compose *śāstra*-s and could speak to

11. *zla-ba-padma.*
12. *ye-śes-byin.* In Tg is attributed to him *Ārya-caturdharmaka-vyākhyāna-ṭīkā* (mDo xxxiv.11).
13. *ye-śes-grags-pa.* In Tg are attributed to him *Tattvāvatārākhya-sakala-sugata-vacasā-tātparya-vyākhyā-prakaraṇa* (rG lxxii.5) and *Pāramitā-yāna-bhāvanākrama-upadeśa* (mDo xxx.15 & xxxiii.79).
14. See Supplementary Note 68.
15. See Supplementary Note 69.
16. See Note 10 of Ch 28.
17. Jinamitra and Dānaśīla were among the compilers of *Mahāvyutpatti* (mDo cxxiii.44). For Sarvajñadeva, see Supplementary Note 69.
18. Mentioned variously as Tailika-pāda, Tilo-pā, Telo-pā, Taili-pāda, snum-pā, dhe-li-pā. See Supplementary Note 70.
19. *rnam-rig-dbu-ma-pa.* See Supplementary Note 12.
20. *pañca-vidyā-sthānāni,* viz. *śabda-vidyā, hetu-vidyā, adhyātma-vidyā, cikitsā-vidyā* and *śilpasthāna-vidyā.* See Roerich SW 506n.
21. *rab-'byor-bskyaṅs.* In Tg is attributed *Homa-vidhi* (rG lvii.10) to him.
22. *sbyaṅs-pa'i-yon-tan-bcu-gñis*—see D 939 on the *dhūta-guṇa*-s. S tr 'he practised the two highly renowned virtues'.
23. S Mahādharmadhātu-maṇḍala.

the tutelary deity personally as it were.

[**Fol 112A**] After he became an adept in magic spells, he easily acquired the power of all *karma-sambhāra*-s. When he was about to attain *siddhi*, his fame reached *ācārya* *Prajñāpālita,[24] who came from the *madhya-deśa* to listen to the Doctrine from him. He then conferred *abhiṣeka* on him (Prajñāpālita) and explained to him the *Tattva-saṃgraha*. For this *ācārya*, he (Ānandagarbha) composed the Vajrodaya.[25]

When he (Prajñāpālita) expounded this in the *madhya-deśa*, the king *Mahīpāla asked him, 'From whom did you receive this text ?'

'Do you have no knowledge even of one who lives in your own kingdom ? I have received this from *ācārya* Ānandagarbha, who resides in *Bhaṃgala.'

Full of reverence, the king invited him to the monastery of *Otsayana-cūḍāmaṇi near Jvālā-guhā[26] in the south of *Magadha. The number of the listeners to the Guhya-samāja became vast. He composed many *śāstra*-s, like the *Tattva-āloka-karī*[27] the great commentary on the *Tattva-saṃgraha*.[28]

King *Vīrācārya of *Oḍiviśa, who was like a real brother to[29] king *Mahīpāla, invited him to a *vihāra* which was situated at the place where previously lived King *Muñja. He first composed the great commentary on the *Śrī-paramādi(-vivaraṇa)*.[30] He [Ānandagarbha] also composed[31] a commentary on the Guhya-samāja and on many other Tantras. According to some of the

24. See Supplementary Note 71.
25. See Supplementary Note 66.
26. *'bar-ba'i-phug*.
27. In Tg is attributed to *ācārya* Ānandagarbha *Sarva-tathāgata-tattva-saṃgraha-mahāyāna-abhisamaya-nāma-tantra-vyākhyā-Tattvālokakarī-nāma* (rG lii-liii).
28. *Sarva-tathāgata-tattvasaṃgraha-nāma-mahāyāna-sūtra*—Sendai Cat No 479. Not to be confused with Śāntarakṣita's *Tattva-saṃgraha* (mDo cxiii.1), nor with another work having the title *Tattva-saṃgraha* and attributed to Ghaṇṭā-vajra (rG lxxxiv.7).
29. *pha-spun-du-'gro-ba. pha-spun*, lit. 'brothers and sisters of the same father' and *du-'gro-ba*, lit' 'one who moves'. S tr 'who moved about with Mahīpāla as a father moves with the son'.
30. See Supplementary Note 66.
31. *ib*.

Tibetans, he composed commentaries on one hundred and eight Yoga-tantras. But it is doubtful if there existed at that time even twenty Yoga-tantras in India.[32] Further, as correctly said by the scholars, there is no basis to say that he composed two commentaries on each of the Yoga-tantras, one big and the other small. Hence it is clear that it is wrong to consider the number to be even a hundred.

[Fol 112B] During this period lived an *ācārya* called *Bhago,[33] who attained *siddhi* by the Vajrāmṛta-tantra.

Previously in Kashmir a **paṇḍita* called Gambhīravajra[34] propitiated Vajrasūrya by the Śrī-sarva-buddha-samayoga-tantra[35] in the crematorium of Śitavana. He had at last the vision of Vajra-amṛta-mahā-maṇḍala and attained the *sādhāraṇa-siddhi* under its blessings.

He prayed, 'Please grant me the *parama*[-*siddhi*]'.

'Go to the *Urgyana country and there in a place called *Dhūmasthira ask for it from a woman who has the complexion of an **utpala* and who bears an emerald-like mark on the forehead.'

This being done, he received it [the *siddhi*]. This *ḍākinī* conferred on him the *abhiṣeka* of Catuḥ(-vajra)-amṛta-maṇḍala. She herself explained to him the Tantras and gave him the treatises on these. Among these, he meditated on *Heruka and attained *mahā-mudrā-siddhi*. After this, he resided in *Mālava. He came across eight beggars and, finding them fit, conferred *abhiṣeka* on them and led them to meditation. The *ācārya* himself attained *siddhi* of eight *vetāla*-s in the crematorium and gave a *vetāla* to each of them. All of them also attained *mahā-siddhi*. He also made a gift of his *sādhāraṇa*

32. S tr 'But this is improbable, inasmuch as up to that period only twenty Yoga-tantras had originated in the *ārya-deśa*.'
33. In Tg is attributed to *siddha-mahācārya* Bhago *Śrī-vajrāmṛta mahātantrarājasya-ṭīkā* (rG xxiv.3).
34. *zab-pa'i-rdo-rje*. In Tg is attributed to *mahāmudrā-siddhācārya* Gambhīravajra of Urgyana a commentary on the *Mahāmudrā-tilaka* called *Śrī-guhyārtha-prakāśa-mahādbhuta-nāma* (rG xx.2).
35. *dpal-saṅs-rgyas-thams-cad-mñam-par-sbyor-ba'i-rgyud*.

siddhi to others. Though there were many who attained *siddhi* for themselves, it is said that only the greatest among the great *siddha*-s could make a gift of their *siddhi* to others.

Further, this *ācārya* had once four disciples. He led each of them to meditation on the Catuḥ-amṛta-maṇḍala. [**Fol 113A**] He also preached *sampannakrama* to each of them and thus they attained Vajrakāya and became invisible. Later on *ācārya* Amṛtaguhya[36] became his disciple. He conferred *abhiṣeka* on him and preached to him the Tantras. After this he went to the realm of the gods to work for the welfare of the living beings.

Ācārya Amṛtaguhya also attained *siddhi* and he was a *mahā-yogī*. He attained the *siddhi* of the *aṣṭa-kośa-kalasa* and satisfied all the poor people. He received wealth from the god of the sky and maintained without interruption eight big centres for the Doctrine.

There is no definite account of the king to whose period they belonged. But by collating the different reports, it becomes clear that they lived after king *Devapāla.

Ācārya *Bhago was his (Amṛtaguhya's) disciple. He also attained *vetāla-siddhi*. With its aid he succeeded in many auspicious *kośa-kalasa-sādhana*. He satisfied everybody all around and built a big temple of Pañcagotratathāgata near the city of *Prayāga and also a big temple of Vajrāmṛta in *Karṇāṭa in the south. He preached the Tantras to **paṇḍita* Vimalabhadra[37] and many others.

It is said that under the auspices of these *ācārya*-s, this Tantra was widely spread also in *Magadha.

The thirtyfirst chapter containing the account of the period of king Masurakṣita [? Vasurakṣī] king Vanapāla and the great king Mahīpāla.

36. *bdud-rtsi-gsaṅ-ba*.

37. *dri-med-bzaṅ-po*. In Tg are attributed to him *Śrī-vajrāmṛta-pañjikā* (rG xxiv.1) and *Vajrāmṛta-tantra-ṭīkā* (rG xxiv.2).

CHAPTER 32

ACCOUNT OF THE PERIOD OF THE KINGS MAHĀPĀLA AND ŚĀMUPĀLA

His (Mahīpāla's) son king *Mahāpāla ruled for fortyone years. He mainly worshipped the Śrāvaka *saṃgha* in the *Odantapurī *vihāra*.

[**Fol 113B**] He maintained there five hundred *bhikṣu*-s and fifty preachers of the Doctrine. As an annexe to this (*vihāra*), he built a *vihāra* called *Uruvāsa. Here also he provided five hundred Śrāvaka-sendhavas with livelihood. Though allowing *Vikramaśīla to retain its previous position, he made this the centre of great veneration. He established some centres for the Doctrine also in Śrī *Nalendra and many centres for the Doctrine also in *Somapurī, *Nalendra[1] and *Trikaṭuka monasteries.

*Piṭo *ācārya*[2] brought the Kālacakra Tantra during the latter half of the life of *Mahīpāla, but he spread it during the period of this king (Mahāpāla).

The logician Alaṃkāra-upādhyāya *alias* Prajñākaragupta[3] also lived during this period.

1. Though S-ed also contains this repetition of Nālandā, S omits it in his tr.
2. In the account of the spread of Kālacakra given in BA ii.753ff, instead of Piṭo-ācārya, we have the name of the Great Piṇḍo-pā, who first obtained the Kālacakra from Sambhala (BA ii.761). D 782, on the authority of Tāranātha's *bka'-babs-bdun-ldan-gyi-rnam-thar*, mentions Pi-rto-pā as an Indian Buddhist who is said to have visited Sambhala. BA i.371 mentions Bito-pāda, a disciple of Buddhaśrījñāna and BA i. 262 mentions Piṭo-pā as one of the five special (Indian) disciples of Atīśa.
3. See note 65 of Ch 26.

Also lived (during this period) *Yoga-pā,[4] Padmāṅkuśa,[5] *Jetāri[6] the senior, Kṛṣṇasamaya-vajra,[7] *ācārya* *Thagana[8] and others.

The account of *Piṭo *ācārya* is to be clearly found elsewhere. It is clear that his disciple Kālacakrapāda[9] lived sometime during the period of this king.

After the death of this king, his son-in-law *Śāmupāla ruled for twelve years.

Now about *ācārya* *Jetāri among them.

In *Varendra in the east there previously lived a feudatory chief called *Sanātana during the reign of king *Vanapāla. His chief queen was very beautiful and intelligent. He also loved her dearly. Even at the time of her bath, he used to place her on a golden tortoise and allowed none to see her. This king received the *abhiṣeka* of Guhyasamāja from the *brāhmaṇa ācārya* Garbhapāda[10] and offered him as fee this queen, horses, gold, elephants, etc.

4. S takes it as an adjective of Padmāṅkuśa and tr : 'Padmāṅkuśa, well-versed in the Yoga'. But in the account of the 84 *siddha*-s, Yogi-pā (Ayogi-pā) is mentioned as the 53rd one : he was a *ḍoma* by caste, belonged to Udantapurī (? Odantapurī) and a disciple of Śabara-pā. —see R. Sankrityayana *Purātattva-nibandhābali* 152. In Tg is possibly attributed to him *Vāyusthāna-roga-parikṣā-nāma* (rG xlviii. 81).

5. In Tg the Tibetan form of his name is given as *padma-lcags-kyu* and three Tāntrika works are attributed to him (rG lxix.169-71).

6. See Supplementary Note 72.

7. *nag-po-dam-tshig-rdo-rje*. S Kālasamayavajra. In Tg one Tāntrika work is attributed to Samaya-vajra or Kṛṣṇa-samaya (rG xxxiv.3) and four to Kṛṣṇavajra (rG xxii.34 ; xxiii.18 ; xlvii.44 & lxxxvi.71).

8. In the account of the 84 *siddha*-s, Thagana-pā is mentioned as the 19th : he was a *śūdra* by caste, belonged to eastern India and was a preceptor of Śānti-pā. BA ii.847 mentions a *brāhmaṇa* Thagana. Tg contains one work (rG xxi.30) by *mahā-brāhmaṇa* Thakkana or Thagana of Urgyana and three works (rG xxxv.3 ; xxxiv.16 & xlviii. 16) are attributed to Thagana, the last of these being *Dohākoṣa-tattva-gītikā*.

9. See Supplementary Note 73.

10. *sñiṅ-po'i-shabs*. In Tg are attributed to him *Vajrayāna-mūlāpatti-ṭīkā* (xlviii.144) and *Kalpokta-mārīcī-sādhana* (rG lxxi.228).

[**Fol 114A**] Gambhīrapāda had a son with auspicious marks born of her. At the age of seven he was sent to an elementary school of the *brāhmaṇa*-s. The other *brāhmaṇa* boys beat him saying, 'You are born in a low family.' When he asked the reason for this, they said, 'Being a Buddhist Tāntrika your father gave the Śūdra queen a higher status and, while worshipping, he does not distinguish between the low and high castes and allows these to mix.'

Thus they persecuted him so much that he returned home weeping. On being enquired by the father, he said all that had happened.

'So they are to be subdued.' Saying this he conferred the *abhiṣeka* of Mañjughoṣa on him and led him to meditation with proper instructions.

After the completion of about a year, he sank deep into the *śuddha-pratibhāsa-samādhi*[11] and had the signs of the approaching *siddhi*. Both inside and outside the cottage, the beam of golden yellow light was spread everywhere. When his mother brought food for him, she saw this and thinking that the cottage had caught fire started crying. This interrupted his meditation and the rays vanished.

His father said : 'He would have himself become equal to Mañjughoṣa only if he could continue to remain in this *śuddha-pratibhāsa* [*-samādhi*] for seven days. But some obstruction is caused to this. Anyhow, he will have great intelligence and will have free access to all the spheres of learning.'

And it happened like that. He learnt without studying the scripts, all the fine arts, prosody, *śabda-vidyā* etc. He became the lord of the great scholars by learning many branches of knowledge only with a single reading and by studying only once or twice even the subjects that were most difficult.

11. V n *'tiṅ-ṅe-'dsin-gyi-gsal-snaṅ*. S mentions that here this should be taken to mean *snaṅ-ba-gsal-ba-nas-bya-ba'i-tiṅ-ṅe-'dsin*, i e. *śuddha-pratibhāsa-samādhi* mentioned in the *Mahāvyutpatti*. In Tantras, this radiation is one of the highest states of *samādhi*, which indicates that the objective is approaching.'

[Fol 114B] He remained an *upāsaka* throughout his life. With his father he studied whatever he (the father) knew—the Guhyasamāja, Cakrasamvara, Hevajra, etc. He also took resort to many other teachers. But he had the special privilege of listening to all the doctrines from Mañjughoṣa himself.

From the time of the death of his father *brāhmaṇa* Garbhapāda to the period of king *Mahīpāla, he did not receive the **patra*.[12] So he went round many places to worship at various temples and to compete with the **paṇḍita*-s in learning. Once he went to *Khasarpaṇi. In front of the gate he saw the image of the fierce Acala and taking it for that of a *rākṣasa*, he had disrespect for it. In a dream he saw many Acalas coming out of the heart of the Great Sage and suppressing all the wicked people. So he wanted to atone for the sin of showing disrespect to the contrivance of the Buddha himself and, as a result, had a vision of Tārā.

She said, 'Compose many treatises on Mahāyāna. That will remove your sin.'

Later on, during the period of king *Mahāpāla a good residence called *Vṛkṣapurī and also the **patra* conferring on him the status of a **paṇḍita* of *Vikramaśīla were offered to him. He delivered many sermons on the Doctrine and his fame spread more and more. He composed[13] short commentaries on the *Śikṣā-samuccaya*, *Caryāvatāra*, *Ākāśagarbha-sūtra* etc. In general, he composed about one hundred *śāstra*-s on many *sūtra*-s and *tantra*-s.

Now about Kṛṣṇasamaya-vajra.

He belonged to the lineage of *ācarya* Buddhajñānapāda. [Fol 115A] In a solitary place of *Rā-ra,[14] he hung up a picture of Hevajra and sat in deep meditation. After many years, when he himself intensely concentrated on the Prati-

12. S-ed *satra*, P-ed *patra*—the letter conferring the title of *paṇḍita*. V n 'S tr diploma and assumes that this is a corruption of the word *patra*.'
13. See Supplementary Note 72.
14. S Chagala, V 'Rāḍa (? Chagala).' The word *ra* in Tibetan means goat.

bhāsa-samādhi of the Maṇḍala, his consort[15] saw a certain object lying reclined[16] in front of the picture. When she told this to the *ācārya*, his meditation was interrupted. He touched the object lying reclined and found it to be a corpse. He realised that it was an article needed for the *siddhi* and gobbled it up without hesitation. After spending seven days in the *sukha-śūnyatā-samādhi*,[17] when he woke up he had the direct vision of the Hevajra-maṇḍala and attained unlimited power.

The thirtysecond chapter containing the account of the period of kings Mahāpāla and Śāmupāla.

15. S 'mother of knowledge'. This is because he reads the word as *rig-ma* ('mother of Veda, Gāyatrī', etc), which should better be read here as *rigs-ma* (consort). V consort.
16. S unclean. But the text has *yor-yor-ba* (reclined).
17. *bde-stoṅ*, an abbreviation of *bde-ba-daṅ-stoṅ-pa-ñid*—see D 669.

CHAPTER 33

ACCOUNT OF THE PERIOD OF KING CANAKA

After this, *Śreṣṭhapāla, the eldest son of king *Mahāpāla, ascended the throne and died after three years. As he left 'no mark of his hands' [i.e. built no monastery etc] he is not counted among the Seven (Pālas).

On a rough calculation, the second half of the life of king *Mahāpāla synchronised with the 'Subsequent Propagation of the Doctrine in Tibet'.[1] To this period also belonged *brāhmaṇa* Jñānapāda.[2] It is said to have been the period also of the latter half of the life of Kṛṣṇācārya the junior.[3]

As the younger son (of Mahāpāla) had not yet attained seventeen[4] years, his maternal uncle *Canaka ruled during the intervening period.

During his (Canaka's) period, *ācārya* *Śānti-pā[5] and others were invited. From this period on, the designation Six Door-keeper Scholars[6] was introduced.

He (Canaka) ruled for twentynine[7] years and, in a war, won victory over the *Turuṣka king.

[Fol 115B] The *Bhaṃgalas once revolted and came to wage war in *Magadha. The Bali-ācārya of *Vikramaśīla prepared *mahā-bali*[8] for Acala. When he put it into the *Gaṅgā, many boats carrying the *Turuṣkas from *Bhaṃgala were drowned.

1. i.e. the revival of Buddhism in Tibet after the persecution by gLaṅ-dar-ma ; the persecution took place in A.D. 901 (or A.D. 841). See A. Chattopadhyaya AT 282.
2. *ye-śes-shabs.*
3. *nag-po-spyod-pa-chuṅ-ba.* BA i. 372 mentions Balin-ācārya, a contemporary of Nāro-pā and also known as Kṛṣṇapāda, the Junior.
4. S-ed *bdun* (seven), P-ed *bcu-bdun* (seventeen). V & S seven.
5. See Supplementary Note 74.
6. i.e. of the Vikramaśīla-vihāra.
7. *ñi-śu-rtsa-dgu* (29). S twentyeight. V twentynine,
8. *gtor-chen*—D 527.

The king had the honour of winning the war. He subdued them (i.e. the Turuṣkas from Bhaṃgala) and restored peace in the kingdom.

After this, his nephew *Bheyapāla, the younger son of king *Mahāpāla,[9] ascended the throne. He (Canaka) lived in *Bhāṭi[10] a small island near the confluence of the *Gaṅgā and the sea in the east of *Bhaṃgala and died there after five years.

During this period, among the Six Door-keeper Scholars the eastern door-keeper was *ācārya* Ratnākaraśānti-pā.[11] His account is to be found elsewhere.[12]

Now about the southern[13] door-keeper Prajñākaramati.[14] He was a scholar in all the branches of learning and had the direct vision of Mañjuśrī. At the time of having debates with the *tīrthika*-s, the moment he worshipped Mañjuśrī and prayed to his picture, the appropriate answers to all the arguments offered by the *tīrthika*-s used to occur to him. It is said

9. S-ed Mahāpāla, P-ed Mahīpāla. The former reading followed.
10. V Bhāṭi.
11. See Supplementary Note 74.
12. V n 'According to the account of the 84 *siddha*-s Śānti was a *brāhmaṇa* by caste. During the time of Dharmapāla, he was a teacher in Bikramaśīla (? Vikramaśīla) and from there was invited to Ceylon by king Ghavin. After three years, on his way back to Vikramaśīla he met Koṭali and gave him *upadeśa*. After twelve years, when Koṭali attained *siddhi*, he (Koṭali) came to pay his respects to Śānti. He found that his teaching could lead to nowhere and hence he took to *sādhana*. In twelve years he attained *mahā-mudrā*, lived for 700 years (? ! !) and went to heaven.'
13. *lho-sgo* (southern gate). But BA i.206—'the six Gate-keeper Paṇḍitas of Vikramaśīla : at the eastern (gate) Śānti-pā, at the southern gate Vāgīśvarakīrti, at the western gate Prajñākaramati, at the northern gate *mahā-paṇḍita* Nāro-pā, in the centre Ratnavajra and Jñānaśrī', cf also the colophon of Prajñākaramati's *Abhisamayālaṃkāravṛtti-piṇḍārtha* (mDo vii.4), where he is mentioned as the western door-keeper (*nub-kyi-sgo* i.e. *apara-dvāra-kapāṭaka*) of Vikramaśīla. But see Tar Fol 117B.
14. *śes-rab-'byuṅ-gnas-blo-gros*. In Tg are attributed to him *Abhisamayālaṃkāra-vṛtti-piṇḍārtha* (mDo vii.4), *Bodhicaryāvatāra-pañjikā* (mDo xxvi.2) and *Śiṣyalekha-vṛtti* (mDo xciv.37).

that after this, when the debate resumed, his victory was a certainty.

Misled by the name Prajñākara, I have found many to commit the mistake of confusing Prajñākaramati with Prajñākaragupta.[15] But it is well-known among the scholars that he (Prajñākaramati) was in rank a *bhikṣu* while Prajñākaragupta was only an *upāsaka*.

Now about the western[16] door-keeper scholar *ācārya* Vāgīśvarakīrti.[17] Born in *Vārāṇasī, he was by caste a Kṣatriya and was ordained in the sect of the Mahāsāṃghika. **[Fol 116A]** He received the name *Śīlakīrti from the *upādhyāya*. When he became a profound **paṇḍita* in grammar, logic and in many other *śāstra*-s, he received the Cakrasamvara from one *Hāsavajra,[18] a follower of Jayabhadra[19] of *Koṅkana. While meditating somewhere in *Magadha, he received in dream his (Cakrasamvara's) vision. He examined the prospect of attaining *siddhi* in Vāgīśvara-sādhana and found the answer in the affirmative.

He meditated on the bank of the *Gaṅgā and dropped a red *Karavīra flower into the *Gaṅgā, which emanated sound and illumination. In a moment it was carried away many *yojana*-s afar and floated back again. He swallowed it up with the water and became a great *siddha* of Vāgīśvara. He came to be called Vāgīśvarakīrti as a result of acquiring the intelligence by which he could completely master everyday the words and imports of a *śāstra* containing a thousand *śloka*-s. He became a vast scholar of the *sūtra*-s, *tantra*-s and all the other branches of knowledge and he found no difficulty in the three, namely exposition, disputation and composition. He

15. *śes-rab-'byuṅ-gnas-sbas-pa*, See Note 65 of Ch 26.
16. *nub-sgo* (western door). But see note 13 of this chapter
17. *ṅag-gi-dbaṅ-phyug-grags-pa*. See Supplementary Note 75.
18. BA i.103 refers to the commentary on the Guhya-samāja by Vajrahāsa and to 'the chapter on the system of Vajra-hāsa'. Tg contains a work (rG lxxv.12) attributed to Hāsavajra.
19. *rgyal-ba-bzaṅ-po*. S & V Jinabhadra. Tg contains a number of works on Cakra-samvara by Jayabhadra of Ceylon—see note 139 of Introduction. & Fol 126B.

frequently received the vision of *āryā* Tārā in particular, who solved all his problems. Thus he acquired the proficiency of defeating many *tīrthika* rivals while going about many places and his fame grew more and more.

The king invited him to *Nalendra and appointed him as the western gate-keeper of *Vikramaśīla.[20] He obtained wealth from Gaṇapati and always worshipped at many temples and *saṃgha*-s. He built many centres for the Doctrine. These included the eight centres for Prajñāpāramitā, four for the teaching of the Guhyasamāja [**Fol 116B**] and one seat [?] each for the teaching of Hevajra, Cakrasamvara and *Māyā [?][21] and also one particularly for the Madhyamaka-pramāṇa.

He made various preparations of elixir[22] and gave these to others. By these one could reach the age of one hundred and fifty and the old man became young. In this way he caused welfare to about five hundred ordained monks and pious householders. He used to preach constantly the Vidyāsambhāra, Prajñāpāramitā, Sūtrālaṃkāra, Guhyasamāja, Hevajra, Yamāri, Laṅkāvatāra, etc, and many other *sutra*-s. He also delivered many sermons on the Doctrine.

As he had a sharp intellect for silencing the *tīrthika*-s, he defeated about three hundred rivals who came from

20. S tr 'The king invited him to become the western gate-keeper of Nalendra and Vikramaśīla.' See note 13 of this chapter.
21. S proposes to read the text somewhat differently : instead of *bde-dgyes-gdan-gshi* as *bde-dgyes-gdan-bshi*, S tr 'Receiving treasure from Gaṇapati, he regularly brought offerings to many temples and *saṃgha*-s, established eight teaching centres of the Prajñāpāramitā, four centres for the teaching of the Guhyasamāja, one centre each for the teaching of the Tantras, namely Sambara, Hevajra and Catuḥpīṭhī'. V tr is similar and he adds in note that there are works in Kg & Tg on Catuḥ-pīṭhī Tantra. In P-ed, however, the word *māyā* occurs in transliteration, instead of which S-ed has *gsum* (three).
22. V n *'bcud-len* ; S mentions that in Tg there is a work on *Mṛtyu-vañcana-upadeśa* ascribed to Vāgīśvara'. cf Tg rG xxvi.68 ; lxxxi.21 & lxxxii.35.

the west. He could make the water in a vessel boil by concentrating for a moment on it. When he consecrated (literally infused life : *prāṇapratiṣṭhā*) an image, it used to move.

Once he drew up *a maṇḍala* for the sake of the king. A devastating flood came near the *maṇḍala*. As he protected it with his concentration, the flood receded from its fringe. He showed many miraculous feats like these on different occasions.

He was once having a discussion on the Doctrine with a *bhikṣu* called *Avadhūti-pā. When he (Avadhūti) quoted Vasubandhu, he (Vāgīśvara) made sarcastic remarks on the use of corrupt (*apabhraṃśa*) words by Vasubandhu. In the same night his tongue swelled and he became incapable of preaching the Doctrine. He suffered from this for several months and on praying to Tārā was told : 'This is the result of your disparaging remarks on *ācārya* Vasubandhu. Therefore, compose *stuti*-s for this *ācārya*.' Accordingly, as soon as he composed the *stuti*, he was cured of the disease.

[Fol 117A] He then worked in *Vikramaśīla for the welfare of all living beings for many years. In the latter part of his life, he went to Nepal. He remained mostly in meditation there, though he preached a little of the Tantra-yāna. But he preached hardly any other aspect of the Doctrine. As he had many consorts most of the people thought that he was incapable of maintaining the conduct of a monk.

The king once built a temple of Cakrasamvara in *Śāntapurī. After its consecration, he got many Tāntrikas to assemble outside the temple for holding a big *gaṇa-cakra*. He sent a messenger to the *ācārya*, inviting him to act as the chief (of the *gaṇa-cakra*). There was a voluptuous dancing girl at the entrance of the cottage of the *ācārya*. There was also a black and violent woman. When (the messenger) asked, 'Where is the *ācārya* ?', they said 'He is inside the cottage.' Then he entered the cottage and said, 'The king requests you to come and act as the chief of the *gaṇa-cakra*.'

'Go back quickly. I shall soon be there.' As he (the messenger) was returning quickly, the *ācārya* along with his two consorts had already reached the cross-road near *Śāntapurī and said, 'We are waiting for you for a long time.'

When the main consecration followed by the big *gaṇa-cakra* came to its end, there remained within the temple only three, i.e. the *ācārya* and his two consorts.[23] He entered the temple with more than the share for sixty participants of the *gaṇa-cakra*. The king thought : 'There are only three within the temple. What then could be the use for so much provisions of the *gaṇa-cakra* !' So he peeped through the door **[Fol 117B]** and saw sixtytwo deities of Cakrasamvara-maṇḍala sitting there and enjoying the provisions of the *gaṇa-cakra*.

In the same place also sat the *ācārya* who had attained the rainbow body.

In the Tibetan account, Vāgīśvarakīrti is said to have been the southern door-keeper and Prajñākara the western door-keeper. What I have written here is based on a consensus of three Indian sources.[24]

The northern door-keeper was *Nāro-pā[25]. His account is to be found elsewhere.[26]

*Śānti-pā, the omniscient of the Kali era (*kali-kāla-sarvajña*) listened to the Doctrine from this *ācārya*.

Along with his disciples, *ācārya* *Śānti-pā was once engaged

23. S tr 'He remained inside the temple along with the father and mother'. The text has *yab-yum* which, though literally means 'father & mother', is also used in the Tāntrika context as honorific for the Tāntrika and his consort—see D 1129.
24. See note 13 of this chapter.
25. See Supplementary Note 76.
26. V n 'Nāro-pā was a wood-seller in Pāṭaliputra in eastern India. Having met the *siddha* Tailo-pā in a crematorium, he served him for 12 years in spite of various quarrels with him and collected alms for him. Finally he brought for him the delicious food of *sdobatapa* (?) and received from him the initiation in Vajravārāhī. In Kg there are two works of this Tantra, viz. *Kriyā-vajravārāhī* (vol *ga* 215-222) and *Jñāna-vajravārāhī* (vol *na* 82-95). In six months, Nāro-pā attained *siddhi* and from his heart came out light, which remained visible for a month, He lived for about 700 years and went to heaven with this body'.

in an act of worship. He sent one of his disciples with offerings, who saw a terrible-looking *yogī* on the *bali* altar. He was panic-stricken and just threw the offerings, came back and reported it to the *ācārya*. The *ācārya* realised that this must have been *Nāro-pā and so he invited him. He sat at his feet and received many *abhiṣekas*, sermons and explanations of the sermons etc. He bowed down before him again and again.

Later on, when *Śānti-pā was about to attain *siddhi*, *Nāro-pā was begging with a skull as his begging bowl. A robber dropped a small knife into the skull. *Nāro-pā cast his magic stare at it and it melted like ghee. He swallowed it and went away.

There was a body of a dead elephant on the cross-road. He performed the rite of entering into it[27] and it walked to the crematorium. When *Śānti-pā came across 'it, *Nāro-pā's voice said, 'Such is the mark of my being a *yogī*. **[Fol 118A]** Will not the great scholar also show some such mark ?'

Ācārya *Śānti-pā said, 'What can a person like me perform afterall ? However, if permitted by a person like you, I may perform something.'

Some people were approaching the place with pitchers full of water. By his magic spell, the water was transformed into liquid gold. He then distributed it among the monks and *brāhmaṇa*-s.

For some years *Nāro-pā also acted as the northern door-keeper. After that he went over to *caryā*.[28] He was succeeded by *sthavira* Bodhibhadra.[29]

(Now about Bodhibhadra).

Born in a Vaiśya family of *Oḍiviśa, he was a perfect *bodhisattva* in his conduct (*caryā*). He was a scholar of the Vidyā-sambhāra, Caryā-sambhāra and specially of the Bodhisattva-bhūmi. He had a vision of *ārya* Avalokiteśvara and

27. S tr 'He let it enter into a village'. The text has *groṅ-'jug*, 'bringing life to a dead body'—see D 250.

28. S '*yoga*', because S-ed has *rnal-'byor-pa* (*yoga*). P-ed has *spyod-pa* (*caryā*).

29. *byaṅ-bzaṅ*. See Supplementary Note 77.

directly listened to the Doctrine from him.

Now about *brāhmaṇa* Ratnavajra,[30] the first great Central Pillar (of Vikramaśīla). A *brāhmaṇa* of Kashmir once propitiated Maheśvara and it was predicted that all his descendants were going to be famous scholars. This came true. The first twentyfour of his descendants were *tīrthika*-s. The twentyfifth of them was *brāhmaṇa* *Haribhadra, who, being defeated in a debate by the Buddhists, was converted into an insider. In this debate he staked his own creed. He became a **paṇḍita* with profound knowledge of the Doctrine. His son was *brāhmaṇa* Ratnavajra.

[Fol 118B] He (Ratnavajra) was an *upāsaka* in rank. He studied in Kashmir up to the age of thirty and learnt by heart the *sūtra*-s, *tantra*-s and all the branches of knowledge. He next came to *Magadha to continue his studies further. He meditated in Vajrāsana and had the vision of Cakrasamvara, Vajravārāhī and many other deities. The king conferred on him the **patra* of *Vikramaśīla. He expounded there mainly the Tantra-yāna, the Seven Treatises on Pramāṇa, the Five Works of Maitreya, etc. After working for the welfare of the living beings for many years, he went back to Kashmir. He defeated many *tīrthika*-s in debate and converted them into the followers of the Law of the Buddha. He established a number of centres for the study of Vidyāsambhāra, Sūtrālaṃkāra, Guhyasamāja, etc. During the latter part of his life, he went to *Urgyana in the west.[31]

There lived a *brāhmaṇa* in Kashmir, who was a scholar of the *tīrthika* philosophies. He had the vision of *īśvara* (God). His own deity[32] (i.e. *īśvara*) instructed him : 'Go to *Urgyana and you will have great success.' So he went to *Urgyana and met *brāhmaṇa* Ratnavajra. They entered into a debate by staking their creeds. Ratnavajra was victorious and converted him into the follower of the Law of the Buddha and

30. *rin-chen-rdo-rje*. See Supplementary Note 78.
31. V & S omit 'in the west', though the text has *nub-phyogs* (in the west).
32. S-ed *khoṅ-ra'i-lhas*. P-ed *khoṅ-ri'i-lhas*, The former followed.

gave him the name *Guhyaprajña. He learnt the Tantra-yāna and eventually attained *siddhi*. He was the person who went to Tibet and came to be known as the Red *Ācārya.[33]

According to the Kashmiris, *brāhmaṇa* Ratnavajra received the rainbow body in *Urgyana itself. Ratnavajra's son was *Mahājana[34] [**Fol 119A**] and his son was *Sajjana.[35] Tibetan religious tradition owes much to them.

Now about *Jñānaśrīmitra,[36] the second great Central Pillar [of Vikramaśila]. He was the author of *śāstra* Free From The Two Extremities. He was also a very kind teacher of Śrī *Atiśa.[37]

He (Jñānaśrīmitra) was born in *Gauḍa. He was earlier a **paṇḍita* of the Śrāvaka *Sendhavas and a scholar of their Tripiṭaka. Later on, he had reverence for the Mahāyāna and thoroughly studied all the *śāstra*-s of Nāgārjuna and Asaṅga.[38] He also knew many Guhya-tantras and, while listening extensively to the *sūtra*-s and *tantra*-s, he always meditated on the Bodhicitta. He had repeated visions of the three, namely *bhagavān* Śākyarāja, Maitreyanātha and Avalokiteśvara. He attained the unlimited *abhijñāna*.

Once, while he was residing in *Vikrama(-śila), he told a novice monk, 'Start immediately so that you can reach the city of *Gayā by to-morrow noon. A *brāhmaṇa* has invited there all the monks with the priests in charge of the temple of Vajrāsana to a seasonal feast. The *Gaṇḍola containing the Mahābodhi will be damaged by fire. Take them along to put the fire out.'

He went to *Gayā and, as predicted, met the residents of Vajrāsana. He said, 'My *guru* has predicted thus. So please

33. *ācārya dmar-po*. See A. Chattopadhyaya AT 292.
34. See Supplementary Note 79.
35. In Tg is attributed to him *Putra-lekha* (mDo xciv.32). The colophon of this as well as of mDo xxiv.2 ; xliv.5 & 6 refer to Sajjana as the son of Mahājana and Mahājana as the son of Ratnavajra, their family being that of great Indian scholars.
36. See Supplementary Note 80.
37. See A. Chattopadhyaya AT 68, 93, 139, 295.
38. V omits Asaṅga, though the text has *thogs-med* (Asaṅga).

return (to Vajrāsana).' Half of them did not believe him and stayed back.

[**Fol 119B**]When he reached Vajrāsana with the other half of them, the *Gaṇḍola of Vajrāsana had already caught fire. Both the interior and the exterior were aflame. They extinguished the fire with prayer to the deity and thus the temple was saved from further damage. The *ācārya* arranged for the restoration of the damaged paintings and the renovation of the wooden structure.

Moreover, in both *Bhaṃgala and *Magadha he renovated numerous older and damaged centres for the Doctrine. He also built many new ones.

These Six Door-keeper Scholars belonged to the first half of king *Bheyapāla's reign.

Though king *Canaka rendered great services to the Law, he is not counted among the Seven (Pālas) because he did not belong to the line of the *Pālas.

From this period on, the study of logic became wide-spread in Kashmir. The logician Ravigupta[39] also belonged to this period.

The thirtythird chapter containing the account of the period of king Canaka.

39. *ñi-ma-sbas-pa*—cf Stcherbatsky BL i.44.

CHAPTER 34

ACCOUNT OF THE PERIOD OF KINGS BHEYAPĀLA AND NEYAPĀLA

Then king *Bheyapāla ruled for about thirtytwo years. He maintained the older tradition, but excepting this did nothing significantly new for the Law. He conferred *patra-s on only seventy *paṇḍita-s of *Vikramaśīla. So he is also not counted among the Seven *Pālas.

After the Six Door-keeper Scholars had passed away, during the period of this king, *Dīpaṃkara *Śrījñāna, famed as Jo-bo-rje[1] dPal-ldan *Atīśa (*prabhu śrī atīśa*) was invited to be the *upādhyāya* (of Vikramaśīla). He also looked after *Odantapurī. Soon after this, the activity of the powerful *Maitrī-pā[2] became wide-spread. When *Maitrī-pā returned from the Śrī Parvata, the period of the Six Door-keeper Scholars like *Śānti-pā was already over by a few years.

[Fol 120A] In the confused account of the previous preachers of *Dohā,[3] there is no substance. Further, in the corrupt history of *Dohā, *Maitrī-pā is called an incarnation of Kṛṣṇācārya. Depending on this, much confusion is created about Jvālapati and the *caryā-dhara* Kṛṣṇa.[4] The firm belief resulting from a bias for such corrupt and confused account that there was somebody called *caryā-dhara* Kṛṣṇa as distinct from Kṛṣṇācārya is completely baseless. The confusion will be removed by consulting the few brief treatises by *ācārya*

1. lit. *prabhu*, the typical Tibetan form of referring to Atīśa.
2. V 'Maitrī-pā (Maitrīnātha)'. cf BA ii. 841f—born in A.D. 1007 or 1010 and passed into *nirvāṇa* at the age of 78.
3. V n 'S remarks that in Tanjur vol *ci*, there are several collections of Dohā under the name Dohākoṣa. Besides, there are many Dohās ascribed to well-known celebrities. In vol *lu*, at the end of the account of the 84 *siddha*-s, there is a collection of Dohās followed by their explanations.'
4. *'bar-ba'i-gtso-bo-spyod-'chaṅ-nag-po.*

Amitavajra.[5]

King *Bheyapāla's son was *Neyapāla. In the authentic biographies, it is stated that he became the king shortly before Jo-bo-rje left for Tibet. There also exists a letter sent (by Atiśa) to him from Nepal.[6] He ruled for thirtyfive years. Nine years after he became the king, the powerful *Maitrī-pā passed away.

This king worshipped one famous as the Mahā-vajrāsana.[7] When an *ūpāsaka*, his name was *Puṇyaśrī. His ordained name was *Puṇyākaragupta.

To his period belonged *Amoghavajra,[8] *Vīryabhadra[9] of the east with *abhijñāna*, *Devakāracandra,[10] *Prajñārakṣita[11] and also most of the direct disciples of *Nāro-pā.

Of the direct disciples of *Nāro-pā, the account of Śrī Śrī *Dombi-pā[12] and of *Kaṇṭa-pā are to be clearly found elsewhere.[13]

5. *dpag-med-rdo-rje.* Apart from a work on the Cakrasamvara (rG xiii. 53) in Tg is attributed to him a commentary on the Dohākoṣa of Kṛṣṇavajrapāda (rG lxxxv.19).
6. *Vimala-ratna-lekha* (mDo xxxiii.103=xciv.33). Eng tr A. Chattopadhyaya AT 520f.
7. *rdo-rje-gdan-pa-chen-po.*
8. See Supplementary Note 81.
9. See Supplementary Note 82.
10. In Tg three Tāntrika works (rG xliii.93; lxi.3 & lxxxiii.31) are attributed to Devākaracandra. Lalou 167 equates the name to Śūnyatā-samādhi, to whom are attributed 3 works in Tg (rG xiv.29; 31; lxxvi. 87 [75]).
11. In Tg 7 Tāntrika treatises are attributed to him—rG xiii.12-6 ; 20 ; lxxiii.12 : lxxxiii.69.
12. The text has Tombhi-pā.
13. S n 'In the account of the 84 *siddha*-s, where the name of the last is Kha-ndi-pā, one can easily recognise the word *khaṇḍa*'. V n 'Dombi was engaged in laundry-work in Śālipura-nagara and received ordination from a *yogī*. The *upadeśa*-s that he received, in the terminology of his profession, are : with the hot water *mudrā* wash the impurity of the body, with the water of words the tongue, and by union of father and mother the soul. In 12 years, he attained *mahā-mudrā*'.

Now about *Kasori-pā. He propitiated Vajrayoginī alone. She appeared through an opening of the cloud and asked, 'What do you desire ?'

'I have the desire to attain the same status as that of yourself.'

As he said this, she melted into his heart. **[Fol 120B]** Immediately he attained many *siddhi*-s. In the crematoriums even the tigers, jackals, etc worshipped him dancing around. People without fortune could see this from a distance. As they approached near, however, the scene vanished.

Now about *Ri-ri-pā.[14]

His textual knowledge was limited. Śrī *Nāro-pā gave him few instructions on the *utpanna* and *sampanna krama*[15] of Cakrasamvara. He meditated on these, attained *siddhi* and acquired unfettered proficiency in all subjects. He could summon the rhinoceros and other wild animals of the forest and move about on their back.

At that time came the Gar-log army. On the street somewhere on the west of *Vārāṇasī, he performed a magical rite. When the Gar-log-s reached there, they saw only dead bodies and the ruins full of stones and wood and the soil upturned. So they went back.

Both of them (Kasari-pā and Ri-ri-pā) attained the rainbow body.

Now about *Prajñārakṣita.

He was a great **paṇḍita* monk. He listened to many theories on Pitṛ-tantra-s and Mātṛ-tantra-s for twelve years from *Nāro-pā and became a special scholar of Matṛ-tantra, particularly of Cakrasamvara. He learnt by heart the four systems of exposition (*catuḥ-ṭīkā-vidhi*),[16] and many systems of instruction (*upadeśa-vidhi*) and many other systems. He meditated for five years in a small holy place near *Odantapurī and had the vision of innumerable tutelary deities like

14. S n 'perhaps a corruption of Tiṇṭiṇi or Tiḍhivi'.

15. V tr 'ways of generation and accomplishment (*utsakrama* and *utpan.ıakrama*)'.

16. viz. *ūha, apoha, rakṣā* and *āgama*.

Mañjuśrī and those of the Carkasamvara-maṇḍala and Kālacakra etc. It is said that he received as many as seventy *abhiṣeka*-s of the Cakrasamvara and became extremely powerful. [Fol 121A] When *Vikramaśīla was once attacked by the *Turuṣka army, he made big offerings to Cakrasamvara and the army was struck by terrible thunder four times. This killed their chief and many brave soldiers and thus they were repelled.

Eight *tīrthika* rivals came to challenge him in debate. When he cast his magic stare from the seat of the debate, six of them turned dumb and two blind. Later on he released them.

After working extensively for the welfare of the living beings mainly according to the Cakrasamvara, he passed away in a forest near *Nalendra, leaving the instruction for the disciples : 'Do not remove my dead body for seven days.' This was accordingly done and in seven days his relics vanished.

*Ri-ri-pā was born in a low Caṇḍāla family. He was highly delighted whenever he saw the great *Nāro-pā. In profound reverence, his body used to become stiff and unconscious. He became a *yogī*. After acquiring immense wealth (as the preceptor's fee), he received *abhiṣeka* of Cakrasamvara from *Nāro-pā and meditated with intense concentration.

When he meditated on the *utpanna-krama*, his *vāyu-citta* got fixed on the *madhyamā*. It is said that the bliss of enjoying the Caṇḍālī brought an end to the residue of his previous *karma*. He soon attained the highest *siddhi*. Even while moving about as an attendant of *Nāro-pā, he used to listen to the Doctrine. He remained mostly invisible and made himself visible only when necessary.

Ācārya Anupamasāgara[17] also lived during this period.

[Fol 121B] He was a monk **paṇḍita* and, though a specialist of the Kālacakra, was vastly learned in all the branches of knowledge. He relieved himself of all distractions and in *Khasarpaṇi intensely propitiated *ārya* Avalokiteśvara for twelve years. Still he had no sign of success. While asleep, he once received the prediction in dream : 'Go to

17. *dpe-med-mtsho*.

*Vikramapurī.' Accompanied by his disciple Sādhuputra,[18] he went there. In the city he witnessed a grand dramatic performance that formed part of the seasonal festival.[19] As a result, he attained the *samādhi* and saw everything as *māyā*. At midnight his tutelary deity appeared in the from of *Avadhūti-pā and said, 'Oh son, this is the ultimate truth (*tathatā*).' The moment this was said, he attained the *mahā-mudrā-siddhi.*

He composed a few treatises for his disciples. It is said that all his disciples attained either the *yoga-samādhi* with its six components or the (miraculous) power of recollection.

To this period also belonged the logician Yamāri[20]. He was a great scholar in all the branches of learning and was a specialist in grammar and logic. Though his family consisted of only three persons inclusive of the son and wife, he was too poor to maintain it.

A *yogī* from the east, on his way to Vajrāsana, asked from him shelter for a night. So he told him about his own poverty. The *yogī* said, 'Being a **paṇḍita*, you have contempt for the *yogī* and so you have not asked for any instruction. But I know the way (rite) to obtain wealth.'

'So, please get me some.'

'Keep ready the *Pi-cu-ra[21] fruits and sandal paste. On my way back from Vajrāsana, I shall perform (the rite).'

On his way back, he conferred on him the blessings of Vasudhārā. **[Fol 122A]** He propitiated (Vasudhārā)[22] and the same year the king made a gift of a large property to him. He also received the highly distinguished **patra* of *Vikramaśīla.

At about this period, a *brāhmaṇa* called Śaṃkarānanda[23]

18. Tg contains two works on Kālacakra (rG iv. 6 & 7) attributed to Sādhuputra and mentioned as written for *mahā-paṇḍita* Dharmākaraśānti.
19. S tr 'a festival in the city, where dancing was going on in a grand scale'.
20. Tg contains his enormous commentaries on *Pramāṇavārtika* (mDo civ.-cv).
21. see Monier-Williams 624.
22. In Tg *Śrī-devī-vasudhārā-stotra* (rG lxxii.48) is attributed to Yamāri.
23. See Note 66 of Ch 26.

lived in Kashmir. He was a scholar of the *śāstra*-s in general and was specially proficient in logic. So he thought of composing a new treatise on logic in order to refute the views of Dharmakīrti. Mañjuśrī told him in a dream, 'Dharmakīrti was an *ārya* and so it is not possible for you to refute him. The faults that you imagine to be there in his views are due to your own wrong understanding.'

So he made amends and composed commentaries on the Seven Treatises. It is said that he became highly prosperous and happy. In the gloss on Dharmottara's commentary it is said that Śaṃkarānanda belonged to a much earlier period. This mistake is the result of the error occurring in the footnote in Parahitabhadra's[24] work.

The thirtyfourth chapter containing the account of the period of kings Bheyapāla and Neyapāla.

24. S misunderstands the name *gshan-phan-bzaṅ-po* or Parahitabhadra, a scholar of Kashmir, to whom are attributed many works in Tg (mDo xlviii 1; rG xxvi.27; mDo xxiv.5); he is also mentioned as the translator of many works, inclusive of Śaṃkarānanda's *Sambandha-parīkṣānusāra* (mDo cxii.2). S tr 'in the gloss on the Good Illustrations for the Welfare of others'. V tr 'As regards the commentary, it is said that in the statements and writings of Dharmottara, Śaṃkarānanda's texts have appeared only because they have been inserted as commentaries as examples of service to others'.

CHAPTER 35

ACCOUNT OF THE PERIOD OF ĀMRAPĀLA, HASTIPĀLA AND KṢĀNTIPĀLA

*Āmrapāla, the son of *Neyapāla, ruled for thirteen years. During his period *ācārya* *Ratnākaragupta[1] was the *upādhyāya* of Vajrāsana.

At the time of *Āmrapāla's death, his son *Hastipāla was too young to rule. So his four ministers, along with the child, ruled the kingdom for eight years. After that, *Hastipāla ascended the throne and ruled for about fifteen years. After him, his co-uterine brother[2] *Kṣāntipāla ruled for fourteen years.

During their period, lived *Ratnākaragupta in *Sauri. Some of the *ācārya*-s already discussed under the account of the period of *Neyapāla lived **[Fol 122B]** during the reign of these two kings,. namely *Maitrī-pā and the disciples of *Dīpaṃkara-śrījñāna, i.e. his 'five spiritual sons'[3] called the great *Pi-ṭo-pā, *Dharmākaramati,[4] Kṣitigarbha (Bhūmigarbha),[5]

1. In Tg are attributed to him rG lix.9 ; lxxi.96 ; lxx.8 ; lxxii.57 & mDo xxxiii.64.
2. *ma-spun*—D 799 & J 330. V 'brother from the mother'.
3. cf BA i.261-2 : 'The five special disciples of the Master were—the *mahā-paṇḍita* Piṭo-pā ; Dharmākaramati, the Lion of the Mādhyamika ; Mitraguhya ; Jñānamati and the *paṇḍita* Kṣitigarbha'. In Tār's list, however, Jñānamati is absent and Madhyamakasiṃha (see note 6 of this chapter) appears as a separate name.
4. In Tg is attributed to Dharmākaramati-pāda rG lxxi.296.
5. *sa'i-sñiṅ-po*, who accompanied Atīśa to Tibet. See A. Chattopadhyaya AT 314. In BA ii,842 he is mentioned as an elder brother of Vajrapāṇi, who was born in A.D. 1017 (BA ii.855ff). Tg contains two works (rG xlv.21 & xv.2) translated by him. V 'Bhusuku' and adds in note, 'the heart of earth (? Kṣitigarbha). S finds the form Bhusuku (Bhu-su-ku) as the name of the 41st *siddha* from among the 84 mentioned in Tanjur'. Such conjectures about *sa'i-sñiṅ-po* are plainly baseless.

Madhyamakasiṃha[6] and Mitraguhya.[7]

This was the period when thirtyseven **paṇḍita* preachers of the Doctrine like *Jñānaśrīmitra and others worked for the welfare of the living beings.

This was also clearly the period when *Maṇikaśrī,[8] Bodhibhadra[9] in Kashmir, the *Pham-thiṅ brothers[10] in Nepal, Jñānavajra,[11] Bhārata-paṇi[12] and others worked for the welfare of the living beings.

Also lived during this period Rāhulamitra,[13] who wrote the principles of the Guhya-samāja-maṇḍala on cloth, and *Nāropā's disciple known in Nepal as the Indian *Dārika-pā, who wrote on *Lui-pā's system of *abhiṣeka.* These (two) are sometimes identified with Rāhula, the direct disciple of Āryadeva, and the great *siddha* *Dārika-pā (respectively). In spite of doubts, it is foolish to try to be categorical in matters concerning identification simply on the strength of imagination.

*Sthirapāla in particular, i.e. the great **paṇḍita* *Sthirapāla, *alias* *Trilakṣa,[14] elaborately explained the Prajñāpāramitā in *Vikramaśīla. There were moreover innumerable others who

6. *dbu-ma'i-sen-ge.* In Tg is attributed to him *Saṃkṣipta-nānā-dṛṣṭi-vibhāga* (mDo xxix.6), a work summing up the different opinions expressed by the *paṇḍita*-s in a grand debate.
7. *bśes-gñen-gsaṅ-ba.*
8. See Supplementary Note 83.
9. See Supplementary Note 77.
10. cf BA i.227-8 ; 380-4 and ii.402.
11. See Supplementary Note 84.
12. See Supplementary Note 85.
13. *sgra-gcan-'dsin-bśes-gñen.*
14. *'bum-phrag-gsum-pa.* In Tg is attributed to him *Ārya-tārā-stotra* (rG lxxi.393) and he is also mentioned as the translator of rG lxviii.19 ; lxxxii.70 & mDo vi—the colophon of the last work mentions him as *mahā-paṇḍita* Dhīrapāla (Sthirapāla), famed as *dvi-lakṣa-granthālaṃkṛta-grīva, alias* Trilakṣa Sthirapāla. V n 'The Sanskrit name Sthirapāla is given in the text itself, which also gives corresponding Tibetan name *brtan-skyoṅ.* To the latter, however, is also adjoined *'bum-phrag-gsum-pa* (Trilakṣa), which is not given in Sanskrit. S remarks that in Tg vol *zu* Tantras one finds the name *'bum-phrag-gsum-pa,* as that of a translator (and hence of a Tibetan ?)'.

are considered as *siddha* **paṇḍita*-s. But it seems that none of them became very famous.

During the period of these three kings the Law was nourished as before. But they are not counted among the Seven (Pālas) because they did nothing spectacular (for the Law).

The thirtyfifth chapter containing the account of the period of Āmrapāla, Hastipāla and Kṣāntipāla.

CHAPTER 36

ACCOUNT OF THE PERIOD OF KING RĀMAPĀLA

King *Rāmapāla was the son of *Hastipāla. **[Fol 123A]** Though he ascended the throne at an early age, he extended his power widely by virtue of his exceptional intelligence.

Shortly after he became king, the great *ācārya* *Abhayākaragupta[1] was invited to act as the *upādhyāya* of Vajrāsana. After many years, he was appointed as the *upādhyāya* of *Vikramaśila and *Nalendra. By this time, the older tradition of these centres had changed.

One hundred and sixty **paṇḍita*-s and about a thousand monks permanently resided in *Vikramaśila. Even five thousand ordained monks assembled there for occasional offerings. In Vajrāsana forty Mahāyanīs and two hundred Śrāvaka *bhikṣu*-s were maintained by the king as the permanent residents. Occasionally even ten thousand Śrāvaka monks congregated there. In *Odantapurī also permanently lived a thousand monks belonging to both Hīnayāna and Mahāyāna. Occasionally even twelve thousand monks congregated there.

Among the Mahāyānīs of the time, the foremost was *ācārya* *Abhayākara[gupta]. Even the Śrāvakas had high regard for him as an expert in Vinaya. The account of this *ācārya* is to be found elsewhere. Of particular significance was the reformation of the Law by him, and the *śāstra*-s he composed were widely read in the later period. Among the Mahāyānīs of India are still found his *śāstra*-s as unaffected by the various distortions due to dialects etc of the intervening period.

The two *ācārya*-s, namely this *ācārya* and *ācārya* *Ratnākaraśānti-pā, **[Fol 123B]** who came later, were comparable in qualities to the older *mahā-ācārya*-s like *Vasubandhu and

1. See Supplementary Note 86.

others, though by the influence of time there was difference in the magnitude of their contributions to the Law and in the welfare caused by them to the living beings.

Already after the death of king *Dharmapāla, the number of *tīrthika*-s and *mlechha*-s gradually increased in the kingdom of *Bhaṃgala, in Ayodhyā etc on the north of the *Gaṅgā and in all the regions on the east and west of the *Yamunā—from *Vārāṇasī to *Mālava, *Prayāga, Mathurā, *Kuru, Pañcāla, *Āgrā, *Sagari, *Dilli, etc. The number of *tīrthika*-s became numerous in *Kāmarū(pa), *Tīrahuti, *Oḍiviśa, etc. In *Magadha the Buddhists were greater in number than before, because of the increase of the *saṃgha*-s and *yogī*-s. It is remarked that this *mahā-ācārya* Abhayākara was practically the last among the most famous great *ācārya*-s who fully nourished the Law with their scholarship, compassion, power and wealth. And this is true. Hence he is to be viewed as having transmitted the thoughts of the *jina* and his spiritual sons to the later living beings. Therefore, his works should be respected more than those of the *ācārya*-s that came after the Six Jewels. His greatness is obviously proved by his holy words.

This king *Rāmapāla reigned for about fortysix years, inclusive of some years after *ācārya* *Abhyākara[gupta] passed away.

[Fol 124A] Before he died, his son *Yakṣapāla was placed on the throne. Three years after that *Rāmapāla died. After this, *Yakṣapāla ruled for only one year, when his minister *Lavasena usurped the throne.

During their period, *ācārya* *Śubhākaragupta[2] was in *Vikramaśila and in Vajrāsana the chief was Buddhakīrti.[3]

2. In Tg are attributed to him rG xiv.64 & lxvi.5. The colophon of the latter mentions him as the preceptor of Śākyaśrī and that this work was composed in the Jagaddala-vihāra.

3. *rdo-rje-gdan-na-rtsa-mi-saṅs-rgyas-grags*, i.e. Buddhakīrti, the chief of Vajrāsana. cf Roerich SW 498 : 'the famous *tsa-mi-saṅs-rgyas-grags-pa*, a Tibetan-Sanskrit scholar who attained the high distinction of being appointed one of the *dvāra-paṇḍita*-s of the *vihāra* of Vikıamaśīla, and some of whose Sanskrit compositions are still extant.' See Tg rG lxxxvi.36 ; xxvi.90 ; lxxxiii.11-19.

According to the current account given by rGa lo[-tsā-ba],[4] *Abhayākara was still alive when he (rGa) was about to return to Tibet. He (rGa) first visited *Abhayākara but did not have the time to study under him for a long time. *Lava-sena was on the throne at the time of his going back to Tibet.

After *Yakṣa(-pāla and Lava-) *sena,[5] many were born in the royal line of the *Pālas and some of them may be still living. But none of them became king. The *Pāla dynasty is also called the Sūrya dynasty[6] while the line of the *Senas was originally the same as that of the Candras.[7]

The thirtysixth chapter containing the account of the period of king Rāmapāla.

4. In Tg. rGa lo-tsā-ba, the translator of rG lxxxiii.25 & 26, is mentioned as *maula* Buddhakīrti.
5. V & S Yakṣa-sena, which occurs in the text, though obviously as a corruption.
6. *ñi-ma'i-rigs.*
7. *zla-ba'i-rigs.*

CHAPTER 37

ACCOUNT OF THE PERIOD OF THE FOUR SENA KINGS AND OTHERS

*Lavasena's son was *Kāśasena. His son was *Maṇitasena. His son was *Rāthikasena. I have not come across any clear account of how many years each of them ruled. Anyway, the four of them taken together did not rule for more than about eighty years.

During their period, the Law was nourished by many scholars and *siddha*-s like *Śubhākaragupta,[1] *Raviśrījñāna,[2] *Nayakapaśrī,[3] *Daśabalaśrī[4] and, shortly after them, by Dharmākaraśānti,[5] Śrī Vikhyātadeva,[6] *Niṣkalaṅkadeva,[7] *Dharmākaragupta and many other followers of *Abhayākara.

To the period of king *Rāthikasena [**Fol 124B**] belonged many with strong moral vows, *vajradhara*-s and vast scholars of scriptures like *mahā-*paṇḍita* *Śākyaśrībhadra[8] of Kashmir,

1. See note 2 chapter 36.
2. In Tg is attributed to him two commentaries on *ṣaḍaṅga-yoga* (rG iv. 15 & 34) and one on *ārya-nāma-saṃgīti* (rG v. 8).
3. BA ii.1053 mentions the Nepalese *paṇḍita* Nayaśrī, a contemporary of Daśabalaśrī, under both of whom the Tibetan scholar sTeṅs-pa lo-tsā-ba (born A.D. 1107) studied.
4. In Tg mDo cxxviii.2 is attributed to Daśabalaśrīmitra. cf BA ii.801 & 1053.
5. *chos-'byuṅ-shi-ba.* In Tg are attributed to him two works on Kāla-cakra (rG iv.6 & 7). cf BA ii.761, 764 & 800.
6. *dpal-rnam-par-grags-pa'i-lha.* Tg contains a work *Paṇḍita-vikhyā-tadeva-mahākāruṇika-siddhilābhākhyāna* (mDo cxxiii.39). cf BA ii.801. V Śrīviśrutadeva.
7. Apart from a number of translations, in Tg are attributed to him xlviii.122-23 and lxxi.104, where his name is given also as Ajitamitra-gupta. cf BA ii.1055 : Chag dGra-bcom (born A.D. 1153) studied unde- him.
8. See Supplementary Note 87.

*Buddhaśrī[9] of Nepal, *mahā-ācārya* *Ratnarakṣita,[10] the great scholar *Jñānākaragupta,[11] the great scholar *Buddhaśrīmitra, the great scholar *Saṃghamajñāna, *Raviśrībhadra, *Candrākaragupta and others. They were famous as the twentyfour great **mahānta*-s.

Among them, the account of *mahā-*paṇḍita* *Śākyaśrī is widely known and is to be accepted as such. *Buddhaśrī of Nepal acted for a short time as the *sthavira* of the Mahāsāṃghikas in *Vikramaśīla. He returned to Nepal and extensively preached the Prajñāpāramitā, Guhyatantra, etc. From the point of view of practices, he lived *ad libitum*.[12]

Now about the great *ācārya* *Ratnarakṣita.

He was known as equal to *Śākyaśri in the knowledge of the Prajñāpāramitā-yāna and other general branches of learning, though, *Śākyaśrī specialised in logic and he (Ratnarakṣita) in Tantra. The two were equal in their occult power and in receiving blessings.

He (Ratnarakṣita) was ordained in the Mahāsāṃghika sect and was the Tantra-ācārya of *Vikramaśīla. He had visions of many tutelary deities like Cakrasamvara, Kālacakra and Yamāri.

When the Nāgas and Asuras were once playing the musical instruments for worshipping Avalokiteśvara in *Potala, the sound conveyed to him the essence of the doctrine of the sixteen *śūnyatā*-s. Everytime he conferred an *abhiṣeka*, he could infuse the spirit of the deity into the initiated.[13] His offerings

9. In Tg is mentioned Buddhaśrī as the corrector of the translation of rG lxxi.345 and Lalou 156 adds that Buddhaśrī of Nepal went to Tibet in A.D. 1198. cf BA ii.709, 1033, 1055-6 : the Tibetan scholar Chag dGra-bcom (born A.D. 1153) studied under him.

10. See Supplementary Note 88.

11. Tg mentions him as author of rG xliii.82 ; lxxii.14 & 15. In BA i.260 is said that after the death of Atīśa, Tshul-khrims-rgyal-ba (Jayaśīla) translated some works (rG xxi.13 etc) under him. The name is missing in V tr.

12. *ci-bder*. See D 381.

13. S tr 'During *abhiṣeka*-s, he could infuse knowledge into logic.' This is perhaps because of misreading *tshad-la* as *tshad-ma* (logic).

were directly received by the *ḍākinī*-s. He could immobilise mad elephants with magic stare. He predicted the fall of *Magadha two years earlier. Some of his disciples with real faith in him went to Kashmir and Nepal.

At the time of the fall of *Magadha, he went to the north. A wild buffalo attacked him near *Tīrahuti. He subdued it with his magic stare [**Fol 125A**] and it began to lick his feet. It also carried him one *yojana* afar.

After working extensively for the welfare of living beings in Nepal, he also went to Tibet for a short period. He composed the *(Cakra-)samvara-udaya-ṭīkā*[14].

About *Jñānākaragupta : He had the direct vision of Maitreyanātha.

About *Buddhaśrīmitra : In a dream, he listened to the Doctrine from Vajravārāhī. He acquired wonderful *siddhi* and with it could perform the feats like subduing an elephant with each hand.

I find that all of them were scholars in all the branches of learning, had visions of the tutelary deities and attained the special merits of *sampanna-krama*. I cannot write more of them, because I have neither read nor heard in details about any of them.

About *Vajraśrī. He was a disciple of Daśabala.[15] He was already one hundred years old during this period and after this period he lived for another hundred years. He worked exetnsively for the welfare of the living beings and never looked old. In the south, he led many thousands of fortunate ones to liberation through the practice of the Tantra-yāna.

During the time of these four *Senas, the number of *tīrthika*-s went on increasing even in *Magadha. There also came many Persian[16] followers of the *mleccha* view. To protect *Odantapurī and *Vikramaśīla, the king even converted these partially into fortresses and stationed some soldiers there. The Mahāyānīs did not have any special importance in Vajrāsana,

14. See Supplementary Note 89.
15. *stob-bcu*.
16. *stag-gzig*—D 548.

though some of the *yogī*-s and Mahāyānis continued to preach there. During a *varṣāvāsa*, about ten thousand Śrāvaka Sendhavas congregated there. While the other centres for the Doctrine became practically extinct, though it is said that the number of monks both in *Vikramaśīla and *Odantapurī remained as it was during the time of *Abhayākara.

[**Fol 125B**]After the death of *Rāthikasena, the few years of *Labaṃsena's[17] reign were peaceful. Then came the *Turuṣka king called the Moon[18] to the region of *Antaravedi[19] in-between the *Gaṅgā and the *Yamunā. Some of the monks acted as messengers for this king. As a result, the petty *Turuṣka rulers of *Bhaṃgala and other places united, ran over the whole of *Magadha and massacred many ordained monks in *Odantapurī. They destroyed this and also *Vikramaśīla.

The Persians at last built a fort on the ruins of the *Odanta-vihāra. **Paṇḍita* *Śākyaśrī went to *Ja-gar-da-la (Jagaddala) in *Oḍiviśa in the east. He spent three years there and then went to Tibet.

The great *Ratnarakṣita went to Nepal. Some of the great **paṇḍita*-s like the great scholar *Jñānākaragupta, along with a hundred minor **paṇḍita*-s went to the south-west of India. The great scholar *Buddhaśrīmitra and Daśabala's disciple *Vajraśrī, along with many minor **paṇḍita*-s, fled far to the south. The sixteen [remaining] **mahānta*-s including the scholar *Saṃghamaśrījñāna, *Raviśrībhadra, *Candrākara-gupta, along with two hundred minor **paṇḍita*-s, went far to the east to *Pu-khaṅ,[20] *Mu-naṅ, *Kamboja and other places. Thus the Law became almost extinct in *Magadha.

There is no doubt that many *siddha*-s and *sādhaka*-s lived at this period. But since the *karma* of the people in general

17. Both P-ed and S-ed Lavaṃsena in transliteration. V & S Lavasena. This is most confusing, because in Tār's account Lavasena cannot be later than Rāthikasena.
18. *zla-ba*. V & S Candra.
19. D. C. Sircar CGEIL 170.
20. See chapter 39.

was unalterable, all these could not be prevented.

At that time, most of the *yogī followers of *Gaurakṣa (Gorakṣa) were fools and, driven by the greed for money and honour offered by the *tīrthika* kings, became the followers of Īśvara.[21] They used to say, 'We are not opposed even to the *Turuṣkas.' **[Fol 126A]** Only a few of them belonging to the *Naṭeśvarī-varga remained insiders.

*Lavaṃsena. His son was *Buddhasena.[22] His son was *Haritasena. His son was *Pratītasena. And others. They had to obey the *Turuṣkas and did not have much of royal power. According to their limited power, they also worshipped the Law a little. Particularly, during the period of Buddhasena, the great *paṇḍita* *Rāhulaśrībhadra resided at *Nalendra. There were then about seventy listeners to the Doctrine.[23]

After him lived *Bhūmiśrībhadra and, after him, Upāyaśrībhadra and others. Sometimes during their period, *Karuṇāśrībhadra, *Munīndraśrībhadra and others also carefully nourished the Law of the Sage.

After the death of *Pratītasena, their line came to an end. Some minor kings are sometimes mentioned as having respect for the Law, but I have not come across any original account of them.

After about a hundred years of *Pratītasena's death, *Ciṅgalarāja[24] became very powerful in *Bhaṃgala. He brought under control all the *Hindus and *Turuṣkas up to *Dili (Delhi). He was originally a devotee of the *brāhmaṇa*-s. Under the influence of his queen, however, he changed his faith and became a devotee of the Buddhists.

He made lavish offerings in Vajrāsana, renovated all the temples there and properly rebuilt the upper four storeys of the nine-storied *mahā-gaṇḍola* which was destroyed by the *Turuṣkas. He established there a centre for the Doctrine under

21. *dbaṅ-phyug.*
22. cf Altekar in Roerich SW 472ff and Roerich SW 499f, 522.
23. cf Roerich SW 548 : Chag lo-tsā-ba gives exactly this account.
24. P-ed Ciṅgala. S-ed Tsa-ga-la. V Chagala-rāja.

paṇḍita *Śāriputra.[25] He made lavish offerings in the temple of *Nalendra, but built no big centre for the Doctrine.

This king was very long-lived. After his death, one hundred and sixty years have passed away.[26] But I have not heard of any king of *Magadha [**Fol 126B**] who lived in this period and was a devotee of the Doctrine. I have neither heard of any with strong moral vow or of any well-versed in the Piṭakes.

Later on, king *Mukundadeva of *Oḍiviśa occupied most of the territory of the *madhya-deśa.* He established no centre for the Doctrine in *Magadha. In *Oḍiviśa, he established the temple for the insiders and also a number of smaller centres for the Doctrine. Thus the Law was spread a little.

Thirtyeight years[27] are known to have passed since the death of this king.

The thirtyseventh chapter containing the account of the four Sena kings and others.

25. In Tg are attributed to him rG lxxiv.3 ; lxxxii.25-6.
26. Tār writes this in A.D. 1608.
27. *Ib.*

TĀRANĀTHA'S

SUPPLEMENT TO THE HISTORY OF BUDDHISM IN INDIA

Though in the Tibetan text itself there is actually no such division, Vasil'ev rightly comments that the History of Buddhism as narrated by Tāranātha actually ends with the previous chapter. Tāranātha also clearly says that in the remaining few chapters he is going to narrate certain minor details relating to the Doctrine.

CHAPTER 38

ACCOUNT OF THE SUCCESSION OF TEACHERS AT VIKRAMAŚĪLA

I shall now relate some other minor details.

During the period of the five successive kings beginning with king Śrī Dharmapāla and till the period of *Canaka, a number of great Tāntrika Vajrācāryas looked after the Law at *Vikramaśīla.

During the earlier period of the rule of king *Dharmapāla, *ācārya* Buddhajñānapāda—and after him Dīpaṃkarabhadra[1]—looked after the Law. The account of this is to be found elsewhere.

*Laṅkā-jayabhadra belonged to the period of king *Masurakṣita [? Vasurakṣī]. This *ācārya* was born in *Laṅkā, i.e. *Siṅgala. There he became a *bhikṣu *paṇḍita*, versed in all the Śrāvaka Piṭakas. Then he came to *Magadha, studied the Mahāyāna thoroughly and became a scholar particularly of the Guhya-tantra. He meditated on Cakrasamvara at *Vikramaśīla and received the vision [of the deity]. Once he went to *Koṅkana in the south. In this region there was the famous *Mahābimba *caitya*, which was unapproachable but the miraculous reflection of which could be seen in the sky. He lived in that country and preached the Guhya-tantra-yāna thoroughly to some of the disciples. He composed the commentary on the *Cakrasambara* etc, [**Fol 127A**] and acquired such miraculous power that when attacked by a wild buffalo, he simply raised the index finger at it and it dropped dead.

Then he became the Tantra-ācārya of *Vikramaśīla. He was succeeded by the *brāhmaṇa ācārya* Śrīdhara,[2] whose account is to be found elsewhere. When he (Śrīdhara) acquired fame as a preacher of the Mahā-māyā in the south, he was

1. See Supplementary Note 89.
2. See Supplementary Note 90.

invited to *Vikramaśīla. From the treatises on the Rakta and Kṛṣṇa Yamāri Tantra composed by him, it is clear that he belonged to the lineage of *ācārya* Jñānapāda. The Tibetans imagine that he was a direct disciple of *ācārya* Kṛṣṇācārya, but the periods of their coming to the mortal world were different and hence he could have been his disciple when, in the later period, he received his vision.

While practising intense meditation, *brāhmaṇa* Śrīdhara one morning went out to collect[3] flowers etc used for worship and saw a majestic *yogī* at his door. He recognised him as Kṛṣṇācārya, bowed down at his feet and prayed, 'Please lead me to succeed in the Vidyā-mantra.' He (Kṛṣṇācārya) gave him instructions of the Sarasvatī-mantra-japa and vanished. Immediately, he had the vision of Sarasvatī[4] on the north-western side of the *maṇḍala* and soon attained *siddhi*.

He was succeeded by *Bhavabhadra.[5] Broadly speaking, he was also a scholar of all aspects of the Doctrine. He studied in particular Vijñāna-vāda[6] and acquired proficiency in about fifty Tantras. He received the blessings of Cakra-saṁvara in dream and also had the vision of Tārā. He practised the Guṭikā-siddhi and attained success. [**Fol 127B**] Later on, he attained success in the practice of alchemy etc, which proved highly beneficial for himself and for others.

He was succeeded by Bhavyakīrti,[7] a profound scholar of the Tāntrika scriptures. He is said to have attained unfettered *abhijñāna*.

He was succeeded by *Līlāvajra, who attained Yamāri-siddhi. It appears that the *Bhairava-aṣṭa-vetāla-sādhana*, which is extant in Tibetan translation, was composed by him. At

3. S-ed *gśig*. P-ed *gśegs-su* (remove). The former reading followed.
4. *dbyaṅs-can-ma*. D 913 : the goddess of learning of both the Hindus and Buddhists.
5. See Supplementary Note 91.
6. *rnam-rig*. S 'the Nyāya system'. But see D 761.
7. *skal-ldan-grags-pa*. Tg contains his commentary (rG xxxiv.1) on Nāgārjuna's *Pañcakrama*, chapters 9-17 of his *Pradīpodyotana-nāma-ṭikā* (rG xxxi), [the first eight chapters of which are attributed to Āryadeva] and another of his work on *Cakrasamvara* (rG vii.1).

this time, he heard the rumour of an impending *Turuṣka invasion and defeated their soldiers by drawing the Yamāri-cakra. After reaching *Magadha, the soldiers became dumb and inactive and remained so for a long time. Thus they were turned away.

He was succeeded by Durjayacandra,[8] whose account is to be found elsewhere.

He was succeeded by Kṛṣṇa-samaya-vajra,[9] whose account is already given.

Then came Tathāgata-rakṣita,[10] who attained power by the *vidyā* of Yamāri and Samvara.[11] He attained the special power of learning the languages of the different peoples and animals and also the *śāstra*-s that he had never studied, immediately after concentrating on his different *dhamanī*-s.

Next came Bodhibhadra[12], who was a great scholar of all the Guhya-mantras of both the insiders and outsiders. By rank he was an *upāsaka* and he attained the direct vision of Mañjuśrī. It is said that by virtue of his *siddhi* in Nāma-saṃgīti, he attained *samādhi* on the name of each deity. **[Fol 128A]** To this period belonged many with the name Bodhibhadra. In Tibet he [i.e. Bodhibhadra under discussion] did not evidently have much fame in the earlier period.

He was succeeded by *Kamalarakṣita.[13] In rank this *ācārya* was a *bhikṣu*. He was a scholar in all *sūtra*-s and *tantra*-s, specially in the Prajñāpāramitā, Guhya-samāja and Yamāri. When he attained *siddhi* of Yamāri in the *Aṃda-giri[14] to the south of *Magadha, he was confronted with various miraculous obstructions. He meditated on *śūnyatā* and all these subsided. Then Yamāri appeared before him and asked, 'What do you desire ?'

8. See Supplementary Note 92.
9. *nag-po-dam-tshig-rdo-rje*. cf BA i.360. In Tg are attributed three Tāntrika works to him (rG xxxiv.3 ; lxxiv.21 & 28).
10. See Supplementary Note 93.
11. S tr 'who attained control of Yamāri and Samvara'. This is because the word *mkhas-la* does not occur in his edition.
12. See Supplementary Note 77.
13. See Supplementary Note 94.
14. V 'Aṅgiri (Aṅga-giri)'.

'Please make me identical with yourself.' As he said this, he (Yamāri) melted into his heart. After this, the moment he thought of anything, he succeeded in it, inclusive of the great *siddhi*-s. It is said that Yamāri Vajradhara appeared before him every night and he used to listen to the Doctrine from him.

He once thought of holding a *gaṇa-cakra* in the crematorium of *Vikrama. Along with many Tāntrika disciples, he brought there the materials for *sādhanā* carried by the *yoginī*-s.[15] On the way they encountered the minister of the *Turuṣka king of *Karṇa of the west, who was then proceeding to invade *Magadha with five hundred *Turuṣkas. They (Turuṣkas) plundered the materials for *sādhanā*. When, however, they came near the *ācārya* and his attendants, the *ācārya* became angry and threw at them an earthen pitcher full of charmed water. Immediately was generated a terrible storm and black men were seen emerging from it and striking the *Turuṣkas with daggers in hand. **[Fol 128B]** The minister himself vomited blood and died and the others were afflicted with various diseases. Excepting one, none of them returned to their country. This made both the *tīrthika*-s and *Turuṣkas terror-stricken.

He performed many other *abhicāra*-s, but for which he could have attained the rainbow body. It is said that the *abhicāra*-s caused some obstacles even for a great *yogī* like him.

This *ācārya* was a kind teacher also of Jo-bo-rje (Atīśa) and Khyuṅ-po-rnal-'byor-pa.[16] It is said that in the latter part of his life, he lived in a forest near *Nalendra, fully absorbed in meditation mainly on *sampanna-krama*.

Except the first two of the twelve *ācārya*-s, each of them acted as the chief of the centre for twelve years. Thus it is said.

After *Kamalarakṣita came the Six Door-keeper Scholars. After them separately came many *ācārya*-s of Tantra.

Dīpaṃkara Jñāna and others did not break the tradition of those who nourished the Law in the general sense [? without

15. S tr 'a few *yogī-s*'. But the text has *rnal-'byor-ma* (*yoginī*).
16. See Supplementary Note 95.

being exclusively Tāntrikas].

After the Six Gate-keeper Scholars, there was no continuity in the succession of *upādhyāya*-s for some years. Then came *upādhyāya* Dīpaṃkara-śrī-jñāna. After him, there was no *upādhyāya* for seven years. Then Mahāvajrāsana[17] became the *upādhyāya* for a short period. After him one called *Kamalakuliśa[18] became the *upādhyāya*. The name of the next *upādhyāya* was *Narendra-śrī-jñāna. He was succeeded by *Dānarakṣita.[19] After him *Abhayākara acted (as *upādhyāya*) for a long time. He was succeeded by *Śubhākaragupta. **[Fol 129A]** Next was *Nayakapaśrī[20] and after him Dharmākaraśānti, who was succeeded by *Śākyaśrī, the great **paṇḍita* of Kashmir.

After him, there was the end of *Vikramaśīla.

The thirtyeighth chapter containing the account of the succession at Vikramaśīla.

17. *rdo-rje-gdan-pa-chen-po.*
18. cf BA i.372.
19. cf BA i.105.
20. cf BA ii.761, 764 & 800, V Sunayakapaśrī, and adds in note 'S remarks that Tg mentions Sunayaśrī and Sunayaśrīmitra, who probably were one and the same person.

CHAPTER 39

ACCOUNT OF THE SPREAD OF THE DOCTRINE IN THE KO-KI COUNTRY IN THE EAST

Eastern India consists of three parts. Of these, *Bhaṃgala and *Oḍiviśa belong to Aparāntaka and are hence called the eastern Aparāntaka. In the north-east,*Kāmarū(-pa), *Tripurā, *Hasama are called *Girivarta, i.e. surrounded by mountains. Proceeding further east from this region, (one reaches) *Naṃga-ṭa on the slopes of the northern mountains. Bordering on the sea are *Pukhaṅ, *Balaku, etc,—the country of the *Rākhaṅ—and *Haṃsavatī,[1] *Mar-ko etc, the country of *Muñaṅ-s. Further, *Cak-ma,[2] *Kam-bo-ja etc. All these are collectively called *Ko-ki.[3]

From the time of Aśoka, *saṃgha*-s were established in these *Ko-ki countries. Later on, these gradually grew large in number. Before the time of Vasubandhu, these were only of the Śrāvakas. Some of the disciples of Vasubandhu propagated the Mahāyāna (in these places). For sometime, the continuity of this tradition just survived. However, from the time of king *Dharmapāla on, there were in *madhya-deśa* many students from these places. Their number went on increasing so that during the time of the four *Senas about half of the monks of *Magadha were from *Ko-ki. Thus, in these countries the Mahāyāna was widely spread and the difference between the Hīnayāna and Mahāyāna disappeared, as it had happened in the kingdom of Tibet.

From the time of *Abhayākara [**Fol 129B**] the influence of the Mantrayāna went on increasing. As most of the scholars of the *madhya-deśa* went to these countries after the invasion of *Magadha by the *Turuṣkas, the Law extensively spread there.

1. V Pegu.
2. V Campā. S-ed *tsa-kma*, P-ed *tsa-ka-ma*.
3. V n 'This name is probably derived from the Chinese word *tszyao-chzhi*'.

At that time lived king *Śobhajāta. He built many temples and established about two hundred centres for the Doctrine.

Next came king *Siṃhajaṭi.[4] He also helped the spread of the Doctrine, and the Law became more extensively widespread in all these countries. It is said that even now during the occasional congregations (there), the number of *bhikṣu*-s reaches twenty to thirty thousand, not to speak of course of the numerous *upāsaka*-s.

From these countries came the later **paṇḍita*-s like Vanaratna,[5] who visited Tibet.

In the later period, there was a king there called *Bālasundara. Though in these countries, the Vinaya, Abhidharma and the Mahāyāna *śāstra*-s were very popular, the Guhyamantra-dharma—excepting a few like the Kālacakra and Trayavṛttamālā[6]—had become extremely rare. So he (Bālasundara) sent about two hundred **paṇḍita*-s to *mahā-siddha* Śāntigupta[7] and others in Dramila and *Khagendra in the south to learn the practice of the Guhya-mantra and restore these in these countries. His (Bālasundara's) sons *Candravāhana now[8] resides in *Ra-khaṅ, *Atitavāhana rules *Ca-gama (? Cākmā), *Bālavāhana rules *Mu-ñaṅ and *Sundara-ha-ci rules *Naṃ-ga-ṭa. (In these countries) the Law remains extensively spread till now according to the older tradition.

The thirtyninth chapter containing the account of the spread of the Doctrine **[Fol 130A]** *in the Ko-ki country in the east.*

4. V n 'I have read *saddajaṭi*'.
5. See Supplementary Note 96.
6. *phreṅ-ba-bskor-gsum*.
7. *shi-ba-sbas-pa*. In Tg are attributed to *mahā-siddha* Śāntigupta five Tāntrika works (rG lxxiv.31 ; 50 ; lxxxiii.32 ; lxxxvi,88 & lxxiv.32).
8. i.e. A.D. 1608 ?

CHAPTER 40

ACCOUNT OF THE INTRODUCTION OF THE LAW INTO THE SMALLER ISLANDS AND OF ITS REVIVAL IN THE SOUTH

In the smaller countries [lit islands] like the *Siṅgala-dvīpa, Yavadvīpa,[1] Tāmradvīpa,[2] Suvarṇadvīpa,[3] *Dhanaśrī-dvīpa and *Pa-yi-gu the Law was spread in an early period and remains widely prevalent till now. Though there are a few Mahāyānīs in the *Siṅgala-dvīpa, the large majority (of the monks there) are Śrāvakas. Even now, about twelve thousand *bhikṣu*-s congregate there during the *Śrī-pādukā ceremony of (worshipping) the foot-print of the Teacher. Most of them are Śrāvakas. In *Dhanaśrī and *Pa-yi-gu, the Mahāyānīs are only a few in number. In the other smaller islands mentioned above exist only the followers of the Śrāvakas.

In the Dramila country [lit island], the Law in its purity did not previously exist. It was first introduced by *ācārya* Padmākara.[4] Dīpaṃkara-bhadra also went there. After that, numerous Vajradharas from *Magadha, *Urgyana and Kashmir extensively spread the Mantrayāna there for about a hundred years. The Tantras which were previously kept secret during the time of king *Dharmapāla and were eventually lost in India and the Tantras brought from *Oḍiyāna but lost in India survive here. Even now, the four classes of Guhya-mantra in their pure teachings are widely current here, as these were in the earlier times. Also partly survive here the Vinaya, Abhidharma and the Prajñāpāramitā-śāstras.

After the *Turuṣka invasion of *Magadha, in the southern

1. *nas-gliṅ*.
2. *zaṅs-gliṅ*.
3. *gser-gliṅ*.
4. *padma-'byuṅ-gnas*. In Tg are attributed to *ācārya* Padmākara seven Tāntrik^ works (rG xlv.37 ; lxvi.9 ; lxix.110 ; lxx.47 ; lxxi.5 ; 145 ; lxxii.2).

parts of India like *Vidyānagara, *Koṅkuna, [**Fol 130B**] *Ma-lyāra and *Ka-liṅ-ga were established some centres for the Doctrine, though these were not very big and the number of the followers of the Doctrine was not very large. Yet there was no break in the tradition of the purity of the teaching and *sādhana*.

In *Kaliṅga, which is included in *Triliṅga, there lived a famous **paṇḍita* called Narasūrya.[5]

Similarly, from the time of the establishment of the Law in the south-western kingdoms by king *Karṇa until the *Turuṣka invasion of *Magadha, it (the Law) was widely propagated by *Jñānākaragupta[6] and others. Many centres for the Doctrine were established in the countries like *Maru, *Me-vā-ra, *Cita-vara, *Bi-tu-va, *Ābhu, *Saurāṣṭra, *Gujiratha etc. Even now many *saṃgha*-s survive in these places.

In the later period, particularly because of the blessings of the *mahā-siddheśvara* Śāntigupta,[7] the Law was revived in *Khagendra and the Vindhyācala.

The *saṃgha*-s were elaborately worshipped during the time of king *Rāmacandra. His son *Bālabhadra built many temples and monasteries in *Śrī *Ratnagiri, *Jitā, *O-ja-na, *U-r-vā-si, etc. He also established in all possible ways many centres for the Doctrine in these places. It is said that the number of even the newly ordained monks there is about two thousand.

The Law in its purity, along with the study of both *sūtra* and *tantra*, became widespread.

The fortieth chapter containing the account of the introduction of the Law in the smaller islands and of its revival in the south.

5. *mi'i-ñi-mar-grags-pa.*
6. V Dīpaṃkaragupta. But the text has Jñānākaragupta in transliteration.
7. See note 7 of ch 39.

CHAPTER 41

ACCOUNT OF THE SPREAD OF THE DOCTRINE IN THE SOUTH AS RELATED IN THE "GARLAND OF FLOWERS"

I have not seen any comprehensive work on the royal **[Fol 131A]** chronology of south India[1] and of the *Ko-ki countries. However, the work called the Garland of Flowers[2] composed by the *brāhmaṇa* *Manomati—which contains a brief account of those kings that helped the spread of the Doctrine in the south and excellently worked there for the welfare of the living beings—gives the following account.

During the period of *Śuklarāja and *Candraśobha—the kings of *Kāñcī in the south—the Garuḍa and other common birds of the small island were brought under control and these birds used to bring medicine, gems and various marine creatures. With these treasures, each of the kings worshipped two thousand monks.[3] A temple was later built for the birds and it was called the *Paṅkhi-tīrtha[4] temple, where a few birds from the small island still come and live.

During the period of the three kings Mahendra [? Maheśa], Kṣemaṅkara [? Śaṃkara] and Manohara [? Manoratha], a thousand *caitya*-s were daily worshipped each with an umbrella (*chatra*) and various other articles immeasurable in quantity.

Further, during the time of the three kings *Bhoga-subāla and his son Candrasena and his [Candrasena's] son Kṣemaṅkara-siṃha [? Śaṃkara-siṃha], each suppliant used to be paid a **dināra* of alchemical gold. To the *bhikṣu*-s and *upāsaka*-s that approached them, they used to give articles worth five

1. P-ed 'the royal chronology of Kashmir and South India'. But S-ed omits Kashmir. The latter reading followed.
2. *me-tog-phreṅ-ba*, evidently not the *Puṣpa-mālā* (mDo lxxxix.1), which is a Vinaya work of the Sarvāstivādins.
3. V *saṃgha*-s. The text has *dge-'dun*. See D 270f.
4. See *Imperial Gazetteer of India* (1908) xxiii.392.

hundred silver *paṇa-s. The place where they lived is not quite clear, though it appears that they belonged to *Koṅkuna.

[Fol 131B] Kṣemaṅkarasiṃha (? Śaṃkara-siṃha) had three sons. The eldest of them was called *Vyāghrarāja, because he had eyes and stripes like those of a tiger. He ruled *Tala-koṅkuna and built two thousand temples there.

The second of them was called *Buda (Budha), i.e. the planet mercury. He ruled *Upara-koṅkuna and *Tu-lu-rā-ti. He used regularly to worship five thousand monks.

The youngest of them was *Buddhaśuca. Expelled from his own country, he eventually became the ruler of *Dravali. He used always to entertain ten thousand *brāhmaṇa*-s and ten thousand Buddhist teachers.

Now, there was a young king called Ṣaṇmukha[5] in the Vindhyācala region. He obtained inexhaustible food and clothes by attaining *siddhi* in the Vasudhārā-mantra. This king thrice liquidated all the debts in the whole of the southern region. He gave one cloth to each of the poor people. It is said that for twenty years he provided about eighty thousand poor people and beggars and other paupers with clothes and food.

Each of the kings of *Malyara belonging to the four generations—namely Sagara, Vikrama, Ujjayana and Śreṣṭha—established five hundred centres for the Doctrine and built a corresponding number of temples.

King Mahendra ruled in the *Karṇāṭa and *Vidyānagara regions. His son was Devarāja, whose son, again, was Viśva. Under the royal command of these three kings, the *kṣatriya*-s and *brāhmaṇa*-s were to worship only the Three Jewels. Each of them ruled for thirty years. King Viśva had three sons. The eldest of them called Śiśu [Fol 132A] ruled for three years. The second son Pratāpa ruled for only one month. Fifty temples were built by each of the two. Pratāpa took the vow : 'I shall kill myself if I ever worship any god other than the Buddha.' He had once to worship the *Śiva-liṅga and so he threw himself into a pit full of sharp razors. The youngest

5. *gshon-nu-gdoṅ-drug*. ? Kumāra-ṣaṇmukha. V 'The young Six-faced One'.

son *Nāgarāja-bhagavān left the country with ten thousand attendants and sailed eastwards to subdue the enemies near *Pu-khaṅ. He conquered the place, worshipped the Buddha and worked elaborately for the Law.

The account of king *Sālavāhana is already given.

Brāhmaṇa *Balamitra was born in *Kaliṅga. He filled with *caitya*-s the land between the two seas.

The triangular region of the south is like a long beak. The apex projects into the south and the base extends towards the *madhya-deśa.* At the extremity of the apex is *Rāmeśvara. The sea on its eastern side is called *Mahodadni and the sea on its western side is called *Ratnagiri. Although the line of demarcation is not visible in the ocean, **[Fol 132B]** as demarcated by the triangular region, however, the colour of the sea along the whole length of the southern coast looks different up to a long distance. The place of the meeting of the waves of the two sides appears to have a higher altitude.

He (Balamitra) built a *caitya* in each city up to the point where met the *Mahodadhi and *Ratnagiri. This was predicted in the *Mañjuśrī-mūla-tantra* as : 'The Doctrine will spread in the land up to the shores of the two seas...

Another *brāhmaṇa* called *Nāgaketu made a lakh of images of the Teacher and offered ten forms of worship[6] to each of these.

Further, there was the *brāhmaṇa* called **Vardhamāla. He prepared ten thousand copies of the works containing the Words (of the Buddha), worshipped each of these in fifteen forms and regularly maintained four thousand *bhikṣu*-s and *upāsaka*-s who were to preserve, listen to and preach these.

The Mahāyāna *ācārya* *Gaggari was a *śruti-dhara* and possessed the power of reading others' thoughts. By his preachings, one thousand disciples attained the stage of *dharma-kṣānti*[7].

6. V n 'These ten forms of worship are regarded as : flowers, garlands, candles, *ghee*, clothes, decoration, umbrella, corn, banner and ornaments'. cf D 439.

7. *chos-la-bzod-pa.*

*Kumārananda was a *gomī upāsaka. As a result of his preaching to five thousand upāsaka-s, all of them became versed in the Prajñā-pāramitā.

There was a householder upāsaka called **Matikumāra. As a result of his preaching the Doctrine, about ten thousand in all—inclusive of the young boys and girls—attained samādhi in Mahāyāna.

[**Fol 133A**] Further, *bhikṣu* **Bhadrānanda, by the mere utterance of the Truth, used to cure the diseases of everybody in the city and save them from the influence of the evil stars. He used to live in the company of twenty monks of extremely pure moral conduct. It is said that when the other monks started harassing him, he flew to the Tuṣita with his mortal body.

There lived two *upāsaka*-s called **Dānabhadra and *Laṅkādeva. They painted ten thousand pictures of the Tathāgata and made ten thousand images with each of the materials like stone, wood, clay and gems. They built an equal number of *caitya*-s and offered ten banners to each of these.

For fifteen years, *upāsaka* *Bahubhuja offered gifts of grain, food, clothes, gold, horses and cattle etc to the suppliants all around. At last he donated his male and female servants—even his son, his wife and his house—meditated in a forest and attained the stage of *anutpattikadharma-kṣānti*. It is said that after preaching the Doctrine to his disciples he went to the Sukhāvatī with his mortal body.

Then, there was the *upāsaka* called *bhaṭṭāraka* Madhyamati.[8] He used to go to the *tīrthika*-s in their guise and, to start with, used to preach them their own scriptures. [**Fol 133B**] In the course of this, he surreptitiously preached the doctrine of *anātma* and *mahā-karuṇā-mārga-krama*. Thus their views were gradually changed without their being aware of it. In this way, he converted them into Buddhists. Since he could assume various forms simultaneously, he managed to lead

8. *dbu-ma'i-blo-gros.*

about ten thousand *tīrthika*-s to the Law of the Buddha.

It seems that these *ācārya*-s appeared shortly before Nāgārjuna. It is at least certain that they lived during the period intervening between the beginning of the spread of the Mahāyāna and the time of Dharmakīrti. The exact period of these above-mentioned *ācārya*-s, however, cannot be definitely ascertained.

The fortyfirst chapter containing the account of the spread of the Doctrine in the south as related in the work 'The Garland of Flowers'.

CHAPTER 42

SOME DISCUSSION ON THE FOUR SECTS

All the *saṃgha*-s discussed so far were divided either in four or in eighteen sects.[1] To discuss these in brief:

There is no difference of opinion as to the theories and practices of these eighteen sects. But there is difference of opinion as to how the division took place.

According to the Sthaviras, the first division was that between the Sthaviras and Mahāsāṃghikas. The Mahāsāṃghikas, again, were divided into eight sub-sects, namely, the Mūla-mahāsāṃghikas,[2] Ekavyavahārikas,[3] Lokottaravādins, Bahuśrutīyas, Prajñaptivādins, Caityakas, Pūrvaśailas and Aparaśailas. And the Sthaviras also were divided into ten sub-sects, namely Mūla-sthaviras, [**Fol 134A**] Sarvāstivādins, Vātsīputrīyas, Dharmottarīyas, Bhadrayānīyas, Sammitīyas, Mahīśāsakas[4] (? Bahuśāsakas), Dharmaguptikas,[5] Suvarṣakas and Uttarīyas.

According to the Mahāsāṃghikas, the first division was into three, namely the Sthaviras, Mahāsāṃghikas and Vibhajyavādins. Then the Sthaviras, again, were divided into two, namely the Sarvāstivādins and the Vātsīputrīyas. The (Sarvā-) stivādins also were divided into the Mūla-sarvāstivādins and the Sūtravādins.[6] And the Vātsīputrīyas were divided into Sammitīyas, Dharmottarīyas, Bhadrayānīyas[7] and Ṣaṇṇāgarīyas. The Mahāsāṃghikas were divided into eight, namely

1. S n 'In the following account, I have mainly followed Vasil'ev. *Der Buddhismus*, p. 247ff, where in the notes, the Tibetan translations of the different names occur. I have also followed Stanislas Julien, *Listes diverses des noms des dix-huits ecoles schismatiques qui sont sorties du Bouddhisme*, in *Journal Asiatique* 1859 p. 327-361'.
2. V Mahāsāṃghika Proper.
3. V Vyavahārika.
4. *mań-ston-pa*—see BA i.27.
5. V Dharmaguptakas.
6. *mdo-sde-smra-ba*. V Sautrāntikas.
7. This name does not occur in V tr.

the Mahāsāṃghikas proper, Pūrvaśailas, Aparaśailas, Rājagirikas, Haimavatas, Caityakas, Siddhārthakas,[8] and Gokulikas. The Vibhajyavādins were divided into four, namely the Mahīśasakas, Kāśyapīyas, Dharmaguptikas and Tāmraśāṭīyas.

According to the Sammitīyas, the first fundamental division was into the Mahāsāṃghikas, Sarvāstivādins, Vātsīputrīyas and Haimavatas. Of these, the Mahāsāṃghikas were divided into six, namely the Mahāsāṃghikas proper, Ekavyavahārikas, Gokulikas, Bahuśrutīyas, Prajñaptivādins and Caityakas. And the (Sarvā-)stivādins were divided into seven, namely the Mūla-sarvāstivādins, Vibhajyavādins, Mahīśāsakas (? Bahuśāsakas),[9] Dharmaguptikas, Tāmraśāṭīyas, Kāśyapīyas and Saṃkrāntikas. And the Vātsīputrīyas were divided into four, **[Fol 134B]** namely Mūla-vātsīputrīyas, Dharmottarīyas, Bhadrāyaṇīyas and Sammitīyas. There was no subdivision of the Haimavatas.

Following the view of the Sarvāstivādins, it is said in Vinītadeva's *Samayabhedoparacanacakra*[10] that the Pūrvaśailas, Aparaśailas, Haimavatas, Lokottaravādins and the Prajñaptivādins were the five main branches of the Mahāsāṃghikas. The Mūla-sarvāstivādins, Kāśyapīyas, Mahīśāsakas, Dharmaguptikas, Bahuśrutīyas, Tāmraśāṭīyas and the Vibhajyavādins were called the Sarvāstivādins. The Jetavanīyas, Abhayagirivāsins, Mahāvihāravāsins were *sthaviras*. The Kaurukullakas, Āvantakas and the Vātsīputrīyas were the three branches of the Sammitīyas. (Thus these were) eighteen in all, differing among themselves in their places of residence, their theories and their teachers.

In this view, the eighteen sects originated from the four principal ones. Many Tantras mention only four original sects. Though disagreeing with the view of the Vātsīputrīyas, this principle of counting the four is acceptable. It is more so, because it is based on the statement of *ācārya* Vasumitra.[11]

8. V Saṃkrāntikas. V n 'Arthasiddhakas ?'
9. V Bahuśrutīyas.
10. by Vinītadeva—Tg mDo xc.13.
11. See *Samayabhedoparacanacakra* by Vasumitra (Tg mDo xc.11).

In the *Bhikṣuvarṣāgrapṛcchā*,[12] the four original sects are mentioned according to this, though there are some differences like dividing the Mahāsāṃghikas into six and [**Fol 135A**] the Sammitīyas[13] into five. However, the above view should be accepted.

There are many discrepancies in the enumeration of the names given before. But most of these are cases of the same sects being mentioned under different names. Some real discrepancies are also to be found in these enumerations.

The Kāśyapīyas, for example, were none but the dissenting disciples of the later *arhat* Kāśyapa ; they are also mentioned as the Suvarṣakas. Similarly, the Mahīśāsakas, Dharmaguptikas, Tāmraśāṭīyas, etc were thus called according to the names of their respective Sthaviras. The Saṃkrāntikas, Uttarīyas, Tāmraśāṭīyas are but the same sect (under different names). So also were the Caityakas and Pūrvaśailas (but names of) the same sect and they were the followers of the wandering mendicant Mahādeva.[14] From them branched off the Siddhārthakas and the Rājagirikas. Accepting this view, these two cannot be counted among the eighteen (sects). The Lokottaravādins and Kukkuṭagirikas[15] (bya-gag-ri-pa) were the same. The Ekavyavahārika is also said to have been the general name of the Mahāsāṃghikas. The Kaurukullaka is translated (into Tibetan) as Sa-sgros-ripa. The Vātsīputrīyas, Dharmottarīyas, Bhadrāyaṇīyas and the Ṣaṇṇāgarīyas are to be roughly taken as being the same.

The *saṃgha*-s of the *ārya-deśa* and the smaller islands are to be clearly regarded as originating from and belonging to the four principal and distinct sects. The scriptural works of the eighteen sects [**Fol 135B**] still survive. But there is practically none following any one of these theories today who do not mix these up with those of others.

It is clear that during the period of the seven *Pāla kings

12. Tg mDo xc.21—attributed to Padmākaraghoṣa. But see BA i.30 & n attributed to Padmasambhava.
13. V Vātsīputrīyas.
14. *lha-chen-po*. V n 'see *supra* ch 9'.
15. V Kaukuṭapāda.

only seven of these sects survived. Among the Śrāvaka-sendhavas this tradition still survives.

Broadly speaking, the four (original) sects exist in their purity. Besides these, there survive only two branches of the Sammitīyas, namely the Vātsīputrīyas and Kaurukullakas, two of the Mahāsāṃghikas, namely the Prajñaptivādins and Lokottaravādins and two branches of the Sarvāstivādins, namely the Mūla-sarvāstivādins and the Tāmraśāṭīyas.[16]

The sect earlier known as the Dārṣṭāntikas was that of the Sautrāntikas which branched off from the Tāmraśāṭīyas. Hence, it is not to be separately counted among the eighteen.

In the older days, when the Law of the Śrāvakas alone was current, there surely existed the followers of the views of these different sects. Since the spread of the Mahāyāna, all the Mahāyāna-saṃghas belonged to one or the other of these sects, though these upheld the Mahāyāna alone and were not influenced by the different views of the earlier sects. Similarly the Śrāvakas also for a long time upheld their own views in their purity and only later their views were influenced by those of the others.

In spite of adhering to the views of either the Hīnayāna or Mahāyāna, all of them wanted to remain pure in the practices and applications of the Vinaya. Nevertheless, the division into the four sects is to be understood as resulting from the differences in the understanding of the practices of the Vinaya. As it is said,

> 'The sayings of the Buddha are to be properly understood as blissful in the beginning, in the middle and in the end, and as being characterised by the three marks and as delivering the threefold teaching.'

[Fol 136A] Following this, profound reverence (for the sayings of the Buddha) should be aroused in everybody.

The fortysecond chapter containing some discussion on the four sects.

16. V n 'The seven schools—if the author had this number in mind—should probably be taken as Sthaviras'.

CHAPTER 43

A BRIEF DISCOURSE ON THE ORIGIN OF THE MANTRA-YĀNA

Now, I find some conceited people who, in spite of being full of doubts, consider themselves to be extremely ambitious. However, their muddled view of the different origin of the Mantra-yāna[1] needs to be examined.

Generally speaking, each of the Sūtras and Tantras has its respective source-book (*nidāna*).[2] Hence, the history of the Sūtras is certainly different from that of the Mantra-yāna. Let us not discuss each of these separately. Speaking in general, the Sūtras and Tantras cannot be differentiated in respect of their place, time and teacher. As to how these reached the human world, (it is to be understood) that most of the Tantras appeared simultaneously with the *Mahāyāna-sūtra*-s. Many of the profound Yoga and Anuttara Tantras, being separately obtained[3] by the different *siddhācārya*-s, appeared gradually. As for example, Sri *Saraha obtained the *Buddha-kapāla*,[4] *Lūi-pā obtained the *Yoginī-saṃcaryā*,[5] *Lva-va-pā and Saroruha obtained the Hevajra, Kṛṣṇācārya obtained the *Sampuṭa-tilaka*,[6] *Lalitavajra obtained the three parts of the *Kṛṣṇa-yamāri*, Gambhīravajra[7] obtained the Vajrāmṛta,[8] *Kukuri-pā obtained the *Mahāmāyā, *Piṭo-pā obtained the Kālacakra.[9]

Earlier, it was wrongly claimed by some that the account of the origin of the Mantra(-yāna) was contained in the

1. *snags-kyi-theg-pa.*
2. *gleṅ-gshi.*
3. *spyan-draṅs.* Lit. invited.
4. *saṅs-rgyas-thod-pa.*
5. *rnal-'byor-ma-kun-spyod.*
6. *kha-sbyor-thig-le.*
7. *zab-pa'i-rdo-rje.*
8. *rdo-rje-bdud-rtsi.*
9. *dus-kyi-'khor-lo.*

commentary on the Sahaja-siddhi.[10] But there exists a history of the Sahaja-siddhi by the great scholar Bu-ston, who compiles in it the account available in all the commentaries[11] on the Sahaja-siddhi. **[Fol 136B]** In this he shows that these (commentaries) contain only the history of Sahaja-siddhi, but not of the Guhya-mantras in general.

'Gos lo-lsā-ba gshon-nu-dpal,[12] though fully aware of all these, wanted to bring life into the dead issue and gave an elaborate account of the Sahaja-siddhi. Let us even assume that the farmer Padmavajra mentioned in it is the same person as *Padmavajra the Great.[13] However, connecting on this basis the history of Sahaja-siddhi with that of Sapta-siddhi[14] and presenting all these as a wonderful account of the origin of the Mantras in general is baseless and fanciful. (Both) Sahaja-siddhi and Sapta-siddhi were practised only by some of the *guhya* Tāntrikas. But this was not true of all. Hence it is extremely confusing to speak of their lineage alone as the lineage of Mantra(-yāna) in general.

So there must have been an amazing account of the history of the Mantra(-yāna) as such, which is not practised by the vast majority of the Tāntrikas of India and Tibet and the lineage of which cannot and should not be considered as their lineage. I say this merely as a joke.

Following this, and depending mainly on fancy, some people invent an account of the first preaching of the Mantra(-yāna) based on incomplete and incorrect citations from the *Tattva-saṃgraha*[15] and the *Krodha-trailokya-vijaya-nirmita-bhāṣā*.[16] originating from Vajracūḍā.[17]

Accepting such a version of the commentary on the Sahaja-

10. *lhan-cig-skyes-grub-kyi-'grel-pa.*
11. See Supplementary Note 97.
12. i.e. the author of *The Blue Amnals.*
13. see BA i.363.
14. *grub-pa-sde-bdun.*
15. *de-ñid-bsdus-pa.*
16. *khro-bo-khams-gsum-rnam-rgyal-sprul-bśad.*
17. *rdo-rje-rtse-mo.*

siddhi, one has to consider wrongly king Śūravajra[18] as the preceptor of *Āryadeva and to identify *kumārī* Sukhalalitā[19] with 'the Yoginī born of the Nāgas'[20] and to include her in the lineage of *ārya-viṣayaka*[21] etc. Further, identifying ḍākinī Subhagā[22] with Matibhadrā,[23] it is baseless and empty babble to say that she belonged to the lineage of the Four Precepts.[24]

[Fol 137A] It is well-known among the scholars that Śrī Dhānya-kaṭaka was the place where Mantra-yāna was originally preached. But what is written in the glosses by some older Tibetan scholars in defiance of this is unknown in India. To write that this place—the name of which should be known even to the foolish Tibetans—was called Saddharma-meghaviśālagañja[25] is due only to a bias for what is baseless and to the tendency of placating (the older scholars). This is nothing but the way in which the fools befool other fools. Sensible persons do not take it as a serious statement at all.

The account in the commentary on the Sahaja-siddhi represents the correct tradition and its *upadeśa* may also contain some significance concerning all the Tantras. But why should the preachings and *śāstra*-s of Sahaja(-siddhi) be considered as preachings and *śāstra*-s of Lakṣmī[26] (Lakṣmīṅkarā) alone ? Besides, (the commentary on) Sahaja-siddhi composed by *Dombī *Heruka enumerates seven or eight *siddhi*-s.

Though the traditions of these are different in both India and Tibet, there is also some similarity between these. But it is ridiculous to be misled by this similarity and proudly proclaim that the two are identical.

18. *dpa'-bo'i-rdo-rje.*
19. *bde-ba'i-rol-pa-mo.*
20. cf BA i.361.
21. *'phags-skor*
22. *skal-ba-bzaṅ-mo.*
23. *blo-gros-bzaṅ-mo.*
24. *gdams-ṅag-bka'-bshi.*
25. *chos-bzaṅ-spriṅ-gyi-yaṅ-rdsoṅ.* V 'The Castle of the Cloud of Faith'.
26. *dpal-mo.*

The origin of the Mantra-yāna is to be understood on the basis of its *śāstra*-s and by compiling the original account coming from their traditions. All these are briefly stated in my *rin-po-che'i-'byuṅ-gnas-lta-bu'i-gtam,*[27] which should be consulted.

Who can give a full account of all the *siddha*-s of the *ārya-deśa* ! **[Fol 137B]** It is said that only the *siddha*-s of the Tārā-mantra system belonging to the period of Nāgārjuna alone numbered five thousand. The number of the followers of *Dārika-pā and Kṛṣṇācārya reaches beyond comprehension. Thus it is to be understood.

The fortythird chapter containing a brief discourse on the origin of the Mantra-yāna.

27. i.e. *Ratnākara-sadṛśa-kathā*.

CHAPTER 44

THE HISTORY OF IMAGE-MAKERS

In the ancient period, the human artists possessed miraculous power and their artistic creations were astounding. In the Vinaya-vastu etc, it is clearly said that the statues made and pictures drawn by them created the illusion of being the real objects. For about a hundred years after the *parinirvāṇa* of the Teacher, there were many artists like them.

As afterwards there was none of them any more, the celestial artists appeared in human guise and made eight wonderful images for worship in *Magadha, like those of the Mahābodhi and Mañjuśrī-dundubhīśvara.[1] The *caitya*-s of the eight sacred places and the inner boundary walls of Vajrāsana were built by the Yakṣa artists during the period of Aśoka and the Nāga artists built many (images) during the time of Nāgārjuna.

The (images) thus made by the Deva-s, Nāga-s and Yakṣa-s created the illusion of the real objects for many years. In the later period, under the influence of time such creations were no more and there remained practically none with the knowledge of the technique concerned.

After that, for a long time there developed the traditions of different artistic techniques depending on the individual talents of various artists. There remained no uniform tradition of the technique (of image-making).

[Fol 138A] Later on, during the period of king Buddhapakṣa there lived an artist called *Bimbasāra, who produced the most wonderful architectural sculptures and paintings: these could be compared to those of the celestial artists of the earlier period.

Numerous artists became his followers. This artist was born in *Magadha. Therefore, the artists following his school

1. *'jam-dpal-rṅa-sgra.* D 367—an epithet of Buddha Amoghasiddha.

were said to belong to the school of the *madhya-deśa* art, wherever they might have been born.

During the period of king Śila, there was an extraordinarily skilled icon-maker called *Srigadharī, who was born in the region of *Maru. He made many sculptures and paintings in the tradition of the Yakṣas, The school following his technique is known as the school of old western art.

During the time of king *Devapāla and Śrī *Dharmapāla, there lived a highly skilled artist called *Dhīmān in the *Varendra region. His son was called *Biṭpalo. These two followed the tradition of the Nāga artists and practised various techniques like those of metal-casting, engraving and painting. The tradition of the technique of the father became different from that of the son. The son used to live in *Bhaṃgala. The cast-images made by the followers of both of them were called the eastern icons, wherever these followers might have been born.

In painting, the tradition of those that followed the father was called the tradition of eastern paintings, while those who followed the son were known as belonging to the school of the *madhya-deśa* painting, because this was widespread mainly in *Magadha.

In Nepal also the earlier tradition of art was similar to the old western (style of Indian art). The paintings and bell-metal castings (of Nepal) of the middle period are said to belong to the Nepalese school, though these resemble the eastern (Indian art).

No distinct (tradition) is found (in Nepal) in the later period.

[Fol 138B] In Kashmir also was followed the tradition of the early central art and of the old western [Indian] art.. In the later period one called *Hasurāja introduced new technique both in sculpture and painting. It is now called the art of Kashmir.

Skilled image-makers abounded in every place wherever the Law of the Buddha flourished. In the regions that came under the influence of the *mleccha*-s declined the art of image-making and the regions under the influence of the *tīrthika*-s had only inferior image-makers. That is why, practically nothing survives today of the tradition of those mentioned above.

In *Pu-khaṅ and southern India still thrives the tradition of image-making. But it is clear that their tradition of art did not reach Tibet in the past.

In the south, there exist numerous followers of the three, namely **Jaya,[2] **Parojaya and **Vijaya.

The fortyfourth chapter containing the history of the image-makers.

2. V Nijaya.

[ON THE SOURCES ETC.]

The account compiled here, if well understood, will remove all the baseless and erroneous ideas. Thus, some of the highly renowned scholars of Tibet say that Nāgārjuna and others came immediately after the seven hierarchs (of the Law) of the Teacher. They think that the *Candra kings ruled shortly after king Aśoka and they claim that during the reign of the fourteen kings—namely the seven *Candras and the seven *Pālas—lived all the *ācārya*-s from *Saraha to *Abhayākara. But since this period was too short to allow all these to have happened and finding the periods preceding and following the *ācārya*-s become extremely brief, they extend the duration of the life of all **[Fol 139A]** and thus try to extend the period as a whole.

Now, it may be asked what the sources of this compilation are. In Tibet there exist many fragmentary narrations as well as compilations of the history of the Doctrine. But I have not seen anything chronologically complete.

I have not written anything except that which is absolutely authentic. I have gone through the work containing two thousand verses compiled by **paṇḍita* Kṣemendrabhadra of *Magadha,[1] in which is narrated the history of the incidents up to the period of king *Rāmapāla. Besides, I have listened to some **paṇḍita* teachers (of India). I have followed here mainly all these and have moreover read the work called the **Buddhapurāṇa* containing one thousand and two hundred verses and composed by the Kṣatriya **paṇḍita* Indradatta.[2] In this are exhaustively mentioned the incidents of the period up to the four *Sena kings. The account of the succession of the *ācārya*-s by the *brāhmaṇa* **paṇḍita* *Bhaṭaghaṭi is similar in length. I have extensively used here both these works.

These three authorities are practically unanimous excepting on certain minor points related to the dates of the different

1. *magadha'i-paṇḍita sa-dbaṅ-bzaṅ-po.*
2. *dbaṅ-pos-byin.*

individuals. I find them mainly describing the way in which the Law was spread in the kingdom of Aparāntaka. But I have not read or heard of any detailed account of how the Law was spread in Kashmir, *Urgyana, Thogar, south India, *Ko-ki and the smaller islands. Hence I could not write about these (in details).

The account of the different incidents of the later period (given by me) **[Fol 139B]** have not come down in writing. In spite of being transmitted only orally, these are authentic. I have also included here the narratives from *The Garland of Flowers*.

[EPILOGUE]

This pleasing garland made by suitably stitching the wonderful account with the string of simple words is being dedicated to decorate the necks of the highly intelligent persons. It is designed to invoke great reverence for those excellent persons who worked for the Law of the Jina. This will also help to differentiate the baseless works (from the correct account). This will greatly enhance the reverence for the Doctrine by helping the correct understanding of the extremely important and admirable activities of those scholars and *siddha*-s that upheld the Law. Its purpose is to arouse reverence for the saints and their Path and thus finally to attain Buddhahood by following the True Doctrine.

Such is the purpose of this composition. By its merit let all the living beings attain the *anuttara* Buddhahood following the path of the practice of virtue. Let them be decorated with merit in all forms.

COLOPHON

With the purpose of causing welfare to the living beings and on the request of some seekers of the Truth, rGyal-khams-pa Tāranātha has composed this work at the age of thirty-four[1] in the Earth-Male-Monkey year[2] or the Bṛhaspati year at the Brag-stod-chos-kyi-pho-braṅ (The Religious Palace of Brag-stod). It is called the dGos-'dod-kun-'byuṅ and contains the clear account of how the True Doctrine—the precious, the glorious and the sources of all glories—was spread in the *ārya-deśa*.

COLOPHON OF THE POTALA-EDITION

[Fol 140A] Let the precious Law spread in all directions for a long time. Thus was written the authentic history of Buddhism in India by the all-knowing Tāranātha of Jo-naṅ. Since the printing blocks of this work were damaged and worn out at the rTag-brtan-phun-tshogs-gliṅ (The Perfect and Eternally Firm Island) of Jo-naṅ, in the Fire-Dog year of sixteenth rab-byuṅ[3] is prepared a fresh block-printing under the state management at the great printing house at Shola [i.e. the administrative section of the palace of the Dalai Lama at the base of Potala in Lhasa] by the profound desire for working for the Law and the welfare of the living beings on the part of the great **paṇḍita* sTag-brag, the preceptor of Śaraṇyanātha-śāsana-pālaka (i e the Dalai Lama). Let this bring welfare to all the living beings.

1. *lo-sum-cu-so-bshi-pa.*
2. i.e. A.D. 1608. S n 'In the year 1608 or 1610, inasmuch as the chronology of the Tibetans as known through Csoma is two years in arrear of the Chinese ; cf Schlaginweit BT 278'. But, thanks to the work of P. Pelliot and others, the uncertainty about Tibetan calendar is now removed—see A. Chattopadhyaya AT 563ff.
3. i.e. the year A.D. 1946.

SUPPLEMENTARY NOTES

1. THE PATRIARCHS

Przyluski's thesis (LEA 1-60) concerning the growth of the later legends about the patriarchs has some interesting light to throw on the possible sources on which Tāranātha depends particularly in the earlier chapters of his work.

As Buddhism outgrows the narrow circle of the early Magadhan communities and expands to the north-west, the need is felt for new legends to justify the authority of the new communities and the māhātmya of their new centres. The most prominent of these new centres are Mathurā and Kashmir. Mathurā is the centre of the Sarvāstivādins and Kashmir that of those who call themselves the Mūla-sarvāstivādins. The typical literary product of the monks of Mathurā is the *Aśokāvadāna* and the most archaic form of this, according to Przyluski, is the *Aśoka-rāja-sūtra*, now preserved in Chinese translation as *A-yü-wang-king*. The typical literary product of the monks of the north-west (Kashmir) is the *Vinaya* of the Mūla-sarvāstivādins (henceforth referred to as VMS).

The first point to be noted about Tāranātha's account is his total indifference to Upāli. Upāli's name occurs nowhere in his *History*, though, according to the Pali sources and the *Vinaya* of the Mahāsāṃghikas (Przy 52), Upāli is the first to be entrusted with the responsibility of the Law. As against this, both *Aśokāvadāna* and VMS claim that the Buddha entrusts Kāśyapa or Mahākāśyapa (who presides over the First Council) with the responsibility of the Law and that Ānanda succeeds Mahākāśyapa. Evidently, therefore, Tāranātha's account of the patriarchs—beginning as it does with Kāśyapa and Ānanda—draws on the tradition recorded in the *Aśokāvadāna* and VMS.

Przyluski argues that this shift of emphasis from Upāli to Ānanda is indicative of a shift of emphasis from the Vinaya to the Sūtra. In the First Council, Ānanda recites the Sūtra while Upāli the Vinaya. Thus, Ānanda is the first of the *bahu-śruta*-s, Upāli the first of the *śīla-dhara*-s (Przy 54). This difference between the traditions of the *bahu-śruta*-s and *śīla-dhara*-s becomes one of basic importance for the subsequent history of Buddhism. The *Aśokāvadāna*—therefore, the Mathurā school of the Sarvāstivādins—strongly champions the former. Hence is the importance attributed in it to Ānanda and this to the exclusion of Upāli. Further, the same work describes the Buddha as first going to Mathurā and then to Kashmir, and this as accompanied by Ānanda. As accompanied by Upagupta, again, Aśoka is described in the *Aśokāvadāna* as making the grandest offering to the *stūpa* of Ānanda. All these are indicative of how Ānanda, Upagupta and the region of Mathurā are glorified in the *Aśokāvadāna*. But the devotion to Ānanda is probably more fervent during the Mathurā phase than during the Kashmirian period (Przy 29). Thus the Mûla-sarvāstivādins of Kashmir—also champions of the tradition of the *bahu-śruta*-s—show the tendency of pushing Ānanda to the background, inasmuch as the VMS describes the Buddha making journey to Mathurā and Kashmir accompanied by Yakṣa Vajrapāṇi instead of Ānanda.

From this point of view, Tāranātha's glorification of Ānanda is indicative of the influence of the Mathurā school. This is further indicated by his account of the conversion of Upagupta by Śāṇavāsika, also an apostle of Mathurā. By contrast, VMS attributes this conversion to Madhyāntika, the apostle of Kashmir, (though, notes Przyluski, the text contradicts itself by also quoting a prophecy concerning the conversion of Upàgupta by Śāṇavāsika : Przy 4). At the same time, Tāranātha's account of the conversion of Kashmir by Madhyāntika is fully in accord with the tradition recorded in the VMS.

Tāranātha disapproves of the view of including Madhyāntika in the list of the hierarchs and admits of only seven in the line of succession. The tradition of admitting only seven hierarchs accepted by Tāranātha occurs in the *Vinaya-kṣudraka*, which is also quoted by Bu-ston ii.108 : 'Kāśyapa, Ānanda, Śāṇavāsika, Upagupta, Dhītika, Kṛṣṇa and Mahāsudarśana—these are the seven hierarchs.' *This is exactly the list of the VMS only with this difference that the VMS adds Madhyāntika to it.*

Interestingly, the *Aśokāvadāna*, which from the point of view of Przyluski's argument need not show any special zeal of including Madhyāntika in the list of the hierarchs, does include him : where it differs from the VMS is that it is yet to add to the list the names of Kṛṣṇa and Mahāsudarśana. These two names are perhaps later added by the monks of Kashmir, particularly because of Sudarśana's connection with Kaniṣka (Tār Fol 31A, Przy 53).

Though the list of the seven hierarchs given in the *Vinaya-kṣudraka* seems to acquire decisive authority for the Tibetan scholars, Bu-ston ii.108, true to his great erudition in the later Buddhist literature, goes on quoting other sources on the patriarchs, showing thereby that some of these sources vitally differ in enumerating the names of the patriarchs—a circumstance which by itself is indicative of these lists being the results of after-thought prompted largely by the later and local needs—but indicating further the more striking point that according to some of these sources the later custodians of the Law are definitely considered as exercising authority only in certain restricted regions. Thus Bu-ston ii.109 : 'It is said in the *Mahākaruṇā-puṇḍarīka* in answer to the question, "Who is to be the guardian of the Doctrine after the Teacher has passed away ?",—"Oh Ānanda, the monk Kāśyapa and thyself, ye two are to guard the Highest Doctrine for 40 years and more. Then, in the city of Mathurā on the mountains Gandhamādana and Mahāpārśva, in the grove called Paṅkavatī, there is to appear the monk Ślaṇavāsa, and, in the same place, the monk Nandin. —On the mountain Uśira, there are to appear 44,000 monks. In the city of Pāṭaliputra, in the Mārgārāma, there will be a monk called Aśvagupta and, in the same city, in the grove of the ducks, the monk called Uttara. —In the country of Aṅga, during the five years' feast, 13,000 Arhats are to arise. —In the city of Suvarṇadroṇa, two monks called Vijña and Sañjaya, in the city of Sāketana—the monk Mahāvīrya, and on the northern border-land of Gandhāra—the monk Kāśyapa, are to appear. All these monks are to be greatly renowned for their miraculous achievements, their great power of faculties... These are to be the propagators of my Teaching." '

Modern scholars are on the whole inclined to view the later legends of the hierarchs exercising an overall authority on the later Buddhist communities as being without any historical foundation (see N. Dutt AMB 16ff and Przyluski 1-60 in particular). 'It should be observed,' remarks N. Dutt, 'that though the Theravādins speak of the line of disciples (*ācariya-paramparā*) from Upāli to Sāriputta, there is no idea of patriarchal succession. In the *Majjhima Nikāya* it is expressly stated that in the Buddhist Saṃgha there is no recognised head. The Tibetan and Chinese traditions have, in fact, given currency to the idea of patriarchal succession.' Observes Przyluski (p.50), 'Kern has shown in his *History of Buddhism* that the lists of patriarchs contradict one another.' There is 'no common element in this matter' in the Sinhalese tradition and in the traditions recorded in the works translated into Chinese and Tibetan. For this and other reasons Kern suspects 'the lists of patriarchs and regards these as apocryphal.' Przyluski adds, 'One may go further ; it is doubtful that at any time after the Nirvāṇa of the Buddha the authority of a single savant had been recognised by all the Buddhists together. This happens to throw doubt on the very existence of the patriarchate.'

Nevertheless, as Przyluski says, the study of the later legends of the patriarchs is not without its own interest, for these have light to throw on 'the real tendencies of the important rival communities, namely the Sthaviras, the Sarvāstivādins and the Mahāsāṃghikas.'

Here is how Przyluski (p.52f) sums up the different accounts of succession that we come across in the different sources :

Works written in Pali : Upāli, Dāsaka, Sonaka, Siggava, Candavajji, Tissa, Moggaliputta. ('The series continues after the conversion of Ceylon').

Vinaya of the Mahāsāṃghikas : the first five savants are—Upāli,, Dāsabala, Jyotidarśa(?), Jita(?), Sense-protected (? Indriya-rakṣita).

Aśokāvadāna : Mahākāśyapa, Ānanda, Śāṇavāsa and

Madhyāntika, Upagupta and Dhītika.

VMS : Mahākāśyapa, Ānanda, Śāṇika and Madhyāntika, Upagupta, Dhītika, Kṛṣṇa and Sudarśana.

Fu-fa-tsang-yin-yuen-king (Nanjio 1340 : a work that 'belongs undoubtedly to the Sarvāstivādin group'—Przy 53) enumerates 23 patriarchs, beginning with the list of the *Aśokāvadāna*, though omitting Madhyāntika.

Thus, while the lists of the Sthaviras and Mahāsāṃghikas begin with Upāli and Dāsaka, those of the Sarvāstivādins begin with Mahākāśyapa and Ānanda. Przyluski (p. 54) argues that of these two lists, the second is earlier, because all the accounts of the First Council—inclusive of those of the Sthaviras and Mahāsāṃghikas—mention Kāśyapa and not Upāli as presiding over the Council. Thus, the first tendency to formulate a definite list of patriarchs manifests itself among the Sarvāstivādins.

Now, 'Śāṇavāsa is the apostle of Mathurā ; Madhyāntika is the ascetic who converts Kashmir. Both were extolled among communities of the west and it had to be early acknowledged that they were the disciples of Ānanda' (Przy 55.) This becomes the pattern of the entire western communities. Upagupta being the immediate disciple of Śāṇavāsika, the spiritual family of Ānanda is formulated as follows :

Ānanda succeeded by Śāṇavāsa and Madhyāntika and Śāṇavāsa succeeded by Upagupta.

'The bifurcation of the genealogical line after Ānanda was an inconvenient complication.' This is sought to be solved by 'the process of arbitrary simplification.' Thus, the author of the *Aśokāvadāna*, failing to separate Śāṇavāsa and Upagupta (both monks of the Naṭa-bhaṭa monastery), is obliged to narrate the life of Madhyāntika before Śāṇavāsa, violating thereby 'the chronological order', since 'the conversion of Madhyāntika is posterior to the entry of Śāṇavāsa into the faith'. The author of the *Fu-fa-tsang-yin-yuen-king* solves the problem by simply dropping the name of Madhyāntika.

'The *History* of Tāranātha,' observes Przyluski (p.56), 'is more complex and hence more instructive. The Tibetan chronicler who appears to have had access to diverse sources endeavours sometimes to notice the synchronism of events.' While 'following the development of Buddhism in the west, Tāranātha does not lose sight of the eastern communities.' Thus, on the one hand he follows the series of the Sarvāstivādins (Mahākāśyapa, Ānanda, Śāṇavāsika, Upagupta, Dhītika), while on the other hand he 'informs us that king Mahendra and his son Camasa reigned in the country of Aparāntaka during the partiarchate of Upagupta, and during the same epoch Arhat Uttara lived in the east. The inhabitants of Bagala built the monastery of Kukkuṭārāma for the latter, and the greatest disciple of Uttara was Arhat Yaśas.'

Now, according to the Pali *Cullavagga,* among the monks that sat in the Second Council (of Vaiśālī) are Sabbakāma, Uttara, Śāṇavāsī and Yaśas. Further a story of the Second Council—which, according to Przyluski (p. 57) was somehow 'inserted' into the VMS but which nevertheless includes 'archaic fragments anterior to the...very formation of Sarvāstivādin group'—mentions that 'at the time of the Council of Vaiśālī, Yaśas had as his teacher Sarvakāma, who himself was a disciple of Ānanda. During the same time, the ascetic Uttara lived in the town of Lieu-chuan (Śrughna). (Przy 56)

From these evidences Przyluski concludes that 'Madhyāntika at Kashmir, Śāṇavāsa and Upagupta at Mathurā, and Uttara, Sarvakāma and Yaśas in the east, were all personages pretty nearly contemporary (Przy 56).' Of these, Madhyāntika, Śāṇavāsa and Upagupta are the heads of the Western Church ; Sarvakāma, Uttara and Yaśas are the heads of the Eastern Church. The authors wanting to glorify the Western Church are the first to draw up for this purpose a rigid list of patriarchs by totally eliminating the heads of the Eastern Church.

From the point of view of this argument we have to conclude that though Tāranātha is fully aware of the developments in the eastern region evidently on the basis of some other tradition (see Supplementary Note 2 : on the possible implications of Tār's reliance on the Śrāvaka-piṭakas and Kṣemendra's works), when it comes to the question of formulating the list of the patriarchs he wants to subscribe to the tradition recorded in the *Aśokāvadāna* and the VMS and at the same time, for reasons not yet clear to us, drops the name of Madhyāntika from the list.

2. THE AŚOKA LEGENDS

'We are yet in the dark', remarks N. Dutt (AMB 19) 'about the part played by Aśoka in the propagation of Buddhism... Throughout his exhortations, so far as they have been found in the Edicts, there is not the slightest hint of his actively helping the propagation of Buddhism. His Edicts refer to the *dhammavijaya* as opposed to conquest by arms, but by *dhamma* he does not mean Buddhism. His *dhamma* consisted of maxims for leading an ideal life and performing meritorious acts which make a person happy in this world as well as the next. The Edicts do not contain a single reference to Nirvāṇa or Śūnyatā, Anātma or Duḥkha, while on the other hand they speak of heaven, and happiness in a heavenly life, which was never an ideal of early Buddhism, for it considered existence in any of the three dhātus, Kāma, Rūpa and Arūpa, to be misery (*duḥkha*).'

It is difficult to overlook the main point of this argument, howevermuch violently it may go against the usually accepted idea of Aśoka being a committed Buddhist [see e.g. Vincent A. Smith in ERE ii.125f]. At the same time, without admitting Aśoka's patronage of Buddhism in some form or other, it is impossible to explain the tremendous enthusiasm with which the later Buddhists wanted to look back at him. This is not denied by N. Dutt. 'But it must be admitted,' he continues, 'that when an emperor like Aśoka shows a bias for a particular religion and even proclaims himself to be a Buddhist upāsaka and pays visits to the monasteries or sacred places of the Buddhists, the religion automatically receives an impulse, and its propagation by the Buddhist monks then becomes easy. So we may regard Aśoka as a passive propagator of Buddhism, and, during his rule, the religion probably made its way throughout his kingdom, also reaching places beyond his dominion.' (AMB 19-20).

The result was the fabrication by the later Buddhists of an enormous mass of legends about Aśoka. These legends became all the more complicated, because the later Buddhists—themselves divided into different sects and having their centres in different regions—went on spinning these often with the specific purpose of glorifying their own centres with little scruple for history and sometimes even reckless of the question of internal consistency of these legends.

One has only to glance through the travel-notes of the famous Chinese pilgrims—Fa-hien, Yuan-chuang and I-Tsing—to see how the country became eventually full of legends concerning Aśoka. Nothing was too extravagantly fanciful—too quaint or too grotesque—to their authors, so long as these served their basic purpose of glorifying the Doctrine by way of glorifying its great patron.

Like these Chinese pilgrims, Tāranātha himself is a devout follower of later Buddhism and, therefore, is expected to show no more critical attitude to these legends than the Chinese pilgrims. Nevertheless, Tāranātha is also confronted with a special problem. The Chinese pilgrims recall these legends piecemeal, usually in connection with what is shown to them as the monuments built by Aśoka in the different parts of the country. They have therefore no problem of bringing all these into a systematic or orderly form. For Tāranātha, however, it is quite different. A history of Buddhism in India is evidently inconceivable for him without a substantial account of Aśoka. At the same time he finds himself confronted with an enormous mass of the legends about Aśoka, which he has to retell in a brief chapter and at least with some semblance to a logical sequence. For this purpose, he has got to be selective ; he has to rely more on some of the *sources* and reject some others.

What interests us in particular about his account of Aśoka, therefore, is the question of his sources for it.

Unlike most of his other chapters, the one on Aśoka is concluded by Tāranātha with the enumeration of the main sources on which it is based. These are :

1) the Avadāna texts,

2) a historical work (now lost to us) by sa-dbaṅ-bzaṅ-po,

3) the *Kalpalatā* and

4) the *Śrāvaka-piṭakas.*

Sa-dbaṅ-bzaṅ-po is usually taken as the Tibetan form of the name of the celebrated Kashmirian writer Kṣemendrabhadra who lived in the 11th century, though there are some difficulties about this identification. Thus,

i) Tāranātha himself knew his sa-dbaṅ-bzaṅ-po as a paṇḍita of Magadha (Fol 139A).

ii) the Indian equivalents of sa-bdaṅ-bzaṅ-po given in Tg are Mahīndrabhadra or Bhūmīndrabhadra, which also better correspond to the literal meaning of the name given in Tibetan [see our note 36 of Ch 4].

iii) the Tibetan equivalent given in Tg of Kṣemendra's name is dge-ba'i-dbaṅ-po (and not sa-dbaṅ-bzaṅ-po) [see our note 60 of Ch 6].

Przyluski himself does not note these difficulties and argues, 'The historical work of Kṣemendra mentioned by Tāranātha has not come down to us for all we know. But there cannot have been any doubt regarding the identity of its author. He is the celebrated Kashmirian writer who lived in the eleventh century' (Przy LEA 108).

The work referred to as the Kalpalatā is taken by Przyluski to be the *Avadāna-kalpalatā* by the same Kṣemendra and on which Tāranātha evidently depends for certain features of the Aśoka legends.

Przyluski argues that since Tāranātha depends so much on Kṣemendra for his version of the Aśoka legends, tne general tendency of Kṣemendra himself has some important light to throw on Tāranātha's account of Aśoka, and though Kṣemendra's major historical work (presumably containing a full biography of Aśoka) is lost to us, Kṣemendra's general tendency can be well-judged from his surviving work, namely the *Avadāna-kalpalatā*. 'Drawing heavily from earlier literature, he had never any scruple about mixing up heterogeneous traditions. Pallavas 70-72 of the *Avadāna-kalpalatā* refering to Śāṇavāsa, Madhyāntika and Upagupta, appear to be inspired by the section on the lives of the saints in the *Aśokāvadāna* while the next two Pallavas are borrowed from quite a different redaction of the Aśoka-legend. Written in the north-western region of India during an epoch when Buddhism was in full decadence, the *Avadāna-kalpalatā* is the meeting ground of two traditions. With a biography of Aśoka drawn from a canonical text it mixes a number of narratives inspired by the *Aśokāvadāna*. Similarly, in the body of Tāranātha's comparatively modern account we can point through the medium of Kṣemendra, to a class of much earlier writings.' (Prz. 108-9)

But what is the significance of Tāranātha's reference to the *Śrāvaka-piṭakas* ? Przyluski answers : 'Just as a section of the *Aśokāvadāna* has ultimately been incorporated into the *Saṃyuktāgama* of the Sarvāstivādins, it is possible that another redaction of the Aśoka-legend—the same that Tāranātha summarises—has been inserted into the canon of another sect. This is what the reference to the *Śrāvaka-piṭakas* appears to imply.' (p. 108). What, then, was this 'other sect' ? Przyluski thinks that it had presumably its centre in Campā or the eastern regions between Magadha and the sea (p. 112), for certain peculiarities of the Aśoka-legends as told by Tāranātha show a preference for this region.

To sum up Przyluski's argument (pp. 112 & 123) : The stories forming the Cycle of Aśoka-legends were originally elaborated by the Buddhist communities in the neighbourhood of Pāṭaliputra. From there it spread to two opposite directions, *viz.* a) towards the west, taking roots first at Kauśāmbī (the centre of the Sthaviras) and then at Mathurā (the centre of the

Sarvāstivādins) and finally in Kashmir (the centre of the Mūlasarvāstivādins) ; and 2) towards the east in the region between Magadha and the sea, near Campā ; 'it was there enriched by new elements from the folk-lore of the neighbouring provinces... it has been incorporated into the canon of the local sects [*Śrāvaka-piṭaka*-s] and transferred afterwards to Kashmir where it was set in verse by Kṣemendra.' (p. 112).

Drawing heavily as he does on the *Śrāvaka-piṭakas* and on Kṣemendra's work, though at the same time relying on the *Aśokāvadāna*, Tāranātha gives us a conglomeration of the Aśoka-legends that developed differently in the different regions. Thus, Tāranātha's version of 1) the youth of Aśoka, 2) his conversion, 3) subduing the Nāgas, 4) erection of the stūpa-s, 5) conveying the assembly of the monks and 6) offerings to the saṃgha-s 'correspond in spite of acute differences to chapters 1, 2, 3 and 6' of the Chinese translation of the *Aśokarāja-sūtra* (which, according to Przyluski, contains the Aśoka-legends in their earliest forms). At the same time, in Tāranātha's account *arhat* Yaśas 'belongs to the basic framework of the legend', while Piṇḍola and Upagupta, the saints specially eulogised by the monks of Kauśāmbī and Mathurā respectively, are conspicuously absent : Tāranātha nowhere mentions the name of Piṇḍola and he speaks of no connection between Aśoka and Upagupta, though the writers of Mathurā are specially anxious to emphasise such a connection. (Prz. 69).

In the following characteristics also, the Aśoka-legends of Tāranātha show a decisive influence of the eastern regions (i.e. derived from the *Śrāvaka-piṭakas* of Campā). Thus : a) Tāranātha says that Aśoka was the son of a king of Campā, 'a singularly audacious alteration of historical truth' which 'could have been imagined only by a story-teller belonging to a country east of Magadha' (p. 111). Again, though according to the *Aśokāvadāna*, Aśoka subdues during his youth the Khasas and the country of Takṣaśilā, in Tāranātha's narrative he subdues the Khasas and the people of Nepal, here too the tradition deviating towards the east.

At the same time, argues Przyluski, such eastern elements

introduced by Tāranātha into his account of Aśoka are indicative of a more developed form of the Aśoka-legends. Thus, while in the *Aśokāvadāna* the Nāga kings of Rāmagrāma do not oblige Aśoka by allowing him to take the relics of the Buddha, in Tāranātha's work the account of subduing the Nāgas is elaborately told and the gradual progress of Aśoka's power fully illustrated. To begin with, Aśoka is the master only of the region between the Vindhyas and the Himālayas without any control over the Nāgas. 'But his power increases along with his merits and he finishes by bringing under his subjection the whole universe including the Nāga kings of the ocean ......Judged by the versions of Tāranātha and the *Avadānakalpalatā*, the legend inserted in the *Śrāvaka-piṭakas* is thus more developed than that of the *Aśoka-sūtra*' (Przy.110).

C. D. Chatterjee (in JAIH i. 114f) comes out rather sharply against Przyluski's thesis that the earliest form of the Aśoka-legends is to be found in the *Aśoka-rāja-sūtra* (which survives for us only in a Chinese translation : *A-yü-wang-king*). On the contrary, argues Chatterjee, the tendency to fabricate such legends finds its earliest expression in the *Kalpanāmaṇḍitikā* of Kumāralāta (c. A. D. 150), the founder of the Sautrāntika school and a native of Takṣaśilā. The author of the *Aśoka-rāja-sūtra* presumably collected the Aśoka-legends from Kumāralāta's work. But 'the legends of emperor Aśoka, as recorded in both these works are so fantastic and imaginary (*kalpanāmaṇḍita*) that they are far away from the bonds of sober history. Aśoka-legends also appear in certain Pali chronicles and commentaries composed in Ceylon ; but they are not so obviously fabricated and preposterous as we find them in the Avadāna texts composed in Sanskrit'. (*ib.*) 'Such fabricated stories in the Avadāna texts, as also in the *Kalpanāmaṇḍitikā*, only tends to show that the evolution of Aśokan legends, as delineated in them, took place at a period that is far remote from the time of the ruler, to which they relate' (*ib.* 126).

3. 'TEN PROHIBITIONS' AND THE SECOND COUNCIL

According to the Pali *Cullavagga* (xii.1.1 ; Eng. tr SBE xx.386f), the Ten Prohibitions violated by the monks of Vaiśālī are : 1) carrying salt in a horn, 2) taking meals when the shadow is two fingers broad, 3) going to another village and taking a second meal there, 4) observance of the *uposatha* ceremonies in various places in the same parish, 5) obtaining sanction for a deed after it is done, 7) drinking butter-milk after meals, 8) drinking toddy, 9) using a rug without a fringe and 10) acceptance of gold or silver.

According to the *Vinaya-kṣudraka* (quoted by Bu-ston ii.91), these are : 1) exclamation of astonishment (*aho* !), 2) rejoicing, 3) digging ground, 4) using the sacred salt, 5) eating on the way, 6) taking the food with two fingers, 7) eating not at due time, 8) taking intoxicating drink, 9) making a new rug without stitching to it a patch of an old one and 10) begging for gold or silver.

Vasil'ev gives another list from the Chinese translation of the *Vinaya* of the Mahīśāsakas. cf also BA i.24.

But whatever might have been the actual list of these prohibitions, there are grounds to think that by violating these the Vaiśālī monks were working for their material prosperity. As it is said in the *Vinaya-kṣudraka*, 'And from the city of Dhanika there came an *arhat* called Yaśas with five hundred attendants who had made a turn through the country. Having arrived at Vaiśālī, they found that the monks had a large income, and they themselves obtained a great share. Having asked the reason of this, they came to know that the ten prohibited points were admitted'. (quoted by Bu-ston ii.91).

Connected with these Ten Prohibitions is the question of the Second Council. Bu-ston ii.95-6 asserts that the alms-giver of this Second Council was the pious king Aśoka (*mya-ṅan-med*), that it took place after 100 years of the Buddha's nirvāṇa with the aim of the exclusion of the ten inadmissible points, and that it was the Council of 700 *arhat*-s mobilised mainly by Yaśas and culminating in the expulsion of the Vaiśālī monks. Tāranātha's account of the Second Council agrees with all these excepting one vital point. Tāranātha asserts that the Second Council was organised 'at the Kusumapurī-vihāra under the patronage of king Nanda (*dga'-byed*), a Licchavi by birth' (Fol 22A). Thus, both Bu-ston and Tāranātha are referring to the same Council, though, according to the former, its patron was Aśoka, while, according to the latter, a Licchavi king called Nanda or *dga'-byed.*

Vasil'ev, therefore, asks in the note : Could this word *dga'-byed* be a Tibetan translation of Piyadasī ? In other words, he suggests the possibility of construing from the Tibetan form in which the name is given by Tāranātha an epithet of Aśoka, so that the discrepancy between the two accounts is somehow or other removed. But the problem is not so easily solved, for Tāranātha also asserts that this *dga'-byed* is Licchavi by birth.

In the statement of Tāranātha, therefore, Kern sees only a tissue of errors (see Filliozat SAI 6), moreover because, as Kern thinks, by the Kusumapurī-vihāra is to be understood Kusumapura or the town of Pāṭaliputra, where the Ceylonese sources place the Third Council.

However, Filliozat argues that this is misunderstanding the real point of Tāranātha. As a matter of fact, the problem of the Second Council is connected with that of the two Aśokas and hence also with the two chronologies. 'The longer one, that of the Pali tradition, places the Second of the Great Councils under the first Aśoka, Kālāśoka, at Vaiśālī, one hundred years after the death of the Buddha, and the Third of the Great Councils at Pāṭaliputra under the second Aśoka [Aśoka Maurya], two hundred and thirtysix years after the death of the Buddha. The shorter chronology, in its most well-known form, places a Council at Vaiśālī or at Pāṭaliputra a hundred years after the death of the Buddha under a unique Aśoka.'

In the background of this, Filliozat proposes to understand the real significance of the statement of Tāranātha : 'Tāranātha is perfectly in accord with the Sinhalese sources in stating that at the time of the Second Council, the reigning king at Pāṭaliputra was a Licchavi. The *Vaṃsaṭṭhappakāsinī*, commenting on the *Mahāvaṃsa* iv.6, in fact calls Kālāśoka, who was reigning at Pāṭaliputra (cf *Mahāvaṃsa* iv.31), the son of Susunāga of the Licchavi family. From the outset one must ask if Nandin (*dga'-byed*) of Tāranātha should not be identified with Kālāśoka. Bu-ston had spoken of Aśoka, while Tāranātha has given the Tibetan equivalent of Nandin, and on the other hand *nandin*, or The Happy One, is the synonym of Aśoka, "without chagrin". Tāranātha, far from furnishing an aberrant fact, thus corresponds well with the Pali sources. We have already remarked that to the Kālāśoka of the Pali sources, corresponds, in the *Aśokāvadāna*, Kākavarṇin, whose name is a synonym of Kāla, since it means "the colour of a crow", whereas *kāla* signifies "black". In Tāranāth awe simply find a synonym of the other part of the name of Kālāśoka. Kālāśoka is the same as Kākavarṇin and Nandin at the same time, and Tāranātha, who simultaneously knew both Nandin and Aśoka Maurya, thus knew, as did the Pali sources, two Aśokas, Kālāśoka and Aśoka Maurya. The distinction between these two Aśokas does not have to be a fallacious doubling by the Pali tradition of Theravāda of a single Aśoka. From this it follows that the hypothesis of the real existence of two Councils under these two kings becomes now considerably reinforced, and it will have to be admitted that the sources that knew only one of these kings and councils are those which are in error.' (Filliozat SAI 6-7).

Such a solution of the problem, however, leaves a number of points unexplained. First, Tāranātha shows no awareness at all of any Council having been convened under the patronage of the pious king Aśoka or Aśoka Maurya. Instead of that, he passes on to the account of the Third Council held under the patronage of king Kaniṣka (Fol 31ff). Secondly, Tāranātha himself is fully aware of the difficulties of the two chronologies connected with the question of the Second Council and he tries to solve the problem at best with some questionable success (Fol 22Bf) : the suggestion of counting a half year as one year and the pedantic discussion on the meaning of the word *yadācit*. Thirdly, the sources like *Mahāvaṃsa* with which Tāranātha is alleged to agree mention the venue of the Second Council as Vālukārāma and not Kusumapurī-vihāra. And so on.

In view of these difficulties, therefore, it appears to be safer to think that Tāranātha, being a very late compiler of the Buddhist legends, allows various traditions to get mixed up in his account, though he tries somehow or other to evolve a rationalised version of the Second Council out of these. In this circumstance, instead of either summarily discarding Tāranātha's version of the Second Council as fanciful (Kern) or of fully defending it (Filliozat), we can perhaps try to understand the peculiar problem with which Tāranātha finds himself confronted. This is best done by recalling the different traditions of the Second Council as recorded in the different Buddhist sources. Vallée Poussin in ERE iv. 183 sums these up :

'According to a tradition fully developed in *Cullavagga* xii and common at least to several sects, there was held in the year 100 or 110 after the nirvāṇa a Council to examine and condemn ten extra-legal practices of the monks of Vaiśālī'. *Cullavagga* gives the date as 100 years after the Buddha's nirvāṇa ; but it is completely silent about the reigning king and also about any subsequent Council. According to the tradition of the Mahiśāsakas, Dharmaguptikas and Sarvāstivādins, the Council took place 110 years after the nirvāṇa, though these traditions also are equally silent about the reigning king and about any subsequent Council. Fa-hien and Yuan-chuang (see Watters ii. 73ff) also mention the time of the Vaiśālī Council as 110 years after the nirvāṇa. Thus, Bu-ston's date of 100 years after the nirvāṇa agrees more with the tradition recorded in the *Cullavagga*, while Tāranātha's date of 110 years agrees more with the other traditions.

'Pali later sources (Sinhalese sources) know the name of the sovereign, Kālāśoka, and they add that the Vesālian schismatics (Vajjiputtakas) in their turn held a Council, the Great Assembly, whence issued the sect Mahāsāṃghika, "of the great assembly",—while the Mahāsāṃghikas are said by other sources to maintain that this Great Assembly was held immediately after the Rājagṛha Council.'

Incidentally, Tāranātha does not speak of the Great Assembly convened by the expelled monks of Vaiśālī and Watters ii. 76-7 comments : 'Very little is told in any treatise about the effect of the Council's action on the Sinning Brethren, but we are left to infer that they submitted to authority and returned to orthodox practices. There is nothing whatever to indicate that they seceded and formed a great sect or school.'

Vasumitra, the famous author of the treatise on the sects, asserts that 100 years after the nirvāṇa, a Council was held in Pāṭaliputra under the patronage of Aśoka ; but the agenda of this Council was the consideration of 'the five points' of Mahādeva and Bhadra and that this 'Council resulted in the division between the Church and the Mahāsāṃghika sect.'

Bhavya relates the tradition of the Sammitīyas that a Council was held 137 years after the nirvāṇa at Pāṭaliputra under the patronage of kings Nanda and Mahāpadma (to consider the 'five points'). According to the same authority the Sthaviras say that a Council was held 160 years after the nirvāṇa at Pāṭaliputra under the patronage of Aśoka to consider certain controversial questions and that it resulted in the Mahāsāṃghika schism.

Tāranātha, however, does not at all connect the Second Council with the 'five points' of Mahādeva and Bhadra. According to him, the confusion created by these 'five points' were cleared up in the Third Council held under the patronage of king Kaniṣka.

'Sinhalese sources : a Council in A. B. (After Buddha) 236 at Pāṭaliputra under Aśoka (Dharmāśoka), which proclaimed the orthodoxy of the Vibhajjavāda ('doctrine of the distinction') to which belongs the Pali or Sinhalese Church and authenticated the last of the Pali Abhidhamma treatises, the *Kathāvatthu.*'

On the basis of the above, Vallée Poussin proposes to reach the following conclusions :

1. Though the Sinhalese sources identify the Vaiśālī monks expelled by the Second Council with those that founded the Mahāsāṃghika sect, there is no evidence in favour of this identification. Other sects claim that the Mahāsāṃghikas originated out of the dispute over 'the five points' and it is certain that 'they admitted the five points'. The Mahāsāṃghikas themselves claim their sect to be ancient and orthodox.

2. 'There was a tradition of the Veśālin Council on Ten Points ; date uncertain, no mention of king.'

3. There was also a 'tradition of a council on "some controverted question" more precisely on "five points" ; date uncertain and probably no mention of king.'

4. In spite of the claim of the monks of Ceylon that their *Kathāvatthu* is an ancient text 'preached mysteriously by the Buddha,' the text is actually comparatively modern.

5. Because Aśoka was viewed later as the second mover of the Dharma-cakra, it was natural to try to place all the important events concerning the history of Buddhism as taking place under him. The later monks did this. They were also eager to describe Pāṭaliputra as the place of the meetings. 'Our northern documents are scanty and conflicting, but they give the impression that there was no certain tradition of the date of Aśoka : 100, 110, 137 or 160 After Buddha are figures out of which no chronology can be extracted.'

6. 'Sinhalese tradition places the Vaiśālī Council in 100 (after Nirvāṇa) under Kālāśoka and the Pāṭaliputra Council in 236 under Dharmāśoka. Besides the "northern" figures for Aśoka (100, 110, 137, 160 years after Nirvāṇa), there was a fourth figure 237 After Buddha (17 or 19 years after his coronation in 217, 219 After Buddha). We are not concerned with the question whether these were fanciful or traditional computations. In fact, the authors of the ecclesiastical history "concocted" in Ceylon admitted this figure without troubling themselves very much to adjust it to some other chronological details of their own ; and as they maintained the

canonic date of Vaiśālī and were at a loss to name the sovereign reigning in 100 After Buddha, they imagined a Black Aśoka (Kālāśoka)—a mere *idolum libri.*'

4. TIṢYARAKṢITĀ AND THE KUṆĀLA LEGEND

Though this legend of the erotic attachment of Tiṣyarakṣitā or Tiṣyarakṣā for Kuṇāla is persistently told in the Avadāna texts, C. D. Chatterjee in JAIH i. 125f draws our attention to a completely different version of the story of Tiṣyarakṣā as preserved in the *Mahāvaṃsa*: 'It tells us that the wicked Tiṣyarakṣā, who was the last chief queen of Aśoka, grew impatient at her husband's paying regular visits to the Boddhi-tree and lavishly spending money for its worship and also at the bestowal of the costliest gifts upon it on these occasions. Being of perverted mentality, she began to compare in her mind how much her husband was spending on the Bodhi-tree and how much on her. Thus, torturing herself in her own mind, she became extremely jealous of that sacred tree and conspired with some officers, who were loyal to her, for its destruction. The Bodhi-tree undoubtedly showed signs of withering away because of the mischief done, but was resuscitated after some time through the mystic power of some members of the Saṃgha.' In the Avadāna texts, by contrast, 'Tiṣyarakṣitā's traditional wickedness has been sought to be proved... by representing her as a notorious woman given to sensual pleasure, who, failing to get any response from her stepson for her illicit love, ultimately got him blinded in taking revenge'.

Cf also G. M. Bongard-Levin & O. F. Volkova, *The Kuṇāla Legend* p. 6 for another version of the legend given by the Jaina poet Hemacandra : 'The legend of Kuṇāla is presented in quite a different light in the Jain tradition reflected in Hemacandra's work, the *Pariśiṣṭaparvan.* First, there is no mention of Tiṣyarakṣitā, one of the main characters of the legend, who is present in all the versions of the legend cycle known to us. Instead of the passionate and insidious Tiṣyarakṣitā, who took revenge on Kuṇāla for her rejected love, Hemacandra mentions only one of Aśoka's wives, who blinded Kuṇāla with the help of forgery in order to assert the right of her son to the throne. It shows that the basic conflict—the clash between Tiṣyarakṣitā and Kuṇāla rejecting her love—which can be traced throughout all the versions of the legend, acquires quite a different aspect with Hemacandra : Kuṇāla is presented as an eight-year old child and the conflict is caused not by amorous passion but by the desire of one of the king's wives to make her son the heir to the throne instead of Kuṇāla. Hemacandra's narration of the legend seems to fall into two parts : 1) the blinding of Kuṇāla and the sending of his rival—the queen's son—to Ujjain ; 2) the birth of Kuṇāla's son, Kuṇāla's wanderings, his coming to Pāṭaliputra and the appointment of Kuṇāla's son—Samprati— the heir to the throne. In the *Pariśiṣṭaparvan*, Takṣaśilā—the principal scene of action in the legend—is not even mentioned. Nothing is said about the rebellion. Ujjain, the capital of north-western India, and not Takṣaśilā, occupies the central place in the story. According to Hemacandra, Kuṇāla was brought up there. The king's forged order to blind Kuṇāla was sent to Ujjain. From Ujjain, the blind Kuṇāla set out for the capital of the empire... All this makes it possible to suppose that in his version of the legend, Hemacandra relied not on the northern versions of the legend, which served as the basis for *Divyāvadāna*, Kṣemendra and Tāranātha, but on some other—probably southern—version, which, unfortunately has not reached us. Hemacandra does not mention the episode of the restoration of Kuṇāla's eyesight as the reward for his virtuous behaviour. Another thing was more important for the Jaina chronicler : to show how Samprati (who, according to the Jain tradition, was a zealous follower of Jainism) made his way to the throne... In the sources of the northern Buddhist tradition Kuṇāla is described as an object of the action of *karma*, as an embodiment of Buddhist virtue and as a true follower of Buddhist *dhamma*; in the Jain *Pariśiṣṭaparvan* the plot develops more vigorously: there are no homilies on Buddhist morals and more room is allotted to the story of how the blinded Kuṇāla was unable to become the heir to the throne and how Samprati became heir in his place. That is why Hemacandra does not describe how eyesight was restored to Kuṇāla'.

5. MAHĀDEVA AND HIS 'FIVE PRINCIPLES'

Watters i.267-270: 'According to the Abhidharma work, Mahādeva was the son of a Brhāmin merchant of Mathurā. While still a very young man, he took advantage of his father's prolonged absence from home on business and formed an incestuous connection with his mother. When his father returned, Mahādeva murdered him, and soon afterwards he fled with his mother. Finding that a Buddhist arhat had an inconvenient knowledge of his guilty life, he promptly killed the arhat. Then finding that his mother was not true to him, he murdered her also. By thus taking the lives of his parents and an arhat, he had committed three unpardonable offences; in the technical language of Buddhism he had "made three immediate *karma*-s", three *ānantarya karma*-s. Stung by conscience and ḥaunted by fear, he now skulked from place to place until he reached Pāṭaliputra. Here he resolved to enter religion, and he easily persuaded a monk of the Kukkuṭārāma-vihāra to have him ordained. He now devoted all his energies and abilities to his new profession and having zeal and capacity, he soon rose to be the head of the establishment, and the leader of a large party in the church at Pāṭaliputra. His intellectual abilities were much above those of the ordinary brethren, but his orthodoxy was doubtful, and his moral character was not above suspicion. Mahādeva claimed to have attained arhatship, and he explained away circumstances which seemed to be destructive of his claim. In answer to queries from younger brethren, he enunciated five dogmas, or tenets which led to much discussion, and at length to open dissension. These tenets were: 1) an arhat may commit a sin under unconscious temptation, 2) one may be an arhat and not know it, 3) an arhat may have doubts on matters of doctrine, 4) one cannot attain arhat-ship without the aid of a teacher, 5) the "noble ways" may begin by a shout, i.e. one meditating seriously on religion may make such an exclamation as "How sad!" and by so doing attain progress towards perfection. These five propositions Mahādeva declared to be Buddha's teaching, but the senior Brethren declared them to be Mahādeva's invention and opposed to the orthodox teaching. There were at the time four "sects" or "parties" of Buddhists at Pāṭaliputra, and these had bitter controversies about the five propositions. When dispute ran high the king, on Mahādeva's suggestion, called an assembly of all the monks to have an open discussion and vote on the subject, the king being a friend and patron of Mahādeva. When the assembly was summoned it was attended by a number of senior Brethren, who were arhats, and by an immense number of ordinary ordained members of the church. The superior Brethren argued and voted against the five propositions, but they were far outnumbered by the inferior members who were all friends of Mahādeva. When the discussion and voting were over the wrangling still continued, and the king ordered all the brethren to be embarked in rotten boats and sent adrift on the Ganges; by this means he thought it would be shewn who were arhats and who were not. But at the critical moment five hundred arhats rose in the air, and floated away to Kashmir. Here they dispersed, and settled in lonely places among the vales and mountains. When the king heard what had occured he repented, and sent messengers to coax the arhats to return to his capital, but they all refused to leave. Hereupon he caused five hundred monasteries to be built for them and gave the country to the Buddhist church. These five hundred arhats introduced and propagated the Sthavira school in Kashmir and the majority of inferior brethren at Pāṭaliputra began the Mahāsāṃghika school.

'It will be noticed that in this account we have neither the name of the king nor the date of the schism. But in the *I-pu-tsung-lun* and the *Shi-pa-pu-lun* the king is Aśoka, and the time above hundred years after Buddha's decease. Additional information on the subject will be found in Wassiljew's *Buddhismus* and in Schiefner's *Tāranātha*. In the *Shan-chien-lu-vibhāṣā* and in the passages of the Pali works referred to in connection with Madhyāntika we find mention of a Mahādeva at Pāṭaliputra. But this man lived apparently a good and pious life, and he was sent by Tissa as a missionary to the Andhra country. He preached (or composed) the *Devadūta-sūtra*,.. and seems to have been successful in propagating Buddhism. This may be the Mahādeva of the northern treatises, the popular and influential abbot of Pāṭaliputra. But the latter dies, and is cremated with peculiar circumstances at the capital, and there is no mention of his mission to Andhra. On the other hand it seems possible that the Brethren, sent away in different directions as apostles, were men who had taken prominent part in the controversies which had arisen among the Buddhists of Pāṭaliputra. All accounts seem to agree in representing their Mahādeva as a man of unusual abilities and learning; and the story of his great crimes as a layman, and his unscrupulous ambition as an abbot related in the Abhidharma treatises are probably the malicious inventions of enemies.'

6. KANIṢKA'S COUNCIL : YUAN-CHUANG & BU-STON

Watters i. 278 : 'It is to the statements made by our pilgrim about Kaniṣka's Council that we are indebted for nearly all our information about the Council.' Yuan-chuang's account (Watters i. 270f) is as follows : 'Our pilgrim next proceeds to relate the circumstances connected with the great Council summoned by Kaniṣka. This king of Gandhāra, Yuan-chuang tells us, in the four hundredth year after the decease of Buddha, was a great and powerful sovereign whose sway extended to many peoples. In his leisure hours he studied the Buddhist scriptures, having a monk everyday in the palace to give him instruction. But as the Brethren taught him different and contradictory interpretations, owing to conflicting tenets of sectarians, the king fell into a state of helpless uncertainty. Then the Venerable Pārśva explained to His Majesty that in the long lapse of time since Buddha left the world, disciples of schools and masters with various theories had arisen, all holding personal views and all in conflict. On hearing this the king was greatly moved, and expressed to Pārśva his desire to restore Buddhism to eminence, and to have the Tripiṭaka explained according to the tenets of the various schools. Pārśva gave his cordial approval of the suggestion, and the king thereupon issued summons to the holy and wise Brethren in all his realm. These came in crowds, from all quarters to Gandhāra, where they were entertained for seven days. They were far too numerous, however, to make a good working Council, so the king had recourse to a process of selection. First all had to go away who had not entered the saintly career—had not attained one to the four degrees of perfection. Then of those who remained all who were arhats were selected and the rest dismissed ; of the arhats again those who had the "three-fold intelligence" and the "six-fold penetration" were retained ; and these were further thinned out by dismissing all of them who were not thoroughly versed in the Tripiṭaka and well learned in the "five sciences". By this process the number of arhats for the Council was reduced to 499. Yuan-chuang goes on to tell that the king proposed Gandhāra as the place of meeting for the Council, but that this place was objected to on account of its heat and dampness. Then Rājagaha was proposed, but Pārśva and others objected that there were too many adherents of other sects there, and at last it was decided to hold the Council in Kashmir. So the king and the arhats came to his country and here the king built a monastery for the Brethren. When the texts of the Tripiṭaka were collected for the making of expository Commentaries on them, the Venerable Vasumitra was outside the door in monk's costume. The other Brethren would not admit him because he was still in the bonds of the world, not an arhat. In reply to his claim to deliberate, the others told him to go away and come to join them when he had attained arhatship. Vasumitra said he did not value this attainment a spittle—he was aiming at Buddhahood and he would not have any petty condition ("go in a small path") ; still he could become an arhat before a silk ball which he threw in the air fell to the ground. When he threw the ball, the Devas said to him so as to be heard by all—"Will you who are to become Buddha and take the place of Maitreya, honoured in the three worlds and the stay of all creatures,—will you here realise this petty fruit ?" The Devas kept the ball and the arhats made apologies to Vasumitra and invited him to become their President, accepting his decisions on all disputed points. This Council, Yuan-chuang continues, composed 100,000 stanzas of *upadeśa-śāstra*-s explantory of the canonical *sūtra*-s, 100,000 stanzas of Vinaya-vibhāṣā-śāstra-s explanatory of the Vinaya, and 100,000 stanzas of Abhidharma-vibhāṣā-śāstra-s explanatory of the Abhidharma. For this exposition of the Tripiṭaka all learning from remote antiquity was thoroughly examined ; the general sense and the terse language (of the Buddhist scriptures) were again made clear and distinct, and the learning was widely diffused for the safe-guiding of disciples. King Kaniṣka had the treatises, when finished, written out on copper-plates, and enclosed these in stone boxes, which he deposited in a tope made for the purpose. He then ordered the Yakṣas to keep and guard the texts, and not allow any to be taken out of the country by heretics ; those who wished to study them could do so in the country... Kaniṣka renewed Aśoka's gift of all Kashmir to the Buddhist church.'

However, to the Tibetan historians of much later period came down a confused account of various traditions concerning what they knew the Third Council, and Bu-ston simply compiles these without much of critical comment. Thus, Bu-ston ii.96f : '(The account of this third rehearsal) is not to be found in the Vinaya and therefore we meet here and there with disagreeing points. According to some, 137 years after the Teacher had passed away, at the time when kings Nanda and Mahāpadma were reigning, and when the elders Mahākāśyapa, Uttara and others were residing at Pāṭaliputra, Māra the Evil One, having assumed the form of a monk named Bhadra, showed many miraculous apparitions, sowed disunion amongst the clergy and brought confusion into the Teaching. At that time, when the elders Nāgasena and Manojña were living, (the clergy) became split into (various) sects. On the 63rd year (after this division had taken place), the Teaching was rehearsed by the elder Vātsīputra. According to others, 160 years after the Teacher had passed away, at the time when king Aśoka began to reign in the city called Kusumavistara (?), the Arhats were reading the word of the Buddha in (4 different languages), viz. Sanskrit, Prakrit, Apabhraṃśa and Paiśācika. Accordingly, the pupils (of the different Arhats) formed separate fractions, and this gave origin to the division into the 18 sects. In the philosophical views (of the different sects) there were many disagreeing points which brought confusion into the Church. —It was for this reason that Arhats and ordinary learned monks, having assembled in the monastery of Jalandhara, rehearsed (Scripture) for a third time. This took place 360 years after the Teacher had passed away. We read however in the *Karuṇā-puṇḍarīka* the following prophecy :— One hundred years after I have passed away, there will appear in Pāṭaliputra a king named Aśoka of the Maurya dynasty. This king will cause to worship the 84,000 monuments containing my relics in a single day. And in the *Prabhāvatī* it is said :— Thereafter the king Dharmāśoka died, and the arhats, in order to put an end to the practice of reciting (Scripture) in Prakrit, Apabhraṃśa and in a dialect of intermediate character, gradually rehearsed (the canonical texts) according to other methods. These new texts were like the sūtras which were compiled in Sanskrit. (Thereafter) the Teaching assumed 18 different forms. — I am of the opinion that (the statement of the authority just mentioned) disagrees with the texts I have quoted before.

'Others (speak about the 3rd council) as follows :—The aim of it was to clear the doubts of the 18 sects as regards the spurious texts of scripture. The time was 300 years after the Teacher had passed away. The place was the country of Kashmir and the monastery of Kuvana, and the alms-giver was Kaniṣka, the king of Jalandhara. The members of the council were 500 Arhats with Pūrṇika at their head, 500 Bodhisattvas, Vasumitra and others, and 250 or 10,000 ordinary Paṇḍitas. After a recitation (of the texts) had been made, it was settled, that the texts acknowledged by the 18 sects were all of them the Word of the Buddha.'

Though neither in the account of Yuan-chuang nor in those quoted by Bu-ston is there any part being played by Aśvaghoṣa in Kaniṣka's Council, the *Life of Vasubandhu* (see Watters i. 278) assigns a prominent role to Aśvaghoṣa in this Council.

7. VARARUCI

The following works are attributed to Vararuci in Tg :

Mahākāla-sādhana. rG xxvi.78 ; lxxxii.69 ; lxxxii.74-5 ; lxxi.81
Mahākāla-stotra. rG xxvi.88.
Mahākāla-abhiṣeka-vidhi. rG xxvi.80
Mahākālī-devī-stotra-aṣṭaka. rG xxvi.91
Mahākāla-karma-guhya-sādhana. (by mahāśmaśāna-siddhi-sampanna mahā-brāhmaṇa Vararuci) rG lxxxii.71
Mahākāla-bali-vidhi. rG lxxxii.76
Mahākāla-stotra. rG lxxxii.77 ; 82
Mahākāla-stotra-mālā. rG lxxxii.78
Devī-kālī-stotra. rG lxxxii. 84 ; 85
Karmakara-stotra. rG lxxxii.91
Yakṣa-kāla-stotra. rG lxxxii.92

Mahākāla-kila-sādhana. rG lxxxii.103
Mahākāla-stotra-ākṣepa. rG lxxxiii.3 ; mDo cxvii.2
Śatagāthā. mDo cxxiii.30

8. SARAHA

The following works are attributed in Tg to Saraha, *alias* Rāhula, Rāhulabhadra and Sarahapāda.

Vajrayogini-sādhana. rG xiv.71
Buddhakapāla-tantrasya pañjikā jñānavati-nāma. rG xxiv.4
Buddhakapāla-sādhana. rG xxiv.7
Sarva-bhūta-vali-vidhi. rG xxiv.8
Buddhakapāla-nāma-maṇḍala-vidhi-krama-pradyotana. rG xxiv.9
Dohā-koṣa-giti. rG xlvi.9
Dohā-koṣa-nāma-caryā-giti. rG xlvii.4
Dohā-koṣa-upadeśa-giti. rG xlvii.5
Kakhasya-dohā. rG xlvii.7
Kakhasya-dohā-ṭippaṇa. rG xlvii.8
Kāya-koṣa-amṛta-vajra-gitā. rG xlvii.9
Vāk-koṣa-rucira-svara-gitā. rG xlvii.10
Citta-koṣa-aja-vajra-gitā. rG xlvii.11
Kāya-vāk-cittamanasikāra. rG xlvii.12
Tattva-upadeśa-śikhara-dohā-giti. rG xlvii.17
Saraha-gitikā. rG. xlviii.14 ; 15
Mahāmudrā-upadeśa-vajra-guhya-giti. rG xlvii.100
Trailokya-vaṃśakara-lokeśvara-sādhana (Oḍḍiyāna-udbhava-krama). rG lxx.25 ; 26 ; lxxi.66 ; 122 ; 123
Adhiṣṭhāna-mahākāla-sādhana. rG lxxxii.107
Mahākāla-stotra. rG lxxxiii.5
Sarahaprabhu-maitripāda-praśnottara. (mahābrāhmaṇa Sarahapādaprabhu Maitripāda mahāmudrā-praśnottara) rG lxxxv.18

Dvādaśa-upadeśa-gāthā. rG xlvii.15
Svādhiṣṭhāna-krama. rG xlvii.16
Bhāvanā-dṛṣṭi-caryā-phala-dohākoṣa-gītikā. rG xlviii.5

9. NĀGĀRJUNA : BIOGRAPHICAL

The most remarkable of the recent studies in Nāgārjuna being K. Venkata Ramanan NP, the points discussed in it about the life of Nāgārjuna are summed up below.

K. Venkata Ramanan NP 336 points out that our main sources for the traditional account of the life of Nāgārjuna are :

In Sanskrit :
1. *Laṅkāvatāra* (Sagāthaka)
2. *Mañjuśrīmūlakalpa*
3. *Harṣacarita* (Bāṇa)
4. *Rājataraṅgiṇī* (Kalhaṇa)

In Chinese :
1. Biography of Nāgārjuna attributed to Kumārajīva
2. Yuan-chuang's account (Watters ii.100-2 ; 200-8)

In Tibetan :
1. Account of the 84 Siddha-s, where Nāgārjuna is mentioned as the sixteenth.
2. Bu-ston ii.122-130
3. Tāranātha's work, (though in the present *History* Tār does not discuss the life of Nāgārjuna, because, as he says, he has discussed it elsewhere)
4. Sum-pa's dPag-bsam-ljon-bzaṅ.

The different versions of the life of Nāgārjuna given in these are so full of palpable legends—often in violent disagreement with each other—that a review of these leads Max Walleser (*Life of Nāgārjuna from Tibetan and Chinese Sources*, Asia Major 1923) to 'strike a very sceptical note not only in regard to the different and sometimes conflicting traditional accounts of the life and work of this Buddhist master but also in regard to the very question of his having ever existed.' (Venkata Ramanan NP 25). As against this Venkata Ramanan (NP 25ff) argues that certain works are indisputably to be attributed to Nāgārjuna and this proves his historicity. 'Furthermore the recent archaeological discoveries at Amarāvatī corroborate to some extent certain broad facts about Nāgārjuna's life on which his traditional biographies agree, these facts being his friendship with a Śātavāhana king and his having spent the latter part of his career in the monastery built for him by this king at Bhramaragiri (Śrī-parvata).'

The traditional account agrees that Nāgārjuna was born as a Brahmin in south India, though, on the question of what led him to the Buddhist Order, the Chinese sources differ from the Tibetan ones. After entering the Order, he is said to have thoroughly studied the Buddhist scriptures then available. But he failed to be satisfied with these and started searching for more texts. Thus he eventually obtained the Prajñāpāramitā-sūtras (Kumārajīva's Vaipulya-sūtras) from a Nāga. These texts fully satisfied him and he devoted the rest of his life to the propagation of their teachings. 'As regards the Nāga from whom Nāgārjuna is said to have obtained the Prajñāpāramitā-sūtras, Kumārajīva speaks of the Nāga chief (Mahānāga), who led him into the sea and opened up for him the Treasury of the Seven Jewels (Saptaratnakośa). Nāgārjuna read the Vaipulya (Mahāyāna) Sūtras, which the Mahānāga selected for his reading, and having read them he deeply penetrated into their meaning. He told the Mahānāga that what he already read there was ten times of what he had read in Jambudvīpa, and eventually brought away with him a boxful of them.'

Nāgārjuna's friend, the Śātavāhana king to whom Nāgārjuna wrote the *Suhṛllekha* (Tg mDo xxxiii.32=xciv.27) and the *Ratnāvalī* (see JRAS 1934 pp. 307-325 ; 1936 pp. 237-252, 423-435), according to Venkata Ramanan, was presumably Gautamīputra Śātakarṇi, who ruled, according to one view, during A.D. 106-130, and according to another view, during A.D. 80-104. Yuan-chuang says that Nāgārjuna was a contemporary of

Aśvaghoṣa, who, again, was a contemporary of Kaniṣka. According to the *Rājataraṅgiṇī*, Nāgārjuna was a contemporary of Huṣka, Juṣka and Kaniṣka. The first two names probably referred to Huviṣka and Vajeṣka, the contemporaries of Kaniṣka II, who was ruling in the year 41 after the accession of Kaniṣka I. 'If the latter's accession is assigned to 78 A.D., the Kaniṣka II should be considered as ruling in 119 A.D.; and if the later date be accepted for Gautamīputra, he would be a contemporary of Kaniṣka II.' Still Venkata Ramanan thinks that, assuming Nāgārjuna to have lived a long life (about 100 years), the possibility of his contemporaneity with Kaniṣka I need not be rejected. Concludes Venkata Ramanan, 'it could perhaps be taken as a highly probable working hypothesis that the upper and the lower limits of the philosophical activity of Nāgārjuna lay somewhere between 50 A.D. and 120 A.D.'

As for the Tibetan sources, Venkata Ramanan p. 336 comments that these 'mix up the two Nāgārjunas, the Mādhyamika philosopher at the beginning of the Christian era and the Siddha Nāgārjuna coming some four hundred years later.' This confusion 'hardly pertains to the Chinese sources which are earlier.'

10. WORKS OF NĀGĀRJUNA

In Tg about 180 works—on all sorts of subjects—are attributed to Nāgārjuna. Bu-ston i.50f, however, mentions six main treatises of Nāgārjuna : 'The six main treatises of the Mādhyamika doctrine (by Nāgārjuna) demonstrating, that which is expressed by the *sūtra*-s directly or otherwise, the essential meaning (of the Doctrine). These works are :

'The *Śūnyatā-saptati*, expounding the theory of the relativity of all elements of existence, devoid of the extremities of causality and pluralism, and

'The *Prajñā-mūla*, denying the reality of origination from self and non-self;

'These two works (are to be regarded as) the fundamental or principal. 'Next come :

The *Yukti-ṣaṣṭikā*,—containing a logical vindication (of the theories).

'The *Vigraha-vyāvartanī*, refuting the challenges of antagonists,

'The *Vaidalya-sūtra*, demonstrating the methods of controversy with adversaries and logicians (in general) and

'The *Vyavahāra-siddhi*, showing that from the point of view of the Absolute Truth—Non-substantiality—and from the empirical standpoint—worldly practice—go along together.'

On the basis of a critical survey of the works associated with the name of Nāgārjuna in Chinese and Tibetan traditions, K. Venkata Ramanan NP 36-7 concludes that the works that can be attributed to Nāgārjuna are :

'I. Texts that constitute chiefly a critical examination of other schools, specially of the Sarvāstivāda doctrine of elements : i) *Madhyamaka-śāstra* (Mādhyamika-kārikā), ii) *Vigraha-vyāvartanī*, iii) *Ekaśloka-śāstra* and iv) *Dvādaśa-mukha-śāstra*. v) *Śūnyatā-saptati* also perhaps belongs to this class.

'II. Texts chiefly expository : i) *Pratītya-samutpāda- hṛdaya-śāstra*, is an exposition of the twelve-linked chain of the course of phenomenal existence, which constitutes the subject-matter of *Kārikā* xxvi ; ii) *Yukti-ṣaṣṭikā* is a short compendium on the basic tenets of Mahāyāna ; iii) *Bodhisattva-pātheya-śāstra* is a short exposition of the factors of the Great Way.

'III. Commentaries or/and Records of Oral Instruction (Upadeśa) : i) *Mahā-prajñā-pāramitā-śāstra* and ii) *Daśabhūmi-vibhāṣā-śāstra* are the two important works that belong to this class ; iii) *Bhava-saṅkrānti-śāstra* and iv) *Ārya-dharmadhātu-garbha-vivaraṇa* also perhaps belong here ; v) perhaps *Vaidalya* which has a *sūtra* and a *prakaraṇa* also belongs here.

'IV. Devotional verses. i) *Niraupamya-stava*, ii) *Lokātīta-stava*, iii) *Acintya-stava*, iv) *Stutyātīta-stava*, v) *Paramārtha-stava*, vi) *Dharmadhātu-stava*.

'V. Letters : i) *Suhṛllekha* and ii) *Ratnāvalī*.

'VI. To these there can perhaps be added the collection of sūtras (Sūtra-samuccaya) on the authority of Śāntideva's *Bodhicaryāvatāra* ; the work is, however, not extant.'

11. ĀRYADEVA

In Tg are attributed a large number of Tāntrika works to Āryadeva : rG xxiii. 3 ; 6 ; xxx ; xxxi ; xxxiii. 8-13 ; xlviii. 117 ; lxxiv. 29 ; 41 ; lxxxiii. 70-74 ; 76 ; xxiii. 5 ; 7 ; 8 ; lxviii. 10. Of these, Bu-ston ii. 131 considers the following to be really the works of Āryadeva : Caryā-melāyana-pradīpa (rG xxxiii. 8), Citta-āvaraṇa-viśodhana (rG xxxiii.9), Catuḥ-pīṭha-tantra-rāja-maṇḍala-upāyikā-vidhi-sāra-samuccaya (rG xxiii.6), Catuḥ pīṭha-sādhana (rG xxiii. 3), Jñānaḍākinī (rG xxiii.5), Ekadruma-pañjikā (rG xxiii. 7) and doubtfully also Pradīpa-uddyotana-abhisaṃdhi-prakāśikā-vyākhyā-ṭīkā (rG xxx & xxxi).

These apart, to Āryadeva are attributed in Tg the following works :

Ārya-prajñā-pāramitā-mahāparipṛcchā-nāma. mDo cxxviii.8
Hastabāla-prakaraṇa-nāma. mDo xvii.22=xviii.3
Vṛtti on above, mDo xvii. 23=xviii.4
Catuḥśataka-śāstra-kārikā. mDo xviii.1
Skhalita-pramathana-yukti-hetu-siddhi. mDo xviii.2
Jñāna-sāra-samuccaya. mDo xviii.6
Madhyamaka-bhramaghāta. mDo xviii.5

The colophon of the last mentions that it was composed at the grand vihāra of Nālandā at the request of Jambudvīpa-rāja Sukhācārya, *alias* Udayī, Sadvaha.

12. OBERMILLER'S NOTE ON THE MĀDHYAMIKA ĀCĀRYAS AND THEIR DIFFERENT POINTS OF VIEW

Obermiller (Bu-ston ii. 135n) : 'In the work of Tsoṅ-kha-pa's pupil Khai-ḍub (mKhas-grub) called stoṅ-thun-bskal-bzaṅ-mig-'byed (Tsaṅ edition Vol i, 37a 1 sqq) we have a short account concerning the Mādhyamika *ācārya*-s and their different points of view. It is said as follows :—The standpoint of Nāgārjuna and Āryadeva was that of the Prāsaṅgikas. However (in their works) no direct discrimination between the Svātantrika and Prāsaṅgika points of view and no refutation of the former has been made. Subsequently, the teacher Buddhapālita composed his commentary on the Mūla-mādhyamika and explained the theory of Nāgārjuna and Āryadeva from the Prāsaṅgika standpoint. After that the teacher Bhāvaviveka likewise composed a commentary on the Mūla-mādhyamika (the *Prajñā-pradīpa*) and made many refutations concerning the points commented by Buddhapālita. It is he who has first founded the Svātantrika system. The followers of each of these two (schools i. e. of Buddhapālita and Bhāvaviveka) are accordingly called by the earlier Tibetan authors "the Mādhyamikas adhering to the different fractions" (pakṣa-grāhiṇo-mādhya-mikāḥ). Bhāvaviveka has moreover composed independent works of his own, namely the main aphorisms of the *Mādhyamika-hṛdaya* with the auto-commentary *Tarkajvālā*. In this he has expounded the Svātantrika theories and the activity of the Bodhisattvas in detail. Thereupon the teacher Jñānagarbha composed the Svātantrika work *Mādhyamika-satya-dvaya* (or Satya-dvaya-vibhaṅga). This teacher, as well as Bhāvaviveka are the representatives of the system which maintains the reality of external objects from the empirical standpoint and does not admit the existence of introspective perception (*sva-saṃve-dana*). Thereafter the teacher Śāntirakṣita composed the *Mādhyamika-alaṃkāra* and laid the foundation to another school of the Mādhyamikas which denies the empirical reality of the external world, acknowledges the introspective perception, but on the other hand does not consider consciousness to have an ultimate reality (differing in this from the Yogācāra-vijñānavādins). The *Mādhyamika-ālokā* and the three *Bhāvanā-krama* of Kamalaśīla, as well as the texts of Vimuktasena, Haribhadra, Buddha-jñānapāda, Abhayākaragupta, etc agree with Śāntirakṣita in the main standpoint (which is that of the Yogācāra-mādhyamika-svātantrika, whereas Bhāvaviveka and Jñānagarbha express the point of view of the Sautrāntika-mādhyamika-svātantrikas). As we have seen, Bu-ston counts Jñānagarbha among the Yogācāra-mādhyamikas.'

13. NĀGABODHI

In Tg the following works are attributed to Nāgabodhi, *alias* Nāgabuddhi, Nāgabuddhi-pāda, Nāgamati etc.
Samāja-sādhana-vyavasthāvalī. rG xxxiii.14
Kramāntarbhāva-upadeśa-nāma-prakaraṇa. rG xxxiii.17
Karmāntavibhaṅga. rG xxxiii.16
Guhyasamāja-maṇḍalopāyikā-viṃśavidhi. rG xxxiii.15
Pañcakrama-ṭikā-maṇimālā-nāma. rG xxxiv.2
Sarvatathāgata-stava. rG lxxiii.3
cf Bu-ston ii.132

14. ŚĀKYAMITRA

In Tg the following works are attributed to Śākyamitra :
Mahāmudrā-yoga-avatāra-piṇḍārtha. rG lxxii.68
Ārya-bhadra-caryā-praṇidhāna-rāja-ṭikā. mDo xxxviii.4
Caryā-melāyana-pradīpa-nāma-ṭikā. rG xxxiv.8
Kosala-alaṃkāra-tattva-saṃgraha-ṭikā. rG l-li
Ārya-vajra-krodha-mahābala-sādhana. rG lxxi.32

15. ŚABARA-PĀDA

Tg contains the following :

Śri-sahaja-upadeśa-svādhiṣṭhāna-nāma. Text expounded by Mahā Śabara. rG xiii.4

Śrī-sahaja-sambara-svādhiṣṭhāna-nāma. Text expounded by Mahā Śabara. rG xiii.5

Rakta-vajra-yoginī-sādhana by Śrī Śabareśvara. rG xiv.26

Śrī-vajra-yoginī-sādhana by Śabareśvara. rG xiv.28

Dohākoṣa-nāma-mahāmudrā-upadeśa by Śrī Mahā Śabara Saraha. rG xlvii.13.

Sārdha-pañca-gāthā by ācārya Nāgārjunagarbha. Text expounded by bhaṭṭāraka Śabara at Śrī-giri. Afterwards transmitted to Karma-pāda and at last to bhaṭṭāraka Nāro-pā. rG xlvii.19.

Śrī-sabara-stotra-ratna by Śrī Vanaratna-pāda. rG lxxxvi.12.

16 MĀTṚCEṬA

The following works are attributed to Mātṛceṭa in Tg.

Varṇanārha-varṇane-bhagavato-buddhasya-stotre-aśakya-stava-nāma. bsTod.29.

Tri-ratna-maṅgala-stotra. bsTod.30

Samyak-sambuddha-keta-stotra (Mahākavi Maticitra) bsTod. 31

Ekottarikā-stotra. bsTod.32

Sugata-pañcatriṃśat-stotra-nāma-ratnamālā-nāma. bsTod. 33

Tri-ratna-stotra. bsTod.35.

Miśraka-stotra-nāma (Mātṛceṭa and *ācārya* Dignāga) bsTod.41

Ārya-tārā-devī-stotra-sarvārtha-sādhana-nāma-stotra-rāja. rG xxvi.21.

Ārya-tārā-stotra. rG lxxi.392

Mahārāja-kaniṣka-lekha. mDo xxxiii.34=xciv.29

Catuḥ-vipa.yaya-(parihāra)-kathā. mDo xxxiii.48=xciv.14

Kaliyuga-parikathā. mDo. xxxiii.49=cxiv.15
Aṣṭāṅga-hṛdaya-saṃhitā-nāma (Pitṛceṭa) mDo. cxviii.4
Aṣṭāṅga-hṛdaya-nāma-vaidūryaka-bhāṣya (Pitṛceṭa). mDo. cxviii.5.-cxix

17. AŚVAGHOṢA & MĀTṚCEṬA

Following are in brief the results reached by M. Anesaki (in ERE ii.159f) and F. W. Thomas (in ERE viii.495f) about Aśvaghoṣa and Mātṛceṭa.

Anesaki on Aśvaghoṣa : The Tibetan colophon of the *Buddhacarita* and the *Life of Vasubandhu* mention him as a native of Sāketa. The latter source further asserts that Aśvaghoṣa was summoned to Kabul by Kātyāyaniputra to cooperate in the compilation of the Mahāvibhāṣā—a compilation which according to Yuan-chuang took place under the patronage of king Kaniṣka. *The Records of the Patriarchs* also mentions Aśvaghoṣa as a contemporary of Kaniṣka. 'We are told that Aśvaghoṣa was a learned but haughty man, who was at last converted to the Buddhist faith in the non-entity of the phenomenal world.' The agent in his conversion was Pūrṇayaśas, a disciple of Pārśva, who is said to have presided over the compilation of the above-mentioned great commentary (*Mahāvibhāṣā*). After 'his conversion, Aśvaghoṣa worked eagerly for the propagation of the Buddha's teaching in Kusumapura (modern Patna), not only as a preacher, but also as a poet and musician. When that town was taken by the army of Candana Kaniṣṭha, the king of the Yueh-chis, Aśvaghoṣa was carried away to their country in the north as a portion of the tribute paid to the conqueror by the Magadhans.' These traditions about Aśvaghoṣa, authenticated as these are by the oldest sources of our knowledge of him, may be accepted as more or less dependable. 'But when we take up many other writings which bear his name, we find ourselves in the dark as to the identity of the person. And the matter is made no clearer by the Tibetan tradition, which applies many epithets to him. This tradition dates from the 16th cent. and itself seems to be the result of confusion.'

Thomas on Mātṛceṭa : 'Mātṛceṭa is the name of a Buddhist author identified by the Tibetan historian of Buddhism, Tāranātha, with Aśvaghoṣa'. However, only Tāranātha identifies the two, while the much earlier Chinese pilgrim I-Tsing 'plainly distinguishes the two authors.' The main ground of this identification is that 'both writers stood in relation to Kaniṣka'. But 'nothing is more certain concerning Aśvaghoṣa than that he was a figure at the court of Kaniṣka, whereas we have an epistle from Mātṛceṭa declining, upon grounds of old age and sickness, to visit the king. Perhaps this is the reason why Tāranātha, identifying the two poets, makes an untenable distinction between Kaniṣka of Aśvaghoṣa and Kanika of Mātṛceṭa.'

18. ŚURA

The following works are attributed to Śūra in Tg. :

Pāramitā-samāsa. mDo xxxi.6
Subhāṣita-ratna-karaṇḍaka-kathā. mDo xxxiii.47=xciv.13
Jātaka-mālā. mDo xci.1
Bodhisattva-jātaka-dharma-gaṇḍī. mDo xciv.2
Supatha-deśanā-parikathā. mDo xciv.20

19. AŚVAGHOṢA

The following works are attributed to Aśvaghoṣa in Tg. :

Śata-pañcāśatka-nāma-stotra. bsTod.38
Gaṇḍī-stotra-gāthā. bsTod.40

Mahākāla-tantra-rudra-kalpa-mahāśmaśāna-nāma-ṭikā. rG xxvi. 72
Vajrayāna-mūlāpatti-saṃgraha. rG xlviii.135
Sthūlāpatti. rG xlviii.136
Maṇidvīpa-mahākāruṇika-pañca-deva-stotra. rG lxviii.35
Guru-pañcāśikā. rG lxxii.17
Daśa-akuśala-karma-patha-nirdeśa. mDo xxxiii.39=xciv.23
Śoka-vinodana. mDo xxxiii.41=xciv.22
Aṣṭākṣaṇa-kathā. mDo xxxiii.46=xciv.12
Pariṇamanā-saṃgraha. mDo cxxxvi.36
Buddhacarita-nāma-mahākāvya (Suvarṇākṣī-putra bhikṣu ācārya mahākavi vādin bhadanta Aśvaghoṣa of Sāketa-deśa, probably Ayodhyā). mDo xciv.1
Vajra-sattva-praśnottara. (ācārya Śrīghoṣa, probably Aśvaghoṣa) rG lxxxv.52

20. LUI-PĀ

The following works are attributed to Lūi-pā in Tg :
Bhagavad-abhisamaya. rG xii.8
Vajra-sattva-sādhana. rG xiii.1
Tattva-svabhāva-dohākoṣa-gītikā-dṛṣṭi-nāma. rG xlviii.2
Lūhipāda-gītikā. rG xlviii.27
Buddhodaya. rG xlvii.41
The above text revised by Taṅkipāda. rG lxxiii.62

21. ASAṄGA

The following works are attributed to Asaṅga in Tg :
Yogacaryā-bhūmi (col : pañca-bhūmyādivarga-yogacaryā-bhūmi-bahubhūmika-vastu *alias* yogācāra) mDo xlix

Yogacaryā-bhūmau Śrāvaka-bhūmi. mDo l
Yogacaryā-bhūmau Bodhisattva-bhūmi. mDo li
Yogacaryā-bhūmi Nirṇaya-saṃgraha. mDo lii-liii.1
Yogacaryā-bhūmau Vastu-saṃgraha. mDo liii.2
Yogacaryā-bhūmau Vinaya-saṃgraha. mDo liv.1
Yogacaryā-bhūmau Paryāya-saṃgraha. mDo liv.2
Yogacaryā-bhūmau Vivaraṇa-saṃgraha. mDo. liv.3 (According to the colophon of the present text the *Pañcabhūmi-varga* [*sa-sde-lṅa*] is composed by ārya Asaṅga)
Dharmakāya-āśraya-asāmānya-guṇa-stotra. bsTod. 7
Prajñā-pāramitā-sādhana. rG lxxi.246
Ārya-maitreya-sādhana. rG lxxi.345
Ārya-sandhi-nirmocana-bhāṣya. mDo xxxiv.1
Buddha-anusmṛti-vṛtti. mDo xxxiv.2
Dharma-anusmṛti-vṛtti. mDo xxxiv.3
Saṃgha-anusmṛti-vyākhyā. mDo xxxiv.4
Mahāyāna-uttara-tantra-śāstra-vyākhyā. mDo xliv.6
Mahāyāna-saṃgraha. mDo lvi.1
Abhidharma-samuccaya. mDo lvi.2
Dhyāna-dīpa-upadeśa-nāma. mDo lxi.4

22. MAITREYA

The following works are attributed to Maitreya in Tg.
Mahāyāna-sūtra-alaṃkāra-kārikā. mDo xliv.1
Madhyānta-vibhaṅga. mDo xliv.2
Dharma-dharmatā-vibhaṅga. mDo xliv.3
Dharma-dharmatā-vibhaṅga-kārikā. mDo xliv.4
Mahāyāna-uttara-tantra-śāstra. mDo xliv.5
Abhisamaya-alaṃkāra-nāma-kārikā-prajñā-pāramitā-upadeśa-śāstra. mDo i.1

cf Bu-ston i.53f : 'The works of the Lord Maitreya, which are—the *Sūtrālaṃkāra*, the *Madhyānta-vibhaṅga*, the *Dharma-dharmatā-vibhaṅga*, the *Uttara-tantra*. Some authorities say that the first two of these four (treatises) belong to the Abhidharma Code, the latter two to the Sūtra Code, and the *Abhisamayālaṃkāra* to the Vinaya Code. I however see no reason (for such a classification). The *Sūtrālaṃkāra* contains an exposition of all the Mahāyānistic doctrines in abridged form...The *Madhyānta-vibhaṅga* : *Anta*—"extremity", means the extremities of realism and nihilism, or otherwise those of eternalism and materialism. *Madhya*—"the middle", is the middle way shunning both these extremities. The treatise, as it gives an analysis (*vibhaṅga*) of both these points, is called *Madhyānta-vibhaṅga*...The *Dharma-dharmatā-vibhaṅga* : *Dharma* are the elements of existence that belong to the phenomenal world and are influenced by defiling agencies. *Dharmatā* is the true essence of all the elements—nirvāṇa. The work, being an investigation of these two principles, bears the name, *Dharma-dharmatā-vibhaṅga*. The *Uttara-tantra* is called so, because it is the highest (*uttara*) of the series (*tantra*) of the Mahāyānistic teachings, it consequently contains the highest of doctrines... Having adjoined (to these four works) the *Abhisamayālaṃkāra* (mentioned before), we shall have all the five treatises of Maitreya.'

23. VASUBANDHU

The following works are attributed to Vasubandhu in Tg.:

Pratītyasamutpādādi-vibhaṅga-nirdeśa. (commentary on Kg. mDo vol. *tsha* xviii.11) mDo xxxvi.1

Tri-ratna-stotra. bsTod 37

Ārya-ṣaṇmukhī-dhāraṇī-vyākhyāna. rG lxviii.1

Sapta-guṇa-parivarṇana-kathā. mDo xxxiii.43=xciv.8

Śīla-parikathā. mDo xxxiii.44=xciv.9

Sambhāra-parikathā. mDo xxxiii.45=xciv.11

Pañcavidha-kāma-guṇa-upālambha-nirdeśa. (mDo xxxiii.59=xciv.25

Sapta-guṇa-varṇanā-kathā. mDo xxxiii.85

Buddha-anusmṛti-ṭīkā (commentary on Tg mDo xxxiii.56) mDo xxxiv.7

Eka-gāthā-bhāṣya (commentary on Kg mDo vol. *sa* xxviii.23) mDo xxxiv.8

Ārya-caturdharmaka-vyākhyāna (commentary on Kg. mDo vol. *za* xxii.8) mDo xxxiv.10

Ārya-gayāśirṣa-nāma-sūtra-vyākhyāna (commentary on Kg. mDo vol. *ca* v.4) mDo xxxiv.12

Ārya-daśa-bhūmi-vyākhyāna (commentary on Kg. Phal-chen 31 vol *ji* xxxvii.1) mDo xxxiv.14

Ārya-akṣayamati-nirdeśa-ṭīkā (commentary on Kg. mDo vol. *ma* xvi.4) mDo xxxv

Ārya-bhadracaryā-praṇidhāna-ṭīkā. mDo. xxxviii.6

Sūtra-alaṃkāra-bhāṣya (commentary on Maitreya's Mahāyāna-sūtra-alaṃkāra-kārikā. Tg mDo. xliv.1). mDo. xliv.7

Madhyānta-vibhaṅga-ṭīkā (commentary on Maitreya's Madhyānta-vibhaṅga mDo. xliv.2) mDo xlv.1

Dharma-dharmatā-vibhaṅga-vṛtti (commentary on Maitreya's Dharma-dharmatā-vibhaṅga. mDo xliv.3). mDo xlv.2

Mahāyāna-saṃgraha-bhāṣya (commentary on Asaṅga's Mahāyāna-saṃgraha. mDo lvi.1) mDo lvi.3

Vivṛta-gūḍhārtha-piṇḍa-vyākhyā (incomplete commentary on the first part of Asaṅga's Mahāyāna-saṃgraha. mDo lvi.1). mDo lvi.5

Triṃśaka-kārikā = Vijñaptimātratā-siddhi = Sarvavijñāna-mātra-deśaka-triṃśaka = Vidyāmātra-siddhi-triṃśat-śāstra-kārikā. mDo lviii.1

Viṃśaka-kārikā = Vāhyārtha-nirodhaka-viṃśaka. mDo lviii.2

Viṃśaka-vṛtti = Viṃśaka-sva-vṛtti. mDo lviii.3

Tri-svabhāva-nirdeśa. mDo lviii.4

Pañca-skandha-prakaraṇa. mDo lviii.5

Vyākhyā-yukti-sūtra-khaṇḍa-śata = Yukti-sūtra-khaṇḍa-śataka. mDo lviii.6

Vyākhyā-yukti. mDo lviii.7

Karma-siddha-prakaraṇa. mDo lviii.8

Mahāyāna-śata-dharma-prakāśa-mukha-śāstra = Dharma-vidyā-dvāra-śāstra [col. A : Vasubandhu (acc. to Chinese index). A : Śrīmad Dharmapāla (acc. to Tibetan tradition)] mDo lviii.9

Abhidharmakośa-kārikā. mDo lxiii.1

Abhidharmakośa-bhāṣya (col. auto-commentary). mDo lxiii.2-lxiv.1

Gāthā-saṃgraha-śāstra-nāma. mDo lxxii.4

Gāthā-saṃgraha-śāstrārtha-nāma (col. auto-commentary). mDo lxxii.5

cf Bu-ston i.56f : 'The eight treatises of Vasubandhu are as follows. The *Triṃśaka-kārikā-prakaraṇa*, teaching that all the elements of existence are but modes of one conscious principle. The *Viṃśaka-kārikā prakaraṇa*, a vindication of this theory by means of logic. The *Pañcaskandha-prakaraṇa*, a vindication of the theory of the five groups of elements which is the foundation of logic. The *Vyākhyā-yukti*, vindicating the possibility of studying and preaching (the Doctrine), in conformity with the theory of idealism. The *Karma-siddhi-prakaraṇa*, vindicating the acts of the three media (from the same standpoint). These five works are independent. Next come interpretations of other works as follows :—The commentary on the *Sūtrālaṃkāra*, vindicating the practice of the six transcendental virtues. The commentary on the *Pratītya-samutpāda-sūtra*, vindicating the twelve-membered formula of the evolution of individual life, and the commentary on the *Madhyānta-vibhaṅga*, a vindication of the three aspects of reality. Such are these eight works, according to the tradition. Some authorities say that since this teacher has composed many more treatises—including the commentary on the *Daśabhūmaka-sūtra* etc—the limitation of their number to eight is incorrect, and so is likewise that of twenty treatises connected with the teaching of Maitreya. Those that insist on a definite number with regard to the latter, count the five volumes of the *Yogacaryā-bhūmi*, the two summary works, the five books of Maitreya and the eight treatises (of

Vasubandhu). The treatises elucidating the practical part of the doctrine are the *Bodhisattva-samvara-viṃśaka*, etc.'

24. VASIL'EV ON 'THE TWO VIBHAṄGA-S'

V n : 'viz. the Madhyānta-vibhaṅga-ṭīkā and Dharma-dharmatā-vibhaṅga-vṛtti. Both are available in Tanjur (vol *bi*). cf *Journal Asiatique* 1849, p.405, No. 455. Madhyānta-vibhaṅga considerably differs from the Sūtrālaṃkāra and belongs to a much later period. The word *dharma* means everything belonging to saṃsāra and by *dharmatā*—nirvāṇa. The author [Tār] wants to say that either the number of prakaraṇa-s is less or they have been lost. We have already noted above that for the Tibetans the five books, unknown to the Chinese, are the teaching of Maitreya. Besides, among the Yogācāra canonical works, they enumerate the seven works of Ārya Asaṅga : the five sections of the Yogacaryā-bhūmi considering these as separate works, the Abhidharma-samuccaya and Mahāyāna-saṃgraha. After this, came the five prakaraṇa-s or original works (rab-tu-byed-pa) of Vasubandhu. These are : 1) Vyākhyā-yukti, 2) Karma-siddhi-prakaraṇa, 3) Viṃśaka, the twenty-śloka treatise on idealism, 4) Triṃśaka, about the emptiness of dualism of self, 5) Pañca-skandha-prakaraṇa, on the five skandha-s. Besides, among the same prakaraṇa-s, however, are also enumerated 1) commentary on Sūtrālaṃkāra, 2) commentaries on the two vibhaṅga-s (according to some). According to others (Bu-ston) these two commentaries are taken as one work and the other one is the commentary on Pratītya-samutpāda.'

25. DĀRIKA-PĀ

The following works are attributed to Dārika-pā in Tg. :

Kālacakra-tantrarājasya-seka-prakriyā-vṛtti-vajrapada-udghāṭi-(nī)-nāma. rG iv.3

Cakra-samvara-sādhana-tattva-saṃgraha-nāma. rG xii.9
Cakra-samvara-maṇḍala-vidhi-tattva-avatāra-nāma. rG xii.10
Cakra-samvara-stotra-sarvārtha-siddhi-viśuddha-cūḍāmaṇi-nāma. rG xii.11
Yogānusāriṇī-nāma-vajrayoginī-ṭikā. rG xiv.43
Vajrayoginī-pūjā-vidhi. rG xiv.45
Kaṅkāla-tāraṇa-sādhana. rG xiv.46
Oḍḍiyāna-vinirgata-mahā-guhya-tattva-upadeśa. rG xlvi.6
(A : a disciple of Līlāvajra, who, again, is the disciple of princess Lakṣmiṅkarā)
Saptama-siddhānta. rG xlvi.46
Tathatā-dṛṣṭi. rG xlviii.48
Prajñā-pāramitā-hṛdaya-sādhana. rG lxiii.14

26. STHIRAMATI

The following works are attributed to Sthiramati in Tg. :
Sūtra-alaṃkāra-vṛtti-bhāṣya (commentary on Vasubandhu's Sūtra-alaṃkāra). mDo xlvi-xlvii
Triṃśaka-bhāṣya (commentary on Vasubandhu's Triṃśaka-kārikā). mDo lviii.10
Pañca-skandha-prakaraṇa-vaibhāṣya (commentary on Vasubandhu's Pañca-skandha-prakaraṇa). mDo lix.1
Abhidharmakośa-bhāṣya-ṭikā-tattvārtha-nāma (supra-commentary on Vasubandhu's Abhidharmakośa). mDo cxxix-cxxx
Madhyānta-vibhaṅga-ṭikā (commentary on Maitreya's Madhyānta-vibhaṅga). mDo xlviii.3
Ārya-mahāratnakūṭa-dharma-paryāya-śata-sāhasrikā-parivarta-kāśyapa-parivarta-ṭikā (commentary on Kg Ratnakūṭa, vol. *cha* vi.8). mDo xxxvii.12
Paramālaṃkāra-viśva-paṭala-vyūha-nāma. rG lxiii.34=lxxv.39
Prakaraṇa-ṭikā-viśeṣa-vyākhyā. rG lxxv.37

Bodhicitta-druma. rG lxxv.38
Samaya-aṣṭaviṃśa-mūla-vṛtti. rG lxxvi.45
Samaya-ratnanidhi. rG lxxvi.46
Sūtra-pañjikā. rG lxxvi.123
Yāna-uddyotana-pradīpa (col. probably of Sthiramati). rG lxxvi.124

27. DIGNĀGA

The following works are attributed to Dignāga in Tg. :
Miśraka-stotra (Mātṛceṭa and Dignāga). bsTod 41
Guṇāparyanta-stotra-ṭīkā (commentary on Ratnadāsa's Guṇāparyanta-stotra, bsTod 44=mDo xxxiii.96) bsTod 45 =mDo xxxiii.97
Guṇāparyanta-stotra-pada-kārikā bsTod 46=mDo xxxiii.98
Eka-gāthā-ṭīkā. bsTod 64
Ārya-mañjughoṣa-stotra. rG lxviii.20
Ārya-prajñā-pāramitā-saṃgraha-kārikā. mDo xiv.2=cxxviii.7
Yoga-avatāra. mDo xxx.12
Samantabhadra-caryā-praṇidhānārtha-saṃgraha. mDo xxxviii.3
Abhidharmakośa-vṛtti-marma-pradīpa-nāma. mDo lxx.2
Pramāṇa-samuccaya. mDo xcv.1
Pramāṇa-samuccaya-vṛtti (col. auto-commentary). mDo xcv.2-3
Ālambana-parīkṣā. mDo xcv.4
Ālambana-parīkṣā-vṛtti (col. auto-commentary). mDo xcv.5
Trikāla-parīkṣā. mDo xcv.6
Nyāya-praveśa-nāma-pramāṇa-prakaraṇa. mDo xcv.7
Nyāya-praveśa-nāma-pramāṇa-śāstra. mDo xcv.8
Hetu-cakra-ḍamaru. mDo xcv.9

28. BHAVYA OR BHĀVAVIVEKA

The following works are attributed to Bhavya or Bhāvaviveka in Tg :

Pradīpa-uddyotana-nāma-ṭikā (chapters 1-8 *ācārya* Āryadeva and 9-17 *mahācārya* Bhavyakīrti). rG xxxi

Pañca-krama-pañjikā-nāma (commentary on Nāgārjuna's Pañcakrama). rG xxxiv.1

Prajñā-pradīpa-mūla-madhyamaka-vṛtti (commentary on Nāgārjuna's Prajñā-nāma-mūla-madhyamaka-kārikā. mDo xvii.1) mDo xviii.8

Madhyamaka-ratna-pradīpa-nāma. mDo xviii.9

Madhyamaka-hṛdaya-kārikā. mDo xix.1

Madhyamaka-hṛdaya-vṛtti-tarka-jvālā. mDo xix.2

Madhyamaka-artha-saṃgraha. mDo xix.4

Nikāya-bheda-vibhaṅga-vyākhyāna. mDo xc.12

29. CANDRAKĪRTI

The following works are attributed to Candrakīrti in Tg :

Pradīpa-uddyotana-nāma-ṭīkā (commentary on Guhya-samāja-tantra). rG xxviii.1

Gaṇapati-samaya-guhya-sādhana. rG lxxxiii.60

Ṣaḍaṅga-yoga-nāma-ṭīkā. rG xxviii.2

Yukti-ṣaṣṭikā-vṛtti. mDo xxiv.1

Bodhisattva-yogacaryā-catuḥ-śataka-ṭīkā (commentary on Āryadeva's Catuḥ-śataka-śāstra-kārikā). mDo xxiv.2

Pañcaskandha-prakaraṇa. mDo xxiv.3

Śūnyatā-saptati-vṛtti. mDo xxiv.4

Mūla-madhyamaka-vṛtti-prasannapadā-nāma. mDo xxiii.1

Madhyamaka-avatāra-kārikā. mDo xxiii.2

Madhyamaka-avatāra. mDo xxiii.3
Madhyamaka-avatāra-bhāṣya. mDo xxiii.4
Madhyamaka-prajñā-avatāra. mDo xxiii.5
Tri-śaraṇa-(gamana)-saptati. mDo xxxii.9=xxxiii.101
Vyākaraṇa-liṅga-avatāra (Attributed to Thon-mi-sambhoṭa, section 6 of which is Samanta-bhadra-vyākaraṇa attributed to Candrakīrti). mDo cxxiv.4
Amṛta-siddhi-maṇḍala-vidhi (*mādhyamika* Candra, probably Candrakīrti). rG lxxv.49

30. CANDRAGOMĪ

In Tg are attributed over sixty works to Candragomī, a large number of which are Tāntrika treatises and *stotra*-s of Tārādevī. Specially interesting, however, appear to be the following works on medicine, grammar and ethics.

Akāla-maraṇa-nivāraṇa-upāya. rG lxix.145
Kuṣṭha-cikitsā-upāya. rG lxix.151
Jvara-rakṣā-vidhi. rG lxix,155
Paśumārī-rakṣā-vidhi. rG lxix.156
Puṣṭi-vaśī-homa. rG lxix.159
Siddhi-sādhana-anusāreṇa-mṛtavatsā-cikitsā. rG lxix.160
Āyuḥ-vardhanī-tārā-kalpa. rG lxxi.363
Candra-vyākaraṇa-sūtra. mDo cxvi.1
Viṃśati-upasarga-vṛtti. mDo cxvi.2
Varṇa-sūtra. mDo cxvi.3
Candragomi-vṛtti. mDo cxxiii.38
Uṇādi. mDo cxxxii.7
Śiṣya-lekha. mDo xxxiii.33

There is also one work attributed to him having the title Lokānanda-nāṭaka-nāma (mDo xcii.2), a drama with a Jātaka theme consisting of 4 acts and a prologue.

31. DHARMAPĀLA

As is evident from the use of the expression 'it is said', Tāranātha hesitates to subscribe fully to the view that ācārya Dharmapāla of the period under discussion actually visited Suvarṇadvīpa in the later part of his life. Still, this reference to such a hearsay is interesting and it indicates that among the Tibetan scholars this view somehow or other gained ground. There is no doubt, however, that the view itself is due to a confusion. There was actually another Dharmapāla—also an outstanding Mahāyāna ācārya—who lived in Suvarṇadvīpa and is usually referred to as the *guru* of Suvarṇadvīpa (*gser-gliṅ-pa*). But he belonged to a much later period, because Atīśa spent a considerable period studying the Mahāyāna texts under him—see A. Chattopadhyaya AT 84ff.

Ācārya Dharmapāla referred to by Tāranātha as a disciple of Dignāga and the successor of Candrakīrti at Nālandā must have been the same ācārya as mentioned by Yuan-chuang and I-Tsing. Yuan-chuang's own preceptor Śīlabhadra was a disciple of this Dharmapāla. See Watters i.372, 374, ii.109, 165, 168, 215, 226ff and I-Tsing (Takakusu) xiv, xxvi, lvii. lviii, 179, 181.

Strangely, however, it is difficult to trace with certainty the works of this Dharmapāla in the Tg, most of the Mahāyāna texts attributed to Dharmapāla in Tg being the works of the *guru* of Suvarṇadvīpa. Yet the Chinese pilgrims speak of Dharmapāla of the period under discussion as 'an author of repute and wrote treatises on etymology, logic and the metaphysics of Buddhism' (Watters ii.228).

However, the works of ācārya Dharmapāla, the preceptor of Śīlabhadra, survive in Chinese translation : 'The translations of 4 works attributed to Dharmapāla all date A.D. 650 to 710—see Nanjio Cat. Apppendix i, 16.' [Takakusu (I-Tsing) lvii].

Incidentally, another Buddhist ācārya called Dharmapāla visited Tibet on the invitation of king Ye-śes-'od ten years before Atiśa went to Tibet—see BA i.69 ; 83-6.

32. VIRŪ-PĀ

The following works are attributed to Virū-pā in Tg :

Rakta-yamāri-sādhana. rG xliii.96
Rakta-yamāntaka-sādhana. rG xliii.97
Bali-vidhi. rG xliii.98
Prabhāsa-udaya-krama. rG xliii.99
Suniṣprapañca-tattva-upadeśa. rG xliii.100
Rakta-yamāri-sādhana-vidhi. rG xliii.101
Yamāri-yantrāvalī. rG xliii.102
Amṛta-adhiṣṭhāna. rG xliii.125
Śrī-virūpa-pada-catuḥ-aśiti. rG xlvii.23
Dohā-koṣa. rG xlvii.24
Mārga-phalānvita-avavādaka. rG xlvii.25
Amṛta-siddhi-mūla. rG xlvii.27
Karma-caṇḍālikā-dohākoṣa-gīti. rG xlviii.4
Virūpa-vajra-gītikā. rG xlviii.16
Virūpa-gītikā. rG xlviii.29
Chinnamuṇḍā-sādhana. rG xiv.33
Uḍḍiyāna-śrī-yogi-yoginī-svayambhū-sambhoga-śmaśāna-kalpa-nāma. rG xxvi.63
Guhya-abhiṣeka-prakriyā. rG lxxiv.25
Amara-siddhi-vṛtti-(sanātana-siddhi) (commentary on rG xlvii.27). rG lxxxiv.14
Amṛta-siddhi. rG lxxxv.21

33. ŚĀNTIDEVA

The following works are attributed to Śāntideva in Tg :
Sarasvatī-pūjā-vidhi. rG lxxi.400
Cakra-samvara-ṭīkā. rG lxxiii.59
Cakra-samvara-sādhana. rG lxxiii.60
Bodhisattva-caryā-avatāra (in 2 parts containing 1000 śloka-s, 10 chapters). mDo xxvi.1
Śikṣā-samuccaya-kārikā. mDo xxxi.1=xxxiii.86
Śikṣā-samuccaya. mDo xxxi.2
Tathāgata-hṛdaya-pāpa-deśanā-vidhi-sahita-śatākṣara-rakṣā (extract from Śikṣā-samuccaya). mDo xxxi.3=xxxiii.61
Ārya-atyaya-jñāna-(nāma)-mahāyāna-sūtra-vṛtti. mDo xxxvii.7
Kevalī. mDo cxxiii.15
Bhodhisattva-caryā-avatāra-udbhava-praṇidhāna. mDo cxxxvi.31

34. DOMBĪ HERUKA

The following works are attributed to Dombī Heruka in Tg:
Guhya-vajra-tantra-rāja-vṛtti (Dombi, the king of Magadha), rG ix.3
Ekavīra-sādhana. rG xiii.11=lxxiii.19
Daśa-tattva. rG xxi.11
Yogi-yoginī-nāma-sādhāraṇa-artha-upadeśa. rG xxi.12
Gaṇa-cakra-vidhi. rG xxi.13
Tri-krama-upadeśa. rG xxii.4
Nairātmya-yoginī-sādhana. rG xxi.17
Ārya-tārā-kurukullā-stotra. rG xxi.30
Śrī-sahaja-siddhi. rG xlvi.8
Nāma-saṃgīti-vṛtti. rG lix.8
Sastotra-kurukullā-sādhana. rG lxxiv.49
Mṛta-vidhi. rG lxxxi.29
Śrī-gaṇapati-cakra-sūrya. rG lxxxiii.48

35. VAJRAGHAṆṬA

In Tg the following works are attributed to Vajraghaṇṭa (rdo-rje-dril-bu) :

Cakrasambara-seka-prakriyā-upadeśa. rG xii.12
Cakrasambara-sādhana. rG xii.13
Cakrasambara-pañcakrama. rG xii.14=lxxiii.21
Sambara-kāya-maṇḍala-abhisamaya. rG xii.15
Cakrasambara-pañcakrama-vṛtti. rG xii.16
Sahaja-sambara-sādhana. rG xii.17
Bhagavat-cakrasambara-sādhana-ratna-cintāmaṇi. rG xii.18
Dvibhuja-sahaja-sambara-sādhana. rG xii.19
Gaṇacakra-vidhi. rG xii.20
Maṇḍala-deva-stotra-ratna-māyādāna. rG xii.22
Vajra-vārāhī-sādhana. rG xiv.49
Ekavīra-sādhana. rG xxi.8
Abhiṣeka-vidhi-ratnamālā-sannibha. rG lxxxiii.21

36. RATNAKĪRTI

In Tg the following works are attributed to Ratnakīrti (rin-chen-grags) :

Yoga-caturdeva-stotra. bsTod 59
Śāsana-sarvasya-nāma-sādhana. rG xl.25
Prajñā-pāramitā-maṇḍala-vidhi. rG lxiii.18
Sarva-dhāraṇī-sādhana-krama-dvaya. rG lxix.196
Sarva-dhāraṇī-maṇḍala-vidhi. rG lxix.197
Sarva-sādhana-karman. rG lxix.198
Vajra-vidāraṇī-sādhana. rG lxxxii.55
Vajra-vidāraṇī-snāna-vidhi. rG lxxxii.56
Abhisamaya-alaṃkāra-vṛtti-kīrtikalā-nāma. mDo viii.4
Kalyāṇa-kāṇḍa-prakaraṇa. mDo lxi.11
Dharma-viniścaya-prakaraṇa. mDo lxi.15

37. DHARMAKĪRTI

Bu-ston i.44ff: 'The Seven Treatises (of Dharmakīrti) consist of the three main works, which may be compared to a body, and four supplementary, which act as its members.' The three main ones are:

Nyāya-bindu. mDo xcv.12
Pramāṇa-viniścaya. mDo xcv.11
Pramāṇa-vārtika. mDo xcv.10

The four supplementary works are:

Hetu-bindu. mDo xcv.13
Sambandha-parīkṣā. mDo xcv.14
Vādanyāya. mDo xcv.16
Santānāntara-siddhi. mDo xcv.17

These apart, Tg contains—

Pramāṇa-vārtika-vṛtti (auto-commentary on Pramāṇa-vārtika and supra-commentary on Pramāṇa-samuccaya) mDo xcv.18. According to the Tibetan tradition, the first *parivarta* is Dharmakīrti's auto-commentary and from 2-4 by his contemporary Devendrabuddhi.

Sambandha-parīkṣā-vṛtti. (auto-commentary on the Sambandha-parīkṣā) mDo xcv.15.

Jātaka-mālā-ṭīkā. (commentary on Śūra's Jātaka-mālā). mDo xci.2.

Buddha-parinirvāṇa-stotra. bsTod 47

In Tg the following Tāntrika works are also attributed to him:

Hevajra-mahātantrarājasya-pañjikā-netra-vibhaṅga. rG xvii.6
Sūtra-vidhi. rG li.6
Sarva-durgati-pariśodhana-mara-homa-maṇḍala-upāyikā. rG lxiii.10
Vajraḍākasya-stava-daṇḍaka. rG xii.23

38. KAMBALA

In Tg the following works are attributed to Kambala :

Ārya-prajñā-pāramitā-upadeśa. rG lxxxvi.33 ; lxiii.15 ; mDo xxx.11

Bhagavat-hevajra-sādhana-tattva-caturakrama. rG xxi.31

Asambandha-dṛṣṭi. rG xlviii.38

Asambandha-sarga-dṛṣṭi. rG xlviii.39

Maṇḍala-vidhi. rG lxxii.54 ; mDo xxxiii.66

Bhagavatī-prajñā-pāramitā-nava-śloka-piṇḍārtha. mDo xvi.1 ; xvi.3 ; cxxxiii.10

Commentary on above. mDo xvi.4

Sādhana-nidāna-nāma-śrī-cakrasamvara-pañjikā. rG vi.2

Bhagavat-śrī-cakrasamvarasya-sādhana-ratna-cūḍāmaṇi. rG xii. 24

Cakrasambara-maṇḍala-upāyikā-ratna-pradīpa-uddyoṭana-nāma. rG xii.25

Kambala-gītikā. rG xlviii.30

Cakrasambara-abhisamaya-ṭikā. rG lxxiii.58

Ārya-sapta-ślokikā-bhagavatī-prajñā-pāramitā-nāma-sūtra. mDo cxxxiii.11

cf BA ii.753 : 'ācārya Nāgārjuna and his disciples obtained the Yoga-tantras, including the Guhya-samāja and others (the Anuttara-yoga-tantras were also called Mahā-yoga-tantras) and preached them. They spread from the south. After that from the west Śrī Kambala (dPal La-ba-pa) and others discovered the Yoginī-tantras in the country of Oḍḍiyāna. They also spread towards Madhyadeśa.'

BA ii.731 Ni-gu-ma (sister of Nāro-pāda) said, 'Except myself and Kambala-pāda (La-ba-pa) no one else knows the precepts of the Six Doctrines.'

Kambala is also called the Sleeping Bhikṣu, because he is said to have slept for three years at the gate of king Indrabhūti's palace—BA i.362.

39. INDRABHŪTI

In Tg the following works are attributed to Indrabhūti :

Sarvabuddha-samayoga-ḍākinī-jāla-samvara-tantrārtha-ṭīkā. rG xxiv.11

Cakrasamvara-tantra-rāja-samvara-samuccaya-nāma-vṛtti. rG viii.1

Cakrasamvara-stotra. rG xii.21

Cakrasamvara-anubandha-saṃgraha. rG xiii.2

Siddha-vajrayoginī-sādhana. rG xiv.23

Śukla-vajrayoginī-sādhana. rG xiv.27

Ḍākinī-vajra-pañjara-mahātantrarājasya-pañjikā. rG xxiii.3

Sampuṭatilaka-nāma-yoginī-tantrarājasya-ṭīkā...rG xviii.6

Ānanda-puṣpa-mālā. rG xxii.50

Tattvāmṛta-upadeśa. rG xxii.51

Sarvabuddha-samayoga-nāma-tantra-pañjikā. rG xxv.1

Sarvabuddha-samayoga-gaṇa-vidhi. rG xxv.12

Vajrasattva-upāyikā. rG xxv.20

Jñānasiddhi-nāma-sādhana-upāyikā. rG xlvi.3

Sahaja-siddhi. rG xlvii.1

Tattva-aṣṭaka-dṛṣṭi. rG xlviii.42

Ratnacakra-abhiṣeka-upadeśa-krama. rG xlviii.132

Ājñā-vinivarta-gaṇapati-sādhana. rG lxxii.36

Vajrayāna-mūlāṅgāpatti-deśanā. rG lxxiii.23

Guhyagarbha-kramadvayoddeśa. rG lxxvi.17

Ratnacakra. rG lxxvi.32 (41)

Jñānāloka. rG lxxvi.32 (42)

Ratnamālā. rG lxxvi.32 (43)

Aparājitā-meruvarābhadraṅkara-ratnasādhana. rG lxxxi.43

Aparājitā-ratnabhadra-sādhana. rG lxxxiii.62

Cittaratna-viśodhana. rG lxxxiv.16

Kurukullā-sādhana. rG lxx.75

Aṣṭabhuja-kurukullā-sādhana. rG lxxi.268

Vajrayoginī-mantratattva-svādhiṣṭhāna-nirdeśa. rG xiv.24

There is also a work attributed to 'king Middle Indrabhūti' (*rājā-madhyama-indrabhūti*)—Sahaja-samvara-svādhiṣṭhāna rG xiii.6. For Middle Indrabhūti, see note 68 of ch 26. Cf. BA ii. 553 for other legends about Indrabhūti.

40. KUKURI-PĀ

The following works are attributed to Kukuri-pā in Tg :
Vajra-sattva-guhyārtha-dhara-vyūha. rG xxv.4
Vairocana-guhyārtha-dhara-vyūha. rG xxv.5
Vajra-heruka-guhyārtha-dhara-vyūha. rG xxv.6
Padma-nartteśvara-guhyārtha-dhara-vyūha. rG xxv.7
Vajra-ratnaprabha-guhyārtha-dhara-vyūha. rG xxv.8
Sughoṭa-lalita-guhyārtha-dhara-vyūha. rG xxv.9
Sarva-maṇḍala-anusāreṇa-pañca-vidhi. rG xxv.10
Sarva-buddha-samayoga-maṇḍala-vidhi. rG xxv.11
Mahāmāyā-tantra-anusāriṇī-heruka-sādhana-upāyikā. rG xxiii.21
Vajra-sattva-sādhana. rG xxiii.22
Moha-taraṇa-kalpa. rG xxiii.23
Mahāmāyā-sādhana-maṇḍala-vidhi. rG xxiii.24
Mahāmāyā-maṇḍala-deva-stotra. rG xxiii.25
Tattva-sukha-bhāvanā-anusāri-yoga-bhāvanā-upadeśa. rG xlviii.65
Srāva-paricchedana. rG xlviii.66
Mahāmāyā-vali-vidhi. rG lxxvi.28

41. SARORUHAVAJRA

The following works are attributed to Saroruhavajra in Tg :
Gīti-tattva. rG xx.9
Hevajra-sādhana. rG xxi.1

Hevajra-maṇḍala-vidhi. rG xxi.4
Samvara-cakra-īśvara-ālikāli-mahāyoga-bhāvanā. rG xlviii.80
Hevajra-tantra-pañjikā-padminī-nāma. rG xv.2
Hevajra-maṇḍala-karma-krama-vidhi. rG xxi.2
Hevajra-pradīpa-śūlopama-avavādaka. rG xxi.3
Homa-vidhi. rG xxi.5
Hevajra-bhaṭṭāraka-stotra. rG xxi.7
Hevajra-maṇḍala-karma-krama-vidhi. rG xxii.1
Guhya-kośa-nāma-mantra-śāstra. rG lxxiv.22
Amṛta-srava. rG lxxv.1

42. LALITAVAJRA

Vajrabhairava-bali-vidhi, rG xliii.73
Bhairava-maṇḍala-vidhi. rG xliii.74
Vajrabhairava-sādhana. rG xliii.72
Vajrasattva-sādhana-vṛtti. rG xxxiv.10
Yamāri-maṇḍala-upāyikā-yamāntakodaya. rG xliii.4
Caitya-sādhana-piṇḍīkṛta-vidhi. rG xliii.5
Kṛṣṇa-trimukha-ṣaḍbhuja-sādhana. rG xliii.41
Kṛṣṇa-yamāri-homa-vidhi. rG xliii.44
Vajra-bhairava-caturyoga-niyama. rG xliii.84
Karma-yama-dharmarāja-sādhana. rG xliii.127
Kṛṣṇa-yamāri-nāma-cakra. rG lxxxi.11
Samaya-amṛta-svāda. rG lxxxi.12
Cakra-nāma. rG lxxxi.13
Vajra-bhairava-tantra-vṛtti-alaṃkāra-upadeśa-nāma.
rG lxxxi.14
Vajra-bhairava-sādhana-upāyikā. rG lxxxi.16
Vajra-bhairava-samaya-maṇḍala-vidhi. rG lxxxi.17
Mahā-vajra-bhairava-māraṇa-cakra. rG lxxxi.22
Kālacakra-riṭiti-sahaja-sādhana-nāma. rG iv.10
Bhagavat-ekajaṭa-sādhana. rG xliv.33

Besides, about sixteen Tāntrika works are attributed to Mitrayogī or Jagat-mitra-ānanda—probably the same as Lalitavajra : rG xliv.35 ; 39 ; 40 ; 47 ; xlviii. 126-31 ; lxviii. 161-2 ; 164 ; lxxxiv. 9-10. The other name by which Lalitavajra is mentioned in Tg is Ajita-mitra-gupta (rG xliv. 33)

cf BA i. 367—Buddhajñānapāda heard many Kriyā and Yoga Tantras from Lalitavajra, who was born in Maṇidvīpa.

43. JĀLANDHARI-PĀ

The following works are attributed to Jālandhari-pā in Tg :
Cakra-samvara-garbha-tattva-siddhi. rG xiii.3
Vajra-yoginī-sādhana. rG xiv.48
Vimukta-mañjarī. rG lxxiii.49
Mahā-kāruṇika-abhiṣeka-prakaraṇa-upadeśa. rG lxxxii.8
Bhagavat-samvara-stotra. rG lxxiii.24
Hevajra-sādhanasya-ṭippaṇī-śuddhi-vajra-pradīpa. rG xxi.19
Huṃkāra-cittabindu-bhāvanā-krama. rG xlviii.72

44. KṚṢṆĀCĀRĪ

cf. the prophecy quoted by Bu-ston ii.120 : 'And in the country of Oḍiviśa there will appear a man possessed of the faculty of mystic meditation which he will exercise with great energy. He will be a follower of the precepts of Rāmaṇi. His name (is spelt as follows) :—The letter *Ka* of the first phonetic class is adorned with the first vowel (i.e. *A*). Then comes the fourth letter of the seventh class (*Ha*), being as if slightly mounted on the letter *Na*. This unique and powerful Yogin will secure the eight great principal magical properties.

The person spoken of here is Kāhna-pā or Kṛṣṇacārin (nag-po-spyod-pa-pa). The six pupils of the latter are to secure the Great Seal (Mahā-mudrā) by means of which everything which has a separate and physical reality will be rejected.'

Tg contains a large number of works—over 150 in all—attributed to nag-po-spyod-pa-pa, Kāhnapāda, Kṛṣṇapāda, Kṛṣṇācārya, Kṛṣṇapaṇḍita, Kāhna-pā, nag-po('i)-shabs, etc.

cf BA ii. 754 : regarding the appearance of Kālacakra in the Ārya-deśa, 'Gos lo-tsā-ba remarks—'after Ghaṇṭapāda (came) Kūrmapāda, he (transmitted it) to Jālandharapāda ; the latter to Kṛṣṇapāda, the latter to Bhadrapāda ; the latter to Vijayapāda ; the latter to Tilli-pā ; the latter to Nāro-pā. Thus from Ghaṇṭa(pāda) till Nāro-pā, there have been eight teachers in the line.' BA i. 385 also mentions Kṛṣṇapāda coming next to Jālandharapāda in the lineage.

45. SAHAJALALITA

Following works are attributed to Sahajalalita in Tg :

Hevajra-tantra-krameṇa-svādhiṣṭhāna-kurukullā-sādhana. rG xxii.26

Ārya-tārā-maṇḍala-sādhana-vidhi. rG xxvi.23

Samanta-mukha-praveśa-raśmi-vimala-uṣṇīṣa-prabhāsa-sarva-tathāgata-hṛdaya-samaya-vilokinī-nāma-dhāraṇī-vivṛti. rG lxvi.18

Hevajra-udbhava-kurukullā-sādhana. rG xxii.28

Hālāhala-sādhana. rG lxxi.25 ; 29 ; 116

Khasarpaṇa-sādhana. rG lxxi.26

Ārya-avalokiteśvarasya-ṣaḍakṣarī-sādhana. rG lxxi.27

Hari-hari-harivāhana-udbhava-avalokiteśvara-sādhana. rG lxxi.28

Uḍḍiyāna-mārico-sādhana. rG lxxi.39

Ārya-ṣaḍakṣarī-mahāvidyā-sādhana. rG lxxi.100

Oḍḍiyāna-mārīcī-sādhana. rG lxxi.225

Kurukullā-sādhana. rG lxxi.263

Ārya-amoghapāśa-sādhana. rG lxxxii.12

46. VINĪTADEVA

In Tg the following works are attributed to Vinītadeva, whom Vidyabhusana HIL 320 proposes to place in c A.D.700.

Prakaraṇa-viṃśaka-ṭikā. (commentary on Vasubandhu's Viṃśaka-kārikā). mDo lviii.11

Triṃśaka-ṭikā. (commentary on Vasubandhu's Triṃśaka-kārikā). mDo xli.1

Vinaya-stotra-pada-vyākhyāna. (commentary on Dharmaśreṣṭhī's Vinaya-stotra). mDo lxxviii.5=xc.10

Triṃśata-kārikā-vyākhyāna. mDo lxxxix.4

Vinaya-vibhaṅga-pada-vyākhyāna. (commentary in 5,100 śloka-s on Kg Vinaya). mDo lxxx.

Commentary on Vasumitra's Samaya-bheda-uparacana-cakra. mDo xc.13

Tantrāntara-siddhi-ṭikā. (commentary on Dharmakīrti's Santānāntara-siddhi). mDo cviii.1

Nyāyabindu-ṭikā. (commentary on Dharmakīrti's Nyāyabindu). mDo cxi.1

Hetubindu-ṭikā. (commentary on Dharmakīrti's Hetubindu). mDo cxi.5

Sambandha-parīkṣā-ṭikā. (commentary on Dharmakīrti's Sambandha-parīkṣā-prakaraṇa). mDo cxii.1

Vādanyāya-ṭikā. (commentary on Dharmakīrti's Vādanyāya-prakaraṇa). mDo cxii.3

Ālambana-parīkṣā-ṭikā. (commentary on Dharmakīrti's Ālambana-parīkṣā). mDo cxii.5

47. *Jñānagarbha*

The Mādhyamika works attributed in Tg to Jñānagarbha appear to be—

Satya-dvaya-vibhaṅga. mDo xxviii.1

Auto-commentary on the above called Satyadvaya-vibhaṅga-vṛtti Satya-dvaya-viniścaya, mDo xviii.2, which was commented upon by Śāntarakṣita, mDo xxviii.3

Bhāvanā-yoga-mārga. mDo xxx.2

Ārya-sandhi-nirmocana-sūtra-ārya-maitreya-kevala-parivarta-bhāṣya. (Partial commentary on Kg mDo Vol *ca* v.1-2)

These apart, certain Tāntrika works and commentaries on Dhāraṇīs are attributed to Jñānagarbha : rG xxi.58 ; xli.13 ; lxviii.2-3. Tg also contains a considerable number of works translated by Jñānagarbha of India.

Mar-pa is mentioned as a disciple of Jñānagarbha, under whom he translated some works contained in Tg—see Roerich BA ii.417n.

48. *Buddhajñāna*

cf Bu-ston ii,159f—Buddhajñāna, a disciple of Haribhadra and a preceptor of Guṇamitra. He composed 14 works on Guhya-samāja and also 'works on offerings, burning sacrifices, worship, magic circles, the propitiation of the Lord of the Water, etc, as runs the tradition.'

In Tg about 50 works are attributed to Buddhajñāna.

'Gos lo-tsā-ba (BA i.367ff) gives a long account of the Tāntrika career of Buddhajñāna.

49. ŚĀNTARAKṢITA

In Tg the following works are attributed to Śāntarakṣita, Śāntirakṣita or Śāntijīva, about whom see A. Chattopadhyaya AT 228ff :

Vajradhara-saṃgīta-bhagavat-stotra-ṭīkā. bsTod.52

Aṣṭa-tathāgata-stotra. bsTod.55

Hevajra-udbhava-kurukullā-pañca-mahā-upadeśa. rG xxii.29
Tattvasiddhi-nāma-prakaraṇa. rG lxxii.4
Satyadvaya-vibhaṅga-pañjikā. mDo xxviii.3
Madhyamaka-alaṃkāra-kārikā. mDo xxviii.4
Madhyamaka-alaṃkāra-vṛtti. mDo xxviii.5
Samvara-viṃśaka-vṛtti. mDo lxi.13
Vādanyāya-vṛtti-vipañcitārtha. mDo cviii.2=cxii.4
Tattva-saṃgraha-kārikā. mDo cxiii.1
Daṇḍa-hasta-lekha. rG lxxvi.32

50. HARIBHADRA

In Tg the following works are attributed to Haribhadra (seṅ-ge-bzaṅ-po) :

Pañcaviṃśati-sāhasrikā-prajñā-pāramitā. mDo iii-v. The text is different from the Prajñā-pāramitā of Kg.
Ārya-aṣṭa-sāhasrikā-prajñā-pāramitā-vyākhyāna-abhisamaya-alaṃkāra-āloka-nāma. mDo vi.
Bhagavat-ratna-guṇa-sañcaya-gāthā-pañjikā-nāma. mDo vii.1
Abhisamaya-alaṃkāra-nāma-prajñā-pāramitā-upadeśa-śāstra-vṛtti. mDo vii.2

51. YAŚOMITRA

In Tg the following works are attributed to Yaśomitra :

Abhidharmakośa-ṭikā Sphuṭārthā-nama. mDo lxv-lxvi. Commentary on Vasubandhu's Abhidharmakośa.
Bodhisattva-bhūmi-śīla-parivarta-ṭikā. mDo liv.7
Abhidharma-samuccaya-bhāṣya. mDo lvii.1
Abhidharma-samuccaya-vyākhyā. mDo lvii.2

Also two *stotra*-s are attributed to *ācārya* Jinaputra (rgyal-ba'i-sras-po), probably the same as Yaśomitra :

Tathāgata-nāma-saṃgīti-kalpika-bhadrālaṃkāra-mālā. bsTod 58
Tri-ratna-stotra-vṛtti bsTod 36

52. ŚĀKYAMITRA

BA i. 359 mentions Śākyamitra as one of the four disciples of Nāgārjuna. Another Śākyamitra is mentioned in BA i. 310 who was evidently in Tibet in A. D. 1387. The works of Śākyamitra catalogued in Supplementary Note 14 are perhaps those of the former.

53. KALYĀṆAMITRA

In Tg the following works are attributed to Kalyāṇamitra, mentioned as a Sautrāntika ācārya :
Pratimokṣa-vṛtti-pada-premotpādikā. mDo lxxviii.3
Śramaṇera-śikṣāpada-sūtra. mDo xc.4
Vinaya-praśna-kārikā. mDo xc.7
Vinaya-praśna-ṭīkā. mDo xc.8
Vinayottara āgama-viśeṣa-āgama-praśna-vṛtti. mDo lxxxi.2
Vinaya-vastu-ṭīkā. mDo lxxix.2

54. DAṂṢṬRĀSENA

The following works are attributed to Daṃṣṭrāsena (mche-ba'i-sde) in Tg :
Ārya-śata-sāhasrikā-pañcaviṃśati-sāhasrikā-aṣṭādaśa-sāhasrikā-prajñā-pāramitā-vṛhat-ṭīkā. mDo xiv
Śatasāhasrikā-prajñāpāramitā-vṛhat-ṭīkā. mDo xii-xiii.

The name occurs in various forms : *ācārya* Dıṣṭasena, Daṃṣṭasena, Daṃṣṭasyana, etc.

55. *Mañjuśrīkīrti*

In Tg the following works are attributed to Mañjuśrīkīrti :
Vajrayāna-mūlāpatti-ṭīkā. rG xlviii.146
Sarvaguhya-vidhi-garbhālaṃkāra. rG xlviii.148
Ārya-mañjuśrī-nāma-saṃgīti-ṭīkā. rG lviii.3
Dharmadhātu-vāgīśvara-mañjuśrī-maṇḍala-vidhi. rG lx.50
Ārya-sarva-dharma-svabhāva-samatā-vipañcita-samādhirāja-nāma-mahāyāna-sūtra-ṭīkā-kīrti-mālā-nāma. (commentary on Kg mDo vol *da*—Sendai Cat. 127). mDo xxxviii.1
Syādyanta-prakriyā. (Sans. Title *Kalāpasyādi*) mDo. cxvi.12

56. LĪLĀVAJRA

Fortyseven works are attributed in Tg to Līlāvajra, Līlāvajrapāda, Vilāsavajra, Varabodhi, Viśvarūpa : rG xxi.66 ; xxii.35 ; xli.7 ; 10 ; xlii.5 ; xliii.4-5 ; 90 ; xlvi.5-6 ; lviii.2 ; lxxii.18-38 ; lxxiv.12 ; lxxv.3 ; 8 ; 23 ; 26 ; 29 ; 33 ; lxxvi.9 ; lxxxi.4 ; 23 ; xxxiii.19 ; xlv.27 ; lxxvii-lxxx ; xliv.4 ; lviii.2

57. Paṇḍita RĀHULA

The following works are attributed in Tg to *paṇḍita* Rāhula :
Utpādanasamāpi-nāma-nairātmya-ekavīra-sādhana. rG xxii.22
Acintya-paribhāvana. rG xlviii.73
Dharma-caryā-aparādha-svayaṃ-mukti. rG lxxiii.33
Vajra-khecarī-sādhana. rG lxxxii.102
Nātha-samaya-stotra. rG lxxxiii.4

58. KALYĀṆAGUPTA

In Tg the following works are attributed to Kalyāṇagupta, *alias* Vākgupta, Vākpraja, Kuśalarakṣita, Kalyāṇarakṣita :
Sarvajña-siddhi-kārikā. mDo cxii.7
Vāhyārtha-siddhi-kārikā. mDo cxii.8
Śruti-parīkṣā-kārikā. mDo cxii.9
Anya-apoha-vicāra-kārikā. mDo cxii.10
Īśvara-bhaṅga-kārikā. mDo cxii.11

59. PRABHĀKARA

The following works are attributed in Tg to Prabhākara :
Nāma-saṃgīti-sādhana. rG lxi.25
Hayagrīva-sādhana. rG lxix.117
Caṇḍa-mahāroṣaṇa-sādhana. rG lxix.123
Sarva-tantra-hṛdaya-uttara-hayagrīva-sādhana. rG lxxi.319

60. BUDDHAGUHYA

The following works are attributed to Buddhaguhya in Tg :
Durgati-pariśodhana-artha-vyañjana-vṛtti. rG lxi.54
Dhyānottara-paṭala-ṭīkā. rG lxvi.1
Ārya-suvāhu-paripṛcchā-nāma-tantra-piṇḍārtha. rG lxvi.2
Ārya-vajra-vidāraṇī-nāma-dhāraṇī-ṭīkā-ratna-ābhāsvarā-nāma. rG lxvi.10
Sarva-durgati-pariśodhana-maṇḍala-vidhikrama. rG lxiii.9
Vairocana-abhisambodhi-vikurvita-adhiṣṭhāna-mahā-tantra-vṛtti. rG lxv.1
Vairocana-abhisambodhi-tantra-piṇḍārtha. rG lxv.2

Vairocana-abhisambodhi-tantra-vṛtti. rG lxiv. 2
Citta-piṇḍārtha-dhyāna. rG lxxvi.32(108)
Cittārtha-prakaraṇa. rG lxxvi.32(109)
Yoga-bali-krama. rG lxxvi.32(112)
Caturapramāṇa-ṭīkā. mDo xxx.6
Maṇḍala-kriyā-vidhi. mDo xxxiii.62
Yogi-kalpa-vighna-nirvahaṇa. mDo xxxiii.72 = rG xlviii.116
Bhoṭa-svāmi-dāsa-lekha. (Letter addressed to Khri-sroṅ-lde-btsan, king of Tibet and his subjects, the Tibetan devotees). mDo xciv.39
Vajrasattva-māyā-jāla-prabhā-krama. rG lxxv.16
Sūkṣma-jāla. rG lxxv.19
Tattva-āloka-karma-alaṃkāra. rG lxxv.20
Mārga-vyūha. rG lxxv.21
Citta-bindu-upadeśa. rG lxxv.23
Krodha-māyā-abhiṣeka-maṇḍala-vajra-karmāvali. rG lxxvi.7
Māyā-abhiṣeka-āvaśyaka-mūla-vṛtti. rG lxxvi.8
Vibhāga-vṛtti. rG lxxvi.32(2)
Bindu-piṇḍārtha. rG lxxvi.32(24)
Śānti-krodha-utpādana-samāpana-upadeśa. rG lxxvi.32(81)
Māyā-prabhāvali. rG lxxvi.32(82)
Heruka-kāya-vāk-citta-sādhana. rG lxxvi.32(98)
Krodha-mudrā-dhyāna. rG lxxvi.32(99)
Vairocana-abhisambodhi-tantra-piṇḍārtha. rG lxiv.1
Karma-upāya. rG lxviii.241
Vajrapāṇi-sādhana. rG lxviii.173
Vajra-vidāraṇī-nāma-dhāraṇī-sādhana-ekavīra-sādhana. rG lxviii.238
Ārya-vajra-vidāraṇī-nāma-dhāraṇī-bali-vidhi-krama. rG lxviii.239
Ārya-vajra-vidāraṇī-nāma-abhiṣeka-vidhi. rG lxviii.242
Dharma-maṇḍala-sūtra. rG lxxii.1
Maṇḍala-kriyā-vidhi. rG lxxii.55
Māyā-jāla-vajra-karma-krama. rG lxxv.5
Vajrasattva-māyā-jāla-abhiṣeka-āvaśyaka. rG lxxv.6
Abhiṣeka-artha-nirbheda. rG lxxv.7

61. VAIROCANABHADRA

Tg contains a number of works translated by Vairocana of India (rG xlvii.24 ; lxxxiii.47 ; 57 ; 60), by Vairocanarakṣita (rG xxi. 31 : xlvii.13 ; lxiii. 13 ; lxxxiv.7 ; lxiii. 55)

Besides these, Tg contains the following by Vairocanarakṣita of Vikramaśīla :

Bodhisattva-caryā-avatāra-pañjikā. mDo xxvii.30
Śiṣyalekha-ṭippaṇa. mDo xciv.36
Śikṣā-kusuma-mañjarī. mDo xxxi.5

The same Vairocanarakṣita appears to be the author of a number of Tāntrika works (rG xliii.91 ; 92 ; 112).

62. KAMALAŚĪLA

The following works are attributed to Kamalaśīla in Tg :

Ārya-sapta-śatika-prajñā-pāramitā-ṭikā. mDo xvi.6
Āya-vajra-chedikā-prajñā-pāramitā-ṭikā. mDo xvi.7
Prajñā-pāramitā-hṛdaya-nāma-ṭikā. mDo xvi.12
Madhyamaka-alaṃkāra-pañjikā. mDo xxviii.6
Madhyamaka-ālokanāma. mDo xxviii.7
Tattva-āloka-prakaraṇa. mDo xxviii.8
Sarva-dharma-abhāva-siddhi. mDo xxviii.9
Bhāvanā-krama. mDo xxx 7, 8, 9.
Bhāvanā-yoga-avatāra. mDo xxx.10=mDo xxxiii.74
Ārya-avikalpa-praveśa-dhāraṇī-ṭikā. mDo xxxvii.3
Ārya-śāli-stambaka-ṭikā. (commentary on Kg mDo vol. *tsha* xviii.10) mDo xxxvii.4
Śramaṇa-pañcāśatka-kārikā-pada-abhismaraṇa. mDo xc.2
Aṣṭa-duḥkha-viśeṣa-nirdeśa. mDo xciv.38
Śraddhā-utpāda-pradīpa. mDo xciv.40
Nyāya-bindu-pūrvapakṣa-saṃkṣipti. mDo cxi.3

Tattva-saṃgraha-pañjikā. mDo cxii.2-cxiv
Citta-sthāpanā-sāmānya-sūtra-saṃgraha. mDo cxxvii.3
Praṇidhāna-paryanta-dvaya. mDo cxxxvi.39

63. DHARMOTTARA

The following works are attributed to Dharmottara in Tg :
Pramāṇa-viniścaya-ṭīkā. mDo cix-cx.1
Nyāyabindu-ṭīkā. mDo cxi.2
Pramāṇa-parīkṣā. mDo cxii.12, 13
A-(nyā)-poha-prakaraṇa. mDo cxii.14
Paralokasiddhi. mDo cxii.15
Kṣaṇabhaṅga-siddhi. mDo cxii.17

64. VIMALAMITRA

See BA i. 191f : 'Vimalamitra was also a direct disciple of Buddhaguhya. Buddhaguhya taught the Māyā Cycle to Vimala and the latter to rMa Rin-chen-mchog. Now, it is stated in ancient records about the ācārya Vimalamitra that there had been two Vimalamitras, the Earlier and the Later, during the reigns of the religious kings Khri-sroṅ-lde-btsan and mÑa'-bdag Ral-pa-can. The Earlier lived during the reign of the religious king Khri-sroṅ-lde-btsan. He did not dress in monastic robes but went about attired as a Yogin. The king and his ministers expressed doubt as to whether he was a heretic or a Buddhist. Doubts were also expressed, because while making obeissance, he had broken an image of Vairocana. In order to remove the doubts of the ministers, he composed the *ṣaḍaṅga-śaraṇa*, in which he said : "The king and ministers did not trust me, so I compose the rite of the six Branches of the Refuge-taking Ceremony. He also composed an extensive commentary on the *Prajñā-hṛdaya* and *Sakṛtprāveśikanirvikalpa-bhāvanārtha*. To judge from the method employed in these books he must have lived after the ācārya Kamalaśīla. The Later Vimalamitra is the author of an extensive commentary on the *Pratimokṣa-sūtra* in fifty chapters (*Pratimokṣa-sūtra-ṭīkā Vinayasamuccaya*). He should be regarded as a monk. The Earlier Vimala taught the precepts of the sÑiṅ-thig to the king and to Myaṅ Tiṅ-'dzin-bzaṅ-po. Then Vimala proceeded to China.'

Roerich adds in note BA i. 119n : rDsogs-po-chen-po-sñiṅ-thig [i.e. the Doctrine of Māha-śānti] is the 'name of a mystic doctrine of the rÑiṅ-ma-pas [i.e. followers of the old Tantras] said to have been founded by Vimalamitra .. The philosophic background of the system is the Mādhyamika doctrine.'

Tg contains over eighty works of which Vimalamitra is mentioned either as the author or the translator.

For Vimalamitra, see also BA i. 106-8 ; 197 : ii. 491 ; 497.

65. DHARMĀKARA

The following works are attributed to Dharmākara in Tg :

Vajra-tārā-sādhana. rG lxxi.185

Dhvajāgra-keyūra-sādhana. rG lxxi.296

Tg also contains the following works as translated by Dharmākara : mDo xxiii.38 ; lxxii.4, 5 ; xc.7, 8, 11 ; xciv.24

66. ĀNANDAGARBHA

The following works are attributed to Ānandagarbha in Tg :

Sarva-kalpa-samuccaya-nāma-sarva-buddha-samayoga-ḍākinī-jāla-samvara-uttara-uttara-tantra-ṭīkā. rG xxv.2

Śrī-guhya-samāja-pañjikā. rG xlii.1

Sarva-tathāgata-tattva-saṃgraha-mahāyāna-abhisamaya-nāma-tantra-vyākhyā-tattvālokakarī. rG lii-liii

Paramādi-vṛtti. rG liv.1
Paramādi-ṭikā. rG liv.2 ; lv ; lvi.1
Māyājāla-mahātantra-rāja-ṭikā. rG lvi.2
Vajra-dhātu-mahāmaṇḍala-upāyikā-sarva-vajrodaya. rG lvii.1
Vajra-sattva-udaya-nāma-sādhana-upāyikā. rG lvii.2
Vajra-sattva-sādhana-upāyikā. rG lvii.3
Ārya-tattva-saṃgraha-tantra-uddhṛta-śrī-trailokya-vijaya-maṇḍala-upāyikā. rG lvii.4
Paramādi-maṇḍala-vidhi-nāma. rG lvii.5
Pratiṣṭhā-vidhi. rG lvii.6, 7
Sarva-durgati-pariśodhana-tejorājasya-tathāgatasya-arhataḥ-samyak-saṃbuddhasya-nāma-kalpa-ṭikā. rG lxiii.1
Sarva-durgati-pariśodhana-mahāmaṇḍala-sādhana-upāyikā. rG lxiii.3 ; 4
Sarva-durgati-pariśodhana-preta-homa-vidhi. rG lxiii.5
Sarva-durgati-pariśodhana-āgame Śava-śuddhi-saṃskāra-sūtra-piṇḍita-vidhi. rG lxiii.6
Sarva-durgati-pariśodhana-maṇḍala-vidhi. rG lxiii.8
Sarva-durgati-pariśodhana-nāma-saṃkṣipta-prakriyā-vidhi. rG lxiii.12
Prajñā-pāramitā-maṇḍala-upāyikā. rG lxiii.18
Mārīcī-devī-sādhana. rG lxxi.358
Mahāvatyāli. rG lxxvi.32(52)
Śrī-guhya-samāja-mahātantra-rāja-ṭikā. rG lxxvii-lxxx

67. PARAHITA

The following works are attributed to Parahita in Tg :
Maṇḍala-abhiṣeka-vidhi. rG xxvi.27
Śūnyatā-saptati-vivṛti. mDo xxiv.5
Sūtra-alaṃkārādi-śloka-dvaya-vyākhyāna. mDo xlviii.1

Tg also contains more than twenty works as translated or corrected by Parahita.

See BA i. 87—Parahita of Kashmir who went to Tibet and assisted Mahājana and other Tibetan scholars in translating the Buddhist scriptures.

68. JINAMITRA

A large number of works in Kg and Tg remain preserved as translated by Jinamitra, who went to Tibet during the reign of king Ral-pa-can and took part in the large-scale and authentic translation of the Buddhist texts. cf. Bu-ston ii.196-97 : Ral-pa-can found the earlier translations of the scriptures partly unintelligible. 'Besides, different translations were made from the Chinese, from the language of Li and Sahor etc. Owing to this there were many different rendering of words and the study of the Doctrine became very difficult. Seeing this, the king issued the following order : "The Aparāntaka teachers Jinamitra, Surendrabodhi, Śīlendrabodhi and Bodhimitra, the Tibetan teachers Ratnarakṣita and Dharmatāśīla, the skilful translators Jñānasena, Jayarakṣita, Mañjuśrīvarman, Ratnendra-śīla and others are to translate the Hīnayānistic and Mahāyā-nistic Scriptures directly from Sanskrit."'

69. *Sarvajñadeva*

Tg contains more than twentythree works as translated by Sarvajñadeva, inclusive of the works by Mātṛceṭa, Dignāga, Āryadeva, Śāntideva, Nāgārjuna, Candragomī and others.

70. TILLI-PĀ

The following works are attributed to Tilli-pā in Tg:
Tattvacaturopadeśa-prasanna-dīpa-nāma. rG xxi.24
Antara-vāhya-viṣa-nivṛtti-bhāvanā-krama. rG xlviii.88
Bodhicitta-vāyu-caraṇa-bhāvanā-upāya. rG xlviii.92
Ṣaḍ-dharma-upadeśa. rG lxxiii.27
Acintya-mahāmudrā. rG lxxiii.32
Guru-sādhana. rG lxxxiv.2
Vāhya-siddhi-pratītya-samutpāda, rG lxxxiv.3

71. *Prajñāpālita*

The following works are attributed to Prajñāpālita in Tg:
Pratiṣṭhā-vidhi. rG lvii.9
Thirtyseven (or thirtysix) works on Yamāri-tantra beginning with Rakta-yamāri-karmāvali-sādhana-cintāmaṇi-nāma (rG xliii.129) and concluding with Yamāri-cintāmaṇi-mālā-nāma-sādhana (rG xlviii.165): these 37 (or 36) works are mentioned as forming a continuous one, rG xliii.129 being the introduction and rG xlviii.165 the conclusion.

72. JETĀRI

The following works are attributed to Jetāri in Tg:
Hevajrasya-seka-niścaya. rG xxi.48
Daśa-krodha-vidyā-vidhi. rG xxi.49
Catuḥ-pīṭha-tattva-catuṣka. rG xxiii.14
Nātha-akṣobhya-sādhana. rG lxiii.30
Aparimita-āyuḥ-stotra. rG lxviii.6
Ārya-aparimita-āyuḥ-jñāna-sādhana. rG lxviii.7

Aparimita-āyuḥ-jñāna-vidhi. rG lxviii.8
Ārya-lokeśvara-cintāmaṇi-cakravarti-sādhana. rG lxviii.156
Caṇḍa-mahāroṣaṇa-sādhana. rG lxix.124
Śītavatī-sādhana. rG lxix.182
Mahāpratisarā-cakra-lekhana-vidhi. rG lxix.186
Vajra-śṛṅkhalā-sādhana. rG lxxi.360
Maṇḍala-vidhi. rG lxxii.56=mDo xxxiii.63
Sugata-mata-vibhaṅga-kārikā. mDo xxix.7=mDo xxxiii.84, cxxviii.4 & 5
Bodhyāpatti-deśanā-vṛtti-bodhisattva-śikṣā-krama-nāma. mDo xxxvii.9
Bālāvatāra-tarka-nāma. mDo cxii.26
Hetutattva-upadeśa. mDo cxii.24
Dharma-dharmi-viniścaya. mDo cxii.25
Bodhicitta-utpāda-samādāna-vidhi. mdo xxxii.6=mDo xxxiii.29
Māyā-jāla-krama-avalokiteśvara-sādhana. rG lxxi.94
Catuḥ-mudrā-sādhana. rG lxxiv.24
Ādi-karmika-bhūmi-pariṣkāra. mDo xxxi.7=mDo xxxiii.30
Citta-ratna-viśodhana-krama-nāma-lekha. mDo xxxiii.31= mDo xciv.30

73. KĀLACAKRAPĀDA

The following works are attributed to Kālacakrapāda in Tg:
Nakṣatra-maṇḍala-sādhana-ekādaśa-aṅga-nāma. rG iv.5
Ārya-kālacakrapāda-sampradāya-nāma-ṣaḍaṅga-yoga-upadeśa. rG iv.19
Kālacakra-supratiṣṭhā-upāyikā-vidhi. rG v.5
Kālacakra-gaṇacakra-upāyikā-vidhi. rG v.6
Kālacakra-homa-upāyikā-vidhi. rG v.7
Padminī-nāma-pañjikā. rG iii.3
Kālacakra-upadeśa. rG iv.13
Seka-uddeśa-ṭīkā. rG iv.1

See BA ii.765 : there were two Kālacakrapādas, one Senior and the other his disciple, Kālacakrapāda the Junior.

74. ŚĀNTI-PĀ

The following works are attributed to Śānti-pā in Tg :
Sukha-duḥkha-dvaya-parityāga-dṛṣṭi. rG xlviii.37
Madhyamaka-alaṃkāra-vṛtti-madhyamaka-pratipadā-siddhi-nāma. mDo lxi.3
Prajñā-pāramitā-upadeśa. mDo lxi.9
Prajñā-pāramitā-bhāvanā-upadeśa. mDo lxi.7, 10= mDo xxxiii.82
Vijñaptimātratā-siddhi. mDo cxii.22
Antar-vyāpti. mDo cxii.23
Ārya-aṣṭa-sāhasrikā-prajñā-pāramitā-pañjikā-sārottamā-nāma. mDo x.1
Sūtra-samuccaya-bhāṣya-ratnāloka-alaṃkāra-nāma. mDo xxx.30
Madhyamaka-alaṃkāra-upadeśa. mDo lxi.16
Chandaḥ-ratnākara. mDo cxvii.4 & 5 ; cxxxiii.7
Vajra-tārā-sādhana. rG lxxi.186=rG xxii.38

75. VĀGĪŚVARAKĪRTI

The following works are attributed to Vāgīśvarakīrti in Tg :
Samaya-tārā-stava. rG lxxxii.48
Mṛtyu-vañcana-upadeśa. rG xxvi.68=lxxxi.21
Sapta-aṅga. rG xl.17
Tattva-ratna-āloka. rG xl.18
Vajrapāṇi-sādhana. rG xlviii.197
Pratiṣṭhā-vidhi. rG lxix.190
Tattva-ratna-āloka-vyākhyāna. rG lxxi.6
Mṛtyu-vañcana-piṇḍārtha. rG lxxxi.19
Siddha-ekavīra-mañjughoṣa-stotra-suvarṇa-mālā-nāma. rG lxxxii.6

In BA are mentioned three Vāgīśvarakīrtis—1) the famous door-keeper scholar of Vikramaśīla (i.206), 2) the younger Pham-mthiṅ brother also known as Vagīśvara (i.384) and 3) one named Piṇḍo-ācārya, famed as Vāgīśvarakīrti in the Madhya-deśa (ii.757f).

76. NĀRO-PĀ

Over thirty works are attributed in Tg to Nāro-pā, Nāḍa-paṇḍita, Nāḍa-pāda, Nāro-pa'i-shabs, Nāro-tapa, Nāro-panta.

In BA, Nāro-pā is said to have been a disciple of Tilli-pā (i.361, 380), a teacher of Atīśa (i.243) and of the Kashmirian Jñānākara (i.361). He was 'the guardian of the northern gate of Vikramaśīla. The ācārya Śānti-pā (Ratnākaraśānti) and the venerable Maitrī-pā heard the Tantra from him' (i.380). Pham-mthiṅ-pā attended on Nāro-pā for seven years and Pham-mthiṅ-pā's younger brother for five years. Mar-pa Do-pa received Nāro-pā's blessings in Tirhut (i.383). The Six Doctrines were bestowed by Nāro-pā on the Master Mar-pa (ii.728).

77. BODHIBHADRA

The following works are attributed to Bodhibhadra (the disciple of Mahāmati of Somapurī) in Tg :

Rahasya-ānanda-tilaka. rG xxii.59
Yoga-satya-lakṣaṇa. rG xlviii.118=mDo xxxiii.73
Jñāna-sāra-samuccaya-nibandhana. mDo xviii.7
Samādhi-ambhāra-parivarta. mDo xxx.18=mDo xxxiii.67
Bodhisattva-samvara-vidhi. mDo xxxii.5=mDo xxxiii.27
Bodhisattva-samvara-viṃśaka-pañjikā. mDo lxi.14

78. RATNAVAJRA

The following works are attributed to Ratnavajra in Tg :

Heruka-sādhana-nāma. rG xiii.26
Cakra-samvara-maṅgala-gāthā. rG xiii.27
Cakra-samvara-maṇḍala-devagaṇa-stotra. rG xiv.10
Cakra-samvara-stotra. rG xiv.11
Bali-karma-krama. rG xxii.11
Hevajra-stotra. rG xxii.16
Mahāmāyā-sādhana. rG xxiii.28
Sarva-buddha-samayoga-ḍākinī-jāla-samvara-mahā-tantrarāja. rG xxv.19

Tg also contains seventeen other works composed or translated by him.

79. MAHĀJANA

In Tg Mahājana is mentioned as the author of Prajñā-pāramitā-hṛdaya-artha-parijñāna (mDo xvi. 15). His name also occurs as the translator of sixteen works inclusive of some by Candragomī, Vasubandhu, Nāthamaitreya and others.

80. Jñānaśrī

BA i.206 & 372 refers to Jñānaśrī as one of the Six Door-keeper Scholars of Vikramaśila. Jñānaśrīmati is mentioned as one of the teachers of Atīśa—BA i.243. Cf also BA i.70, 85,347,355 : the great Paṇḍita Jñānaśrī of Kashmir who went to Tibet without having been invited. Sum-pa 118 mentions Jñānaśrī as one of the four eminent disciples of the *guru* of Suvarṇadvīpa (Dharmakīrti or Dharmapāla).

Tg contains works by Jñānaśrī, Jñānaśrīmitra of Kashmir,

Jñānaśrībhadra and Jñānamitra. Of these, a number of works on Vajra-vidāraṇī-karma (rG lxviii.232-35) mentions mahā-paṇḍita Jñānaśrī as author and translator, the name occurring also as the translator of a number of other treatises (rG lxviii.225-31). Besides these Tg contains :

Sūtrālaṃkāra-piṇḍārtha (mDo xlviii.2) by ācārya mahā-paṇḍita Jñānaśrī.

Kāryakāraṇabhāva-siddhi (mDo cxii.29) by mahā-paṇḍita Jñānaśrīmitra.

Śīla-saṃvara-samaya-avirodha-nāma (rG lxxii.19) by Jñānaśrībhadra of Kashmir.

Pramāṇa-viniścaya-ṭikā (mDo cx.2) by Jñānaśrībhadra of Kashmir.

81. AMOGHAVAJRA

Tg contains over a hundred works of which Amoghavajra is mentioned as the author or translator. These include a considerable number of works on Amṛtasiddhi, composed by him in Tibet : these mention Virū-pā as the ācārya of Amṛtasiddhi : rG lxxxv. 22-9 ; 38-47. BA ii. 1042 mentions him as a disciple of Mitrayogin and according to BA i. 162 he visited Tibet soon after A. D. 1086. See also Supplementary Note 95.

82. VĪRYABHADRA

Apart from a few translations attributed to him, Tg contains his work Pañcakrama-Pañjikā Artha-prabhāsa-nāma (rG xxxiv.4). Besides, the colophon of the Bodhisattvāvadāna-kalpalatā of Kṣemendra (mDo xciii) mentions that it is edited on the basis of the manuscripts obtained from India, Kashmir, Khotan, Nepal and China and that the edition is guided by the research of Vīryabhadra, the date of the completion of the work being probably A. D. 1052 in the month of Vaiśākha on the birth anniversary of the Buddha.

83. *Maṇikaśrī*

The following works are attributed to Maṇikaśrī in Tg :
Ekavīra-sādhana. rG xiii.29
Cakra-samvara-ekala-vīra-sādhana. rG xiv.17

He is also mentioned as the translator or corrector of a number of works. BA i. 385 mentions him as an exponent of Cakrasamvara and as belonging to the lineage of Lūi-pā, Deṅgi-pā, La-va-pā, Indrabhūti, etc.

84. *Jñānavajra*

In Tg Jñānavajra of Nepal is mentioned as the translator of six works : rG xiv. 3-7 ; 24 ; 61 ; lxxiii.22. Besides these, he is mentioned as the author of
Sādhana-caryā-avatāra. rG xxxiii.32
Ārya-jambhala-stotra. rG lxxii.45

A large number of Tāntrika treatises are also attributed in Tg to Jñānavajra of Oḍḍiyāna, *alias* Advaya-jñānavajra.

Tg mDo xliii (a commentary on the Laṅkāvatāra) is attributed to Jñānavajra of China.

85. BHĀRATA-PĀṆI

Also known as bodhisattva Vajrapāṇi. Tg contains a number of his works inclusive of:

Bhagavatī-prajñā-pāramitā-hṛdaya-ṭīkā-artha-pradīpa-nāma (mDo xvi. 10)—text expounded to the Tibetan kalyāṇamitra-s at Lalitapattana in Nepal.
Ṣaḍaṅga-yoga rG. iv.11
Lakṣa-abhidhāna-udhṛta-laghu-tantra-piṇḍārtha-vivaraṇa. rG vi.1
Tattvagarbha-sādhana. rG xii.7
Nīlāmbaradhara-vajrapāṇi-yakṣa-mahārudra-vajra-agnijihva-tantra-vṛtti. rG xliv.73

cf BA ii. 843 : 'This Vajrapāṇi (Phyag-na) was born in the Fire-Female-Serpent (year : A. D. 1017). From childhood he had sharp intellect and was learned in all the heretical and Buddhist sciences, as well as in many sections of the Tantras of the Mantra-yāna. He specially mastered the Cycle of Dohā (Saraha's Dohā).' He was a younger brother of Kṣitigarbha, (who accompanied Atiśa to Tibet)—BA ii. 842. He is mentioned as one of the Four Great Disciples of Maitrī-pā (born A.D. 1007 or 1010), the other three being Na-te-ka-ra, Devākaracandra and Rāmapāla—BA ii. 842. He was invited to Tibet by 'Brog Jo-sras and he composed the Vajra-pāda-nāma—BA i. 857. Tg contains a considerable number of works translated by him.

86. ABHAYĀKARAGUPTA

V n 'According to *Thob-yig*, Abhayākaragupta was born in eastern India as the son of a chief of all the Brahmins. A young *yoginī* sent him to Magadha for being ordained in the

Law of the Buddha. He came to Bhaṃgala and became a *śramaṇera.* Thereafter in Vigamala (?) vihāra, he studied logic, Tripiṭaka, Madhyama, Pāramitās and became the *gaṇa-pati* of the *saṃgha*-s and taught logic. For studying the *siddhāntas*, he went to the teacher Ratnākaragupta in a cave of the city of Be'u. When his fame spread far and wide, the Magadharāja Rāthika made him the chief of all the *paṇḍita*-s and gave him as gift the Indrauli garden. He freed from the prison a little over hundred persons whom the king Carasinda wanted to offer as sacrifice, drove away the Turuṣka army etc. His works related to the commentaries on 8,000 Pāramitās, Vinaya, Logic and Madhyama. On Tantras, his works which are particularly famous are: 1) a commentary on Sampuṭa known under the name Upadeśa-mañjarī, 2) the Sea of Siddhāntas, where all the precepts for propitiating various deities are collected at one place, 3) Vajra-mālā, where all the *maṇḍala*-s of *sādhana* are described.'

BA i. 32 quotes from his Muni-matālaṃkāra (mDo xxix.10) and BA i. 371 refers to his Vajrāvalī and Vajrāvalī-nāma-maṇḍala-sādhana. In Tg are attributed about 50 works to him.

BA i. 219—rMa lo-tsā-ba (born in A. D. 1044) studied in India under Abhayākara.

87. ŚĀKYAŚRĪ

BA ii.599—there exists a biography (rnam-thar) of Śākyaśrī of Kashmir by Khro-phu-lo-tsā-ba (byams-pa'i-dpal), who invited him to Tibet. He visited the Tibetan monasteries in A.D. 1208—BA i.306. He 'ordained many monks in Tibet including the Sa-skya Pan-chen and others... The great *bhadanta* Tsoṅ-kha-pa also obtained monkhood through the lineage of Śākyaśrībhadra.' In BA i.35 is quoted the prophecy of Tārā to Śākyaśrībhadra about his becoming tne Buddha Bhāgīrathī of the Bhadra-kalpa (i.e. one of the Thousand Buddhas of the Bhadra-kalpa). Cf also BA ii.1062ff : Śākyaśrī was born in A.D. 1127, ordained in 1149, came to Tibet in his 78th year (A.D. 1204), stayed there for ten years and left for Kashmir in A.D. 1214. He passed away in Kashmir at the age of 99 in A.D. 1225.

In Tg are attributed to him the following works :

Kalpa-pūjā-mahā-catuṣka-kārikā. bsTod 62
Ārya-tārā-bhaṭṭārikā-upadeśa-āśraya-āsanna-maraṇa-āmnāya. rG xxvi.39
Viśuddha-darśana-caryā-upadeśa. rG xlviii.124
Mañjuśrī-cala-cakra. rG lxviii.13
Siṃhanāda-rakṣā-cakra. rG lxviii.167
Saṃkṣipta-amoghapāśa-sādhana. rG lxviii.168
Amoghapāśa-bali-vidhi. rG lxviii.169
Poṣadha-karaṇīya. rG lxviii.170
Ārya-amoghapāśa-poṣadha-vidhi-āmnāya. rG lxviii.171
Ārya-maitreya-sādhana. rG lxxi.344
Ārya-tārā-sādhana. rG lxxi.395
Ārya-kṛṣṇa-jambhala-sādhana. rG lxxii.43
Ārya-amoghapāśa-sādhana. rG lxxxii.10
Bodhisattva-mārgakrama-saṃgraha. mDo xxxii.15
Mahāyāna-upadeśa-gāthā. mDo xxxii.20
Saptāṅga-saddharma-caryā-avatāra. mDo xxxii.14

88. RATNARAKSITA

The following work is attributed to Ratnarakṣita in Tg :

Samvara-udaya-mahātantrarājasya-pañjikā-padminī-nāma. rG xii.1

He is also mentioned as the translator and corrector of a large number of works.

89. *Dīpaṃkarabhadra*

In Tg Dīpaṃkarabhadra is mentioned as the author of a large number of Tāntrika works. These include—

Guhya-samāja-maṇḍala-vidhi. rG xxxix.13
Aṣṭa-krodha-maṇḍala-abhiṣeka. rG lxix.7
Ārya-vajra-vidāraṇī-pratiṣṭhā. rG lxix.20

He is also mentioned as the translator of rG xl.8

90. ŚRĪDHARA

In Tg more than thirty Tāntrika works are attributed to Śrīdhara, which include :

Kṛṣṇa-yamāri-sādhana. rG xliii.1
Kṛṣṇa-yamāri-maṇḍala-upāyikā. rG xliii.2
Rakta-yamāri-sādhana. rG xliii.103
Caturyoga-tattva-nāma-svādhiṣṭhāna-upadeśa. rG xliii.105
Kṛṣṇa-yamāreḥ-rakta-yamāreśca-pūjā-vidhi. rG xliii.109

Besides, two works on lexicon are attributed to one Śrīdhara of Nepal (mDo cxxxiii.2 ; 3)

91. BHAVABHADRA

The following works are attributed to Bhavabhadra (Bhavabhaṭṭa) in Tg :

Cakra-samvara-pañjikā-nāma. rG vi.3
Vajra-ḍāka-nāma-mahātantrarājasya-vivṛti. rG ix.1
Hevajrasya-vyākhyā-vivaraṇa-nāma. rG xv.3
Catuḥ-pīṭha-tantrarājasya-ṭikā-smṛti-nibandha-nāma. rG xxii.60
Catuḥ-pīṭha-sādhana-upāyikā. rG xxiii.9

Catuḥ-pīṭha-jala-homa. rG xxiii.10
Maṇḍala-avatāra-saṃkṣipta-kalpa. rG lxxi.372
Cintāmaṇi-tārā-nāma-sādhana. rG lxxi.374=lxxi.381
Tārā-dhāvana-vidhi. rG lxxi.375
Poṣadha-vidhi. rG lxxi.376

92. DURJAYACANDRA

In Tg the following works are attributed to him :
Ratnacchaṭā-nāma-pañjikā. rG vi.4
Saptākṣara-sādhana. rG xiii.8=lxxxvi.67
Cakrasamvara-sādhana-amṛtākṣara-nāma. rG xiii.9
Kaumudī-nāma-pañjikā. rG xvii.1.
Ṣaḍaṅga-nāma-sādhana. rG xxi.21
Sarvabhūta-bali. rG xxi.23
Nairātmya-sādhana. rG xxii.18
Nairātmya-devī-pañcadaśa-stotra. rG xxii.19
ḍākinī-vajrapañjara-pañcaḍāka-sādhana. rG xxii.35
Mahāmāyā-tantrasya-pañjikā-māyāvatī-nāma. rG xxiii.16
Suparigraha-nāma-maṇḍala-upāyikā-vidhi. rG xxi.22

93. TATHĀGATARAKṢITA

In Tg the following works are attributed to him :
Ubhaya-nibandha. rG vii.5
Yoginī-saṃcaryā-nibandha. rG xii.3
Śmaśāneṣṭa. rG xxii.43
Sragdharā-sādhana. rG xxvi.15
Śūnyatā-bhāvanā. rG xxvi.16
Kudṛṣṭi-dūṣaṇa. rG xxvi.17
Corabandha. rG xxvi.18

Vidyāvardhana. rG xxvi.19
Mṛtyu-kāpaṭya. rG xxvi.20
Vajrasattva-sādhana-bhāṣya. rG xxiv.9
Vajrabhairava-hastacihna-viśuddhi. rG xliii.81
Caturmukha-samaya-siddhi-sādhana. rG lxxxii.73

94. KAMALARAKṢITA

The following works are attributed to him in Tg :
Kṛṣṇa-yamāri-sādhana. rG. xliii.10
Maṇḍala-vidhi. rG xliii.12
Kṛṣṇa-yamāri-sādhana-maṇḍala-vidhi. rG xliii.32
Vajra-bhairava-sādhana-udbuddha-kamala-nāma. rG lxxxi.15

Kamalarakṣita was a contemporary of Atīśa, to both of whom the guru of Suvarṇadvīpa (Dharmapāla or Dharmakīrti) expounded the following works : mDo xxvi.6 ; 7 ; xxxi.4 ; xxxiii.87—see also A. Chattopadhyaya AT 93 ; 479f ; 484 ; 491.

95. KHYUṄ-PO-RNAL-'BYOR

BA ii.728f 'I shall now tell the story of the Lineage of the Six Doctrines founded by Ni-gu-mā, sister of Nāro-pā. Its Lineage and of Guidance and Initiation : the introducer of the doctrine (to Tibet) was the *siddha* Khyuṅ-po-rnal-'byor. He belonged to the Khyuṅ-po clan and was born at sÑe-mo-ra-maṅs in the Tiger Year (1086 A.D.) as son of father sTag-skye and mother bKra-śis-skyid. Soon after his birth, the Indian *siddha* Amogha came there and uttered an auspicious prophecy about him. At the age of ten, he mastered reading the Indian and Tibetan alphabets. He became proficient in the Kālacakra. At the age of thirteen, he studied with the *ācārya* gYuṅ-druṅ-rgyal-ba the Bon doctrine and preached it to others, and about seven hundred scholars (possessing manuscripts of the text) attended his class. He then studied extensively the Cycle of the rDsogs-chen-sems-sde with the bla-ma 'Byuṅ-gnas-seṅ-ge, and then preached it. During that time also he gathered about seven hundred disciples... Having taken with him a considerable quantity of gold, he journeyed to Nepal and studied there the work of a translator with the *paṇḍita* Vasumati .. He was well-received by Atulyavajra and met rDo-rje-gdan-pa. He became a novice (attendant of rDo-rje-gdan-pa—Amoghavajra) and heard many doctrines. He then heard many Tāntrika doctrines from Śrī Bhadrasajjana, Vairocana .. After his return to Tibet... he secured more than a thousand golden *sraṅs*... After that he journeyed again to Nepal and obtained from Pham-mthiṅ-pa the Samvara-mūla-tantra and the gdan-bshi. After that he proceeded to India and offered to rDo-rje-gdan-pa a hundred golden *sraṅs*. He heard many doctrines at Nālandā from Dānaśīla, a disciple of Nāro-pā, Sumatikīrti, Rāmapāla, Natekara, the venerable Ratnadevī of Kaṃ-ka-ta, and from the *siddha* Sūryagarbha, a disciple of Kukuri-pā. He met also Maitrī-pā and obtained from him many Tantras, and offered him seven *sraṅs* of gold.' He is said to have met Ni-gu-mā, the sister of Nāro-pā, Lalitavajra, Āryadeva, *ḍāki* Sumati, *ḍākinī* Sukhasiddhi, a disciple of Virū-pā, Gaṅgādharā Samantabhadrī, Sukhavajra, Advayavajra, etc, and presented gold to 150 teachers. After his return to Tibet, he met Atīśa at mÑa'-ris. 'Some of his own Indian (Sanskrit) manuscripts being slightly damaged, he restored them after collating them with the manuscripts in Atīśa's possession.'

In Tg rG lxxiii.30 : 34 ; 36 ; 39-41 are mentioned as works exposed by Ni-gu-mā to Khyuṅ-po-rnal-'byor, *alias* Garuḍa-yogī or Garuḍa-bhaṭṭa. Tg lxxxii.104 is exposed by Maitrī-pā to him.

96. VANARATNA

BA ii. 797ff : 'The Precious Great *paṇḍita* was born [in 1384 A. D.—Roerich n] as the son of a king in the town of Sadnagara in eastern India [Chittagong District, East Bengal]. At the age of eight, he received the noviciate from one named Buddhaghoṣa.' At the age of 20, he received the final monastic ordination under Buddhaghoṣa and Sujātaratna. 'Then having become an ascetic he journeyed to Ceylon. He spent six years there.' Next he journeyed to Kaliṅga in southern India. 'There a great *paṇḍita* called Narāditya (*mi'i-ñi-ma*) famed as a scholar in Jambudvīpa praised him...Again he proceeded towards Śrī Dhānyakaṭaka Mahācaitya and stayed for some time in the hermitage of Nāgabodhi...Then while *en route* to Magadha, he studied with the heretical *paṇḍita* Harihara the book *kalāpa*.' In the *vihāra* called Uruvāsa 'a miraculous stone image of Ārya Avalokiteśvara spoke to him : "Go to Tibet ! After attending on a king, you will be of benefit to many !" In accordance with this prophecy, he first proceeded to Nepal...He reached Tibet in the year Fire-Male-Horse' (A. D. 1426 : Vanaratna is often called "Paṇḍita-mtha'-ma" or the Last Paṇḍita).

In Tg are preserved over 40 works written or translated by him. BA ii. 801 : he belonged to the lineage of Abhaya, Nāyakapāda. Daśabalaśrī, Śrībhadra, Lalitavajra, Dharmagupta, Ratnākara, Padmavajra, etc.

'Gos lo-tsā-ba, the author of the *Blue Annals*, was himself a student of Vanaratna (BA i. 380), about whom therefore 'Gos lo-tsā-ba shows the highest regard : 'He seems to have been the most popular among the paṇḍita-s who visited Tibet in later times' (BA ii. 802) and 'Therefore, he became our highest and only refuge' (BA ii. 805).

97. SAHAJA-SIDDHI

Tg contains a considerable number of works on Sahaja-siddhi. Thus :

Sahaja-siddhi by the king Indrabhûti. rG xlvii.1
Sahaja-siddhi-paddhati (commentary on the above) by Lakṣmīṅkarā. rG xlvii.2
Sahajānanda-dohākoṣa-gītikā-dṛṣṭi by Bhadhe (Bhāṇḍārin). rG xlviii.8
Sahaja-aṣṭaka by Maitrī-pā. rG xlvi.17
Sahaja-samvara-svādhiṣṭhāna by Mahā Śabara. rG xiii.5
Sahaja-samvara-svādhiṣṭhāna by rājā madhyama Indrabhūti. rG xiii.6
Sahaja-maṇḍala-traya-āloka-saṃjanana-nāma by Jñānaśrī. rG xiv.20
Sahaja-gīti by Śāntideva. rG xlviii.1
Sahaja-rati-saṃyoga by Ratnākaraśānti. rG xxi.28
Sahaja-ānanda-pradīpa-nāma-pañjikā by Vajragupta. rG xx.4
Sahaja-ananta-svabhāva by Kanthālin. rG xlviii.90
Sahaja-samvara-svādhiṣṭhāna by Tilo-pā. rG xiii.24
Sahaja-tattva-āloka by Kuśali-pā. rG xiii.55
Sahaja-āmnāya by ācārya Medinī. rG xlviii.76
Sahaja-yoga-krama by Ratnākaraśānti. rG xxi.29
Sahaja-sadyoga-vṛtti-garbhaprakāśikā-nāma by ācārya Thagana. rG xxi. 30
Sahaja-siddhi by Samayavajra. rG lxxiv. 28

98. THE TURUSKA KING "MOON" [FOL 125B]

[Note contributed by Harbans Mukhia]

It is nearly impossible to identify the owner of the name 'the Moon' with certainty, for no known name among the Turks mentioned in this context corresponds to this word. One could, however, stretch the meanings of some of the names and try to narrow the gap between them and the Moon. Shihab-ud-din Muhammad Ghori, for instance.

Minhaj-us-Siraj has included 'Adwand-Bihar' among the conquests of Shihab-ud-din. (*Tabaqat-i-Nasiri*, tr. H. G. Raverty, Vol. I, London, 1881, p. 491). 'Adwand-Bihar' is obviously a corrupt form of 'Odantapurī-vihāra' or 'Uddaṇḍapura-vihāra.' Considering that the word 'Shihab' means 'a bright star', (Steingass, *Persian-English Dictionary*, s.v.) it is possible that the reference to 'the Moon' might have been intended for him. Tāranātha's reference to the region of the 'Antaravedi' (Fol. 125B) is not very helpful either. Prof. S. C. Sarkar suggests that the reference might have been meant for either Shihab-ud-din or Qutb-ud-din Aibak, the word 'Qutb' signifying the pole-star. (S. C. Sarkar, 'Some Tibetan References to Muslim Advance into Bihar and Bengal and to the state of Buddhism thereafter', *Proceedings of the Indian Historical Records Commission*, vol. xviii, 1942, pp. 138-52, n. 10).

There could be little doubt, however, that the person who was directly responsible for the destruction of the Odantapurī and Vikramaśīla monasteries was Ikhtiyar-ud-din Muhammad bin Bakhtiyar Khalji, the dubious credit for whose accomplishment was passed on to his master Shihab-ud-din (certainly by Minhaj, probably also by Tāranātha). Odantapurī or Uddaṇḍapura was the ancient name of the city of Bihar or Vihāra and it was situated very close to Vikramaśīla. (A Cunningham, *Reports of the Archaeological Survey of India*, vol. viii, p. 75 ; also vol. xi, p. 185, where this point has been further reinforced. In vol. iii, pp. 128-29 Cunningham had suggested that Uddaṇḍapuradeśa was the name of a district and the place was the modern Tandwa, also called Bishenpur Tandwa where considerable Buddhist remains still exist). These monasteries were destroyed around 1203 A.D. (The date is inferred indirectly —see A.B.M. Habibullah, *The Foundation of Muslim Rule in India*, 2nd. edn., Allahabad, 1961, p. 84, notes 78 and 79). Tāranātha's account of this destruction largely tallies with the one given by Minhaj. (Minhaj, *op. cit.*, pp. 551-52). Minhaj had as his informants two of the 'holy warriors' who had themselves participated in the venture under the leadership of Ikhtiyar-ud-din Khalji and had shared the booty. The greater number of the inhabitants of Odantapurī were shaven-headed Buddhist monks whom Minhaj (and presumably his informants) mistook to be Brahmans. They were all slain. Minhaj, however, states that Ikhtiyar-ud-din and his companions had attacked the place under the impression that it was a fortress. It was only when they noticed books and became acquainted with their contents that they realized what they had destroyed were monasteries and libraries.

Tāranātha's allusion to 'the petty Turushka rulers of Bhaṃgala and other places' (Fol. 125B) raises an interesting question. While the king of Bengal at this time was Lakṣmaṇasena (Tāranātha's Labaṃsena ?), could it be that the Turks had already established themselves at some levels of administration and, on the arrival of Ikhtiyar-ud-din, got united, presumably under his leadership, and 'ran over the whole of Magadha ..' etc. ? There is no evidence to this effect from the other sources and Tāranātha's evidence, not fully reliable, is inadequate for arriving at so vital a conclusion. For, if true, this would suggest that the process of the establishment of the Turkish rule in Bengal stands exactly reverse to the similar process in North India, or indeed, the whole of India excluding Bengal. In North India the Turks captured and controlled only the higher echelons of administration, the lower ones being left almost entirely in the hands of the Hindus from the beginning to the end of the medieval period of Indian history. (Prof. S. C. Sarkar has drawn the following conclusion from Tāranātha's allusion which appears to be a little far-fetched : This reference to the existence of 'Turki Muslim puppet kings of Bhaṃgala [i.e. East Bengal] and other adjacent regions' [tr. Prof. Sarkar's] is an important revelation ; they evidently acknowledged the suzerainty of the Turushka power of Upper India. The question is how and when were these Muslim principalities founded : probably Turki adventurers seized the Arab-Persian [Tajik] trading settlements in the Gangetic ports and deltaic regions which could easily have come into existence in the preceding few centuries,—and these Turki adventurers would subsequently affiliate themselves to the main Turki state of Delhi in the same way as Md.-ibn-Bakhtiyar did. The Senas, as patrons of 'Tajiks' would, of course, tolerate these principalities as allies, [*op. cit.*, Fn 12]. Prof. Sarkar does not take into account the possibility that Tāranātha might have been misinformed). Tāranātha's mention of monks acting as the messengers of the Turks, if true, could similarly point to a very interesting line of inquiry into the social and political conditions of the region. The burden of available evidence, however, does not appear to support Tāranātha. (Prof. Sarkar similarly appears to read too much into this reference by Tāranātha : This Tibetan allusion raises the point whether the invasion of Bihar and Bengal, 1199-1203, was due only to the stray adventures of Md.-ibn-Bakhtiyar or was planned under the direct leadership of the Delhi kingdom in support of Buddhist Dissenters and of the Senas who patronized Islam and Brahmanical reaction against Buddhism. [*op. cit.*, Fn 10]).

99. ON HISTORY OF IMAGE-MAKERS

[Note contributed by Pranabranjan Ray]

Tāranātha's 'History of Image-makers' will remain a somewhat enigmatic source of information for the students of Indian art history. Myths and dogmas so shroud whatever he has recorded here that it becomes difficult to correlate his account with known historical facts and art objects at hand. In a sense the sections on arts and crafts in Ābul Fazl's *Āin-i-Ākbari*, though attempt to give less information in time-span, are much more dependable for their objectivity and understanding.

In the opening paragraph, Tāranātha says something about the human artists of the "ancient period" who flourished within about a hundred years of Buddha's *pari-nirvāṇa*. Archaeological evidence about art of the period referred to are conspicuous by their absence. Can Tāranātha's account be taken as a literary reference that fills up a gap in our knowledge ?

Tāranātha's naivette about stylistics makes it difficult to accept many of his assertions about the art styles removed from him in time-span. Tāranātha, for instance, extols the Yakṣas —as also the Nāgas and Devas—for having been successful in creating illusions of real objects. Excepting the Gandhāra art we know of no other art style that could be remotely called realistic.

Tāranātha's account assumes importance when he mentions the names of individual artists. For instance he speaks of an artist called Bimbasāra, during Buddhapakṣa's (a late Gupta ?) reign. It is of some significance, since we know that by the end of the Gupta period the unified style of the high classical art of the Gupta era was giving way to local variations, one of which the late R. D. Banerjee termed as the Eastern School of Gupta art.

Tāranātha mentions another sculptor called Srigadhari in the region of Maru, that is either Rajasthan or Gujarat. Till about the end of nineteenth century there had never been any art object in India which bore the impression of a purely individual style (with the possible exception of some paintings of a few masters like Mansur). So Srigadhari, was either a pioneer or an acknowledged master of a stylistic trend, which itself possibly evolved out of some older stylistic trend through certain innovations made by certain individual artist.

Of greater significance are the names of Dhīman and Bitpalo, the two artists, who flourished in Varendra during the reign of Devapāla and Dharmapāla, who were, by implication, the innovators of the Pāla idiom of sculpture and painting. But from the known examples of the Pāla period, sculptures and tempera paintings on wooden manuscript covers, it is very difficult to notice any difference between the father's and the son's stylistic structures. Tāranātha even mentions their engraving (!).

Tāranātha has perhaps rightly pointed out an affinity between Nepalese and western Indian art, even if one disagrees with his main contention about the decisive influence of the latter over the former. In absence of detailed information about the time and the sort of stylistic change Hasurāja brought about in Kashmiri art, it is not possible to vouch for the veracity of Tāranātha's statement about him.

Despite the various shortcomings of Tāranātha's history,—largely motivated by his sectarian zeal—Tāranātha has done one singular service to the historiography of Indian art. Tāranātha in this little chapter has concentrated his attention on high arts, which according to Stella Kramrisch's characterization are 'time-bound' arts, as against the folkish or 'time-less' art forms. These high arts, were essentially urban in origin and depended on the patronage of courts, reflecting the fashions and attitudes of the ages in which these were created. And as such, individual innovators and improvisers had great roles in the shaping and enrichment of these systems. Though each of these systems had to work within the framework of iconographic canons and certain other *a priori* canons of beauty etc., as also within the conventions set up by the individual systems themselves. Yet, within the systems individul artists could improvise and innovate unlike that in folkish modes. But unfortunately few texts have recorded the names of these innovators and improvisers.

APPENDIX

V. P. VASIL'EV AND A. SCHIEFNER ON TĀRANĀTHA'S HISTORY OF BUDDHISM IN INDIA

[In 1869 was published from St. Petersburg a German translation of *Vasil'ev's Introduction to Tāranātha's History of Buddhism in India* by A. Schiefner along with Schiefner's Foreword to it. In this Appendix is given Schiefner's *Foreword* first and then Vasil'ev's *Introduction*. The German Foreword is translated by Prof. Haridas Sinharay and Vasil'ev's Introduction is translated from the Russian original by Sri Harish Chandra Gupta.]

FOREWORD

To the Introduction of the Russian Translation of Tāranātha's History of Buddhism in India by Professor Wassiljew (Vasil'ev)

A. SCHIEFNER

Translated from the German by Professor Haridas Sinharay

During my journey through Berlin in June 1860, I presented a copy of the recently published German translation of Professor Wassiljew's *Buddhismus* Part I to Carl Friedrich Koeppen, who was already famous for his profound work on the religion of the Buddha. I received from him a highly original and complimentary letter, in which he expressed himself as follows:

> 'Please accept at least my thanks for your present which I hardly deserve and the seed of which falls upon a barren soil, inasmuch as for a full year I have completely given up my investigations into the Buddha and His Holiness and have given over my few Buddhist books to the dealers in antiquities. In spite of this and in spite of my reluctance, an old passion has swayed me to devour the work of Wassiljew. This has convinced me that I have so long written as a blind man does on colours and in this I am thoroughly convinced. I shall regard it as my last duty towards the Buddha and His Holiness to acknowledge this conviction openly, i.e. to prove to the best of my ability the profound significance of this work and the advancement in Buddhistic research which it shows in any of the critical journals like the *Brockhausschen Blaettern*, should my publisher take the trouble.'

I am not aware if this project has taken shape. However, I hold it as my duty to reiterate the judgement of this profound scholar who mentions in the letter his own work as a theory of the blind on colours. I had an opportunity to publish a few words on the work of Professor Wassiljew published by the Academy, and in this to mention my relation to his work. To begin with, I have, on January 7, 1854, reported in brief in the *Bulletin Hist. Phil.* (Vol xi.p.380) on the works on Buddhism discovered by Professor Wassiljew during his stay for ten years in Peking. I have already expressed my wish there that he should not delay any more the publication of Tāranātha's *History of Buddhism in India* written in the Tibetan language, along with his annotations and explanations worked out from Tibetan and Chinese sources. In the same month, I placed before the Academy a German translation of his highly learned article on the works relating to Buddhism in the University Library of Kazan (*Bulletin Hist. Phil.* Vol xi, pp.337-365). In my report on the above-mentioned work on Buddhism that I submitted on April 4, 1856 (*Bulletin Hist. Phil* Vol xiii, pp.348-352), I have clearly stated how the leading western scholars on ancient India—Lassen, Roth and Weber—could expect a widening of our knowledge of Buddhism from the scholarship of Wassiljew, and how the published work justified this expectation to a high degree. That is the reason why I immediately thought of bringing out an edition of this work in the French or the German language. After I had supervised and brought to an end the printing of the Russian edition in 1857 of this work, I prepared a literal French translation of it. However, this could not be published because of comments against its French style. Thus I held it all the more as my duty to persuade a noteworthy expert in ancient India to translate this work into German. The printing of this translation appeared in 1860 and has been supervised by me. In certain passages where a greater exactness was desired, I have to acknowledge entirely the services of Wassiljew.

As a continuation of this work, Professor Wassiljew placed before the Academy on April 19, 1866, his Russian translation of the History of Buddhism in India written by the Tibetan scholar Tāranātha at the beginning of the seventeenth century. This circumstance gave me the chance to publish the Tibetan original, the expenses for it being borne by the Academy. For editing this text I have collated four manuscripts. Two of these belong to our University Library, one—which is very corrupt—to the Asiatic Museum of the Academy of Sciences and the fourth to Professor Wassiljew. As I have clearly noted in the Latin Foreword to this edition of the text published in 1868, the Russian translation of Professor Wassiljew has served me substantially in the restoration of the correct reading of some of the corrupt passages.

With the editing of the Tibetan text, I simultaneously undertook a translation of the work in German. And as I had a Russian translation before me, I hope I have thereby profited by his knowledge. The printing of this translation I began simultaneously with the printing of the Russian translation, and could continue it uninterrupted till May 1868. I had, however, to wait for a full year for the publication as Professor Wassiljew had been hindered by other works to devote his energy to the printing of the Russian translation. Due to this delay, the world of learning has gained, inasmuch as it was possible for me to incorporate into my German translation as a supplement a major portion of the notes taken from the rich treasure of his studies in the Tibetan and Chinese literature on Buddhism, which Professor Wassiljew added during the printing of his translation.

I want to be fully clear about this in the present Foreword to his Introduction. If I have made this Foreword shorter than had been my original purpose and have taken a few notes on the life of Tāranātha from the Introduction of Professor Wassiljew's Russian translation, it is partly explained by the circumstance that I planned to publish my German translation as a commemoration of the 550th Jubilee of the Ritter und Domschule at Reval, on June, 19. And thus it was that the content of the Russian Introduction could not be given in detail. On the express wish of Professor Wassiljew who lays quite rightly a special worth on his Introduction, I hold it as my duty to take up the publication of the same in the form of a postscript in order that I may be nearer the points in which I have differed from him.

A. Schiefner

St. Petersburg,
September 30, (October 12), 1869.

INTRODUCTION

TO THE RUSSIAN TRANSLATION OF TĀRANĀTHA'S HISTORY OF BUDDHISM IN INDIA

V. P. VASIL'EV

Translated from the Russian by Sri Harish Chandra Gupta

The learned world—better than us—will evaluate the merits of this work translated by me, though *prima facie* it is not going to meet the expectations that its high-sounding title holds : *History of Buddhism in India.* Tārānātha's account is not a faithful exposition of something unknown. As it is, it rather needs a tremendous amount of investigation and explanation. It is merely some new material which can put off the spark of doubts and perplexities, which, considering the present state of our knowledge of Buddhism, can hardly be extinguished altogether. We are, however, sure that the learned world will not refuse either to collate or to annotate and investigate this material, for it will be in a better position than ourselves.

These remarks about the inadequacy of Tāranātha concern, of course, the early centuries of Buddhism, about which we know much even from other sources. However, we are sure that the learned world will pay attention to the fact that whatever the period in which the Buddha might have lived—a thousand years and odd before Christ as the Chinese think, or two or more as the Tibetans think—in the whole span of this period, in all the Buddhist accounts—or better, legends—we find the same personalities and the same events. And now, when we have before us a full survey of this History by Tāranātha—for which the learned world would find it easier than ourselves to give a fairly definite or at least an approximate chronology—it turns out, if Tāranātha is to be trusted, that this history did not begin so many years before our era. We are sure that the scholars will not ignore our note that there hardly existed two

Aśokas, for it was not Kālāśoka but Dharmāśoka, the builder of monuments and the acknowledged patron of Buddhism, who lived, as generally admitted 116 years after the Buddha. We can hardly say anything about the assumption that by the well-known Piyadasi is meant Aśoka and not Ajātaśatru, whom our author calls 'Gifted with Auspicious Vision' (mthoṅ-ldan-dge-ba : *kṣemadarśin*).[1] In that case, it would be necessary to recollect the legend of the well-known drama of Virūdhaka, the companion of Sandrakotta and the murderer of Artha-siddha (as Śākyamuni was called) and who, according to the Buddhist legends appears as the annihilator of all the Śākyas. Besides in the Chinese text on Nirvāṇa, Ajātaśatru consults Śākyamuni for a war with *Yue-ci*-s, in which, because of wrong understanding of Chinese texts from the so-called Tibet minor, one must see a corruption of either the word for Greeks or Bactrians (under a general and most ancient name Yakṣa ?). Since in Tāranātha's account, instead of two Aśokas there appear two Kaniṣkas, of whom the latter has of course a better claim to historicity, it can be shown that the well-known kieu-tsieu-kio is rather not Kaniṣka but Aśoka, who conquered all lands west of the Indus and built monuments there and whom our author does not at all link with Ajātaśatru. This of course he would not have done for the reason that for a Buddhist it would be more pleasant to consider the noble king related to the patron of the founder of the Doctrine (probably some data were available for this purpose).[2] Then, even the appearance in Kuśavana of Dhītika—having greater claim to contemporaneity with Aśoka than Upagupta—would have given some grounds for consideration.

In general the scholars will elucidate better than us the question as to whether the Buddhist account has an archaeological and antiquarian aspect, besides having the

1. Sum-pa in his *History* calls him simply "gifted with vision" (mthoṅ-ldan).
2. Sum-pa also takes the name Tharu for that of a tribe which Aśoka came from.

legendary one. In other words, on the expiry of a long time after its foundation, when attempts began to be made to explain this foundation, did the Buddhists not encounter the Greek accounts of their previous connections with India ? Did they not come across the monuments left by the linc of Piyadasi—the significance of which could be understood also by them as obscurely as by the present scholars—and did they not try to link their account with all these ?[3]

Similarly, we shall not undertake to decide as to what authenticity should be ascribed to Tāranātha's account of the later appearance of Pāṇini. According to the general tone of Buddhism, this date would not appear to be a later one, for the use of the script unknown to him in the beginning could not have been mastered by him later than others—because the religion itself required it. The scholars will not, of course, ignore [without proper attention] Tāranātha's legend of Aśoka's sending a letter to the Nāga-s. They will judge better than ourselves whether or not one should see in this legend the impression which the importance of reading and writing (hitherto unknown to them)—which has the power to order the return of the seized treasures—might have created on the people. The scholars also, of course, know what power, in the mystic teaching, the letters of alphabet—their contemplative movement, their absorption inside oneself—have. It is left to them to decide whether this again is not due to the first acquaintance with reading and writing—which to the Indians, though unfamiliar with it, but much advanced in thought and civil development—must have appeared in its time, a more remarkable invention than wireless to the present-day crowd, which they credit to supernatural power.

3. Generally speaking, Ajātaśatru, Aśoka and Kaniṣka appear before us in the same light. All of them patronised (Buddhism), built monuments and monasteries.—which nevertheless judging from the initial asceticism of the Buddhists, could not have appeared either under the first or the second king. All the three took part in convening Councils while the same history represents them elsewhere as not having taken part in these events. This raises doubt even about the historicity of the Councils themselves (i.e. at least of the first two).

As regards the non-Buddhist personalities included by Tāranātha in his account, we must make one general remark. The author has not done so on purpose ; they had to appear in the legends (or biographies) of those Buddhist personalities with whom they had some connections. Buddhism is not at all alien to historiography because it found in history a means for its own exaltation. The general character of the peoples of the East, who even today believe in the personality of the Chinese emperors (who officially announce miracles taking place in their empires) and who believe in everything miraculous, provided the Buddhists with an opportunity to convert history into legend—a fact that has always been of use to religion. There is not a single famous Lama or Hoshang now who dies without his biography being written or his sayings recorded. But this is so from the very beginning of Buddhism. We have legends not only about persons who lived in the period most close to that of Śākyamuni but also about those who have lived much later. Probably, in their time, these individual legends were far too many. Though our author mentions that he has drawn not upon the legends about individual persons but upon whole histories, it is now seen from the tone of his exposition that even these histories from which he took material were compiled from various individual biographies. From the language and tone, it is now clear that this work includes biographies written in their time in different schools with different beliefs and notions. It can also be noticed that the biography of a much later person was written earlier than that of another who might have lived earlier. Anyone—whatever his acquaintance with the Buddhist legends—can see this from the tone and subject-matter of the legend and its language. The question as to how these should be identified in a history compiled by one person is very simple : the Eastern writers never try to pass on anything read by them in their own words ; the earliest text, as originally written, is reproduced *in toto* from one work to another.

By this, we do not at all mean to say that the legends given by Tāranātha have reached us without any interpolation. On the contrary, these must be seen from various angles. We should not forget that our history is written in Tibet, which imported Buddhism in its stage of latest development, i.e. mysticism called Tantras. That is why not only the Mahāyāna but also Hīnayāna personalities are here mostly Tāntrikas. This does not prevent one from seeing various strata of legends on the earliest soil of the ancient texts. Thus, Aśvaghoṣa, a protagonist of Hīnayāna, is converted first into a Mahāyānist and then into a Tāntrika. We may nevertheless remark that by Tāntrika legends we do not mean the miraculous as such ; miraculous stories appear no less in Hīnayāna.

Another legendary aspect lies in the tendency to carry everything to antiquity ; the facts of a later period are attributed to a remote period. For example, the author begins the history of mysticism from a period almost contemporary to Nāgārjuna. The actual appearance of personalities, who have published some work on mysticism, is almost always preceded by a reference to a person who was supposed to be acquainted with this work. But this too is typical not of mysticism alone. The whole Buddhist literature, for instance, was so compiled. The mystics, passing their Tantras for something preached by the Buddha, at least do not conceal the fact of their later appearance in the world. We can even determine, approximately though, the very period of their appearance, if we can follow the method of fabricating their legends. However, about the Mahāyāna works, we only know that Nāgārjuna brought to light the Prajñā-pāramitā, though it is not known in which redaction.

The author also mentions the time of the appearance of the *Aṣṭa-sāhasrikā-prajñā-pāramitā*. By comparing the Mahāyāna literature in Chinese and Tibetan, we can also infer that Maitreya's works did not appear at the same time. Nevertheless, the Mahāyāna literature that have come down to us in Chinese and Tibetan translations are enormous ; when did all these works appear ? The only thing that can be asserted by us is that according to the data available to us—and as per remarks just made by us on Tāranātha—the fabrication of Mahāyāna works attributed to the Buddha continued until Mahāyāna itself was overcome by mysticism. Besides many canonical Mahāyāna works were written when several commentaries had already been produced on each of the other works that had appeared earlier. The same can be said of the Hīnayāna works ; their redactions changed continually. Thus the Tibetan Vinaya is not what the Vinayas of all the four schools known in Chinese translation are.

Not to speak of the Abhidharmas, even the Sūtras were subjected to change. We have indications that 800 years after the death of the Buddha there was a collection of works of the Sammitīya school. Probably the other schools also did not lag behind.

Our main concern, however, is the question of the literature. With the classics before us, there is a possibility of following and analysing critically the sequence in which the works appeared and even the reasons for their appearance. All this would not obstruct the understanding of Tāranātha, more so because his *History* is full of the names of works attributed to the Buddha as well as with works of other individuals. But this has to be left to the work of future scholars.

While reading Tāranātha, we must be aware also of the same tendency to carry back to antiquity even the names of places and persons.

The main historical merit of Tāranātha's work indisputably is that this work acquaints the learned world for the first time with personalities totally unknown till now and with those from a period which can unmistakably be called "historical". If this period cannot be so considered from the time of Nāgārjuna, it can in any case begin from the time of Ārya Asaṅga. The span of time covered by this period till that of the total extinction of Buddhism from the Madhya-deśa should be assumed to be more than a thousand years. Till now we know practically nothing about this period, particularly about all that had happened after the visit of the famous Yuan-chuang who also alludes to various personalities.

The learned world would, we think, compare the suggestions of Yuan-chuang with Tāranātha's account, establish identity between persons mentioned perhaps under different names by both the authors, and thus facilitate the study of this period. We know for the first time only from Tāranātha about the sequence in which the most notable ones accepted Buddhism, the names of their patrons and enemies and the trends of their theological activities. It is not for us to suggest to the learned world that if the Siddha-s represented by our author as enwrapped in legends—that appear ridiculous to us—be unmasked, they will turn out to be workers, writers, etc, though traversing a totally new path purified from the one followed earlier by the other leading Buddhists. We speak of mysticism in its full and extraordinary development as the so called principles of meditation.

The information communicated by Tāranātha on this period has all the appearance of authenticity. He knows the scholarly method of ascertaining the relative period of a particular person from his works and from the references to him by others. Probably in this case the account used by him had, as their sources, individual biographies. We do not know what the learned world will surmise from these legends for a history of India of that period, but it will nevertheless make use of Tāranātha's account. Perhaps Tāranātha's last chapter alone—that on the artists—will be regarded as a great contribution redeeming all other shortcomings of his *History*.

As regards the period preceding Ārya Asaṅga, one must treat it with a greater caution. If from the account of the later period we note for instance how the legends about Ārya Asaṅga, Vasubandhu or Guṇaprabha as given by Tāranātha differ from those given by Yuan-chuang, and how the ones given by the latter vary from those in the still earlier sources,—what then should we surmise about the legends pertaining to a more remote period ?

If our comment that Nālandā which later became so famous

had been an insignificant place at the time of Fa-hien is justified, what should one think of the anecdotes which Tāranātha links with this place alone ? And these fancies of Tāranātha automatically lead one to think whether similar accounts of other places and personalities should not be looked upon with the same distrust. We see for example that Nālandā claims all the celebrities of Buddhism. Even Vasubandhu, Ārya Asaṅga and Nāgārjuna had to live there. This is fully refuted by the other documents. We clearly see from this work of Tāranātha that the monasteries tried to link their legends with well-known personalities. That is why the biographies of the latter take them from one place to another. And Tāranātha repeatedly refers to the founding and restoration of religious centres. If so, how can one avoid doubting that Śāriputra and Maudgalyāyana, in whose birthplace Nālandā was built, were direct disciples of Śākyamuni ? More so, because the well-known Abhidharmas are attributed to them. This further leads one to assume that they could have been born in the north-western India, the home of the Abhidharmas. This fact alone leads to many historical absurdities. The names of these teachers are closely linked with the works attributed to the Buddha. In almost each of these—even including the Hīnayāna works—one of them is either putting questions to the Buddha or teaching in his stead. This means that we must look from a different angle at the redaction of these very works. The dogma founded in these is concerned with a local problem — so much so that what the work frequently has in view is not the dogma but the place and the person concerned. Again, the very facts about the place where the Buddha attained enlightenment,—the famous Vajrāsana,—the time of the building of the Mahābodhi image, the place of the abode of Kapila (which the well-known great Tibetan scholar places at some point further to the west) are doubtful. If in investigating the possible origin of the legends about Śāriputra and Maudgalyāyana, by examining all the places and chronological points, we come to the conviction—or at least to the assumption—that these teachers, who had actually lived much later, had to be dated by the followers to the earliest possible period, we surmise that Buddhism moved not from east to west but in the reverse direction.

In any case, when as a result of the spread of the written language (for which Tāranātha mentions the approximate period too), Buddhism took to recording its history, it had already digressed from its original character. Having spread over a vast area, it continued in many places in the form of monastic life, which presupposed statutes and legends. This resulted in diversity and discord, though not in the form in which it is represented by the Buddhists. This would rather give some grounds for agreement and reconciliation which was expressed in the basic similarity of the directions of the Vinaya as well as in the tradition of the original teachings of the Buddha and in its subsequent fate. We think that we cannot look on ancient Buddhism except through the prism of the so-called Third Council—historically the first in our opinion—and again one held in the west!

And so Tāranātha's *History* is not a history as such but only a document which calls for further research into history and provides for this some remarkable and rare facts. Besides, this *History* becomes all the more valuable as it gives the hope of discovering still more ancient histories. We already know from Yuan-chuang that neither historiography nor a description of the country was unknown to the Indians. Tāranātha positively refers to three hitherto unknown historical works compiled veritably in India. There is no doubt that these will be searched out. If the author had them at his disposal at the beginning of the 17th century, they could not have become extinct thereafter. These are to be searched for not only in Tibet but also in Nepal. It is a pity that our scholars have not so far known what to look for, or the scholars going there were not learned enough.

It will not be out of place to mention that the rare honour of acquainting the academic world with Tāranātha fell to our lot almost unexpectedly. At a time when we had just taken up the study of Oriental languages at Kazan, one Lama Nikituyev

—who had come in 1835 from Transbaikal—was the first person to inform our most respected and well-known Professor, O. M. Kovalevsky, of the existence of this history. The manuscript itself was soon procured from the Kalmuk steppes. As Professor Kovalevsky was not good at Tibetan, Lama Nikittuyev (with whom we used to live for our practice in Mongolian language) translated, right before us, the entire work of Tāranātha into Mongolian language for our honourable professor. We were absolutely sure that the honour of acquainting the academic world with this work would sooner or later go to this professor of ours. The idea of superceding him did not even occur to us, not only because we were aware of the gap between his and our capabilities, but also because it would have been extremely indelicate and too ungracious of us to go ahead of a scholar who was going to honour us by taking the lead. Another factor that weighed with us was that in Mongolian language we possessed then few—or almost none—monumental works that it would have been sinful to snatch away this material from the hands of our professor.

Therefore, on arrival in Peking in 1840, when we easily procured a Tibetan copy of Tāranātha (and showed it to father Avvakum, who brought the copy for the Asiatic Department),[4] we did not at all think of making a complete translation of this whole work. We made only some brief excerpts for personal use,—which we tried to supplement in the course of our subsequent studies, though only for a knowledge of the subject and not for publication. It was only in the last year of our stay in Peking,—when we had already compiled a lexicon of the Dogma, the *Mahāvyutpatti,* made translations of (the treatise on the) various sects, surveyed the Buddhist literature and system,—that we realised that all these works together with the translation of Yuan-chuang made by us in 1842 were not

4. This is what *paying attention* is ! One may pass by rare works and not know their worth ! Professor Kovalevsky had also been in Peking. Because of his acquaintance with Minjnl Khukutu (whom we did not find alive any more), it would have been easier for him to procure all sorts of histories, had he only known their Tibetan titles.

by themselves adequate (for our purpose) without the history of Tāranātha. It was then that we started making a complete translation of Tāranātha, though without the slightest idea of getting it published. This is also seen from the first part of our *Buddhism*—though, from a different aspect—where, with a long list of the contents of Tāranātha's work, we seem to have asked of the learned world the question: "Does this work deserve to be translated in full ?"

Although at the time of our stay for ten years in Peking, we made a comprehensive study of Buddhism from the Chinese and Tibetan sources, and prepared many works,—which we hoped to finalise on our return to Russia with the help of European sources and European scholars,—we, on our return, got an absolutely different assignment which diverted us from Buddhism. Besides, our colleagues were so little interested in this subject that when, because of the truly learned participation of Mr. Schiefner, the first volume of our work on Buddhism was published, the criticism in Russia was considerably colder than in the foreign press. Only when our *Buddhism* was translated into French (though not without mistakes, as in the German translation) and we saw that even after a decade of its publication, our work was often arousing the interest of scholars, who nonetheless continued to refer to it and draw materials from it, did we think of our previous works lying in abeyance. In particular, when there started appearing references even to Tāranātha from whom we had only quoted some short extracts, it naturally occurred to us that it would be better to publish the whole of Tāranātha's work. These were the ideas expressed by us in our well-known letter to Schiefner—printed in *St. Petersburg News* (No. 141 of May, 26 1866).

There was now hardly any hope of Professor Kovalevsky publishing his translation from the Mongolian. It was almost fifteen years he had left the faculty. Besides, when we now took up this work, we realised what it meant to publish Tāranātha in a manner worthy of the learned world and that our learned professor (Kovalevsky) did not wish to risk his reputation by publishing it in the form in which we are doing.

True, a scholarly treatment of the history of Buddhism demanded not only a good study of all that had been written in Europe but a much more profound study of all the Buddhist works. We fully admit that we do not fulfil these prerequisites and are no more than mere translators. We cannot even vouchsafe that our translation is throughout faultless. The few translations from the Tibetan that have so far appeared in Europe are largely those of the Buddhist Sūtras—which are not so difficult in language and the translations of which could be checked either with their Sanskrit originals or with other translations available in the Chinese and Mongolian languages. Any one studying the Tibetan text of Tāranātha published by Mr. Schiefner will well understand that the language here is considerably different, for the understanding of which there exists an entirely different grammar totally unknown to Europe and for which the lexicons published so far are inadequate. Above all, nothing can be done if one does not really know what is discussed and what is not discussed by Tāranātha !

Besides, we must confess that we did not make the resumption of the study of Buddhism or the continuation of the work started a prerequisite for our wish to publish Tāranātha. This would have diverted us from our immediate responsibilities and would have opened the perspectives of a never-ending labour which, with our present resources, was hardly possible. Hence we are setting some limits and wish to publish only what has already been done. We will consider it a great honour for ourselves and be fully satisfied if we are able to publish all our materials relating to Buddhism even in the form in which it is at present available to us. Now, with the return of Mr. Minaev, who has in Europe made a study of Buddhism from Pali sources, one can hope for the better. But at present nothing can be said of the future. As regards the present work, we must admit frankly and unreservedly that this publication would never have been possible without the participation of Academician Schiefner. The very restoration of Sanskrit proper names would have been impossible for us without him. Besides, the translation made by us was written in free hand and at a time when we had no Tibetan teacher to help us. Some unavoidable slips, therefore, crept in. Besides there are lacunae where the text could not be clearly read or the literal translation seemed absurd.

Mr. Schiefner was the first to set upon the task of publishing the Tibetan text by collating the few manuscripts available in St. Petersburg. And if we can say without vanity,—and Mr. Schiefner will agree (let us hope)—that in many places, our Russian translation served him as an important handbook for publishing the text as well as his translation into German, we must also say—not out of sheer false courtesy—that we have been checking our own translation with the text published by Mr. Schiefner and with his translation printed before ours. Else, our mistakes would have been too many. If at certain places, our translation varies from the German translation, we have retained our version largely for future research and consideration of the learned scholars. In our translation, we did not stick everywhere to literal accuracy. To express the ideas of the author more clearly, we have made some additions in parentheses. We must also, therefore, remark that Mr. Schiefner's translation is marked by greater accuracy. Whatever the case may be, we nonetheless must mention to our readers—and the whole European academic world will, of course, agree—that taking into consideration the present knowledge and resources of the European scholars, Tāranātha's work could be translated at present in our St. Petersburg alone.

We are not after fame and popularity and would, therefore, have easily refused to get our translation of Tāranātha published in the Russian language. Schiefner's German translation rendered it only an extra luxury. But we had regard not only for the Russian sentiment, which wanted that everything published in Russia and with Russian money should be in Russian, but also for the fact that Tāranātha's translation would be a tremendous manual for our missionaries to whom this book could give the best idea of the weak side of the Buddhists, of all their absurdities, of all the distortions made by them in their own religion and of all trash passed on by them as sacred. Of no little use will be the legends quoted in this work to the research scholars on folk-literature in general.

With Schiefner's German translation before us—as we have already mentioned—we have added Schiefner's notes to our translation. Whatever we have added on our own behalf has been done only to make the sense of the translation more intelligible. Nevertheless, in many places, particularly in the account of mystic subjects, the translation still remains obscure. In fact, we intended to give a detailed exposition of the whole Tāntric system because of the newness of the subject in a special article which would have also served as a commentary.

Besides, we also wanted to take this opportunity of putting, in form of appendices, the surveys compiled by us earlier of the Vinaya, Hīnayāna, Yogācāra and Mādhyamika literature —though only in the form in which these were available to us. We also found an old translation of Bhavya on the Hīnayāna schools. To all these, we are sure, the learned world would have given the same indulgence as given earlier to the appendices in the first volume of our *Buddhism*. But since all these additions would have occupied a considerable space besides holding up the very printing of even the German translation of Tārapātha's work—which Mr. Schiefner, with his characteristic sense of modesty, has already held up for a whole year,—we propose to bring these out in the form of a separate monograph.

We must, however, now voice our reservations on some characteristics of the language of translation. First of all, it must be mentioned that the Tibetans often translate into their language not only the dogmatic terms but also the proper names of persons and places. It is only rarely that the real Indian names are also given (in their Indian form). This had to be one big hurdle in the work of the translation. The best thing would have been to translate these proper names also into

Russian : if any scholar happens to come across any name in Sanskrit original, he could, from our translation, guess to whom the reference was. But there lies the rub : the proper names cannot always be translated with accuracy, particularly into our language.

Nevertheless, we have, before us, many Sanskrit words in Tibetan translation. It may be remarked that the Tibetans always translate the same term by certain fixed words. One can, therefore, reconstruct the original Indian name more or less accurately. However, it is possible to depend upon the experience and skill of Mr. Schiefner who undertook this important task. It is our duty to mention this so that the scholars are not faced with any difficulty. As for us, we have tried always to append the original Tibetan words in case of the proper names.

Some scholars will perhaps deem inappropriate the use by us of certain words borrowed from the language of our orthodox religion : for instance, *dukhovnye* [for *saṃgha*-s], *posvyashchenie* [consecration], *blagoslovenie* [blessing] etc. But when a scholar comes across, in the language of another—even heathen—religion, synonymous words, he cannot escape the duty to convey the meaning and the spirit of the author accurately. A scholarly translation is not meant to attract the layman.

Certain Russian words have been used by us in an absolutely new sense. For example. we are always writing : *tri sosuda** [lit. three caskets] in the sense of the three types of Buddhist works. Some scholars do not translate, this term and use the original Sanskrit word *tripiṭaka*. The Tibetans and the Chinese, however, always translate it into their language ; the Sanskrit word would have hardly been understood in Russian. It properly means : three "chests", "baskets", "reservoirs", etc., for it is seen that each type of works, in its time, comprised a "special treasure". It appeared odd to us to translate this term into Russian by the words *tri koroba* or *tri korziny*, for these words do not express the reverence that the Buddhists have for their term.

Another word often used by us is *sovershenie*, *sovershat'* in the sense of attaining a certain supernatural power or calling [propitiating] a certain spirit or deity. Our verb *vyzvat'* [*lit.* to call], we think does not fully express the sense of the Buddhist word. This word does not indicate that "calling" or "attaining" is the consequence of a certain procedure subjected to certain conditions, customs, even continued efforts of spirit and body. This, it appeared to us, is rather expressed by the verb *sovershat'*. The Tibetans and the Chinese convey this sense by using the equivalent words : *siddhi*, *sādhana*, etc. As regards the usual oddities of the language of translation, we feel that these are unavoidable in a translation from the language of subjects which are not very much in vogue in the world of scholarship. In his preliminary draft translation, the translator first sees not to the purity of the syllable but to the accuracy of translation. He tries not to say anything more or less than what is intended by the author. But later, on examining his translation, he is afraid of making any corrections so that he may not damage the sense for the sake of clarity. In our translation, many scholars will of course find many places vague, incomplete and indistinct. But this was not always due to the lack of knowledge of the language. On the contrary, this demanded greater skill because often the authors also express themselves vaguely. In the oriental languages in particular the native writers are not well acquainted with our etymological and syntactical structure.

Now a few words on Tāranātha himself. This name is not very well known among the Lamas. It is known to us more from the time of Urgin rJe-btsun Dam-pa Khutuktu, the incarnation of Tāranātha. Despite this, however, we have very scanty data on the first of all these *Khutuktu*-s. As we shall see, Tāranātha gives the number of years that had passed since his birth when he wrote his work. This year, the Earth-Monkey year,—according to Sum-pa-mkhan-po's "Chronological Table" (available in his "History of Buddhism"),—corresponds to

A.D. 1608. The year of birth, the Wood-Pig year, corresponds to A.D. 1575. From these very tables, we know that the personal name of Tāranātha was Kun-dga'-sñiṅ-po. Properly speaking, this is all that we know of Tāranātha. We do not know whether there is any separate biography of his. However, it is true that there exists a biography of rJe-btsun Dam-pa, which certainly must be containing an account of Tāranātha. But in spite of all our efforts, we could not procure it.

Why Tāranātha is little known among the Lamas of the present day can be explained by the antagonism of the dominant Yellow-cap (dge-lugs-pa) sect of dga'-ldan [monastery] of Tibet and Mongolia—founded by Tsoṅ-kha-pa—towards all other schools or sects formed in Tibet. Tāranātha belonged to one such school called Jo-naṅ, from the place Jo-mo-naṅ. This school had built up a monastery, which gave asylum to one Dolvupa (? grol-grub-pa) who had quit the Sa-skya-pa followers and developed, in his work Ri-chos-ṅes-don-rgya-mtsho, the fundamental teaching of this school about special emptiness (gshan-stoṅ). Although Tsoṅ-kha-pa himself heard the Kālacakra and the Pāramitās from one of the pupils of this Dolvupa and a pupil of this pupil, the theory of special emptiness was refuted by all the Yellow-cap scholars. After Tsoṅ-kha-pa, however, the Jo-naṅ follower Kun-dga'-grol-mchog and particularly his incarnation (skye-ba) Tāranātha—according to the history of Tibetan schools—spread the teaching of this school. The monastery rTag-brtan-phun-tshogs-gliṅ was founded, images were installed, blocks were prepared for the printing of most of Jo-naṅ books. Under the patronage of Rin-spuṅs of Kar-ma-bstan-skyoṅ-dbaṅ-po, the strength of this school doubled. But when the power of Rin-spuṅs declined,—it is said,—that after the death of Tāranātha, the Fifth Dalai Lama converted the Jo-naṅ monasteries into Yellow-cap ones and sealed the blocks. As a result, of the works of Jo-naṅ teaching, only two works of Tāranātha—the *Siddhānta* and *History of Buddhism*—are now known.

To this small piece of information of Tāranātha himself, we can add a little more from the same history of the school. "In

Khal-kha[5], the king (Khan ?) Usutai, after seeing the third Dalai Lama, founded the monastery of Erdeni-Jobo. The son of his grandson Tushiet-khan was an incarnation of Tāranātha—rJe-btsun Dam-pa blo-bzaṅ-bstan-pa'i-rgyal-mtshan, the jewel of Khal-kha, who had earned great honours from the Manchurian Emperor (Kang-hi). He founded the monastery Ri-bo-dge-rgyas-gliṅ and the number of his incarnations has not come to an end now." It is known that the incarnations of Urgin *khutuktu*-s must be looked for in Tibet, the home of Tāranātha.

April 4, 1869 V. Vasil'ev

5. The native name of Mongolia Proper, the country of Jenghis-khan, lit. the sacred enclosure of Khal-kha ; the name applied to Urga in Northern Mongolia, where the incarnation of the Tāranātha Lama resides. The latter is sometimes styled Khal-kha-rje-btsun-ḍam-pa, the Venerable Holy One of Khal-kha : D 143.—Ed. note.

BIBLIOGRAPHY

BA : *The Blue Annals*. The *Deb-ther-shon-po* of 'Gos lo-tsā-ba, translated by G. N. Roerich. 2 vols. Calcutta 1949 & 1953,

Basham, A. L. *History and Doctrine of the Ājivikas*. London 1951.

Beal, S. *Buddhist Records of the Western World*. London 1884.

Bongard-Levin, G. M. & Volkhova, O. F. *The Kuṇāla Legend and an Unpublished Aśokāvadāna Manuscript*. Calcutta 1965.

Bu-ston, *A History of Buddhism*. Translated by E. E. Obermiller. 2 parts. Heidelberg 1931-2.

Chattopadhyaya, A. *Atiśa and Tibet*. Calcutta 1967.

Cordier, P. *Catalogue du fonds tibetain de la bibliotheque Nationale. 2 e partie. Index du bsTan-' gyur*. Paris 1909-15.

Das, S. C. *A Tibetan-English Dictionary*. Reprint Calcutta 1960.

Dutt, N, *Aspects of Mahāyāna Buddhism and its Relation to Hīnayāna*. London 1930

— *Early Monastic Buddhism*. Calcutta 1960.

ERE : *Encyclopaedia of Religion and Ethics*.

Filliozat, J, *Studies in Aśokan Inscriptions*. Translated by R. K Menon Calcutta 1967.

Fa-hien—see Legge.

HB : *History of Bengal*. Vol i, Dacca 1943.

IA : *Indian Antiquary*

IHQ : *Indian Historical Quarterly*.

I-Tsing—see Takakusu.

JAIH : *Journal of Ancient Indian History*. CU.

Jaschke, H. A. *A Tibetan-English Dictionary*. London 1958 ed.

JASB : *Journal of the Asiatic Society of Bengal*.

Keith, A. B. *A History of Sanskrit Literature*. Oxford 1928.

Kushan Studies in USSR. Calcutta 1970.

Lalou, M. *Répertorie du Tanjur d'apres le catalogue de P. Cordier*. Paris 1932.

Legge, J. *A Record of Buddhist Kingdoms*. Being an account by the Chinese Monk Fa-hien of his travels in India and Ceylon (A, D. 399-414) in search of Buddhist Books and Discipline. New York 1965 ed.

Monier-Williams, M. *A Sanskrit-English Dictionary*. Oxford 1899.

Mahāvyutpatti. (Asiatic Society edition).

Nanjio, B. *A Catalogue of Chinese translation of the Buddhist Tripitaka, the sacred canon of the Buddhists in China and Japan*. Oxford 1833.

Przyluski, J. *The Legend of Emperor Aśoka in Indian and Chinese Texts*. Translated by Dilip Kumar Biswas. Calcutta 1967.

Ramanan K. Venkata. *Nāgārjuna's Philosophy as presented in the Mahāprajñāpāramitā-śāstra.* Tokyo 1966.

Roerich, G. N. *Selected Works* (Izbrannye Trudy), Moscow 1967, —see also BA.

Rockhill, W. W. *Life of Buddha.* London 1907.

Sachau, E. C. *Alberuni's India.* Reprint New Delhi 1964.

SBE : *Sacred Books of the East.*

Sankrityayana, R. *Purātattva-nivandhābali* (in Hindi). Allahabad.

Sastri, N. S. *Bāhyārtha-siddhi.* Sikkim 1967.

Sastri, H. P. *Prācina-bāṅgalāra-gaurava* (in Bengali). Calcutta 1963.

Schiefner, *A. Tāranātha's Geschichte des Buddhismus in Indien.* (Tr of Tāranātha's *History* in German). St Petersbug 1869,

—(ed) *Tāranātha'i rGya-ga -chos-'byuṅ.* (Tāranātha's Tibetan text). St Petersburg 1868.

Schlagintweit, E. *Buddhism in Tibet.* London 1863.

Sendai Cat : *A Complete Catalogue of the Tibetan Buddhist Canons, edited by Hakuju, Ui and others.* Sendai 1934.

Sircar, D. C. *Cosmography and Geography in Early Indian Literature.* Calcutta 1967.

Stcherbatsky, Th. *Buddhist Logic.* 2 vols Leningrad 1930-32.

— *Conception of Buddhist Nirvāṇa.* Leningrad 1927.

Takakusu, J, *A Record of the Buddhist Religion as Practised in India and the Malay Archipelago by I-Tsing.* Reprint Delhi 1966.

2500 Years of Buddhism. ed P. V. Bapat. New Delhi 1956.

Vasil'ev (Wassiljew), N. P. *Tāranātha's History of Buddhism in India* (in Russian translation). [*Buddizm : Ego Dogmaty, Istoriya I Literatura.* Pt III—Istoriya Buddizma v Indii, Sochinenie Daranaty.] St Petersburg 1869.

Vidyabhusana, S. C. *History af Indian Logic.* Calcutta 1921.

Watters, T. *On Yuan Chwang's (Yuan-chuang's) Travels in India. (A. D. 629-645).* Reprint Delhi 1961.

Winternitz, M. *A History of Indian Literature.* Vol. ii, Calcutta 1933.

INDEX

[Tāranātha's text only]

I. TEXTS

Abhidharma-dhātukāya-pāda-śāstra 94n
Abhidharmakoṣa 88n, 94n, 174, 181, 212, 227
—bhāṣya-ṭīkā Tattvārtha-nāma 181n
—śāstra-kārikā-bhāṣya 167n, 168n
—mahā-vibhāṣā-śāstra 94n, 96n
Abhidharma-piṭaka 89, 190, 201
—prakaraṇa-pāda-śāstra 94n
—samuccaya 160
Abhiniṣkramaṇa-sūtra 19
Abhisamaya-alaṃkāra 159n, 160-1, 188-9, 191
—vṛtti Piṇḍārtha 295n
Acintya-kramopadeśa 262n
Āgama-gāthā-mālā 92
Ajātaśatru-kukṛtya-vinodana 25n
Ākāśagarbha-sūtra 292
Akṣayamati-nirdeśa-sūtra 169, 172
Amarakoṣa 225n
Amarasiṃha-gītikā 225n
Amṛta-kuṇḍalī-āgama 149n
Apoha-siddhi 240n
Arhat-saṃghavardhana-vyākaraṇa 60n, 116n
Ārya-aṣṭasāhasrikā-prajñā-pāramitā 190, 208, 266n
Ārya-avalokiteśvara-carpaṭi-racita-sūtra 154n
—avataṃsaka-dharmaparyāya-śata-sāhasrikā 98
—buddha-bhūmi-vyākhyāna 260n
—catur-dharmaka-vyākhyāna-ṭīkā 269n, 285n
—cundā-sādhana 257n
—daśabhūmi-sūtra-nidāna-bhāṣya 239n, 260n
—daśabhūmi-vyākhyāna 169n
—gayāśīrṣa-sūtra-miśraka-vyākhyā 239n, 260n
—laṅkāvatāra-pañcaviṃśati-sāhasrikā 98
Ārya-mahāsannipāta-dharma-paryāya-śata-sāhasrikā 103
—maitreya-sādhana 156n
—mūla-sarvāstivadi-śramaṇera-kārikā 168n, 259n
—mūla-sarvāstivādi-vinaya-kārikā 197n
—nāma-saṃgīti 316n
—nandamitra-avadāna 97n
—pañcaviṃśati-sāhasrikā-prajñā-pāramitā-upadeśa-śāstra-abhisamaya-alaṃkāra-kārikā-vārttika 188n
—prajñā-pāramitā-saṃgraha-kārikā-vivaraṇa 178n
—ratnakūṭa-dharma-paryāya-śata-sāhasrikā 98

—ratnakūṭa-samāja 143, 171
—svapna-nirdeśa-nāma-mahāyāna -sūtra 92n
—tārā-stotra 311n
—vasumitra-bodhisattva-saṅgīti-śāstra 94n
Aśokāvadāna 32n, 35n, 38n, 51n, 54n, 55n, 67
Aśoka-vinīta-avadāna 67
Aśokena-nāga-vinīta-avadāna 67
Aṣṭa-bhaya-trāṇa 197n
Aṣṭādaśa-purāṇa 19
Aṣṭa-mahāsthāna-caitya-stotra 62n
Aṣṭa-mahāsthāna-caitya-vandana-stava 62n, 261n
Aṣṭāṅga-hṛdaya 132
Aṣṭa-sāhasrikā-vṛhat-ṭīkā 260
Ātma-yoga-nāma 262n
Avadāna-kalpalatā 43n, 58n, 67, 76n
Avalokiteśvara-sādhana-śataka 207
Avataṃsaka 143, 171

Bahubhūmika-vastu 158n
Bhagavat-śākyamuni-stotra 178n
Bhairava-aṣṭa-vetāla-sādhana 326
Bhārata (Mahābhārata) 19
Bhikṣu-varṣāgrapṛcchā 341
Bhoṭa-svāmi-dāsa-lekha 282n
Bodhicaryāvatāra : see Caryāvatāra
—pañjikā 295n
Bodhisattva-jātaka 93n
—samvara-viṃśaka 207
—yogacaryā-catuḥśataka-ṭīkā 124n, 199, 213, 213n
Brahmajāla-sūtra 93n
Buddha-anusmṛti 172
Buddhapālitā-mūlamadhyamaka-vṛtti 186n
Buddha-purāṇa 70n, 259n, 350
—samayoga 103
—udaya-nāma 178n

Caitya-avadāna 67
Cakra-samvara-udaya-ṭīkā 318
Cāṇakya-nīti-sāra 130n
Candra-pradīpa 207
Candra-vyākaraṇa 84, 84n, 203
Caryāvatāra 218-9, 238, 292
Caryā-saṃgraha-pradīpa 152
Catuḥśataka-vṛtti 124
Caturaśīti-siddha-pravṛtti 235n
Citta-tattvopadeśa-nāma 262n
Cullavagga 20n, 68n, 69n
Cundā-sādhana 257n

Daśabhūmi-sūtra 169, 172, 207
Devātiśaya-stotra 16n, 100n, 101
— — ṭīkā 259n
Devī-vasudhārā-stotra 240n
Dharma-dharmatā-vibhaṅga 159n
Dharma-sañcaya-gāthā-dvādaśa-sāhasrikā 98
Dharma-skandha 87n
Dhātu-kāya 88n
Dhyānottara-paṭala-ṭīkā 282
Dīpavaṃsa 52n
Divyāvadāna 54n, 77n, 93n
Dohākoṣa-tattva-gītikā 290n
Dṛṣṭānta-mālya 92n

Ekottara-karmaśataka 176n

Gaṇḍālaṃkāra 207
Ghana-vyūha-dvādaśa-sāhasrikā 98
Guhyasamāja-Tantra 103, 104, 132, 198n, 241n, 290
Guṇāparyanta-stotra 178n, 190

Homa-vidhi 285n
Hṛdaya-stotra 127

Indra-vyākaraṇa 84, 113
Jātaka-mālā 132, 135n

Kalāpa-vyākaraṇa 113-4
Kalpasūtra 111n
Kalpatraya 243n
Kalpokta-mārīcī-sādhana 290n
Karma-siddha-prakaraṇa 268n
—siddhi-ṭīkā 268n
Kāryatraya-stotra 126n
— — nāma-vivaraṇa 126n
— avatāra-mukha 148n
— vṛtti 268n
Kaṁsadeśa-vyākaraṇa 60n, 116n
Karmasiddhi-prakaraṇa 172n
Kāya-traya-avatāra 207
Kośalālaṃkāra 270, 270n
Kriyā-vajravārāhī 299n
Kṣudra-āgama 69
Kuṇāla-avadāna 67, 76n
Kurukullā-sādhana 129n
Kuṣṭha-cikitsopāya 202n

Lalitavistara 5, 19
Lokeśvara-śataka 271n
Lokeśvara-śataka-stotra 269n
— stotra 153n

Madhyama-āgama 92n
Madhyamaka-alaṃkāra 260, 269, 270
— avatāra-kārikā-nāma 199
— catuḥ-śatikā 213
— mūla 187, 198n, 212, 218
— satya-dvaya 270
Madhyānta-vibhaṅga 159n
Mahābhāṣya 112n, 113
Mahā-mudrā-tilaka 287n
Mahārāja-kaniṣka-lekha 135n
Mahāsamaya-sūtra 171n
Mahāvibhāṣā 88n, 150n
Mahāvyutpatti 46n, 56n, 79n, 98n, 259n, 285n, 291n,
Mahāyāna-saṃgraha 160
Manasāmaṅgala 145n, 146n
Maṅgalāṣṭaka 116n
Manjuśrī-mūla-tantra 6n, 9n, 60n, 83, 97n, 104n, 126n, 137, 154n, 336
Māyājāla Tantra 154
Meghadūta 116
Miśraka-stotra 190-1
Mṛtyu-vañcana-upadeśa 297n
Mūlāpatti 197n

Nāgānanda-nāma-nāṭaka 178n
Nāma-saṃgīti 203, 270, 271, 327
Nyāyālaṃkāra 108, 109

Pañcakrama 326n
Pañcamudrā-sūtra 172
Pañcaskandha-prakaraṇa 172n
Pañca-viṃśati-sāhasrikā 189n
— — — aṣṭa-adhyāya 189, 194-5
Paṇḍita-vikhyātadeva-mahākāruṇika-siddhi-lābhākhyāna 316n
Pāṇini-vyākaraṇa 83, 83n, 84
Paramārtha-bodhicitta-bhāvanā-krama-varṇa-saṃgraha 284
Pāramitā-yāna-bhāvanākrama-upadeśa 285n
Piśāca-pilupāla-sādhana 82n
Piṭakadharamuṣṭi 92
Pradīpa-mālā-śāstra 207
Pradīpa-uddyotana 198n
Pradīpoddyotana-nāma-ṭīkā 326n
Prajñā-mūla 108n
Prajñā-pāramitā-abhisamaya 189
— aṣṭasāhasrikā 90, 171

— pañcaviṃśati-sāhasrikā 172
— saṃgraha 136
— śata-sāhasrikā 105, 108, 171
— sūtra 156, 162, 188, 189, 207
Prajñā-pradīpa-mūla-madhyamaka-vṛtti 260n
Prajñā-pradīpa-ṭīkā 260n
Prajñapti-śāstra 87n
Prakaraṇa-pāda 88n
Pramāṇa-samuccaya 183, 229
Pramāṇavārtika 239n, 308n
— alaṃkāra 239n, 240n
— alaṃkāra-ṭīkā-supariśuddha-nāma 239n
— ṭīkā 240n, 260n
— vṛtti 239n
Praṇidhāna-saptati-nāma-gāthā 136n
Prasannapadā 198, 198n, 199
Pratibandha-siddhi 240n
Pratimokṣa-sūtra 80, 259n
— paddhati 259n
Pratītya-samutpādādi-vibhaṅga-nirdeśa-ṭīkā 212n
Pratītya-samutpāda-sūtra 172
Puṣpamālā 150n, 197, 334n
Putra-lekha 302n

Raghuvaṃśam 19
Rakta-yamāntaka-sādhana 245n
Rakta-yamāri-sādhana 245n
Rāmāyaṇa 19

Saḍaṅga-yoga 316n
Saddharma-puṇḍarīka-vṛtti 261n
Sādhana-mālā-tantra 257n
Samāja-ratna 171
Samantabhadra [-vyākaraṇa] 140-1, 206
Samayabhedoparacanacakra 104, 227, 340
Sambandha-parīkṣānusāra 309n
Saṃkṣipta-nāma-dṛṣṭi-vibhāga 311n
Sāmudrika-nāma-tanu-lakṣaṇa-parīkṣā 262n
Sambandha-parīkṣānusāra 240n
Saṃvṛti-bodhisattvabhāvanopadeśa-varṇa-saṃgraha 284n
Samyak-vāk-pramāṇoddhṛta-sūtra 269n
Saṃyukta-āgama 92n
Sannipāta-sāhasrikā 98
Śāntī-krodha-vikrīḍita 244
Sapta-kalpa-vṛtti 243n
Sarva-devatā-niṣpannakrama-mārga-nāma 262n
Sarvajña-maheśvara-stotra 16n, 100n
Sarva-siddhikara-nāma 154n
Sarvatathāgata-kāya-vāk-citta-kṛṣṇa-yamāri-nāma-tantra 243n
—tattva-saṃgraha-mahāyāna-abhisamaya-nāma-tantra-vyākhyā-tattvālokakarī-nāma 286n
— nāma-mahāyāna-sūtra 90n, 270n, 286n
Śatapañcāśatka-nāma-stotra-ṭīkā 148n
— stotra 133n, 134, 191n
Śata-upadeśa 103
Satya-dvaya-vibhaṅga 270n
Siddha-garuḍa-śāstra 142n
Śikṣā-samuccaya 217-8 2.9n, 292
Siṃhanāda-sādhana 202n
Śiṣya-lekha-ṭippana 209n
— vṛtti 209n, 295n
Sitābhyudaya 227n
Śrāvaka-piṭaka 67, 121, 167-8, 171, 179
Śreṣṭhiputra-sukhadeva-siddhi-lābha-ākhyāna 222n
Śrī-cakra-saṃvara-sādhana 230
Śri-candra-guhya-tilaka-nāma-mahā-tantra-rāja 242n

Śrī-devī-vasudhārā-stotra 308n
Śrī-guhyārtha-prakāśa-mahādbhuta-nāma 287n
Śrī-jñāna-guṇa-phala-nāma-stuti 268n
Śrī-paramādi (-vivaraṇa) 286
Śrī-paramasvarūpa-mahāsukhapada-vajra-nāma-samādhi 153n
Śrī-ratna-mañjarī-nāma-ṭīkā 225n
Śrī-vajraḍākasya-stava-daṇḍaka-nāma 230n
Śrī-vajrāmṛta-mahātantrarājasya-ṭīkā 287n
— pañjikā 288n
Stotra-śata-pañcāśatka 148, 191
Stuti-śata-pañcāśikā 203
Śūnyatā-saptati 108n
Suprabhāta-stotra 261n
Sūtra-aṣṭa-adhyāya 189
Sūtrālaṃkāra 159n, 172
Sūtra-piṭaka 95
Sūtra-samuccaya 217, 219
Suvarṇamālāvadāna 92
Suvarṇavarṇa-avadāna 22
Svarṇa-dāna-avadāna 67

Tanu-vicāraṇa-śāstra 262n
Tārā-sādhana-śataka 207
Tarkajvālā 80n
Tathāgata-hṛdaya-sūtra 127, 143
Tattvasaṃgraha 90
Tattvāvatāra-vṛtti 225n
Tattvāvatārākhya-sakala-sugata-vacasā-tātparya-vyākhyā-prakaraṇa 285n
Tattvaviniścaya 161n
Trayamiśraṇa-mālā 103
Trikāya-stotra 126
Tri-svabhāva-nirdeśa 162
Triṃśaka-kārikā-prakaraṇa 172
Tripiṭaka 92, 124

Udānavarga 91n, 104, 259n
Uṣṇīṣa-vijayā-dhāraṇī 170, 172, 174
Utsava-avadāna 67
Uttaratantra 159

Vaidalya-sūtra 108n
Vairocanābhisambodhi-tantra-ṭīkā 282
Vairocana-māyājāla-tantra 242
Vajra-dhātu-yogāvatāra 282
Vajra-gandhāri-sādhana 167n
Vajrāmṛta-tantra-ṭīkā 288n
Vajrasattva-sādhana 230
Vajrasūci 132n
Vajrayāna-mūlāpatti-ṭīkā 290n
Varṇanārha-varṇana 133n, 134n
Vastu-saṃgraha 158n
Vāyusthāna-roga-parīkṣā-nāma 290n
Vāyutattva-bhāvanopadeśa 227n
Vedas 45, 48, 229
Vibhaṅgadvaya 172
Vibhāṣā 86-88, 89n, 168
Vigraha-vyāvartanī 108n
Vijñāna-kāya 88n
Vimala-ratna-lekha 305n
Viṃśaka-kārikā-prakaraṇa 172n
Vinaya 26n
Vinaya-āgama 108
Vinaya-kārikā 150n
Vinaya-kṣudraka-vastu 20n, 21, 32n, 68n, 69n
Vinaya-saṃgraha 259n
Vinaya-śāstra 19
Vinaya-stotra 82n
Vinaya-sūtra-vṛtti-abhidhānasya-vyākhyā 176n
Vinayavastu 19n
Viśeṣastava 16n, 100n, 101
— ṭīkā 259n
Vivaraṇa-saṃgraha 158n
Vyākaraṇa-liṅgāvatāra 206n

Vyākhyā-yukti 172
— ṭīkā 212n
Vyavahāra-siddhi 108n

Yamāntakodaya 244

Yoga-caryā-bhāvanā-tātparyārtha-nirdeśa 268n
Yoga-pota 271
Yoga-tantra-tattva-saṃgraha 270
Yukti-ṣaṣṭikā 108n
— vṛtti 199

II. PLACES

(including names of monasteries and temples)

Ābhu [Mount Abu] 99, 333
Āgrā 314
Agrapurī, *in* Mathurā 179
Ajantā 132n
Aṃda-giri 327
Amṛta-kumbha *temple* 262
Aṅga 50n, 53, 70, 97
Aṅgiri (Aṅga-giri) 327n *See also* Aṃda-giri
Antaravedi 319
Aparāntaka 38-9, 65-6, 102, 116, 120, 137-8, 256, 330, 351
Arvanti (? Avantī) 249
Ārya-deśa 5, 152, 245, 271, 287n, 341, 346, 352
Aśmaparānta 76-7, 96
Ayodhyā 165, 174n, 175n, 314

Bagala (Bagla) 39, 244
Balaku 330
Bālanagara 224n *See also* Pālanagara
Balapurī 212
Bahlika country 96n
Bengal 259n, 284n
Bhaga-vihāra 180n
Bhaṅgala (Baṅgala ; Bhaṃgala) 10n, 109, 121-2, 127, 144, 153n, 186, 210, 225, 251-3, 255-8, 259n, 268, 285-6, 294-5, 303, 314, 319-20, 333, 348
Bhāṭi *island* 295
Bhiruka-vana 83
Bikramaśīla (?) *See* Vikramaśīla
Bodhimaṇḍa (Vajrāsana) 37
Brag-stod-chos-kyi-pho-braṅ 352

Cak-ma (cākmā ; ca-ga-ma) 330-1
Campā 33, 50n, 51n, 154n, 330n
Campāran 235n
Campāraṇa 50
Candradvīpa 202
Caṭighābo (catigon) 255
Ceylon 18n, 29n, 295n, 296n
Chagala 267n *See also* Rārā
China 29n, 138, 257n
Chittagong 255
Citavara 253, 333
Cūḍāmaṇi 228

Dakṣi-nagara 218n *See also* Śrī Dakṣiṇa

Daṇḍakāraṇya 180
Dantapurī, Danṭapurī 186
dBus [Central Tibet] 282
Devagiri 212, 241n
Devīkoṭa 214, 215
Dhanaśrīdvīpa 332
Dhānya-kaṭaka 107, 192, 209, 345
Dharma-gañja 141, 243
Dharmāṅkura-vihāra 160
Dhūmasthira 287
Di-li (Dilli ; Delhi) 131, 314, 320
Dramila 207n, 331-2
Dravalī 109, 232, 335
Dravida *country* 207

Gajni 149
Gaṇḍakī *river* 252n
Gandhamādana 31, 34n
Gandhāra 34, 59n, 79, 97n, 167n
Gaṅgā 24, 34, 52, 59, 60, 145, 153n, 202, 233, 235, 294-6, 314, 319
Gaṅgāsāgara 268
Gañja *kingdom* 241n
Gauḍa 121, 133, 173, 175, 302
Gauḍapurī (Gauḍapura) 235n
Gayā 131n, 302
Girivarta 330
Gotapuri temple (Gauḍapuri ?) 235
Guhā-vihāra 35n
Gujiratha 235, 333
Gur-pa-parvata 156
Gurva hill 27

Hacipura [Hājipura ?] 252
Hala 224
Haṃsavatī 330
Ha-sa-ma (Assam) 142, 198, 330
Hastināpura *city* 243
Hastināpurī 104
Himālaya (Himālayas) 53, 60, 76, 265, 282

India 5, 18, 39, 68n, 214n, 227n, 287, 290n, 299n, 319, 323, 330, 332, 344-5, 349-50, 351-2
See also ārya-deśa
Indus 29n

Jagaddala-vihāra (Ja-gar-da-la) 314n, 319
Jālandhara 91, 93, 121, 274
Jambudvīpa 15n, 17, 60, 62, 71-2, 124, 192-4, 202, 208, 243
Jetavana 24, 62n
Jītā 333
Jo-naṅ 352
Jvālā-guhā 188, 286

Kaccha *country* 261
Kailāsa
See Ti-se [Kailāsa]
Kaliṅga 218, 237, 333, 336
Kāmaru 268
Kāmarūpa 47, 133, 253, 314, 330
Kāmboja 319, 330
Kaṃsadeśa 60n
Kāñcī 11, 126, 181, 334
Kaṅ-karova 241n
Kapilabhargu (?) 241n
Kapilavāstu 62n, 241n
Kapin
See Kashmir
Karavīra *province* 241n
Karṇāṭa 288, 335
Kashmir 29-31, 32n, 33, 46, 51n, 62n, 65, 71, 80, 87n, 91-2, 137, 149, 167-8, 174, 177, 185, 197, 211, 220, 235-6, 259-61, 266-7, 269-70, 285, 287, 301-03, 311, 316, 318, 329, 332, 334n, 338, 351

Kāśī-Vārāṇasī 82
Kauśāmbī 39n, 68
Khagendra 147, 331, 333
Khorāsāna 118
Khorosan 178
Khoṭen 60n
Ko-ki 330-1, 334, 351
Koṅkana 296, 325
Koṅ-ku-na *country* 199, 333
Kośala 270
Kukkuṭārāma-vihāra 55n
Kuṇḍalavana-vihāra 92n
Kuśavana 73
Kuśīnagara 62n
Kusuma-alaṃkāra monastery 130
Kusumapura 6n, 85, 97, 130
Kusumapurī 68
Kuvana monastery 92n, 93

Lahore 137
Laṅkā 18n
See also Ceylon
Laṅkāpurī 245n
La-tā *city* .196
Lhasa 352
Li-yul 60, 62, 116

Madhima *island* 272
Madhya-deśa 33-4, 121, 137, 164, 168, 188, 213, 217-20, 224, 229, 257, 286, 330, 348
Magadha 18n, 22, 24, 25n, 27, 39, 43n, 52, 57, 62n, 100, 101n, 110n, 111n, 114-15, 121, 133, 138, 165, 168, 173-5, 180, 197, 210-11, 234, 256, 258, 259n, 262, 285-6, 288, 294, 296, 301, 303, 314, 318-19, 321, 325, 327-8, 330, 347-8, 350
Mahodadhi 336
Malapurī 241n
Mālava 47, 49, 68, 108, 131, 179, 210, 249, 287, 314
Malya-ra 186, 333, 335
Maṇidvīpa 272n
Mar-ko 330
Maru 253, 333, 348
Mathurā 30n, 32n, 34, 35n, 45, 60n, 81, 85n, 179, 234, 314
Me-vā-ra 333
Mu-naṅ 319, 330-1
Muruṇḍa 35n
See also Urumuṇḍa
Muruṇḍaka *hill* 244-5

Nāga-loka 265
Nairañjanā *river* 62n
Nalendra [Nālandā] 93n, 99, 101, 106-7, 109, 111, 120, 123, 125-7, 133-4, 136, 138, 141, 167, 171, 175, 182, 187, 197-8, 203, 206, 208-9, 211, 213-5, 218, 220-2, 232, 242, 251, 258, 268, 271, 289, 297, 307, 313, 320-21, 328
Naṃ-ga-ṭa 330-1
Naṭa-bhaṭika *vihāra* 30n, 34n, 35, 37, 87
Nepal 51, 174-5, 256, 271, 298, 305, 311, 317-9, 348

Odantapurī 258, 262-3, 266n, 289, 304, 306, 313, 318-9
Oḍḍīyāna 241n
Oḍiviśa 78, 90, 104, 108-9, 133, 148, 150, 152, 173, 175, 177-8, 182, 184-5, 226, 251, 253, 256, 267-8, 286, 300, 314, 319, 321, 330
Oḍiyāna 332

O-jɛ-na 333
Otsayana-cūḍāmṇi *monastery* 286

Paṅkhi-tīrtha 334
Pāṭaliputra 39n, 52, 57, 62, 64, 66, 69n, 77, 80n, 97, 299n
Pegu 330n
See also Haṃsavatī
Persia 244n
Piṇḍa (Piṇḍaka) *vihāra* 254
Potala 317, 352, 382
Potala *hill* 208, 247, 248, 281
Prayāga 160n, 288, 314
Pu-khaṅ 319, 330, 336, 349
Rāḍha country 109, 267n,
See also Rā-rā
Rājagṛha 20n, 42, 52n, 53, 61, 62n, 167, 174
Rākhaṅ 330-1
Rāmeśvara 336
Rā-rā country 267, 292
Ratnagiri 144, 333, 336
Ratnagupta *monastery* 185
Ṛṣi Mātaṅga 234
rTag-brtan-phun-tshogs-gliṅ 352

Saddharma-megha-viśālagañja 345
See also Dhānya-kaṭaka
Sa-ga-ri (Sāgar ; Saugar ?) 161, 314
Śālipura nagara 305n
Sāketa 82n, 91n, 103, 260n
Samataṭa 198
Sambhala 245n, 289n
Saṃkāśya 69n
Śaṃśa 272n
Samudragupta *temple* 267
Sanava *desert* 241n
Śāntipurī 298
Śarāvatī vihāra 80
Śatapuṣpa *mountain* 191n
Śatruñjaya 191n
Sauri 320
Saurāṣṭra 215, 333
Shola 352
Siṃhala (Siṅgala-dvīpa) 72, 123-4, 202, 207, 325, 332
Sindhu 74
Śira *hill* 34-5
Śīrṣa-parvata 35n
See also Urumuṇḍa
Siṣa 272
Śītavana 32, 287
Somapurī 266-7, 289
Śoṇaka *city* 69n
Sonārgāon 122
Śrāvastī 27, 62n, 79
Śrī-dhana 241n
Śrī Dhānya-kaṭaka
See Dhānya-kaṭaka
Śrī-Nalendra
See Nalendra
Śrīparvata 110, 121-2, 124, 127, 215
Śrī Trikaṭuka
See Trikaṭuka
Sukhāvatī 337
Sumeru 59, 263-4
Suvarṇadvīpa 332

Takṣaśilā 51n, 76n, 77n, 78n, 96n, 116n
Tala-koṅkuna 335
Tāmradvīpa 332
Thogar 46, 65, 96, 117, 149, 253, 351
Tibet 29n, 84, 174-5, 210, 266, 269, 271, 282n, 285, 294n, 302, 305, 310n, 315, 317-9, 331, 344-5, 349-50
Tīrahuti 34, 54, 133, 210, 314, 318
Ti-se [Kailāsa] 282-3
Trikaṭuka *monastery* 266n, 267, 289
Triliṅga 333
Trimalaya 228
Tripura 40, 330
Tukhāristān 46n, 65n, 96n, 176n, 253n
Tu-lu-rā-ti 335
Tuṣita 337

Udantapurī (? Odantapurī) 290n
Udyāna 243n
See also Urgyana
Ujjayinī 45, 49, 52n, 86
Upara Koṅkuna 335
Urgyana 241n, 243-4, 245n, 271-2, 283, 287, 332, 351
Urumuṇḍa hill 34n
Urvā-si 333
Uttara 39, 40
Vaiśālī 20, 24, 25n, 62n, 68-9
Vajracūḍā 344
Vajrāsana 313-4, 318, 320, 347
Vārāṇasī 26, 31, 41, 62n, 103, 114-5, 138, 154, 189, 194, 210, 233, 235-6, 282, 296, 306, 314
Varendra 199, 244, 266, 268, 290, 348
Vidyānagara 333, 335
Vikramapurī 308
Vikramaśīla 18, 93n, 285, 289, 292, 294, 295n, 297-8, 301-2, 304, 307-8, 311, 313-4, 317-9, 325-6, 329
Vindhya 53, 60, 87, 211
Vindhyācala 232, 234, 333, 335
Vistaravatī 96n, 149n
Vṛkṣapurī 292
Yamunā 314, 319
Yavadvīpa 332

III. PERSONS, DEITIES, ETC.

Abhayākaragupta 313-6, 319, 329-30
Abhijña Vajrāsana *guru* 230n
Acala 292, 294
Adarpa 16, 47
Agnidatta 8, 85
Aja 26
Ajātaśatru 6n, 20, 22, 24, 25, 26, 27, 54n, 61
Ajita *bhikṣu* 69n, 205
Ajita *jina* 277
Ajitamitragupta 316n
Ajitanātha 156, 159, 211-2
Ajitakṛṣṇa 123n
Ākāśa 213
Ākāśagarbha 213
Akṣacandra 7, 117, 120
Alaṃkāra-upādhyāya
See Prajñākaragupta
Alāpalu 29n
Al-beruni 111n, 138n
Altekar, A.S. 320n
Amarasiṃha 225, 227
Amitavajra *ācārya* 305
Amoghapāśa 193
Amoghavajra 305
Āmrapāla 8, 310, 312
Amṛtaguhya 288
Ānanda 21-5, 26n, 30, 32n, 33, 68n, 74n, 75
Ānandagarbha 284-6
Anaṅgavajra
See Gorakṣa
Anesaki, M. 130n, 131n, 132n, 133n
Āntivāhana 9n
Anūpa 50n
Anupamasāgara *ācārya* 307
Anuruddha See Rādhagupta
Apalāla 29n
Ardho 119
Arhat *ācārya* 154
Āryadeva 123-9, 136, 151, 186, 188, 311
Ārya-śūra 132, 135n
Āsana-siṃha-koṣa 72

Asaṅga 177, 197, 204-5, 225, 254, 269, 302
Asaṅga brothers 106, 149-75, 185-6
Aśoka 6, 39n, 49-53, 54n, 55n, 57n, 58n, 59, 61, 62n, 66-70, 75-7, 78n, 91n, 135, 330
Aśoka (Aśokaśrī) *ācārya* 201
A-svabhāva 252-4
Aśvaghoṣa 117n, 131n, 132, 135n, 136n, 139n, 148, 190n, 284
Aśvagupta 13, 97
Atīśa (Jo-bo-rje; Dīpaṃkara Srījñāna) 157n, 197n, 213n, 289n, 302, 304-5, 310, 317n, 329
Atītavāhana 331
Auduṣṭa 29
Avadhūti-pā (Paiṇḍapātika) 214n, 308
Avadhūti-pā *bhikṣu* 298
Avalokitavrata (? Avalokiteśvaravrata) 260
Avalokiteśvara 83, 98, 112, 131, 137, 154-5, 201-2, 205, 209, 223, 246-7, 253, 281, 300, 302, 307, 317
Avantaka 14
Avitarka 98, 102
Ayogi-pā *See* Yoga-pā

Bahubhuja 13
Bai-kham-pa 118
Bālacandra 7, 210
Balamitra 12, 336
Bāla-paṇḍita (?) 55n
Bālabhadra 333
Bālasundara 331
Bālavāhana 331
Ban-de-ro *alias* Khuni-ma-mpta 137
Basham, A.L. 20n
Basunāga 164
Behulā 145n, 146n
Bhāḍaghāṭi (Bhaṭaghaṭi) 69
Bhadra 16, 80-2, 85, 94
Bhadrānanda 12
Bhadrapālita 17, 184-5
Bhago 287-8
Bhaṃśacandra (? Vaṃśacandra) 7, 120, 122
Bhaṇṭa (? Bhaṭa) 34
Bharadvāja 23
Bharthari (? Bhartṛhari) 249
Bharṣa (Bharśi; Varṣa ?) 10, 196, 201, 209-11
Bhaṭṭa Ācārya 226
Bhavabhadra 18, 326
Bhāvaviveka (Bhavya) 80n, 177-8, 186-9, 196, 198, 212, 226, 253, 260
Bhavyakīrti 18, 326
Bheyapāla 8, 295, 303-05, 309
Bhīmaśukla 112, 114-5
Bhoga-subāla 11, 334
Bhojadeva 108
Bhṛgu *See* Bhṛku-rākṣasa
Bhṛku-rākṣasa (Bhṛgu) 47-8
Bhṛkuṭī 192-3, 281
Bhṛṅgāraguhya 232
Bhūmigarbha *See* Kṣitigarbha
Bhūmīndrabhadra 43n
Bhūmiśrībhadra 320
Bhusuku (Bhu-su-ku) 310n
Bimbisāra 52n
Bindusāra 6n, 7, 50n, 51n, 52n, 130-1
Bi-śli-mi-lil 118
Bitpalo 348
Bito-pāda 289n
Bodhibhadra 18, 300-11, 327
Bodhivarman 259n
Bongard-Levin, G.M. 52n, 76n, 77n, 78n
Brahmā 154, 226

Bṛhaspati 17, 142, 144, 148
Buda (Budha) 11, 335
Buddhadāsa 150, 177, 188
Buddhadeva 15, 103
Buddhajñānapāda (Buddhajñāna, Buddhaśrījñāna) 260 276, 278, 280, 289n, 292, 325
Buddhaguhya 276, 280, 281, 282
Buddhakapāla 153
Buddhakīrti 257n, 314, 315n
Buddhanandī 74
Buddhapakṣa 9, 138, 139n, 142, 144, 148-9, 155, 190
Buddhapālita 177, 186-8, 197-8, 204, 226
Buddha Samantaprabha 96n
Buddhaśānti 276, 280-3
Buddhasena 320
Buddhasiṃha 161n
Buddhaśrī 317
Buddhaśuca 11, 335
Buddhaśrīmitra 317-9
Burnouf, E. 53n
Bu-ston *passim*

Cakrasamvara 298, 301, 317, 326
Cala 9, 210-1, 223-4
Caladhruva 9, 224
Camaśa 6, 39, 52
Canaka 10, 17, 130, 256, 294-5, 303, 325
Cāṇakya 6n, 130
Caṇḍa-giri (Caṇḍa Girika) 54n
Candanapāla 8, 102, 104
Candrasena 11, 334
Candra-vāhana 331
Candraśobha 11, 334
Caṇḍāśoka *See* Aśoka
Caṇḍikā, *goddess* 106-7
Candragomī 18, 84n, 187, 196, 199, 200-6, 207n, 208-9, 211-2, 222-3, 225-6
Candragupta 6n, 7, 8, 50n, 90n, 123, 130
Candrākaragupta 317, 319
Candrakīrti 124, 187-8, 197-8, 203-6, 208-9, 211-3, 225-7, 230n, 273
Candramaṇi 197
Candrapadma 285
Candrarakṣita 90
Cārin ācārya [? Kṛṣṇācārī] 259
Carpaṭi 153, 154n
Chag dGra-bcom 316n, 317n
Chag lo-tsā-ba 42n, 60n, 205n, 208n
Cakrāyudha 276
Chatterjee, C. D. 50n, 51n, 53n, 60n
Chattopadhyaya A. 175n, 212n, 259n, 260n, 302n, 305n, 310n
Ciṅgalarāja 320
Cundā *goddess* 257-8

Daṃṣṭrāsena 268
Dānabhadra 12
Dānaśīla 259
Dānarakṣita 329
Dārika-pā, Dāri-pāda, Dārika-pāda 178, 230, 311
Darśana 37
Daśabalaśrī (-mitra) 316, 318-9
Datta-trai (Dattātreya) 225
Deki-pā 178n
De, S. K. 102n
Deva Bodhisattva 124n
Devākaracandra 305
Devapāla 8, 153, 261-2, 264-5, 266n, 269, 273, 288
Devarāja 12, 335
Devaśarman (Devaśarmā) 88n, 226n *See also* Devaśrama
Devaśrama 226
Dhaki 178n
Dhanakuṭṭi 178n
Dhanarakṣita 164

Dhanika 50, 69n
Dharmā 51n
Dharma-Aśoka 66
Dharmacandra 7, 8, 137-8
Dharmadāsa 177, 186, 189, 198, 213, 226
Dharmagupta 14
Dharmākaradatta 276
Dharmākaragupta 316
Dharmākaramati 310, 310n
Dharmākaraśānti 308n, 316
Dharmakīrti 211n, 228, 230-2, 248-9, 254-56, 309
Dharmamitra 176n, 253-4
Dharmapāla 8, 266n, 268, 276-8, 283-4, 295n, 314, 325, 332
Dharmapāla *ācārya* 18, 197, 209, 211-2, 213n, 214, 225-6, 229, 260n, 274, 330
Dharmapāla (of Suvarṇadvīpa) 213n
Dharmapālita 225n
See also Dharmapāla
Dharma Sārthavāha 82n
See also Dharmaśreṣṭhī
Dharmaśreṣṭhī 13, 82
Dharmatrāta 15, 91, 94n, 97n, 103, 259n
Dharmika 16, 104
Dhārmika Subhūti 132
Dharmottara 14, 309
Dhīrapāla· *See* Sthirapāla
Dhītika 45-7, 49, 65n, 68-9, 71, 75
Dignāga 148, 176-95, 213, 225-6, 229
Diṅgi-pā, Diṅga-pa 178, 178n, 230
Divyākaragupta 98
Dīpaṃkara-bhadra 18, 325, 332
Dīpaṃkara Jñāna 328
Dombī Heruka 214n, 222, 229, 230, 245, 279, 287
Dombi-pā 305
Drumaripu 231
Durdharṣakāla 123-5, 131-2, 134
Durgā *goddess* 251
Durjayacandra 18, 327
Dutt, N. 49n, 71n, 74n, 93n, 95

Eka-jaṭī 192

Fa-hien 25n, 54n
Feer, L. 29n

Gaggari 12, 336
Gambhīrapāda 291
Gambhīrapakṣa 9, 149-50, 161-2, 176
Gambhīra-śīla 52
Gambhīra-vajra 287
Gaṇapati 297
Gaṇeśa 100
Garbhapāda 290, 292
Gaurakṣa (Gorakṣa) 320
Gāyatrī 293n
Gauḍavardhana 9, 121, 154
Ghadhari *See* Kaudālika
Ghanasa (Ghanasāla) 103
Ghavin 295n
Ghoṣa 78n
Ghoṣaka 15, 96, 103
Ghoṣila 49
Gobicandra (Govicandra) 7-8, 249, 251, 256, 258
Gokarṇa 54
Gopāla 8, 227n, 257-8, 261-2, 264-6
Gorakṣa 227
Gudhari (Guḍarī) *See* Kaudālika
Guhyadatta 150n, 177, 198
Guhyapati 98, 102, 151
Guhyaprajña 302
Guṇamati 210, 212
Guṇamitra 260n
Guṇaprabha 18, 176-7, 179, 197, 210, 254
Gupta 32

Ha-lu-lu 122
Haribhadra 117, 161, 254, 260, 266n, 274, 276-8, 301

Haricandra 7, 104, 117
Harisiṃha 230n
Haritasena 320
Harṣadeva (of Kashmir) 62n, 261
Harṣavardhana Śīlāditya 176n, 178n
Hāsavajra 296
Hastipāla 8, 310, 312-3
Hayagrīva 192
Hemadeva 124
Hermaios 46n
Hiṅgalācī 74
Hoffmann, H. 165n

I-ma-sya 46
Indra 58n, 102
Indrabhūti 152n, 214n, 241, 244
Indradatta *paṇḍita* 70, 259
Indra-dhruva 102
Īśvarasena 211, 229
Īśvaravarman 111n
I-Tsing *passim.*

Jaḥsā 39, 44
Jalandhari-pā 249-50
Jaleruha 150, 177
Jambhala 23n, 278
Jaṭānika 96n
Jaṭi 96
Jaya 16, 39-41
Jayabhadra of (Laṅkā) 296
Jayacandra 7, 117, 120
Jayadeva 197-8, 214, 217
Jayaśīla 317n
Jetāri *the senior* 290
Jina 70
Jinabhadra 296n
Jinamitra 285
Jīvaka 149n
Jīvākara 149
Jñānacandra 148n, 207n, 268
Jñānadatta 285
Jñānagarbha 252-3, 259-60
Jñānākaragupta 317-9, 333
Jñānamati 310n
Jñānapāda 18, 266n, 274, 279, 294
Jñānaśrī 295n, 302, 311
Jñānavajra 311
Jvālapati 304

Kākaṇḍaka 68n
Kakutsiddha (Kakudasiddha ; Kakudasiṃha) 141
Kāla 49n, 68n, 70n, 74n, 132
Kālacakra *deity* 222n, 317
Kālacakrapāda 290
Kālasamaya-vajra 290n
Kalhaṇa 43n
Kālī *goddess* 115-6
Kālidāsa 114-6
Kalyāṇa 16, 39, 41-2, 44, 50
Kalyāṇagupta 276
Kalyāṇamitra 98, 268
Kāmacandra 7-8, 176
Kamalabuddhi 197-8
Kamalagarbha 103
Kamalagomī 246-7
Kamalakuliśa 329
Kamalarakṣita 19, 328
Kamalaśīla 283
Kāmāśoka 53
Kambala-pā 152, 252, 275
Kaṇāda 231
Kaṇādagupta Kaṇadaroru (Kaṇanāda ?) Kaṇagupta 226, 231, 231n, 232
Kanaka 50
Kanaka *Digambara* 53
Kanakavarṇa 22n *See also* Suvarṇavarṇa
Kāṇeripāda 123n *See also* Karṇa-ri-pā
Kanika 9, 131, 135
Kaniṣka 8, 9n, 80n, 87n, 91, 93n, 94-5, 131, 132n, 135n

Kaṇṭa-pā 305
Kapila *sage* 40
Kapila *yakṣa* 72
Karmacandra 7-8, 144, 148-9, 150, 154
Karṇa *king* 333
Karṇa-ri-pā 123
Karuṇāśrībhadra 320
Kāśasena (? Kasasena) 10, 316
Kāśī-jāta 17, 122
Kasori-pā 306
Kāśyapa 14, 79, 81, 139n, 156n, 267
Kātyāyana 86n, 88n
Kaudālika 262
Kauṭilya *See* Cāṇakya
Keith, A.B. 43n
Kern, H. 263n
Kha-ndi-pā 305n
See also Kaṇṭa-pā
Khasarpaṇa *ārya* 194-5, 257
Khri-lde-sroṅ-btsan 259n, 276, 281
Khri-ral (Ral-pa-can) 284
Khuni-ma-mpta *alias* Ban-de-ro 137-8
Koṭali 295n
Krauñci-kumārī 71
Kri-Kri (Kṛkiḥ) 92, 267
Kṛṣṇa 71
Kṛṣṇa *ārya* 49, 68-70, 72-3, 74n, 102
Kṛṣṇa *brāhmaṇa* 183
Kṛṣṇa *caryā-dhara* 304
Kṛṣṇācārin 259
Kṛṣṇācārya *ācārya* 249, 251, 268, 304
Kṛṣṇācārya *the junior* 268, 294
Kṛṣṇa-muni-rāja 183
Kṛṣṇasamaya-vajra 290, 292, 327
See also Samaya-vajra
Kṛṣṇavajra-pāda 305n
Kṣāntipāla 10, 310, 312
Kṣemadarśin (Ajātaśatru) 6, 20
Kṣemaṅkara 116, 334
Kṣemaṅkarasiṃha [? Śaṃkara-siṃha] 11, 334-35
Kṣemendrabhadra 43, 54, 67, 69, 75, 77n, 259
Kṣitigarbha (Bhūmigarbha) 310
Kubjita 69n, 87
Kuku-rāja (Kukura-rāja ; Kutā-rāja) 241-2
Kukkurī-pā (Kukurī-pā ; Ku-khu-ri-pā) 230n, 274
Kulika 16, 98
Kuliśaśreṣtha 226
Kumāralāta (Kumāralābha) 116-7
Kumāralīla 226, 230-2
Kumārānanda 12, 232
Kumārasena 117
Kumāraśrī (of 'Gos) 93
Kumārila 226n, 230
See also Kumāralīla
Kuṇāla 15, 76-7, 117
Kuñjarakarṇa 76
Kuśa-putra [? Kauśika] 53
Kuśala 82n
Kusuma 211n
Kuvera 79

Labaṃsena 319
Lakṣāśva 8, 97-8
Lakṣmaṇa 50n
Lakṣmī 79n
Lakṣmīṅkarā 197n, 214n
Lalitacandra 7-8, 251, 258
Lalita-vajra 241-2, 244-5
Lalou, M. 263n, 305n
Lassen 78n, 123n, 258n, 261n
Laṅkādeva 12
Laṅkā-Jayabhadra 18, 325
Lavasena 10, 314-5
Legge, J. 25n, 32n, 60n, 62n, 76n
Lha-tho-tho-ri-gñan-btsan 175
Līlāvajra 18, 244, 326
Litvinsky, B. A. 46n, 65n, 96n
Lo-dri 278
Lūi-pā 153, 178, 178n, 230, 311
Lva-va-pā 152, 241, 244-6

Madhu 17, 109
Madhyamakasiṃha 310n, 311

Madhyamati 13
Mahādeva *monk* 79-81, 94
Mahādeva *god* 39-41, 53, 70, 100, 133, 225-6
Mahājana 302
Mahākāla 107, 112-3, 125, 267
Mahākāśyapa 21-2
Mahākauṣṭhila 88n
Mahā-koṭali 262 *See also* Kaudālika
Mahākrodha 215
Mahāloma 13, 81-2, 84
Mahā-madhyāntika (Mahā-madhyāhnika) 25
Mahāpadma 6, 85, 90, 94
Mahāpāla 289, 292-5
Mahā Śākyabala *See* Śākya Mahābala
Mahāsammata 177
Mahāsena 10
Mahāsudarśana 69
Mahātyāga 13, 85
Mahā-vajrāsana 305, 329
Mahāvīrya 103
Mahendra 6, 11-2, 38-9, 334-5
Maheśvara 39n, 125, 219n, 301
Mahīndrabhadra 43n
Mahīpāla 8, 266n, 284, 286, 289, 292, 295n
Mahīśāsaka 14
Maitrīnātha 304n *See also* Maitri-pā
Maitrī-pa 304-5, 310
Maitreya 42n, 98, 156-9, 189, 301-2
Makṣika 17, 173
Mālikabuddhi 140
Mā-ma-thar 118
Maṇikaśrī 311
Maṇitasena 10
Mañjughoṣa 204-5, 243, 291-2 *See also* Mañjuśrī
Mañjuśrī 90, 98, 107, 139, 182, 184, 186, 204, 215-7, 242-3, 280, 282, 295, 307, 309, 327
Manohara (? Manoratha) 11, 334
Manomati 334
Māra 35-7, 80-1, 90, 118, 279
Masurakṣita 325
Mātaṅgī-pā 129, 139n 273,
Mātaṅgarāja 179
Maticitra (*See also* Mātṛceṭa) 132, 135n, 139
Matikumāra 12
Mātṛceṭa 9n, 123n, 126n, 130-6, 139n, 191n, 253
Matsyendra, Matsyanātha, Mīnanātha 153n
Maudgalyāyana 20n, 21, 88n, 89, 101
Menandros 46n
Mīmāṃsaka 259n
Mīnanātha 153n
Mi-nar 46
Ming-ti, *Chinese Emperor* 139n
Mīna-pā 154n
Mitracita (Maticitra; Mātṛceṭa) 133n
Mitraguhya 310n, 311
Mi-tsche-kia *See* Kāla
Mokṣasena 210n
Monier-Williams, M. 145n, 308n
Mudgaragomin 100
Muditābhabhadra 140
Muktasena 210n, 211n, 212n
Mukundadeva 321
Muñja 108, 286

Nāga, *monk* 82, 85
Nāgabodhi (Nāgabuddhi) 123, 126, 127, 152, 215, 273
Nāgadatta 181
Nāgāhvāya 123, 126 (*See* Tathāgatabhadra)
Nāgakeśa 177
Nāgaketu 12, 336
Nāgamati 127n
Nāgamitra 148, 151, 186, 207n
Nāgarāja-bhagavān 336

Nāgārjuna 9n, 17n, 62n, 98n, 101, 102n, 106-19, 121-4, 126-9, 151, 152, 166, 186-8, 197-8, 204-5, 207n, 302
Nāgeśa 177
Nanda 6, 13, 82-3, 85, 94, 106
Nandamitra 97
Nandapriya 148n
Nandin 13, 68, 81-2
Narada (? Nārada) 262-3
Narasūrya 333
Naravarmā 243
Narendra-śrī-jñāna 329
Nāro-pā 294n, 295n, 299, 300, 305-7, 311
Naṭa 34
Nava 27
Nayakapaśrī 329
Nemacandra 7, 120
Nemita 50, 52
Netā 146n
Neyapāla 8, 304-5, 309-10
Nirāloka 177n

Obermiller, E. E. *passim*

Pacari 154n
Padma 230n
Padmaka 50
Padmākara 332
Padmākaraghoṣa 276
Padmāṅkuśa 290
Padmavajra 152, 242
Paiṇḍapātika *See* Avadhūti-pā
Palladius 79n
Paṇa 27
Pañcadeva 193-5
Pañcagotra Tathāgata 280
Pañcamasiṃha 10, 209-11, 216, 223, 225, 228
Pañcaśṛṅga 124
Paṇi (Pāṇini) 6, 16, 83-4, 112-3, 116n, 202n, 203
Parahita 284
Parahitabhadra 309
Parahitaghoṣa-āraṇyaka 136
Parahita Svarakāntāra 136n
Paramasena 106, 196, 197, 210
Paramāśva 153
Pārśva 13, 87n, 92
Patañjali 112-3
Pathak, S. 102n
Pātra-pāla 10n
Pham-thiṅ *brothers* 311
Phaṇīcandra 7, 120-1
Pi-lu-pa (Pilupāla) 82, 82n
Piṇḍo-pā 289n *See also* Piṭo ācārya
Pi-rto-pā 289n
Pi-ṭo-pā 289n, 310
Pito ācārya 289-90
Pitṛceṭa 130n, 132
Pluto 23n
Posada 13, 78
Prabhākara 276
Prāditya 10n, 175n, 224, 228n, 232n *See also* Pradyota, Prasanna
Pradyota 10, 224, 232 *See also* Prāditya
Prajñāgarbha (? Jñānagarbha) 260n
Prajñākaragupta 289, 296
Prajñākaramati 209n, 295-6, 299
Prajñākīrti 197
Prajñāpāla 82n, 286
Prajñārakṣita 305-6
Prajñāvarman 259
Prakāśacandra 255, 285
Prakāśadharmamaṇi 103
Prakāśasīlā, Prasannaśīla 155
Prasanna 10, 211, 224, 228, 232n
Prasena 210n
Prasenajit 59n
Pratāpa 12, 335
Pṛthivībandhu 261
Przyluski, J. 32n *sqq*
Puṇyākaragupta (Puṇyaśrī) 305

Puṇyakīrti 253, 259
Puṇyaśrī *See* Puṇyākaragupta
Pūrṇa 17, 88n
Pūrṇabhadra 17
Pūrṇavardhana 276
Puṣpa 211
Puṣyamitra 120-1

Rādhagupta 54n
Rāghava 16, 78
Rāhula 17, 273, 311
Rāhulabhadra 101-5, 110, 126, 131, 136, 148, 280
Rāhulamitra 98, 148, 311
Rāhulaprabha 102
Rāhuvratī 232
Rāmacandra 333
Rāmapāla 313-5
Rājyapāla 261n *See also* Rāsapāla
Rakṣita-pāda 273
Rāmapriya 148, 191n
Rāsapāla 261
Ratha 60n
Rathika 50
Rāthika (Sena) 10, 44
Ratnadāsa 178n
Ratnākaragupta 310
Ratnākaraśānti-pā 295, 313
Ratnakīrti 209, 225, 227
Ratnamati 198
Ratnasāgara 141
Ratnavajra 295n, 301-2
Ravigupta 196, 222n, 303
Revata 69n
rGa-lo [-tsā-ba] 315
Ri-ri-pā 306-7
Rockhill, W. W. 69n
Roerich, G. N. *passim*
Ro-ru-nanda 229
Rudra 115

Sabari-pā 128, 151, 290n
Sabbakāmī 69n
Sachau, E. C. 111n, 138n
Sādhuputra 308
Sagadeva (Viśākhadeva) 150n, 177n, 197, 197n
Sāgaramegha 276
Sāgarapāla 265n *See also* Samudrapāla
Sahajalalita 251, 267
Sajjana 302
Śākyadeva 191n
Śākya Mahābala 10
Śākyamati 260
Śākyamitra 128, 128n, 268
Śākyamuni 267
Śākyaprabha 259
Śākyarāja 302
Śākyaśrī 314n, 329
Sālacandra 7, 120, 122-3
Sa-la'i-sto-bas 82n
Sālavāhana 11, 227, 336
Sāgara 11
Samalvāhana (Sātavāhana) 111n
Samaya-vajra (Kṛṣṇasamaya-vajra) 18
Sambhūta 69n
Sambhūti 15, 121
Saṃgamaśrībhadra 168n
Saṃghabhadra 167-8, 174-5
Saṃghadāsa 150, 177, 185, 197-8
Saṃghaguhya (Saṃghagupta, Siṃhagupta) 132, 132n
Saṃgharakṣita 151, 186, 188
Saṃghavardhana 116
Śaṃkara *bhikṣu* 108, 109n
Śaṃkara (? Kṣemaṅkara ; Udayana) 11, 334
Śaṃkarācārya (Śaṅgarācarya) 225-6, 232
Śaṃkaradeva 219n
Śaṃkarānanda 308-9
Śaṃkara [-pati] 16, 100-1
Śaṃkara-gāruḍi (Śaṅku) 145n
Śaṃkarasvāmin 101n

Sampradūta 225
Samudra 55n
Samudrapāla 265
Śāmupāla 10, 289-90, 293
Samyaksatya 106
Samyak-sambuddha 20, 40, 60
Sanātana 290
Śāṇavāsika 24-8, 31-4
Saṅgatala 98
Sañjaya 14
Sañjaya (Saṃjayin) 91
Saṅghavardhana 15
Saṅkajati [Śaṅkhajāti] 223
Śaṅkhika 50
Sankrityayana, R. 152n, 154n, 290n
Śaṅku 17, 142, 144-7
Saṇmukha (? Kumāra-ṣaṇmukha) 11, 335
Saṇmukha-kumāra (*deity* Kārtika) 113
Śāntarakṣita (Śāntijīva) 260, 277
Śāntideva 18, 197, 214-5, 217-8
Śāntigupta 331
Śānti-pā 290n, 294, 295n, 299, 300, 304
Śāntiprabha 253, 259
Śāntisoma 252
Śāntivāhana 112
Śāntivarman 189, 191
Saptavarman (Śarvavarman; Sarvavarman) 111, 113-4, 116
Saraha (*alias* Rāhula) 102n, 104, 151, 152n, 153n
Sarasvatī *goddess* 109, 226, 326
Śāriputra 20n, 21, 87n, 88-9, 101, 321
Saro 144
Saroruha 152n, 241, 242, 246
Sarvajñamitra 211, 220-1
Sarvanivāraṇa-viṣkambhī 103
Sarvakāma 87
Sarvajñadeva 285
Sastri, H. P. 217n
Sastri, N. S. 24n
Sātavāhana 9n, 111n
Śeṣa-nāga (Patañjali) 112, 202n, 203, 208
Siddha 16, 47
Siddhacandra 196, 210
Śīla 8, 196-200, 209-10
Śīlabhadra 212n, 260
Śīlakīrti 296
Śīlapālita 252
Siṃha 9, 196, 209
Siṃhacandra 7, 210n
Siṃhabhadra 175n, 260n
Siṃhagupta 132n
Siṃhajaṭi (Saddajati) 331
Siṃha Sudarśana 91
Siṃha-Koṣa *See* Āsana-Siṃha-koṣa
Siṃhamukha 277
Siṃhanāda 202
Siṅ-khi-pā 127-8
Sircar, D. C. 50n, 130n, 191n, 214n
Śiromaṇi 267
Śiśu 12, 335
Śiva 115
Ślaṇavāsa (*See also* Sāṇavāsika) 13, 79
Śobhajāta 331
Śreṣṭha 12
Śreṣṭhapāla 8, 294
Śrī, *goddess* 79
Śrīcandra 7, 131, 137
Śrīdhara 18, 325-6
Śrīgupta 225, 252-3
Śrīharṣa 8, 176, 178
Śrīkūṭa 135n
Śrīlābha 15, 103, 117
Sroṅ-btsan-sgam-po 175n
Stcherbatsky, Th. 71n, 181n, 303n
Sthiramati 177, 179, 180n, 201, 210n, 212
Sthirapāla (Trilakṣa) 311
Subāhu 6, 26-9
Subhadrāṅgī 51n
Subhagā 124
Śubhākaragupta 314, 329

Śubhaṅkara (? Kṣemaṅkara) 15, 116
Subhūtipālita 285
Śubhamitra 251
Śubhasāra 192
Sudarśana 56n, 73-5, 176n
Sudhanu 6, 29, 31, 33, 38
Śūdra 16, 91
Sudurjaya 182
Sujaya 16, 39-40, 42
Śukāyana 73
Sukhadeva 222-3
Sukhasiddhā *ḍākini* 214n
Śukla (Śuklarāja) 11, 334
Śūlapāṇi 115
Sumana 50n, 51n
Sum-pa 141n, 142n
Sundara-ha-ci 331
Sundaravyūha 276
Supramadhu 17, 109
Śūra 17, 132, 186, 190-1, 259
Śūravajra 345
Sūryagupta 196-7, 222
Suṣīma 50n, 51n
Suvarṇavarṇa 22
Suvarṣaka 14
Suviṣṇu 17, 109
Saraṇa 221

Tailo-pā *siddha* 299n
Tanti-pā 249
Takakusu, J. *passim*
Takṣaka 147
Tāmraśāṭa 14
Taṅki-pāda 178n
Tārā *āryā* 133, 146, 191n, 192-3, 201-2, 206, 208, 212, 215-6, 220-2, 254, 281, 292, 297-8, 326
Tārā *princess* 201
Tathāgatabhadra 123n, 126 (*See* Nāgāhvāya)
Tathāgata-rakṣita 18, 327
Thagana (Thagana-pā ; Thakkana) 290
Thomas, F. W. 126n, 131n, 132n, 134n, 135n, 136n
Thon-mi-sambhoṭa 206n
Tiṅgi 230n
See also Diṅgi
Tissa Ekavihārika 50n, 51n
Tiṣyarakṣitā 76-8
Trilakṣa *See* Sthirapāla
Triratnadāsa 136n, 178, 190-1
Tsoṅ-kha-pa 161n
Turuṣka Mahāsammata 9, 149, 185

Udbhaṭa-siddhi-svāmin, *alias* Mudgaragomin 16, 100-1
Uḍya-upāsaka 264
Umā *goddess* 53-4, 100, 115
Upagupta 32-8, 44-6, 57n, 70, 87, 176n
Uttara 13-4

Vāgīśvarakīrti 295n, 296, 299
Vairocanabhadra 277
Vairocanamitra 209n
Vaiśravaṇa 79n
Vajradhātu-mahā-maṇḍala 282, 285
Vajra-amṛta-mahā-maṇḍala 287
Vajraghaṇṭa 152n, 222, 230
Vajrahāsa 296n
Vajrapāṇi 26n, 29n, 30n, 310n
Vajrasūrya 287
Vajravārāhī 245, 301
Vajrayoginī 250, 306
Vāmana 15, 116
Vaṃśacandra *See* Bhaṃśacandra
Vanapāla 8, 284, 290
Vanāyu 85
Vanaratna 331
Vararuci 16, 85-6, 111-5, 202-3
Vararuci, *the second* 17
Varasena 196n, 210n
Vardhamāla 12, 336

Vāsantī *princess* 114-5
Vāsavadatta 65
Vasubandhu 17n, 85n, 89, 94n, 149-50, 160n, 161-176, 177n, 179-82, 185, 190, 227, 298, 313, 330
Vasunāga 17
Vasumitra 15, 87n, 88n, 93-4, 96, 97n, 103-4, 225, 227, 340
Vāsuki-nāga 146-7, 248
Vasunetra 17, 137
Vasurakṣī (? Masurakṣita) 10
Vasusāra 34
Vatsa, *monk* 71-2
Vatsīputra, Vātsīputrīya 14, 71n, 181, 339-41
Vibharaṭṭa 261
Vidyabhusana S. C. 93n, 131n, 141n, 142n
Vigamacandra 7-8, 176-7
Vigatarāgadhvaja 98
Vigataśoka 6, 66, 76, 78-9
Vijña 16, 82
Vikrama 12
Vikramāditya 123, 139n, 175n
Vikrīḍa 244
Vimalamitra 284
Vimalacandra 7-8
Vimuktasena 177, 188, 190, 196, 210-2, 254
Vinayasena [?] 210
Vinītadeva 82n, 176n, 251
Vinītasena 210-1
Vīrasena 6, 79, 82, 94, 210
Virū-pā 197, 214-5, 222, 245
Virū-pā *the junior* 261
Vīrya 17, 104
Vīryabhadra 305
Viśākhadeva *See* Sagadeva
Viśeṣaka 200
Viśeṣamitra 259
Viṣṇu 9, 53, 70, 115
Viṣṇurāja 224, 249
Viṣṭa-pāla (Veṣṭa-pāla) 180
Visukalpa 104
Viśva 12, 335
Vītaśoka 50n, 51n
Volkova, O. F. 52n, 76n, 77n, 78n
Vṛkṣacandra 7, 150, 176
Vyāghrarāja 335

Watters, T. *passim*
Wilson, W. W. 264n
Winternitz, M. 131n, 132n

Yakṣapāla 8, 314-5
Yamāntaka 130n
Yamāri 215, 245, 280, 308, 327, 328
Yaśaḥ (Yaśa ; Yaśoda ; Yaśano) 13, 39, 55, 57, 58n, 60-1, 66, 68, 69n, 87
Yaśasvin 16, 79, 79n
Yaśika 79n
Yaśomitra 261
Yoga-pā (Yogi-pā ; Ayogi-pā) 290
Yuan-chuang *passim*